SIGNETS

READING H.D.

Signets
Reading H.D.

Edited by

SUSAN STANFORD FRIEDMAN

and

RACHEL BLAU DUPLESSIS

The University of Wisconsin Press

Photographs on pages 8–19, 21–28, 165, 167, and 168 are reproduced courtesy of the Yale Collection of American Literature, Beinecke Rare Book and Manuscript Library, Yale University. The photograph of H.D. on p. 20 is reproduced courtesy of The Schlesinger Library, Radcliffe College. The photograph on p. 166 is reproduced courtesy of the Galleria Schwarz, Milan. Copyright © Hannah Hoch/VAGA New York 1990. Epigraphs and the photo captions on pages 8–28 from the published and unpublished works of Hilda Doolittle, as follows, reprinted by permission of New Directions Publishing Corporation. All rights reserved. *Bid Me to Live.* Copyright © 1960 by Norman Holmes Pearson. *Collected Poems, 1912–1944.* Copyright © 1982 by the Estate of Hilda Doolittle. *The Gift.* Copyright © 1969, 1982 by the Estate of Hilda Doolittle. Copyright © 1982 by Perdita Schaffner. *Hedylus.* Copyright © 1928, 1980 by the Estate of Hilda Doolittle. *Helen in Egypt.* Copyright © 1961 by Norman Holmes Pearson. *Hermetic Definition.* Copyright © 1958, 1959, 1961, 1969, 1972 by Norman Holmes Pearson. *Hermione.* Copyright © 1981 by the Estate of Hilda Doolittle. Copyright © 1979 by Perdita Schaffner. *Tribute to Freud.* Copyright © 1956, 1974 by Norman Holmes Pearson. All previously unpublished material by Hilda Doolittle Copyright © 1990 by Perdita Schaffner. An earlier version of chapter 21 appeared in *Women's Studies* 5:2 (1977). Copyright © 1977 by Gordon and Breach, Science Publishers, Inc.

The University of Wisconsin Press
114 North Murray Street
Madison, Wisconsin 53715

3 Henrietta Street
London WC2E 8LU, England

Library of Congress Cataloging-in-Publication Data

Signets : reading H.D. / edited by Susan Stanford Friedman and Rachel
   Blau DuPlessis.
      506 pp.   cm.
      Includes bibliographical references (p. 455) and index.
      1. H. D. (Hilda Doolittle), 1886–1961—Criticism and
   interpretation.   I. Friedman, Susan Stanford.   II. DuPlessis,
   Rachel Blau.
   PS3507.O726Z86   1990
   811'.52—dc20
   ISBN 0-299-12680-3   90-50088
   ISBN 0-299-12684-6 (pbk.)   CIP

For
Perdita Schaffner

SIGNET—as from sign, a mark, token, proof; signet—the privy seal, a seal; signet-ring—a ring with a signet or private seal; sign-manual—the royal signature, usually only the initials of the sovereign's name. (I have used my initials H.D. consistently as my writing signet or sign-manual, though it is only, at this very moment, as I check up on the word "signet" in my Chambers' English Dictionary that I realize that my writing signature has anything remotely suggesting sovereignty or the royal manner.) Sign again—a word, gesture, symbol, or mark, intended to signify something else. Sign again—(medical) a symptom, (astronomical) one of the twelve parts of the Zodiac. Again sign—to attach a signature to, and sign-post—a direction post; all from the French, *signe*, and Latin, *signum*. And as I write that last word, there flashes into my mind the associated *in hoc signum* or rather, it must be *in hoc signo* and *vinces*.

H.D., Tribute to Freud

Contents

Preface

The signs of H.D.'s presence as a major writer of the modernist period have become strikingly visible through the past two decades. Using "H.D." as her "writing signature" for nearly sixty years, Hilda Doolittle (1886–1961) made her distinctive mark on modern literature as a poet, novelist, essayist, translator, and memoirist. *Signets: Reading H.D.* is a basic collection of essays that traces her presence from the various perspectives and with the differing critical methodologies that have emerged in the last two decades of criticism.

H.D.'s rich and varied oeuvre is an essential part of Anglo-American modernism. In its innovative forms and visions, it is affiliated with the work of other modernist writers — especially Ezra Pound, Marianne Moore, William Carlos Williams, T. S. Eliot, D. H. Lawrence, Gertrude Stein, W. B. Yeats, and Dorothy Richardson, all of whom she knew personally. H.D.'s work is also connected with that of James Joyce, Virginia Woolf, Langston Hughes, Jean Toomer, William Faulkner, and Zora Neale Hurston, most (if not all) of whose work she knew well. Additionally, H.D. was deeply engaged with three currents of twentieth-century thought and culture that influenced literary modernism: psychoanalysis, cinema, and the Harlem Renaissance.

H.D.'s lyrics of the teens (in *Sea Garden*) and her epics of the forties and fifties (*Trilogy* and *Helen in Egypt*) are defining works of modernity. Her translations from the Greek (mainly Euripides and Sappho) were influential transpositions of classical lyrics into the modernist context. Her experimental prose fiction — *Hedylus, HER, Palimpsest, Nights, Bid Me to Live (A Madrigal)* — belongs in the tradition forged by Stein, Joyce, Woolf, and Richardson, all of whom ruptured conventional narrative. H.D.'s essays and memoirs — such as *Tribute to Freud, Notes on Thought and Vision, Advent, End to Torment, The Gift*, and *H.D. by Delia Alton* — present vibrant cultural readings of her various selves interwoven with her times. The historical and spiritual impact of violence and war in their cultural and personal meanings is a central preoccupation of these reflexive texts.

H.D.'s writing is in some measure transcendental, mythic, and "modern"; and in some measure liminal, heterogeneous, and "postmodern." At all points, her work is fundamentally dialogic, reflecting her negotiations as a woman to place herself within and through language in a position of authority—not in the Other place of masculine privilege, but rather in a positionality emergent from her "difference," from what she called in "The Master" the "hardship / of the spirit" that comes with "what it is to be a woman." As Louis L. Martz stated in his introduction to H.D.'s *Collected Poems, 1912–1944*: "Her poetry and her prose, like her own psyche, live at the seething junctions of opposite forces."

Hence H.D. can be located, suggestively, on the borderline of distinctive impulses within twentieth-century modernity: the exhilaration of radical breaks with the past, the uncertainty of separation from cultural certainties; the pleasure and play with the materiality of language, the inadequacy and emptiness of words; the subjectivities of self, time, and space, the fragmentation of identity and reality; the splitting and dispersion of symbolic systems, the indeterminacy of all repatterning; the explosion of desire out of Victorian confinement, the conflict this release brought among and between women and men; the breaking of racial, gender, and class boundaries; the blast of technological progress and futurism, the devastation of war; the search for the sacred, and the secular Death of God. As an inheritor of romanticism adrift in modernity, H.D. proposed powerful syntheses of these forces in structures of resolution. As a harbinger of postmodernism, H.D. saw these solutions unraveling as they were formed in a process of search that was ever fluid, never fixed. As she wrote in a section of *Trilogy* with which she particularly identified her own sensibility:

> *we know no rule*
> *of procedure,*
>
> *we are voyagers, discoverers*
> *of the not-known,*
>
> *the unrecorded;*
> *we have no map;*
>
> *possibly we will reach haven,*
> *heaven.*

The passage on "signs" and "signets" in H.D.'s *Tribute to Freud* from which we have drawn our title has a very distinctive flavor. Its self-reflexivity, its casual, even self-correcting tone is combined with the highest claims. It denies, yet sub rosa asserts "sovereignty" or the "royal manner." The passage makes etymological links among self and culture, webbings of metonymy, and syncretisms, both religious and secular. But most important, the epigraph marks the many ways in which *reading*—interpreting, decoding, reading the writing, and writing a necessary and sufficient "reading"—were central activities for H.D. The psyche (conscious and unconscious), events (the sacred and the historical), writings (past "scribblings" and the "unwritten pages of the new"), and images (personal and mythic)—all produced hieroglyphs to be endlessly read and reread, endlessly woven and rewoven. In this volume, we are "reading H.D.," to read not only her writings, but also her own readings of the already written in culture, in myth, in history.

Reading H.D. has been a historically specific practice. Reflecting the patterns and politics of literary history, H.D.'s work was imperfectly considered and irregularly available in the first era of the academic canon formation of modernism: the 1940s for Eliot, Joyce, and Yeats; the 1950s for Wallace Stevens, Moore, Stein, Lawrence, and Woolf; the 1960s for Pound, Williams, and again, Woolf. The women writers (Woolf, Stein, Moore) were valued, through these decades, only for technical innovation and were scarcely read from informed gender perspectives. While there might be debate about the degree of canonicity accorded these women, there is no doubt that "H.D." ("who was she?" "what is it?") was not known in the fullness and complexity of her achievement, and had even become a kind of modernist embarrassment by not remaining a placeable "imagist." Locked in the limitations of her reputation as "the perfect imagist" and associated mainly with an escapist classicism, H.D.'s epic poems and prose were largely trivialized or ignored by the critics. Most of her work went out of print, and much (particularly her avant-garde prose fiction, memoirs, and last poems) remained unpublished during this period.

While the academic community moved H.D. to the periphery of modernism, some of the innovative poets of the 1950s and 1960s, such as Robert Duncan, Denise Levertov, and Allen Ginsberg, continued to read and deeply admire H.D.'s work. Indeed, Duncan exerted a telling influence on some contemporary scholarship with the publication during the 1960s and 1970s of chapters from *The H.D. Book*, his influential consideration of modern history, consciousness, and poetics (forthcoming from the University of California Press). In a parallel way, L. S. Dembo's chapter on H.D. in *Conceptions of Reality in Modern American Poetry* (1966) and his pioneering issue of *Contemporary Literature* devoted to H.D. (1969) initiated serious and sustained critical scrutiny of her work. H.D.'s friend and first executor, Norman Holmes Pearson, correctly predicted in an interview printed in that issue that "the next half-dozen years will see H.D. discovered, that she will indeed receive the kind of attention that she has long deserved and can withstand."

With the rise of feminism and the advent of women's studies in the late 1960s and 1970s, the context for reading H.D. changed dramatically. Feminist scholarship pioneered these new readings and provided the essential momentum for a major reassessment of H.D.'s work as part of the larger cultural project of recovering forgotten, marginalized, and misappropriated women writers and of reconceptualizing the terms, movements, and figures of literary history. Many feminist poets — Adrienne Rich and Judy Grahn preeminent among them — (re)claimed H.D. as an essential figure of their matrilineage. During the late 1970s and the 1980s, as a result of the urgency and intellectual ferment of feminist approaches to scores of recovered and newly read twentieth-century women writers, the number of readings of H.D. from a variety of critical, biographical, and contextual perspectives rapidly increased. New Directions and Black Swan Books in the United States and Carcanet and Virago in Britain brought out new editions of H.D.'s out-of-print works and published many of her unpublished works. One of her early avant-garde novels — *Asphodel* — is forthcoming from Duke University Press; yet a significant portion of her prose remains unpublished. Perdita Schaffner, H.D.'s daughter and literary executor, has facilitated access to H.D.'s work with extraordinary generosity of spirit. Her illuminating introductions and sketches have accompanied many of H.D.'s recently reissued and newly published texts.

Although some critics like Hugh Kenner and Alfred Kazin continue to see H.D. as a peripheral figure, her work has increasingly been read as central to the literary history and theory of both modernism and women's writing. Seven journals — *Agenda, Sagetrieb, San Jose Studies, Poesis, Iowa Review, Contemporary Literature*, and *HOW(ever)* — published special issues on H.D., and five conferences were held for her centennial in 1986. The *H.D. Newsletter* was founded by Eileen Gregory in 1987. In spite of the continuing controversy her work often elicits, H.D.'s writing does indeed command attention and sustain scrutiny. The arrival of poststructuralist theory onto the American critical scene in the 1980s has added significantly to this new assessment of her place in literary history. Much of H.D.'s probing, endlessly interpretive readings and writings lend themselves particularly well to poststructuralist concepts of textual practice and subjectivity.

Signets: Reading H.D. collects significant essays of the past two decades to constitute a core of H.D. criticism. The book aspires to serve newcomers to H.D. as well as those already familiar with her texts and the major events of her life. We have included many of the most influential articles of recent years and selected those essays that focus on the works of H.D. being read and taught most frequently. The book presents a spectrum of methodologies — including biographical, contextual, textual, new historicist, psychoanalytic, and poststructuralist — many of which have been integrated with a feminist critical foregrounding of gender. Reflecting the period of time in which they were written, these essays mirror the changes in reading practices that have taken place generally in literary studies and demonstrate in particular the increasing intersection of French poststructuralist theory with Anglo-American feminist criticism. While representative, informative, and provocative, this selection cannot pretend to explore the full range of important work on H.D. To keep the size within practical bounds, we have not included book chapters on H.D., articles examining H.D. in relationship to other writers, and highly specialized articles. This volume should be supplemented with the many other excellent articles and full-length book studies on H.D. that are noted in the Selected Bibliography.

As organizing rubrics for the essays in this anthology, we open with *Lives* and continue to evoke words and concepts that were important signets for H.D.: *Images, Palimpsests, Prophecies,* and *Rescriptings.* These rubrics suggest thematic, formal, and personal strategies that tended to crystallize at certain points in H.D.'s development, but that extended throughout her career. In *Lives,* we include pieces that represent different ways of telling lives, in recognition of how various discourses construct lives differently. Rather than foster the notion of a definitive "life" with a single essay or chronology, *Lives* begins with an essayistic memoir by H.D.'s daughter (Schaffner). It continues with a photobiography of her life (Friedman, DuPlessis, and Silverstein); a selection from the poem *Biography* by an H.D. biographer (Barbara Guest) that probes the uncertainties, accommodations, and interiorities endemic in writing biography; chronologies of H.D.'s life (Louis H. Silverstein) and of the production and publication of her work (Friedman); and a new historicist study incorporating cultural paradigms and H.D.'s own life-writing (Adalaide Morris). The subsequent four sections of the book loosely chart the shape of H.D.'s developing oeuvre in an approximate chronological and generic order. *Images* deals primarily with H.D.'s imagist and postimagist lyrics of the teens and twenties. Articles address her contribution to modernist innovation (Cyrena N. Pondrom); her gendered re-vision of romanticism (Cassandra Laity); Sappho's liminal presence in *Sea Garden* (Eileen Gregory); and her postimagist play with imaging and being imaged in a visual medium (Diana Collecott). *Palimpsests* focuses mainly on the layered and experimental prose written in the twenties and early forties. Articles explore textual and psychic resonances between conscious and unconscious subjectivities in *Palimpsest* (Deborah Kelly Kloepfer); the bisexual narrative of *HER* in the context of the *Kunstlerroman*, psychoanalysis, and lesbian issues (Friedman and DuPlessis); reading the textual and political unconscious in the palimpsestic (re)writing of *Paint It To-Day, Asphodel*, and *Bid Me to Live (A Madrigal)* (Friedman); and the interdependence of writing and listening, symbolic and semiotic, in *Tribute to Freud* and her essays (DuPlessis).

Prophecies examines the formation of H.D.'s prophetic voice and magisterial poetry of the forties (especially *Trilogy*). Articles look at the evolution of H.D.'s prophetic voice as it constellated around the concept of projection from the teens through the forties (Morris); the revisionist theology, with its sexual/textual echoes, in *Trilogy* (Susan Gubar); *Trilogy*'s recovery of the personal and divine Mother in the midst of war (Albert Gelpi); the open prosody and conversational poetic of H.D.'s meditative epic (Alicia Ostriker); and H.D.'s sense of the sacred in relation to heterodoxy and poetic quest (Duncan). *Rescriptings* explores H.D.'s revisionary views of myth and modernism predominantly in the fifties (especially *Helen in Egypt*), but also suggests the constant interpretive scrutinies of inscriptions and traditions as a significant act for a female modernist. Articles present *Helen in Egypt*'s re-vision of Homer's *Iliad* and Hitler's fascism in the (re)creation of a matriarchal mythos (Friedman); the resolution of romantic thralldom in cultural and biographical rescriptings of gender relations (DuPlessis); and a poststructuralist reading of *Helen in Egypt* as a critique of specularity in male modernist formalism (Elizabeth A. Hirsh). As Alicia Ostriker has noted about the works of prophecy and rescripting in "The Poet as Heroine: Learning to Read H.D.": "These are works that wrestle with the great modernist issues of faith's collapse and the possibilities of reconstruction; self and society; the nature of language and the value of poetry in history; the meaning of the imagination."

As topical clusters, these sections resonate with each other, and most of the essays weave forward and backward in time and across H.D.'s genres. Closing the volume, the Selected Bibliography presents primary and secondary titles with which we invite our readers to continue their own tracings of the myriad signs of H.D.

Part I

Lives

Are you alive?
I touch you.
You quiver like a sea-fish.
I cover you with my net.
What are you—banded one?
　　　　　—H.D., "The Pool"

CHAPTER 1

A Sketch of H.D.: The Egyptian Cat

PERDITA SCHAFFNER

The turquoise-blue cat had caused considerable anxiety. I now keep her wrapped in cotton wool and tissue paper, in a small box within a larger box, stowed away in the back of the case containing my mother's books — those she wrote, and those she read for research and study, or just for fun. That seems as safe a place as any — way off in our secluded country house in eastern Long Island. When I go away she is on her own, and still more secure than she would be with me, traveling back and forth while changing habitats.

I know nothing of her archeological past, if indeed she has any. H.D. bought her in Egypt in the early 1920s, and brought her home. Genuine artifact, or exquisite facsimile? Experts could tell at a glance. I haven't submitted her to their evaluation, and never will. I don't wish to face up to the responsibility. If she should turn out to be a priceless treasure, I would have to lock her up, or donate her to a museum. Either way — in a bank vault, or in a hall of Egyptology — she would no longer be truly mine. On the other hand, I could never bear to have her diminished. "Sorry, this is just a reproduction." Euphemism for fake. I prefer the mystery.

Genuine or fake, a link with the Pharaohs or merely a souvenir from this century — she is beautiful. She sits inch high, with a proud elongated posture. Her features are finely drawn. They vary — lofty, remote, almost disdainful at times; then tender; then again, inscrutable; always aristocratic. Between her front paws, pressed against her chest, she guards a microscopic replica, her kitten.

Drawing from the occult past, or imitating it, she can behave most unaccountably. She has a life force of her own.

She came to me in a varied bag of H.D.'s possessions, shortly after her death. It's only by chance that I felt something hard and tiny, tucked deep into the lining.

Then I kept losing her. And she always came back. Burglars ransacked our city home, taking everything, so I thought. Months later, my husband spotted a ridge of turquoise between the floorboards. I carried her around in the zippered compartment of my purse after that. Again, she got away—only to turn up in the back of our station wagon.

Long, long ago, she hung on a black velvet ribbon around H.D.'s neck. "This is the cat, and this is the kitten," she would say, pointing out the parallel in our relationship.

H.D. was hardly an archetypal mother, nor would one expect her to be. At the time, I really didn't expect or know anything otherwise. We lived in Switzerland with her friend Bryher, isolated from the world. Visitors came by from time to time; mostly writers, adults only. I never consorted with other children, other families, other mothers. So, for all I knew, everybody's mother was a poet; a tall figure of striking beauty, with fine bone structure and haunting grey eyes; and frequently overwrought, off in the clouds, or sequestered in a room, not to be disturbed on any account.

She was intensely maternal—on an esoteric plane. She venerated the concept of motherhood, but was unprepared for its disruptions. She flinched at sudden noise, and fled from chaos. Mercifully for her, she was well buffered. We had a staff, almost a bodyguard. I could always be removed. *"Madame est nerveuse; viens ma petite!"* Or Bryher would step in and marshal me off. "Your mother's very nervous today." Every day, it seemed. So, fair enough, that's the way it was. A mother was someone who wrote poetry and was very nervous. And who walked alone and sat alone. And was capable of overwhelming affection, but on her own time and terms, preferably out of doors. I accompanied her on her daily walk, clasping a bag full of crusts and crumbs. Always the same time: ten o'clock, when her morning's work was done and put away. The same circuit, down some stone steps to the lake, where we fed the gulls, swans, and ducks. Then she reclaimed her solitude. "Run ahead, run, run, *run!*" I charged along and returned, and cantered around her in circles while she strolled and dreamed.

She spent the afternoons in her room, reading, writing letters, and thinking—concentrating on everything and nothing, in an intense trance-like meditation. The Egyptian cat was her mantra. She sat gazing at it for hours, fingering it, running it up and down the velvet ribbon.

When she left the door ajar, I sidled in and joined her. She never objected; she quietly made room for me in the armchair. And I never wriggled, chattered, or wished I were anywhere else. Those were privileged interludes, all the more so for being surreptitious. I dreaded an outsider barging in, breaking up our rapport, our shared secret.

Then I didn't see the little cat, ever again, in my mother's lifetime. Was it already given to disappearing? Or did its presence suddenly become too hypnotic for comfort? At any rate, it was replaced by a crystal which exerted the same psychic pull. I gazed into it, and only saw our reflections, or warped magnifying-glass views of dress and furniture fabric. But she seemed to see something else. If I sat still enough for long enough, I would see too. I stayed absolutely quiet, mesmerized.

Her work — the actual writing — was, of course, a deeply private matter. Then, the door was always closed. She had no workroom as such, only an alcove in her bedroom, stripped down to essentials: a sturdy table, a gray jar full of pencils, a stack of school exercise books, and a reference book or two. She rose very early, and got straight down to work, filling up the exercise books with tight faint script. She preferred hard pencils; they lasted longer; she didn't have to interrupt herself with the mechanics of sharpening. When she reached a certain point, she closed all the books and put the pencils back in their jar until next morning.

"Like working on a sampler," she confided, years later. "So many stitches and just so many rows, day after day. If I miss even one day, I drop a stitch and lose the pattern and I feel I'm never going to find it again."

And I ask her about all those other times, when she was not at her desk, yet not entirely in this world — the walks along the lakefront, the sessions with the little cat, with the crystal. Was she dreaming, was she in a sense writing? Well, both; and a correlation of the two.

"Evolving. Searching. My past, the past, the past that never was, and making something real of it. And it's always eluding me. I think I've found it, and I find it's wrong. But the wrong way can be illuminating too, it so often points out the right way — ultimately. The idea *behind* the idea is the one I'm really reaching for. Again, it's a bit like exploring a galaxy with a trick telescope, picking out pinpoint constellations, and taking optical illusions for their worth, too. And it's all part of the ragtag-and-bobtail of my sewing basket. Do you follow me?"

Surprising enough, yes. No matter how dizzying her flights and sudden her descents, or mixed and unexpected her metaphors, I could always follow. I just had to grow up first, and find my own bearings.

She didn't always travel in exalted spheres. Fortunately for her, for me, for her whole *entourage*, she had a marvellous sense of humor; and a spontaneous wit which seized the absurdities of life and everyone's foibles, including her own. So she laughed a lot. The quintessential "loner," nonetheless she loved company. She had many friends, young and old, and some very eminent. Violet Hunt, Elizabeth Bowen, the Sitwells — singly, and triply — Ivy Compton-Burnett . . . all came to tea, whenever she was in London. She was equally interested in people with more humdrum lives. She could involve herself in the daily problems of a veterinarian's assistant—or a typist in a secretarial pool. She mixed all her guests together; being a superb catalyst, everybody had a wonderful time. She also enjoyed ordinary pursuits, jaunts: an afternoon at the movies, bus rides, shopping expeditions. She read current best-sellers as well as esoteric tomes. She achieved a perfect balance between anguished sensibility and plain, down-to-earth, everyday life. And, now that the pressures and conflicts of motherhood had ceased, she became a much better mother. We respected each other as individuals. We were adults together, and friends.

And so it is with mothers and daughters, mothers and sons. Another generation has grown up. I've come full circle, with four such friends of my own—who have all played with the Egyptian cat, and admired it.

"But don't worry. Sure you'll lose it again. But it always gets back to you." Possessing an intimate affinity.

This essay previously appeared in H.D., *Hedylus*. Rev. ed. Redding Ridge, CT: Black Swan Books, 1980. 185–94.

CHAPTER 2

A Photobiography of H.D.

SUSAN STANFORD FRIEDMAN,
RACHEL BLAU DUPLESSIS, AND
LOUIS H. SILVERSTEIN

These photos image the narrative of H.D.'s life from childhood to old age. Photos of people who constituted her family at different points in her life have been interspersed in the processus of images. Others to whom she was particularly close at times — like Ezra Pound, William Carlos Williams, D. H. Lawrence, John Cournos, Cecil Gray, Havelock Ellis, Brigit Patmore, Marianne Moore, Robert McAlmon, Dorothy Richardson, Robert Herring, Silvia Dobson, Sigmund Freud, Erich Heydt, and Norman Holmes Pearson — have not been included because we wanted to sustain the focus on a portrait of H.D. moving through time. Captions for these photos are taken from H.D.'s writing, sometimes from contexts that are far from the autobiographical. Each caption is meant to be a suggestive and oblique adjunct to the photo, one that creates a juxtaposed relationship rather than a direct commentary. Dates for the photos are approximate.

Helen Wolle Doolittle, in art class, *circa* 1871

I said painting reminded me of my mother. I told him how as children we had admired her painting and boasted to visitors, "My mother *painted* that." My mother was morbidly self-effacing.

Advent (164)

8

Professor Charles Leander Doolittle, *circa* 1900

Father, aloof, distant, the provider, the protector—but a little un-get-at-able, a little too far away and giant-like in proportion, a little chilly withal.

Tribute to Freud (38)

Gilbert, Harold, and Hilda Doolittle, *circa* 1889

One of these children was called Mignon. Not my name certainly. It is true I was small for my age, *mignonne*; but I was not, they said, pretty and I was not, it was very easy to see, quaint and quick and clever like my brother. . . . It was a girl between two boys; but, ironically, it was wispy and mousy, while the boys were glowing and gold.

Tribute to Freud (101, 107)

Hilda Doolittle, Graduation Photo from Miss Gordon's School, 1901

I have had enough.
I gasp for breath.
. . . .
O to blot out this garden
to forget, to find a new beauty
in some terrible
wind-tortured place.

"Sheltered Garden" (*CP* 19–21)

Hilda Doolittle, early 1900s

In all my life, it seemed, I had never had such a terrible dream. "My mother, my mother."
. . . But she stands grim & forbidding, all the Puritan, her hands folded on the Yale library
case that contains the early MSS and pictures. I do not want to go back to the studio portrait stages or even to the faded photograph of a leggy girl on a black horse. . . . I do not
want to go back at all but the dream impells me & a broken hip that has kept me in bed,
for over nine weeks.

Hirslanden Notebooks (I:3)

12

Charles Leander, Hilda, Charles Melvin (in front), Gilbert, Helen, Harold, Eric, and Alfred Doolittle, *circa* 1907

Why was it always a girl who had died? Why did Alice die and not Alfred? Why did Edith die and not Gilbert? . . . I did not cry. The crying was frozen in me, but it was my own, it was my own crying. There was Alice — my own half-sister — Edith, my own sister and I was the third of this trio, these three Fates. . . . The gift was there, but the expression of the gift was somewhere else.

The Gift (4)

Frances Josepha Gregg, *circa* 1910

A sister was a creature of ebony strung with wild poppies or an image of ivory whose lithe hips made parallel and gave reflection of like parallel in a fountain basin. As sister would run, would leap, would be concealed under the autumn sumac or lie shaken with hail and wind, lost on some Lacedaemonian foothill.

HER (10)

H.D., 1916–1917

She was Medea of some blessed incarnation, a witch with power. A wise-woman. She was seer, see-er. She was at home in this land of subtle psychic reverberations, as she was at home in a book.

Bid Me to Live (A Madrigal) (146)

15

Richard Aldington, *circa* 1916

I love Richard with a searing, burning intensity. I love him and I have come to this torture of my free will. I could have forgotten my pride broken and my beauty as it were, unappreciated. . . . Of my will, I have come to this Hell . . . I believe this flame is my very Daemon driving me to write. I want to write."

Letter to John Cournos, 5 September 1916

H.D. and Frances Perdita, 1919

Perdita gets more charming & that is the trouble. . . . We must have some fun &
some great adventures — I am torn between a desire for any little place with Perdita
& fairy-books & Noah's arks and dolls, and a wild adventure. Perhaps in time, I will
have both.

Letter to Bryher, 19 April 1919

H.D., 1919–1922

Dryads
haunting the groves,
nereids
who dwell in wet caves,
. . . .
The light of her face falls from its flower,
as a hyacinth,
hidden in a far valley,
perishes upon burnt grass.

"Acon" (*CP* 32)

Winifred Bryher, 1920–22

it was beyond any words;
there were no words
even in our glorious speech
that could hint the joy we had then;
how can we to-day in a crude tongue,
in a strange land hope to say
one word that can hint at the joy we had
when the rocks broke like sand under our heels
and they fled?

"I Said" (CP 324)

H.D., by Man Ray, *circa* 1922

Who was there that mattered or cared? Ray Bart a white spirit kept some stronghold of the Spirit, but there was this Raymonde that Ray Bart's few odd admirers did not count on; Raymonde was tenuous, Raymonde was obliterated, but Raymonde had that power, that still assertive quality; forever and forever a Raymonde dwelt secure and tenuous and suave and slightly sentimental within a world of security, tenuous as the golden mist above the Arno.

Palimpsest (128)

H.D., as Helga Doorn in *Wing Beat*, 1927

He cared too much for writing. Words followed him, filled the pallid substance of his skull with fervour. Sometimes he had to shake his dark short curls in running water to wash the words out.

Hedylus (29)

Kenneth Macpherson, 1927–1929

But it is a privilege, in no small way, to stand beside just such rare type of advanced young creative intellectual. . . . Pro patria indeed, if that pro patria is a no-man's land, an everyman's land of such plausible perfection. Mr. Macpherson, like Mr. da Vinci is Hellenic in his cold detachment, his cool appraisal, his very inhuman insistence on perfection.

Borderline (13)

H.D., early 1930s

I wanted to dig down and dig out, root out my personal weeds, strengthen my purpose, reaffirm my beliefs, canalize my energies, and I seized on the unexpected chance of working with Professor Freud himself.

Tribute to Freud (91)

H.D., 1946

We are the keepers of the secret,
the carriers, the spinners

of the rare intangible thread
that binds all humanity

to ancient wisdom,
to antiquity

Trilogy (CP 522–23)

H.D. and Perdita Schaffner, Lugano, 1952

Am I reminded of happy release from pain and the fortunate auspices, predicted for my daughter who arrived in the vernal equinox, and at the high tide of the sun, at noon exactly? Surely the high tide of her stars brought fortune to me.

Advent (137)

H.D., by Bernhard Obrecht, 1956

why must I write?
you would not care for this,
but She draws the veil aside,

unbinds my eyes,
commands,
write, write or die.

Hermetic Definition (7)

H.D. and Bryher, *circa* 1959

when all the others, blighted, reel and fall,
your star, steel-set, keeps lone and frigid trist
to freighted ships baffled in wind and blast.

"To Bryher," *Palimpsest*

H.D., 1959–1960

I feel the lure of the invisible,
I am happier here alone
in this great temple,

with this great temple's
indecipherable hieroglyph

Helen in Egypt (21)

Selection from the Poem Biography

BARBARA GUEST

Three

An itch
              the width of an elbow
an urge
              really to "know"
when the flea entered the garment
anemonies
where were they picked?

Icy shadows
              grapes in the "goblets"
              the fabric ripped

An excellent "e" for evening
when the spicy shrieks sent out alarms,

              then a word like Egypt.

Five

Yet another day
among the boxes
                        what was the year of the prune
                        whose telephone rang in the flat?
Dizziness shared
a hint of disgrace amid the pines,

The card said, "William Blake,"
yet the notes were from another clime.

Birthdates absconding
I read the stars.

This one of mid-morning
weaving its plume from the sky,

Again the Angel descends.

Tomorrows begin to wither
the ashes form their ring
and voices whisper,

There's sobbing too
behind the arras

And nuttiness hits me
a sting like rivers
you forget in the rain
their flash.

       Then you see from the window
       the physical features —
       the bangs, the brow, the frown
       where it lingers on its arithmetic
       of cities, trading symbols

       The Archer, the Virgin, the Twins.

       Mutinies of celebrations
       like birds in aviaries
       or spies at the diaries,

              I read all that.

Eight

Biography a dubious route

  curate's disease
  the offhand way they plunge
  into the locker room

  subsidies for living,
  raven's wings shadowing the wall.

Deadly moon-struck

  weed-stuck
  gardens

the too calm sea.

Nine

A single seeming blinded object
  a sentence a voice
    the throat
then the rushing. Sound rushing dramatic
away from its disability
there's a note selective.

Passage without a pen
through the hurricane
  whorl shell Shade

Fictions dressed like water.

CHAPTER 4

Herself Delineated: Chronological Highlights of H.D.

LOUIS H. SILVERSTEIN

1886   Birth of H.D. (Hilda Doolittle) on September 10 in Bethlehem, Pennsylvania, to Charles Leander Doolittle (1843–1919), professor of astronomy at Lehigh University, and Helen Wolle Doolittle (1853–1927), a Moravian and formerly a teacher of music and art at the Moravian Seminary.

1886–95   Lives in Bethlehem; attends Moravian schools and assimilates Moravian history, culture, and religion, which later infuses her work, especially *The Gift, Trilogy, The Mystery,* and *Helen in Egypt.*

1895   Moves to Upper Darby, just outside of Philadelphia; father becomes professor of astronomy at the University of Pennsylvania and director of the Flower Observatory.

1901–2   Attends Miss Elizabeth Gordon's School (8th grade) in West Philadelphia.

1901   Meets Ezra Pound (1885–1972), a student at the University of Pennsylvania, in October at a fancy dress party at the Burd School in Philadelphia.

1902–5   Attends Friends' Central School in Philadelphia.

1905–8   Becomes engaged, then disengaged, to Ezra Pound, at least twice; Pound nurtures H.D.'s reading, introducing her to William Morris, Balzac, Ibsen, and the Mosher Press edition of *The Romance of Tristan and Iseult*; Pound composes poems to her which are bound up as "Hilda's Book"; these experiences are later described in *End to Torment* and fictionalized in *HER*.

1905　Meets William Carlos Williams (1883–1963), a medical student at the University of Pennsylvania, at a dinner hosted by Pound on April 9; Pound and Williams become frequent visitors at the Doolittle home.

　　　Graduates on June 16 from Friends' Central School; delivers an address at commencement entitled "The Poet's Influence."

1905–6　Attends Bryn Mawr College as a day student for three semesters; Marianne Moore (1887–1972) is a classmate; withdraws, possibly due to ill health, failing grades, and increasing involvement with Pound.

1908–9　Enrolls in the College Course for Teachers at the University of Pennsylvania.

1909–13　First prose publications in syndicated and Presbyterian papers.

1910　Meets Frances Josepha Gregg (1884–1941), a student at the Pennsylvania Academy of Fine Arts; writes poems to Gregg modeled on Theocritus; experiences intense passion for Gregg which is interrupted first by Gregg's brief liaison with Pound and later by Gregg's marriage to Louis Wilkinson; retains intense feelings for Gregg well into the 1930s; later fictionalizes this relationship in *HER*.

　　　Lives in Patchin Place, Greenwich Village, New York City, in the fall; attempts to earn living as writer.

1911　Sails for Europe on July 23 with Frances Gregg and her mother, Julia Gregg.

　　　Spends summer in Paris with the Greggs, sees Walter Rummel whom she met the previous year, and then resides in London where Pound has settled; the Greggs return to America; these experiences are later fictionalized in *Asphodel* and *Paint It To-Day*.

1911–13　Introduced to the literary and cultural circles frequented by Pound; meets F. S. Flint, Ford Madox Ford, Violet Hunt, Wyndham Lewis, Brigit Patmore, Olivia Shakespear, May Sinclair, W. B. Yeats, and Richard Aldington (1892–1962);

studies at the British Museum and travels in Europe, often accompanied by Aldington and sometimes also by Pound.

1912 Receives letter from Gregg announcing that she is to be married in April; the Wilkinsons return to Europe, stopping in London and inviting H.D. to join them on their honeymoon; she accepts but is stopped by Pound.

Goes to Paris in May, joined later by Aldington; meets Margaret Cravens (1881–1912) and is disturbed by her suicide on June 1, an experience which she later fictionalizes in *Asphodel*; learns of Pound's engagement to Dorothy Shakespear.

British Museum tea shop episode involving H.D., Pound, and Aldington occurs in September: Pound edits three of H.D.'s poems in accordance with evolving imagist principles and adds "Imagiste" to H.D.'s initials, then sends them to Harriet Monroe, editor of *Poetry*.

1912–13 Meets her parents in Genoa in October, then travels in Europe with them through July, joined by Aldington for most of the time; later associates her love for Aldington with their travels and courtship in Italy, especially Rome, Naples, Paestum, Amalfi, Capri, Venice, and Florence; meets Phyllis Bottome in Rome.

1913 First known publication of poems ("Hermes of the Ways," "Epigram," and "Priapus") in January in *Poetry*.

Meets John Cournos (1881–1966) and John Gould Fletcher (1886–1950).

Marries Richard Aldington on October 18 in London at the registry office in Kensington; her mother and Pound are witnesses; with marriage automatically becomes a British citizen.

1913–16 Resides in Kensington and Hampstead; writes and translates.

1914 *Des Imagistes: An Anthology* published; includes poems by H.D., Aldington, Pound, and others.

Begins friendship with D. H. Lawrence (1885–1930) and Amy Lowell (1873–1925) in July; meets Frieda Lawrence in August.

1915–17 Exchanges manuscripts with Lawrence with whom she has an intense cerebral relationship; Lawrence includes her in his plans for Ranamin, an ideal community which never materializes; the relationship is broken off by him later for various reasons, including his disapproval of her joining Cecil Gray in Cornwall and becoming pregnant.

Assists in collecting and selecting poems for the 1915, 1916, and 1917 volumes of *Some Imagist Poets: An Anthology*.

1915   Receives the Guarantors' Prize from *Poetry* for "The Wind Sleepers," "Storm," "Pool," "The Garden," and "Moonrise."

Birth of stillborn daughter on May 21.

Resumes contact in August with Marianne Moore who has submitted some poems to the *Egoist*, of which Aldington is an assistant editor; Moore remains an important friend, correspondent, and creative support for life; Moore later serves as H.D.'s literary agent in America during World War II.

Choruses from Iphigeneia in Aulis published in November as no. 3 of the *Poet's Translation Series*.

1916–17   Substitutes for Aldington for one year (June–May) at the *Egoist*; is succeeded by T. S. Eliot.

Primary residence is 44 Mecklenburgh Square, London; later fictionalizes experiences of this period in *Bid Me to Live*; certain events are also fictionalized by Aldington in *Death of a Hero*, by Cournos in *Miranda Masters*, and by Lawrence in *Aaron's Rod*.

1916   *Sea Garden* published.

Resides in Martinhoe, North Devon, from February through mid-July, then follows Aldington to Corfe Castle, Dorset, and returns to London (Mecklenburgh Square) in November.

Aldington enlists as a private in Devon in May, trains near Corfe Castle, is promoted to corporal in November, and is sent to France in December; while in Devon he has an affair with Flo Fallas.

1917   *The Tribute and Circe: Two Poems* published.

Receives Vers Libre Prize from the *Little Review* for "Sea Poppies."

Tendencies in Modern Poetry by Amy Lowell published which contains first critical assessment of H.D.'s poetry in book form.

Resides in London; goes to Derbyshire in July, then to Lichfield from September through November.

Lends her room in Mecklenburgh Square to the Lawrences from October 20 to November 30, after they are expelled from Cornwall, an experience fictionalized by Lawrence in *Kangaroo*.

Aldington returns from France in July, remains in England for officer's training until April 1918 when he returns to France, having received his commission as 2d lieutenant in November; while in England begins his affair with Dorothy Yorke.

1918   Resides in London until the end of March, then goes to live with Cecil Gray at Bosigran near Zennor, Cornwall; becomes pregnant while in Cornwall and later acknowledges Gray as the father of her child; returns to London in mid-August.

Gilbert Doolittle (H.D.'s brother) arrives in France in May; is killed in action on September 25 and buried in St. Mihiel Cemetery, Thiaucourt, France.

Meets Bryher (Annie Winifred Ellerman, 1894–1983) who calls on her with a friend at Bosigran on July 17; this event, which is later fictionalized in *Asphodel* and in Bryher's *Two Selves*, marks the beginning of their lifelong relationship, and this date later becomes one which they celebrate annually; this relationship initially (ca. 1919–23) is extremely intense and erotic but later evolves into a deeply committed and companionate bond which anchors their lives.

Begins correspondence with Bryher which continues for the rest of her life, later writing almost daily and sometimes even more frequently, whenever they are apart.

Informs Aldington of her pregnancy at the beginning of August; he is very ambivalent, sometimes expressing feelings of displacement and at other times supportive, offering advice and assistance.

Shares a cottage in Speen, Buckinghamshire, with a friend from Philadelphia, Margaret Snively Pratt, from September until the end of the year.

1919   Resides in London at Exeter House, 17 Montague Street, during January and February.

Meets Havelock Ellis and introduces Bryher to him.

Aldington returns to London in February after demobilization; Bryher attempts to assist him in finding employment as a writer.

Contracts the war influenza and later credits Bryher with saving her life.

Death of her father on March 2 in Pennsylvania.

Stays at St. Faith's Nursing Home from March to mid-April, with visits from Bryher, Aldington, Pound, and Patmore.

Frances Perdita Aldington is born on March 31 at noon.

Joins Aldington in mid-April at the Hotel du Littoral in London to resume marriage, but they separate within a few days and never live together again; Aldington tells her she must register the child as Gray's and then they will get a divorce, but she goes ahead and registers the child as Aldington's on May 6 and lives with the fear of reprisal for the next decade; consults a doctor who tells her to regard Aldington's behavior as shell shock; Aldington lives with Yorke for the next decade.

Goes to Cornwall and the Scilly Islands with Bryher in June and July; has "jelly-fish" and "bell-jar" experiences described in *Notes on Thought and Vision*; shows these *Notes* to Havelock Ellis and is disappointed by his lack of understanding.

1919–20   Resides at 16 Bullingham Mansions, Kensington, near Perdita who is at the Norland Nurseries.

1920   Travels to Greece and Corfu with Bryher from February through April; Havelock Ellis accompanies them to Athens; meets Peter Rodeck on the ship and is attracted to him but does not have an affair with him, an event recalled in *Advent* and fictionalized in *Hedylus* and *Palimpsest*; has "writing-on-the-wall" experience in Corfu at the Hotel Angleterre et Belle Venise, as described in *Tribute to Freud*.

Travels to America with Bryher and Perdita, arriving September 10; has reunions with Amy Lowell, Marianne Moore, and William Carlos Williams, who introduces them to Robert McAlmon (1896–1956).

1920–21   Moves on to California with Bryher and Perdita, joined by her mother; tries living and writing in Santa Barbara, Carmel Highlands, and Monrovia; returns to New York early in February.

1921–46   Alternates residences between Territet and Burier-La-Tour, Switzerland, where she lives with Bryher, and London, where she usually maintains her own flat; occasional trips to Paris, Berlin, Venice, etc., are interspersed throughout the pre–World War II years.

1921–25   Joined by her mother who lives and travels with them and looks after Perdita.

1921   *Hymen* published.

           Bryher marries McAlmon in New York on February 14.

           Returns to England at the end of February with Bryher, Perdita, and McAlmon.

           Responsible, with Bryher, for arranging with Harriet Shaw Weaver for the publication of Marianne Moore's first book, *Poems*, without Moore's permission or approval.

1922–27   Literary friendships and contacts include Djuna Barnes, Sylvia Beach, Mary Butts, Nancy Cunard, Norman Douglas, Adrienne Monnier, Dorothy Richardson, Gertrude Stein, and Alice B. Toklas.

1922–24   Resides, when in London, in Mayfair at the Washington Hotel.

1922   Travels with her mother and Bryher from February until April in Italy, Greece, and the Asia Minor coast; trip includes sailing past Lesbos and a stop at Constantinople.

1923   Travels with her mother and Bryher to Egypt by way of Italy from January through February; itinerary includes Cairo, Luxor, Karnak, and a cruise down the Nile; on February 2 they observe objects being carried from Tutankhamun's tomb; these experiences are later fictionalized in *Palimpsest*.

           Stays on Capri with Bryher from March until mid-April.

1924   *Heliodora and Other Poems* published.

1925   *Collected Poems of H.D.* published.

Spends June and July in London with her mother looking for a permanent flat; stays at 37 Park Mansions, Knightsbridge.

1925–32   London residence is 169 Sloane Street, Knightsbridge.

Interests in psychoanalysis and in aspects of the occult such as astrology, numerology, and tarot develop and deepen.

1926   *Palimpsest* published.

Meets Kenneth Macpherson (1902–71) in December through Frances Gregg.

1927–33   *Close Up* published by Bryher and Macpherson; includes poems and articles on film by H.D. during 1927–29.

1927–32   Period of relationship with Macpherson; experiences intense affair with him in 1927–28; his affairs with men after 1929 gradually draw him out of the resulting ménage consisting of H.D., Bryher, Perdita, and himself; his relationship with H.D. becomes more distant after 1932, and she turns for companionship to other young men such as Dan Bart, Robert Herring, Stephen Haden-Guest, and Eric Walter White; the experiences with Macpherson are fictionalized in *Narthex, Kora and Ka, The Usual Star*, and *Nights*.

1927   *Hippolytus Temporizes: A Play in Three Acts* published.

Makes her film debut in February in *Wing Beat*, filmed by Macpherson; begins acting in *Foothills*, which continues production into the following year.

Mother dies on March 21.

Leaving one marriage of convenience and entering another, Bryher divorces McAlmon in June and marries Macpherson on September 1; Bryher and Macpherson visit Sigmund Freud (1856–1939) in Vienna with Ellis' introduction.

1928   *Hedylus* published.

Perdita is adopted by Bryher and Macpherson on May 11.

Has abortion in November in Berlin.

1929   Visits Paris and sees Pound and Aldington, who has left Yorke
            and is now living with Brigit Patmore.

1930–31   Bryher and Macpherson build Kenwin, a Bauhaus-style villa,
            in the foothills above Lake Geneva at Burier-La Tour as a home
            for them, H.D., and Perdita.

1930   Stars with Paul Robeson in *Borderline*, a film produced by
            Macpherson in Switzerland; with Bryher, does substantial edit-
            ing of and montage for the film.

            Borderline (pamphlet) published.

1931   *Red Roses for Bronze* published.

            Undergoes psychoanalysis with Mary Chadwick in London at
            26 Tavistock Square; has twenty-four sessions between April
            13 and July 6.

1931–32   Has five psychoanalytic sessions with Hanns Sachs, Bryher's
            analyst since 1928.

1932–34   London residence is 26 Sloane Street, Knightsbridge; flat is
            decorated by Macpherson.

1932   Takes a Hellenic cruise with Perdita and visits Delphi for the
            first time in April.

            Hears in December that she has been accepted for three months
            of analysis with Freud on recommendation of Bryher and Sachs.

1933   In analysis with Freud in Vienna from March 1 through June
            12; leaves without finishing her analysis because of a bomb scare
            on the tracks of a tram on which she is riding.

1934–46   London residence in Flat 10, 49 Lowndes Square, Knights-
            bridge.

1934   *Kora and Ka* and *The Usual Star* published.

            Meets Silvia Dobson in February and invites her to join her in
            Venice for Easter; maintains contact and corresponds with her
            for the rest of her life.

Has a brief but severe breakdown in August after hearing of the death of J. J. Van der Leeuw, whose hour with Freud preceded her own.

Returns to Vienna to complete her analysis with Freud, beginning October 31 and ending on December 2; receives Freud's blessing to give informal "hours" to people, which she does for a few friends in 1935-36.

1935-50   Bryher publishes *Life and Letters Today*; contains poems, reviews, and articles by H.D., including the first publication of *Tribute to Freud* in 1945-46 and sections of *By Avon River* in 1947.

1935   *Nights* published.

1935-38   Continues psychoanalysis with Walter Schmideberg.

1936   *The Hedgehog*, illustrated by George Plank, published.

           Meets Muriel Rukeyser.

1937   *Euripides' Ion* (translation) published.

           Receives a letter in January from Aldington, requesting a divorce so that he can marry Netta Patmore, Brigit's daughter-in-law; initiates divorce proceedings in February; later Aldington asks for financial aid in order to hurry proceedings along so that his and Netta's child can be born legitimate.

1937-38   Travels with Bryher to America in December; stays mostly in New York City; also visits Bethlehem; meets Norman Holmes Pearson (1909-75); leaves for England January 14.

1938   Receives the Levenson Prize from *Poetry* for "Sigel XV" and "Calypso Speaks."

           Sees Aldington at her flat on June 9 when he asks her to pay for the divorce; obtains the final decree of divorce on June 22.

           Begins correspondence with May Sarton in October after reading *The Single Hound*; meets her in the summer of 1939.

           Death of Olivia Shakespear in October; sees Pound in London on November 17 when he comes to clear out his mother-in-law's apartment; never sees him again and, after 1939, does not correspond with him again until August 1948.

1939–61   Interest in the hermetic tradition intensifies and develops; key influences include Robert Ambelain's *Dans l'ombre des cathédrales* (1939) and Denis de Rougemont's *Love in the Western World* (1940); also reads extensively in their other writings, as well as those of Jean Chaboseau, and the tradition of the Kabbalah.

1939–46   Returns to London from Kenwin in November; remains there with Bryher until May 1946, with occasional trips to Cambridge, Kent, Cornwall, and Stratford-on-Avon; writes poetry and memoirs, reliving experiences of World War I and meshing them with those of World War II; literary friendships and contacts include Elizabeth Bowen, Walter De la Mare, John Masefield, Vita Sackville-West, Edith Sitwell, and Osbert Sitwell.

1941–46   Period of intensified interest in spiritualism; joins the Society for Psychical Research; meets Arthur Bhaduri in 1941 and participates in regular seances with him and his mother, May Bhaduri; meets and attends spiritualist lectures by Lord Hugh Dowding, including one on October 20, 1943; is influenced by Dowding's reports of communications through mediums with airmen and believes she receives messages herself from these deceased RAF pilots during seances; these experiences are fictionalized in *Majic Ring* and *The Sword Went Out to Sea*.

1943–45   Pearson based in London with the OSS; has regular Sunday evening suppers with H.D. and Bryher; later he becomes one of H.D.'s strongest supporters, serving in many roles, including adviser, agent, confidant, and editor; later, as her executor, he would strive to keep H.D.'s literary reputation alive and to assure that her unpublished works would be published in accordance with her wishes.

1943   Participates in "A Reading by Famous Poets . . ." at the Aeolian Hall in aid of the French in Great Britain Fund; attended by the queen and the two princesses.

          Has vision of a *héros fatal* on a Viking ship while in a seance on October 29, which later metamorphoses in *Helen in Egypt*.

1944   *The Walls Do Not Fall* and *What Do I Love?* published.

1945   *Tribute to the Angels* published.

         Believes she receives messages about the danger of atomic war-
         fare through table tapping from some of Dowding's RAF pilots
         in a seance on September 3; Dowding rejects these messages,
         questioning their validity and preferring his own later commu-
         nications from these pilots.

         Accepts invitation from Katharine McBride of Bryn Mawr Col-
         lege to give a series of lectures on poetry in 1946; plans later
         canceled because of illness.

1946   *The Flowering of the Rod* published.

         Suffers a major breakdown in the winter brought on by ill health
         (anemia and meningitis), the strain of World War II, her feel-
         ings of rejection by Dowding, and other factors.

         Taken by Dr. Dennis Carroll to Seehof, Privat Klinik Brunner,
         Küsnacht, near Zürich, as arranged by Bryher and Walter
         Schmideberg, and recovers in October but remains there
         through mid-November; treatment includes intravenously in-
         jected shock therapy.

1946–61 Period of intense correspondence with Pearson; resumes and
         maintains regular correspondence with Aldington; corresponds
         less frequently with McAlmon and Pound.

1946–55 Resides in hotels in Switzerland, alternating between Lausanne
         during the winter months and Lugano during the summer
         months; has frequent visits from Bryher; other visitors include
         Perdita, Pearson, Plank, and Schmideberg; literary friends and
         contacts include E. M. Butler and Herman Hesse.

1948–49 Reviews, reworks, and polishes unpublished manuscripts dur-
         ing what she refers to as her "sabbatical year."

1949   *By Avon River* published; this and all other publications through
         1972 are largely due to Pearson's efforts.

         Begins correspondence with Robert Duncan (1919–88), who is
         representative of the younger poets, including Robert Creeley,
         Allen Ginsberg, Robert Kelly, and Denise Levertov, who regard

her as a mentor; Duncan uses her as the significant medium of his own aesthetic philosophy in *The H.D. Book*.

1950   Perdita, who has settled in America, marries John Schaffner in June; has four children: Valentine (b. 1951), Nicholas (b. 1953); Elizabeth Bryher (b. 1956), and Timothy (b. 1960).

1951   Travels to New York in April to see her first grandchild.

1953   Undergoes operation for abdominal intestinal occlusions at the Clinique Cecil in Lausanne in January; leaves in March; returns in June for further treatment.

Travels to New York in April to visit the Schaffners.

Moves in June to the Klinik Brunner in Küsnacht where she stays until June 1954; meets and enters psychoanalytical consultation with Dr. Erich Heydt, the Klinik's "Oberarzt," who regards her as his colleague and friend.

1955   Makes tape recording of selections from *Helen in Egypt* during January and February at Pearson's request.

1956–61 Resides in Küsnacht at the Klinik Brunner.

1956   *Tribute to Freud* published.

Travels with Bryher to New York in September to visit the Schaffners; goes to New Haven to view the exhibition which Pearson has mounted in Yale's Sterling Memorial Library in honor of her seventieth birthday; journeys with Bryher and Pearson to Bethlehem.

Falls and breaks her hip at the Klinik Brunner in November; is taken to Klinik Hirslanden in Zürich where she remains through February 1957.

1957   *Selected Poems of H.D.* published.

1958   Receives the Harriet Monroe Memorial Prize from *Poetry* for "In Time of Gold," "Nails for Petals," and "Sometimes and After."

Takes oath of allegiance on September 13 in order to regain United States citizenship.

1959   Receives the Brandeis University Creative Arts Award for Poetry.

1960   *Bid Me to Live (A Madrigal)* published.

Receives a citation for distinguished service from Bryn Mawr College, the Longview Award for "Regents of the Night," and is the first woman to be given the Award of Merit Medal for Poetry of the American Academy of Arts and Letters, which she accepts in person.

Sees Richard Aldington at Küsnacht several times in March and April as well as his daughter, Catherine, whom she meets in September 1959.

Meets Lionel Durand in April; grants him an interview for *Newsweek*.

Travels to New York to attend the ceremony at the American Academy of Arts and Letters on May 25, where she meets St. John Perse, whose poetry she admires; sees the Schaffners, the Pearsons, Marianne Moore, and other friends; meets Robert Duncan and Denise Levertov; returns to Küsnacht in June.

Begins correspondence with Denise Levertov.

1961   *Helen in Egypt* published.

Moves to the Hotel Sonnenberg in Zürich after the Klinik Brunner is sold in April.

Suffers a stroke in June and is taken to the Roten Kreuz Spital in Zürich, then transferred to the Klinik Hirslanden; a copy of *Helen in Egypt* is placed in her hands by Bryher the day before she dies on September 27.

After cremation in Zürich on October 2, her ashes are flown to Bethlehem where they are interred in the family plot in Nisky Hill Cemetery on October 28.

This chronology is adapted from a work in progress detailing the events in H.D.'s life, a portion of which has been published in the *H.D. Newsletter* 2 (Winter 1988) under the title "Planting the Seeds."

CHAPTER 5

Dating H.D.'s Writing

SUSAN STANFORD FRIEDMAN

The chart below provides dates for the composition and publication of H.D.'s work, including volumes of poetry and translation, book-length poems, novels and novellas, shorter prose fiction assembled into volumes, short stories published in periodicals after 1913, film essays, volumes of personal/meditative essays, and memoirs. It includes published and un-published work, as well as texts that have been destroyed. It does not include the stories H.D. wrote and partially published between 1907 to 1913; her reading notebooks (e.g., for *Helen in Egypt*; on Dante); her brief diaries not prepared for publication (e.g., Paris 1912 diary; Lionel Durand 1960–61 diary); her signed and unsigned book reviews; periodi-cal publication of individual poems; and foreign editions or translations of her work.[1] Republication dates and partial publication information may be incomplete because of the numerous reprintings of H.D.'s work by small, avant-garde presses.

I have determined or estimated dates for the composition, destruction, submission, and rejection of manuscripts from the following sources: (1) dates recorded on manuscripts and published volumes; (2) H.D.'s dat-ing of her own writing in texts like *Autobiographical Notes, H.D. by Delia Alton, Advent, End to Torment, Thorn Thicket, Compassionate Friend-ship*, and *Hirslanden Notebooks*; (3) correspondence, especially letters to and/or from H.D., Bryher, Norman Holmes Pearson, Richard Aldington, John Cournos, Marianne Moore, George Plank, Robert McAlmon, Robert Herring, Viola Jordan, Silvia Dobson, etc.; (4) Louis Silverstein's remark-able *H.D. Chronology*, a work in progress. I have included information about manuscripts destroyed, submitted for publication, and rejected where I have come across such references, but I suspect that more infor-mation will come to light in the future. Question marks indicate uncer-tainty of dating. The chart reflects my best knowledge and estimates as of November 1989 and will undoubtedly need revision as more about H.D.'s life becomes known.

By the forties, H.D. regularly dated her manuscripts and published volumes. But as a note of caution, I would emphasize that she may have fictionalized some dates to give the work a favorable "natal" horoscope. She wrote in *Thorn Thicket*, for example, "I have dated the *Rose* 1948, and to *The Sword went out to Sea* that preceeded [*sic*] in [it?], 1947. I gave *The Sword* dates, Part I (Kusnacht, Lausanne), May 6, Professor Freud's birthday, and to Part II (Lausanne, Lugano), July 17, the annivery [*sic*] of the day that I met Bryher in Cornwall" (28).

The various noms de plume that appeared on H.D.'s manuscripts and publications are an important part of the composition of her texts because each name crystallized a different identity for the writer as she both made and was (re)made by each text. She used the name "H.D." for almost all her published works, with the exception of her pre-1913 stories published under the name Edith Gray; "Pontikonisi (Mouse Island)," by Rhoda Peter; *Nights,* by John Helforth; and "Ear-Ring," by D. A. Hill. A number of manuscripts carried other names on the title page: *Paint It To-Day,* by Helga Dart; *HER,* by Helga Doorn (H.D.'s film name); *Bid Me to Live (A Madrigal), Majic Ring, The Sword Went Out to Sea (Synthesis of a Dream), White Rose and the Red, H.D. by Delia Alton, The Mystery,* and *Magic Mirror,* by Delia Alton. Other manuscripts had no names on the title page, such as *Asphodel* and *Pilate's Wife.* H.D. was dissuaded from using the name "D. A. Hill" for *The Hedgehog* and "Delia Alton" for *Bid Me to Live.*[2]

TITLE	COMPOSITION	PUBLICATION
Sea Garden (poems)	1912–15 or 1916	1916, 1983
Choruses from Iphigeneia in Aulis (translation)	1913?	1916, 1919, 1925, 1983
Choruses from Iphigeneia in Aulis and the Hippolytus of Euripides (translation)	1913?	1919, 1925, 1983
Notes on Euripides, Pausanius, and Greek Lyric Poets (essays, translation)	1916?–18?, fall 1919, fall 1920	Portions: "People of Sparta": 1924; "Choruses from the *Bacchae*": 1931; prose in *Ion*: 1937; "The Wise Sappho": 1982
Notes on Thought and Vision (essay)	July 1919	1982
Hymen (poetry, with prose insets in "Hymen")	1916, 1918?–21	1921, 1925, 1983
Paint It To-Day (novel)	1921	Chaps. I–IV: 1986

TITLE	COMPOSITION	PUBLICATION
Asphodel (novel)	1921–22	———
Untitled "prose work" (three "long short stories" planned as a volume, to include: "Floriel"; "Behind Me a Sword"; "Beryl")	1922	Destroyed
Heliodora (poetry)	1916, 192?–24	1924, 1925, 1983
Collected Poems (poetry and translation)	1912–24	1925
Hippolytus Temporizes (verse drama)	1920, 1922, 1924, 1925	Portion: 1925; Whole: 1927, 1985
Palimpsest (story sequence/novel)		1926, 1968
"Secret Name"	spring 1923	
"Hipparchia" and "Murex"	1924–?	
"Pontikonisi (Mouse Island)" (story)	1924	1932
Niké (novel)	1924–?	Destroyed
Hedylus (novel)	1924–?	Portion: 1925; Whole: 1928, 1980
Pilate's Wife (novel)	1924, 1929, July–Aug. 1934	Submitted and rejected
The Hedgehog ("children's" novel)	1924, 1926–27, 193?	1936, 1988
HER (novel)[3]	1926, 1927?, 1930	1981
Close Up reviews (11 film review essays)	1927–29	4: 1927; 5: 1928; 2: 1929
Narthex (novella)	1927 or 1928	1928
The Usual Star (2 stories)		1934
"The Usual Star"	autumn 1928	
"Two Americans"	1930	1987
Borderline (essay)	1929 or 1930	1930
"Low Tide" (story or novella)	1931 or 1932	Destroyed
Red Roses for Bronze (poetry and translation)	1924–?	1931, 1983
Kora and Ka (includes 2 novellas)	July–Aug. 1930	1934
Kora and Ka		1978
Mira-Mare		
Nights (novella in two parts)		1935, 1986
"Prologue"	summer, Dec. 1934	
"Nights"	Aug.–Sept. 1931	
Euripides' Ion (translation with prose insets)	1916, 1919, summer 1934, Aug. 1935	1937, 1986
"Ear-Ring" (story)	?	1936
The Dead Priestess Speaks (poetry)	1931?–38?	Portions: 1931, 1932, 1933, 1937; Whole: 1983
The Moment (short story volume)	Jan. 1950	———
"The Moment"	1926	
"Jubilee"	1935	
"The Last Time"	1936	
"Hesperia"	1923, 1934, 1948	

TITLE	COMPOSITION	PUBLICATION
"AEgina"	1933	
"The Guardians"	1945	
The Seven or *Seven Stories*[4] (short story volume)	1960	
"Hesperia"	1924, 1934, 1948	
"AEgina"	1932	
"The Moment"	1926	
"Jubilee"	1935	
"The Last Time"	1935	
"The Death of Martin Presser"	194?	1965
"The Guardians"	1945–46	
Bid Me to Live (A Madrigal) (novel)	Feb. 5–Mar. 30 and July 27–Nov. 8, 1939; Autumn/ Winter 1947; Nov. 1948; Dec. 1949–June 1950	1960, 1983
Within the Walls (14 sketches)	summer 1940–spring 1941	1990
The Gift (autobiography)	1941; 1943; 1944	Portions: Chap. 3:
Chapters 1–6	1941?	1969; Chap. 1:
Chapter 7	1943	1981; Chap. 2:
Notes	June, July 1944	1986; Abridged edition: 1982
The Walls Do Not Fall (poetry, vol. 1 of *Trilogy*)	1942	1944, 1973, 1983
Majic Ring (novel)	1943, 1944, Apr. 1954	——
What Do I Love? (poetry)	1941, 1943, 1944	1944, 1983
Tribute to the Angels (poetry, vol. 2 of *Trilogy*)	May 17–31, 1944	1945, 1973, 1983
Writing on the Wall (essay-memoir, later titled *Tribute to Freud*)	Sept. 19–Nov. 2, 1944	1945–46, 1956, 1974, 1985
The Flowering of the Rod (poetry, vol. 3 of *Trilogy*)	Dec. 18–31, 1944	1946, 1973, 1983
By Avon River		1949, 1990
"Good Friend" (poem)	Apr. 23, Aug. 1945?	
"The Guest" (essay)	Sept. 19–Nov. 1, 1946	
The Sword Went Out to Sea (Synthesis of a Dream) (novel)		Submitted and rejected
Part I	Dec. 1946–May 6, 1947	
Part II	May–July 17, 1947	
White Rose and the Red	1947?, summer 1948	Submitted and probably rejected
Advent (journal-essay, later published in *Tribute to Freud*)	Dec. 1948	1974, 1985
H.D. by Delia Alton (journal-essay, titled *Notes on Recent Writing* by Norman Holmes Pearson)	Dec. 12, 1949–June 5, 1950	Portion: 1983; Whole: 1986

TITLE	COMPOSITION	PUBLICATION
Autobiographical Notes (3 chronologies and notes)	1949?	——
The Mystery (novel)		Chaps. 3, 14–19, 1976
Part I	1949	
Part II	1951	
Helen in Egypt (poetry with prose captions)		1961, 1974
"Pallinode"	Sept. 1952–winter 1952–1953	
"Leuké"	Aug. 1953–?	
"Eidolon"	Jan., Sept.–Oct. 1954	
prose captions	1955	
Magic Mirror (novel)	Jan. 1, 1955 or 1956–1956	——
Compassionate Friendship (journal-essay)	Feb. 18–Sept. 21, 1955	——
Selected Poems (poetry)	Selection and correction: 1956	1957
Hirslanden Notebooks (4 journals)		——
I	Jan. 26–Feb. 3, 1957	
II	n.d.	
III	Feb. 4–11, 1957	
IV	Oct. 1958, Feb. 1959, Apr. 1959	
Vale Ave (poetry)	spring 1957	Sections 5, 37: 1958; section 18: 1958; Whole: 1982
Sagesse (poetry, in *Hermetic Definition*)	June 9, 1957–winter 1957	Sections 1–10: 1958; Whole: 1972
End to Torment (essay-memoir)	Mar. 7–July 13, 1958	1979
Winter Love (Espérance) (poetry, in *Hermetic Definition*)	Jan. 3–Apr. 15, 1959	Portion: 1969; Whole: 1972
Thorn Thicket (journal-essay)	Jan. 1–Oct. 27, 1960	——
Hermetic Definition (poetry, in *Hermetic Definition*)		Pirated edition: 1971; authorized edition:
I	Aug. 17–Sept. 24, 1960	1972
II	Nov. 1–Dec. 24, 1960	
III	Jan. 24–Feb. 19, 1961	

NOTES

This chronology is an updated version of "H.D. Chronology: Composition and Publication of Volumes," first published in the *H.D. Newsletter* 1 (Spring 1987): 12–15 and reprinted in *Sagetrieb* 6 (Fall 1987): 51–56.

1 For H.D.'s periodical publications, see Boughn; Bryer and Roblyer. See the Selected Bibliography in this volume for a list of H.D.'s unpublished manuscripts and papers.
2 I discuss the formation and significance of these names at length in *Penelope's Web*.
3 The manuscript is dated in H.D.'s hand as "about 1927," with the "about" crossed out. But *Autobiographical Notes* records as unpublished work for 1926 *Asphodel* and *HER*. A letter of May 14, 1930, from H.D. to Bryher notes that "pages of HER back and am working on that."
4 *The Moment* and *The Seven* (or *Seven Stories*) are basically the same collection, but they were conceived as volumes at different times. *The Moment*, with six stories, was drawn together in 1950 (*H.D. by Delia Alton* 208). *The Seven*, with the addition of "The Death of Martin Presser" to the same six stories, was formulated in 1960 (*Thorn Thicket* 35-37). The dates H.D. provided for the stories differ slightly (see also *H.D. by Delia Alton* 181, 183).

WORKS CITED

Boughn, Michael. "The Bibliographic Record of H.D.'s Contributions to Periodicals." *Sagetrieb* 6 (Fall 1987): 171–94.
Bryer, Jackson R., and Pamela Roblyer. "H.D.: A Preliminary Checklist." *Contemporary Literature* 10 (Autumn 1969): 632–75.
Friedman, Susan Stanford. *Penelope's Web: Gender, Modernity, H.D.'s Fiction* (New York: Cambridge UP, 1990).
Silverstein, Louis H. *The H.D. Chronology*, work in progress.

CHAPTER 6

A Relay of Power and of Peace: H.D. and the Spirit of the Gift

ADALAIDE MORRIS

Three quirks in H.D.'s life have puzzled her readers and resisted the explanatory efforts of her biographers. When judged by contemporary customs, the anomalies in her handling of money, her manipulation of her writing signature, and her management of motherhood appear at best odd, at worst suspicious or even pernicious. Our customs, embedded in a capitalist ethics of having, tending, and augmenting, appear to have little to do with the procedures and beliefs that inform H.D.'s life and work, procedures and beliefs that are, I will argue, much more closely aligned with a different theory of social and spiritual organization. It is not the ethos of an individualistic market economy but the spirit of the gift that gives H.D.'s life and thought its distinctive structure.

The gift economy received its classic elaboration in the work of the anthropologist Marcel Mauss, who first discerned the extent to which primitive societies are organized by obligations to give, receive, and reciprocate.[1] For Mauss, the significance of gift exchange is its creation and affirmation of a social link between gift partners, a link that distributes power and generates peace. Mauss's most striking example is the Pacific island Kula ring, a circular route along which the island tribes pass red shell necklaces clockwise and white shell bracelets counterclockwise. As the gifts travel along the ring, their motion is beyond the individual ego: each bearer is a part of the group and each donation is an act of social faith. This paradigmatic example of gift exchange collapses the precise distinctions so carefully elaborated by capitalist economists, for each gift, as Mauss explains, "is at the same time property and a possession, a pledge and a loan, an object sold and an object bought, a deposit, a mandate, a trust; for it is given only on condition that it will be used on behalf of, or transmitted to, a third person."[2] In the moment of transfer, the self flows toward union with others in a community constituted by reciprocal acts of giving.

In the cultures Mauss describes, gift giving is a wide, enduring, fundamental social contract, an exchange not only of goods, wealth, and property but of "courtesies, entertainments, ritual, military assistance, women, children, dances, and feasts." This system of *total prestations*[3] seems a far cry from the social organization of Pennsylvania, London, and Switzerland, the sites of H.D.'s life. I will argue, however, that H.D.'s handling of three of the commonplace relay points of twentieth-century life — the circulation of money, a name, a child — opens into a larger spiritual economy that provides a ground for the rituals that center her poems, novels, and autobiographical tributes.

Money is our customary medium of exchange, but H.D.'s attitude toward it was consistently eccentric. Though she herself came from a comfortable family, through her association with Bryher she was in touch with one of the largest fortunes in Europe, riches amassed by Bryher's father, Sir John Ellerman, who controlled one of England's greatest shipping fleets, vast holdings in British and continental real estate (including hundreds of acres of London property), the bulk of shares in the London *Times* and Associated Newspapers, and major financial and editorial interest in several leading London magazines. In the 1950s, H.D. had, by Barbara Guest's reckoning, several million dollars in the bank, the fruit of large settlements from Bryher and a family inheritance wisely invested by her brother Harold, yet she lived in modest hotels, ate meagerly, and considered cigarettes an extravagance.[4]

Why did H.D. virtually ignore her money? The interpretation that has tempted H.D.'s biographers is that she thereby bound herself to Bryher in a reciprocal pathology. Janice S. Robinson suggests that Bryher bought not only her two husbands of convenience, Robert McAlmon and Kenneth Macpherson, but also H.D. For her, Bryher was an active, even tyrannical partner demanding allegiance in return for support, so that, for example, H.D.'s copious, tender, full letters to Bryher during her analysis with Freud become extorted documents: "Bryher was paying for the analysis," Robinson explains, "and she demanded a firsthand account of the proceedings."[5] Guest's parallel interpretation depicts H.D. as the passive, dependent partner in the exchange, a woman who "had the mentality of one to whom things are given, but are not earned, nor even rightfully inherited."[6]

These melodramatic explanations depend on the terminology of market exchange — paying, accounting, earning — and their unease derives from

the extension of market practices into the personal sphere.[7] When we look
at the forty-two years of correspondence between H.D. and Bryher, however, we find something quite different: the record of a continuous, large,
vibrant exchange of news, enthusiasm, interest, poems, books, suggestions, irritations, and affection, with very little attention on H.D.'s part
to Bryher's financial arrangements. When she receives a check, she files
it away; when she receives a settlement, she seems mute and discomfited.[8]
The record seems to verify H.D.'s assertion to Norman Holmes Pearson
that she was unlike those who did, in fact, prey on Bryher: "When I met
her first — a little thing, — all tense, dressed like a princess, buns over her
ears — she said to me 'you're the first person who treats me like a human
being. Everyone else looks at me as though they saw just over my head
a funnel out of which pours gold coins.' And I said, 'yes but you should
meet my friends, they're not like that.' But they were like that."[9]

If H.D.'s disinterest in money is a constant, so, in a parallel instance,
is her disregard of her given name. Authors' names are the currency of
accountability, the signatures that stand for their creativity in the same
way paper money stands for value. Though H.D. cherished her writing,
she never signed it, published or unpublished, with her given name. The
early stories appeared under the names "J. Beran" and "Edith Gray," the
poems under the rubric Pound designed, "H.D., Imagiste," and then simply
"H.D." She signed autobiographical novels from the 1920s "Helga Dart"
or "Helga Doorn," fiction from the 1920s and 1930s "Rhoda Peter," "D. A.
Hill," or "John Helforth," and the late prose, including the novel *The
Sword Went Out to Sea*, the text she considered "the reward, the crown
of her achievement, her achievement itself,"[10] "Delia Alton."

The augmentation of a name, of, say, Hilda Doolittle, is an individualistic gesture: the benefits of labor collect and accrue in the name that over
time becomes one's register, record, and reputation. Several explanations
for H.D.'s array of pseudonyms are possible, even plausible. Caution is
one. In a homophobic culture, even before *The Well of Loneliness* trial
in 1928, it was prudent to mask or suppress lesbian material like H.D.'s
unpublished autobiographical novel of 1921, *Paint It To-Day*, signed in
typescript "Helga Dart." Similarly, in a rational and materialistic society,
authors of stories like the psychic extravaganza "Pontikonisi (Mouse
Island)" (1924), which H.D. signed "Rhoda Peter," risk the label of crack-
pot or crank. Though she did suppress the lesbian elements of her autobiography, however, H.D. in her early poetry openly collaborated with
Sappho[11] and freely conjured old and strange gods. However sanctioned
by her classical subject matter, the territory H.D. claimed as her own was
from the first marginal and suspicious.

It might be argued that H.D.'s carefully tended hieroglyphic signature, the figure she termed her "writing signet or sign-manual,"[12] simply substitutes for her given name. As Susan Stanford Friedman maintains, however, this signature was valued precisely because it was without gender, nationality, chronology, or biography.[13] It was an objective correlative for her poetry, as apparently impersonal, transparent, and hard as the verse reviewers loved to call "crystalline."[14]

The word "crystalline" suits the taut early poetry but not the experimental prose signed with other names. The various signatures for these manuscripts participate in the task Friedman finds central to all the prose: "self-creation through the construction of various personae who embodied in coded forms various parts of H.D.'s own life."[15] "Rhoda Peter," thus, was the part of H.D. that mirrored Peter Rodeck, the man whose manifestation sparked the "Pontikonisi" experience, and Helga Dart, like many other of H.D.'s pseudonyms (and titles), expanded the seed crystal "H.D." by following out one possible vector of the initials. Throughout her life, H.D. used her signature not to fix but to extend and disperse her identity.

Both money and a name have market value: we use them to purchase commodities and muster credit. In ignoring her money and rewriting her name, H.D. indicates her allegiance to another economy, an economy that also seems to operate in some of her parenting decisions. Though she was a loving mother to the child conceived with Cecil Gray after separation from Richard Aldington and born almost at the cost of her life, she shared her daughter, first informally, then legally, with Bryher.[16]

A child is a soul we bring into life, a financial, legal, and moral responsibility, and — like money and a name — a force that extends our identity, power, and reach into the future. That H.D. placed her child within a much wider, more rarefied economy is suggested from the first by the name she gave her: Frances Perdita. As Frances, she returns to H.D. her lost companion Frances Gregg; as "Perdita," the lost one, child of Queen Hermione in Shakespeare's *The Winter's Tale*, she is the baby lost in H.D.'s 1915 stillbirth and now found again.[17] The story that informs this circulation from absence back into presence or from death back into life is the myth of Kore's intermittent return to Demeter, a myth that reinforces our sense that a child is a gift bestowed by larger powers. This lesson is central to H.D.'s fictional recreations of her child's conception, all of which portray the apparent father as a veil for the true seed and source, the "Father who art in Heaven," usually named as the sun god Helios/Apollo.[18] "God was the lover and the beloved," H.D. summarizes in *Asphodel*,[19] and his gift is a child who is a visible token of the tie between heaven and earth.

A child is, of course, less ethereally, a being that bonds those who participate in its care. For H.D., the child was never primarily hers, much

less Gray's or Aldington's, but rather the center of the group Rachel Blau
DuPlessis has called her "sufficient family."[20] In naming her daughter for
Frances Gregg and passing her on to Bryher, H.D. bound past and present
together and firmed her new alliance with Bryher by giving Bryher responsibility for the child. When Bryher married H.D.'s lover, Kenneth
Macpherson, Macpherson took the place of the father in this unconventional but tenacious family of four.[21] In many groups outside the white
middle-class hegemonic norm, child–keeping is a shared responsibility,
part of the flux and elasticity of kinship networks. The adults who cared
for Perdita (including, variously, Bryher and her parents, H.D.'s mother
and aunt Laura, Kenneth Macpherson, and Silvia Dobson) constitute
H.D.'s chosen kin.[22]

In one of Perdita Schaffner's superb essays on her childhood, she notes
that H.D. "was intensely maternal — on an esoteric plane" (see above,
p. 4). The level on which H.D. consented to motherhood is, like that on
which she conducted her financial and authorial affairs, abstracted from
the drive that leads us to hold and hoard those things we mark as "ours."
The choices she made suggest that throughout her life H.D. had little sense
of property as we know it. She seems to operate within another economy.

Two parables from *Tribute to Freud* adumbrate some important features
of this economy. The first, from *Advent*, is the story of a trick exchange;
the second, from *Writing on the Wall*, is a tale of a true one. In juxtaposition, they suggest a theme that runs throughout H.D.'s thinking: the
rift between a market economy that works through reason and egotism
and a gift economy animated by imagination and love.

In *Advent*, following a trail of associations from the statue of Pallas
Athene on Freud's desk through the bust in Poe's "Raven" to the cryptic
analyst huddling like an old owl behind the couch, H.D. recalls "a special
gift" from her father. In his study was a large white snow-owl under a
bell jar. Like a hero in training, the child asks the wise father to give her
his owl, for, perhaps, if he is Zeus, the all-powerful one, she could be
Pallas Athene, born from his head with her sigil, the owl. Yes, Professor
Doolittle replies, the owl is hers, hers forever. Announcing that he is not
an Indian giver and won't ask for it back, he adds a rider that reveals
him instead to be a Yankee trader: he gives her the owl on the condition
that it stay where it is (*Tribute to Freud* 124–25).

A gift economy, as Lewis Hyde points out, is precisely the economy
of Indian giving, the opposite of what might be called "white man keeping."[23] White men keepers remove property from circulation. Like Professor Doolittle and his ancestors, the Puritan fathers who fought with
Indians (*Tribute to Freud* 34), they bargain shrewdly and lay up treasures.
Indian givers, in contrast, pass the gift along: it crosses the boundary

between two parties, and in time it or its equivalent is expected to return. If boundaries are unbreached, no one is richer or poorer, no change occurs. As the parable emphasizes, the gift that does not move is not a gift.

The second parable is the story of a cluster of gardenias H.D. sends "to greet the return of the Gods," the arrival in London of Freud's collection of Greek and Egyptian antiquities, Chinese and Oriental treasures, shipped after his flight from Vienna in 1938. Significantly the note is unsigned, but Freud recognizes the giver and in his acknowledgment puts his finger on the key difference between the two economies: what H.D. calls Gods, he notes, " 'other people read: Goods' " (*Tribute to Freud* 11).

The gardenias accomplish a wish framed five years earlier. Recalling his memory of gardenias in Rome, she had scoured Vienna for gardenias for his birthday; not finding them, she gave him nothing. Though she later sent money to a friend in Vienna to find gardenias, her friend heard that Freud liked orchids — " 'people always ordered orchids' " (*Tribute to Freud* 9) — and sent orchids in H.D.'s name. This, too, for H.D., was nothing.

The gift of gardenias so deeply satisfies H.D. because it is a real gift. Unlike the stationary owl, it moves; it comes from love, not calculation; and it is intimate: because Freud had given her the moment in Rome when, he told her, " 'even *I* could afford to wear a gardenia' " (*Tribute to Freud* 9), she could trade not in the conventional token of orchids but in the currency of his desire. But the main point is that the gift entails gods, not goods, that it has a spiritual dimension suggested by two fissures characteristic of the gift economy: the gap in time between the impulse and its accomplishment and the gap opened between herself and Freud by the third term of this exchange, the figure of the returning antiquities.

The story of the gardenias is the initial gesture of H.D.'s *Tribute to Freud*, and it stands in the position of the larger gift to follow: the composition of the tribute itself, completed ten years after H.D.'s second series of sessions with Freud ended in December 1934. The interval between the analysis and H.D.'s tribute is crucial because, unlike Professor Doolittle's, Freud's gift was transformative. The fairy-tale scripts that fill *Tribute to Freud* work because the story H.D. is telling fits the folktale paradigm of the hero in training who asks the master for wisdom and receives a threshold gift, a gift that opens a passage from one state into another. The transfer of the gift from the full to the empty place creates an imbalance, and a stretch of time must intervene before we can right the balance by passing the gift along. In the interval between the moment a gift comes to us and the moment we release and forward it, we suffer what Hyde calls "the labor of gratitude," the struggle to rise to the level of the gift and integrate it with our own vision so that we can give it away again.[24] H.D.'s struggle with Freud's fundamental presuppositions is her work to carry his ideas further, work conducted in the period marked by the gift of gardenias.[25]

The second interval is the space opened in the exchange by the figure of the gods. Gift exchanges characteristic of our culture generally move in reciprocal circuits of two: I give my friend x, she gives me y, and we each privately wonder whether our gifts are commensurate, whether x could be said to equal y. Here giving slides toward bartering, a commodity exchange in which it is important to be precise and even canny. In the exchanges characteristic of a gift culture, however, not only are the bestowals not simultaneous or even predictably related in time but before the return donation the gift leaves the boundary of the ego and circles into mystery.

Lewis Hyde offers an example that clarifies this transit. Maori hunters in New Zealand give a portion of their kill to priests who prepare the birds at a sacred fire, eat a few of them, and return the rest as a gift to the forest. In reciprocating the forest's gift to the tribe, the priests assure continued abundance, but, more important, their presence in the gift exchange opens the circle beyond a simple give-and-take between hunters and forest and moves the transaction from the realm of barter into the realm of the sacred. This hunting ritual may seem exotic, yet, as Hyde points out, it has the same structure as the Old Testament ritual of first fruits.[26] The inclusion of the priests in the cycle redirects gratitude beyond the personal, the temporal, and the quantifiable and makes exactly the point Freud understood H.D. to make: the crux of the matter is gods, not goods.

The middle term in the parable of the gardenias, Freud's collection of antiquities, functions like the priests in the Maori and Hebrew rituals to route the exchange through the sacred. This routing aligns the gift of gardenias, the final interchange with Freud recorded in *Tribute*, with the first, the moment when H.D. entered Freud's study and gazed not at him but at his statues — " 'You,' " he grumbled, " 'are the only person who has ever come into this room and looked at the things in the room before looking at me' " (98). Freud no doubt noted that the gardenias greeted not him but his antiquities, but H.D.'s point remained: for her, the best part of Freud was contained in the treasures of which he was "part and parcel" and which represented "another region of cause and effect, another region of question and answer" (97, 99).

This region of cause and effect anchors H.D.'s complex elaboration of the concept of the gift. Throughout her career, the gift stands in opposition to the marketplace, providing a site from which H.D. could critique and attempt to correct the relations of a capitalist economy that she

believed could only result in what she came to call a "death-cult": the
materialist, strife-ridden, masculinist "iron-ring of the war."[27]

There is no evidence that H.D. ever read the work of Marcel Mauss.
The listing of her library at the Beinecke, however, contains many texts
that align her concerns with his: for example, tomes on the history of
religion and mythology, archeological investigations, and explorations of
the customs of archaic societies. Where Mauss drew on field reports from
places like Samoa, New Zealand, Melanesia, the Andaman Islands, and
Northwest America, H.D.'s interests were in the arc she saw running from
Egypt to Crete into classical Greece, in her ancestral Moravians, and in
the Northeast American Indian tribes that interacted with them. Despite
the differences in the cultures they studied, there are remarkable similari-
ties in the patterns Mauss and H.D. perceive and in their admiration for
them, admiration quickened by an animus against the marketplace and
what they believe to be its inevitable moral and political consequences.
As E. E. Evans-Pritchard points out in his introduction to *The Gift*,
Mauss was Emile Durkheim's nephew and most distinguished pupil. Born
in 1872, he was of the generation immediately preceding H.D.'s, and his
life, like hers, was deeply afflicted by the two world wars. In World War
I, as H.D.'s artistic circle dissolved and dispersed, Mauss lost almost his
entire intellectual group, the team of brilliant younger scholars trained
by Durkheim. During World War II, while H.D. suffered the bombing
of London, Mauss inhabited Nazi-occupied Paris where he not only lost
some of his closest colleagues and friends but, being Jewish, experienced a
terror that contributed to his mental collapse, like H.D.'s, after the war.[28]
Mauss was not only a sociologist but a Sanskrit scholar and a historian
of religions, just as H.D., in her way, was a student of Greek and a
passionate investigator of spiritual and mystical traditions. Their theories
of the gift, consequently, have an archaic and spiritual cast antagonistic
to the assumptions and procedures of modern materialist economies.
Though H.D. lacked the intellectual training that sparked Mauss's brilliant formulations, her Moravian upbringing provided her with a lived
connection to a culture his concepts illuminate. This overlap becomes
apparent in the way a crucial feature of the gift economy, the Maori notion
of the *hau*, passes through ceremonies like the Moravian love feast into
H.D.'s own poetry and poetics.
Marshall Sahlins identifies Mauss's master concept as "the indigenous
Maori idea *hau*, introduced . . . as 'the spirit of things and in particular
of the forest and the game it contains.' "[29] For Mauss, the *hau* is the god
in the goods. It is alive and active, a part of the donor that travels along

with the thing given and that eventually calls the gift or its equivalent back toward its source. The birds the hunters take contain the forest's *hau*, just as, in another register, Freud's analysis of H.D. might be said to contain his. Not to return the gift poisons the recipient and destroys the life-sustaining gift cycle.[30]

Returning to Mauss's Maori source text, however, Sahlins makes a crucial observation. If the *hau* were simply a spirit that compels return, gift exchange would require just two stations; the Maori explanation involves three, the *hau* appearing first in the transition from the second to third. The introduction of the third station demonstrates what for Sahlins is the key fact of gift exchange: the yield, power of increase, or augmentation of the gift as it moves from station to station.[31] The birds the priests return to the forest are more elaborate and complex than the initial gift. This increase is at once environmental (a nourishing of the ecosystem), spiritual (an affirmation of a mutually sustaining connection with nature and the gods), and social (a community bonding).[32] For the Maori, these three aspects overlap and fuse, each implicating and enabling the others. The *hau* of the gift binds the material, spiritual, and social realms that a market economy compartmentalizes and sets into opposition.

Modeled on the early Christian *agapae*, the original Moravian love feasts celebrated not only religious and social occasions but also the start or finish of most economic enterprises: the laying of a cornerstone for an oil mill, for example, or the harvesting of a crop of wheat. These simple meals accompanied by hymn singing passed the yield of the gift back to its source, enacting the *hau* as at once an economic, social, and spiritual increase. The food shared by the worshippers or workers nourished them, affirmed their connections to the land and the Lord, and situated their community within the mutual obligations of giving, receiving, and reciprocating.[33] The *hau* that circulates through a gift economy represents, for Mauss, H.D., and Hyde, the increase of the life force, a circulation of power and affirmation of peace dynamically opposed to the competitive and even death-dealing dynamics of a market economy.

The contrast between the two economies is severe, perhaps, as Mauss, Hyde, and H.D. draw it, too severe, since gift rituals, like turn-of-the-century potlatches, can become extravaganzas of competition and conflict, while even the most wholehearted capitalist economy sustains elements of gift exchange. Each of these thinkers, however, was profoundly moved by the events in their lives—the two world wars and, in Hyde's case, the Vietnam War—toward the conclusion that the bonds a gift economy creates are shattered in a market economy. As they understand it, gift exchange moves from reverence toward abundance and alliance, while market exchange moves from exploitation toward scarcity and conflict. This sequence leads them into their summary oppositions: for Mauss the will for peace against the will to war; for Hyde, the forces of *eros*, "the principle of attraction, union, involvement," against the forces of *logos*, "reason and logic in general, the principle of differentiation in particular"; and for H.D., the animating impulses of *eros* and *eris*, love and strife.[34]

Binary oppositions tend to seem most clear and compelling at the borderlines, the places where two systems intersect or collide. The borderline is the place of maximum difference, maximum tension, and maximum potential for change, and it is here, at the flashpoint of opposition, that H.D. situated many of her poems and much of her life. Her choice to form an alliance with an heir to one of capitalism's great fortunes and yet ignore her own money and live as closely as possible by the dictates of a gift economy could not have seemed as odd to her as it does to her biographers. Not only was it a site for the oppositions she found fruitful but it replicated the intersections of her childhood. The circumstances of H.D.'s birth placed her precisely at the juncture of the two economies: the coexistence in Bethlehem, Pennsylvania, of the Moravian religious community and the Bethlehem Steel Corporation.

Bethlehem was founded by Moravians in 1741. The church, schools, and community buildings that were the scene of H.D.'s early life constitute, according to one architectural historian, "the purest expression of Moravian thought."[35] Moravian doctrine emerges so clearly in architecture because it is less an abstract theology or dogma than a design for living. At its center is the binding power of love Hyde identifies as the heart of the gift culture, an *eros* that determined not only Moravian rituals of connection like the love feast and kiss of peace but also the daily arrangements of their economy.[36]

The economy that formed the town was codified in the Brotherly Agreement of 1754, a pact whose name recalls the church's 1457 founding as the Jednota Bratrska (later the Unitas Fratrum). This contract obligated its members to give, receive, and reciprocate, made no distinction between the material and the spiritual, and, with the sweep of H.D.'s later decisions, also ruled out the key institutions of bourgeois capitalism: private enterprise and the patriarchal nuclear family. The entire community was considered one family, headed by Christ and his bride the Church and embracing all church members. All Moravians worked for the community which, in turn, housed, fed, clothed, and supported them.

Extending along Church Street, where H.D. grew up, were the Church, the *Gemeinhaus*, the First Single Brothers' House, the Sisters' House, and the Widows' House. The *Gemeinhaus* was the settlement's first permanent structure, containing the kitchens and communal dining hall, the chapel, and a dormitory divided into rooms for the groups the Moravians called Choirs (girls, boys, older girls, older boys, single sisters, single brothers, married women, married men, widows, and widowers). Though provisions were made for them to meet privately once a week, in the early years couples lived apart.[37] Children entered the Choirs at eighteen months, were separated by gender at five or six years, were educated and guided into marriage by the Choirs, and inhabited separate structures, buildings like the Sisters' and Widows' Houses on H.D.'s street.

Among other early buildings were a waterworks, a slaughterhouse, oil and grist mills, a tannery, and a blacksmith, locksmith, and nailsmith,[38] structures that indicate the town's function as a center into which the surrounding population funneled materials and from which they took finished articles. By 1759 Bethlehem was capable of sustaining thirteen hundred inhabitants and a corps of missionaries that traveled among the Indians.[39] Though the Brotherly Agreement was abrogated in 1762,[40] the successful meshing of the material and the spiritual continued across the century. It was not until 1844, some forty years before H.D.'s birth, that the settlement and the church were formally separated, their property reallocated, finances decentralized, and communal responsibility for missionary work redefined.[41]

Even after the 1840s, however, the Moravians struggled to preserve the semblance of a gift economy. Wanting to benefit from the rich manufacturing resources of the Lehigh Valley and yet keep their village free of its clatter and its culture, they struck a compromise. To house the blast furnaces, factories, railroads, and secular workers of the industrial economy, they organized a new town across the river, a settlement without Moravians.[42] In South Bethlehem was the Union Paper Bag Machine Company, which produced the paper bags invented by H.D.'s grandfather, the Reverend Francis Wolle, and the Bethlehem Rolling Mill and Iron Company, ancestor of Bethlehem Steel, established by Francis' brother Augustus.[43]

The split between the religious and secular communities, inscribed in the landscape that surrounded H.D., was written as well in the generations of her family. The Wolles were direct descendants of the Unitas Fratrum, part of the leadership of the Moravian community, but the family also included prominent members of the industrial sector. The contrasting pairs begin with her pious and scholarly grandfather Francis and his brother Augustus, reduplicate in Francis' sons J. Fred Wolle, who established the famous Moravian Bach Choir and Festival, and his brother Hartley, a businessman, and reappear in H.D. herself and her brothers Harold and Melvin, both wealthy and successful merchants.[44]

It is not surprising, then, that the two economies collide throughout H.D.'s work, not only in the debate in *Tribute to Freud* over whether

Freud's small statues are "goods" or "gods" or in the quarrel in *Trilogy* over whether poets are "useless" or crucial but in the dramatic juxtapositions of poems like "Calypso" and in the diatribes that end *Sea Garden* and the long sequence H.D. called "The God."

"Calypso"[45] is an angry poem with a taut dialogic structure. Here, Odysseus' words, stripped of the adulatory matrix of Homer, Joyce, or Pound, become merely his version of the encounter and, as Susan Stanford Friedman has noted, "most probably for the first time in cultural history, 'Callypso Speaks' her own story."[46] The variance between the two versions, however, makes the interspersed speeches less a dialogue than two starkly disjunctive monologues. Calypso speaks from a sacred gift economy, Odysseus from the smug and cunning individualism of a market economy.

In the usual recitation of the episode, Calypso is a nymph who welcomes Odysseus to her exotic island, offers her love, and then, after eight years, compelled by the gods, sadly releases him to continue his journey. The two parts of H.D.'s poem elide the story's middle: Calypso's entanglement in the "romantic thralldom" Rachel Blau DuPlessis identifies as a consistent strain in H.D.'s work.[47] This erasure of the conventional story forces our attention to two parallel moments of rapacity: Odysseus' intrusion into Calypso's island paradise and his departure. In the first, he hunts her down and rapes her; in the second, he counts, stashes, and sails away with the magic gifts bestowed by a goddess whose powers regenerate and restore life.

Both parts focus on a disjunction. The first occurs when Calypso identifies herself as "priestess, occult, nymph, and goddess," an important station in the gift economy, but Odysseus can only see her as a commodity. Reasoning through a familiar syllogism, he proclaims that because "a nymph is a woman" and "all men are fathers, / kings and gods," therefore, "you will do as I say." In H.D.'s rewriting, however, he is neither king nor god but a barbarian, an "obscene force" who employs the sort of sexual magic conventionally assigned to Circe to debase her and the culture she embodies.

The second disjunction provides the force of the poem's conclusion. Here H.D. intersperses two rapt and antithetical speeches: Odysseus' litany enumerating Calypso's magic gifts and Calypso's curse marshaling all the forces in her command — sand, winds, waves, and skies — to batter and blight him. The ironically juxtaposed refrains, his "she gave" against her "he took," reiterate the pattern of their interaction.[48] He has treated her gifts as his capital, misused their *hau*, and broken the gift cycle, thus earning the full resonance of Calypso's charge: "man is a devil, / man will not understand." In making this charge by rewriting Odysseus' first appearance in the epic, H.D. suggests that such egotistical profit taking is a primal sin, the evil that exiles him from a fundamentally harmonious and nurturing universe.

"Cities," the final poem of *Sea Garden*, and "The Tribute," conclusion of the 1925 sequence H.D. called "The God," focus on the terrain of exile: the urban, industrial marketplace. These are harsh, uneasy productions that jut away from the preceding poems, poems that are, on the whole, visionary celebrations of giving, receiving, and reciprocating. First published in 1914 and 1917, these poems describe squalid cities in which individuals crowd, swindle, and blight each other, "ring false coin for silver, / offer refuse for meat" (*CP* 59). The erotic ties of community are broken, beauty is banished, and old gods flee. Profit taking replaces poem making and brings what for Mauss and H.D. is its inevitable consequence: the worship of war.

In this capsule history of a market economy, the god that prevails is Mars, apotheosis of H.D.'s blind and brutal Odysseus. He is "a blackened light" (*CP* 62) that reduces the city's multiple, intermingling, and spiritual culture to a masculinist, hierarchical, and literal-minded monotheism.[49] Anger gives these poems a programmatic pitch, but their function is important. They tie what readers might take to be the preceding poems' escapist classical landscape to an urban, industrial, war-ridden present and delineate what H.D. and Mauss experienced as the nightmarish alternative to the spirit of the gift.[50]

Beyond broad oppositional strokes like those in "Calypso," "Cities," and "The Tribute," H.D. ignored market economics and concentrated instead on various manifestations of the spirit of the gift. Her metonymy for the gift is the pearl without price, from the biblical parable that uses the language of the market to tell a tale of the spirit. "The kingdom of heaven," the parable says, "is like unto a merchant man, seeking goodly pearls, who, when he had found one pearl of great price, went and sold all that he had, and bought it" (Matthew 13:45–46). Its great price moves the pearl past all calculations of value, for it is worth, simply, all we have.[51] For H.D. the pearl is "the highest symbol of spiritual attainment, the Gift, the without-price."[52] The realm of the without-price is the terrain of religion and poetry, and it is here, at the center of her work, that H.D.'s theory of the gift becomes most elaborate and compelling.

If the enemies of gift giving are calculation, hoarding, and egotism, for H.D. its champions are those two gods of loosening, circulation, and connection: Eros and Hermes. Eros, as we will see, rules the giftings of eroticism, but he is also in Hyde's sense the affiliator or community builder, the god that compels us to include one another. Violations of this dictate cause consequences much more dire, for H.D., than those provoked by passion's slips and sloppiness. In H.D.'s reading, the cause of the Trojan War is not Helen's wantonness or Paris' desire but Thetis' exclusion of Eris from her wedding feast. "Who caused the war?" H.D. asks. "[Helen] has been blamed, Paris has been blamed but, fundamentally, it was the fault of Thetis." Her act transgresses an important law of the gift culture: in Mauss's formulation, "Everyone who can, will or does attend . . . must be invited. Neglect has fateful results."[53] The attempt to exclude Eris provokes her to toss the golden apple marked "To the Fairest" among those whose contentions for the title will rend the communities of gods and mortals alike.

As if to include strife in his composition, the father of Eros is sometimes said to be Eris' brother, Ares, but in other writings he is Hermes the thief: loosener of property from the hands of the grasper, god of the crossroads, and protector of travelers. In some stories Hermes is merely a cheat, but more often he is a transmitter who, like the Maori hunter, passes on what he takes. The pattern is set in Hermes' very first act when as an infant he steals the cattle of the sun, then sacrifices them to the other gods. This passion for circulation makes him the messenger of Zeus and inventor of the lyre and the alphabet. He and his inventions pass along divine or esoteric secrets, and this, for H.D., merges him with the Egyptian Thoth, with Hermes Trismegistus, reputed author of the *Hermetica*, and with Hermes Psychopompous, conductor of souls into the realm of the gods. "His metal is quicksilver," H.D. writes, with a nod at his Roman incarnation as Mercury, and "his clients, orators, thieves and poets" (*CP* 547). It is Hermes who is the patron of the small band of initiates, the "we" that constitutes the gift community throughout H.D.'s writings.

H.D.'s lyrics have sometimes been read as cries out of a fragile, overwrought isolation, what one critic calls a "loneliness, a metaphysical estrangement that confronts her at every moment with the perilous condition of her own identity."[54] In fact, however, the primary and sustaining pronoun of her poetry is not "I" but "we": the hermetic band, clan, or tribe that submerges the ego in community with others. Even the poems H.D. wrote in the first person singular tend to be social and inclusive. If they do not create an "I" that is one of a chorus, usually they either, like "Calypso," rewrite a shared mythology, or, like many of the poems in *Sea Garden*, enact imperatives toward union — prayers, invocations, or gift rituals designed to draw others into intimate alliance.

When H.D. translates from Greek drama, what magnetizes her is not the speech of the estranged but the talk of the folk who gather to comment on displays of perilous individuality. The Greek "choros" is a group voice: for H.D., "the play's collective conscience" and "a manifestation

of its inner mood." Often wiser than the individuals who carry on before
it, the choros expresses outrage, comments on the power of the gods, and
anticipates the coming action, yet it also speaks the "unconscious" of main
actors too taut and tangled to understand what they feel. The choroses
H.D. chose to translate—choroses from *Iphigeneia in Aulis, Hippolytus,
Ion, The Bacchae, Hecuba*, and *Morpheus*—are spoken by bands of
women who have a strong sense of both the group's wisdom and the
individual's anguish. When a single speaker steps forward from the choros,
she speaks for the group in the same way a soloist sings for the religious
choirs H.D. considered the "direct descendant[s]" of the Greek choros.[55]

To a culture that exalts the lonely or endangered individual, the choros
may seem the least compelling part of the play. To H.D., however, it
offered a model for a community that understands and supports the individuals that constitute it. A number of her poems, like "The Mysteries:
Renaissance Choros" or "Adonis," recreate the band directly; others, like
"Huntress" or "Hymen," find analogous instances in Greek tradition; and
still others, like "We Two," create a diminished but effective private community. Even the exemplary imagist lyric "Oread" invokes ecstasy not for
a lonely individual but for the band: "hurl your green over us," the oread
cries, "cover us" (*CP* 55). The great fissure in H.D.'s work is not between
"I" and others but between "us" and "them," between the initiates of a
gift culture and the "smug and fat," those whose conventionality, materialism, and egotism identify them as part of a market economy (*CP* 511).

H.D.'s "we" has, of course, designs on us, her readers, for it is a per-
emptory inclusion resisted at the risk of becoming one of "them." This
proleptic move assumes we are what she would like us to be, and if we
assent to it, we do in fact receive knowledge that connects us into her
community. Such inclusiveness emerges from Eros, from the "love" H.D.
calls "the motive force, the only true dynamic force that can be employed
or depended on, for true contact," but it circuits through Hermes and,
H.D. continues, its "exact quality . . . would be better described as *recognition*."[56] The bonding of the group occurs through acknowledgment of
a shared hermetic tradition: "We know each other / by secret symbols,"
she explains in *Trilogy*, "though, remote, speechless, / we pass each other
on the pavement" (*CP* 521).

Though much of H.D.'s work rushes into or away from the moment
of transmission, a number of factors charge this moment with danger.
The gift forms a bond between the donor and the recipient and if, as is
almost always the case for H.D., the donor is a figure of great power—a
master, a lover, a god—the recipient may not be able to live up to or
contain the gift and thus risks being consumed, overwhelmed, or driven
mad. In addition, because the gift that must be given and received must

also be reciprocated, it places the recipient under strict obligation to continue the chain of transmission. And, finally, the one who attempts to pass the gift on risks rejection, humiliation, or exclusion, the slammed door H.D. experienced many times in her life.[57]

The successful negotiation of these dangers demands a labor of gratitude that feeds the gift's *hau* and propels it onward. The form this process takes, however, varies according to the nature of the donor, a figure H.D. usually portrays as a teacher, lover, or god. These three aspects frequently conflate or superimpose, so that Freud, for example, becomes Prometheus, or gods manifest as lovers, but it is useful to consider them separately, for each relays a different form of the gift and thereby generates a different sort of increase.

H.D.'s masters were brilliant, magnetic men, men whose ideas hit the twentieth century like "whirlwinds."[58] Preeminent among them were Pound, Lawrence, and Freud, and with each the pattern was similar: intense contact leading to submission, a long period of incorporating and reworking their teachings, and a final tribute releasing her from their power and passing on the gift complicated and enriched by her insight. Each tribute was, as H.D. labeled her memoir of Pound, an "end to torment." This phrase echoes Norman Holmes Pearson's hope for Pound's release from St. Elizabeths Hospital, but it more tellingly applies to H.D.'s hope for release from the grip of her "immensely sophisticated, immensely superior, immensely rough-and-ready" initiator.[59] The gift held corrodes and reduces its recipient; released, it restores the balance and refreshes and extends the gift community.

H.D.'s struggles with Lawrence, recorded in *Bid Me to Live*, are released in *Compassionate Friendship*; the struggles with Pound, recorded in *HERmione*, are released in *End to Torment* and *Winter Love*; and the struggles with Freud, recorded in "The Master," are released in *Tribute to Freud*. Each "tribute" partakes of the doubleness of the word, for it is both a payment levied and a gift rendered, and each honors the word's etymology from the Latin *tribus*, the tribe or community enriched by the gift's circulation. The tribute, one of H.D.'s favorite and finest genres, abides by the gift law she spelled out to Pearson when he protested the title of her poem "Tribute to the Angels": "I must keep *Tribute*," she notes, "as it is a *payment* that I owed them—and I hope [I] did pay!" The "homework" she assigns him is three passages from Numbers, Deuteronomy, and Romans, biblical injunctions to give, receive, and reciprocate.[60]

When H.D. tries to work out Lawrence's place in the sequence of her "initiators," she marks him as the middle of seven: Pound, Aldington, Cournos, Lawrence, Gray, Macpherson, and Schmideberg. In another tally, she counts Peter Rodeck, the Dutchman Van der Leeuw, Freud, and Dowding.[61] To these, we might add the later figures of Erich Heydt and Lionel Durand. It is an odd assortment. Schmideberg and Heydt were analysts, and Van der Leeuw the analysand who preceded her in Freud's hours. Cournos was a close friend; Rodeck, Dowding, and Durand were intense attractions; Aldington, Gray, and Macpherson were lovers. How do such men, figures like Rodeck, Van der Leeuw, Dowding, and Durand whom she barely knew or minor talents like Cournos and Gray, attain the power of Pound, Lawrence, and Freud? In what way could they be called "initiators"? What part do they play in the gift economy of H.D.'s work?

When H.D.'s erotic attachments are subjected to a historical, social, or gender-role analysis, they do indeed reenact the dismal script of obsession, sexual polarization, dominance, submission, and betrayal Rachel Blau DuPlessis calls "romantic thralldom."[62] It is, however, precisely from this point of view that "love-affairs" began to seem to her "rather tiresome and not very important."[63] To comprehend what could become the sublime or numinous consequences of erotic encounters, we need to place them among those moments of gift exchange that are "religious, mythological and shamanistic" because those "taking part are incarnations of gods and ancestors, whose names they bear, whose dances they dance and whose spirits possess them."[64] H.D.'s paradigm is the union of Eros and Psyche: the soul's struggle in the dark with an unseen and unknown sacred force. In such moments the other is not primarily a historical nor even a personal presence, but a momentary incarnation. It is when lovers like Gray or Macpherson or potential lovers like Rodeck or Dowding inevitably fall back into their distracted and distressed humanity that the betrayal occurs.

Like so many of H.D.'s gift rituals, this erotic theophany recalls and recasts Moravian theology. For Moravians, Christ was the Divine Bridegroom of all souls, a metaphor realized or ritualized in the consummations of marriage where the earthly husband as a "Vice-husband" or "Proxy-husband" stood in for Christ in the same way that H.D. experienced Gray standing in for Helios or Macpherson for Hermes.[65] This paradigm moves eroticism from a romantic folly of two toward a spiritual community, a circuit through which gifts pass, knowledge and power are transmitted, and the spirit of the gift is nourished.

This circuit ties the erotic act into the incremental relays characteristic of gift transmission. In H.D.'s autobiographical writings, therefore, Gray appears as a gift from Lawrence and the force he represents, while in *Nights* the lover is "the gift" from the god he incarnates. Like Rodeck in *Majic Ring*, each appears as a "god-send": a messenger, angel, or bearer of divine power.[66] For mythic artists like H.D., the world is imbued with a divine force that is eternally recurrent and that we recognize when it moves toward us because it repeats the primordial paradigms of myth and sacred history, models like the story of Eros and Psyche or the Moravian vision of Christ the Bridegroom. The heterosexual structure of these paradigms leads almost inevitably to a last aspect, one that illuminates an odd and recurrent feature in H.D.'s work: the sudden appearance, often as if from nowhere, of a child.

In H.D.'s writings, the child is the *hau* of the gift, its increase, generated from what she calls in *Narthex* the lover's "soul-sperm."[67] At first, in *Asphodel, Hedylus*, and H.D.'s translation of *Ion*, the child is the issue of sexual union with a lover-god, but later, in *Helen in Egypt, End to Torment, Hermetic Definition*, and *Winter Love*, it arrives from the "inseminating beauty"[68] of a more spiritual meeting and both manifests and projects into the future the increase of the gift. *Helen in Egypt*, the fullest writing of this pattern, culminates with the birth of the double-child Euphorion, essence of Helen and Achilles, brought to birth under the power of "the 'sea-mother' . . . Thetis, Isis or Aphrodite."[69]

It is here at the culmination of this pattern that H.D. solicits and receives the gifts of the goddess in her guise as mother. The masters and inseminating lovers in her life and work were men, but the one that oversees her creativity is female. The sequence is perhaps clearest in *Winter Love* where all Helen's paramours—Menelaus, Paris, Odysseus, Achilles, and Theseus—vanish back into their antecedents and the goddess, here called "grandam, great *Grande Dame*, // midwife and *Sage-Femme*," recalls her from the edge of death to bring forth and nurture her child, *Espérance*.[70] This mother, or grand-mother, stands, as we will see, at the source of H.D.'s creativity in *The Gift*; she is reborn in Bryher, who brought H.D. through the near death preceding her childbirth and then mothered her child; and she reappears in *Winter Love* near the close of H.D.'s work. The generative power she represents, the fruit of the gift economy, is H.D.'s answer to the culmination of the market economy in division and destruction.

The increase from teachers, then, is the tribute, and the increase from lovers, the child. The increase sparked by the final partner in gift exchange, the gods, is more generalized, but it might be thought of simply as writing, the poet's productivity. The gift rituals of the early poems—for example, the rite of first fruits in "Orchard," the "love-offering" in "Holy Satyr," the marriage in "Hymen"—draw the gods closer, repay them, and contribute to their work, but in late poems like *Trilogy* and *Hermetic Definition*, she invokes them to offer homage and receive, in turn, the visions that are the heart of her work. Here the gift as Mauss and Hyde describe it merges both with our more contemporary meaning, her gift or capacity as a poet, and with its special Moravian sense, the gift of prophecy and preaching.[71] The law of the gift culture dictates that what she receives must be disseminated — "write," the goddess tells her in *Hermetic Definition*, "write or die."[72] The gift uncirculated becomes, like the German word *gift*, a toxin or poison,[73] but the gift passed on reaches out, through Eros and Hermes, to gather us into its life-sustaining community.

In H.D.'s work, the primary text of gift exchange, the primer, is *The Gift*. This compelling book, written in London during the Nazi air assaults, returns to her Moravian childhood to bear witness to "a Gift of Vision" and a vision of the gift.[74] Here the command "write, write or die" becomes eerily pertinent, suggesting the perilous urgency with which she labored to pass on her vision: "tap, tap, tap on the machine when the explosions come," Pearson reports, "& Mrs. Asche saying — 'But Madame' + H saying — 'Go away! go away; let me type!' "[75] Like Mauss who suggested that his post–World War I investigations of gift communities pointed the way to better "procedures for our societies,"[76] H.D. proposed her understanding of the Moravian "secret" as a way out of catastrophe into peace.

Preceding *The Gift* were the desolate years of the early 1930s during which H.D.'s writings became fewer and more frenzied, and then, following her analysis with Freud, the first gropings toward release in the translation of Euripides' *Ion* and the draft of *Bid Me to Live*. Robert Duncan sees *Ion* as "a turning point" in H.D.'s work, "the crowning achievement of her first phase" and "the declaration of her later work," and Susan Stanford Friedman marks *Bid Me to Live* as the end of her writing block and the transition into her great period,[77] but it is *The Gift* that stands as the first full writing of the vision that guides her late work, "a vision of power and of peace" (135) that submits contemporary personal, political, and spiritual life to the laws of the gift economy.

If *Ion* is a major draft toward this vision, *Bid Me to Live* steps away from it. Here for the last time in H.D.'s work, characters yield helplessly to world events, reproducing in their sexual and creative lives the competitive egotism of the market. They are Punch and Judy puppets slugging it out against a backdrop of war, "victims, victimised and victimising" who fight "not so much a losing as a lost-battle."[78] In *The Gift* and the writing that follows, the urge is to engage and transform world events. If *The Gift* is a primer, its lesson is that the way toward transformation runs through the rituals of gift exchange inhabiting our childhoods and informing myth, legend, and sacred history. Because some of these rituals are accessible through imagination, *The Gift* combines these two routes to create a mix H.D. named "autobiographical fantasy."[79]

As an autobiography, *The Gift* returns to moments from her childhood, occasions like a parade, a play, preparations for a Moravian Christmas, or a jaunt to a lake packed with water lilies. Part of the delight of these memories is their recovery of childhood's lost particulars — woolen mittens on strings, the crinkled faded paper wrapping Christmas ornaments, the crackle of popcorn at a play — but what compels H.D. in each instance is its link to the general. Each important event is a ritual of giving, receiving, and reciprocating, and each opens back through "inherent or inherited perception" to the experience of "all the children of all the world; in Rome, in Athens, in Palestine, in Egypt" (18).

The push from the particular to the general and through the individual to the cultural accounts for much of the strange power of this text. For H.D. the transition is not metaphoric — a feeling, for example, that her childhood was somehow *like* an Egyptian girl's childhood — but actual, a movement made possible by an inborn "racial and biological inheritance," a part of the brain that "contains cells . . . which can be affiliated to the selves of people, living or long dead" (*M* 70).[80] This theory of inherited memory means that although we live in a secular market economy, we nonetheless have direct access to the kind of sacred experience Mauss records, to traces of a gift culture capable of restoring orientation toward life even in the midst of world catastrophe.

In every chapter there is at least one event that connects with and therefore evokes past cultural rituals, so that, for example, the parade meant to drum up business for a production of *Uncle Tom's Cabin*, a procession of slaves, hounds, a cruel overseer, and a little girl in a golden chariot, "was a Medieval miracle-play procession with a devil, who was Simon Legree, and the poor dark shades of purgatory, who were the negroes chained together, and it was Pallas Athenè, in her chariot with the Winged Victory . . . who was coming to save us all" (18). Each event "comes true" not when the autobiographer discovers some factual confirmation for it — a newspaper account, perhaps, or a contemporary letter — but rather when it coincides with and therefore allows her to relive a moment of gift exchange from myth or sacred history.

By this theory of inborn memory, it is also possible to relive the memories of family members, a possibility H.D. demonstrates in chapter 2, "The Fortune Teller," where she recounts as intimate and immediate experience events lived by her mother before she was born. This is not simple narrative retelling but, we are to believe, an instance in which a cell of inherited memory is fired, "certain chemical constituents of biological or psychic thought-processes are loosed" (*M* 72), and the scene is released into the daughter's consciousness.

This memory-at-one-remove shades into the second major strategy of

The Gift: fantasy, or the imaginative reexperiencing of mythic or legendary events. Here H.D. constructs an elaborately layered scenario through
which, as we will see, she imagines her grandmother recovering and re-
enacting a moment of suppressed Moravian history that she passes on to
her granddaughter who, in turn, reenacts it and forwards it to us. This
is the familiar passage of the gift, the labor of gratitude, and the feeding
of the *hau*, but the lesson is doubled because the "secret" the grandmother
discovers and passes on is, appropriately, the vision, promise, and ritual
of gift giving.

Chapter 5, "The Secret," initiates us into the spirit of the gift, but not
before the preceding chapters have prepared us to understand her instruction. Our identification with the protagonist propels us back into the child's
open-mindedness; the plot moves us back into the child's bonded family,
the first gift community; and the repeated trajectory from the individual
to the cultural exercises, if only at one remove, skills of memory that bring
back rituals of the gift. These lessons, learned through narrative, are reinforced by H.D.'s style, by pronoun and verb constructions and sentence
formations that foil the brain's isolated, analytic, or rational functions
and encourage instead the communal, associative, and symbolic.

The autobiographical "I" is the child Hilda, but the text begins in and
continually returns to her familiar "we" and "our," referring first to the
Doolittle children but then, insofar as we enter her child consciousness
and family traditions, to all the world's children, so that the father becomes not just "my" father or "our father" but finally "your father" and
then "our-father" (60). In the same strategy that created a gift community in *Sea Garden*, H.D. uses direct address to pull us in: "I want you
to know," she writes (*CL* 606), or "you may wonder," "you may know"
(26–27). Or, in a reversed strategy, she joins us, the others, and writes
of herself in the third person as "Hilda" (66). The elastic, permeable self
these constructions presuppose, a self wider than the bounds of the ego,
is a primary precondition for gift exchange.

Linearity, logic, and distance—subverters of the gift—have no purchase
at the text's center. Constantly shifting verb tenses undermine the linear
by circling backward and forward in time, turning the diachronous into
the synchronous and all time into "now." Sentence constructions defeat
the logical by derailing thought trains with *but*, dwelling in paradoxes,
and moving from such childlike openings as "There was," "What he did,
was," or "What it was, was" to assign both fact and myth the status of
"actuality" (25). The measured distances of similes constantly slide into
the superimpositions of metaphor so that *like* collapses into *is*: "This is
not only like that town," she has the founder of the Moravian city ex-
claim, "this is indeed that town, Bethlehem" (*TIR* 28). These strategies

recreate a child's epistemology, a knowing that has not yet exchanged the gift's fairy tales for the market's calculations.

Like Elizabeth and Henri in H.D.'s novel *The Mystery*, the child is tracking a suppressed family and tribal legend, an esoteric secret. The clues are words or *"spells"* (10): letter sequences whose magic incantatory power both compels and eludes her. Some, like *aisle* or *virgin* or *sister*, have both secular and sacred resonance; others, like *Wunden Eiland* or *Gnadenhuetten*, are specific to Moravian history. The most general and powerful clue, however, is the word *gift*, a word that resonates throughout the text and provides the thread that leads to "The Secret."

At first the gift seems to belong to men: her father, the brilliant astronomer, is "gifted" (42), and so is the musician Uncle Fred. But if artists are people with gifts, then ladies too can be gifted (12), yet her mother, both a pianist and a sketcher, lost her gift by allowing her father to frighten her into the role of dutiful daughter, reducing her to a "mechanical" player and "a very good copyist" (*TIR* 32).[81] But then, the child thinks, perhaps her mother gave her musical gift away to Uncle Fred (*M* 63), yet if so her resulting emptiness would contradict the biblical promise: "Give, and it shall be given unto you; good measure, pressed down, and shaken together, and running over" (Luke 6:38, quoted in part in *M* 69). But then perhaps not, because the fortune-teller promised her mother that she would bear a child who would have a gift. Is Hilda, then, the child "marked with that strange thing they called a gift" (11)?

This somewhat condensed line of associations gives the ingredients of the gift: it is alive and mobile, it binds those through whom it passes, it demands a labor of gratitude or creativity, and it follows the injunctions to give, receive, and reciprocate. Yet several questions remain: from whom would Hilda receive the gift, to whom would she pass it, and what is its purpose?

"The Secret" is an intricately staged ritual through which Hilda's grandmother, a grandam or Sage Femme, passes on to her granddaughter the wisdom that could make "a united brotherhood, a *Unitas Fratrum* of the whole world" (135). It is a hot summer night streaked with falling stars: Papa is at his telescope mapping stars; Mama, the aunts and uncles are outside counting and wishing on them; and Hilda and Mamalie are in an upstairs bedroom where Mamalie, in a trance initiated by the phrase "shooting star," describes the event that grounds the text's central palimpsest. This event is a Moravian ceremony with the Indians that took place in 1741, that Mamalie, deciphering secret records, acted out for herself in 1841, and that H.D. herself will reenact at *The Gift*'s close in 1941. The chapter, heavily scored and much reworked in manuscript, is tangled with the complexities of establishing an erased Moravian history through

an ecstatic old woman's murmurings to an enthralled young girl. The device
by which H.D. maintains control of the incident, however, also functions
to turn it into a collaboration: as Mamalie works back into her vision,
then forward from it, she projects onto Hilda the identities of those who
surrounded her in the past, identities Hilda in turn takes up and plays
out to keep Mamalie in her trance.

Mamalie's story is a tale of encounter, mutual recognition, and visionary gift exchange between two cultures, both despised by the canny white
traders. Mamalie emphasizes that the Moravians were not interested in
exploitative exchange: they "had not asked for furs, they had not traded
with the Indians, this in itself was strange," but, in addition, "they had
not taken land," purchasing it from John Penn and then, when asked,
buying it again from the Indians.[82] When they first meet, the tribes, like
the hermetic initiates in *Trilogy*, recognize each other by secret symbols:
the Indians perceive their Great Spirit in the Moravians' music, and the
Moravians recognize their circle, flower, and star in the hieroglyphs on
the Indians' ceremonial belt. When the Indians gave the Moravians the
belt, Mamalie explains, it was, like all true gift exchange, "more than an
exchange of outer civilities, it was an inner greeting and it seemed a pact
had been made."[83]

The pact was a plan to have a meeting at which they would enact one
of the most ancient rituals of connection: the exchange of women. It is
tempting to dismiss such ceremonies as a commodification of women, but
we are dealing here with the gift, not with the market. The exchange H.D.
describes is not social but sacred. As we saw in the escalation toward the
Grandam in her poetry, for H.D., as for other recorders of the gift economy, women seem to embody the spirit of the gift: its bonding into kinship, its life-sustaining mutuality, and its generative power. Those who
operate through *eros* also tend to worship "a special Spirit," a feminine
soul or godhead that H.D. calls variously the *Sanctus Spiritus*, Sophia,
or Holy Wisdom (135).[84] When the Moravian Anna von Pahlen is initiated into the Indian mysteries and the Indian Morning Star is baptized
Moravian, they exchange inner names and the pact between the two tribes
is sealed.[85]

How did the Moravians and Indians recognize each other's secret symbols, deities, and rituals? What was the importance of the ceremony at
Wunden Eiland? For H.D., the meeting marks the confluence of two great
streams carrying the ancient secret of the gift, one flowing eastward from
Asia, China, and Tibet to the Indians, the other flowing westward from
the Knights Templar and Cathars to the Moravians.[86] When the two tribes
merge in an ecstatic talking in tongues, it is the culmination of a long and
perilous passage of the *hau* of the gift toward a moment that "[links] up

all the mysteries through time, in all lands and for all peoples." The secret exchanged at *Wunden Eiland*, "properly directed, might have changed the course of history, might have lifted the dark wings of evil from the whole world."[87]

It might have, but it didn't. The *hau* of the gift was stopped at *Wunden Eiland*, its promise broken both by the more conventional Moravians, who condemned the ceremony as a scandal and burned the records, and by disaffected Indians who subsequently rained burning arrows on the Moravian settlement at Gnadenhuetten. When one hundred years after *Wunden Eiland* Mamalie and her first husband discover and decipher the forgotten scroll, he dies and she burns in the fever that recurs on the night of the falling stars and passes only when she transmits the gift to Hilda, who, in turn, one hundred years after Mamalie's vision, suffers in the *now* of the text the agonies of "the great fires and the terrible bombing of London" (131) and "passionately regret[s] only this. That the message that had been conveyed to me, that the message that my grandmother had received, would again be lost."[88]

Mamalie's terror at the words "shooting star" is her fear that "the papers would be burnt or she would be burnt," and now, H.D. continues in her final chapter, "I would be burnt" by "savages" whose flaming arrows are the bombs falling all around her (131, 99). As the book closes, the "all clear" siren signals the end of the raid and H.D. hears—or acts out for herself—Anna von Pahlen and Shooting Star, the Native American shaman, calling together to the "Great Spirit and the Good Spirit who is the God of the Brotherhood and the God of the Initiates" (142). At this moment, the gift passes on to us and we are left, like Mamalie and then Hilda, holding the future in our hands.

In case we should want to shirk the gift by claiming that we, her readers, are in any case not "savages," H.D. has reminded us "never [to] forget how each one of us (through inertia, through indifference, through ignorance) is, in part, responsible for the world-calamity."[89] We might prefer to consider her story of the gift a literary concoction, a fairy tale, but if so, the text repeatedly emphasizes, it is an ancient story, one whose wisdom we have turned into a "secret" by exalting the individualistic, the rational, and the competitive. Should we take the gift seriously, however, as Mauss, Hyde, and H.D. have done, it would be impossible to remain inert, indifferent, or ignorant. Whatever we might choose to do with it, the responsibility for the gift's increase is now in our hands.

What H.D. chooses to do with the gift is to write it, again and again, into the heart of her texts. The "autobiographical fantasy" that grounds the gift in the circumstances of her life firmly establishes a circuit that connects the personal to the political and the spiritual. The energy of the gift, active in all her late works, organizes relations between persons, events, and ideas along the line of a transmission of knowledge that creates community and assumes responsibility for addressing world crisis. The force that opposes the everyday contentions of the marketplace and the intermittent terrors of war is H.D.'s relay of power and of peace: the spirit of the gift.

NOTES

I am grateful to the University of Iowa for a Faculty Developmental Assignment during which I completed this essay and to Jay Semel and Lorna Olson whose services at University House created a congenial and supportive scholarly environment. This essay previously appeared in *Contemporary Literature* 27 (Winter 1986): 493–524.

1   See Marcel Mauss, *The Gift: Forms and Functions of Exchange in Archaic Societies*, trans. Ian Cunnison (New York: Norton, 1967). My understanding of the spirit of the gift is informed by the commentary of Lewis Hyde in *The Gift: Imagination and the Erotic Life of Property* (New York: Random House, 1983) and Marshall Sahlins in *Stone Age Economics* (Chicago: Aldine-Atherton, 1972). For an excellent exposition of the gift economy in Elizabethan culture, see Patricia Fumerton, "Exchanging Gifts: The Elizabethan Currency of Children and Poetry," *ELH* 53 (1986): 241–78.

2   Ibid., 22.

3   Ibid., 3. On the place of women in the exchange, so central to Lévi-Strauss's theories of kinship, see Gayle Rubin's important essay, "The Traffic in Women: Notes on the 'Political Economy' of Sex," in *Toward an Anthropology of Women*, ed. Rayna R. Reiter (New York and London: Monthly Review Press, 1975), 157–210.

4   Barbara Guest, *Herself Defined: The Poet H.D. and Her World* (Garden City, N.Y.: Doubleday, 1984), 112–13, 295–97. For additional details about the Ellerman fortune, see Janice S. Robinson, *H.D.: The Life and Work of an American Poet* (Boston: Houghton Mifflin, 1982), 262.

5   Robinson, *H.D.*, 278.

6   Guest, *Herself Defined*, 265.

7   The not quite veiled implication here, of course, is that H.D. was, in some sense, kept, an implication H.D. herself nervously parodies in calling Bryher's anniversary gift of a fur coat "the wages of sin" (*Compassionate Friendship*, typescript of the second draft, in the Collection of American Literature, Beinecke Rare Book and Manuscript Library, Yale University, 9). This and other unpublished material are cited with the generous permission of Perdita Schaffner, H.D.'s literary executor, and David Schoonover, Curator of the American Literature Collection at Beinecke.

8   See, for example, H.D.'s letters to Bryher of Feb. 1, 1919; Dec. 26, 1932; Sept.

23, 1945. For confirmation of Bryher's light hand in giving, see Robert Herring's letter to H.D. (dated April? 1933 at Beinecke); Herring writes: "Bryher has been being marvellous to me lately in that kind of anonymous way of hers, which makes it difficult to 'thank' her. She is like a kind note fluttering in through the window . . . the sender has gone, there's just a sentence in one's mind, a white miracle, left" (ellipsis in original).

9 Norman Holmes Pearson, notes toward a life of H.D., written on Hotel Weisses Kreuz letterhead and filed at Beinecke in a folder labeled "H.D. Biog," 4–5.

10 H.D., *H.D. by Delia Alton, The Iowa Review* 16.3 (1986): 186.

11 Susan Gubar, "Sapphistries," *Signs* 10.1 (1984): 53–58. Gubar opposes the "fantastic collaboration" between Sappho and poets like Renée Vivien and H.D. to the "anxiety of authorship" characterizing nineteenth-century women writers' relationships with their male precursors.

12 H.D., *Tribute to Freud* (New York: McGraw-Hill, 1974), 66.

13 Friedman made this point in a lecture at the University of Iowa in the fall of 1983. It forms part of the argument of her essay "Theories of Autobiography and Fictions of the Self in H.D.'s Canon," in *Figuring the Self: Modernism and Autobiographical Writing*, ed. Thomas R. Smith (State College: Pennsylvania State UP, 1991), and of her book *Penelope's Web* (New York: Cambridge UP, 1990).

14 *H.D. by Delia Alton* 184.

15 Prospectus for *Sagas of the Self* [working title of *Penelope's Web*], 4.

16 At the conclusion of H.D.'s autobiographical novel *Asphodel*, the child is exchanged between the H.D. and Bryher characters as part of a mutual pact to live: "If you promise never more to say that you will kill yourself," Hermione says, "I will give you something. . . . I want you to promise me to grow up and take care of the little girl" (ts. part II, Beinecke, 184). Bryher's legal adoption of Perdita occurred in 1928, a period during which H.D. feared the recurrence of Aldington's earlier threats of a perjury suit and "five years penal servitude" for her false registry of the child as his legitimate offspring (*Asphodel*, part II, 176; see also the letter at Beinecke to Brigit Patmore, dated Feb. 18, 1925). Guest mentions the adoption in *Herself Defined* 155, 203.

17 Guest makes this suggestion in *Herself Defined* 111.

18 H.D., *The Hedgehog* (London: Brendin, 1936), 27. The god Helios is the father of Phoebe Fayne in *Asphodel*, of Hedylus in *Hedylus*, and of Ion in H.D.'s recreation of Euripides' *Ion*.

19 *Asphodel*, part II, 91. Here the child's name, Phoebe Fayne, links the Helios mythology to the name given Frances Gregg in both *Asphodel* and *HERmione* (New York: New Directions, 1981).

20 Rachel Blau DuPlessis, *Writing Beyond the Ending: Narrative Strategies of Twentieth-Century Women Writers* (Bloomington: Indiana UP, 1985), 76.

21 Long after the dissolution of this *ménage à quatre*, Macpherson continued to father his adopted daughter. On a trip in 1947, in fact, Kenneth and Perdita encountered Gray and, as Perdita summarizes the tangled moment, "my legal father introduced me to my father. 'Cecil, my daughter Perdita' " (Perdita

Schaffner, "A Profound Animal," in H.D.'s *Bid Me to Live (A Madrigal)* [Redding Ridge, Conn.: Black Swan, 1980] 191–92).

22 For alternate family arrangements, see especially Carol B. Stack's description of the community she calls The Flats in *All Our Kin: Strategies for Survival in a Black Community* (New York: Harper and Row, 1974), particularly chapter 5, "ChildKeeping," 62–89. For a description of Perdita's many family groupings, see Guest, *Herself Defined* 243.

23 Hyde, *Gift* 3–4.

24 Ibid., 47.

25 It must be emphasized that the work H.D. did both assimilated *and* countered Freud's insights. Here, see Rachel Blau DuPlessis and Susan Stanford Friedman, " 'Woman is Perfect': H.D.'s Debate with Freud," *Feminist Studies* 7 (1981): 417–30, and, especially, Friedman's *Psyche Reborn: The Emergence of H.D.* (Bloomington: Indiana UP, 1981), 17–154.

26 Hyde, *Gift* 18–20.

27 H.D., *Helen in Egypt* (New York: Grove, 1961), 99.

28 E. E. Evans-Pritchard, "Introduction," Mauss, *Gift* v–vi.

29 Sahlins, *Stone Age Economics* 149.

30 Mauss, *Gift* 10.

31 Sahlins, *Stone Age Economics* 160.

32 Hyde, *Gift* 37.

33 These obligations are detailed in Mauss, *Gift* 10–11. For a description of the Moravian love feasts, see Gillian Lindt Gollin, *Moravians in Two Worlds: A Study of Changing Communities* (New York: Columbia UP, 1967), 20.

34 Mauss, *Gift* 80; Hyde, *Gift* xiv; H.D., *Helen in Egypt* 115.

35 William J. Murtagh, *Moravian Architecture and Town Planning: Bethlehem, Pennsylvania, and Other Eighteenth-Century American Settlements* (Chapel Hill: U of North Carolina P, 1967), vii.

36 For the best explications of Moravian theology see Gollin, *Moravians in Two Worlds*; and Jacob John Sessler, *Communal Pietism among Early American Moravians* (New York: Henry Holt, 1933). See also two books by Adelaide L. Fries, *The Moravian Church: Yesterday and Today* (Raleigh: Edwards & Broughton, 1926), a book H.D. consulted; and *The Road to Salem* (Durham: U of North Carolina P, 1944), a text she owned, annotated, and cited in her "Notes to 'Dark Room,' " *Montemora* 8 (1981): 73.

37 Gollin, *Moravians in Two Worlds* 85. For information about the Choir system, see 67–89; and Sessler, *Communal Pietism* 93–105.

38 Murtagh, *Moravian Architecture* 13.

39 Gollin, *Moravians in Two Worlds* 198.

40 For a discussion of the complex causes for the dissolution of this Agreement, see ibid., 198–203; and Sessler, *Communal Pietism* 182–212.

41 Sessler, *Communal Pietism* 207.

42 *Bethlehem of Pennsylvania: The Golden Years, 1841–1920* (Bethlehem, Pa.: Lehigh Litho, 1976), 13.

43 Ibid., 28–30.

44 In *The Gift,* H.D. records this split by tracing lines of inheritance: while she

inherits her family's visionary capacities, her brother "Harold will inherit the mills and the steel and numbers too and become a successful businessman like Uncle Hartley" (New York: New Directions, 1982), 66.

45 "Calypso," in H.D., *Collected Poems, 1912-1944*, ed. Louis L. Martz (New York: New Directions, 1983), 388-96. Further citations to this volume, abbreviated *CP*, will appear in the text.

46 Friedman, *Psyche Reborn* 236. "Callypso Speaks" is the apt title Norman Holmes Pearson affixed to the second part of H.D.'s poem in his *Selected Poems of H.D.* (New York: Grove Press, 1957), 59. For H.D.'s strategy of displacing narrative by giving voice to the "other side," the woman's side, see DuPlessis' discussion of H.D.'s "Eurydice" in *Writing Beyond the Ending* 70-71, 109-10.

47 DuPlessis, *Writing Beyond the Ending* 66-83.

48 In Friedman's summary, "she gave and gave and gave; he took and took and left" (*Psyche Reborn* 239).

49 For a fertile elaboration of the differences between polytheism and monotheism, see James Hillman, *Re-Visioning Psychology* (New York: Harper, 1975).

50 H.D.'s review of a collection of Marianne Moore's poems identifies the impulse behind poems like "Cities" and "The Tribute": "[Moore] is fighting in her country a battle against squalor and commercialism. We are all fighting the same battle" (*Egoist* 3 [August 1916]: 19).

51 The distinction between value and worth is Hyde's, though, as he notes, Marx made a parallel distinction by tying "worth" to "use-value" and "value" to "exchange value" (*Gift* 60).

52 *Majic Ring*, second typed draft at Beinecke, 79.

53 *Helen in Egypt* 111; Mauss, *Gift* 38.

54 Joseph N. Riddel, "H.D. and the Poetics of 'Spiritual Realism,' " *Contemporary Literature* 10 (1969): 447.

55 H.D.'s comments on the Greek choros come from the notes to her translation of Euripides' *Ion* (Boston: Houghton Mifflin, 1937), 22, x, 59, 3.

56 *Majic Ring* 35.

57 The metaphor of a door that shut on four "extravagant and illuminating occasions" comes from *The Sword Went Out to Sea*, second typed draft at Beinecke, book I, 83. The epigraph to this lengthy attempt to assuage the pain of rejection and continue the gift cycle is prefaced by Bryher's reassurance: "*It's not lost. This will go on somewhere.*"

58 The metaphor of the "whirlwind" describes Pound's *Cantos*, where for H.D. "the world and time are blasted, dynamited, shattered" (*Compassionate Friendship* 22-23). The language of catastrophe that haunts her descriptions of these men struggles to register their impact on her.

59 H.D., *End to Torment: A Memoir of Ezra Pound* (New York: New Directions, 1979), ix, 3. For the best account of Pound's challenge and H.D.'s response, see Paul Smith, *Pound Revised* (London: Croom Helm, 1983), 110-32.

60 H.D.'s communication to Pearson is dated Oct. 24, 1944, and transcribed in his folder of notes labeled "*Trilogy* (annotated)." The passages to which she refers are Numbers 31:28, Deuteronomy 16:10, and Romans 13:7.

61 *Compassionate Friendship* 35; *The Sword Went Out to Sea*, book I, 83–86, 95.
62 Rachel Blau DuPlessis, "Romantic Thralldom in H.D.," in this volume. See also *Writing Beyond the Ending* 66–83.
63 *Majic Ring* 97.
64 Mauss, *Gift* 36.
65 For the Moravian ritualizations of marriage, see Sessler, *Communal Pietism* 151–52. For the rewritings of Gray as Helios, see especially *Asphodel*, part II, 93–94; for Macpherson as Hermes, see *Narthex* (in *Second American Caravan*, ed. Alfred Kreymborg et al. [New York: Macaulay, 1928]) and *The Usual Star* (Dijon: Darantière, 1934). The most lush and extended descriptions of this hierogamy occur in *Nights*, by "John Helforth" (Dijon: Darantière, 1935). With H.D.'s habit of conflating the figures in her life, the superimpositions can become dizzying; thus, for example, H.D. confesses to her friend George Plank that she had an erotic relationship with Bryher in Greece, "a sort of 'marriage by prozy' [*sic*]," in which Bryher stood in for Rodeck while, as other texts show, Rodeck himself stood in for Helios and thus redoubled the earlier figure of Cecil Gray (letter to Plank, May 1, 1935, 2; *Majic Ring* 156).
66 *Bid Me to Live* 110; *Nights* 105; *Majic Ring* 150.
67 *Narthex* 281. Hyde finds a similar structure in the writings of the fourteenth-century Christian mystic Meister Eckhart, who believed that "when God pours himself into the soul, the Child is born, and this birth is the fruit of gratitude for the gift" (*Gift* 55).
68 *End to Torment* 36.
69 *Helen in Egypt* 299.
70 H.D., *Hermetic Definition* (New York: New Directions, 1972), 115. Excellent scholarship has been done on the maternal influence in H.D.'s work. See particularly Friedman, *Psyche Reborn* 131–54; Deborah Kelly Kloepfer, "Flesh Made Word: Maternal Inscription in H.D.," *Sagetrieb* 3.1 (1984): 27–48; and DuPlessis, *Writing Beyond the Ending* 66–83.
71 A telling definition of the Gift in its Moravian sense comes from the polemics of the eighteenth-century pamphleteer John Roche: when the Moravians found potential converts, Roche fulminates, "then would they tell them they were sure, by many Signs and Reasons they knew, that that Person would soon receive the Gift, and that so soon as they would, they should preach and instruct the people" (*Moravian Heresy, wherein the Principal errors of that Doctrine . . . Are set forth* [Dublin, 1751], 72).
72 *Hermetic Definition* 7.
73 "Gift? *Gift?*" H.D. portrays her mother musing in "The Fortune Teller," "That was the German for poison." "The Fortune Teller," the original chapter 2 of *The Gift*, was excised from the New Directions edition but appeared in *The Iowa Review* 16.3 (1986): 14–41. Quote is on page 31.
74 H.D., *The Gift* (New York: New Directions, 1982), 135. The New Directions edition of *The Gift* not only omits a chapter but cuts or elides other significant portions of the manuscript (for a commentary on the publishing history of this text, see Rachel Blau DuPlessis, "A Note on the State of H.D.'s *The*

Gift," *Sulfur* 9 [1984]: 178–82). Fortunately, three chapters have been published intact: chapter 1, "The Dark Room," *Montemora* 8 (1981): 57–72; chapter 2, "The Fortune Teller," *The Iowa Review*; and chapter 3, "The Dream," *Contemporary Literature* 10 (1969): 605–26. For ease of reference, whenever possible I will cite the page numbers of the New Directions text in parentheses following the quotation. Citations to the *Montemora* material will be preceded by *M*, *The Iowa Review* material preceded by *TIR*, and the *Contemporary Literature* material preceded by *CL*. Other citations will appear in endnotes and, unless indicated, will refer to the final typescript of *The Gift* at Beinecke.

75 From Norman Holmes Pearson's notes at Beinecke, "H.D. Biog."

76 Mauss, *Gift* 69.

77 Robert Duncan, *The H.D. Book*, part II, "Nights and Days," chapter 1, *Sumac* 1 (Fall 1968): 107; Friedman, *Psyche Reborn* 31.

78 *Bid Me to Live* 7, 49.

79 H.D., *H.D. by Delia Alton* 189.

80 This theory echoes Freud's notion that experiences of the ego "when they have been repeated often enough and with sufficient strength in many individuals in successive generations" can "transform themselves . . . into experiences of the id, the impressions of which are preserved by heredity." For this citation and discussion of other Lamarckian traces in Freud's thought, see Ronald W. Clark, *Freud: The Man and the Cause* (London: Jonathan Cape, 1980), 437.

81 Adrienne Rich's contention that "the dutiful daughter of the fathers in us is only a hack" links a "primary intensity" between women to the ability to say "no" to the fathers (*On Lies, Secrets, and Silence: Selected Prose, 1966–1978* [New York: Norton, 1979], 201–2). The contrast between Helen Doolittle's tie to her father and Hilda's tie to her grandmother seems to make a similar point.

82 "The Secret," 33. "The Death of Martin Presser," a short story H.D. considered appending to *The Gift*, makes the same point (*Quarterly Review of Literature* 13.3–4 [1965]: 241–61).

83 "The Secret," 33–36.

84 See "The Secret," first typed draft, 12. Here the "special Spirit" is designated *Mutter* and linked to the deity worshipped by the Crusaders. In this equation, H.D. is drawing on one of her favorite sources: Denis de Rougemont's *Love in the Western World*, a book she read in both the French and English editions and consulted frequently in writing *The Gift* (see, for example, her letter to Bryher of May 25, 1941). For a portrait of H.D.'s *Santa Sophia*, see the central poem of *Trilogy*, *Tribute to the Angels* (*CP* 553–67), and Susan Gubar's analysis in "The Echoing Spell of H.D.'s *Trilogy*," in this volume. For a more general discussion of the feminine deity in gnostic religions, see Elaine Pagels, *The Gnostic Gospels* (New York: Random House, 1979), 48–69.

85 "The Secret," 31–32; see also "Morning Star," 9. With H.D.'s zeal for conflation, she has Hilda, who is at this point playing Mamalie's daughter Aggie, reason that since Anna von Pahlen's inner name was, like Aggie's middle name, Angelica, "I would be part of Anna von Pahlen, too, and I would be part

of the ceremony at *Wunden Eiland* and I would be Morning Star along with Anna" (32). For the exchange of women from the perspective of a market economy, see Gayle Rubin's "The Traffic in Women"; for the exchange of women in the history of gift rituals, see Hyde, *Gift* 93–108.

86   "The Secret," first typed draft, p. 34.
87   "Morning Star," first typed draft, p. 27; "The Secret," first typed draft, pp. 29–30.
88   "Morning Star," 8.
89   "Because One Is Happy," 2.

Part II

Images

This is no rune nor riddle,
it is happening everywhere;

what I mean is—it is so simple
yet no trick of the pen or brush

could capture that impression;
music could do nothing with it,

nothing whatever; what I mean is—
but you have seen for yourself

that burnt-out wood crumbling...
you have seen for yourself.

—H.D., *Trilogy*

CHAPTER 7

H.D. and the Origins of Imagism

CYRENA N. PONDROM

At the conclusion of his book, Noel Stock, the biographer of Ezra Pound, summarized: "With Yeats, Joyce, Lewis and Eliot dead he was the last survivor among the leading men of the formative years of the 'modern movement' in English literature — the movement in which he himself had played an important part, not only as innovator and renewer of language, but as impresario and publicity-agent, fund-raiser and office boy."[1] One could easily conclude from Stock's summation that modernism was a movement which owed its foundation and its characteristics to men alone. His emphasis is hardly atypical, even today, when a rapidly swelling scholarship on women writers makes only the least informed unaware that modernism possessed important women members.

The honor role of modernists who wrote in English must include, of course, Gertrude Stein, Hilda Doolittle, Dorothy Richardson, Marianne Moore, Virginia Woolf, and Edith Sitwell, to name only those leaders whose innovative work began within the period Stock calls "the formative years" of the modern movement. To those must be added the women whose genius lay more in the arenas of "impresario . . . publicity-agent [and] fund-raiser" — Amy Lowell, of course, and the great editors and publishers, without whom the shape and probably even the scope and influence of modernism would surely have been different: Harriet Monroe. Dora Marsden. Harriet Shaw Weaver. Margaret Anderson. Sylvia Beach.

Several of these women — among them Hilda Doolittle and Gertrude Stein — were not merely important participants in the modernist movement, but can claim priority in the creation of some of the literary models from which modernism developed. What is more, a systematic examination of the characteristics of major women modernists would prompt a revision in conventional descriptions of modernist political tendencies, use of myth, and attitudes toward a transcendental ideal, and even in the theory of the nature of the modernist movement itself. Thus in very important ways the literary history of modernism is an account that remains to be written.[2] An appropriate place to begin that reconsideration lies in the origins of imagism.

Most thoughtful students of the origins of modern poetry now recognize that important roots of modern poetry lie in imagism. Although Ezra Pound after 1914 made a number of statements intended to minimize public valuation of the importance of imagism, his own poetry and his theories of poetic form and structure which undergird the modernist long poem grow directly out of it.[3] Consequently, it is of considerable significance to consider how the fundamental elements of the theory of the image and the nature and structure of the imagist poem came into being. A close comparison of the early "theory" of imagism with the actual practice of Ezra Pound, Richard Aldington, and H.D. strongly supports the inference that H.D.'s early poems were models which enabled the precepts of imagism to be defined. To evaluate the evidence for this proposition we must review again the oft-told tale of the beginnings of imagism.

When Hilda Doolittle arrived in London in the fall of 1911, Ezra Pound had already been in Europe three years. He had published six slim volumes of poetry — A Lume Spento (Venice, 1908), A Quinzaine for this Yule (London, 1908), Personae (London, 1909), Exultations (London, 1909), Provença (Boston, 1910), and Canzoni (London, 1911). With this he could claim a volume of comparative scholarship, The Spirit of Romance (London, 1910), and a volume of translations of the poetry of Guido Cavalcanti. H.D. at this time had written (for Frances Gregg) and published, apparently in New York commercial papers in 1910, only a few poems, which she has said were inspired by those in the volume of Theocritus that Pound had given her.[4] Probably it was predictable that critics focused attention primarily on Pound as the originator of imagism.

At the end of 1911 and in the spring of 1912, H.D., Pound, and Richard Aldington lived in adjacent flats in Church Walk, Kensington, and met frequently, along with F. S. Flint, to discuss modern poetry.[5] Flint introduced them to the work of contemporary French poets,[6] and by May H.D., Aldington, and Pound were all three in Paris,[7] then ablaze with groups of poets issuing manifestoes and promulgating "rules" for the revitalization of modern poetry. Typical were the fantaisistes, the unanimistes, the Whitmanistes, the futuristes, the paroxystes and so on, almost ad infinitum.[8] A complete report on this ferment appeared in the August 1912 issue of the Poetry Review, in F. S. Flint's monograph "Contemporary French Poetry."

It was during this exposure to the animated French coteries that the group decided to form a movement themselves: imagisme. "In the spring or early summer of 1912, 'H.D.,' Richard Aldington and myself decided that we were agreed upon . . . three principles," Pound wrote later, ". . . agreeing upon these three positions we thought we had as much right to a group name as a number of French 'schools' proclaimed by Mr. Flint in the August number of Harold Munro's [*sic*] magazine. . . ."⁹

On August 18, 1912, Pound first used the term *imagiste* in writing, in a letter to Harriet Monroe. He agreed to send *Poetry* interesting new work from London and Paris, and he included as a first installment two poems of his own for the magazine: "To Whistler: American" and "Middle-Aged." He called the latter "an over-elaborate post-Browning 'Imagiste' affair."¹⁰ It was probably a month or six weeks later that Pound discovered that H.D. was a poet of real merit. The tale is told in H.D.'s own inimitable words:

"But Dryad," (in the Museum tea room), "this is poetry." He slashed with a pencil. "Cut this out, shorten this line. 'Hermes of the Ways' is a good title. I'll send this to Harriet Monroe of *Poetry*. Have you a copy? Yes? Then we can send this, or I'll type it when I get back. Will this do?" And he scrawled "H.D. Imagiste" at the bottom of the page.¹¹

Pound sent the poems in a letter dated only October [1912]. Pound's letter, like H.D.'s account of the event, clearly implies that little time elapsed between his discovery of her poems and his actually sending them to Monroe. In the letter to her he says, "I've had luck again, and am sending you some *modern* stuff by an American. . . ." A few days later, in a letter dated October 13, he sent some more of his own poems to Monroe with the comment: "You must use your own discretion about printing this batch of verses. At any rate, don't use them until you've used 'H.D.' and Aldington. . . ."¹² He referred to this "batch" of poems as "Contemporania." Pound continued to send poems to Monroe in small batches throughout the fall, and from them she eventually selected a dozen which appeared in the April 1913 issue of *Poetry* under the heading "Contemporania."¹³ We know, thus, that between August 18, 1912, when he first agreed to send material to *Poetry*, and October 13, Pound had sent Monroe poems by H.D. and Aldington, followed by a few poems of his own intended for the series "Contemporania."

Pound's own "imagiste affair," "Middle-Aged," appeared in the first issue of *Poetry*, in October 1912, and the Aldington poems, "Au Vieux Jardin," "To a Greek Marble," and "Choricos," in November 1912. H.D.'s poems—"Priapus" ["Orchard"], "Hermes of the Ways," and "Epigram"— appeared in January 1913. True to Pound's request, Monroe did not publish more of his poems until April 1913, after the poems by H.D. and Aldington had appeared.

In March 1913, however, she published the now famous brief essays by Flint and Pound explaining the principles of imagism. It was there that Pound first defined the "image" as "that which presents an intellectual and emotional complex in an instant of time," and directed his fellow poets—if they would learn from imagism—to

Use no superfluous word, no adjective, which does not reveal something.

Don't use such an expression as "dim lands *of peace.*" It dulls the image. It mixes an abstraction with the concrete. It comes from the writer's not realizing that the natural object is always the *adequate* symbol.

Go in fear of abstractions. . . .[14]

In the same issue, F. S. Flint, always self-effacing, represented himself as the interviewer of an imagist, and summarized as a result of his conversation the familiar "rules" of imagism:

1. Direct treatment of the "thing," whether subjective or objective.
2. To use absolutely no word that does not contribute to the presentation.
3. . . . to compose in sequence of the musical phrase, not in sequence of a metronome.[15]

During the formative months between Pound's first recorded use of the name *imagisme* and the date of the publication of the first descriptions of the movement in March 1913, there were, then, only a handful of poems which Pound had explicitly advanced under the label *imagiste* as the evidence of a new movement: his own "Middle-Aged," the three poems by Aldington, and the three by H.D. A comparison of them offers interesting evidence of the significance of H.D. in creating the models that were to make imagism the foundation of the modern movement in English and American poetry.

Of particular interest is the first poem that Pound labeled *imagiste.* The poem begins with a poeticism of the type imagism rejected, and continues with an explicit comparison which is distinctly not the "super-position" of images, without explanation, that Pound later extolled in writing about his own imagist poem "In a Station of the Metro."[16] The first lines are

'Tis but a vague, invarious delight
As gold that rains about some buried king.[17]

The first line is simple assertion, which equates an unspecified "it" (*'Tis*) with a descriptive complement (*vague, invarious delight*) so intangible that the mind can conjure no clear image. There is an attempt to be more graphic in the next line, with the simile comparing the "delight" to the "gold that rains about some buried king." Such a simile, with the abstract emotion stated first, and then discursively compared by means of "as" to an exotic unrelated object, is almost the antithesis of the technique which

Pound himself endorsed as a hallmark of imagism and source of technical renewal for modern poetry.

"The point of Imagisme is that it does not use images *as ornaments*. The image is itself the speech," Pound wrote in 1914.[18] Applying such a prescription to the poem itself, the critic would expect the concrete image to precede the general statement of feeling and to generate in the reader an emotion which the poet wished to communicate. Only then, if at all, would one expect the poet to use a simile linking his specific image to an abstractly labeled state, such as "the vague invarious delight" of middle-aged desire. (Indeed, if the image "worked," the explanatory simile would be superfluous.) The progress in "Middle-Aged" is the reverse.

The next two stanzas develop two sustained similes which elaborate the scene which produces the "gold that rains about some buried king" and explicitly make the comparison with the "I" of the poem:

> As the fine flakes,
> When tourists frolicking
> Stamp on his roof or in the glazing light
> Try photographs, wolf down their ale and cakes
> And start to inspect some further pyramid;
>
> As the fine dust, in the hid cell
> Beneath their transitory step and merriment,
> Drifts through the air, and the sarcophagus
> Gains yet another crust
> Of useless riches for the occupant,
> So I, the fires that lit once dreams
> Now over and spent,
> Lie dead within four walls . . .

Although these lines present a vivid objective scene, the exact nature of the comparison remains abstract and equivocal: the syntax establishes a comparison between the I-figure and the falling gilt or dust of the pharaoh's tomb, but the sense insists upon a comparison between the (presumably newly middle-aged) persona and the dead king.[19] Eventually the elaborate similes emerge. The speaker is like the dead king, and love seems to him now no more than the dust or gilt which sifts down upon the mummy in his case as the living play above. Love now elicits only "precious metaphors" rather than more robust action, and even these are futile, for the dark (of middle age) hides their beauty even from those with a cat's eyes.

This technique is quite unlike that urged by Pound in his famous explication of his "In a Station of the Metro" as a paradigm imagist poem. There two vivid and explicit images are juxtaposed without syntactical connection explaining the significance of their relationship. The emotion in the poem is perceived by the reader as the product of the interaction of the two images, with their respective emotional weights. Such a perception is, as Pound argued, instantaneous. "Middle-Aged," in contrast, is analytic; reader response is slower and perhaps more cognitive than emotive. In addition, the cadence of the language, although cast in vers libre, is not that of ordinary speech (another precept of imagism), and the poem contains several "poetic" inversions like "the fires that lit once dreams."

Pound, in his cover letter to Monroe, called the poem a "post-Browning" as well as an "imagiste" affair; and in fact the traces of Browning are rather more clear than the imagist tendencies. The poem has some affinities with "Cino," another rather interesting poem that anticipates some of the tendencies of the imagist movement but is clearly in the pre-imagist mode.

Three other poems appeared in *Poetry* under the description "imagist" prior to the publication of the three by H.D. — the Aldington poems Pound apparently sent just before he was shown H.D.'s work. These lyrics are even further from the hard, clear autonomous images of H.D.'s "Hermes of the Ways" or "Priapus." A good illustration is "Au Vieux Jardin":

> I have sat here happy in the gardens,
> Watching the still pool and the reeds
> And the dark clouds
> Which the wind of the upper air
> Tore like the green leafy boughs
> Of the divers-hued trees of late summer;
> But though I greatly delight
> In these and the water lilies,
> That which sets me nighest to weeping
> Is the rose and white colour of the smooth flag-stones,
> And the pale yellow grasses
> Among them.[20]

In this poem the emotion to be conveyed is asserted in a simple declarative sentence in line 1; the images which follow explain the source of the speaker's happiness. As in Pound's "Middle-Aged," the abstract generalization precedes the concrete image, rather than arising from it. The speaker's pleasure in the scene is complex, and reaches an intensity difficult to distinguish from misery. These shifts in emotion are conveyed strictly by declarative statements; an examination of the images alone ("the rose and white colour of the smooth flag-stones") would not lead the reader to a similar affective response.

The language of the poem, although dominated by simple description of natural objects in the manner imagists prized, also exhibits elevated and artificial diction of the kind they sought to discourage. The phrases "green leafy boughs," "divers-hued trees," and "That which sets me nighest to weeping" are all examples. In its choice of a homely and everyday theme, this poem, like Pound's, does reflect a postsymbolist emphasis on the empirical world; but it nevertheless remains a pre-imagist poem.

The other two poems by Aldington published in the same issue in November 1912 use more esoteric settings for more abstract laments. The first, "Choricos," which Charles Norman identified as the poem Aldington began in 1911 in imitation of Euripides,[21] is an address to Death. The poem begins as follows:

> The ancient songs
> Pass deathward mournfully.
>
> Cold lips that sing no more, and withered wreaths,
> Regretful eyes, and drooping breasts and wings —
> Symbols of ancient songs
> Mournfully passing
> Down to the great white surges. . . .[22]

The major characteristic that this poem shares with imagist poetry is its use of free verse. That connection is not insignificant. The battle to free poetry from the demands of an obligatory regular metric was at times a strident one, and it was being aggressively waged by the founders of modernism (and others, like Robert Bridges and Maurice Hewlett) between the years 1908 and 1912. But in other respects, this poem might better be described as a degradation of symbolism. Even though Pound presented it as an example of imagism, it better illustrates his instructions about what not to do enunciated in "A Few Don'ts by an Imagiste" in March 1913.

The poem continues as a song to death, asserting an equation between that abstraction and various natural experiences, as in the sixth stanza:

> O Death,
> Thou art an healing wind
> That blowest over white flowers
> A-tremble with dew;
> Thou art a wind flowing
> Over dark leagues of lonely sea;
> Thou art the dusk and the fragrance;
> Thou art the lips of love mournfully smiling;
> Thou art the pale peace of one
> Satiate with old desires. . . .[23]

One of the most distinctive things about these lines is the absence of clear images. One can imagine a white flower bearing dew, but no visual image

readily arises for "a wind flowing / Over dark leagues of lonely sea."
Similarly, "the dusk and the fragrance" and "the lips of love mournfully
smiling" have insufficient detail for the reader to be moved by a concrete
vision, and Aldington's "pale peace" seems almost to anticipate the "dim
lands of peace" that Pound was so shortly to use as an illustration of what
not to do.[24] These examples are not isolated ones. The poem uses *thou*,
thee, or *thy* seventeen times, and *thou* is accompanied by the archaic form
of the verb: *art, blowest, layest, sealest*. Flowers are "a-tremble," and the
poem is generally beset by "pallid chaplets" and "illimitable quietude."

"To a Greek Marble," the third of the Aldington poems published in
November 1912, "presents / no adjunct to the Muses' diadem." The poem
is a direct invocation of a statue of a Greek goddess, undoubtedly like
those among the marbles in the British Museum where Aldington, H.D.,
and Pound spent so much time in these years. The poem is a lament that
the figure remains silent and unhearing despite the speaker's persistent
whispers of past trysts:

> I have whispered thee in thy solitudes
> Of our loves in Phrygia,
> The far ecstasy of burning noons
> When the fragile pipes
> Ceased in the cypress shade,
> And the brown fingers of the shepherd
> Moved over slim shoulders. . . .[25]

As in the previous poem, the majority of phrases combine an abstraction
with the concrete, with the result that the visual image is imprecise and
the intensity of the lines reduced. A "far" ecstasy is no more vivid than
an ecstasy, and even, by the expression of distance, perhaps somewhat
attenuated in imagined clarity. "Burning noons" approaches cliché, and
"pipes" gain very little in visible characteristics by being "fragile." The effect
of the poem depends more upon the emotive strength of nouns describing states of being than it does upon the reader's reaction to concrete,
vividly imagined objects or scenes.

There is an unstated comparison, however, which is very much in keeping with imagist techniques — comparison of the unresponsive marble
goddess with a real woman. Either the "White grave goddess" (line 2) is
literally the Greek marble of the title and the "loves in Phrygia" metaphoric, or the goddess is metaphor for a woman who remains oblivious
to the speaker's pleas, notwithstanding past intimacies. If the first reading is chosen, the poem deals with the completeness and autonomy of the
work of art, which elicits ecstasy and longing from its human beholder,
who can have neither completeness nor autonomy. If the second reading

is selected, the poem is part of a long tradition of male literary invocations to the beautiful but cruelly unresponsive woman, one who, in this case, is placed quite explicitly on a pedestal. The poem is enriched by the coexistence of these two patterns of meaning, as the suggestion that the words might express human sexual longing intensifies the sense of the observer's longing before the work of art. Conversely, a systematic reading of the poem as revealing the absolute dichotomy between the work of art and the human observer strengthens the apprehension of the remoteness of the human woman to which the marble seems to refer.

The imagist poems of H.D. stand in sharp contrast to these early poems of Pound and Aldington in clarity, sharpness, precision, objectivity, and use of a presentational rather than a discursive style. All three poems that she published in January 1913 use figures drawn from Greek mythology (as does Aldington's "Choricos"), but in a fashion as concrete as the original epics or stories. The poem entitled "Priapus" and subtitled "Keeper of Orchards," for example, begins:

> I saw the first pear
> As it fell.
> The honey-seeking, golden-banded,
> The yellow swarm
> Was not more fleet than I,
> (Spare us from loveliness!)
> And I fell prostrate,
> Crying,
> Thou hast flayed us with thy blossoms;
> Spare us the beauty
> Of fruit-trees![26]

The prayer is to Priapus, the son of Dionysus and Aphrodite, and thus offspring of revelry and love. He is the god of fruitfulness, the protector of the bees, the vine, the garden. He was represented in sculpture as the phallus or as a small garden god with twisted body and huge penis. The poem presents a moment in the orchard at harvest time, a moment fraught with intense and conflicting emotions.

It is the inevitable instant at which the ripeness of the maturing fruit passes from the conclusion of growth to the beginning of decay. It is the moment at which the fruit is at its sweetest. This swelling, fecund fruit is primal—it is the *first* pear—and its fall is primal too. Its uterine shape invokes the female gift for reproduction as the phallic god of the garden invokes the male. The speaker in the poem speeds by sight to the place of fall with the swiftness of the bees ("The honey-seeking, golden-banded, / The yellow swarm"), whom Priapus protects, who come to make honey from the fruit. The very act of seeing is an expression of passionate desire to apprehend that moment—its beauty, its meaning, its fruit. Made analogous to the bees by the identity of action, the speaker too seems about to recreate that moment into something sweet, something with the power to nourish and please. At that very moment of apprehension there is another apprehension, the recognition of the intense experience of plenitude, ripeness (perhaps, in a subtext, even of birth itself) as threat: ("Spare us from loveliness!")

Like the pear, the speaker falls—"prostrate, / Crying." The possible meanings of the fall and tears are many, and all are a part of the exegesis of that moment. The loveliness may be too great, the experience too intense, so that at the moment of its apprehension the ecstasy cannot be distinguished from pain. The moment of fruition may contain the recognition of destruction, and the experience of the greatest loveliness may make the inevitability of its loss through decay unbearable. The fall may be complete submission to the beauty perceived, and the tears the tears of joyous apprehension. Again, the fall may be the primal human fall, brought about by eating of the fruit of the tree of the knowledge of good and evil; the act of seeing the beauty and death in the moment of the pear's fall may be the modern counterpart to that ancient myth of overreaching. The fall may be a sexual fall, and the tears the reflection both of joy at that moment and anguish at its power to flay and to consume. The structure of the poem invites all these suggestions, and the poem derives its significance from the complicated sum of all of these endlessly interacting meanings.

The second stanza identifies this paradoxical moment of conflicting emotions as the peculiar triumph or affliction of the human speaker:

> The honey-seeking
> Paused not,
> The air thundered their song,
> And I alone was prostrate.

The speaker next renews the petition to the "God of the orchard" to "Spare us from loveliness" and pledges an offering. That offering is enumerated in the fourth and final stanza:

> The fallen hazel-nuts,
> Stripped late of their green sheaths,
> The grapes, red-purple,
> Their berries
> Dripping with wine,
> Pomegranates already broken,
> And shrunken fig,
> And quinces untouched,
> I bring thee as offering.

These offerings are of fruits past their prime; the grapes have begun to ferment, the pomegranates are broken, and the womblike fig has lost its ripe fullness. These fruits, like the untouched quinces, were not consumed in their ripeness. They are an appropriate gift from one praying to be spared the moment of consuming intensity.

The implication that the cost of escape from that moment is to die without being savoured again suggests a sexual subtext: the experiences that loveliness brings are anguishing, but the cost of escaping them is barrenness or inutility. In early fall 1912, when H.D. showed this poem to Pound, her own life was fraught with just such anguishing conflicts. Engaged to Pound before he left for Europe in 1908, H.D. in 1910 had become seriously involved with Frances Gregg. It was with Frances and her mother that H.D. had made the journey to Europe in 1911, from which H.D. was never permanently to return to the United States. Pound himself apparently also became involved with Gregg—one friend recalled him as "engaged" to her.[27] Throughout 1912, H.D. was constantly in the company of Pound and Aldington, whom she would not marry until 1913. It seems clear that in 1911 and 1912 H.D. was torn, both between heterosexual and homosexual attractions and between personal poetic creativity and the role of handmaiden and muse which she felt Pound thrust upon her.[28] Each sexual alternative must have seemed to offer anguish which could be escaped only at the cost of physical or poetic barrenness. The intensity of experience which this poem captures, then, has its correlative in H.D.'s own life, but the control she gains through the embodiment of the experience in juxtaposed images epitomizes the "objectivity" which came to be identified as a hallmark of modernism.[29]

Indeed, one of the striking aspects of this poem is the total absence of words which describe an emotion or state of being. Instead H.D. presents an action which embodies a mood. Contrast, for example, Aldington's

> I have sat here happy . . .
>   ("Au Vieux Jardin")
>
> Pity my sadness . . .
>   ("To a Greek Marble")

or Pound's "vague invarious delight" ("Middle-Aged") with H.D.'s

> I fell prostrate,
> Crying

The lines from H.D. are laden with all the ambiguity and radiance of observed experience; the mind returns to them again and again, reinterpreting as the feelings they elicit change with each added detail from the poem. The Aldington lines are simple assertion; if the speaker is not an authority upon whether he is happy or sad, who is? Thus the images that follow are simply elaboration upon the causes of the emotion named. The contrast illuminates with clarity the difference between the image as ornament and the image as speech.

In all three examples from Aldington and Pound, the abstraction precedes the images and controls the way they are understood. In "Priapus" the image, whether object or act, precedes any statement of mood and gives rise to the reader's apprehension of it. This difference has implications for the depth, intensity, and economy of the poem. Because the meaning of the event or image is not constrained by prior abstractions, the poem's interpretations are multiple and paradoxical. In some ways the poem's images and actions are much like a nonliterary event about which we have similar amounts of information. Our experience of the poem is intensified because we identify the emotion by a reflective awareness of our response to our own imaginative enactment of the scene.[30] We grasp the mood not by cognition of an external abstraction but by reflexive inspection of feeling. The poem is economical because each image is itself speech, not ornament; if we were to eliminate a set of images, the meaning of the poem would change. In contrast, in Pound's "Middle-Aged," for example, each of the comparisons which begin stanzas 2 and 3 ("As the fine flakes . . ."; "As the fine dust . . .") is essentially an expansion upon the meaning of the first simile, " 'Tis but a vague, invarious delight / As gold that rains about some buried king."

The same economy, the same precedence of image over abstraction, characterizes the second of the poems by H.D. which appeared in *Poetry* in January 1913. In this poem the crystalline structure is anticipated by the imagery itself. The first part begins:

> The hard sand breaks,
> And the grains of it
> Are clear as wine.
>
> Far off over the leagues of it,
> The wind,
> Playing on the wide shore,
> Piles little ridges,
> And the great waves
> Break over it.[31]

These lines match sound to scene almost to the point of being onomatopoetic. Consider: it/wine/it/wind/wide/piles/little/ridges/it: the *i*'s squeak like sand under foot; the single-syllable words keep time like footsteps.

(Pound said, "I believe that every emotion and every phase of emotion has some toneless phrase, some rhythm-phrase to express it.")[32]

The poem is the first of a powerful series of poems by H.D. that present the speaker buffeted at the boundaries of two colliding worlds. (One thinks, as well, of "Oread," "Evening," "Sea Rose.") At this boundary there is a no-man's-land that seems both land and sea. The wind which tosses the ceaselessly moving sea tosses the sand into small replicas of the waves which break over it. The speaker belongs to this boundary area. The fluid, restless sea, Great Mother, with its "leagues" of distance and depth, its fearsome power, its associations with creativity and psyche, and all the possibilities of its "many-foamed ways," draws her to its edge. The land behind is the sea's reciprocal: stable, sheltering, and safe, but it does not draw the speaker from the shore. Here the speaker finds "him / Of the triple path-ways, / Hermes, / Who awaiteth."

Hermes Trismegistus is the name given by Neoplatonists to the Egyptian god Thoth, whom the Greek Hermes closely resembled. Hermes the thrice great, believed to be the author of books of occult wisdom, was the god of writing, learning, and wisdom ("the triple path-ways"). In Greek mythology he was the inventor of the lyre, the alphabet, numbers, and music. He was both god of eloquence and protector of travelers, and small statues of his figure were set up along the roads. This is the figure who waits for the speaker. Whatever route may bring travelers to this boundary ("Facing three ways, / Welcoming wayfarers"), Hermes proffers the skills by which they may stay. The loneliness of this place, its link to what is primal in experience, its threat, are the speech of the images with which part I of the poem ends:

Wind rushes
Over the dunes,
And the coarse, salt-crusted grass
Answers.

Heu,
It whips round my ankles!

In the second part of the poem, the speaker looks inland from this boundary instead of toward the sea: "Small is / This white stream, / Flowing below ground / from the poplar-shaded hill, / But the water is sweet." Unlike the saltwater of the sea, the land water can sustain life, even though its flow is small in this boundary place. The "sea-orchard" of the first part here bears small, hard fruits, and "The boughs of the trees / Are twisted / By many bafflings." This is no ordinary beauty, for that which lives and grows shows the stress of its place on a boundary. Nonetheless, it stands on a stable place, and the sea does not destroy it:

> Twisted are
> The small-leafed boughs.
> But the shadow of them
> Is not the shadow of the mast head
> Nor of the torn sails.

The poem concludes with an invocation to Hermes, whose protection continues here at this place where the sea meets the land:

> Hermes, Hermes,
> The great sea foamed,
> Gnashed its teeth about me;
> But you have waited,
> Where sea-grass tangles with
> Shore-grass.

There is not a single direct statement of emotion in the poem. No word lays claim to desperation, struggle, fear, courage, or fortitude. Yet the poem communicates all these things and offers a spare and elegant vision of resolve before a challenge that almost overwhelms, and of will that refuses to relinquish two mutually exclusive worlds. Because it does not intrude the personal details of the poet's life, it elicits an intense response from any who have experienced deep conflicts. It is the relationship of the images, the form, which presents the structure of a primal human experience. Pound understood, in 1914, this power of poetry. He wrote:

The statements of [analytic geometry] . . . are "lords" over fact. They are the thrones and dominations that rule over form and recurrence. And in like manner are great works of art lords over fact, over race-long recurrent moods, and over to-morrow.

Great works of art contain this fourth sort of equation. They cause form to come into being. By the "image" I mean such an equation; not an equation of mathematics, not something about *a, b,* and *c,* having something to do with form, but about *sea, cliffs, night,* having something to do with mood.[33]

One can enrich one's understanding of H.D.'s "Hermes" by noting the elements of her own experience which may have given rise to it. An expatriate for only a year's length, H.D. surely stood on the boundary between two cultures. The "sea-orchard" which "shelters from the west" recalls the American heritage which she never relinquished, though she spent most of her adult life abroad. She stood on the boundary between two definitions of her sexual identity, and was shaping with pain an identity which relinquished neither role. She stood poised between a traditional childhood as the daughter of a distinguished professor and the unstable life of the expatriate writer abroad, and she again preserved elements of her heritage in her life and art. She faced the unfathomable depths of her psyche and her creativity, and she drew strength to confront them from her craft as a writer, from her study, and in time from her exploration of the wisdom of the occult. The myth of Hermes embodies those skills to which she turned for the strength to remain at the boundaries of her life.

These biographical details are unnecessary for an accurate reading of the poem, and would even narrow the meaning and intensity of the poem were they present. As it stands, the poem provides the form which readers fill with the comparable intense experiences of their own. In doing so, the poem anticipates more than the prescriptions of imagism. Its method is more fully described by the discussions of poetic form in Pound's essay "Vorticism" than by the early imagist documents, which focus chiefly on metric, economy, the use of ordinary language, the preference for metaphor over simile, and the avoidance of imprecision and abstraction. The way form (or the relationship of the elements of a poem) itself becomes an image is not explicitly considered in the first explanations of imagism in March 1913. Thus these poems do more than offer models for the description of imagism. They actually provide early poetic models for the important transformation of the static form of imagist doctrine into vorticism.

And it was vorticism which offered a description of a dynamic form which itself made a statement; form which could support the long poem with its efforts to offer comprehensive order for experience; form which enabled the poem to make an absolute statement because it imposed the same relationship among the "values" of the poem's "equation" even though readers drew the specific equivalence for each "value" from their own diverse experience; form which supported the multiple simultaneous meanings necessary to present the complexity of the modern world and the relativity of its truth. Thus, H.D. is far more than that relatively "minor" poet offered us by so many literary historians: the most talented imagist in the years of the beginnings of modernism, but a poet whose work remained within what Pound reviled as the creative cul-de-sac of "Amygism." Instead we must view her poems as important not only to the founding but also to the development of the dynamic current of modernism which shaped the nature of a literary generation and beyond.

But the writings about imagism and vorticism are Pound's. What credit is due a poet who does not explain her method or expound its benefits? The record compels one to argue that Pound's own understandings of what modern poetry should be trying to do significantly depended upon the models which H.D.'s poems offered him. The evidence may be summarized as follows.

On August 18, 1912, Pound was prepared to send to Harriet Monroe as "imagist" a poem of his own that met few of the criteria outlined for the imagist poem in "Imagisme" and "A Few Don'ts by an Imagiste" in March 1913. In September 1912 he sent three poems by Richard Aldington which similarly violated many of the precepts laid down six months later. Two of these first four poems, his own "Middle-Aged" and Aldington's "Choricos," he himself excluded from the anthology *Des Imagistes*, which was assembled in the summer of 1913, although it first appeared in February 1914.[34] In their stead he included two poems of his own which had appeared before an imagist school was established: "The Return," published in the *English Review* in June 1912, and "Doria," which first appeared in the *Poetry Review* in February 1912. Of these, the one that genuinely meets the more profound requirements of imagism is "The Return."

Between Pound's application of the word imagism to poems only distantly related to what became that movement's precepts and his enunciation of the characteristics of imagism came his reading of H.D.'s poems "Priapus" and "Hermes of the Ways." That reading led him, the record intimates, to reexamine his own work to find examples that approximated that standard. The result was the exclusion of "Middle-Aged" and the inclusion of "The Return," when he assembled the poems for *Des Imagistes* in spring and summer 1913. The result was also the description in March 1913 of the process by which imagism worked. Whether or not those precepts had been discussed in the spring or early summer of 1912, Pound clearly did not envision fully how they applied to actual poems when he sent "Middle-Aged" and "Choricos" to *Poetry*.

Pound very quickly grasped the first implications of H.D.'s poems — he had an almost unerring eye for poetic brilliance — but what he first saw was more technical than structural. As he reconsidered her work, and similar poems among his own, between spring 1913 and summer 1914, he saw more clearly the dynamic formal, structural principles which underlay such poems. The result of that understanding apears in the significant advance in poetic theory that characterizes the essay "Vorticism," which appeared in the *Fortnightly Review* on September 1, 1914. Preceding the composition of that essay Pound had been exposed to the theories of Bergson[35] and the drive toward abstraction of the cubists, futurists, and abstract expressionists in painting and of Gaudier-Brzeska in sculpture — as well as to the poetry of H.D. In "Vorticism," he stressed the nature of the image as a conception of the mind (with the capacity to be absolute which Bergson attributed to acts of intuition), and sought to explain the formal function of juxtaposed images in the poem as analogous to the "planes in relation" of postimpressionist art. He stressed the concrete and objective nature of the poetic image, even when it expressed a subjective state of mind, and he turned to the language of the geometers of the fourth dimension (then the subject of considerable attention in the popular scientific press)[36] in an attempt to explain how the images of a poem can combine to create a concrete form which cannot be visually represented in two planes. (Like the attempts to represent the fourth dimension by a succession of three-dimensional projections, the total form of the poem emerges from the superposition of a succession of coherent patterns implicit in the relationship of images in the poem and recreated in the mind of the reader.)

The most significant development in this essay is Pound's effort to develop a theory of poetic form and function which accommodates the simultaneously visual and dynamically conceptual character of poetry. He had developed by February 1912, before he encountered H.D.'s poems and described the precepts of imagism, the idea of an absolute rhythm in poetry which makes its statement without interpretation. As Hugh Kenner has argued, it is on this, fundamentally musical, idea that the excellence of "The Return" (June 1912) was based.[37] Now he sought to broaden and expand his theory to reflect in a more sophisticated way than the early precepts of imagism did the visual and conceptual character of poetry as well. In an early version of the essay Pound made explicit the fact that the poems which had prompted these efforts were those of H.D.

The essay "Vorticism," which is widely discussed by Pound critics as central to his mature concepts of poetic form, is an elaboration and expansion of "Vortex. Pound." which appeared in *Blast* 1 (June 20, 1914). Pound concluded that essay thus:

Poetry

The vorticist will use only the primary media of his art.
The primary pigment of poetry is the IMAGE.
The vorticist will not allow the primary expression of any
concept or emotion to drag itself out into mimicry.
In painting Kandinski, Picasso.
In poetry this by, [*sic*] "H.D."

Whirl up sea —
Whirl your pointed pines,
Splash your great pines
On our rocks,
Hurl your green over us,
Cover us with your pools of fir.[38]

The poem, of course, is "Oread," which had apeared in the *Egoist* in February 1914. Significantly, Pound ranges H.D. beside Kandinsky and Picasso as innovators of the modernist form he sought to describe. Clearly the poems of H.D. continued to be examples which served Pound as a basis for the elaboration of his own ideas of poetry.

Pound's poems, as well as his critical writings, changed in the months immediately after his discovery of H.D.'s work. The evidence lies in the poems published as "Contemporania" in the April 1913 issue of *Poetry*. These poems were sent to Monroe in several batches between October 1912 and their appearance.[39] Pound's letter to Monroe on October 13, 1912, appears to be a cover note for the first group of poems; in it he comments specifically on "The Epilogue" and "The Dance" (which may be "Dance Figure") and alludes with some comments about "the 'Yawp' " to "A Pact," a poem addressed to Walt Whitman. These three poems, assembled a few days after he sent H.D.'s poems to Monroe, clearly have not yet made the transition to an imagist method. Pound explicitly is uneasy about them.

One, "A Pact"—a narrative poem with a few telling images—is a pledge to use Walt Whitman's poetic innovations, presumably his everyday diction and free verse, both of which were inspiring Pound's French contemporaries:

> I make a pact with you, Walt Whitman—
> I have detested you long enough.
>
> . . .
>
> It was you that broke the new wood,
> Now is a time for carving.[40]

Given the date of its submission, the poem is a fascinating declaration of a decision to adopt a new language. (It also anticipates Yeats's analogous declaration in "A Coat," which appeared first in *Poetry*, in 1914.) Although more direct and colloquial, it does not itself fully illustrate the new style, since the fundamental statements of the poem are made by direct assertion rather than by image.

Of the other two poems listed in this first batch, "The Epilogue" was never published (the poem by that name in *Collected Shorter Poems* is a different one);[41] and " 'The Dance,' " Pound wrote, "has little but its rhythm to recommend it."[42] If the reference is to "Dance Figure," the judgment was too harsh, and he let the poem appear. In any case, Pound seems to be measuring his poems against a style he could not yet quite command. During the next two months, however, he developed his own version of the directness, the clarity, the economy of imagist statement, which he so much admired in the poetry of H.D.

The most important evidence of this achievement is "In a Station of the Metro," a poem which he used in "Vorticism" to explain his evolution from his pre-imagist to his imagist phase. In the essay, Pound dates that progress as eighteen months earlier. Since "Vorticism" was published September 1, 1914, a year and a half earlier would be March 1913, a month before the poem appeared. (Such a late dating for the poem might be supported by Pound's casual remark in "How I Began" in *T.P.'s Weekly* of June 6, 1913, that he had been trying to write the poem for "well over a year" and had composed its final version "only the other night.")[43] If, on the other hand, Pound meant to date his composition of "Metro" as eighteen months before the time of writing (rather than publishing) the "Vorticism" essay, the poem would have been composed in November or December of 1912, since the publishing history of *Blast* shows that the essay could not realistically have been written earlier than May 1.[44] This would place the writing of "Metro" just before the time Pound sent in the second batch of poems for the "Contemporania" sequence. The poem is commonly associated with the beginnings of imagism and hence is usually treated as if it were prior to H.D.'s poems, or at least simultaneous. In fact, though, it must have been written in the two months after he had sent H.D.'s poems to *Poetry*.

Evidence that Pound sought to develop a more direct, economical style, free from archaism and more reliant on the image, in the three months following his discovery of H.D.'s poems also exists in the language and printing history of "Contemporania." In addition to "Dance Figure," "A Pact," and "In a Station of the Metro," nine other poems made up the "Contemporania": "Tenzone," "The Condolence," "The Garret," "The Garden," "Ortus," "Salutation," "Salutation the Second," "Pax Saturni," and "Commission." Of these, "Pax Saturni" was not reprinted until the 1960s, when it appeared under the title "Reflection and Advice."

Four others were omitted when the sequence was reprinted August 15, 1913, in the *New Freewoman*, accompanying an essay by Rebecca West which summarized key excerpts from "Imagisme" and "A Few Don'ts." She introduced the sequence with the words: "The following poems are written by Mr Ezra Pound since he became an *imagiste*."[45] Interestingly, the poems which were omitted — "A Pact," "The Condolence," "Ortus," and "Commission" — are poems with only limited claim to imagist style. Whether because he no longer thought them excellent or because he was pressed for space, Pound clearly selected for omission the transitional poems which most resembled his earlier work and least resembled the imagism for which, as we have seen, H.D. set the standard. The other poems of "Contemporania" show a new hardness, a new avoidance of abstraction, and a new commitment toward making the image the speech — as well as a satiric thrust which cannot be linked to H.D.'s models at all.

Pound himself described what had happened to his style between Octo-

ber 1912 and early 1913, with these lines from "Salutation the Second"
in "Contemporania":

> Here they stand without quaint devices,
> Here they are with nothing archaic about them.
>
> . . .
>
> Go, little naked and impudent songs,
>
> . . .
>
> Go! rejuvenate things![46]

Finally, there remains the difficult question of the nature of H.D.'s debt
to Pound. With respect to this, practically everyone has taken Pound at
his own estimation. He has claimed that he invented imagism to get H.D.
started.[47] Indeed, the whole circumstances of the fall of 1912 suggest that
Pound's "Ortus," written along with the other poems of "Contemporania,"
should be read as an address to H.D. — and as a claim to have made her:

> How have I laboured?
> How have I not laboured
> To bring her soul to birth,
> To give these elements a name and a centre!
> She is beautiful as the sunlight, and as fluid.
> She has no name, and no place.
> How have I laboured to bring her soul into separation;
> To give her a name and her being!
>
> Surely you are bound and entwined,
> You are mingled with the elements unborn;
> I have loved a stream and a shadow.
>
> I beseech you enter your life.
> I beseech you learn to say "I,"
> When I question you;
> For you are no part, but a whole,
> No portion, but a being.[48]

H.D. was a woman Pound "named," with the initials H.D., and she
lived behind them so completely that some reviewers of *Sea Garden* spoke
of the author as a man. She herself said, in 1958, "The significance of
'first love' can not be overestimated."[49] But she was also developing a life
and identity separate from the powerful personality of a man to whom
she had once been engaged. Some of her poems themselves testify to what
sort of stress was involved for this woman, in 1913, to become, "no part,
but a whole."

Nevertheless, as we have seen, the dates of his own actions belie Pound's claim that imagism was invented to publicize H.D.'s poetry, and the very self-absorption which could lead Pound repeatedly to claim responsibility for her career, and more, was a danger H.D. recognized and from which she withdrew. At some time in London, before his marriage, Pound again proposed to H.D., "Let's be engaged"; when her child was born, Pound appeared, to declare, " 'My only real criticism is that this is not my child.' "[50] But H.D. would not resume the relationship on Pound's terms. Years later she explained:

my poetry . . . was built on or around the crater of an extinct volcano. . . . The vines grow more abundantly on those volcanic slopes. Ezra would have destroyed me and the center they call "Air and Crystal" of my poetry.[51]

There can be no doubt that the relationship with Pound is important to H.D.'s decision to write poetry, and the whole question of H.D.'s debt to Pound is one which merits further attention. But treating H.D. as a poet Pound molded ignores the critical facts that she began her poetic career in the years just after her engagement to Pound ended, and that her first poems — which we do not have — were written for the woman who filled "like a blue flame" the "vacuum" Pound left.[52] (One may wonder if H.D. read "Ortus" with irony, and why indeed Pound chose not to reprint it in England in 1913.)

We cannot know what we would have seen of H.D.'s work without the admiration and encouragement of Pound's astonished, "But, Dryad, this is poetry." Her motivation may have been more than a little the determination to demonstrate her independent skill. But we do know that what she showed Pound was already poetry. That he proposed editorial changes should surprise none; many agree that both Yeats and Eliot profited from Pound's editorial hand, but few would argue that they would have been substantially poorer poets without it. The facts are that H.D. wrote powerful poems which support Pound's definitions of the image and the vortex — *before* he formulated these ideas and before his own poetry showed any consistent effort to achieve these goals. And, in addition, that in the months immediately after H.D.'s poems came into his hands, Pound's practice and his theory rapidly changed in an effort to define and demonstrate these ideals of poetic form. Without minimizing the significance of other figures or the tumultous intellectual currents of the day, we can surely say: H.D. appears to have been the catalyst and her poems the model which set modern poetry on its now familiar way.

NOTES

This essay previously appeared in *Sagetrieb* 4 (Spring 1985): 73–100.

1   Noel Stock, *The Life of Ezra Pound* (New York: Random House, 1970), 460.

2   I am now at work on a study entitled *Women and the Rise of Modernism* that will consider the contributions of H.D., Stein, Moore, Sitwell, Woolf, and Richardson to modernism, and the revisions in literary history and theory of the movement which their achievements imply.

3   Hugh Kenner discusses at length the significance of the doctrine of the image and notes that "Imagist propaganda merged into the Vorticist." He refers to Pound's transfer of attention from imagism to vorticism as a "change in terminology" through which Pound continued to elaborate the basic ideas which had been apparent in the essential elements of imagism. See *The Pound Era* (Berkeley: U of California P, 1971), 180–86, 191. Kenner does not, however, acknowledge the importance of H.D.'s work at critical moments in the development of the theory of the image. Kenner also takes at face value Pound's self-aggrandizing claim that the origin of imagism was a moment of casual generosity intended to get H.D.'s poems published, when the record is clear that he was trying to form a literary movement under the label of "imagism" before he had seen her poems. (See *Pound Era* 177.) For other recent critics giving due weight to the significance of imagist ideas in the rise of poetic modernism, see John T. Gage, *In the Arresting Eye: The Rhetoric of Imagism* (Baton Rouge: Louisiana State UP, 1981), 7 and passim, and Peter Jones, Introduction in *Imagist Poetry* (London: Penguin, 1972).

4   H.D., *Autobiographical Notes*, cited in Susan Stanford Friedman, "Hilda Doolittle (H.D.)," *Dictionary of Literary Biography*, Vol. 45: *American Poets, 1880–1945*, 1st ser., ed. Peter Quartermain (Detroit: Gale Research, 1986), 115–49.

5   Cyrena N. Pondrom, *The Road from Paris: French Influence on English Poetry, 1900–1920* (Cambridge: Cambridge UP, 1974), 20.

6   Pound to Isabel W. Pound, February 21, 1912, cited in Pondrom, *Road* 19.

7   Postcard, May 9, 1912, in "Selected Letters from H.D. to F. S. Flint," ed. Cyrena N. Pondrom, *Contemporary Literature* 11.4 (Fall 1969): 559. See also Stock, *Life of Ezra Pound* 116.

8   Pondrom, *Road* 22–23, 82–83.

9   Ezra Pound, "A Stray Document," *Make It New* (London, 1934), 335.

10 Pound to Harriet Monroe, August [18], 1912, *The Letters of Ezra Pound*, ed. D. D. Paige (London: Faber, 1951), 44.

11 H.D., *End to Torment: A Memoir of Ezra Pound*, ed. Norman Holmes Pearson and Michael King (New York: New Directions, 1979), 18.

12 Pound, *Letters* 46.

13 Ellen Williams, *Harriet Monroe and the Poetry Renaissance: The First Ten Years of "Poetry," 1912–22* (Urbana: U of Illinois P, 1977), 43.

14 Ezra Pound, "A Few Don'ts by an Imagiste," *Poetry* 1.6 (March 1913). Rpt. in Pound, *Literary Essays*, ed. T. S. Eliot (London: Faber, 1954), 4–5.

15 F. S. Flint, "Imagisme," *Poetry* 1.6 (March 1913). Rpt. in Pound, *Literary*

Essays 3. These two brief articles were the first printed explanations of the imagist movement.

16 "Vorticism," *Fortnightly Review*, September 1914, reprinted in *Gaudier-Brzeska* (New York: New Directions, 1970), 89.

17 Ezra Pound, *Collected Shorter Poems*, 2d ed. (London: Faber, 1968), 252.

18 Pound, "Vorticism," 88.

19 Janice S. Robinson, in *H.D.: The Life and Work of an American Poet* (Boston: Houghton Mifflin, 1982), 45–46, asserts that Pound's "Middle-Aged" was written in response to H.D.'s "Priapus" and "Hermes of the Ways," which he recognized as superior to his own poems. Such homage might be refreshing, but in this case must be untrue, since Pound sent "Middle-Aged" to Monroe on August 18, 1912 (see note 10, above). H.D. indicated in her unpublished *Autobiographical Notes* that Pound's reading of the two poems occurred in autumn, and internal evidence in Pound's letters suggests a date between the third week in September and the first week of October (Pound, *Letters* 44–45). Thus one must conclude that Pound had not seen the poems by H.D. at the time he composed "Middle-Aged."

20 *Poetry* 1.2 (November 1912). Reprinted in *Des Imagistes*, ed. Ezra Pound (1914; rep. New York: Frank Shay, 1917), 11.

21 Charles Norman, *Ezra Pound* (New York: Macmillan, 1960), 89.

22 *Des Imagistes* 7.

23 *Des Imagistes* 7–8.

24 As N. Christoph de Nagy has pointed out, the phrase "dim lands of peace" which Pound cited as a negative example actually may be found in "On a Marsh Road," a poem in the Ford Madox Ford (né Hueffer) volume *The Fear of the Night* (1904). See de Nagy, *Ezra Pound's Poetics and LIterary Tradition: The Critical Decade* (Berne: Francke Verlag, 1966), 58, 116. He acknowledges the reference in the midst of an argument insisting that it was Ford whose critical (as opposed to poetic) writings "freed Pound from the stilted archaic language of his early volumes." De Nagy attributes the influence particularly to the ideas contained in the preface to Ford's *Collected Poems*, an essay for which an early draft appeared as "Impressionism — Some Speculations" in *Poetry* in August and September 1913. Pound wrote Harriet Monroe announcing his discovery of the piece in May 1913 (see *Letters* 56–57), a month after the appearance of the two essays describing imagism and nearly eight months after his discovery of H.D.'s poetry. De Nagy treats H.D. largely as Pound's creation, and seeks to justify the priority he ascribes to Ford's influence by asserting the significance of 'man to man' discussion" (13).

25 *Poetry* 1.2 (November 1912). Reprinted in *Des Imagistes* 10.

26 *Poetry* 1.4 (January 1913). Reprinted in *Des Imagistes* 24–25. In later printings, the title is "Orchard."

27 Charles Norman cites an interview with Margaret Widdemer. See his *Ezra Pound* 6. For other discussions of the ambiguities and internal conflict of this period see H.D., *End to Torment* 17–19; Friedman, "Hilda Doolittle (H.D.)"; Barbara Guest, *Herself Defined* (New York: Doubleday, 1984), 32–39.

28   H.D., *End to Torment* 35.

29   Pound called for a verse "free from emotional slither" as early as February 1912, in the *Poetry Review* (rpt. *Literary Essays* 12), and T. S. Eliot made the idea of objectivity a touchstone of modern poetry for the next few years with his doctrine of the "objective correlative" in "Hamlet and His Problems" in 1919.

30   Put in the language of Bergson, we know the feeling directly and absolutely, for we enter it and grasp it from within, by intuition. The assertion *about* feeling, the abstraction, we know only relatively, for it is external to our mind, and we approach it only through the succession of points of view given to us by analysis. See Henri Bergson, "Introduction to Metaphysics," in *The Creative Mind* (Totowa, N.J.: Philosophical Library, 1965), 159–62. This classic essay, translated by fellow imagists T. E. Hulme and F. S. Flint in England in 1912, provides a philosophical rationale for many of the important goals and techniques of imagism. The fact that the poets did not use the philosophy systematically or acknowledge its significance openly does not undercut its importance in understanding the rise of modernism.

31   "Hermes of the Ways," *Poetry* 1.4 (January 1913). Reprinted in *Des Imagistes* 21–23.

32   Pound, "Vorticism," 84. Pound made comparable assertions as early as the beginning of 1912.

33   Pound, "Vorticism," 91–92.

34   Alfred Kreymborg says he received the poems for *Des Imagistes* before the end of the summer, 1913. See *Troubadour: An American Autobiography* (New York: Sagamore Press, 1957), 158. Stock says word of the anthology was circulating in London by June 22 (*Life of Ezra Pound* 139). Definite plans for publication were forthcoming by November, but Pound added at least one more poem — Joyce's "I Hear an Army Charging" — in early January 1914.

35   Stock (*Life of Ezra Pound* 106) says Pound attended a series of lectures on Bergson given by T. E. Hulme in November and December 1911, which probably included "Bergson's Theory of Art" and "The Philosophy of Intensive Manifolds."

36   Linda Dalrymple Henderson, "A New Facet of Cubism: 'The Fourth Dimension' and 'Non-Euclidean Geometry' Reinterpreted," *Art Quarterly* 34.4 (Winter 1971): 42. *Scientific American* actually held a contest in 1909 for submission of the best description of the fourth dimension. The author presents diagrams of mathematicians' efforts to represent the fourth dimension by a series of projections in three-dimensional space. I am grateful to Professor Barbara Buenger, Department of Art History, UW-Madison, for calling this reference to my attention.

37   Kenner, *Pound Era* 189–91.

38   *Blast* 1 (June 20, 1914): 154 (rpt. Santa Barbara: Black Sparrow Press, 1981).

39   Stock (*Life of Ezra Pound* 134) says the poems were sent "in two lots in October and December 1912." Williams (*Harriet Monroe* 43) says, "The group was selected out of a number of poems that Pound sent in several batches in 1912."

40 Pound, *Collected Shorter Poems* 98.

41 K. K. Ruthven, *A Guide to Ezra Pound's* Personae (1926; Berkeley: U of California P, 1969), 266.

42 Pound to Harriet Monroe, October 13, 1912, in *Letters* 45.

43 Ezra Pound, "How I Began," *T.P.'s Weekly*, June 6, 1913, 707.

44 The first plans for *Blast* did not use the label "vorticism." As late as April 15, 1914, the *Egoist* carried an advertisement for the first number, announced for April, which said the journal would discuss imagisme in verse, as well as cubism and futurism in art, but made no reference to vorticism. Kenner (*Pound Era* 238) says it was Pound who coined the phrase, and "held up [the review] some weeks" so that pages containing the vorticism manifesto could be added to those already printed. The first number did not come out until June 20. Clearly, Pound would not have drafted the essay for *Fortnightly* explaining vorticism before he had written the pages for *Blast*. Thus, May 1 is a practical earliest date at which the essay could have been drafted, a date which would place the composition of "Metro" in November. The likelihood is that Pound wrote the essay for *Fortnightly* after the appearance of *Blast* had caused so much fuss, and thus that "Metro" should be dated slightly later.

45 Rebecca West, *New Freewoman* 1.5 (August 15, 1913): 87.

46 Ezra Pound, "Salutation the Second," *Poetry* 2.1 (April 1913). Rpt. in *Collected Shorter Poems* 94–95.

47 For example, Pound to Glenn Hughes, September 26, 1927, in *Letters* 288. The same assertion, repeated in *Ezra Pound: Dichtung und Prosa*, figures in H.D.'s memoir of Pound, *End to Torment*, e.g., see page 4.

48 Pound, *Collected Shorter Poems* 93–94.

49 H.D., *End to Torment* 19.

50 Ibid., 30.

51 Ibid., 35.

52 Ibid., 8. I am very grateful to my colleague, Professor Susan Stanford Friedman, for urging me to examine the significance of Gregg in this connection, as well as for her thoughtful reading of this manuscript and her other very helpful comments on it.

CHAPTER 8

H.D.'s Romantic Landscapes:
The Sexual Politics of the Garden

CASSANDRA LAITY

The summer H.D. began *Helen in Egypt* she wrote exuberantly to Norman Holmes Pearson of the unpublished novel by Swinburne, *Lesbia Brandon*, which Bryher had recently sent her, "Oh this book is really the turn of the tide. I mean I have waited for the 'romantics' to come really back. . . . So now I can just get caught up in the tide, no more swimming against the breakers" (letter to Pearson, Aug. 8, 1952, Beinecke). As H.D. suggested, the antiromanticism of her male contemporaries had constrained her throughout her career. Critics such as Douglas Bush misread and dismissed H.D.'s poetics as a "fundamentally precious and romantic" Victorian Hellenism (Bush 505), leveling at her work the traditional charges against women's poetry—escapism, effeminacy, sentimentalism—in the name of a pernicious "romanticism." However, H.D. did not attempt to disguise her lifelong debt to the romantics. Pound had introduced her to Rossetti, Swinburne, Blake, and Morris during her adolescent apprenticeship in poetry. Together they read Swinburne almost obsessively in the early years of their brief engagement, and the Victorian-romantic is persistently echoed throughout *HER*, H.D.'s fictional autobiography of her sexual and aesthetic awakenings. Looking back in *End to Torment*, H.D. indirectly described both herself and Pound as a synthesis of London and America, "Mark Twain and William Morris" (*End to Torment* 40). And in her late Pre-Raphaelite novels, H.D. recreated both Morris and Swinburne as, respectively, father and brother figures to her autobiographical heroines, revealing her debt to the father and brother precursors of her mature poetics.[1] H.D.'s enthusiasm over the anticipated "turn of the tide" in favor of the romantics at the peak of her career indicates that she did not share her male contemporaries' anxiety of influence toward the ro-

110

mantic past; rather H.D. strongly identified with the outcast, "effeminate" tradition.[2]

Far from escapist and sentimental, H.D.'s transformed romanticism drew upon the romantics' preoccupation with the split between eros and spirituality projected in the dialectical landscapes of romantic quest romance. As with the romantics, H.D.'s search for a "lost land" she called "Hellas" ("Note on Poetry," 1287) signifies the inward quest for a reconciliation of sexuality and spirituality: the quest pattern of her psychic landscapes imitates the structure of romantic quest romance, as described by Harold Bloom, which frequently recounts a journey through "crisis" and despair in the "lower paradise" of sexual thralldom to a regenerate paradise of love where eros and creative autonomy are triumphantly reunited.[3] However, both the fallen and regenerate paradises of romantic tradition assume a poetics of male desire, which H.D. necessarily transformed, I suggest, to express the obstructed or liberated forms of desire within the female imagination. The sensuous trap or "Venusberg" typified by such poems as Keats's "La Belle Dame Sans Merci" or Swinburne's "Laus Veneris," in which the knight is doomed to endure the embrace of Venus for all eternity, projects specifically male anxieties about female domination. The moment of "crisis" for the male quester occurs when he becomes "feminized," and surrenders his sexual and imaginative freedom to a female principle of manipulative power; decadents such as Swinburne were labeled "effeminate" by male modernists Eliot and Yeats for their fascination with the overflowered love bower and its resident dominitrix.[4] Male modernists were more tolerant of the early romantics who reasserted sexual difference and male privilege in regenerate bowers of love such as Shelley's Hellenic paradise in *Epipsychidion*, where Shelley's quester projects a union with his beloved Emily.[5] Bloom's description of the consummated romantic quest as "a dialectic of love . . . uniting the imagination with its bride" envisions a hierarchical relation between the sexes in which the quester is male and the object of his quest is female ("Internalization," 17). While the romantic tradition provided H.D. with a form for her own debate about the possibilities of achieving a union of erotic fulfillment and creative autonomy, it inadequately expressed that conflict within the female imagination.

As Susan Friedman, Rachel DuPlessis, and others have shown, H.D.'s profoundly revisionary poetics continually redefined the tropes of male literary tradition in terms of the gender issues that must arise for the woman poet and visionary.[6] Shifting the focus of romantic quest to the female imagination, H.D. revised the tradition, I suggest, to create a poetics of female desire which both used and critiqued the conventions of romanticism. The overflowered, lower paradises of sexual appropriation in works such as "Hyacinth" and "Murex," I hope to demonstrate, describe the loss of female power to patriarchal conceptions of femininity and sexuality: H.D.'s enchantresses and female questers frequently decline in the sensuous trap of a consuming male desire. The way out of the morass explores alternatives to the romantic thralldom[7] that distracts the female imagination from intellectual and creative rigor. H.D.'s contrastingly spare and embattled "Hellas," I suggest, envisions a realm of homoerotic passion and sympathetic love between androgynous male and female spirits which disrupts the strict sexual differences of the male tradition by urging self-identification rather than polarization as a means to psychic completion. As with the early romantics, therefore, H.D.'s regenerate landscapes celebrate a triumphant union with the beloved as the fulfillment of the quest, but her displacement of the romantics' male poetics of sexual difference with the brother or sister bond disrupts the traditional "marriage plot" of romantic quest romance.[8] Similarly, while H.D. found affirmation for her exploration of same-sex love in the more homoerotic emphasis of decadents such as Swinburne, she forged her own poetics of desire from the Victorian-romantics, redeeming "forbidden" sexuality from its place in the appropriately "decadent" lower paradise to create a triumphant myth of female visionary and erotic power.

H.D.'s resulting poetics of desire bears out recent theories of a "female aesthetic" which elaborate on Nancy Chodorow's model for the social construction of female identity and sexuality. Chodorow's theory that male self-definition is constructed by insistence on separation from the mother and strict sexual difference, while female autonomy proceeds from connection and the mother-daughter bond, has been extended by DuPlessis, Elizabeth Abel, and others to define a female aesthetic of fluid boundaries and self-identification.[9] H.D.'s condemnation of the Lawrentian exaltation of sexual polarity in the "man-is-man, woman-is-woman" aesthetic (*Bid Me to Live* 136) manifests itself in her fallen bowers where the female victim frequently languishes in psychic thralldom to a male principle of power or self-destructs in the predatory politics of conventional male-female relationships. Alternatively, H.D. emphasizes "sameness" or the breakdown of gender difference in her "Greek" landscapes which frequently celebrate the sister bond. Significantly, even H.D.'s male homoerotic pairings in poems such as "Hyacinth" encode the sister bond in the apparently male myth. H.D.'s aesthetic of sameness also extends to heterosexual relationships, as I hope to show, where the sympathetic love is metaphorically projected as a "homoerotic" or "sister" bond in a symbolic Greek landscape.

Before examining works such as "Hyacinth" and "Murex" which integrate the dialectic of landscapes in H.D.'s evolving poetics of female desire, it will be useful to trace the early influence of the romantic landscapes H.D. found in Swinburne, particularly, on her first volume, *Sea Garden*.

I

The early imagist landscapes of H.D.'s *Sea Garden* demonstrate her debt to the romantic overflowered paradise and regenerate landscape as projections of obstructed or liberated states of mind. *Sea Garden* establishes a dialectic between the dense "sheltered garden" that "chokes out life" and the dynamic "wind-tortured" seascapes of triumphant, glinting flowers and distant rock terraces. In poems such as "Garden" and "Sheltered Garden," H.D. images the psychic paralysis traditionally associated with the romantic Venusberg. Usually oversweet, overflowered, and located in an enclosed space — a garden, bower, or glade — the romantic fallen paradise of love from Keats through the Pre-Raphaelites, decadents, and early Yeats conceals a deadly trap behind its apparently safe, sensuous refuge. Its dense, enclosed atmosphere proves stifling rather than protective; frequently overripe, the lush vegetation suggests the cloying sweetness of decay. Despite its sensuous promise, the love bower is actually sterile and blighting in its all-consuming torpor which anesthetizes its victim, overpowering all generative impulses, including sexual desire. As a metaphoric projection for mental processes, the garden signifies stasis, escapism, and psychic fragmentation rather than process, intellectual striving, and psychic unity.

H.D.'s oversweet, suffocating paradises introduced in *Sea Garden* illustrate Harold Bloom's description of the "lower paradise": "Where there is languor, the sense of the autumn of the body, there is always a suggestion of danger and limitation, particularly to the imagination" (*Yeats* 109). Although the "I" throughout most of H.D.'s *Sea Garden* is deliberately androgynous, she/he perceives the overflowered paradise as a sensuous trap. "I have had enough / I gasp for breath," cries the speaker in "Sheltered Garden," oppressed by the stifling enclosure of "border-pinks, clove-pinks, wax-lilies, / herbs, sweet-cress // . . . border on border of scented pinks" (*CP* 19). In poems such as "Garden" and "Orchard," the hot, overripe late-summer/autumnal paradises with their "grapes, red purple . . . dripping with wine" evoke the cloying sweetness of the lower paradise (*CP* 29). The atmosphere of the sheltered garden, like the Venusberg, suggests stasis and torpor: "this beauty . . . without strength chokes out life"; "fruit cannot drop / through this thick air" (*CP* 20, 25). H.D.'s speakers long to break out of their psychic paralysis and escape to the heady freedom of the alternate stormy landscape:

> O to blot out this garden
> to forget, to find a new beauty

in some terrible
wind-tortured place.

(*CP* 21)

The only gendered poem in *Sea Garden*, "The Gift," reveals H.D.'s association of the sheltered garden with the traditional romantic Venusberg. In
that poem H.D.'s tormented speaker suffers under the influence of a sensuous "Venus" whose garden is "over-sweet . . . strangling / with its myrrh-
lilies" and imaginatively frees herself in a sparse, tranquil seascape (*CP* 18).

The alternative, spare seascapes of *Sea Garden* derive in part from
Sappho,[10] but the embattled displaced flowers and stark beauties of H.D.'s
psychic landscapes also respond strongly to the romantic visionary tradition of the "sublime."[11] Although H.D.'s first volume appears to reject
the excesses of romanticism for the "dry hardness" of classical art
celebrated by T. E. Hulme in his program for a more "realistic" and concrete modernist poetics (126), H.D.'s use of classical landscape to convey
heightened states of consciousness finds a source in romantic visionary
tradition. The clash of elements and the dangerous heights of *Sea Garden*'s "terrible wind-tortured place" suggest Edmund Burke's definition
of the sublime literary landscape which "excite[s] the ideas of pain and
danger" and is therefore "productive of the strongest emotion which the
mind is capable of feeling" (58). While H.D.'s speakers languish in the
sheltered garden, her sea flowers flourish in the harsh assault of the elements. Poems such as "Huntress" and "Pursuit" evoke the heady dangers
of a chase through wild territory. The famous confusion of sea and land
in later imagist poems such as the much-quoted "Oread" — "Whirl up, sea —
/ whirl your pointed pines" — suggests psychic process rather than stasis
in the uncertain flux of the landscape. Unlike the torpid sheltered garden,
the galvanizing sea garden images psychic power, mental clarity, and the
battle of contraries which brings all faculties to bear.

Swinburne, perhaps the chief poet among H.D.'s early masters, appears
to have exerted the strongest influence on H.D.'s conception of the dual
romantic landscapes in *Sea Garden* and her later work. H.D. read Swinburne not as a perverse, "decadent" poet, but as a romantic mythmaker
of psychic landscape who also explored alternate forms of desire. Pauline
Fletcher traces Swinburne's recovery of the romantic sublime in poems,
such as "Thalassius," which describe the poet-speaker's progress from the
stifling love bower to the purgative influence of the wild seascape (Fletcher
191–223).[12] H.D. would have encountered Swinburne's decadent, scarlet
love bowers in the erotic *Poems and Ballads*, which she and Pound read
to each other in the early years of their courtship, and which she read
to her friend and lover Frances Gregg. The late summer love bowers of

poems such as "The Two Dreams" recall H.D.'s stifling gardens in *Sea Garden*:

> Even this green place the summer caught them in
> Seemed half deflowered and sick with beaten leaves
>
> . . .
>
> The trees' weight burdening the strengthless air.
>
>   (Swinburne 2:19)

In *HER*, H.D.'s fictional account of the adolescent experiences that shaped her poetics, Swinburne's lines continually prompt Hermione's meditations; and Swinburne himself is read, discussed, and invoked throughout the novel.[13] H.D. was clearly attracted to Swinburne's disruptive, stormy landscapes. While Hermione leafs through her Swinburne in *HER*, she vents her restlessness with familial and romantic constraints in her yearning for a snowstorm — "I'd give anything to see snow against swirling waters" — and subsequently quotes Swinburne's allusion to a spare snowy landscape in "Before the Mirror" (*HER* 126, 127). Lines from Swinburne's *Atalanta in Calydon* suggestive of the chase and spring renewal, "the hounds of spring are on winter's traces," consistently express Hermione's desire to escape her home and run freely by the sea, recalling poems such as "Pursuit" in *Sea Garden*.[14] Later, H.D.'s notes for her unpublished Pre-Raphaelite novel, *White Rose and the Red*, draw attention to Swinburne's childhood love of the sea and its significance as the expression of his mythology. She notes, "Buffeted by the sea . . . struggle, caused young S. pleasure. Cruelty and beauty in S., as in the sea. S. stoicism face of elements. His own mythology vs. religious instruction" ("Notes on Pre-Raphaelites," 28). H.D. clearly identified with Swinburne's rejection of external constraints in his passionate mythology of the elements.

The wind-buffeted flowers and seascapes of *Sea Garden* demonstrate a clear debt to Swinburne's similarly purgative, transplanted sea gardens. H.D.'s "The Gift" may have been directly influenced by Swinburne's "Laus Veneris," which was among H.D.'s favorites: like H.D.'s speaker, Swinburne's knight is ensnared by Venus' "hot" overflowered bower and imagines freedom "where tides of grass break into foam of flowers" — the mixed metaphor of sea and land also recalling H.D.'s later "Oread." Further, H.D.'s triumphant displaced flowers in *Sea Garden* may have drawn from Swinburne's stoic sea gardens which are also more beautiful for their triumph over the elements: like H.D.'s "Sea Rose" — "more precious than a wet rose / single on a stem" — Swinburne's "foam flowers endure when the rose blossoms wither" (Swinburne 3:18). In poems such as "The Triumph of Time" (among Pound's favorites), Swinburne's sea flowers feed on the searing energy of the sun: "with lips wide open and face burnt blind / the strong sea-daisies feast on the sun."

However, Swinburne did not specifically link his well-known celebration of Sapphic love with the regenerate seascape; rather he included homoeroticism among the range of "decadent" preoccupations pictured in the lower paradise which prompted his tormented personae to long for refuge and self-contemplation in the cleansing wash of the sea. H.D. would transform Swinburne's lonely seascapes into Sapphic communities of creative power,[15] disregarding at once both the immoral connotations of Swinburnian "decadence" and the stoic resignation of his world-weary, fin-de-siecle romanticism.

II

Following *Sea Garden*, H.D. evolved from the androgynous, fragmented quest pattern of her early imagism toward a reintegration of the dual romantic landscapes in a more distinctive poetics of female desire. H.D.'s later poem "Hyacinth" draws upon the romantic tradition of opposing landscapes to debate the issues of gender and sexuality and their relation to creative autonomy that would preoccupy her more mature poetics. Ostensibly a dramatic monologue in which the bereaved Apollo rejects the advances of a fiery temptress for love of the beloved boy Hyacinth he accidentally killed in a discus contest, "Hyacinth" 's fallen overflowered love bower and contrastingly sparse mountain haunt illustrate the tension between an obliterating, predatory heterosexuality and a "pure" inspiring homoerotic love within a single consciousness. Although the consciousness is male (Apollo), and the alternative sexuality he claims on the sparse mountainside describes the father-son or male homoerotic relation between Apollo and the young Hyacinth, H.D. uses the male mask, I suggest, to assert the female aesthetics of "sameness" as described above. While the homoerotic myth may encode H.D.'s own lesbian desires, and particularly her relationship with Bryher, there is evidence to suggest that H.D. uses the man-boy relation in "Hyacinth" to project the spiritual bond H.D. believed she had shared with Richard Aldington — a sympathetic love that was painfully severed by his preference for the "feminine" and sexually vital "temptress," Dorothy Yorke. However, before discussing the autobiographical dimensions of "Hyacinth" 's love triangle, I will establish the poem's debate between the two forms of desire projected in its dialectical romantic landscapes.

Apollo's monologue moves from his rejection of the debilitating "lower paradise" inhabited by the temptress to an imaginative projection of the purgative mountain haunt where he will remain faithful to the memory of Hyacinth. From the opening of the poem, in which Apollo reveals his preference for Hyacinth over the outraged seductress, Apollo's enraptured meditation on his homoerotic passion establishes a clear dichotomy between the two forms of desire as debilitated or empowered states of being. Apollo begins,

> Your anger charms me,
> and yet all the time
> I think of chaste, slight hands,
> veined snow;
> snow craters filled
> with first wild-flowerlets;
> glow of ice-gentian. . . .

The rush of associative imagery which merges the contraries of scarlet heat with "white" intensity in Apollo's contemplation of Hyacinth's hands encodes his homoerotic desire as a merging of both physical and intellectual passion. Similarly, the landscapes which dominate the poem assign the unity of sexuality and spirituality to the mountain- and seascape where Apollo imaginatively retreats from the stifling lower paradise. As in Swinburne's "Laus Veneris," or H.D.'s earlier "The Gift," the speaker's meditation progresses from the deadly lower paradise to an imaginative projection of his purgative retreat. However, "Hyacinth" 's celebration of homoerotic love redefines the romantic poetics of male desire, I suggest, revealing H.D.'s mistrust of the prevailing sex-gender system. Whereas "Hyacinth" 's lower paradise with its "feminine" and fiery temptress condemns the passion that depends on power play and sexual difference, the poem's regenerate mountain "garden" urges the disruption of gender roles and celebrates the eros of self-identification and "sameness" associated with the female aesthetic.

"Hyacinth" therefore enacts a drama of imprisonment and escape in its romantic landscapes whereby the questing Apollo rejects the predatory passion of the love bower for the unconventional territory of same-sex love. A classic Venus figure with "red lips" and "russet hair," the seductress inhabits an enticing garden which like the Venusberg of romantic tradition conceals a subtext of death and decay in its imagery of confinement, stagnation, and finally extinction. The bereaved Apollo both perceives and rejects the lurking threat to his psyche posed by the overripe overflowered love bower she offers to him:

> Take the red spoil
> of grape and pomegranate

the red camellia,
the most, most red rose;
take all the garden spills,
inveterate,
prodigal spender. . . .

(*CP* 202)

The garden associated with the temptress' charms shares the highly charged color and sensuous glut of late summer paradises such as "Garden" in the earlier *Sea Garden*. Like the romantic Venusberg, the paradise approaches putrefaction: overripeness to the point of rottenness is latent in images such as "red spoil," with its double meaning as both the trophy of sexual conquest and its assured decay, and "garden spills," which are at once overluxuriant plants and discarded "slops." In the remaining lines of Apollo's description, the dense catalogue of "heavy" petaled and strongly perfumed flowers which overaccumulate to the point of suffocation suggests the torpor and cloying sweetness of the romantic Venusberg, recalling Venus' love bower in Swinburne's "Laus Veneris" — "her beds are full of perfume and sad sound":

prodigal spender
just as summer goes,
the red scales of the deep in-folded spice,
the Indian, Persian and the Syrian pink,
their scent undaunted
even in that faint,
unmistakable fragrance
of the late tuberose,
(heavy its petals,
eye-lids of dark eyes
that open languorous
and more languorous close — the east . . .)
take these.

(*CP* 202)

The garden's narcotic influence is suggested in the image of closed eyes that concludes the passage. Further, images of confinement accumulate in the "deep in-folded spice," the later "whorls" of "clustered peonies," and other references to the garden's dense vegetation. Apollo's allusion to the love bower as "swales" or swamplands in his angry injunction "keep all your riot in the swales below" clearly reveals his perception of the garden as a realm of psychic stagnation and corruption, located, significantly "below." Finally, he recognizes the annihilating force of the garden's deceptively "safe" refuge in his parting threat to the doomed temptress — "you have your short / tense space of blazing sun" — who will self-destruct like the autumnal paradise in the caustic sun of her passions. Similarly, H.D.'s "Hymen," described by Susan Gubar ("Sapphistries," 55) as a "somber meditation on the predatory nature of heterosexuality," dramatizes a suggestively violent form of sexuality in its "hot sheltered glen." The metaphorical "rape" which climaxes the poem's marriage ceremony projects the bride's initiation into eros in a colorfully charged love bower where the "plunderer" bee "slips / between the purple flower-lips" as "the sun lies hot across his back."

"Hyacinth" 's alternative landscape of mountain and sea ledge to which Apollo imaginatively retreats forms an exhilarating contrast to the stasis he perceives in the deathly "swales below" of predatory heterosexual passion. Apollo's visionary landscape associates the upper regions, both high and expansive, with the inviolate homoerotic attachment to Hyacinth; and his reverie generates images of transformation, creative intensity, and renewal. While Apollo complains that Hyacinth's death has left him feeling "worthless / weary, world-bedraggled," "nevertheless," he asserts that in the

> mountains
> still the rain
> falls on the tangle
> of dead under-brush,
> freshens the loam,
> the earth and broken leaves
> for that hoar-frost
> of later star or flower,
> the fragile host
> of Greek anemones.
>
> (*CP* 204–5)

The lower paradise is merely seasonal, but the mountain haunt perpetually renews itself: apparently cast out, "dead under-brush," Apollo will be reborn, as loam gives way to "later star or flower." Images of elemental change — rain becomes hoarfrost — and dazzling contrasts, as frost and flower give the appearance of stars, project the process of ontological change. Like H.D.'s imagist poem "Oread," and Swinburne's imagined seascape in "Laus Veneris," "where tides of grass break into foam of flowers," H.D.'s rendering of Apollo's preferred mountain landscape confuses images of the sea and land in a dynamic interchange:

> all, all I gladly give
> who long but for the ridge,
> the crest and hollow,

the lift and fall,
the reach and distant ledge
of the sun-smitten,
wind-indented snow.

(*CP* 206)

The impression of expanding rather than confining space created by the rapid ebb and flow of the landscape in the superimposition of wave and mountain ridge inscribes Apollo's psychic regeneration beneath the passage's apparent self-effacement.

Having rejected the lower paradise, Apollo does not forfeit eroticism like Swinburne's solitary questers in poems such as "Thalassius," but explores another mode of desire in the vision of the mountainside where he maintains his loyalty to Hyacinth. Apollo asserts the triumph of his homoerotic passion over the temptation of "the swales below" in his reference to the memory of Hyacinth as "one last flower" "upon the mountain slope" which endures, even "cleaves" to "the wet marge of ice." (Apollo, of course, preserved the memory of Hyacinth in the hyacinth flower which he created from the boy's blood.) Defying the temptress' solicitations, Apollo continues, "you and autumn yet / can not prevail / against that flame, that flower / (ice, spark or jewel) / the cyclamen, / parting its white cyclamen leaves" (*CP* 204). The iced cyclamen hearkens back to the glinting, salt-encrusted sea flowers of *Sea Garden*; but here the triumphant cyclamen appears to image the flowering and opening of homoerotic desire, as Apollo celebrates his enduring attachment to Hyacinth over the blighted sexuality of the temptress and the suffocating design of her contrastingly "in-folded" flowers.

While "Hyacinth" may well encode H.D.'s bisexuality in the homoerotic coupling of the poem,[16] there is also evidence that H.D. uses the homoerotic myth and the hyacinth flower frequently found in her regenerate "Greek" paradises to evoke the spiritual communion she shared with Richard Aldington, which H.D. believed had been shattered by the "temptress" Dorothy Yorke.[17] H.D. uses the Hyacinth myth elsewhere to encode her "homoerotic" attachment to Aldington prior to his sexual betrayal with the passionately "female" Dorothy Yorke. In *Hipparchia*, a deliberate fictionalization of the Aldington-Yorke triangle, H.D.'s autobiographical heroine, Hipparchia, assumes the mask of the boy Hyacinthus slain by Apollo during her lovemaking with the virile Marius (based on Richard Aldington). The fluid, transformative nature of their sexual intimacy is imaginatively rendered through the homoerotic myth as Hipparchia recreates herself in the image of Hyacinthus, "with mouth caught inward by a firm line of white teeth, it was a boy, stricken in adolescence. . . .

Hipparchius slain by Helios" (*Hipparchia* 29, 30). Later, in the company of the scarlet courtesan Olivia (based on Dorothy Yorke), who has seduced Marius from Hipparchia, Marius recalls the more subtle and protean power of Hipparchia's "homoerotic" sexuality in the "vision" of the slain boy, "underlip caught inward by a firm line of white teeth," that "for a moment challenged the vulgarity of the new shade of scarlet" (31). H.D. consistently depicted Yorke as a classic "harlot," "doomed to self-extinction," as Julia remarks of Arabella in *Bid Me to Live* (8); and throughout *Hipparchia* she emphasizes her heroine's resemblance to the hyacinth, "honey flower." The similarly drawn opposition between the shallow eros of the enflamed seductress in "Hyacinth" and the homoerotic intensity of the bond between Hyacinth and Apollo suggests that H.D. encodes in the poem her conviction that Aldington's sexual betrayal had violated their sacred, sympathetic union for a self-destructive passion. In *Hipparchia*, Marius recognizes too late that the courtesan merely satisfies his body, while Hipparchia touches his soul; "Hyacinth" may therefore be H.D.'s revenge on Yorke—the poem enacting H.D.'s fantasy in which Aldington rejects Yorke for the sympathetic bond, now hopelessly severed.

Further, the encoding of the Aldington-Yorke-H.D. triangle in "Hyacinth" explains Apollo's puzzling lament to the temptress, "take all for you have taken everything," which implies that the femme fatale and her luxuriant paradise have come between himself and his inviolate love for Hyacinth—the Greek myth did not include a third. There is strong textual evidence to suggest that H.D. had both Aldington and her precursor, Swinburne, in mind when she wrote those lines. Apollo's anguished refrain, particularly in the lines "take all . . . but do not let me see you taking this," is a conscious borrowing from Swinburne's similar refrain in his "Hymn to Proserpine" (Swinburne 1: 67–73)—"wilt thou take all Galilean / but these thou shalt not take"—which H.D. quotes specifically with reference to her loss of Aldington in the unpublished autobiographical novel *Asphodel*. There, Hermione uses Swinburne's lines to address an apparently malevolent deity who has "taken" her unfaithful husband, "Darrington": mourning her loss, Hermione quotes from two of Swinburne's poems in succession, "O sister my sister . . . will you yet take all Galilean . . ." (34). Finally, the lines from Swinburne's "Itylus," "O sister my sister," which precede the echo of his "Hymn to Proserpine," lend credence to the argument that H.D. fictionalized her bond with Aldington as a homoerotic attachment. Earlier in *Asphodel* during the courtship between Hermione and Darrington (Aldington), Hermione recalls Swinburne's lines—"O sister my sister"—as she recognizes in him the kindred "sister" spirit she seeks. The lines from "Itylus" (Swinburne 1: 54–56) would resonate throughout H.D.'s works for the rest of her career, always evoking the higher love between equals she sought in both men and women.

H.D. seems to have preferred to imagine her relationships with men in terms of a "homoerotic" connection—in poems such as "Towards the Piraeus" for example—which would not conflict with her creative autonomy. Whereas, H.D. believed, the conventional gender roles polarized the sexes and effaced the woman artist, an imagined "homoerotic" relation in which she assumed the mask of "boy" left her free for her art. H.D. uses the homoerotic myth of Hyacinth and Apollo elsewhere to signify a heterosexual love that disrupts conventional gender roles. In *Hippolytus Temporizes*, the androgynous Artemis suggests that the dying Hippolytus be transformed into a flower, like "Hyacinth," "as a symbol of my love" (128). Realizing that he is "lost" to the temptress Phaedra, Artemis abandons the idea. By donning the mask of "boy," H.D. was, perhaps, able to overcome the fear of psychic appropriation and maintain the appropriately worshipful, even desiring and passive relationship without endangering her art. If the homoerotic myth in "Hyacinth," therefore, recasts Aldington's sexual betrayal as the accidental slaying or severing of the sympathetic bond with H.D., the poem disassociates H.D. entirely from the predatory heterosexuality represented by the romantic Venusberg and thus affirms a poetics of "sameness" as opposed to the polarizing sexuality figured in the lower paradise.

H.D.'s "Murex," the second novel of her prose trilogy, *Palimpsest*, directly transposes the romantic dialectic of landscapes into the female visionary imagination without the mediation of a male mask. In this woman artist's narrative, H.D.'s poet heroine, Raymonde Ransome, painfully breaks through her self-obliterating romantic thralldom to patriarchal conceptions of beauty and sexuality and reconstructs a female aesthetic that will enable her to write. Raymonde Ransome's emergence from the psychic trap of her marriage and its dissolution during the war years are metaphorically rendered by her struggle to get "behind" the obscuring vision of Botticelli's overflowered *Primavera* to the "Greek" Delphic city of prophecy and creative inspiration. Again, H.D.'s transformation of romantic landscape redefines the lower paradise as a realm of predatory heterosexuality and recreates the regenerate paradise as the locus of a female aesthetics of self-identification—this time in the sister bond. Raymonde Ransome is unable to confront or escape her sense of sexual inadequacy at the loss of her husband to the more "feminine" and sexually vital Mavis Landor until she meets Ermentrude Solomon, the similarly unconventionally androgynous beauty who has also lost her husband to Mavis Landor. Raymonde discovers in Ermy her twin "sister" whose classic "Artemisian" beauty startles Raymonde out of her paralyzing endorsement of the sensuous feminine ideal Freddie prefers. Raymonde's homoerotic self-identification with Ermy's stark, androgynous beauty thus returns her symbolically to the Delphic city of a rigorous and uncompromising female creativity formerly blocked by the overflowered *Primavera* of female thralldom.

While "Murex" is set in London a decade after the war, the war-torn city figures less prominently in the narrative than the obscuring vision of Botticelli's *Primavera* which hovers insistently before Raymonde Ransome's mind's eye, imaging the apparently calm but inwardly devastated condition of her psyche. The overflowered paradise of romantic tradition in this self-consciously female narrative answers to Rachel DuPlessis' description of the "romantic thralldom" that characterized H.D.'s relationships with men: "an all-encompassing, totally defining love between unequals . . . which has the high price of self-obliteration and paralysis . . . and insists upon the differences between the sexes" ("Romantic Thralldom in H.D.," 406 below). H.D.'s overflowered *Primavera*, then, transforms the conventional lower paradise of male sexual anxiety to recreate the woman artist's uniquely female anxieties about the dangers to the psyche posed by female thralldom. Further, Raymonde's description of her own self-deceiving "charm" as the legacy of "the overflowered 1890s" and of the London artists as a "second flowering of the already overflowered 1890s" ("Murex," 125) suggests that H.D.'s evocation of wartime male sexual politics deliberately creates a network of associations with the sensuous but deadly floral landscapes of the romantics.

The image of Botticelli's *Primavera* provides an apt metaphor for Raymonde's romantic thralldom to her husband, conjuring up both the paradisal Italian landscape of her honeymoon in Florence, and the Italianate paradises of the British romantics — Keats, Shelley, Byron, and Landor — which she associates with London throughout the narrative. Conscious that in marrying Freddie she has surrendered her artistic identity, Raymonde laments, "she had not wanted so simply to marry Freddie. She had wanted to be free and wild and to find beauty on her own, on its own" (128). Raymonde remembers the Italy of "that past layer of consciousness that was life to her with Freddie" as a floral landscape of "almost oriental beauty . . . of self-effacement, of obliteration" (128). Like the conventional Venusberg, the *Primavera*, which conflates Raymonde's honeymoon and the London of the war years, projects a deceptively safe and sensuous but deadly refuge from reality. Raymonde's repeated references to the psychic trap of Botticelli's spring paradise — "the wonder of the Botticelli was simply that those creatures stood so static" — describe her own state of emotional and psychic paralysis. Raymonde unconsciously reflects upon her drugged, sensuous daze when she muses, "people in

Botticelli . . . moved in a mist, moved in some region of supersensuous beauty. Beauty to be understood . . . by the senses" (103, 104). Like the waxed sheltered garden of *Sea Garden*, Raymonde's *Primavera* is "artificial," "highly sensuous," and soporific with its "obvious dimmed pink pincushion roses and the obvious dimmed heavy shade of evergreens and the devious slightly sentimental turn of the head of the flaxen transparence of the elongated limbs of Flora" (125). Flora, the central "Venus" figure which inhabits the spring paradise, is a projection of Mavis Landor, the feminine ideal which Raymonde has failed to achieve and which she still, bitterly, endorses in her persistent thralldom to Freddie. Raymonde's constant refrain, "Behind the Botticelli there was another Botticelli, behind London there was another London that was clear and stark," reveals her struggle to strip away the obscuring palimpsest of the false and predatory eros represented in the blighting artifice of the lower paradise and discover a new form of desire that will release her creative energies — "Behind an Italian background of small and precise little pincushion pink roses, there was another Italy, another Venus."

The other Venus or female muse arrives in the form of Ermentrude Solomon, also mourning the loss of her husband to the femme fatale Mavis Landor. Once again H.D. equates the symbolic realm of inspiration and eros with the disruption of gender roles and conventional sexuality. Ermy's stark, Artemisian beauty, unacknowledged by male desire, attunes the drifting Raymonde to her slumbering powers and transports her symbolically to Delphi, the realm of a similarly androgynous and powerful female aesthetic. Raymonde's self-identification with Ermy's classic stature — "so tall / and narrow at the hips / with just such eyes" — sparks the rigorous and confrontational process H.D. associated with female creative energy and returns Raymonde to "another Raymonde," the relentless woman poet within her, "Ray Bart" (159). Disrupting the passive complacency of the Botticelli, Raymonde is irresistibly drawn behind the lower paradise to the "city" of creative energy inhabited by her relentless poet self:

Far and far and far and far — further than. . . . Flora with transparent draperies, spilled crocus, hyacinth, smaller unfamiliar herbs from South Italian meadows . . . another Raymonde . . . Ray Bart, held a gate-way to a city . . . [where] Ray Bart would always sleuth and trail and track her. (127)

Significantly, "Murex" concludes with Raymonde's decision to leave the London "mists and drift of anodyne" for the mountainous retreat Cret-d'y-Vau, where she will be forced to write: "the clear Alpine air inevitably focused, brought her mind to almost clairvoyant intensity of vision" (98).

As I have attempted to demonstrate, H.D.'s Hellas was not a fixed psychic or erotic territory; rather she reshaped the romantic visionary tradition to imagine new liberating possibilities which shifted with the changing patterns of her life and thought. H.D. used the Sapphic landscape to encode a range of relationships and forms of desire, from the heterosexual agenda of "Hyacinth" to the less erotic sister bond of "Murex," and the overtly lesbian desire projected in works such as *Hipparchia*. At the conclusion of that quest narrative, the Sapphic island paradise which Hipparchia apprehends in the young Julia's eyes "as in a sorcerer's crystal" recasts the romantic regenerate paradise as the locus of a triumphant lesbian love.

H.D.'s unique transformation of romanticism may account for the uncharacteristic exuberance of her modernist poetics. Struggling to break with the "effeminate," "escapist" tradition of the past, H.D.'s most antiromantic contemporaries preoccupied themselves with the urban wasteland, while the several forms of H.D.'s Hellas continued to generate new fictions from romantic explorations of gender and sexuality.

NOTES

This essay previously appeared in *Sagetrieb* 6 (Fall 1987): 57–76.

1 Swinburne is an imagined twin brother to H.D.'s red-haired Elizabeth Siddall in *White Rose and the Red*, and Morris her fatherly protector. H.D. repeatedly asserted that Morris would have been a more appropriate father than her scientist father, and adopted Morris as her "spiritual father" in *The Sword Went Out to Sea*. See my essay "H.D. and A. C. Swinburne: Decadence and Modernist Women's Writing," *Feminist Studies* 15 (Fall 1989), for more on H.D. and Swinburne.

2 H.D. does not appear to have shared the antagonistic relation to the past described by Harold Bloom in his analysis of the male tradition's "anxiety of influence."

3 See Harold Bloom's definition of romantic quest in his "The Internalization of Quest Romance."

4 Yeats described his own early poetry in the 1890s as "effeminate" and "womanish." He cautioned George Russell against succumbing to the influence of a decadent poetics, "that region of brooding emotions . . . which kill the spirit . . . [and whose dwellers] speak with sweet, insinuating feminine voices" (*Letters* 435).

5 In Yeats's "The Philosophy of Shelley's Poetry," he looks favorably on the female figures in Shelley's poetry which he perceives as images for beauty and art within the male imagination.

6 Susan Friedman explores H.D.'s revisionist mythmaking in her groundbreaking *Psyche Reborn* which focuses on H.D.'s transformation of Freud's influ-

ence. Rachel Blau DuPlessis' recent inquiry into H.D.'s feminist enterprise in *The Career of That Struggle* explores how H.D. claims "cultural authority, authority of otherness / marginality, gender authority, and sexual / erotic authority" (xiii).

7 Here I use Rachel DuPlessis' term, "romantic thralldom," in her discussion of the predatory pattern of H.D.'s relationships with men ("Romantic Thralldom in H.D.," in this volume).

8 See Rachel DuPlessis' *Writing Beyond the Ending* which explores twentieth-century women writers' revision of the conventions of narrative and particularly the "ending" of the romance.

9 See Rachel Blau DuPlessis' "For the Etruscans" and Elizabeth Abel's "(E)merging Identities: The Dynamics of Female Friendship in Contemporary Fiction by Women."

10 See Eileen Gregory's essay "Rose Cut in Rock: Sappho and H.D.'s Sea Garden," in this volume.

11 See Adalaide Morris' discussion of H.D.'s conception of "projection," and particularly her exploration of H.D.'s visionary interaction with her imagist landscapes in *Sea Garden*, in this volume.

12 See also David Riede's *Swinburne: A Study of Romantic Mythmaking*.

13 See Friedman and DuPlessis' discussion of H.D.'s rejection of an oppressive heterosexuality for self-identification with a sister-muse in *HER* (" 'I had two loves separate,' " in this volume). H.D.'s allusions to Swinburne in *HER* continually affirm the central homoerotic relationship between Hermione and Fayne Rabb.

14 Susan Friedman links H.D.'s allusions to oppressive heat and stagnant water in *HER* to "Garden" and H.D.'s stifling relationship with Pound; while she perceives the "Greek" poems in *Sea Garden* such as "Huntress" and "Pursuit" as expressive of H.D.'s liberation in the "sister-love" she found with Gregg ("Palimpsest of Origins," 70).

15 Adalaide Morris discusses the communal nature of H.D.'s visionary poetics in both her discussion of H.D.'s *The Gift*, "Autobiography and Prophecy: H.D.'s *The Gift*," and her essay on the "gift-economy," "A Relay of Power and of Peace: H.D. and the Spirit of the Gift," in this volume.

16 Friedman suggests that the reference to Hyacinth is an encoding of H.D.'s relationship with Bryher, noting images associated with Bryher — specifically hands and smallness — in the opening of the poem (review of *Hedylus*, 330).

17 I am indebted to Barbara Guest's biography of H.D., *Herself Defined: The Poet H.D. and Her World*, for the biographical information in this essay.

WORKS CITED

Abel, Elizabeth. "(E)merging Identities: The Dynamics of Female Friendship in Contemporary Fiction by Women." *Signs* 6 (Spring 1981): 413–35.

Bloom, Harold. *The Anxiety of Influence.* New York: Oxford, 1973.

Bloom, Harold. "Internalization of Quest Romance." *Romanticism and Consciousness: Essays in Criticism.* New York: Norton, 1970.

Bloom, Harold. *Yeats.* Chicago: U of Chicago P, 1970.

Burke, Edmund. *A Philosophical Inquiry into the Origin of Our Ideas of the Sublime and Beautiful.* New York: Garland, 1971.

Bush, Douglas. *Mythology and the Romantic Tradition in English Poetry.* Cambridge: Harvard UP, 1937.

Chodorow, Nancy. *The Reproduction of Mothering.* Berkeley: U of California P, 1987.

DuPlessis, Rachel Blau. *H.D.: The Career of That Struggle.* Bloomington: Indiana UP, 1986.

DuPlessis, Rachel Blau. "For the Etruscans: Sexual Difference and Artistic Production — the Debate over a Female Aesthetic." In *The Future of Difference,* ed. Hester Eisenstein and Alice Jardine, 128–56. New Brunswick: Rutgers UP, 1985.

DuPlessis, Rachel Blau. *Writing beyond the Ending: Narrative Strategies of Twentieth-Century Women Writers.* Bloomington: Indiana UP, 1985.

Fletcher, Pauline. *Gardens and Grim Ravines: The Language of Landscape in Victorian Poetry.* Princeton: Princeton UP, 1983.

Friedman, Susan Stanford. "Palimpsest of Origins in H.D.'s Career." *Poesis* 6 (Fall 1985): 56–73.

Friedman, Susan Stanford. *Psyche Reborn: The Emergence of H.D.* Bloomington: Indiana UP, 1981.

Friedman, Susan Stanford. Review of H.D. *Hedylus. Sagetrieb* 4 (Fall/Winter 1985): 325–34.

Guber, Susan. "Sapphistries." *Signs* 10 (Autumn 1984): 43–62.

Guest, Barbara. *Herself Defined: The Poet H.D. and Her World.* New York: Doubleday, 1984.

H.D. *Asphodel.* Beinecke Library, Yale University.

H.D. *Bid Me to Live (A Madrigal).* Redding Ridge: Black Swan Books, 1983.

H.D. *Collected Poems: 1912–1944 (CP).* Ed. Louis L. Martz. New York: New Directions, 1983.

H.D. *End to Torment.* New York: New Directions, 1979.

H.D. *Hedylus.* Redding Ridge: Black Swan Books, 1980.

H.D. *Helen in Egypt.* New York: New Directions, 1961.

H.D. *HERmione.* New York: New Directions, 1981.

H.D. *Hippolytus Temporizes.* Redding Ridge: Black Swan Books, 1985.

H.D. Letter to Norman Holmes Pearson, Aug. 8, 1952, Beinecke Library, Yale University.

H.D. "A Note on Poetry." In *The Oxford Anthology of American Poetry,* Vol. 2, ed. William Rose Benet and Norman Holmes Pearson, 1287–88. New York: Oxford UP, 1938.

H.D. *Notes on Pre-Raphaelites.* Beinecke Library, Yale University.

H.D. *Notes on Recent Writing* (1949). Beinecke Library, Yale University.

H.D. *Palimpsest*. Carbondale: Southern Illinois UP, 1968.

H.D. *Trilogy*. New York: New Directions, 1973.

H.D. *White Rose and the Red*. Beinecke Library, Yale University.

Hulme, T. E. "Romanticism and Classicism." *Speculations: Essays on Humanism and the Philosophy of Art*. London: Routledge and Kegan Paul, 1958.

Laity, Cassandra. "H.D. and A. C. Swinburne: Decadence and Modernist Women's Writing." *Feminist Studies* 15 (Fall 1989): 461–84.

Morris, Adalaide. "Autobiography and Prophecy: H.D.'s *The Gift*." In *H.D.: Woman and Poet*, ed. Michael King. Orono, ME; National Poetry Foundation, 1986.

Riede, David G. *Swinburne: A Study of Romantic Mythmaking*. Charlottesville: U of Virginia P, 1978.

Swinburne, Algernon Charles. *Collected Poetical Works*. Vols. 1–6. New York: Harper & Brothers, 1925.

Yeats, W. B. *The Letters of W. B. Yeats*. Ed. Allen Wade. New York: Macmillan, 1955.

CHAPTER 9

Rose Cut in Rock:
Sappho and H.D.'s Sea Garden

EILEEN GREGORY

A familiar shade has haunted the female lyricist and the perception of her work throughout this century—the specter of the Poetess. Within recent tradition the Poetess is identified with the prolific, sentimental "songbird" of nineteenth-century romanticism. Engraved in popular iconography through imaginary and legendary figures such as Emile Grangerford and Elizabeth Barrett Browning, this woman appears as pale and withdrawn, sensitive to the point of neurosis and hysteria, passionate, ecstatic, and morbid. Such a cultural image, surviving into the twentieth century, has negatively affected the critical assessment of women poets. The female lyricist, Theodore Roethke said, is generally considered to suffer from certain "aesthetic and moral shortcomings": limitation of range, triviality, superficiality, vapid repetition of themes, moral cowardice and inauthenticity, misplaced eroticism, and "lyric or religious posturing" (133–34). The Poetess has received ample enough scorn from female poets and critics as well. A modern woman writer must shun this specter, fearing that she be seen as a love poet, "a reincarnation of Edna St. Vincent" (Sexton 80, 40), or a poet of "bland ladylike archness or slightness" (Plath 172); and she must distance herself from the company of other "female songbirds" (Bogan, *What the Woman Lived* 86). If the Poetess is a figure of disdain to male poets and of shame to women poets, she represents oppressive limitation to some feminist commentators, who see her poetic postures and themes as somewhat neurotic strategies of response to a male culture with a reductive view of female destiny.[1]

The rejection of the Poetess, then, has some historical justification. But the consistent distaste for this figure goes beyond such a clear critical ground. Moreover, the dismissal of the female lyricist cannot be entirely

129

explained as an ambivalent response to a woman's assuming a male role.[2]
The antipathy is more fundamental — a suspicion of the latent power of
the Poetess, and of the woman poet's access to a potent lyric voice. The
capacity for "perfect and poignant song," Louise Bogan claims, is the
special province of the woman poet; and "when this song comes through
in its high and rare form, the result has always been regarded not only
with delight but with a kind of awe" ("Heart and Lyre," 429). Though
Bogan herself, having great ambivalence toward the role of woman poet,
suffered from the shame attending such a poetic voice, her remarks here
show distinct insight into a lyric mode that she knew intimately and consistently honored. She here names the awesomeness of the Poetess that
lies beyond the diminished images we inherit.

Much of the ambivalent response to H.D.'s poetry has come from the
presence of this cultural figure. Critics have continued to admire the early
imagist poems and ignore subsequent work because, as Susan Stanford
Friedman says, the "short, passionate lyric has conventionally been thought
appropriate for women poets if they insist on writing, while the longer,
more philosophic epic belongs to the real (male) poet" ("Who Buried
H.D.?" 807). Thus to point exclusively to the excellence of the Poetess
is already to condemn with faint praise, to admire, as Ezra Pound said
of H.D., the "refined, charming, and utterly narrow minded she-bard"
(157). In the past few years critics have rightly attempted to redress the
exaggerated emphasis on representative "imagist" poems of H.D. with
studies of her fiction and of the long poems of her middle and late life.
But this recovery of her stature is made in part out of aversion to the specter
of the Poetess, the limited lyricist. In this approach the early lyrics are
understood in terms of a developmental reading of H.D.'s career, so that
they necessarily appear to demonstrate limitation she would later
transcend, incipient vision that would gain scope and substance.[3] Recent
remarks take this reversal in the valuation of H.D.'s work almost to the
point of putting away the early achievement as relatively "trivial" (Grahn
27, 101). A recent study of the "nightingale" tradition among American
women poets consistently views H.D.'s poems, especially the early lyrics,
as continuous with the self-limiting postures of her predecessors (Walker
142ff.).

Thus the early poems have been admired in the past for the same reason
that they have lately been ignored: they point to the limitation of the
Poetess. From the beginning of her career, H.D. indeed takes the Poetess
as a guide. As a presence in her poetry, however, this figure suggests not
limitation but scope, not shallowness but depth of erotic experience, not
shamefulness and cowardice but deliberate courage. I attempt here to
recover something of the complexity of vision informing H.D.'s first book

of poems, *Sea Garden* (1916). In reading this work I am not primarily interested in H.D.'s place within modern poetic movements, or with the way in which these poems encode private or social history. I approach her as a great lyricist, a great love poet, at once in the mainstream and at the margins of lyric traditions in Western poetry. In her early poems, as much as in the explicitly mythical and occult work of her middle and late career, H.D. establishes herself within an archaic lyric tradition in which the voice of the woman poet has distinct potency.

Just as feminists have reclaimed such marginal figures as the Spinster and the Witch, so we need now to recover proper awe for the Poetess. In this attempt I follow Robert Duncan in his *H.D. Book*, who, in fidelity to H.D.'s poetic achievement, reverses the accepted reading of this figure.[4] The Poetess, he claims, the woman in whom daimonic genius resides, is "an enormous persona like the hieratic figures of women in the major arcana of the Tarot." The general disdain for the woman poet, Duncan implies, is a response to the ambivalent power she carries, "the genius of a woman that men would propitiate or exorcise" (39). When the Poetess, the daimonic psychic woman, is present in a male poet, she is highly suspect, and the poet, especially the modern poet, often feels shame at his own "feminine" gift (79–80). But when this Poetess *is* a woman, then the defense against the disturbing authority of her voice is more virulent: "Aroused to battle by the claims of genius wherever they are made — for *genius* is itself of the old titanic order — male guardians of the literary Olympus have been the more aroused when the titaness appears, with the sense that 'it is unseemly that a woman / appear disordered, dishevelled' " (55).

The reclamation of this figure of the Poetess has great implications. It pertains to the question of the "Muse" of the woman poet, which some are beginning to explore (Rich 162–66; Diehl; DuPlessis). Duncan would agree with Mary J. Carruthers, who suggests that women poets gain unusual power when they accept the Muse, the imagined source or inspiration of their work, as a female figure. When the woman takes the Muse as female, Carruthers says, "she is not Other but Familiar, maternal and sororal, a well-known face in the poet's immediate community." This myth of the female Muse "seeks to recreate and remember wholeness . . . through a meeting of familiars which recalls a completeness that is present but forgotten or suppressed by history" (295–96). She sees the power arising from this "familiarization of the muse" in "Lesbian" poets, taking that term in the large sense that Adrienne Rich defines. Rich says that *lesbian* was for her not a simple sexual identification but an "elusive configuration" that she always sought: "It was a sense of desiring oneself; above all, of choosing oneself; it was also a primary intensity between women, an intensity which in the world at large was trivialized, caricatured, or invested with evil" (200). Such an awareness on the part of the poet, Carruthers asserts, means an affirmation of women's community and of erotic connections between women past and present, and an acceptance of an essentially marginal place in relation to culture at large, with a view to the psychic regeneration of that world in terms of a "metaethic" of personal integrity (294–95, 321–22).

H.D. always imagined herself as Poetess in the sense that Duncan describes and that Carruthers suggests in speaking of the woman's Muse. Her early work is continuous with the later explicitly visionary poems in seeking a recovery of "the Sceptre, / the rod of power" of the poet-goddess (*CP* 512), in proposing a hieratic role for the poet, and in affirming the healing power of poetry. In *Sea Garden* in particular she attempts to recover the imagination of goddess-centered Lesbos. The sea-washed landscape she renders here is, as Rich has described the lesbian "configuration," the place where the virginity of the soul is achieved, an integrity born of "choosing oneself." Though it does not explicitly affirm bonds between women in a community set apart, it is nevertheless in conversation with such a world. In *Sea Garden* the poet has "familiarized" the Muse, has fully acknowledged a female source of poetic potency, insisting on a radical valuation of the world within the intense clairvoyance and vulnerability of erotic feeling.

In the polytheistic world of the sea garden there is no one figure of god or goddess who represents a Muse. But beyond the figures within the poems there is a latent mythic presence: Sappho herself, the first love-possessed lyricist, who carries for H.D. an authority for her own marginal explorations, for her sustained spiritualized eroticism.[5] While many women poets have avoided the Sapphic inheritance, seeing it as representing narrow "feminine" lyricism (Gubar 59), H.D. takes this Poetess as a crucial source of lyric power. From the very beginning of her career she possessed a keen instinct leading her toward the "maternal and sororal" image at the origin of her poetic gift. With the restraint of one who knows her familiar spirit intimately, H.D. recovers the memory of Lesbos obliquely, through radical austerity. Faithful to her guide, she understands that this intimate landscape is communicable only as it is interiorized and recreated in spirit.

If we accept Sappho as a great erotic poet, Paul Friedrich suggests, "then her body becomes an icon for a myth of the inner life" (113). What are the contours of the myth seen through this female "body" of language? What is that interior landscape of Lesbos, and how is it present in H.D.'s *Sea Garden*? I would like to evoke Sappho herself, as her poetry—in translation—can render her presence, and to evoke as well H.D.'s Sappho. H.D.'s specific meditation on the Greek poet, recently published as "The

Wise Sappho," has great resonance in the world of *Sea Garden*.[6] Here
H.D. shows keen awareness of Sappho's poetry, and at the same time sees
the Greek poet through the lens of her own alienation from the island
and her longing as lover and poet for such a place.

Perhaps the most remarkable quality of Sappho's imagined Lesbos is
the "liminality," the threshold quality, of its central mysteries, all of which
reflect the goddess Aphrodite whom Sappho both serves and embodies
in song.[7] Aphrodite's theophany occurs within mood, in the state of *aphrodite*, an interiorized quality of feeling indistinguishable from the numinous
presence of the goddess herself (Friedrich 97, 124). Aphrodite dissolves
boundaries between inner and outer, between self and other. In the same
way the central values of Sappho's world are at once deeply subjective
and radically impersonal (god-given); they represent a deep interiority in-
fusing an outward shape or motion, making it vibrant and golden. The
quality of grace, or *charis*, which the goddess and the poet cultivate, is
a refined excellence at the center of life, a revelation, through one's whole
presence—in movement, speech, action—that one shares in the life of the
gods (Friedrich 106–7). A similar quality of exquisiteness (*habrosune*) is
the very texture of aphroditic/sapphic vision (Friedrich 122–23). Sappho
says in one fragment (Lobel and Page no. 58), "But I love [the exquisite],
. . . this, and yearning for the sun has won me Brightness and Beauty"
(trans. Nagy 176). This delicacy and refinement, like the quality of grace,
is present both in the outward richness of the other and in the vision that
endows it with beauty. Aphrodite stands within and between seer and seen,
speaker and spoken, giver and given. And the poet through the liminal
rite of the poem makes the moment of her theophany a communal event.

One Sapphic fragment especially points to the nature of Aprhodite and
to some of the images surrounding her. In fragment LP 2, Sappho summons Aphrodite to come to a sacred grove and participate in ritual festivi-
ties in her honor:[8]

You know the place: then

Leave Crete and come to us
waiting where the grove is
pleasantest, by precincts

sacred to you; incense
smokes on the altar, cold
streams murmur through the

apple branches, a young
rose thicket shades the ground
and quivering leaves pour

down deep sleep; in meadows
where horses have grown sleek
among spring flowers, dill

scents the air. Queen! Cyprian!
Fill our gold cups with love
stirred into clear nectar

Sappho invokes the goddess to leave her island and come to this intimate place; but the sensuous, incantatory poem itself manifests her presence. For both Aphrodite and poetry have each the power of *thelxis*, enchantment, manifest in bodily response (Segal 144). In the erotic charm of the poet's language, Aphrodite enters the body and soul, awakening the motions of desire. The rich and dense fragrance of frankincense mingles with the delicate odors of flowers, and the murmur of cold water through graceful trees blends with the exquisite shadowing of roses. This complex heightening of senses is climaxed, when from quivering leaves — kindled and alive, as are body and vision too — a *koma*, an enchanted sleep, descends. The spell complete, the entranced eyes open to the larger animation of burgeoning spring, to feeding horses, to a meadow of blossoms, through which move refreshing breezes. When Sappho calls, finally, "Queen! Cyprian! / Fill our gold cups with love / stirred into clear nectar," the goddess is with these words no longer latent but suddenly manifest. Having already awakened the suppliant to the fresh yet erotically charged life within her presence, she crowns the moment as Divine Queen. As if among the imperishable gods, she pours out into gold cups immortal nectar mingled with the lucid joy of this consummated mortal rite.

What is this rite, and where does it take place? An altar has been prepared, and perhaps a feast as well, but no one is present; nothing is present except the longing voice of Sappho and the images by which she gives body to longing. This sacred place where the goddess enters is intimate and interior: it is, Thomas McEvilley suggests, "the imagination of the poet, the grove of transformations in which visions are seen and the breaches in reality are healed." Moreover, the "sacred grove" is the poem itself, creating in the reader through the speech of the poet "the trance of paradise" in which the goddess is entertained ("Fragment Two," 332–33).

This poem also suggests a set of images that are central to Sappho's world. One of these is the spatial image of a "private space." Lesbos itself — or Sappho's *thiasos* or group of young girls — is such an insular space, a liminal "island" set apart from ordinary life, within which a ritual passage is experienced.[9] But there are still other distinct spaces within the daily life of the *thiasos*, Eva Stehle Stigers says, such as the "invisible bond or . . . single enclosure, impenetrable by others" wherein two women are united in intimacy. The private space in Sappho's poetry "is a metaphor

for emotional openness in a psychological setting apart . . . from everything experienced by a woman in the ordinary course of life" ("Private
World," 56–57). These spaces often enclose one another within imagination and memory, as in LP 96, when Sappho in an intimate moment with
Atthis comforts her for the loss of a friend, creating the space of the
remembered *thiasos* as well as the imagined solitary moment when her
separated friend in Lydia now longs for her. Likewise in LP 2, the space
of the grove is interiorized to become the space of the longing body and
the innermost shrine of the goddess. Through the poems, however, this
private space is communal space, the very matter of intimacy celebrated
within the *thiasos*.

This "emotional openness" so necessary to the growth of the young
woman is also at the basis of two other mysteries: the figure of the bride
or *nymphe*, and the image of the flower. These recurring presences point
to the paradoxical, threshold quality of Sapphic eroticism, both virginal
(cold streams through apple branches, the meadow of spring flowers, fresh
breezes) and sensually charged (smoking incense, shadows of roses, quivering leaves, the gold cup waiting to be filled).

The young women on Lesbos are virgins being prepared for marriage.
The nuptial moment is a threshold state, and the bride is a figure of passage. For the Greeks, the bride or *nymphe* denotes a woman at the moment of transition from maiden to wife and mother. Aphrodite, who is
herself a Bride, guides these women in the refinement of their grace and
in the cultivation of desire. The threshold of the bridal moment, sacred
to the goddess, represents then a moment of fullness in beauty, of openness to the demands of Eros. That very openness carries intense potency;
mythically the bride or nymph is associated with an ambiguous, aphro-
ditic state of delicate yet awesome erotic potential.[10] The name of nymph
is also given to the goddesses who inhabit the wild regions of nature. They
too are elusive and liminal figures, being, like aspects of elemental nature
itself, both inviolate and erotically suggestive.

The flower is a natural image for the young girls of Sappho's Lesbos,
for the delicacy and beauty of youth coming to distinct perfection at the
moment of opening. The brief time of the opened flower is another liminal moment; and it is the major image attending descriptions of the community of girls surrounding the poet. But in Sappho's poetry—contrasting
markedly, as Stigers shows, with a male poet's use of the image—the flower
represents not an incomplete process of development, but rather a specific kind of fullness possible in the *thiasos*, wherein a "maiden's delicate
charm" and her "youthful, self-celebrating erotic drive could find expression without compromise of . . . her emotional freshness" ("Retreat from
the Male," 92).

That flower and maiden are at the center of Sappho's world points to an obvious lyric preoccupation: loving and witnessing to the ephemeral. These two images represent "that brief moment when the beautiful shines out brilliantly and assumes, for all its perishability, the stature of an eternal condition in the spirit if not in the body" (McEvilley, "Sapphic Imagery," 269). Because they represent the gracious time of the union of souls in beauty, flowers carry the remembrance of the bonds within the *thiasos* of maidens. In one fragment (LP 94) Sappho recalls her parting words to a woman: " 'If you forget me, think / of our gifts to Aphrodite / and all the loveliness that we shared / all the violet tiaras, / braided rosebuds' " (trans. Barnard no. 42). The garlands of flowers are woven times of the animated body, woven graces. Sappho's poems, recalling that unfading beauty in the heart, are themselves such moments, such woven roses (McEvilley, "Sapphic Imagery," 269).

Though H.D. understands fully her distance from this religious and mythic world of Lesbos, she nevertheless claims it in her way. She drew at least as much guidance from her study of Greek lyric poetry as from any contemporary influence or immediate tradition. That she absorbed aspects of craft and conception from these sources seems evident in her early poetry, in the choric voice, in rhythms associated with dance and erotic enchantment; in the figure of the nymph and the image of the flower; and in the image of the marginal space of erotic intimacy. Furthermore, like Sappho's lyrics, the early poems are forcefully ritualistic and liminal, demanding that the reader surrender ordinary orientation and participate in the erotic ordering of the poem. Jean Kammer has seen H.D.'s early poems as resting in a certain poetic mode which, unlike other forms of metaphor, does not move from concrete to abstract, but which rests in juxtaposition and suspension of concrete poetic elements in a configuration. Kammer says that the "absence of a named feeling . . . force[s] us to search for other, less rational entries into the poem." This form of speech turns the metaphoric activity inward, so that "the reader is forced *through* the singular experience of the poem" (158).

H.D.'s poetic affinities with Sappho, however, are more fundamental than any external influences. They rest ultimately, one might say, in the kind of "goddess" they each imagine serving, and in the kind of lyric necessities that service entails. Sappho has Aphrodite at the center, and H.D. a more complex, syncretic figure drawing together qualitites of Aphrodite, Artemis, and Athene. It is not so important to name this figure as to recognize her powerful, shaping presence. She insists upon the primacy of Eros as a ground of value and vision, and thus upon the worth of the animated mortal body. She promises within the experience of passion not only suffering but grace and loveliness, and a certain kind of purity and wisdom. This figure compels an ever deepening interiority as the matter of poetic exploration, so that a moment of mood comes to reveal its lucid truth, and the ephemeral becomes the god-given, oracular substance upon which the poetess works. Finally, this goddess by her liminal nature, her movement under and between cultural fixities, bequeaths to the lyricist her paradoxical role as a threshold figure, pointing inward to the truth of intimacy and suggesting withdrawal, while at the same time inviting public celebration.

H.D. in her essay "The Wise Sappho" might be describing this veiled and complex figure who gives sanction and potency to her lyric song. She calls upon the memory of Sappho's creation in a meditation upon the question of poetic and psychic survival. H.D. opens her reflection with the remark of Meleager of Gadara about the poems of Sappho that he gathered in his *Garland*: " 'Little, but all roses' " (*Notes on Thought and Vision* 57). Her whole meditation plays upon this phrase. H.D. at first negates, then qualifies and turns, then finally returns at the end of the essay to affirm his statement. But what accounts for her continuous metamorphic word play? *Not* roses, not *all* roses, not roses *at all*; not flowers — but rocks, island, country, spirit, song (57–58). This rhetorical process is necessary in order for H.D. to articulate the network of association defining for her the nature of Sappho's immortality. In this essay the Greek poet serves as a guide to her in working through what is essentially her own puzzle: what is the durable matter of fragile lyric song, what is the principle of durability within one's openness to the suffering of Eros? In other words, how does the rose survive, how is the rose a rock? One thing is certain: upon Sappho's endurance as the image of woman/poet/lover somehow depends her own.

In "The Wise Sappho" H.D. places herself implicitly in the position of Hellenistic Meleager, who lived, like the modern poet, in a mongrel and graceless age. In the proem to his *Garland*, Meleager says that he has gathered "flowers" from the ancient poets, adding his own, to weave a "garland" for his friends, though "the sweet-speaking garland of the Muses is common possession of all the initiated" (*Palatine Anthology* 4.1 [Paton 1]; my translation). In her work H.D., too, in a sense, gathers those flowers, the woven roses of Sappho and others, transmuted into her own severe poems; and they too are for an implied audience of friends and *mystai*, those within the mysteries of Eros.

But H.D. in this essay seems also to identify herself with Sappho — like the ancient poet she fashions roses with stubborn endurance in time. In that transmission/transmutation of Sappho into a new time, H.D. would not choose roses as the sign of Sapphic power and beauty: "I would bring orange blossoms, implacable flowerings made to seduce the sense when every other means has failed, poignard that glints, fresh sharpened steel:

after the red heart, red lilies, impassioned roses are dead" (57). H.D. here reveals her literary place in relation to Sappho: after the "impassioned roses" are dead—after the living poems are lost, after the passionate life they represent is inaccessible—she would offer through her poetry what Sappho's fragments also seem to offer—other "implacable flowerings" that would "seduce the sense," almost through violence, within the extreme numbness of modern life.

Though little remains of Sappho's work, H.D. reflects, it is durable matter: her fragmentary, "broken" poems are not lush roses, not flowers of any color, but rocks, within which "flowers by some chance may grow but which endure when the staunch blossoms have perished." The fragments, in other words, are a ground, an enduring subtext, for imagination. More durable than individual poems is this rock-world: "Not roses, but an island, a country, a continent, a planet, a world of emotion, differing entirely from any present day imaginable world of emotion" (58).

What are the qualities of Sappho's Lesbos that flourish in imagination? H.D. remembers it in terms of its grace, its ample loveliness. Yet more than this she emphasizes the deep bitterness, "the bitterness of the sweat of Eros," within which Sappho suffered (59–62). That suffering is essential to Sappho's "wisdom"—which H.D. understands not as an abstract, Platonic wisdom, not Greek *sophrosyne* or Christian constancy, but one gained within the nets of devastating feeling (63–64). The wisdom of Sappho's poetry, H.D. suggests, came from "the wind from Asia, heavy with ardent myrrh," but tempered with a Western wind, "bearing in its strength and salt sting" the image of Athene (63). It is, in other words, characterized by its sensuous immediacy, but also by its questing spirit, its penetrating consciousness, its clarity and control. Sappho was "emotionally wise," capable in her simplicity of seeing within the momentary awkward gesture of a girl "the undying spirit of goddess, muse or sacred being." Sappho's wisdom is a concrete, human love which merges "muse and goddess and . . . human woman" in the perception of grace and beauty (64–65).

"Sappho has become for us a name." As a cultural and artistic figure, H.D. finally implies, she is one with her poems and one with the power of her poems: she is "a pseudonym for poignant human feeling, she is indeed rocks set in a blue sea, she is the sea itself, breaking and tortured and torturing, but never broken." She is an island "where the lover of ancient beauty (shipwrecked in the modern world) may yet find foothold and take breath and gain courage" (67). For this reason the puzzle of Sappho's mortal durability is significant—her poetry, rose/rock/island/ sea, is the timeless *matter* of ephemeral feeling and ephemeral speech at the basis of lyric expression. In this sense—that Sappho *is* feeling, *is* a rocky island retreat for the lover of beauty—she *is*, I suggest, H.D.'s "sea garden." She is the mythic figure at the ground of H.D.'s world of fragile sea- and rock-roses. She is the goddess who guards it, the sea that washes it, and the spirit informing the poet who suffers her ecstasies within it.

I suggest that *Sea Garden* is a consciously crafted whole, with studied consistency in landscape, voice, and theme. The landscape is a sufficiently constant feature among the poems that we get the sense of a finite place: desolate sandy beach strewn with broken shells, large promontories and rocky headlands; inland, a barren stretch of sparse but hardy vegetation beyond the beach, and low wooded hills nearby; deeper inland, the marshes and places of luxuriant or cultivated growth. The voice in these poems also possesses consistency. All the speakers have a similar tone and intensity, even in poems dealing with specific dramatic situations and appearing to have sometimes male and sometimes female speakers.[11] This voice is similar to that in H.D.'s translations of Euripidean choruses. Though few of the poems speak of "we," the collective voice is suggested; the "I" dissolves within the pervasive sense of generalized suffering and exaltation, like the single voice in the chorus of tragedy. The poems are often addressed to another person or to a god, and, in a few instances, they are simple meditations. But the most representative address, occurring in more than a third of the poems, is the apostrophe, the vocative voice. It seems in part to function as prayer or supplication, summoning presences, as do some of the poems in the *Greek Anthology*. More than this, the apostrophe, as Jonathan Culler points out, serves to create "a detemporalized immediacy, an immediacy of fiction." The "apostrophic" force is central to lyric power, creating "a fictional time in which nothing happens but which is the essence of happening" (152). The voice of these poems, then, is hermaphroditic, collective, and atemporal. The poem is, in a sense, a liminal state without ordinary determinations of gender, person, or tense.[12]

The poems of *Sea Garden* appear to have been selected and arranged quite deliberately. The separate lyrics are not presented in chronological order, though their order is clearly not random. Furthermore, the volume does not represent merely a gathering of H.D.'s already published poems, for many of the best of these—for instance "Oread," "Sitalkas," and "The Pool"—do not appear until her third collection, *Heliodora and Other Poems*. The unity of *Sea Garden* is not immediately apparent; nevertheless the work gives a singleness of affect. It is this affective coherence that first led me to contemplate the possibility of hidden authorial motives.[13]

I find evidence of self-conscious crafting not only in the consistency of landscape and mood but in several details of structuring as well. Simi-

lar poems, such as the encounters with gods, the intense dramatic monologues, and especially the five sea-flower poems, are spaced evenly throughout the work, giving the impression of rhythmic or cyclic recurrence of
moods and images. Furthermore, there is slight but deliberate progression in the poems depicting times of day (midday, evening, and night),
and another, more subtle, progression in the placement of the precincts
of the chief gods (the "shrine" at the beginning, the "temple" in the center,
the "herm" as a boundary marker at the end). But to perceive the most
significant instances of artistic choice in arrangement requires that one
grasp the ritual intent of the whole volume: that one enter the sea garden,
a world ritually set apart, as an initiate in its mysteries. Seen in this light
the volume has a group of three initiatory poems that move us immediately and deeply into the mysteries of the sea garden, and three poems
of closure that allow reflection upon the marginal nature of that world
and the cultivation of the soul's beauty it allows. Considering first the
governing images and themes of the book as a whole, I wish to treat the
initiatory poems, others that suggest the character of the sea garden experience, and finally the poems of closure.

The title of the collection points to the governing experience in all its
poems. The *garden* is traditionally the place of consummation of love.
In H.D.'s poems the garden is still the place of love, but love washed with
salt. It is a *sea* garden, inimical to all but the most enduring. The sea
represents here the harsh power of elemental life, to which the soul must
open itself, and by which it must be transformed or die. H.D. need not
have known, but probably did, that sea/salt is the arcane alchemical substance linked to the mysterious bitterness and wisdom essential to spiritual
life. "Without salt," it is said, "the work [the alchemical *opus* of trans-
formation] has no success" (Jung par. 329). To experience sea/salt is to
be within the visceral elements of bodily life, the "common salts" (Hillman,
"Salt," 117). It is to feel open wounds, to suffer desire without fulfillment,
to be made aware of vulnerability and fear. More important, the psychological experience of salt *specifies* and *clarifies* pain: "No salt, no experiencing—merely a running on and running through of events without
psychic body. Thus salt makes events sensed and felt, giving us each a
sense of the personal—my tears, my sweat and blood, my taste and value"
(Hillman, "Salt," 117). It gives ground and substance to subjectivity, to
feeling and desire.

This salt experience and the wisdom and beauty born of it are the central mysteries to which H.D.'s *Sea Garden* allows access. C. G. Jung associates alchemical salt with the sea, thus with Luna and with the "feminine,"
with Eros and feeling (par. 330). One need not fix its mysterious character in Jung's terms. But nevertheless it is clear that for H.D. these associ-

ations — marah ("bitter"), mar, mer, mater, Maia, Mary — to some degree
pertain. Indeed, they are at the heart of the network of imagery informing her longer works and centering in the Goddess, who is both hetaira
and mother, who is "sea, brine, breaker, seducer, / giver of life, giver
of tears" (*CP* 552). Working the mystery of salt, H.D. in *Sea Garden*
explores in a deeply interiorized and careful way the very matter of
subjectivity.

In the opening three poems we move from an intense, static focus upon
a mysterious icon ("Sea Rose"), to a choice for movement and engagement
with the sea ("The Helmsman"), and, finally, to a ritual passage of entrance into the sacred mysteries of the sea garden ("The Shrine").

H.D.'s flowers, like Sappho's, represent a moment when a certain
poignant beauty takes on "the stature of an eternal condition in the spirit"
(McEvilley, "Sapphic Imagery," 269). "Sea Rose" (*CP* 5) immediately
reveals to the reader the necessity to *look through* the image to read that
eternal condition. The initiate's work begins with learning *clairvoyance*.
This "harsh" rose, "marred and with stint of petals, / meagre . . . thin,
/ sparse of leaf," has no conventional worth, but, marked by the inimical
elements, is altogether poor. Yet it is "more precious / than a wet rose
/ single on a stem." Here the typical standards of beauty are reversed,
and in the last stanza the "spice-rose" is deficient for not possessing the
"acrid fragrance" of this harsh flower. The relentless elements in action
are annihilating ("you are caught in the drift . . . you are flung on the
sand"); yet they exalt ("you are lifted / in the crisp sand / that drives in
the wind"). The beauty is in the mark of sea torture.

This movement in the wash of waves, in the near annihilation of elemental power, is repeated in many poems, especially in "Storm" and in
the flower poems, which end frequently, as this one does, with an exalted
moment, a movement upward — you are caught, flung, *lifted*. In "Sea Lily,"
too, the flower is "lifted up," though the wind hisses "to cover [it] with
froth" (*CP* 14). And in "Storm" a leaf is "broken off . . . hurled out, /
whirls up and sinks" (*CP* 36; emphasis added). The ecstatic image at the
end of "Sea Violet" is even clearer: "Violet / your grasp is frail . . . but
you catch the light — / frost, a star edges with its fire" (*CP* 26). This exaltation belongs to a "virginal" ecstasy of salt, to the "fervor of salt" associated, James Hillman suggests, with a psychological desire for purification
through the impure element of salt, through the intensity of subjective
experience ("Salt," 130–36). "Sea Rose" and these other poems reveal the
spiritual potency residing in a surrender to the process of "sea-change."
The flowers represent, like those of Sappho, a pure openness to life; however, rather than the fresh, natural virgin threshold of the young girls in
Lesbos, these show a virginity, an integrity, *achieved* within desire. More-

over, in these key recurring poems the voice itself reveals its radical openness, its own movement in the wash of feeling. The dominant voice in
Sea Garden comes from within the sea-washed flower.

This first poem in *Sea Garden* gives an image of the soul's sea torture
and the second (*CP* 5–7) calls upon the sea guide, the steersman, within
it: "O be swift— / we have always known you wanted us." The "we" of
this poem is one of only a few in the volume, but here as elsewhere it is
ambiguous. The intensity of the voice suggests that if it is not a single
person speaking as many, it is a group of initiates speaking as one: it is
a choric voice. The mystery of "The Helmsman" is in its opening cry. With
this we know we are in an ominous yet exuberant territory where knowledge ("we have always known") and desire ("you wanted us") work in
inevitable, reciprocal concert. The Helmsman seems to have initiated desire, and the initiate seems to have avoided that call. She has gone inland,
"cut off from the wind / and the salt track of the marsh," as she has been
enchanted with the tangles, brambles, knotted roots of earth, "the feel
of the clefts in the bark, / and the slope between tree and tree" leading
her further on. Indeed the greatest part of the poem is the joyous recollection of the adverse path: "we loved all this." But she has returned, for
the love of inland places, though rich, leaves the soul in suspension, a
static, becalmed state, while the sea love is connected with motion and
impetus:

> But now, our boat climbs—hesitates—drops—
> climbs—hesitates—crawls back—
> climbs—hesitates—
> O be swift—
> we have always known you wanted us.

To the initiate, one who knows she is called to it, the choice for sea experience comes with a mysterious inevitability. For there is never any
question that the Helmsman, whom she has always known to want her,
will have her. It is only a question of time, until the rich openness to life
which his love initiates has run its course, through her growing awareness, back to him. The initiate, caught in desire and knowledge, has no
choice. The Helmsman is in a sense like the Greek figure of the personal
daimon who is connected with one's character and fate, the invisible presence who steers one toward a destined end.[14] She cannot leave the sea
behind, for her experience, even on land, is one of passionate immersion—"we parted green from green . . . we dipped our ankles"—and sharp
tactile rhythmic apprehension. Fleeing the sea brings her to it—since the
sea that brought her in motion informs her every movement.

If the initial poem opens vision, and the second awakens desire for destined motion, then the third brings holy dread. "The Shrine" (*CP* 7–10) imitates a rite of passage into the sacred place of the goddess. It does not seem to matter precisely who this figure is, whether Artemis or Aphrodite,[15] for to H.D. the two were often fused. The goddess is simply "She [who] watches over the sea," the primary power within this cosmos. Whoever approaches must overcome inward and outward voices of resistance and accept what is then given.

Just as in Sappho's poems, H.D.'s shrine of the goddess is both inside and outside, and the goddess' presence is manifest as the desire for her is more evident. The initiate at first resists the claim of the goddess, assuming the skepticism of the landsmen. Even as she resists, she is drawn inexorably forward, and as she comes nearer her desire increases, even as her awareness of danger grows. Addressing the goddess (present in her shrine on a promontory), the speaker demands for her to reveal herself: is she, or is she not, evil? "Quiet men" seek a secure headland, yet she treacherously gives no shelter from wind and tide, exposing the staggering ships to tumult. The goddess does not answer such profane questions. Still in turmoil, the initiate suddenly remembers the goddess, as though she were indeed intimate with her, and only now after long exile were returning to her:

> You are not forgot,
> O plunder of lilies,
> honey is not more sweet
> than the salt stretch of your beach.

The goddess embodies the sweetness of salt, the sensual ecstasy (plunder) of the inviolate (lilies). These qualities, uniting bodily and spiritual desire, are essential within the sea garden. That desire *is* the goddess, and *is* the ritual experience of her power.

Approaching the shrine, the initiate feels the goddess' paradoxically destructive and creative brilliance, both "sparks that unknot the flesh" and "splendour athwart our eyes." After this terrible ascent of the initiate to her precincts, however, the goddess reveals herself in her deep sympathy and tenderness. For all her terribleness, she has "touched us":

> your eyes have pardoned our faults,
> your hands have touched us —
> you have leaned forward a little
> and the waves can never thrust us back
> from the splendour of your ragged coast.

Opened to the initiate as she enters the sacred space of the shrine is the revelation of the goddess as only those know who have seen her. It is the image of a mother, intimate and tender, who leans to join herself with her suppliant. The speaker's choice to serve the "splendour of [the] ragged coast" embodies the desire within the whole of this volume; it is analogous to the poet's resolution to write *Sea Garden*, to serve her austere and dangerous calling. This passage to the shrine represents in other terms the longing of the soul to meet the familiar "maternal or sororal" face at its center, to join oneself to oneself.

The quest underlying the poems of *Sea Garden* entails acceptance of one's given destiny and responsiveness to the sacred presences that appear to shape and guide. For the initiate who speaks in these poems, a governing destiny compels the endurance of distinct intensities. We might speak of different aspects of erotic suffering within *Sea Garden* in terms of distinct figures, all of which converge in the choric voice of the initiate: the lover, in ecstasy within the suffering of external bondage or necessity; the nymph, in her experience of wild spirits; the poet, in her endurance of the process of creation; and the seer, in her surrender to her clairvoyant gift.

The three poems speaking through the figure of the lover—"Acon," "Prisoners," and "Loss"—are alike in one respect: they each show human desire as it becomes transmuted within the experience of death; and the clear image of the beloved crystallizes within the suffering of harsh necessity. In "Acon" the lover, with the image of his dying Hyella, "whom no god pities," gathers flowers and calls upon nymphs to bear them to her, for "The light of her face falls from its flower, / as a hyacinth . . . perishes upon burnt grass" (*CP* 32). In "Loss" the lover, himself about to die, remembers his perished comrade and imagines the beauty of his cleansed, sea-washed body: "your white flesh covered with salt / as with myrrh and burnt iris" (*CP* 22). And in "Prisoners" the lovers incarcerated, crushed by fate, have distilled their desire; the speaker at the moment of going to his death recalls how his lover once picked up a flower: "and it flamed, the leaf and shoot / and the threads, yellow, yellow— / sheer till they burnt / to red-purple" (*CP* 35). These are extreme instances of love, yet they share the same essential code as "Sea Rose"—the torture and transfiguration of the soul within the suffering of elemental salt.

The group of poems exploring the figure of the nymph—"Pursuit," "The Wind Sleepers," "Huntress," and "Sea Gods"—are remarkable in sharing a certain puzzling ambiguity: for in them it is difficult to distinguish the god from natural effects. These poems ask for our participation in a moment in which wildness dissolves the boundaries between human and non-human, or in which a wild domain is reinhabited by its gods through the summoning of the poem. "Pursuit" and "Huntress" share the same landscape of woodlands, the same action of the hunt. In the first a frenzied lover pursues someone through the land, someone, however, who is never visible except in the signs of violence, the crushing of flowers and snapping of branches, left in his/her track. The lover reads in these signs evidence of desperate flight, but when the trail simply ends he/she imagines that a "wood-daemon" has saved the fleeing figure (*CP* 12). The drama here is simply the speaker's merging with the wildness of another creature, who, whether human, animal, or spirit, is absorbed into the element of nature, like a dryad into a tree. The "Huntress" too, whether god or human, is the very spirit of wind, of animal instinct and abandon; and the speaker here is one of a band like Artemisian nymphs or Dionysian Maenads, merged with the nature of their god (*CP* 24).

In the other two poems of the nymph — "The Wind Sleepers" and "Sea Gods" — the nature of our participation is more complex. Here the sea presences in wind and wave have lost their power: the wind sleepers, unable to endure the wind, have retreated into the city walls; the sea gods, now mangled and broken by the sea, are "no stronger than the strips of sand / along your ragged beach" (*CP* 30). This is to say that the gods are overwhelmed by their own elements: gods of wind and sea succumb to the *mere* (literal) wind and sea. The recovery of the elemental gods from this naturalistic oblivion is through a conjuration, a summoning of song. For the wind sleepers one must "pour meted words / of sea-hawks and gulls / and sea-birds that cry / discords" (*CP* 15): one must imitate the animated life of the sea air. For the sea gods, however, the nymph conjures through the offering of masses of violets, hoping that "you will answer our taut hearts, / you will break the lie of men's thoughts, / and cherish and shelter us" (*CP* 31). The violets serve in this summoning because their brilliant and lovely colors return to the sea its delicate animation, and because they show the "taut hearts" of those open to the presence of the gods.

The figure of the poet, too, has distinct encounters, which take place in the "private space" of imagination, the cultivated garden or orchard. Within the "sea garden" itself are two other gardens, both of which taken together define clearly the exigencies of creation in this marginal world. In "Sheltered Garden" (*CP* 19–21), the speaker is within a place containing masses of perfect fragrant flowers (pure "essences"); it is enclosed and tranquil. Yet this kind of beauty inspires, in the speaker, the panic of suffocation ("I have had enough. / I gasp for breath"), and entrapment ("Every way ends, every road, / every foot-path leads at last / to the hill-crest"). She desires a sharp astringent aroma, a "scent of resin" or a "taste of bark," and exposure to wind and cold: "For this beauty, / beauty without strength, / chokes out life." Finally she wishes to destroy the garden ("I want wind to break, / scatter . . . snap off . . . fling . . . leave half-trees, torn, twisted"). A strange instinct conceives of the need for extreme change:

> O to blot out this garden
> to forget, to find a new beauty
> in some terrible
> wind-tortured place.

The soul needs terribleness (awe, intensity, excess) and torture (tension, strife) in order to possess vitality or to achieve its distinctive beauty. Where these are not present, as in a sheltered garden, the soul is threatened with death and responds desperately with a desire for violence.

"Garden" (*CP* 24–25), a poem in two parts, describes not a place anti-thetical to life and creation but one essential to it. In a sense it defines the "aesthetic" of creative apprehension and suffering within the sea garden. In the first part of the poem, a rose is again an image of beauty, but here it carries a sense of power as the untouchable, inaccessible thing that the poet desires, like the adamantine "rock roses" in H.D.'s essay on Sappho: "You are clear / O rose, cut in rock, / hard as the descent of hail." The rose "cut in rock" (growing in the crevice of a rock, or made precise by the background of rock) is clear and "hard as the descent of hail" (sharp, cold, relentless). The austerity and clarity of the image are compelling, and the speaker is drawn to its force. She imagines what she "could" do, what her power could be before this image, with increasingly conditional claims, until she admits her powerlessness before it. She "could scrape the colour / from the petals," seize the image directly and violently, but to do so would destroy and denature the rose; to do so would be to have it only as "spilt dye from a rock." The speaker cannot possess the rose, and cannot break its crystal, because this would involve superhuman strength ("If I could break you / I could break a tree"). She ends with the strange conditional statement: "If I could stir / I could break a tree — / I could break you." Before the image of the rose she cannot even stir; so much less can she break a tree, or, indeed, assert her mastery at all.

In this poem the rose is *image*, the object of the poet's desire; yet she cannot touch or possess it, cannot shatter its ice, but only witness to its radiance. Thus the poem dramatizes the aesthetic of H.D.'s early work: poetry is the evocation and reenactment of the experienced power of the image. The knowledge of her weakness before the image is a refined salt experience — the consciousness of longing in the presence of a beautiful but unyielding object. A similar though more satisfying longing is shown in "The Contest" (*CP* 12), where the human athlete also represents the image — but here one that is humanly crafted. As image, the male figure is highly liminal; his aspects of grace and power, as experienced by the poet, reside between nature and human artifice. This image has the "rare silver" of a resolved epiphany.

The second part of "Garden" is the familiar poem "Heat." It is tied to the first enigmatic part by the common theme of longing within the process of creation, and by the sense of stasis and need for release. In both poems, too, the endurance of the moment is part of the necessary process of insight and making. The speaker asks the wind to "rend open the heat," cut it, plough through it, so that ripe fruit can drop. The heat is a palpable force that "presses up and blunts / the points of pears." In this imagined op-pression of unbearable pregnancy she prays for a deliverance from the process of gestation and ripening, though even her own metaphor acknowl-edges that without the force of heat the growing and ripening fruit would not assume its proper shape. Thus in this essential garden both poems speak of salt suffering in terms of creative process, within which it is hard to bear attention to the potency of specific image and to be patient in the heated forging of the destined shape. The poem "Orchard," too, extends the image of the cultivated place of creation. It seems, in a sense, to con-tinue the agony of creation: the pears are ripe, the bees are animated, but the poet cannot bear "the beauty / of fruit trees" (*CP* 28). They signify a fruition difficult to embrace, unless she acknowledge the elemental power who governs the process of natural growth.

The voice of the seer in the sea garden has a different agony than that of others. She must endure the revelations that the strange light of the sea garden gives, and these are not always without their terror and danger. A group of poems, "Mid-day," "Evening," and "Night," shows a proces-sion in the light of the day, and the seer's intense awareness makes these passages difficult. The too-brilliant noon exacerbates the mind and dissi-pates the body, and the speaker longs for the deep-rooted, shady poplar on the hill (*CP* 10). In the more liminal light of evening body and soul are awake and clairvoyant. Yet in "Evening" that intense consciousness brings a vision of the obliteration of identity, as gradually when night comes the shadows fold flower and bud and grass stem in upon them-selves until everything is lost, moving inward to obscurity (*CP* 18–19). The intensity of clairvoyance, strangely, brings one close to death. In "Night" (*CP* 33) the relentless darkness that takes apart, undoes, the petals is the inexorable force of dissolution leading to death, connected with the mechanism of linear time. After the rose is finally disintegrated by night, the "stark core" is left to perish—an image not only of mortality but of the loneliness of a being held in a dead absence within time.

Two other poems deal with the seer's clairvoyance in a particular way: one of these, "The Gift," shows a woman coming to understand the necessities that her visionary "gift" demands; another, "The Cliff Temple," shows the longing of a woman for the god of light. The woman in "The Gift" (*CP* 15–18) suffers from her clairvoyance, finding that like a curse it brings isolation and confusion to her attempt to love another. In this intensely rendered address, the seer/poet, shaken by an intimate encounter with a woman she loves, offers her the "gift" of this poem. This gift honors the woman, yet while doing so it shows the necessity of the seer's withdrawal. Just as in "Sheltered Garden," so here too the beauty of the woman, her luxuriant garden, her rich loving, are too much to bear: "The house, too, was like this, / over painted, over lovely." Yet the unendurable quality of the woman's beauty, it is important to notice, comes from her unreflective and careless regard for it: having so much, her beauty means too little. She is innocent: "The world is yet unspoiled for you, / you wait, expectant," as children wait for random, insignificant favors to fall to them.

To the seer, however, beauty is so potent and portentous that it puts her in danger. "Sleepless nights, / I remember the initiates, / their gesture, their calm glance," she explains, but though she lives as these *mystai*, she lives without the containment of a ritual. She yearns for another life, where beauty does not "crowd / madness upon madness," where "a still place," the barren seascape, would allow peace. The seer intuits that in that "still place" "some hideousness" is necessary in order "to stamp beauty, / a mark . . . on our hearts." Beauty, visionary beauty, must be brought to the body and felt by its deep impression. The speaker's gift to the woman expresses the nature of her pain; it lies in her "gift" of vision, which demands retreat, austerity, and care.

"The Cliff Temple" (*CP* 26–28) renders the sometimes precipitous passion within the seer's dedication to the god of light. The god of the temple seems to be both Apollo, who had a cliff shrine on the Greek island Leukas, and the sun god Helios. Just as H.D. conflates Aphrodite and Artemis, so she sees these gods as one. As in "The Shrine," here too the suppliant summons the god through her own desire, invoking first the distant heights themselves — the high rock pillar — which somehow *is* the god; and, doing so, she is suddenly *with* the god. In this poem the god's temple, the "Great, bright portal, / shelf of rock . . . clean cut, white against white," has about it that clarity and perfection of form (as in "O rose, cut in rock") associated with Apollo. At this height "next to the sky" one experiences the sense of sublimity, distance, removal from strife ("the terrible breakers are silent / from this place"), aspects of Apollo's nature. Yet the place carries its own tumult — the wind "booms" and "thunders," as though one with the violent breath of the god. The aspiration for the sanctum of Apollo is for lucid vision, oracular power, and, aesthetically, for measure and formal control.

But the sky temple seems an image as well of the Gate of the Sun—
"you lift, you are the world-edge, / pillar for the sky-arch"—through which
Helios passes. Helios, as distinct from Apollo, has an erotic aspect, as
well as vibrancy and immediacy. The seer, while sensing the peace of the
place, is also frenzied in pursuit of the elusive god—"for ever and for ever,
must I follow you / through the stones? . . . I wondered at you. . . .
dear—mysterious—beautiful." The madness of loving the sun was known
to Aphrodite, who threw herself from the White Rock of Leukas for love
of Phaethon, son of Helios; and also to Sappho, who jumped from the
same rock in a related story, and who says of herself that "yearning for
the sun has won me Brightness and Beauty."[16] The speaker of this poem,
like Aphrodite and Sappho, so longs for the unattainable lover that she
also asks, "Shall I hurl myself from here, / shall I leap and be nearer you?"
But unlike the goddess of "The Shrine," this power never welcomes, but
only beckons, ever beyond and upward. The experience of the ascent to
the heights, then, is clear vision, sublimity, and quiet, yet also an agonized erotic possession. The allusion here to the fall from the White Rock
of Leukas points to the hidden danger within clairvoyant ecstasy, in part
explaining the sinister quality that may accompany the seer's gift: the
visionary and erotic intoxication has a deathly counterpoint—the plunge
into salty depths.

The closing poems of *Sea Garden* establish a complex passage out of
this marginal world, marking its boundaries ("Hermes of the Ways"),
affirming its splendid illusion ("Pear Tree"), and framing it in relation to
the modern world ("Cities"). This passage of closure brings us again, as
with "The Shrine," to a god who can lead one at this threshold; and to
a clairvoyant image, like that in "Sea Rose," iconic of the soul's state. It
adds, however, as a way to define the necessity for the garden, a vision
of a world in which spirit and beauty can live only as they are marginal
and sequestered.

"Hermes of the Ways" (*CP* 37–39) speaks of the god of the crossroads,
who stands at boundaries. His power is important in seeing the "marginal"
nature of the "sea garden." Hermes marks the boundary to this world,
standing in the place of the "sea garden" itself, the place of severe exposure between the sea and land where wind, water, and sand buffet and
score the "sea" flowers. At this very edge one meets "him / of the triple
path-ways, / Hermes, / who awaits." This god attends souls at such
thresholds, "Dubious, / facing three ways, / welcoming wayfarers." He
stands with the sea orchard to the west, the sea wind approaching from
the east, and the great dunes before him. This is the *cosmos* of *Sea Garden*
in miniature, the place between the terrible sea and the "poplar-shaded
hill." There the twisted trees produce hard and small fruit, "too late

ripened / by a desperate sun / that struggles through sea-mist." Here Hermes waits to welcome those who enter this place "where sea-grass tangles with / shore-grass." Only to those journeying, in process of change, he allows his power, giving not certainty but only steadiness and patience.

"Pear Tree" (*CP* 39) follows "Hermes of the Ways" and precedes the last poem, "Cities." If I am justified in seeing the selection and placement of the poems as deliberate, reflecting a ritual awareness on the poet's part, then "Pear Tree" is somewhat puzzling. In the whole of the volume there is no other such unqualified beauty or such unqualified ecstasy as we find here. This image seems in some sense outside the ordeal of the sea garden. And indeed it is outside—past the boundaries marked by the god of thresholds. I suggest that in terms of *Sea Garden* the pear tree becomes an image of the soul's completion or fullness, an image of the transformed soul, as well as an image of the poetic illusion, the transforming artifice, of *Sea Garden* itself.

Some of these possible meanings reside in part in the white/silver images of the poem. The tree is "Silver dust / lifted from the earth." Its white flowers open, parting "silver / from . . . rare silver." It floats like a body of air, or like the bright moon; yet it is air with substance: "you front us with great mass." In the alchemical language of transformation, silver represents a high moment of fulfillment: it is the recovery of the "second whiteness," of innocence and virginity, at the culmination of a tortuous and intense process; it is the full light of the moon, wherein soul and imagination are solidly realized; and finally white/silver is a state-between, a liminal state, often referred to as bride, dawn, or dove (Hillman, "Silver (1)," 22–24; "Silver (2)," 21). These occult senses seem coincident with the images and themes of *Sea Garden* and appropriate to the joyous moment rendered in the poem. As a spiritual image, the blossoms of the pear, like other flowers in the sea garden, carry the paradox of virginity: white and inviolate, yet with purple at the heart. Moreover, this brilliant flowering of white and silver has issue as part of a generative process: the flowers "bring summer and ripe fruits / in their purple hearts." The blossoming pear tree is a new beginning after the arduous process of fertility and growth shown in the sea garden.

In another occult sense white/silver is essentially associated with the imagination: silver is the moon's "subtle air body," nourishing the soul with the "continual generation of images" (Hillman, "Silver (1)," 24). The pear tree, like the moon's air body, is the poetic illusion itself. It is a seeming that is real: it is dust, yet it is a "great mass"; it hardly occupies space, yet it fills space brilliantly. On another level the tree, like the rose cut in rock, represents the awesomeness, the otherness, belonging to the *image*; yet here that power seems miraculous, rather than inexorable. This poem serves to mark the completion of the ritual of the sea garden with pleasure, aspiration, and hope.

The last work, "Cities" (*CP* 39–42), breaks dramatically with the preceding ones in subject and tone. Its placement at the end of the volume is deliberate, serving as a kind of epilogue to speak of the nature of the poetic work that it completes. It recalls the context of the disfigured modern city in terms of which the marginal world of the "sea garden" takes on vital significance. The city *necessitates* the sea garden, a place of seclusion where intense desire is felt; and its hideousness focuses the value, the "rare gold," of recollected beauty. We are told that those who serve the old splendor of cities in the context of the swarming squalor of the new city are given their animation through the still vital *"spirits, not ghosts"* that people the city: *"their breath was your gift, / their beauty, your life."* This concluding poem of the book tells us what we have experienced in the sea garden, a place distinct from, yet within, the city—like old cells of honey in a new hive—where beauty is remembered. It also presents explicitly the figure of a guardian and speaker—the voice in the poems of *Sea Garden*—who is given the gift of utterance through the breath of spirits, ancient *daimones*. In this context the sea garden is a sacred place where the ever-present voices are entertained, where the work of spirit, marginal yet essential to life, can continue.

Sappho's "emotional wisdom," as H.D. saw it, rested in her capacity to love and to transfigure the mortal gesture within the lucid, uncompromising light of imagination. Such wisdom, too, H.D. possesses. In *Sea Garden* Sappho is "She [who] watches over the sea," moving one inward to her severe salt domain. H.D., serving this mortal Muse, makes of the ephemeral rose the durable substance of rock. Like Meleager she shapes and gives a "sweet-speaking garland" to initiates who wish experience of the common mysteries.

NOTES

Portions of this paper were delivered at the Twentieth Century Women Writers International Conference, Hempstead, New York, November 7, 1982; and at the South Central Modern Language Association, Tulsa, Oklahoma, November 8, 1985. Research and writing time in the summer of 1985 were supported by a grant from the National Endowment for the Humanities. This paper previously appeared in *Contemporary Literature* 27 (Winter 1986): 525–52.

1   See, for example, the discussion of Dickinson in Gilbert and Gubar 582–86ff. An extended treatment of the self-limiting postures of female poets is that of Walker.

2   Gilbert and Gubar (539–49ff.) persuasively argue such a position.

3   Two thoughtful developmental readings of the early poetry are those of Friedman in *Psyche Reborn* 3–10; and Ostriker 30–33.

4   The essay of Duncan from which I here draw is a rich meditation on the nature of the genius and the muse; I have attempted not to distort his thought in converting it into linear argument.

5   Two critics, Gubar (46–47, 53) and Grahn (5–8), make this point in their studies of Sappho as a source of poetic and religious authority for H.D. and other women — especially lesbian — writers.

6   The manuscript of *The Wise Sappho* (also entitled "The Island: Fragments of Sappho") is not precisely dated, though evidence would suggest that it was written in 1920 at Carmel Highlands in California. Though *Sea Garden*, then, would seem to have preceded H.D.'s essay on Sappho, both come from the same imagination of the island experience, of which Lesbos served as a configuration.

7   My understanding of Aphrodite and of the liminal qualities of Sappho's world has been greatly shaped by Friedrich, especially chaps. 5 and 6.

8   In the major points of my interpretation of this poem I am indebted to McEvilley, "Sappho, Fragment Two."

     Because of its grace, and not because of its literal accuracy, I quote here the version of Barnard. Here is my own literal rendering of the fragment: Come from Crete, for my sake, to this holy temple, where is the lovely grove of apple-trees, and where altars are smoking with frankincense; therein cold water murmurs through apple branches, and the space is all shaded over with roses, and from quivering leaves an enchanted sleep descends; therein a meadow where horses feed has blossomed with spring flowers, and soothing breezes blow. . . . there . . . Cypris, pour gracefully in golden cups nectar mingled with these festivities.

9   For a discussion of rites of passage see Turner 94ff.

10   Two important elaborations of the significance of the *nymphe* are those of Winkler 77–78; and Detienne 102–3.

11   Ostriker (30) notes the androgyny of the speaker.

12   See Turner (96, 102–3, 106) for discussion of timelessness, anonymity, and sexlessness in liminal states.

13   Fraistat (4–21) discusses the dynamics of reading a collection as a single work. See as well Rosenthal and Gall, who, in making a case for the "poetic sequence" as a modern genre, give brief notice to *Sea Garden* (477–78).

14   See Dodds (42ff.) for a discussion of the individual daimon.

15   Swann (30) claims that the poem refers to the shrine of Artemis at Leukas. But Aphrodite too was known as guardian of seafarers, and H.D. would have known a poem in the *Palatine Anthology* by Anyte (9.144 [Paton 3]) speaking of a sea shrine of Aphrodite.

16   See Nagy's essay exploring the connection of Sappho and Aphrodite with the sun god and the White Rock of Leukas. This is his translation of Sappho's fragment (176).

WORKS CITED

Bogan, Louise. "The Heart and the Lyre." *A Poet's Alphabet: Reflections on the Literary Art and Vocation*, ed. Robert Phelps and Ruth Limmer, 424–29. New York: McGraw, 1970.

Bogan, Louise. *What the Woman Lived: Selected Letters of Louise Bogan, 1920–1970*, ed. Ruth Limmer. New York: Harcourt, 1973.

Carruthers, Mary J. "The Re-Vision of the Muse: Adrienne Rich, Audre Lorde, Judy Grahn, Olga Broumas." *Hudson Review* 36 (1983): 293–322.

Culler, Jonathan. "Apostrophe." *The Pursuit of Signs: Semiotics, Literature, Deconstruction*, 135–54. Ithaca, N.Y.: Cornell UP, 1981.

Detienne, Marcel. "The Myth of 'Honeyed Orpheus.' " *Myth, Religion and Society: Structuralist Essays by M. Detienne, L. Gernet, J.-P. Vernant and P. Vidal-Naquet*, ed. R. L. Gordon, 95–109. Cambridge: Cambridge UP; Paris: Editions de la maison des sciences de l'homme, 1981.

Diehl, Joanne Feit. " 'Come Slowly—Eden': An Exploration of Women Poets and Their Muse." *Signs* 3 (1978): 572–87.

Dodds, E. R. *The Greeks and the Irrational*. Berkeley: U of California P, 1951.

Duncan, Robert. "The H.D. Book: Part Two: Nights and Days, Chapter 9." *Chicago Review* 30 (Winter 1979): 37–88.

DuPlessis, Rachel Blau. "Family, Sexes, Psyche: an essay on H.D. and the muse of the woman writer." *Montemora* 6 (1979): 137–56.

Fraistat, Neil. *The Poem and the Book: Interpreting Collections of Romantic Poetry*. Chapel Hill: U of North Carolina P, 1985.

Friedman, Susan Stanford. *Psyche Reborn: The Emergence of H.D.* Bloomington: Indiana UP, 1981.

Friedman, Susan Stanford. "Who Buried H.D.? A Poet, Her Critics, and Her Place in 'The Literary Tradition.' " *College English* 36 (1975): 801–14.

Friedrich, Paul. *The Meaning of Aphrodite*. Chicago: U of Chicago P, 1978.

Gilbert, Sandra M., and Susan Gubar. *The Madwoman in the Attic: The Woman Writer and the Nineteenth-Century Literary Imagination*. New Haven: Yale UP, 1979.

Grahn, Judy. *The Highest Apple: Sappho and the Lesbian Poetic Tradition*. San Francisco: Spinsters, Ink, 1985.

Gubar, Susan. "Sapphistries." *Signs* 10 (1984): 43–62.

H.D. *Collected Poems, 1912–1944 (CP)*, ed. Louis L. Martz. New York: New Directions, 1983.

H.D. *Notes on Thought and Vision & The Wise Sappho*. San Francisco: City Lights Books, 1982.

Hillman, James. "Salt: A Chapter in Alchemical Psychology." *Images of the Untouched: Virginity in Psyche, Myth and Community*, ed. Joanne Stroud and Gail Thomas, 111–37. Dallas: Spring, 1982.

Hillman, James. "Silver and the White Earth (Part One)." *Spring: An Annual of Archetypal Psychology and Jungian Thought* (1980): 21–48.

Hillman, James. "Silver and the White Earth (Part Two)." *Spring: An Annual of Archetypal Psychology and Jungian Thought* (1981): 21–66.

Jung, C. G. *Mysterium Coniunctionis: An Inquiry into the Separation and Synthesis of Psychic Opposites in Alchemy*. Trans. R. F. C. Hull, 2d ed. New York: Princeton UP, 1970. Vol. 14 of *The Collected Works of C. G. Jung*, ed. William McGuire et al. Bollingen Series 20. 20 vols. 1953–1979.

Kammer, Jean. "The Art of Silence and the Forms of Women's Poetry." In *Shakespeare's Sisters: Feminist Essays on Women Poets*, ed. Sandra M. Gilbert and Susan Gubar, 153–64. Bloomington: Indiana UP, 1979.

Lobel, Edgar, and Denys Page, eds. *Poetarum Lesbiorum Fragmenta*. 1955. Oxford Clarendon-Oxford UP, 1968.

McEvilley, Thomas. "Sapphic Imagery and Fragment 96." *Hermes* 101 (1973): 257–78.

McEvilley, Thomas. "Sappho, Fragment Two." *Phoenix* 26 (1972): 323–33.

Nagy, Gregory. "Phaethon, Sappho's Phaon, and the White Rock of Leukas." *Harvard Studies in Classical Philology* 77 (1973): 137–77.

Ostriker, Alicia. "The Poet as Heroine: Learning to Read H.D." *American Poetry Review* 12.2 (1983): 29–38.

Paton, W. R., ed. *The Greek Anthology*. 5 vols. 1916. Loeb Classical Library. Cambridge: Harvard UP; London: William Heinemann, 1969.

Plath, Sylvia. *The Journals of Sylvia Plath*. Ed. Frances McCullough and Ted Hughes. New York: Dial, 1982.

Pound, Ezra. *The Letters of Ezra Pound 1907–1941*. Ed. D. D. Paige. New York: Harcourt, 1950.

Rich, Adrienne. *On Lies, Secrets, and Silence: Selected Prose, 1966–1978*. New York: Norton, 1979.

Roethke, Theodore. "The Poetry of Louise Bogan." *On the Poet and His Craft: Selected Prose of Theodore Roethke*, ed. Ralph J. Mills, Jr., 133–48. Seattle: U of Washington P, 1965.

Rosenthal, M. L., and Sally M. Gall. *The Modern Poetic Sequence: The Genius of Modern Poetry*. Oxford: Oxford UP, 1983.

Sappho. Trans. Mary Barnard. Berkeley: U of California P, 1958.

Segal, Charles. "Eros and Incantation: Sappho and Oral Poetry." *Arethusa* 7.2 (1974): 139–60.

Sexton, Anne. *Anne Sexton: A Self-Portrait in Letters*. Ed. Linda Gray Sexton and Lois Ames. Boston: Houghton, 1977.

Stigers, Eva Stehle. "Retreat from the Male: Catullus 62 and Sappho's Erotic Flowers." *Ramus* 6.2 (1977): 83–102.

Stigers, Eva Stehle. "Sappho's Private World." In *Reflections of Women in Antiquity*, ed. Helene P. Foley, 45–61. New York: Gordon and Breach Science, 1981.

Swann, Thomas Burnett. *The Classical World of H.D.* Lincoln: U of Nebraska P, 1962.

Turner, Victor. *The Ritual Process: Structure and Anti-Structure*. 1969. Symbol, Myth, and Ritual Series. Ithaca, N.Y.: Cornell Paperbacks-Cornell UP, 1977.

Walker, Cheryl. *The Nightingale's Burden: Women Poets and American Culture before 1900*. Bloomington: Indiana UP, 1982.

Winkler, Jack. "Gardens of Nymphs: Public and Private in Sappho's Lyrics." In *Reflections of Women in Antiquity*, ed. Helene P. Foley, 63–89. New York: Gordon and Breach Science, 1981.

Images at the Crossroads:
H.D.'s "Scrapbook"

DIANA COLLECOTT

THE SCRAPBOOK

> Greece, Greece, people, faces. Egypt . . . Face upon face, impression upon impression and all of modernity (as she viewed it) was as the jellified and sickly substance of a collection of old colourless photographic negatives through which gleamed the reality, the truth of the blue temples of Thebes, of the white colonnades of Samos . . .
>   — H.D., "Murex," *Palimpsest*

H.D., like her modern persona in *Palimpsest*, was an inveterate collector of photographs — and she did not discard their negatives, despite frequent changes of address. The photograph boxes at the Beinecke Library are replete with snapshots and portraits of her family and friends. They also contain picture postcards of places and works of art, many of which reflect her vivid interest in mythology and iconography. Entering this private ground, the student of H.D. may be forgiven for imagining, with Raymonde, that the "reality" or "truth" of her subject may be glimpsed through this lifetime's accumulation of photographs. Yet the belief in a transcendent realm of value is as outdated as the notion that a photographic portrait is a "mirror of the soul," or a landscape a "window on the world." Contemporary criticism casts a cold eye on such nostalgic realism: "Notions of truth and reality are based on a longing for an unfallen world in which there would be no need for the mediating systems of language and perception but everything would be itself, with no gap between form and meaning."[1]

Yet it might be possible — might it? — to enter an artist's imaginary, to go through the looking-glass with her into that "unfallen world" and yet retain, like a Golden Bough in Elysium, some sense of difference; to re-

155

sist identification, remain a sympathetic interpreter but not a naive reader. For even if a photographic image is not simply "a picture" in the traditionally representative sense, it is nevertheless "a means of saying something," even a kind of writing.[2] Photographs were a form of communication, even a currency, between H.D. and the members of her intimate circle in the late 1920s and early 1930s. "I am involved with pictures," she wrote in 1929, referring to the movies she was making with Bryher and Kenneth Macpherson.[3] The movies produced stills which were eagerly shown to directors such as Pabst and circulated amongst the contributors to *Close Up*.[4] Macpherson, who was H.D.'s lover at the time of his marriage to Bryher in 1927, shared their pictorial enthusiasms and brought to them a sophisticated sense of the ways in which photographic images could be composed into complex messages. Postcards from art galleries became semantic units in their private language. Receiving a selection of these from H.D. one Easter, he acknowledged the fact that, when read in sequence as she intended, they acquired new meanings. "And the surrealists pretend to be new!" he wrote, ". . . Not painting but the juxtaposition of paintings surely is the soul of wit."[5]

In the Norman Holmes Pearson Collection at Yale is a splendid photograph album, in a brown leather portfolio, known as H.D.'s "Scrapbook." Its most interesting pages bear, not the randomly associated pictures we expect of a scrapbook, but carefully composed images. They juxtapose photographs of H.D. herself with photographs of Greek architecture and sculpture, some acquired on site during H.D.'s visits to Greece and others culled from brochures and from museums elsewhere.[6] (In one letter to H.D., Macpherson promised to "bring back armfuls of Greek stuff" from Berlin, no doubt with the album in mind). H.D.'s initiation into Greek art had taken place at a succession of shrines to high culture. First, the old Philadelphia Academy, among whose plaster casts Thomas Eakins had photographed his students in Greek costume as living models.[7] Then the Musée du Louvre in Paris, where she beheld the Victory of Samothrace which appears in the album and features in the text of *Asphodel*. Next, the British Museum in London, where the Elgin Marbles from Athens offered "Classical Fragments," to be reworked in her early story "The Greek Boy" and in poems such as Richard Aldington's "To a Greek Marble."[8] Only after this aesthetic pilgrimage did she actually reach Greece: in 1920, she was herself photographed among the monumental ruins of the Athenian Acropolis; in 1932, she attained the shrine to Apollo at Delphi. But she was already familiar, from photographs, with the statues and temples of these sites, and she was aware, from Pausanias' *Guide to Greece*, that such shrines had also been, since ancient times, treasure houses and art galleries.

The Scrapbook, then, is both ancient and modern. The "Greek stuff" testifies to the preoccupation with ancient Greece that informs not only H.D.'s poetry, but also her perceptions of modern phenomena such as the cinema. The modernity of the Scrapbook is implicit in its recognition that the photograph does not distinguish between images of different origin or date, and that photographs can be multiplied, reproduced, and recycled. Hence, in this album, "images of real things are interlayered with images of images."⁹ Photographic images, no less than paintings, are subject to the operations of the fantasizing mind; composite images, on the page as well as on the screen, may be structured in the complex mechanisms that Freud showed to be at work in speech and the dream. Like dreams, these pages of the album offer cryptic texts or *palimpsests* whose meanings are not available to the uninitiated.

The privilege of photography was vastly extended in the twenties and thirties by advertising and the cinema: the realistic representation of fantasy worlds on screen was supported by magazine images of movie stars, dream homes, and exotic places. It became a fashionable pastime to cut out such pictures and paste them into scrapbooks as scenarios for snapshots of oneself and one's friends. By this time, however, *photomontage* had developed as a sophisticated art form with a firm basis in popular culture. The use of composite photographs had been common in propaganda postcards of the First World War. It excited the German Dadaists who saw, not merely a new technique, but "a technique in which the image would *tell* in a new way."¹⁰ Hannah Höch and John Heartfield used photomontage to disrupt assumptions about reality and to shock the spectator into political recognitions. The essential method was to separate and recombine elements of several pictures in order to draw extra meaning from them. Their works sometimes gained effect by seeming to obey the rules of scale and perspective that photography had inherited from academic painting, sometimes by flaunting them.¹¹ Blander styles of photomontage were common in film publicity, but the cover of the pamphlet to promote Macpherson's *Borderline* used a collage of black and white faces from the movie similar to some of Heartfield's work. Macpherson would have been exposed to this work during his frequent visits to Berlin with Bryher, between 1927 and 1933, as editor of *Close Up*. Their visits synchronized with the hot debate in the magazine about styles of *montage* in the cinema, in which he took an eclectic position allowing for a range of effects "from sharply contrasted construction to 'transfusion.' "¹²

The "Greek" photomontages in H.D.'s Scrapbook were not made by the poet. On the first page, which is also the first photomontage, Pearson's penciled inscription confirms one's intuition: "made by Kenneth." The internal evidence suggests that Macpherson composed these images during the time of his closest intimacy with H.D. and Bryher in 1927–28. He may have set the album aside during the filming of *Borderline*, 1929–30, in which all three were involved, and taken it up again in 1930–31.[13] The photomontages that interest us are at the beginning of the album. They all incorporate pictures of a naked H.D., taken some years before it was made. Pearson's inscription (probably dictated by Bryher many years later) indicates the place, "California," and ascribes a date, "1921." The actual date of the photographs was almost certainly 1920, when the two women, together with H.D.'s mother and daughter, spent the autumn months at Carmel Highlands near Monterey on the spectacular coast of Northern California. This offered the privacy of log huts "hidden in the pines" and a warm climate in which to go naked.[14] Carmel Highlands Inn is a few miles south of Carmel-by-the-Sea, which was fast becoming a retreat for artists and writers at that time. In a letter to Alida Monro written shortly after their arrival, H.D. admits to being happier at Carmel than in New York: "here on the very edge of the world — pine-woods back of the cottage and the sea with real breakers facing us."[15] This sense of being on the edge of the known is present in the palimpsest of Kenneth's photomontages: if the Californian coastline was Bryher's *West*, it was H.D.'s *Hesperides*.[16]

The six nude photographs of H.D. in the Scrapbook were taken out of doors in different poses and different locations: three in the Carmel pinewoods and three on rocks at the sea's edge.[17] Two nude photographs of Bryher, both taken on the shore, complete the group, though only one of them is used in the photomontages.[18] The settings of these photographs, whether Greek, Californian, or Cornish, are often meeting points between earth and sea. They anticipate H.D.'s lines in *Trilogy*: "we are at the crossroads, / the tide is turning. . . ."[19] Bryher must have been well aware, even when writing *West*, that this vital interface could also be used to signify that crossing of the lines of sex and gender that informs the text of Kenneth's montages and the context of their three lives. It is hard to say how conscious H.D. was of these meanings. The word *palimpsest* suggests simultaneously certain erasures of awareness and a commitment to recover what is lost. H.D.'s novel *Palimpsest* was the first of her works to be seen by Macpherson, and his familiarity with the world of male homosexuality may have made him less inhibited than she about the meanings it encoded. Moreover, with Kenneth as male lover, H.D.'s bisexual identity was secure. Macpherson's ability to share with H.D. and Bryher sexually ambivalent perceptions, not to mention his access to their lives and writings, uniquely qualified him to work on their album of photographs.

In 1928, H.D. would characterize Kenneth as "Narthex" or "Eleusinian wandbearer," the *narthex* being the plant stalk carried by initiates or the wand used by magicians. In the same text, she describes her own *persona* as "slim intellectual wandbearer, herself narthekophoros."[20] It is tempting to assume, with Freud, that the wand or stalk symbolizes the phallus and that H.D. was here phallicizing or fetishizing herself. More resonant, however, is Juliet Mitchell's suggestion that the simple upright is the sign of the *i*—a mark that predates, in the development of the personality, awareness both of the separate ego and of gender division, just as it predates the act of writing itself.[21] This sign is carried into the actual writings of H.D., Bryher, and Macpherson with typical syncretism. Describing her first meeting with H.D., Bryher offers this metaphor for the poet's tall figure: "a spear flower if a spear could bloom."[22] The tooled leather cover of H.D.'s Scrapbook also bears a design of "spear flowers"; these resemble the pattern incised on the outer walls of the Egyptian temple of Dendur, where long-stalked lotuses seem to stand guard over the mysteries within.[23] A similar motif of "a sceptre / and a flower-shaft / and a spear" is central to H.D.'s poem "The Mysteries," celebrating the rebirth of Adonis (*CP* 301). The spear flower of Adonis and the flower stalk of the Eleusinian wandbearer thus mark the line between the sacred and the profane. H.D.'s Scrapbook is itself a realm of female mysteries which Kenneth Macpherson was privileged to enter. When his compositions incorporate the photographs of H.D. in the Carmel pinewoods, they confirm intimations of a sacred grove dedicated to the goddess and associate it with the temple architecture that evolved from such natural locations. When they use the photographs taken on the shore, they endorse earlier readings of H.D. as "Oread" or rock nymph. Though paying tribute to the Hellenism or romanticizing of the classics in which H.D.'s poetic sensibility was formed, they share her sure-footed sense that the ancient sculptures of gods and goddesses were carved out of the rock of Greece itself.

Before and during her first visit to Greece, H.D. was contemplating the role of artistic representation in the relationship between the human and the divine. In her *Notes on Thought and Vision*, written in 1919, she argued: "The best Greek sculpture used the bodies of young athletes as Lo-Fu used the branch of the fruit tree," that is, "as a means of approach to ecstasy."[24] At Athens in 1920, she identified a statue of a naked youth as a site of transformation, and beauty as a crucial link in the chain of being:

The statue of Helios on the Olympic frieze, as the beautiful personality that once charmed us, acts as a go-between. The youth is a link between men (let us say) and statues. The statue is a link between the beauty of our human lovers and the gods. (*CP* 327)

In the texts of Bryher and Macpherson, as well as H.D., the athletic body is always a meeting point, between temporal and spiritual, nature and art, male and female. The archetypal "go-between" linking the realms of mortals and immortals was "the winged messenger, Hermes of the Greeks, Mercury of the Romans."[25] Depicted as a beautiful youth, he belonged to the place of intersection and was commemorated at crossroads. H.D. had celebrated him in "Hermes of the Ways" and would do so again when she and Kenneth were "involved with pictures." "Projector," which was published in *Close Up*, is a paean of praise to the divine magician of cinematography and gives him the attributes of Hermes:[26]

> master of shrines and gateways
> and of doors,
> of markets
> and the cross-road
> and the street;

> (*CP* 349)

When, in the photomontages, Kenneth juxtaposes the Bryher/H.D. photographs with pictures of Greek temples and sculptures, he is placing them at a crossroads. The image marks an intersection that is also a site of meaning. "An image at the crossroads": the phrase recurs in H.D.'s prose, referring both to Her's perception of Fayne as Hera,[27] and also to the writer's reading of her own childhood:

There we sit . . . making a little group, design, an image at the crossroads. It appears variously in Greek tragedies with Greek names. . . . (*Tribute to Freud* 28–29)

The name from Greek tragedy central to Freud's account of childhood was that of Oedipus, who killed his father at a crossroads. If, as Elizabeth Wright argues, "the Oedipus complex is for Freud the nucleus of desire, repression and sexual identity" in the child's relationship with the father, then its twin, the castration complex, is the nexus of the child's relationship with the mother.[28] Freud's thinking was firmly within the patriarchal tradition that defined women as castrated men and censured them for "penis envy." His theories were available to Bryher's circle via Hanns Sachs (whom she met in 1927) well before Freud insisted to H.D. that the statuette of Athene was imperfect because "she has lost her spear" (*Tribute to Freud* 69). H.D. refutes this reading with *"woman is perfect"* (*CP* 455). Her stone imagery of this period is suggestive not of castration, but of sacrifice. In a 1927 piece tellingly entitled "Restraint," she argues for a significant classicism in the cinema in these terms: "our least set should have its focus of simplicity, its as it were altar block, should mean something."[29]

In the first photomontage, H.D.'s body lies like an "altar block" heavy with meaning, between two Greek temples.[30] On the left is the ruined Doric temple of Poseidon at Sounion, which H.D. and Bryher had visited in 1920. On the right is the Ionic temple of Athene Nike, the Wingless Victory, close by the Parthenon, which H.D. revisited with Perdita in 1932. She returns to it twice in the cinematic flashbacks of *Writing on the Wall*: "the tiny Temple of Victory that stands on the rock of the Acropolis, to your right as you turn off from the Propylaea . . . ," "the little temple to your right as you climb the steps to the Propylaea on the Acropolis of Athens" (*Tribute to Freud* 56, 69). The precise directions show the subject ("I" or "you") to be in a familiar landscape—the kind that recurs in dreams. We are reminded, too, of the physical *presence* of Greek architecture even in ruin, the sureness with which these temples site themselves between physical bodies and the idea of the gods.

H.D. identified herself with Athene Nike, while Kenneth seems to have associated himself with Poseidon.[31] Athene's birth and her contest with Poseidon for the right to name the city are commemorated on the pediments now displayed among the Elgin Marbles in the British Museum, which H.D. knew well. Are we presented, in this photomontage, with what Eisenstein would have called "*montage* for conflict," or is it an image of reconciliation? If the dialectic of gender difference is represented in the temples, it is also resolved pictorially in the central, mediating figure between them. Athene was victorious in her struggle with Poseidon, and the Attic collaboration between goddess and god, earth and sea, was thus celebrated in an image of female perfection: Athene Nike. She "combined the most active qualities of the old goddess and the young male gods who had partly superseded her."[32] This harmonizes with Kenneth's visions of H.D. as an adorable androgyne; he wrote her, in the dawn of their love affair: "I knew I had seen god or goddess in you then." At about the time when the Scrapbook was made, H.D. announced that she was enjoying a "very static and 'classic' and peaceful relationship with Bryher and Macpherson."[33] This too might be written into the symmetry of the first photomontage, which is composed like an upturned triangle, with its base connecting the temples and its apex in the image of H.D. Such a reading is possible if we separate the characters of Nike and Athene and associate the latter with Bryher. Her reciprocal relationship with H.D., as a lover of the same sex, would justify this. Moreover, as H.D.'s patron and the adoptive mother of her daughter, Bryher combined the active and protective roles of the goddess: in "Helios and Athene," H.D. wrote of "the massive shield-rim of Athene, guardian of children, patron of the city" (*CP* 326).

In modern terms, the placing of an image of H.D. at the "crossroads" between these two symbols recalls Edward Carpenter's designation "the intermediate sex."[34] His was a more positive interpretation of homosexuality than that of Havelock Ellis, whom Bryher and H.D. consulted in London and took with them to Greece in 1920. Ellis's notion of the *invert* influenced Radclyffe Hall's novel *The Well of Loneliness*, published (and censored) in 1928, close to the time when H.D. suppressed the text of *HER* and Bryher contracted a "white" marriage with Macpherson.[35] Nevertheless, in the privacy of their Scrapbook, Kenneth may well be alluding to H.D.'s bisexuality, and the first photomontage can be read as an attempt to transcend the tension of the poet's "I had two loves separate" (*CP* 453) in a composition that resonates with the triumphant conclusion of "Helios and Athene":

> Athene, the maiden, Parthanos, is doubly passionate.
>
> (*CP* 330)

Parthanos or *parthenos*, from which "Parthenon" derives, means virginal, inviolate, entire. The early images of Pallas Athene, known as *palladia*, were carved from single blocks of stone found lying on the ground; these were supposed to have fallen from the sky and to have their power from heaven. H.D. associated her own power with the earth; she would adopt Freud's metaphor of archeological recovery when writing of her work with the unconscious:

The Gift was there, but the expression of the gift was somewhere else.
  It lay buried in the ground; in older countries, fragments of marble were brought to life again after long years. On these altars, flowers had lain. . . .[36]

In these lines, Philadelphian gravestones are transformed into Greek altars. The motif of rebirth echoes H.D.'s call, on her first visit to Athens, for a renaissance of Greek studies: "the time has come to build up a new approach to Hellenic literature and art" (*CP* 328). Her early writings resound with the building of temples and setting up of statues and altars. By the late 1920s, the same motif would recur in H.D.'s writings on the cinema. There are hints in them of Abel Gance's manifesto, "The Time of the Image Has Come," where he says: "all legends, all mythologies and all myths, all founders of religion and the very religions . . . await their exposed resurrection [on film]."[37] Rebirth was also a theme in H.D.'s work with Sigmund Freud who, moving toward his writing of *Moses and Monotheism*, accused her of wanting to "found a new religion" (*Tribute to Freud* 51).

For Freud, as archimago and interpreter of images, H.D.'s feeling for her mother was the clue to her mystery. She wrote to Bryher: "F. says . . . 'back to the womb' seems to be my only solution. Hence islands, sea,

Greek primitives and so on. . . ."[38] For us, opening H.D.'s Scrapbook, the word *matrix* can act as a key to unlock its complexities. In Webster's dictionary, the primary sense of matrix is the womb; its secondary sense is "that within which or . . . from which, something originates and develops"; third, matrix indicates the substance between cells of a plant or tissue; fourth, in mathematics, it means a grid of intersections. As another poet writing of H.D. has said: "the pattern can't be 'read' or deciphered completely, but only expressed in statements which are declarations of relationships between things. The most abstract hieroglyphs are the most simple memories. . . ."[39] To go back, then, to simple memories: the original meaning of *matrix*, the maternal womb, has both a time and a space dimension. Turning to the photomontages, we can identify a double matrix, in which the moment of California, 1920, is reunited with the moment of Greece, 1920, when Bryher and H.D. made their first journey together. Macpherson, sensitive to the women's shared experience, has replaced Bryher's photographs of H.D. in their imaginative matrix. The initial effect of the photomontages is to make the spectator believe that the photographs of the women, like those of the scenes beside them, were taken in Greece. Next comes the realization, signified by the third sense of matrix, that meaning is interjacent and lies between the distinct elements that make up the whole. Another time/place factor was present in the making of the photomontages: that of France around 1930, when the Mediterranean setting and the warmth of Kenneth's devotion to H.D. seem to have evoked the first flame of her love for Bryher. Thus the heterosexual eroticism of the H.D./Kenneth relationship, evident elsewhere in the Scrapbook, acts as a matrix in which the homosexual eroticism of the H.D./Bryher relationship is celebrated. At the same time, Kenneth's compositions are products of the bisexual triad of which the H.D. figure in *Narthex* declares: "We're not three people. We're just one."

Now the mathematical meaning of matrix comes into play, for we are clearly dealing with more variables than those of time and place. Beside the literal values of geography and chronology, we are already taking account of symbolic meanings. Each of the locations mentioned connotes specific valences of freedom, ranging from the hedonism of the French Riviera for well-to-do expatriates in the late twenties and early thirties, back through the naturism, wish fulfillment, and relative sex equality of California some years before, to the liberation from the homosexual taboo that these three associated with ancient Greece.[40] As we have seen, *texts* are crucial to these meanings; equally important is the notion of *intertexts*. Michael Riffaterre defines the intertext as "any one of the various matrices that is active in the writing of the passage and vital to the reading of it."[41] Students of H.D.'s writings are well aware of the range of matrices that must be activated in the reading of her work: geographical, temporal, spiritual, mythological, biographical, and psychoanalytical as well as literary, they interact in such formulations as "psychomythology." The very plurality of these systems of meaning argues against the practice of "decoding" H.D. as if there were a single objective key to her meaning and as if we, her readers, were not ourselves implicated in a network of relations to others. Her own practice should remind us that the subject or self is not the fixed innate entity assumed in classic semiotics, but is a function of textual operations, an endless process of becoming.[42] Post-structuralist semiotics has had wider application in the field of cinema and photography than in that of literature. It is striking, however, that some of these developments in the science of meaning were anticipated by H.D. and Macpherson around 1930 owing to the conjunction in their work between modernist poetics, psychoanalysis, and cinematography. It is therefore appropriate to consider the theoretical context of the photomontages at two discrete but related historical moments: the one in which they were created (1920s–1930s) and the one in which they may now be interpreted (1980s–1990s).

HOW DO WE READ A PHOTOGRAPH?

> The "photographic text," like any other, is the site of a complex "intertextuality," an overlapping series of previous texts "taken for granted" at a particular cultural and historical conjuncture. These prior texts, those *presupposed* by the photograph, are autonomous; they serve a role in the actual text but do not appear in it, they are latent to the manifest text and may only be read across it "symptomatically" (in effect, like the dream in Freud's description, photographic imagery is typically *laconic* . . .).
>
> —Victor Burgin, *Thinking Photography*

Behind Victor Burgin's account of the "photographic text" is Roland Barthes's resonant question, "How do we read a photograph?" His own answer was: "Thanks to its code of connotation the reading of a photograph is . . . always historical; it depends upon the reader's 'knowledge' just as though it were a matter of a real language [*langue*], intelligible only if one has learned the signs."[43] Exploring the ways in which photographic signs acquire meaning, Barthes uses the term *syntax* to refer to the placing of photographs in sequence so that the whole has a connotative value higher than that of the individual parts. Subsequent semioticians—notably Umberto Eco—have distinguished between Barthes's notion of a "code of connotation" and the idea of "rhetorical" codes, arising from the juxtaposition of elements within a photograph as well as between different but adjacent photographs. This thinking draws not only on structural lin-

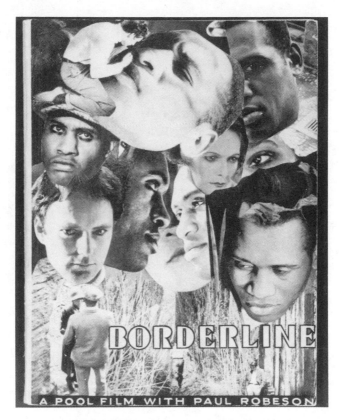

1. *Borderline* photomontage. Photo courtesy of Beinecke Rare Book and Manuscript Library, Yale University.

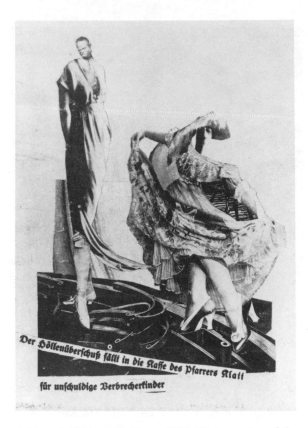

2. Hannah Höch, *Dada-Dance*, 1922. Photo courtesy of the
Galleria Schwarz, Milan.

3. Between Poseidon and Athene. Photo courtesy of Beinecke Rare Book and Manuscript Library, Yale University.

4. The Blameless Physician. Photo courtesy of Beinecke Rare Book and Manuscript Library, Yale University.

5. Nike, Victory. Photo courtesy of Beinecke Rare Book and Manuscript Library, Yale University.

6. At the Hesperides. Photo courtesy of Beinecke Rare Book and Manuscript Library, Yale University.

168

guistics, but also on Freud's observation of the close relationship between language phenomena and the unconscious. According to Jacques Durand, "The rhetoricized image, in its immediate reading, is heir to the fantastic, the dream, hallucinations. Metaphor becomes metamorphosis, repetition, seeing double, hyperbole . . . etc."[44] Durand defines rhetoric as "the art of fake speech" and uses the Freudian concepts of *desire* and *censure* to explain why, in photographic media such as advertising and the cinema no less than in literature, literal meaning so often gives way to deliberate artifices such as the conceit. If we were to adopt the language of rhetoric in discussing Macpherson's photomontages, we might well wish to refer to them as complex images or *conceits*. They not only exploit the interchangeability, in the photographic medium, of people and statues, but play with the meanings of *metaphor* and *metamorphosis*.

The theories summarized here were anticipated by the pioneers of modernism early in the twentieth century. As editor of *Close Up*, which claimed with justice to be "the only magazine devoted to film as art," Kenneth Macpherson was alert to the controversies of the cinematic avant-garde. He also acted as go-between in what Anne Friedberg has called "the striking liaison between cinematic and psychoanalytic theory" that produced *Borderline*.[45] Foremost among the film directors influenced by Freud was G. W. Pabst, whom the H.D. triad greatly admired. Through him, they came into contact with Hanns Sachs whose "Film Psychology" was published in *Close Up*. Introducing this article, Macpherson referred to "the psychological process known as displacement," thus anticipating the use of this term by post-Freudian literary critics.[46] *Close Up* also created a space in which modernist writers and cinematographers could pool their ideas. Macpherson's awareness that the cinema could learn from literature at a structural level, rather than that of imitative effects, was reflected in his article "*Close Up* and Film Structure."[47] His mentor in this respect was the revolutionary Soviet filmmaker Sergei Eisenstein, who would argue that "cinematography is for the first time availing itself of the experience of literature for the purpose of working out its own language, its own speech, its own vocabulary, its own imagery."[48] In 1930, *Close Up* published Eisenstein's crucial articles entitled "The Fourth Dimension in Kino," in which he presented his own theory of montage as a grammar of this new language.[49] Eisenstein's method of editing disposed of the illusion of logical continuity or simple narrative and arose from the recognition that "any two pieces of film stuck together inevitably combine to create a new concept, a new quality born of that juxtaposition. . . ."[50]

"Juxtaposition" accurately describes the practice of joining pieces of celluloid edge to edge when editing, but it also applies to the succession of scenes on film. Macpherson describes the effect on the spectator of Eisenstein's practice:

Imagine any point where two scenes are jointed together, between the relinquishing of the old and the acceptance of the new, there will be a kind of mental "re-
snapshotting."[51]

The expression "re-snapshotting" indicates an ability to translate modernist theory into terms an amateur photographer can understand. Its applica-
bility to the techniques of photomontage, as Macpherson witnessed them
in Berlin, is obvious; with hindsight, it might also be applied to the verbal
experiments of the Imagists. Cyrena N. Pondrom has argued convincingly
that Ezra Pound's theoretical accounts of both Imagism and Vorticism
were inspired by H.D.'s early poetic practice: "In 'Vorticism,' he [Pound]
stressed the nature of the image as a conception of the mind . . . and sought
to explain the formal function of juxtaposed images in the poem as analogous to that of the 'planes in relation' of postimpressionist art" (see above,
p. 100). Alternatively, Pound described the "one-image poem" as "superposition" or "one idea set on top of another."[52] *Superposition*, or the
placing of one image on top of another, might be described as H.D.'s
characteristic method, just as *juxtaposition* or side-by-side construction
is Kenneth Macpherson's. Quite early on, she lit on the word *palimpsest*
to indicate both the narrative construction and the local method of her
prose fiction. The one page in the Scrapbook that we can confidently assign to her is a welter of superimposed images: photographic prints and
newspaper cuttings of the faces of Richard Aldington and D. H. Lawrence at different dates have been stuck on, torn off, recovered and set
on top of one another. The manuscript of *Madrigal* or *Bid Me to Live*
apparently went through similar palimpsestic erasures and revisions.[53]

In *Writing on the Wall*, both techniques are vividly in evidence: the dense
layering of material from different moments in the writer's history, and
the discursive conjunction of images from memory and dream, art and
literature, involve the reader in a vertiginous process of "re-snapshotting."
From her poetic apprenticeship, H.D. was accomplished at assembling
discrete particulars into new wholes strong in connotation. Freud's associative procedures enriched and extended her craft as an Imagist and
naturally invoked visual analogies; recalling analysis with him, she writes,
"We . . . patiently and meticulously patch together odds and ends of our
picture-puzzle" (*Tribute to Freud* 119). Similar expressions occur in the
1930 *Borderline* pamphlet, which has been ascribed to H.D.[54] It says
Macpherson's *montage* is "the meticulous cutting of three and four and
five inch lengths of film and pasting these tiny strips together," and describes the technique as "almost that of superimposition but subtly differing from it." Is there a hint here of H.D.'s longing for the *whole* that
"superimposition" promises to satisfy by leaving nothing out? The tech-

nique of her mature writing shares with our habits of viewing the capacity to invest individual items of meaning with that wholeness, identity, and sense of being which mere "juxtaposition" leaves in question. Yet, as the pamphlet points out, the difference between these two structural principles is subtle, and the examples of both Pound and Eisenstein demonstrate that juxtaposition can be a means to quite elaborate ends.

"Superimposition" for H.D. is a means of reading one thing or category in relation to another: it is above all a mental operation. Thus she records in her diary that she experienced Egypt visually, in terms of the Gustav Doré illustrations in her childhood Bible.[55] Macpherson's use of juxtaposition belongs to the physical rather than the mental sphere, but its effects are both complex and poetic. The separate elements of the composition are pieced together in ways that recall H.D.'s metaphor of patchwork and the "picture-puzzle." Image 6, for instance, is composed of two photographs: of H.D. in full frontal nudity, Venus-like among the rocks, and of a stone metope from Olympia which depicts Heracles handing the apples of the Hesperides to Athene, while Atlas resumes his burden. The photograph of the metope has been cut like a jigsaw, and the two pieces have been separated or displaced so as to "reveal" the picture of H.D. In the original photomontage the use of disparate materials is explicit, but there is an element of fake in the jagged cutting that makes the worked stone resemble rock and thus effects a transition between the two photographs. Moreover, an illusion of perspective occurs because of the difference in scale between the figures on the metope and that of H.D. The photographs appear to be placed on two distinct planes, though they are attached to the single plane of the album page. The spectator seems to be peering down at the figure of H.D. and at the same time seeing her momentarily through the sliding screen created by the parted metope. These teasing allusions to the peepshow were doubtless intended by Macpherson; they involve the onlooker in the spectacle, while insisting on his or her distance from it. As Burgin puts it: "To look at a photograph beyond a certain period of time is to court frustration: the image which on first looking gave pleasure has by degrees become a veil behind which we now desire to see."[56] In this case, the forward movement of desire is checked by the parted metope, and the inevitable frustration is marked by the way the image of H.D. is literally "framed" by the classical sculpture. This has the effect of aestheticizing the woman's nakedness and also rendering it sexually ambiguous by placing it in the context of Greek male nudity.

The snapshot of H.D. is also framed ideologically by the mythological imagery, which multiplies its capacity for connotation. The actual context of the classical sculpture is identified in writing on the page of the Scrapbook: the temple of Zeus at Olympia where, Pausanias records, "most of the labours of Heracles are represented." In his eleventh labor, "The Apples of the Hesperides," Heracles is most closely associated with the goddess Hera, for the earthly paradise in the far west was hers. Heracles was named for Hera, as her foster child; according to some readings of the myth, he was also her consort, as an incarnation of Zeus, and remarried each year the virgin form of the goddess, who was reborn like Aphrodite by immersion in holy waters.[57] Thus, behind father Zeus is mother Hera, just as (H.D. would later write) "there is, beneath . . . every temple to God-the-father, the dark cave or grotto . . . to Mary, Mère," the mother goddess.[58] Does Image 6 offer us, beyond the peep show of Beauty at her toilette, a glimpse into the birth cave? In the photomontage, H.D.'s image not only complements that of Athene in the metope, but also recalls the birth of Venus and Hera as divine mother:[59] both Hera and Venus meet is Hespera, the Evening Star, and are thus connected with the Hesperides. These meanings resonate with the text of *HER*, where the heroine is "like a star invisible in the daylight," where (in the Academy) "there was a picture of a naked woman standing on a sea shell," and where Fayne (the other Her) is seen, like Hera, as "an image standing by a crossroad" (*HER* 225, 136, 121).

Such depths of connotation are achieved by Macpherson with the surface techniques of an art that Pound described, in his essay on Vorticism, as "planes in relation." Through illusions of movement and three-dimensionality, he gives us a sense of the "fourth dimension" that Eisenstein claimed for his cinematic montage and H.D. pursued in her writing.[60] The sliding screen of Image 6 is comparable to the lifted wing and dynamic draperies of Image 5. There is an equally interesting suggestion of movement in Image 2: here the cut-out photograph of H.D. seated on a rock is apparently in front of, but actually on top of, the photograph of a frieze from Epidauros depicting Nike, Hygeia, and Asklepios. As a static image, this has a heiratic quality which evokes H.D.'s devotion to Freud, her "blameless physician" (*Tribute to Freud* 101): she seems to have placed her head on his knee. Yet the seated figure in the foreground might equally well be "at the pictures" watching projections on a screen above her eye level. The two readings elide with one another when we recall Freud's discussion of the daydream and its continuing influence on cinematic theory, especially in the recent concern with scopic pleasure. We may also recall that Asklepios' cure, like Freud's, involved the interpretation of dreams. If H.D. is depicted here as "the dreamer," then she is also the visionary. The three figures she sees belong literally to the stone frieze; but symbolically they represent the supranatural plane "above her head," resembling thus the divine triads of *Trilogy*. They seem to be moving, as if on a cartoon or primitive filmstrip, from right to left, so that the angelic wings and fluttering draperies of Nike bring back H.D.'s vision of her at Corfu. H.D. would refer to this experience as a kind of supranatural cinema: "the series of shadow—or of light—pictures I saw projected on the wall" (*Tribute to Freud* 41). She also describes the successive images of her vision as moving upward, as the frames move in projection, and adds of Nike: "She is a moving-picture" (*Tribute to Freud* 55).

The illusion of dimensionality in these photomontages attracts analogies with landscape painting and theater design, as well as with the cinema. As we have seen, Image 3 arranges a photograph of a recumbent H.D. between those of two Greek temples. The one on the left is edge to edge with the picture of her; that on the right overlaps it like a stage flat, suggesting again a reading from right to left (like some ancient scripts) and a perspective that recedes in the same direction from foreground to background. H.D.'s nude body is thus at the center of all three axes— height, breadth, and "depth." The photographs that make up these suggestive and witty constructions are themselves "tricks of imagery and light," to quote Macpherson's *Poolreflection*.[61] But they have not been retouched in the studio or subjected to other technical effects such as soft focus to enhance their strength of connotation. Nor should the photomontages be categorized as trick photography. Rather, Macpherson's art belongs to the category of *trompe l'oeil*, which does not aim to deceive, since it announces its intention to do so; to quote Riffaterre, it is "the marker of the make-believe." Kenneth's photomontages may be seen as artful hallucinations, film-world fantasies, or the magical exercises of a "neophyte narthex." The album indicates a range of sensibility that can catch H.D.'s highest aspirations and also perform conjuring tricks. The privacy of the parlor game should not be overlooked: H.D.'s Scrapbook was never intended to be seen outside an intimate circle.

If the photomontages are theatrical conceits or feats of prestidigitation, what of the photographs themselves? For in Kenneth's tableaux or moving pictures, the image of H.D. is the star attraction, the center of attention. These photographs of H.D. appear to have been taken by Bryher herself; it would follow that those of Bryher were taken by H.D. Their intimate character suggests that no third person was present, though we have recently discovered some photographs of both women naked together. It is characteristic of Bryher, the silent editor of two successful journals, not to identify herself as photographer in her glosses on the album for Norman Pearson, though she names Kenneth as artist of the photomontages. Bryher had her "Kodak" with her in California; she was among the amateur photographers on the Carmel beach during a dramatic episode in the shooting there of a film starring Mary Pickford. In the chapter of

West that tells this tale, Bryher insists that H.D., not she, was "keen on the movies," and refers to her companion as "Helga Doorn," the Garboesque sobriquet that H.D. used as a star of *Borderline*.[62] It is surprising, perhaps, that H.D. could perform as well as Bryher on the other side of the camera. However, snapshots taken in Cornwall and California, which show the women individually (though often in similar poses, clothes, and settings) suggest that this mutual image making was part of their relationship.[63] Marianne Moore, who herself acquired a "vest-pocket Kodak" at about this time, was in close touch with the two women during their visit to the United States. In *West*, Bryher refers to her as the "Dactyl." This is the signature on a letter to H.D., in which Moore mentions her mother's delight "when I tried to describe to her, some of your snapshots in the woods."[64] Since Moore associates these pictures with William Carlos Williams "cavorting about naked for the fun of it," she must be referring to the nudes; H.D. had probably shown them to her on their return journey through New York in February 1921. Although the photographer Imogen Cunningham complained (with reference to her series of pictures of John Butler, "On Mount Rainier") that 1915 was "a little late to be chasing a naked husband around, even in California," 1920 was apparently not too late for Bryher and H.D. to photograph each other naked there or to show these pictures to their closest friends.

If these exceptional photographs *were* taken by the women themselves, then they express a reciprocity between artist and subject rare in the history of photography. The pictures themselves are an actual trace of the quality of feeling between Bryher and H.D. in the early days of their relationship. Lesbian imagery of this period is largely inaccessible, and what *is* known — the graphics of Djuna Barnes, for example — often shares the pictorialism of masculine decadence. By contrast, the Bryher/H.D. photographs may be compared to the active collaboration between Anne and Elizabeth Brigman in 1903–13. Anne Brigman's photographs of her sister as a naked dryad or hamadryad are especially interesting in view of Ezra Pound's early representations of H.D. and her own use of his nickname "Dryad" in their later correspondence. They were taken among the trees and rocks of the Californian High Sierras — a place quite distinct from the Parisian milieu of Djuna Barnes, which H.D. and Bryher would encounter after their sojourn in America. Bryher may have seen Brigman's photographs in *Camera Work*.[65] Both in process and as products, they differ from many of the nude studies of the female body made by male photographers. These frequently mimic the dominant/submissive pattern of male/female relationships. The photographer imposes uncomfortable positions on his model and often uses aggressive close-up, which gives the effect of dismembering her body. Some of Man Ray's *Women* of the 1920s show this treatment, and Edward Weston's *Nudes*, taken on the beach at Carmel, exemplify the objectification that characterizes much pictorial representation of women's bodies.[66]

In such pictures, it has been argued, the gaze of the man composing the photograph colludes with that of the man beholding it; their combined gaze deletes the female subject of whom the image is made and substitutes an object. Laura Mulvey, whose work on visual pleasure in the cinema has been highly influential, identifies this effect of the male gaze with Freud's notion of fetishism.[67] In the cinema, the whole female body may be phallicized or made into an unthreatening fetish, and some critics have seen this as the basis for the cult of the "screen goddess." (It is worth noticing here that, while H.D. enjoyed acting in movies, it was Kenneth Macpherson who attempted to promote her as a star.) The notion of fetishism is especially controversial among feminists. H.D.'s poem "The Master," which arose from her analysis with Freud, has been read on the one hand as a powerful assertion of female sexuality and on the other as a phallicizing of the female body.[68] The crucial lines for the second reading are:

> for she needs no man,
> herself
> is that dart and pulse of the male,
> hands, feet, thighs,
> herself perfect.

> (*CP* 456)

Whatever interpretation is placed upon these lines, it can be said that the verbal signs of "The Master" belong to the same discourse as the visual signs of the nude photographs. In them, whether the female body is active or passive, erect or recumbent, we are invited to acknowledge its autonomy, its freedom from the male gaze.

In *Women and Film*, Ann Kaplan asks, "Is the gaze *necessarily* male? . . . Could we structure things so that women own the gaze? If this were possible, would women want to own the gaze?"[69] These questions are relevant to the Bryher/H.D. photos. In her biography of the poet, Barbara Guest alludes to Bryher's request that H.D. seek nude photographs of film actresses for her in Vienna as "a masculine taste for pornography"; she also highlights H.D.'s "Confession" — "I am very vain and have an inordinate inferiority complex" — as a clue to her character.[70] Guest apparently wants to cast Bryher in the role of voyeur and H.D. in the role of exhibitionist, assigning to one and the other the active and passive "perversions" designated by Freud. Implicit in this casting is a commitment to culturally defined gender stereotypes (male = active, female = passive) and a conventional perception of homosexuality as perverse. At the very least, we can see from the evidence of the Californian photographs of the two women that these roles were interchangeable and not gender-defined. We can go further and participate in a fluid realm of female looking: a mutual beholding which celebrates the object as subject. Meryl Altman's comment to mc, about these images of H.D., that "the gaze is present *in* the photograph," strengthens my own sense that there is a world of difference between the eroticism of these photographs and the kinds of gratification described by Freud.

NOTES

I am grateful to all who have helped me with corrections and developments of the original drafts of this article, especially those who attended the symposium for H.D.'s centenary at the University of Maine at Orono. This essay is adapted from an article in *H.D.: Woman and Poet*, ed. Michael King. Orono, ME: National Poetry Foundation, 1986. 319–68.

1   Jonathan Culler, *Structuralist Poetics* (London: Routledge and Kegan Paul, 1975), 132.

2   Jean-Louis Swiners, cited by Victor Burgin,*Thinking Photography*, ed. Burgin (London: Macmillan, 1982), 70.

3   "Confession/Answer to a Questionnaire," *Little Review* 12.2 (May 1929): 38–40.

4   Macpherson's generous use of movie stills was a significant feature of *Close Up*. In a letter of this time, H.D. asks Robert Herring for stills of Garbo used in the magazine.

5   The letters between Kenneth Macpherson and H.D. in the Beinecke Library at Yale are mostly undated, so it is hard to be precise on chronology; the Easter in question may have been 1932 or 1933. I shall not normally document subsequent references to this correspondence.

6   The photomontages are reproduced here in the order in which they occur in H.D.'s "Scrapbook." I shall refer to them by numerals in the text of this article, but offer the following captions of my own:

    3   Between Poseidon and Athene
    4   The Blameless Physician
    5   Nike, Victory
    6   At the Hesperides

I am most grateful to Perdita Schaffner, by whose kind consent these illustrations appear, and to the trustees of the Beinecke Rare Book and Manuscript Library of Yale University for permitting their publication.

7   In *HER*, the "old Academy" is the setting of Fayne's appearance in *Pygmalion* ([New York: New Directions, 1981], 134), which is discussed in the third section of my original essay: see Michael King, ed., *H.D.: Woman and Poet* (Orono, ME: National Poetry Foundation, 1986), 351–52. Eakins' photographs are

reproduced in E. C. Parry and R. Stubbs, *Photographer Thomas Eakins* (Philadelphia: Olympia Galleries Ltd., 1981).

8   The ts. of "The Greek Boy" by Hilda Doolittle is in the Collection of American Literature, Beinecke Library. Aldington's "To a Greek Marble" appeared in *Poetry* 1. 2 (Nov. 1912).

9   Susan Sontag, *On Photography* (New York: Delta Books, 1977), 175 et passim.

10   See Dawn Ades, *Photomontage*, rev. ed. (London: Thames and Hudson, 1986), 20.

11   David Evans and Sylvia Gohl, *Photomontage: A Political Weapon* (London: Gordon Fraser, 1986), 28–29.

12   Kenneth Macpherson, "An Introduction to the 'Fourth Dimension in the Kino,' " *Close Up* 6.3 (March 1930): 174–75.

13   The latest material in the Scrapbook dates from 1930–31: photographs of Perdita between ten and twelve years old, and of Kenwin under construction. There are also numerous holiday snapshots of H.D., Macpherson, Herring, and others in the South of France (in 1931, H.D. and Mary Chadwick joined Kenneth and his new lover Toni Slocum at Monte Carlo). I am grateful to Louis Silverstein, of Yale University Library, for helping me with these identifications, as with so much else.

14   Bryher gives a thinly veiled account of their stay there in chapter 4 of *West* (London: Jonathan Cape, 1925). Barbara Guest says that Bryher and H.D. spent Thanksgiving and Christmas with H.D.'s Howard cousins in Monrovia and went north to Carmel via Santa Barbara in January 1921, returning east in February. *Herself Defined: The Poet H.D. and Her World* (New York: Doubleday, 1984), 134–35. But according to the H.D. letters cited in this article they were at Carmel by the beginning of October 1920, having already visited Santa Barbara, and H.D.'s Blue notebook, in the Beinecke Library, is inscribed "Carmel Highlands—autumn 1920." H.D.'s later *Autobiographical Notes* for Normal Pearson, in the Beinecke Library, indicate that they traveled from Carmel to Monrovia for Thanksgiving and that the Howards joined them at Carmel for Christmas.

15   H.D. to Alida Monro, October 1, 1920, Department of Special Collections, University of California, Los Angeles. The Carmel Highlands Inn is still in business but, according to the *New York Times* travel section (July 1, 1984) "has lost some of its old charm" through being remodeled.

16   The text of *Bid Me to Live* ([Redding Ridge, CT: Black Swan, 1983], 36, 50) recalls Robert Herrick's use of *Hesperides* as the title of his collected works; the meaning behind this is the Greek myth of the earthly paradise in the far west, to which Image 6 alludes.

17   The seaside photographs may have been taken at Point Lobos, a few miles south of Carmel, or possibly in Cornwall, which H.D. and Bryher visited in the summers of 1919 and 1920. Since this essay was first published in 1986, a number of nude photographs have come to light in Perdita Schaffner's Bryher archive, and I am grateful to Virginia Smyers for drawing my attention to them.

18   There appears to have been an earlier album devoted to these nude photographs: three brown pages, each bearing a single matt enlargement in sepia tones (two are of H.D., the third is of Bryher) are attached to the center of the later black-leaved album known as the "Scrapbook." For the photomontages in the later album, Kenneth has used high-quality trimmed prints of smaller size, in grey matt tones matching those of the other pictures he has used.

19   H.D., *The Collected Poems, 1912–1944*, ed. Louis L. Martz (New York: New Directions, 1983), 524.

20   H.D., *Narthex, The Second American Caravan*, ed. Alfred Kreymborg et al. (New York: Macaulay, 1928), 225–84.

21   Juliet Mitchell, "The Letter *i*," *Oxford Literary Review* 8.1–2 (1986). This paper took as its starting point Derrida's references to Melanie Klein in "Freud and the Scene of Writing," *Writing and Sexual Difference*, trans. Alan Bass (Chicago: U of Chicago P, 1978), 196–231.

22   W. Bryher, *Two Selves* (Paris: Contact Editions, 1923), 126. Julie Abraham discussed this recognition image in her paper "The History of the Player's Boy: Bryher's Lesbian Writing," Sixth Berkshire Conference on Women's History, 1984. I am also indebted to her for the connection between it, the cover of the Scrapbook, and the Temple of Dendur now in the Metropolitan Museum of Art, New York.

23   In *Narthex* we learn that Gareth (Bryher) disliked tooled leather, but Raymonde (H.D.), browsing among the boutiques with Daniel (Kenneth) during their shared honeymoon in Venice, bought a florentine portfolio for herself. Another H.D. persona, Hermione, associates the later binding of her Temple Shakespeare with "the temple on the Nile" (*HER* 82).

24   H.D., *Notes on Thought and Vision* (San Francisco: City Lights Books, 1982), 46–47.

25   H.D., *Tribute to Freud* (New York: New Directions, 1984), 7.

26   Bryher expressed similar cinematic perceptions in a more modern idiom: for her, "the hall of a hotel" with its comings and goings "always suggested some casual sequence in a movie": "An Interview: Anita Loos," *Close Up* 2.4 (April 1928): 12. The equation Macpherson = Hermes/Mercury is backed up by his own use of the pseudonym "Mercurius" for an article on *Close Up* (see note 47 below). One of Bryher's London subsidiaries was the Mercury Press.

27   H.D., *HER* 10.

28   See Elizabeth Wright, *Psychoanalytic Criticism* (London and New York: Methuen, 1984), 15.

29   H.D. "The Cinema and the Classics II," *Close Up* 1.2 (August 1927): 32.

30   Walter Burkert makes the point that Greek altars were often placed in the open, cult stones thus imitating altars of natural rock, and "the temple facade . . . as a rule, forms the background." *Greek Religion*, trans. John Raffan (Oxford: Basil Blackwell, 1985), 87.

31   On one page of the Scrapbook, Kenneth combines a snapshot of himself with three prints of the same view of the ruins at Sounion; on another, he juxtaposes a temple from Paestum in Italy (then thought to be dedicated to Poseidon) with a sculpted male gazing at his own "pool reflection."

32 Vincent Scully, *The Earth, the Temple and the Gods*, rev. ed. (New Haven and London: Yale UP, 1979), 155. I have benefited from Scully's poetic understanding of Greek landscape, mythology, and architecture.

33 H.D. to Ezra Pound, March 1928, Beinecke Library.

34 Carpenter's *The Intermediate Sex* was published in 1908; he knew Havelock Ellis and influenced D. H. Lawrence. See Emile Delavenay, *D. H. Lawrence and Edward Carpenter* (London: Heinemann, 1969); also Sheila Rowbotham and Jeffrey Weeks, *Socialism and the New Life: The Personal and Sexual Politics of Edward Carpenter and Havelock Ellis* (London: Pluto Press, 1977).

35 See Susan Stanford Friedman and Rachel Blau DuPlessis, " 'I had two loves separate': The Sexualities of H.D.'s *HER*," in this volume. Ellis' theory of *inversion*, and its influence on Hall, is discussed by Lillian Faderman in *Surpassing the Love of Men* (London: Junction Books, 1981), 317–20.

36 H.D., *The Gift* (New York: New Directions, 1982), 4.

37 Abel Gance, "Le temps de l'image est venu," *L'art cinématographique* 2 (1927), cited by Walter Benjamin in *Illuminations*, ed. Hannah Arendt (London: Fontana, 1977), 224.

38 H.D. to Bryher, March 23, 1934, Beinecke Library.

39 Leslie Scalapino, "Re-Living," *Poetics Journal* 4 (March 1984): 53.

40 In Macpherson's correspondence with H.D., "Saph" is shorthand for lesbian, while he apparently insisted on using "Athenian" for male homosexual; see Peggy Guggenheim, *Out of This Century* (New York: Universe Books, 1979), 292. This adds another dimension to the remark of Raymonde that "Athens was somehow Daniel" (*Narthex* 256). Judith Hallett has found that in England and in the United States, "Sapphism" was replaced by "lesbianism" only in the twenties and thirties: "Sappho and Her Social Context," *Signs* 4 (1979): 447–64.

41 Michael Riffaterre, "The Semiotic Approach to Literary Interpretation," paper delivered at the Georgetown Conference on Literary Criticism, 1984. See Riffaterre's *Semiotics of Poetry* (Bloomington: Indiana UP, 1978), passim.

42 This argument draws on Burgin, *Thinking Photography* 145; the same writer warns us that this version of the subject "evicts the familiar figure of the *artist* as autonomous *ego*, transcending his or her own history and unconscious."

43 Roland Barthes, "The Photographic Message" (1961), *Selected Writings of Roland Barthes*, ed. Susan Sontag (London: Fontana, 1983), 207.

44 Cited by Burgin, "Photographic Practice and Art Theory," *Thinking Photography* 71; this essay informs my account.

45 Anne Friedberg, "Approaching *Borderline*," *Millenium Film Journal* 7–9 (1980–81): 130–39; revised version in Michael King, ed., *H.D.: Woman and Poet* (Orono, ME: National Poetry Foundation, 1986), 369–94.

46 *Close Up* (Nov. 1928): 8–15. Sachs's "Day-Dreams in Common" appeared in the *International Journal of Psychoanalysis* in 1920, and Friedberg ("Approaching *Borderline*") tells us that his book on the subject appeared in German in 1924. She also points out that Freud's 1908 essay "The Relation of the Poet to Day Dreaming" deeply influenced other writers on film. Adalaide Morris, in "The Concept of Projection: H.D.'s Visionary Powers"

in this volume, demonstrates the extent of metaphors from film in H.D.'s accounts of the poetic process.

47 Kenneth Macpherson, "*Close Up* and Film Structure," *Architectural Review* 68. 408 (Nov. 1930): 221ff.

48 Sergei Eisenstein, *The Film Sense*, trans. and ed. Jay Leyda (New York: Harcourt Brace, 1947), 166–67. An application of this idea can be found in the title of Oswald Blakeston's article on continuity devices, "Punctuation Marks," *Close Up* 11. 4 (April 1928): 42–44.

49 Sergei Eisenstein, "The Fourth Dimension in Kino," *Close Up* 6.3 and 6.4 (March and April 1930): 184–94 and 253–68. H.D. was probably indebted to Eisenstein for her idea of the "fourth dimensional," which occurs in section III of the MS of *The Gift*, Beinecke Library: see H.D., "The Dream," *Contemporary Literature* 10.4 (1969): 606; "dimensional" was Macpherson's formulation in his editorial introduction to the Eisenstein articles.

50 Sergei Eisenstein, "Montage in 1938," *Notes of a Film Director*, trans. Danko (New York: Dover Publications, 1970), 63.

51 Kenneth Macpherson, "An Introduction to 'The Fourth Dimension in Kino,' " *Close Up* 6.3 (March 1930): 175–84.

52 Ezra Pound, "Vorticism," *Fortnightly Review* (1914), rpt. in *Gaudier-Brzeska: A Memoir* (New York: New Directions, 1961), 88. See also note 58 below.

53 The final revision of *Madrigal* occurred in the late forties: it is possible that the Aldington/Lawrence page of the H.D. Scrapbook is a silent testimony to the crisis which, according to Barbara Guest, led H.D. to tear out her bookplates.

54 *Borderline* (London: Mercury Press, 1930). Charlotte Mandel attributes this pamphlet to H.D. in "Garbo/Helen: The Self-projection of Beauty by H.D.," *Women's Studies* 7. 1/2 (1980): 127–35.

55 Entry for March 2, 1933: "He [Freud] said how fortunate I had been to discover reality 'superimposed' (his word) on the pictures." (*Tribute to Freud* 119). Contrast the quotation from "Murex" at the beginning of this article.

56 Burgin, *Thinking Photography* 152.

57 See Barbara G. Walker, *The Woman's Encyclopedia of Myths and Secrets* (San Francisco: Harper and Row, 1983), 392–94.

58 Ts. of *The Gift*, Beinecke Library. H.D.'s belief coincides with Jane Harrison's theory that "In Olympia . . . the ancient Heraion where Hera was worshipped alone long predates the temple of Zeus." *Prolegomena to the Study of Greek Religion* (1903; rpt. London: Merlin Press, 1980), 315. In the same chapter, Harrision uses the term "superposition" to describe the triumph of patriarchal over matriarchial religion at Olympia.

59 In "The Making of a Goddess," Jane Harrison writes: "We have seen one woman-form take various shapes as Mother and Maiden, as duality and trinity; we have seen these shapes crystallize into Olympian definities as Athene, as Aphrodite, as Hera, and as it were resume themselves again into the great monotheistic figure of Venus Genetrix." *Prolegomena* 21.

60 Eisenstein may well have revitalized H.D.'s interest in the "fourth dimension," which had been under discussion by artists and scientists since the publica-

tion of Einstein's theories early in the century and informed Pound's 1914 essay on Vorticism: see Pondrom, "H.D. and the Origins of Imagism," in this volume.

61 Kenneth Macpherson, *Poolreflection* (Territet, Switzerland: Pool, 1927).

62 Bryher, *West* (London: Jonathan Cape, 1925), 61. Bryher maintains here that her own interest in the incident was that of a journalist; she may have acquired her skill as a photographer in preparation for this role.

63 The photographs of this period were probably taken on the Folding Pocket Kodak, which was introduced in 1903 and sold in Britain and the United States until 1934; this was popular because it produced "postcard-sized" prints, whose cost was included in the price of the Kodak film. The Cornish and Californian photos conform to these measurements (3½ × 5⅜ inches), as does Beinecke's only original of the H.D. nude used, same size, in the first photomontage. Information from E. S. Lothrop, *A Century of Photography* (Dobbs Ferry, NY: Morgan and Morgan, 1973).

64 Marianne Moore to H.D., March 21, 1921, Beinecke Library.

65 They appeared in *Camera Work* in 1909 and 1912. See Thérèse Thau Heyman, *Anne Brigman* (Oakland, CA: Oakland Museum, 1974).

66 See Janet Malcolm's discussion of this subject in *Diana and Nikon: Essays on the Aesthetic of Photography* (Boston: David R. Godine, 1980), 23–24. It is ironic to reflect that the anonymous female models of both male photographers were themselves outstanding photographers: Lee Miller for Man Ray and Tina Modotti for Edward Weston.

67 See Laura Mulvey, "Visual Pleasure and Narrative Cinema," *Screen* 16.3 (1975): 6–18. On fetishism and film, see also Claire Pajakowska, "The Heterosexual Presumption," *Screen* 17.1 (1981): 79–92. Freud's essay "Fetishism" dates from 1927.

68 Compare Rachel Blau DuPlessis and Susan Stanford Friedman, " 'Woman is Perfect': H.D.'s Debate with Freud," *Feminist Studies* 7.3 (1981): 417–30, with Claire Buck, "Freud and H.D.: Bisexuality and a Feminine Discourse," *M/F* 8 (1983): 53–65.

69 Ann Kaplan, *Women and Film* (London/New York: Methuen, 1983), 24.

70 Guest, *Herself Defined* 210.

Part III

Palimpsests

There were shrines, shrines in spite of what people said. There were shrines beyond shrines, feet beyond feet, faces beyond faces. Faces overlaid now one another like old photographic negatives and faces whirled on and on and on, like petals down, down, down as if all those overlaid photographic negatives had been pasted together and rolled off swifter, swifter, swifter from some well controlled cinematograph. Her mind behind her mind turned the handle (so to speak) for a series of impressions that devastated her with their clarity, with their precision and with their variety.

—H.D., *Palimpsest*

CHAPTER 11

Fishing the Murex Up:
Sense and Resonance in H.D.'s Palimpsest

DEBORAH KELLY KLOEPFER

> how can you scratch out
> indelible ink of the palimpsest
> of past misadventure?
> —H.D., *The Walls Do Not Fall*

A palimpsest is a parchment that has been written over several times, earlier versions having been imperfectly erased. It creates a strange, marginal writing that is both intentional and accidental; it must be excavated, sought after, at the very moment that it is seeping through unbidden. Coincidentally and rather remarkably, the word is an anagram, a "text" containing/concealing another text; rearranged, the letters read "simple past." "Palimpsest," then, actually enacts its own functioning, both erasing and engaging the "past" that engenders it. This overwriting/underwriting suggests two contradictory impulses — it creates both an augmented or extended text and a reduced or narrowed one; it accommodates multiplicity and yet, in the privacy of its intersections, creates a cryptic and distorted space as well.

In 1926, H.D., highly attuned to the resonances of this ancient form and its parallels to consciousness, published an important work called *Palimpsest*. This "rather loosely written long-short-story volume" (*Tribute to Freud* 148), as she called it, is difficult, disorienting, and often irritating. It is "un-even" and "badly punctuated" (*Compassionate Friendship* 28), according to its author. "It is hallucinated," she writes, "and I must become hallucinated in order to cope with it." Nonetheless, years later H.D. found that it "held and astonished" (*Compassionate Friendship* 29) her much as it continues to hold and astonish; it is extraordinarily compelling both as a text and in the place it occupies in the canon of her work, falling midpoint between 1919 and 1934 and thus serving as a kind of fulcrum for the psychic and literary period bounded by H.D.'s childbirth breakdown and by the termination of her analysis with Freud.

As various critics have observed, 1919 marked a turning point for H.D. "The previous years had been a period so filled with both achievement and anxiety, so critical and traumatic that she would spend the rest of her life mythologizing it: rehearsing it in verse, in prose, in direct auto-biography and in historical and legendary personae, again and again seeking to unriddle her destiny as woman and poet" (Gelpi 7). Indeed, after her break with Pound and imagism, the loss of a child, the deaths of her brother and father, the dissolution of her marriage to Richard Aldington, the trauma — particularly strong for H.D. — of world war, and her illness following the birth of her daughter, H.D., at thirty-three, became understandably preoccupied not only with unriddling her destiny, but also with making some sense of her past.[1]

During the fifteen artistically frustrating years which followed, novels and their sequels or "pre-quels" appeared rapidly, eclipsing the poetry.[2] The early autobiographical "fiction" is marked by a feverish, hallucinatory intensity alternating with an extraordinary detachment. One has the sense that H.D. never really comes to terms with any of the material, hence her need to act it out — textually — over and over, revising, altering, intensifying, disclaiming, but never exhausting her obsession with the forces of her early life.

Palimpsest surges with this psychological and textual confusion. It is a text superimposed as if "photographic negatives had been pasted together and rolled off swifter, swifter, swifter from some well controlled cinematograph. Her mind behind her mind turned the handle (so to speak) for a series of impressions that devastated her with their clarity, with their precision and with their variety" (*Palimpsest* 157). She has reentered the past and reengaged it, releasing herself into it as she eventually released herself into her work with Freud, until she understood that the transformation spiritually, psychologically, and textually of the simple past into palimpsest would reflect and encompass all the significant aspects of her voice and vision: division of selves and consciousness, the layering or embedding of language, the seepage of past into present, hermeticism, and revisions and palinodes as impulses.[3]

It is difficult to know where or how to enter this "devastating" text as *Palimpsest* rolls forward, subverting and concealing the generating units and frames on which it is nonetheless dependent. The text, like the consciousness that creates and is created by it, is a kind of hallucinated, layered cinema: a film frozen, a film melting with the heat of an incandescent brain, a film rewound, a film reversed, a film alternately speeded up and slowed in motion; to read the text is also somehow to view it.[4] There is, consequently, because of both its structural convolutions and its reliance on image, no sense of determining syntax here, no familiar structure that consistently constructs the direction of the reading.

Despite H.D.'s abandoning of conventional structure and syntax, however, it is possible to locate oneself within the textual topography. *Palimpsest*, like a number of H.D.'s works, is a trilogy, a form that was highly attractive to her throughout her career. There is, for example, the work finally called *Trilogy*, composed of *The Walls Do Not Fall* (1944), *Tribute to the Angels* (1945), and *The Flowering of the Rod* (1946); there is *Helen in Egypt* (1961) structured as "Pallinode," "Leuké," and "Eidolon"; there is the tripartite *Hermetic Definition* (1973) written as "Red Rose and a Beggar," "Grove of Academe," and "Star of Day." All of these published works consciously use a tripartite structure as a controlled and controlling device. Among the unpublished work, however, there are trilogies less intentional, more obsessive, generated by the impulse to retell "the story," to do it right or more clearly wrong, to reveal it finally or to disguise it more completely. These series are more triptychs than trilogies, perhaps, as they do not move forward from the initial telling but rather back inside it, altering the landmarks but never leaving the original "scene." One might group, for instance, the three novels surrounding *Palimpsest*—*Paint It To-Day* (1921), *Asphodel* (1921–22), and *HERmione* (1981; written as *HER* in 1927)—which process and reprocess H.D.'s pre-1920 relationships; one might also take as a unit *The Sword Went Out to Sea* (1946–47), *White Rose and the Red* (1948), and *The Mystery* (1949–51), novels that, according to Janice Robinson, H.D. "conceived of . . . as a prose trilogy" (343). I would suggest rather that H.D. *recognized eventually* the connections among these novels, for in her prose, H.D. does not "conceive" trilogies. She conceives such structural strategies in the poetry, but in the novels she discovers them after the fact just as she discovered in analysis that she functioned psychologically in triangles.[5] This is perhaps part of the reason she was drawn to the trilogy as form—because it acted out early relationships in a kind of prose compulsion which she did not get control over, understand, or use to her real advantage until the poetry after analysis. Suffused also with mystical, numerological, and Delphic associations, the trilogy accommodated both emotional triangles and arcane trinities, offering H.D. the textual space in which she could work both the psychic and spiritual aspects of her vision.

The trilogy *Palimpsest* occupies an unusual and important position in the canon in the sense that it is prose, but prose conceived and published as a triad. The text is divided into three distinct spaces. "Hipparchia: War

Rome (*circa* 75 B.C.)" centers on a vanquished Greek living in Rome as a poet and courtesan. The "plot" is interior, the only external markings being Hipparchia's movement among villas. H.D.'s focus is on Hipparchia's struggle to reclaim and renounce her mother, to embrace and repudiate several lovers, and to maintain the Hellenic spirit in the Roman mosaic. Part II, "Murex: War and Postwar London (*circa* A.D. 1916–1926)," works around a split figure, Raymonde Ransome/Ray Bart, a poet whose task it is to forget utterly the trauma of her past. Through a teatime encounter with a jilted friend, her own history—loss of a lover, death of a child—is unearthed against her will, brought up from the depths of her subconscious despite all her linguistic and psychological defenses, until everything is "altered horribly" (117). "Secret Name: Excavator's Egypt (*circa* A.D. 1925)" centers on Helen Fairwood, a "high-class secretary" to a famous archeologist, who finds herself at liberty for several days in Luxor. Involved in a brief relationship with Rafton, an ex-captain on his way to Assuan, and in indulging a visiting American parvenue and her daughter, Helen moves from temple to tomb, attempting to "keep her . . . balance" suspended between two "antagonistic worlds" (176).

Despite the differences in character, chronology, and plot, there are important connections among the sections. On the most basic level there is the shared juxtaposition of past and present, always the basic division in H.D.'s work. There are, for H.D., in fact, always two pasts—her own and the historical past, antiquity. Just as her own past compelled her, the classical world had an intense and unabating attraction for H.D., archetypal and mythological figures providing a clarity and order that the war-torn twentieth century could not. One of the attractions was, I think, the fact that although antiquity itself was "split," the split was very clear. The essential division, as H.D. saw it, did not involve the schisms and rifts of world war or the gaps and chasms of madness; the split was neither among men nor within man but between gods and men, between this world and another, a split that was irrevocable but somehow negotiable. And the far past, for H.D., was more "helpful" than the present—it participated in psychic life; it offered signs, omens, auguries, visions, voices, which the poet could borrow or translate to close the gap. It is not difficult to understand H.D.'s intense connection to and affection for the classical and preclassical world when we understand that her lifelong project was to cross the gulf, to learn the language of repair, to close the gap both within and between past and present: "I mend a gap in time" ("May 1943," *CP* 492). Ironically, H.D. found it easier to undertake the repair of the split between Earth and Olympus, between life and death, than the breaks in her own past; the classical division somehow allowed her a safer and more manageable prototype for dealing with her own life.

All other polarities are subsumed under this initial way of dividing experience: "Her mind was a glass that was set between this world, this present and the far past that was eternal. A glass, a lens, a living substance lies between ourselves and our final attainment. Antiquity" (*Palimpsest* 163). The far past is clearly a privileged and invested space; the present distorts and dilutes experience and vision:

all of modernity . . . was as the jellified and sickly substance of a collection of old colourless photographic negatives through which gleamed the reality, the truth of the blue temples of Thebes, of the white colonnades of Samos. . . . Modernity was unfamiliar and semi-transparent and it obscured antiquity while it let a little show through, falsified by the nervous movement of its transparent surface. Falsified by the nervous erratic jerks of its deep-sea members. Modernity was the unfamiliar, always baffling substance. (158)

In *Palimpsest*, each section operates individually around the tension between these two spheres: Hipparchia is haunted by her own past and by ancient texts; Raymonde Ransome is consumed by the split between her present and her past and by some ancient past that informs her own; Helen Fairwood searches for herself in an ancient mystery that she invokes to clarify both modernity and herself.

At the same time, however, H.D. attempts to "close the gap" both within each section and in an intertextual project that appears in early allusions to later textual spheres as she structures a triad that erects boundaries of time and space and then abandons them. In part I, for example, the discourse becomes increasingly suffused with images of Egypt, anticipating part III. Hipparchia, in a delirious state that ruptures boundaries between reason and madness, perception and imagination, self and other, senses everywhere "Egypt in the shadow" (47) and feels herself suffocating under "some Egyptian coffin lid" (81). She merges Aphrodite and Isis (80); believes herself to *be* Isis; believes that Isis has come finally to recall her (92). She endows her lover, Verrus, with "late-Egyptian tendencies" (51), then merges him with a hallucinated vision of Osiris. Similarly, part II presages the excavations in part III as Raymonde Ransome identifies her visitor Ermy with "some unearthed Queen Nefertiti" (126) and listens to her story as to "some past Egyptian's odd and sorry history" (108). And just as Hipparchia feels the presence of ancient tombs, Raymonde thinks of her past as "far and far and far as far as a buried Egyptian's neatly painted coffin" (110) — "that long pre-Egyptian past of 1917" (109). These are more than random images; they form the connective tissue of the text, images that will be retrieved in the actual Egypt section and then wash backwards to redetermine "Hipparchia" and "Murex" like a sea that is both eroding and increasing the shoreline. This is the functioning of the palimpsest which simultaneously erases and glosses the earlier texts.

Once H.D. has set this tide into motion, it works in both directions; images initially engendered in "Hipparchia" resurface in "Murex" and "Secret Name." Raymonde Ransome, for example, is flushed with the "lightning of vivid thought that was her Athenian inheritance" (171). She imagines her ex-husband with hair "like a conqueror's helmet" (134). She, like Hipparchia, writes, knowing that the "Greek formula must not be forgotten" (155). Helen Fairwood, similarly, "[thinks] across toward Athens" (173). Scarabs make her imagine "some exquisite, incredibly slender Graeco-Egyptian, some incredibly carnal Roman" (179), images that invoke Hipparchia and her lover Verrus as if Helen Fairwood were privy to their past as well as her own. Her companion, Rafton, seems to her a conqueror, "authentic, Roman, officer of one of the flashy and distinguished legions of the middle-ageing procrastinator, Caesar" (175). Captain Rafton has merged momentarily with Verrus, just as Verrus earlier became Osiris — ancient Rome and Egypt, both modern and encrypted, washing together through time and space so that "the present and the actual past and the future were . . . one. All planes were going, on, on, on together" (166).

Hipparchia, Raymonde Ransome, and Helen Fairwood — like many of H.D.'s protagonists — are also linked by being writers. All produce texts, and their relationships to these texts and to the surrounding discourse are central to an understanding of this work. All three sections early on establish the failure of the spoken word to translate inner states adequately. Language, on one level, becomes a system of checks and "counters" used only to parry, to keep others at a distance, to defend oneself against the rising of buried material: "in their static and exact speech they questioned and they answered. Each knew the other perfectly versed in this common practice of speaking one way and of thinking other. . . . There was no arrière-pensée. Simply a simple knowledge that all she said was falsehood" (32). Raymonde Ransome, similarly, engages in conversation "holding to the letter of the talk, thinking, as was her manner, elsewhere. She had trained herself . . . to carry on her apparently eager and ecstatic conversation and to stand posed, apart, sustained in some other region" (102). And Helen Fairwood likewise carries on "a merely outer shell of conversation" (231).

Speech to these women seems to be connected to obligation, a kind of social contract they fulfill but in which they do not really participate. As writers, translators, and transcribers, they are compelled by text; through them H.D. explores the struggle to form a relationship between psychic life and the written word, a relationship beyond Helen Fairwood's "heavy and weary research into Graeco-Roman texts for . . . tiresome facts, for authentic and tiresome information on lost fragments" (189).

Of the three women, Hipparchia's immersion in manuscripts is perhaps the most consuming. As poet and translator, she is involved in finishing a book begun by her dead uncle, a scientific book on plants which she is suddenly compelled to transform into "a fervid compilation of poetry, religion and ethics" (71). In her project to work Greek poetry into Latin, she is torn between intense labor with "odd untranslatable fragment[s]," which become "set, stubborn, unmalleable metal in her head," and "the sudden appearance, from nowhere, of some magic turn of speech," some "authentic metre" (77). Hipparchia discovers translation to be a "desecration," "the dark sputtering of an almost extinguished wick in an earth bowl which before had shown rose in alabaster" (72). She begins to realize that if she creates not an actual translation but a palimpsest, a text that does not replace the original but allows and invites the struggling of the over-writing/underwriting, there is an entirely different result. She finds that "the Greek words, inset in her manuscript, would work terrific damage" (73). The Greek in this context—she is translating Sappho and Moero—is associated with antiquity and her own past, while the Roman, for Hipparchia, is the present; thus her own manuscript echoes the larger one and H.D.'s belief that the past can be called upon both to disrupt and redeem the present.

This same impulse reappears in Raymonde Ransome, linked to Hipparchia both through avocation and through language as she "grub[s] at odd manuscripts" (116) with "paper and pencil. Parchment and stylus" (151). The real connection between the two women, however, surpasses a lexical one. Each exists in a kind of split self—Hipparchia as herself and as a replication (both solicited and repudiated) of her dead mother, Raymonde Ransome as her public self and as Ray Bart, her poetic alter ego. Both women have an ambivalent relationship to their work, both riveted to it and repelled by it. At various points they burn with the intensity of it; at others they disclaim it and try—unsuccessfully—to extract themselves from it. Hipparchia's relationship to writing is complicated by its association with her mother, who wandered off renouncing her family, pleasure, beauty, and her body for the intellect. Hipparchia, an intense, icy courtesan, courts the sensuous as a way of separating herself from her mother, but she is continuously drawn back to poetry and language, never able to escape from her vulnerability to the mother who surfaces as a phantom throughout the text to "plague" her (78).[6] Similarly for Raymonde Ransome, writing often appears unbidden: "Why was it . . . when she especially repudiated her genius, it so came to plague her?" (150).

H.D. uses a rather astonishing image to further bind the projects of these two women separated by two thousand years. When Raymond feels the presence of her poet self overtake her, it appears as a very particular sensation:

With the very pencil she held poised, she tried to fend off her recurrent metres. . . . The icy glamour of the thing she knew was Ray Bart's helmet closed above her. Above Raymonde's forehead (where she would have worn some slight and fragrant but soon withering little crown of field flowers) Ray Bart's helmet rested. (147–48)

Not only does the imagery here suggest the diadem and the Roman helmets that fill part I, but the sense of a head constricted as a prelude to creative release is also an echo of Hipparchia's own sense of the "high-water mark of intellectual achievement" (35):

The mind developed beyond normal, developed and tyrannized, must again flow back and back or else a string bound tight about a frozen skull will, by just one minute hair-breadth of a tightening, cut through; cut (she visualized it) a skull neatly like a thread dividing a round cheese or ripened melon. Her head was about to be split like some ripe fruit overweighted on its trellis. (35)

What H.D. creates here is a kind of double palimpsest. Within each section the images are layered — Ray Bart overlaying Raymonde Ransome; Hipparchia the mother rising up through Hipparchia the daughter — and then both sections are superimposed like negatives, the images bleeding through time and space.

It is not just through overlaid images or impulses that H.D. works her palimpsest, however; it is also extraordinarily integrated into the structure of the language itself. The narrative voice, for example, is layered, a conflation or alternation of interior monologue, indirect discourse, and omniscient third person, moving through dialogue, turning back on itself, amending, confirming, repeating: " 'You see, they're always funny. They amuse me.' They amused her. They were funny" (102). In each section, stories are told in layers of present conversation, private perception, retrieved memory and hallucination coded in italics, interrupted clauses, and parentheses:

He spoke, though she hardly heard his utterance, something far and far — "when all these Mithradatean blusterings are over — Capua — the villa — " something about Hipparchia being set, as any gem more suitably, something from far and far and far about some suave and golden Eros — "a child sometime" — and feel sleeping — down and down into some apprehended beauty, some world of suave utterance and of chaste renewal. *Couches spread in the palace of Zeus.* So Hebe removing affectedly small dainty bracelets (she thought of Hebe with small bracelets) held close her giant lover. (36–37)

Hallucinated sections such as these, imitating the intrusions and convolutins of consciousness, appear throughout *Palimpsest*, as it ruptures itself, rises up from within itself, spills over, broken open by images, desires, voices, other times and space.

The linguistic palimpsest operates not only out of disturbed syntax but through a series of embedded refrains. Some of them are intratextual, lines that, once engendered, reappear over and over in a particular section. In "Hipparchia," for example, phrases and questions such as "Greece dissociated from any central ruling," and "since when . . . has one been able to escape the dead?" become a cadence to the surrounding discourse, an insistent throbbing which beats like the metronome Ray Bart hears inside her head. Initially these phrases are marked off from the surrounding text, but eventually italics and quotation marks disappear until whole sections (79), beating with an almost unbearable intensity, are formulated entirely of reconstituted refrains, until the present of the text is simultaneously its past. Like so many of the visual images, these auditory ones, which initially seem confined to their generating sections, cross textual boundaries resonating in other sections until we are hearing "from far and far and far and far," "feet — feet — feet — feet — feet" — soldiers' feet, metrical feet — an endless process of synthesis and return not unlike Hipparchia's description of her own work: "Things formed and reformed and when finally discarded (it had so often happened) had a strange way of reappearing in third startling manifestation" (77).

A second kind of "refrain" takes the form of disembodied poems written or remembered or translated by the women whose discourse they interrupt. In a replication of the intensely complicated functioning of consciousness, they break through the text and then, once having appeared, split and reappear in fragments. "Murex" is interrupted, for example, by poetic texts in the form of Ray Bart's developing poem, the lines of which accumulate through additions and revisions as Raymonde Ransome/Ray Bart offers successive drafts of a poem centered on her confrontation with the woman who releases her own repressed past. H.D. accomplishes this process initially through repetitions; subsequently she recasts and splinters the verses, annotating them line by line (153) until finally the annotations themselves become refrains of earlier lines (164), no longer quoted but thoroughly integrated so that the text is constantly washing through both other texts and itself.

Hipparchia, similarly, offers "crude beginning" (40) of her own poetry and then revises, correcting the original, subsequent versions replacing the engendering poems. The text is also punctuated by two poems by Antipater of Sidon, one on the fall of Corinth and the other on the death of Hipparchia's mother. H.D. uses these poems in curious ways, offering them in pieces — entire verses "forgotten" and then remembered later — floating in the text and then dissociated, like the Greek cities, from any central ruling, to reappear as refrains. The text is layered further by translations of Moero's grape song (71) and of Euripides, verses that Hipparchia then borrows for her own verse until she is "dazed, drugged and drunk . . . with the new Alexandrians" (77). Something remarkable is going on here as Hipparchia "borrows" not only her own verse but H.D.'s as well, incorporating Sapphic fragments and Euripidean choros, the very verses, some of them, that H.D. was herself writing and translating several years earlier in *Hymen* (1921) and *Heliodora* (1924). The text, then, is marked by intact first drafts evolving into revisions which then begin to merge into a true palimpsest—not poems set off typographically, but fragments "imperfectly erased" which appear throughout the larger text. At the height of her delirium, the lines of poetry couple with each other and with Hipparchia's (and H.D.'s) own story until there are no longer boundaries between her own work, her translations, her revisions and palinodes, and her subconscious: "Which was actual communion, . . . which was poetry? Metres, memories formed and reformed" (76).

H.D.'s pervasive sense of and preoccupation with the "ineffable quality of merging" that underlies palimpsest has particular interest for her in the realm of consciousness; it is not, in fact, retraced and overlaid imagery that compels the imagist poet—it is the palimpsest of perception, selves, intellect, and vision(s).

H.D., decades prior to her analysis with Freud, was intensely taken with the idea and experience of levels of consciousness, levels to which she gains access if she will "let go perception, let go arrow-vibrant thought" (95). She finds an "inner world," "a scroll that unwinds before shut eyes" (82), a kind of Freudian subconscious which "was shifted, was opened up as if a layer of hardened, protective sand and lava had been sifted. Behind that layer, the things that had been (really because of that layer) blighted were, by the same token, now fresh" (143). But H.D. also identifies a kind of other-consciousness, a "super-sense" (65) that is associated not primarily with memory, repression, and desire but with "vision."

A difficulty in writing about *Palimpsest*—or much of H.D.'s work—is that she often operates out of a private lexicon, the terms of which are variously evolving and abandoned.[7] The distinctions she makes, for example, between mind, intellect, perception, and vision are at certain times and in certain works essential; at other times she rather casually conflates them, and it is not always clear when the terms are interchangeable. One cannot read *Palimpsest*, for example, without hearing echoes of *Notes on Thought and Vision*, which H.D. wrote in 1919, attempting to distinguish among states of consciousness.[8] The earlier work is close to *Palimpsest* both chronologically and psychologically; in it, H.D. hypothesizes "three states of manifestations—sub-conscious mind, conscious mind, over-conscious mind" (49). This overconsciousness—also called "over-mind" and "over-brain"—functions through a kind of "thought" that is "vision," the vision of the artist, a kind of "waking dream" (49). These terms can seem suddenly rather manageable, but just as suddenly, theory and text wash apart as imagining, vision, thought, and perception begin to intersect.

It is clearly very difficult to talk about consciousness in H.D., a poet dependent on the enmeshment of "arrow-vibrant thought," "frozen intensity," hallucination, dream, visitation, "lotus vision," and "actual image," in some vastly complicated palimpsest of insight and despair; an interesting point of departure, however, which spans in some way the contradictions and convolutions is "bicamerality," in the sense that Julian Jaynes uses it in *The Origin of Consciousness in the Breakdown of the Bicameral Mind*. Bicamerality refers, by definition, to two-chamberedness; in Jaynes's terms it refers to a mind with no "analog I," which operates nonetheless as self and other with no "consciousness" of either and no ability to narratize. He offers a flawed but compelling model for reflecting on a number of modernist texts, particularly those of H.D., for her concept of the function and locus of poetic consciousness is very close to Jaynes's notion of bicamerality. Jaynes suggests that ancient men, until a certain point of linguistic inscription, operated through a mind one hemisphere of which responded to the instruction or admonition of the other through the mediation of hallucinated voices—the muses, gods, and goddesses of ancient texts. This "otherness," which was really "other chamberedness," is perceived as external and divine (although how men without the ability to create analogs, recognize otherness, or narratize could conceive of the "divine," Jaynes leaves unclear).

Jaynes attributes the "appearance" of bicamerality to the acquisition of language (speech) and the disappearance of bicamerality (the emergence of consciousness) to the development of language into written text, which both localized and therefore disempowered the auditory hallucinations and author(iz)ed the analog self. As we know from poststructuralism, once there is the written sign, the ability—the need—to represent, there is by definition a loss, a gap, a split between the "I" and the narratizable "me," between self and other, between signified and signifier; the sign, we know, is the mark of absence.

But to H.D.—and this is crucial to an understanding of every word she wrote—the sign is the mark not of absence but of presence. This is why she grapples to textualize "the story," this is why she works her experiences and relationships through verse and prose, obsessively, because in the word she finds not the sign of the gap but the way to close the gap— *In the beginning was the Word*.[9]

Jaynes's model offers a way of understanding this sense of presence.

Whether what he says is "true" is irrelevant here—what is important is that H.D.'s work functions "as if" it emerged out of or returned to a bicamerality, a state in which language does not represent loss but rather speaks presence. The fact that this "presence," according to Jaynes, is a neurological phenomenon in no way dilutes the intensity of the experience; it is "as if" there were an "over-consciousness" (notice how easily H.D.'s own vocabulary intersects Jaynes's) that gave voice to poetry, that offered a gift and was the gift and was the giving. Jaynes, in fact, suggests that poetry, by nature, is a memory, a nostalgia (374) for that "space," for those voices—that poetic creation is, almost by definition, bicameral (373). In a sense it is this very phenomenon that H.D. tries to explain in her not altogether successful attempts at theory. What she calls "over-mind" is what Jaynes calls "voice of the gods"; although he cautions against a topography of consciousness, he nonetheless creates one, a split "world" bridged by voices not unlike H.D.'s mapping of "The intellect, the brain, the conscious mind [as] the bridge across, the link between the subconscious and the over-conscious" (*Notes on Thought and Vision* 49). H.D. had some instinctive sense of this strange psychic "space" that "spoke" to some other "space"; the one difference between what Jaynes describes and what H.D. experiences is that H.D.'s split world is colored by the consciousness of it. In Jaynes's view, bicamerality disappears with consciousness, but one of the ways, perhaps, of understanding H.D.'s vision is to imagine her in possession of both, existing always, writing always with the conscious sense of a "preconscious" experience. This sense of conflicting spheres into which one abandons oneself and yet which one somehow mediates is central to her work and her attempts to comprehend and codify what links varying "states of manifestations" and to close the gap between them. The bicameral mind is another version of what she calls palimpsest, a mind that has simultaneously expanded and limited itself.

All these convolutions of engendering and retrieval and layering of text and consciousness can be seen within the boundaries of *Palimpsest*; I would now like to move outside the text to explore how this form functions as a paradigm of an intertextual process throughout H.D.'s canon as her earliest struggling with language and consciousness, her earliest attempts to translate psychic life into text, appear and reappear.

The particular connection I would like to look at is the one between *Palimpsest* and *Tribute to Freud*, H.D.'s account of her analytic sessions in 1933 and 1934.[10] This later work is itself a kind of palimpsest, composed as it is of *Writing on the Wall* and *Advent*, two separate records of her relationship with Freud, the first, oddly, written ten years after analysis (1944) without the aid of the journal (1933) on which the text of the "addendum" (actually composed in 1949) is based. It is in keeping with the convolutions of the form that *Advent* appears after *Writing on the Wall*, the generating forms always surfacing last in H.D.'s work as the symptoms give way to the underlying events and images that engendered them.

The title *Writing on the Wall* refers to visions that II.D. saw projected on a hotel wall in 1920 during a trip to the Greek islands with her companion Bryher. Much of her "tribute" to Freud is devoted to a description of these images that surfaced in her consciousness and that resurface in the text as hieroglyphs, ancient writing psychically excavated. H.D. herself recognized the quality of palimpsest in her attachment to these images. In 1944 she writes:

But there I am seated on the old-fashioned Victorian sofa in the Greek island hotel bedroom, and here I am reclining on the couch in the Professor's room, telling him this, and here again am I, ten years later, seated at my desk in my own room in London. But there is no clock time, though we are fastidiously concerned with time and with a formal handling of a subject which has . . . no time-barriers. (*Tribute to Freud* 47)

H.D. connects here 1920, 1933, and 1944; the connection she does not make is to 1926, although she echoes Raymonde Ransome's experience of "over-consciousness" to explain her own "symptoms" as "over-thought" (51) and borrows the topography of *Palimpsest* to locate her Corfu vision: "But symptom or inspiration, the writing continues to write itself or be written. It is admittedly picture-writing, though its symbols can be translated into terms of today; it is Greek in spirit, rather than Egyptian" (*Tribute to Freud* 51). Its form, then, is Egyptian, its spirit Hellenic, its translation modern.

The reason H.D. instinctively reaches into the 1926 text to articulate the 1944 one is, I think, that both texts are concerned with the Greek experience. As Susan Gubar has pointed out, the first section of *Palimpsest* makes allusions to H.D.'s trip with Bryher: like H.D., Hipparchia is ill and exhausted; like H.D., she is "rescued" by a younger woman who woos her back to health with the promise of a "regenerative voyage" to Greece (53). I would go further, however, and suggest that decades before they are inscribed deliberately in *Writing on the Wall*, the "picture writing" images are acted out through Hipparchia, Raymonde Ransome, and Helen Fairwood, all of whom are women prone to "constant aberrations, these psycho-hysterical visionary sensations" (*Palimpsest* 187).[11] There is a strange double convolution, then, for the initial writing — on the wall — preceded *Palimpsest*, seeped into it, and then was "erased," so that by the time H.D. finally transcribes the vision for the "first" time it is really a second draft, *Palimpsest* revealing itself to be an engendering text of *Tribute to Freud*.[12]

To understand how this intertextual palimpsest functions, we need first look at the images themselves. The first projection H.D. sees in Corfu is the head of a visored soldier or airman, "a silhouette cut of light" (*Tribute to Freud* 45). Before she can assess it carefully, it gives way to "the conventional outline of a goblet or cup" which suggests "the mystic chalice" (45). Almost immediately the third image draws itself — "a three-legged lamp stand," a familiar object that H.D. associates with the tripod of Delphi. H.D. calls these first three projections "cards" (48) alluding to tarot figures, but the "reading" is suddenly broken "as if there were a slight question as to the conclusion or direction of the symbols" (46). During the pause, H.D. fears that her "mind may not be equal to the occasion" (47); she describes the experience to Bryher, who is standing near her, and asks her whether she should go on. While H.D. hesitates "there is a sort of pictorial buzzing" emanating from "small creatures . . . in black . . . [like] very small half-winged insects" (48), which then seem "tiny people," but Bryher encourages her to continue, and the buzzing ceases. As the first three pictures remain "static," dots of light appear forming lines that constellate excruciatingly slowly into a ladder, "Jacob's ladder if you will" (54). The intense concentration required seems almost unbearable, but fortunately, the last figure forms quickly, H.D. reports, manifesting itself as an angel, "Niké. Victory" (54), who floats up the ladder past a series of half-*S* patterns, a kind of scrollwork. She moves toward "a series of tent-like triangles" (55), at which point H.D. "shut[s] off, 'cut[s] out' before the final picture" (56), disturbed at the premonition of war but assured by Victory, H.D.'s "own especial sign" (56). H.D. is exhausted; she has had "maybe just a little too much" (56). Bryher, however, takes over and "reads" the final image, "a circle like the sun-disk and a figure within the disk; a man, she thought, was reaching out to draw the image of a woman (my Niké) into the sun beside him" (56).[13]

Freud considered these images to be H.D.'s "most dangerous" symptom (*Tribute to Freud* 41); I find this fascinating because in a sense the vision at Corfu marks rather her release from symptoms and her entry into signs. Corfu represents an intermediate moment, a moment in which H.D. projects "visionary sensation" and conflates it with text. What she sees is different from her other reported "visions" precisely because it is "written." H.D. suggests that we can read the writing, even "the fact that there was writing" (51), in several ways. In Freud's view, she reports, it suggests "megalomania"; a "suppressed desire for forbidden 'signs' " (51). What disturbed Freud, one supposes, is that unlike the poetic visions that she "created," the Corfu vision appeared to her ready-made. Moreover, she

interpreted it, in part, as belonging to "a tradition of warnings or messages from another world or another state of being" (50). When H.D.
thinks through Freud, she sees the experience as "freakish" and "dangerous," thought "that had got out of hand, gone too far" (51). Her own
inclination, however, is to read the writing-on-the-wall as "an extension
of the artist's mind . . . projected from within (though apparently from
outside), really a high-powered *idea*, simply over-stressed, *over-thought*,
you might say" (51). Her description of the experience resonates with the
experiences she tried to explain — and understand — in *Notes on Thought
and Vision*; knowing what we do about her sense of levels of manifestations, it is not difficult to understand her to have been that late afternoon
in a state of "over-consciousness." Julian Jaynes's idea that "bicameral
men did not imagine; they experienced" (371) is also helpful in trying to
understand what was happening to H.D. as she stared at the hotel room
wall. She did not "imagine" or "create" the signs at Corfu but *experienced*
them as if they had been given to her; rather than a pathological moment,
it was a bicameral one.

There is a fine line, however, as Jaynes continually intimates, between
pathology and bicamerality: in the modern world we are expected to function consciously; severe or prolonged aberrations move us from art to
madness. What salvages the Corfu experience, what saves H.D., continually, is projection into text. This is why she textualizes — to both register
and repair the rifts, the gaps, the losses, the aberrations: "my thought /
would cover deplorable gaps // . . . reveal the regrettable chasm, / bridge
that before-and-after schism, // . . . in an endeavour to make ready, //
as it were, the patient for the Healer" (*Walls Do Not Fall* 54). Textualization is the way that H.D. heals herself and the world: writing as sign
replaces the symptom as sign; sickness is transformed into signifier.

One important aspect of *Palimpsest* is that it is the space in which she
explores this process and begins to close the gap opened at Corfu. Reading H.D.'s account of her experience in *Writing on the Wall*, one is struck
not only by the intensity of the experience or the nature of the images
but by the fact that the same "vision" washes through the 1926 novel.

The first image, the visored soldier, is reflected in the helmeted men
who appear throughout *Palimpsest* — ex-captains, World War I airmen,
and the Roman soldiers who surround Hipparchia. The chalice is central
in Hipparchia's image of her head as a "chaste goblet" filled with a "subtly
dangerous" "bubbling fire," "bubbling wine" (35) and also in her distorted
reflection in a "chased pure metal goblet" (69), which, like "an enchanter's
crystal," also offers images of the dead. The motif of triangles appears
in references to Egyptian pyramids and Roman tents; the black flies appear
insistently as Hipparchia's sense of "small insinuating black-winged mon-

sters . . . her just realized fearful suspicion of an inimical dark world buzzing beneath her amethyst water-clear indifference" (43). Nike is recuperated both in the phantom Nike birth house Helen Fairwood hallucinates in the desert and in Hipparchia's sense of herself as "Delphic priestess" reaching out toward "a just-invisible and just not-embodied Helios" (41), impossible to dissociate in his various manifestations in *Palimpsest*—all three women are preoccupied with him—from the last image in Corfu, "invisible" to H.D. until "seen" through Bryher.

Moreover, in *Writing on the Wall* H.D. describes the entire experience in a passage that is remarkably similar to passages in *Palimpsest*, a passage worked in images reappropriated from the earlier text as if the experience were somehow the same, as if securing the vision in Corfu were related to Helen Fairwood's need "to dive deep, deep, courageously down into some unexploited region of the consciousness, into some common deep sea of unrecorded knowledge and bring, triumphant, to the surface some treasure buried, lost, forgotten" (179). In *Tribute to Freud* H.D. writes:

I have the feeling of holding my breath under water. As if I were searching under water for some priceless treasure, and if I bobbed up to the surface the clue to its whereabouts would be lost forever. . . . I . . . am in . . . another element, and as I seem now so near to getting the answer or finding the treasure, I feel that my whole life, my whole being, will be blighted forever if I miss this chance. (53)

Raymonde Ransome, faced with the "writing on the wall," the inevitability of her own past bleeding through "faces, people, London. People, faces, Greece. Greece, people, faces. Egypt" (157), plunges underwater in the same search:

On, on, on, on, and out of it like some deep-sea jewel pulled up in a net squirming with an enormous catch of varigated [sic] squirming tentacled and tendrilled memories, just this, this—*who fished the murex up?* (157)

What is it, then, the women in *Palimpsest* are looking for? What is it H.D. finds in Corfu?—"just this, this." The line from Robert Browning's "Popularity" becomes one of the most important refrains washing through the text, one from which H.D. takes the title of the second section, and one which becomes an emblem of the palimpsest. Beyond the "sense" of Browning's tribute to Keats exploring the psychic and material price of the writing life, there is the central image of the murex, the mollusk that yielded to the Greeks their coveted purple dye. Drawn up from antiquity, drawn up from the sea, drawn up from another poet's poem, it is a living link between present and past, the "liquor filtered by degrees" that H.D. draws on "to paint the future from the past" (Browning 217). The nature of the murex undoubtedly appealed to H.D., encoding as it does both poles she worked around in the poetry—air and crystal, sea and jewel, form and essence. A shell enclosing mysterious substance, a substance that had to be distilled and refined almost alchemically, is a sign for H.D. of the pulse she felt so intensely, the pulse between the tightening helmet and the diadem, between arrow vibrance and release. Like the jewel in *The Flowering of the Rod* that opens into infinity and releases for Kaspar "the whole secret of the mystery" (152), the shell that releases a suffusion of purple provides the way of closing the gap, for the murex is the sign of the inner spaces of both consciousness and language: "Verses, verses, verses. *Who fished the murex up?* Verses were the murex. They dyed all existence with their colour" (160). This treasure, then, "buried, lost, forgotten" is both memory and meter, repressed biographical material and the poet's language itself. In a similar way, the vision on Corfu is also the murex, and "Herself . . . sunk, down, down to some unexplored region of the consciousness" (221) is the murex as vision, verses, identity merge into one so that "she herself is the writing," is the shattered poem, is the voices, is the writing on a hotel wall.

Text becomes, then, both what is sought and the means of seeking it(self). In H.D.'s palimpsest of language and desire, she excavates earlier texts—both psychic and literary—to release the writing that will initiate/ has initiated the excavation. The extraordinary importance of *Palimpsest* is that it both generates and recuperates the mode so central to H.D.'s aesthetics and psychology. It is a hermetic text that nonetheless spills out of itself freely. It opens into the future and into the past and then conflates both impulses in the present. As a vastly underestimated modernist murex, it explores the relationship between language and consciousness through images and strategies that connect three minds as if we were in the presence of one layered consciousness, a textual consciousness that is the reflection of H.D.'s lifelong literary and personal struggle to "[merge] and [make] one all the selves, the self of the slave locked into the silver barred and shimmering intellect, the slave more languorous . . . , the other, the slave that held, a solid link, her everyday self, enslaved to both these others" (*Palimpsest* 212).

NOTES

This essay previously appeared in *Contemporary Literature* 27 (Winter 1986): 553–73.
1   For fuller discussion of the impact of these events on H.D.'s life and work,

see Robinson; Barbara Guest, *Herself Defined: The Poet H.D. and Her World* (Garden City, N.Y.: Doubleday, 1984); and, particularly, Friedman.

2   Only three novels of this period have been published: *Palimpsest* (1926); *HER* (1927) (published as *HERmione* in 1981); and *Hedylus* (1928). The others, including *Paint It To-Day* (1921) and *Asphodel* (dated 1921–22) remain in typescript at Beinecke Rare Book and Manuscript Library, Yale University.

3   Understanding H.D.'s "voice and vision" is obviously a complicated undertaking. Susan Stanford Friedman's *Psyche Reborn* remains the definitive comprehensive text that opens into biography, psychoanalysis, sexuality, mysticism, and aesthetics. The work of Rachel Blau DuPlessis is also focused with an unerring sense of H.D.'s psychic and artistic struggling. See "Family, Sexes, Psyche: An Essay on H.D. and the Muse of the Woman Writer," *Montemora* 6 (1979): 137–56; *H.D.: The Career of That Struggle* (Harvester, 1986); and "Romantic Thralldom in H.D.," in this volume. In regard to the notion of palimpsest as metaphor in H.D., the most specific discussions are found in Friedman, who discusses the process in terms of H.D.'s personal history, traumas, and breakdowns (29–30); and Joseph Riddel, who discusses palimpsest in terms of the enactment of *Ur*-patterns in "H.D. and the Poetics of 'Spiritual Realism,' " *Contemporary Literature* 10 (1969): 447–73.

4   For a discussion of film as "psychic medium" in H.D., see Adalaide Morris, "The Concept of Projection: H.D.'s Visionary Powers," in this volume.

5   Various critics and H.D. herself constantly return to the sense of "triangles" in her psychological functioning. There is, for example, always "mother-self-father"; Adalaide Morris quotes H.D. from a letter to Bryher (March 23, 1933) as saying, "My triangle is mother-brother-self." As Morris suggests, "The records of analysis swarm with formulae as Freud and H.D. decipher originary patterns beneath a palimpsest of repetition" (p. 287 below).

6   The issue of Hipparchia's relationship to her mother and to language is explored more fully in my "Flesh Made Word: Maternal Inscription in H.D.," *Sagetrieb* 3.1 (1984): 27–48.

7   In regard to the notion of "projection" in H.D., Adalaide Morris notes that the "meaning [of the word] alters subtly and sometimes confusingly" (see below, p. 275); Morris clearly has a sense of this lexical shifting in H.D.'s work.

8   A useful discussion of the relationship between H.D.'s several visionary experiences and *Notes on Thought and Vision* is found in Morris, "Concept of Projection," in this volume. See also Robinson 230–34.

9   Norman Holland also discusses H.D.'s search "to close the gap with signs," although his emphasis is on her need to "concretize" rather than "textualize." See "H.D. and the 'Blameless Physician,' " *Contemporary Literature* 10 (1969): 474–506.

10 I am looking at a very limited portion of a very rich document. For broader discussions of this work, see Friedman; DuPlessis and Friedman, " 'Woman is Perfect': H.D.'s Debate with Freud," *Feminist Studies* 7 (1981): 417–30; and Joseph Riddel, "H.D.'s Scene of Writing—Poetry As (And) Analysis," *Studies in the Literary Imagination* 12.1 (1979): 41–59; and Holland.

11 Several critics have alluded to the fact that H.D. reprocessed hallucinated material in her 1920s novels. Adalaide Morris focuses primarily on another vision, the apparition of "Peter Van Eck" (Peter Rodeck) on the deck of the *Borodino* during the trip to Greece, suggesting that H.D. "struggled to tell the story" for more than twenty years (see below, p. 280). Janice Robinson writes that "a particularly vivid re-creation of the central images associated with the Corfu vision appears in *Hedylus*" (251), but after identifying Helios in the 1928 novel, she does not pursue this suggestive train of thought.

12 Adalaide Morris makes a fascinating observation that adds yet another layer to the palimpsest: she traces the images of the Corfu vision to an earlier text, the poem "Helios and Athene," written during the trip to Greece just after H.D. and Bryher were denied access to Delphi and just before their arrival in Corfu. According to Morris, "the Corfu vision is structured like a hermetic re-creation of the Delphic session" ("Reading H.D.'s 'Helios and Athene,' " 162) which, denied in one space, H.D. first imagines into text and then projects into vision.

13 Various critics have discussed these images. Morris reads them in terms of a pervasive "projective process" in H.D. (p. 274, below). Holland looks at H.D.'s vision in terms of "mother fixation," megalomania, and castration complex, and as a symbolic intermediary "to close the gap with signs" (492); Riddel reads the Corfu experience as a "dream" centered on "a question of the sign" (56). Robinson discusses them as an "omen of apocalyptic catastrophe" (303), and Friedman suggests that Corfu represented H.D.'s confirmation of "an artistic destiny in which she would write prophecy, art, and healing into a message of resurrection for the modern 'city of ruin' " (186).

WORKS CITED

Browning, Robert. "Popularity." *Robert Browning's Poetry*, ed. James F. Loucks, 215–17. New York: Norton, 1979.

Friedman, Susan Stanford. *Psyche Reborn: The Emergence of H.D.* Bloomington: Indiana UP, 1981.

Gelpi, Albert. "The Thistle and the Serpent." In *Notes on Thought and Vision*, by H.D. San Francisco: City Lights Books, 1982.

Gubar, Susan. "Sapphistries." *Signs* 10.1 (1984): 43–62.

H.D. *Collected Poems 1912–1944*. Ed. Louis L. Martz. New York: New Directions, 1983.

H.D. *Compassionate Friendship*. Typescript. Beinecke Rare Book and Manuscript Library. Yale University, New Haven, Conn.

H.D. *The Flowering of the Rod. Trilogy*. New York: New Directions, 1973.

H.D. *Notes on Thought and Vision*. San Francisco: City Lights Books, 1982.

H.D. *Palimpsest*. 1926. Carbondale: Southern Illinois UP, 1968.

H.D. *Tribute to Freud*. 1956. New York: McGraw-Hill, 1974.

H.D. *The Walls Do Not Fall*. *Trilogy*. New York: New Directions, 1973.

Jaynes, Julian. *The Origin of Consciousness in the Breakdown of the Bicameral Mind*. Boston: Houghton Mifflin, 1982.

Morris, Adalaide. "Reading H.D.'s 'Helios and Athene.' " In *Extended Outlooks*, ed. Jane Cooper, et al., 155–63. New York: Macmillan, 1982.

Robinson, Janice. *H.D.: The Life and Work of an American Poet*. Boston: Houghton Mifflin, 1982.

CHAPTER 12

"I had two loves separate": The Sexualities of H.D.'s HER

SUSAN STANFORD FRIEDMAN AND
RACHEL BLAU DUPLESSIS

By the 1920s, a decade after her earliest success as a poet, H.D. had begun to feel that the public figure of "H.D., Imagiste," created in part by
Pound's promotion of her work, had forged a cage of poetic and critical
expectation that did not allow her to develop. She was at the same time
a close friend and admirer of Dorothy Richardson, and an avid reader
of both Joyce and Woolf. Possibly influenced by her contemporaries, and
motivated by a desire for artistic growth, H.D. embarked on an exploration of the possibilities offered by fiction to render the subjective realities
of the psyche. The published results of her early experimentation were
Hedylus (1928), her novel about a Greek boy, and *Palimpsest* (1926), a
work composed of three stories about three seemingly different women
whose lives at different historical eras in fact constitute versions of the
same life story—near H.D.'s own.

The fiction which H.D. published, however, is only a small part of what
she actually wrote. Beginning in 1920, and continuing through the decade,
H.D. experimented with the novel in ways typical of high, formalist modernism, with its development of interior monologues, its deemphasis on
external plot to emphasize interior action, and its breakup of sequential
chronology. The unpublished texts she produced during this period of
experimentation are *Paint It To-Day* (completed in 1921), *Asphodel* (written in 1921–22), *Pilate's Wife* (begun in 1924 and finished in 1934), and
HER (completed in 1927), the most significant and finished of this cluster.[1]
In these works, H.D.'s unique stamp on the surfaces of modernist form
evolved out of the austere poetics of imagism, in which she sought objective correlative for emotion, and out of her deep commitment to both

205

cinema and psychoanalysis, which offered her ways of focusing on the fleeting subjectivities of consciousness.[2]

Although H.D.'s texts might indeed have constituted significant chapters in the history of the novel, they had no chance of being influential because they simply were not published. Why didn't they reach the public? What are the reasons motivating — at the same time — innovative expressions and repressive silences? Rightfully, we must ask if H.D.'s texts are "finished," "polished," or even "good," and whether H.D. wanted or even tried to publish them. Certainly *Asphodel* and *Paint It To-Day* read as completed drafts — with sections of brilliant writing interspersed among sections that could have benefited from revision. H.D. even wrote on the manuscript copy of *Asphodel*, "Early edition of MADRIGAL, DESTROY," an order which, luckily, neither she nor her literary executor, Norman Holmes Pearson, carried out. *Pilate's Wife* is important for H.D.'s canon, but it is hardly her best prose writing; however, she considered it finished and was disappointed in its rejection by at least one publisher. There is no evidence at this point to suggest that H.D. tried to publish *HER*. But the typescript of *HER* was made under the direction of Pearson and had been carefully revised by H.D., whose handwritten corrections appear throughout. In fact, at the time of his death in 1975, Pearson was preparing both *HER* and H.D.'s coherent and exacting autobiographical memoir *The Gift* (1941–43) for publication.[3]

The ultimate answers to questions about expression and repression are, however, far more complex than these speculations about literary value or publishing difficulties suggest. The reasons both reflect and illuminate the anomalous position of H.D. — as well as other women writers — on the fringes of the modernist mainstream. H.D.'s novels are highly autobiographical, far more explicitly so than even Woolf's *To the Lighthouse* and *Orlando*. While not every detail may be biographically accurate, it is clear that these works illuminate her life. Publication of these frank romans à clef meant virtually absolute self-disclosure. And what of that, a modernist scholar might well ask, thinking of Joyce or Lawrence? But unlike Joyce and Lawrence, H.D. anchored her fiction in a life that contained the culturally forbidden love of woman for woman. Central dramatic and lyric moments in all of these texts are lesbian — explicit, not coded, celebratory, not ultimately condemnatory, and rich with the problematic of any relationship, including the issue of betrayal. The persona, always a mask for H.D. herself, experiences a fusion of erotic and spiritual passion for another woman, a bond associated with H.D.'s centered identity as both woman and artist. These woman-identified relationships appear within the context of H.D.'s equally intense but even more ambivalent emotional and sexual entanglements with a series of men, relationships which she simultaneously sought and retreated from precisely because of their threat to her identity as woman and artist.

With the exception of *Pilate's Wife*, in which H.D.'s relationships with women and men are encoded in the historical setting of a novel about Jesus and a priestess of Isis, H.D.'s unpublished novels of the twenties belong to a sequence that she called her "madrigal cycle." *Bid Me to Live (A Madrigal)*, written in 1939, is the only published volume in this series of texts, each recounting an overlapping part of her life from about 1906, when she flunked out of (or withdrew from) Bryn Mawr College, to 1920, after the birth of her daughter, Perdita.[4] The text of the madrigal novels is a story which invariably follows some version of this biographical sequence: H.D.'s love for and engagement to Pound; her parallel and competing love for Frances Josepha Gregg, the friend of a schoolmate at Bryn Mawr; the disintegration of her engagement; her voyage to Europe with Gregg in 1911; Gregg's return to America and sudden marriage to Louis Wilkinson; H.D.'s life as a woman in the European artistic milieu; her first publication as "H.D., Imagiste," under Pound's aegis in 1913; her marriage to Richard Aldington later that year; her first pregnancy ending traumatically with a stillborn child in 1915; the First World War; Aldington's enlistment and the dissolution of the imagist circle; Aldington's and H.D.'s affairs and the disintegration of their marriage in 1917 and 1918; H.D.'s relationship with Winifred Ellerman (Bryher) established during the months of her second pregnancy in 1918; H.D.'s illness (the influenza of 1919), the birth of her baby, and paternity questions about her child in 1919; Bryher's role as rescuer, her promise to take H.D. to Greece, and their idyllic month in the Scilly Isles (June 1919) that created a bond to be maintained until H.D.'s death in 1961. This story moves from intense love of both man and woman, centers in the experiences of loss and betrayal engendered by heterosexual relationships in a patriarchal context, and ends in the celebration of a love for a woman and the birth of a girl child. Underlying the entirety of this lived experience was H.D.'s commitment to her art. This formative arc of years indeed served as the "hieroglyph" to be interpreted and thus in some measure to be controlled in her novels. Fiction became the arena in which H.D. could both reflect upon and plot to resolve the conflicts that had repeatedly torn her life apart.

Yet to construct the one novel which she did publish from this "madrigal cycle," H.D. took a cut from the story's center only. *Bid Me to Live* is about romantic thralldom and cultural struggles for voice, validation, and space as a woman artist in relation to such male figures as Richard Aldington, D. H. Lawrence, and Cecil Gray. In what she chose to publish, H.D. excised or deflected attention away from Gregg and Bryher, both of whom played crucial roles in H.D.'s personal and poetic development.[5]

Virtually all of H.D.'s published works (and many of her unpublished ones) drastically underplay her status as a companionate woman and her connections through Bryher with homosexual and lesbian circles in Europe. At the same time, the narrative of heterosexual attraction, betrayal, and victimization was a recurrent feature of her writing. Both her fiction and poetry frequently express her need to be delivered from the cultural scripts of romantic thralldom in which she repeatedly immersed herself.[6] Many of these narratives represent her attempt to transpose the sexual politics of the love plot into a series of relationships in which she has transcended victimization. But still the narrative strategies of published works like *Bid Me to Live, Helen in Egypt, Winter Love*, and *Hermetic Definition* continue to operate with a heterosexual context.

In print, therefore, H.D. could examine her identity as a tormented heterosexual seeking nonoppressive relationships with men, the culturally approved love objects for women. In focusing on the heterosexual script, she muted often to the point of invisibility her lesbian bonds with women. In private, however, in unpublished manuscripts "safe" as the diary where so many of women's forbidden thoughts have found a half-life of secret articulation, H.D. explored her passion for women and its relation to her artistic identity.

In these slightly franker times, we should not underemphasize the totality and the ferocity of the taboo against same-sex relationships. Just after H.D. finished *HER*, the initial publication of *The Well of Loneliness* (1928) produced a storm of abuse against its author, Radclyffe Hall, and the ultimate banning of her literary plea for tolerance of her "God-given difference." When asked recently if H.D. and Bryher were concerned about Hall's fate, a close friend of H.D.'s said: "Oh yes, very much so. We didn't call ourselves homosexuals in those days. We had to be very, very careful."[7] Bryher herself married twice to maintain social convention and financial ties to her family, especially to her father, Sir John Ellerman, the wealthy British shipowner. The power of convention for both Bryher and H.D. may also have been internalized to some degree. It is possible that the writer's block which plagued H.D. during the thirties was related to internalized norms of compulsory heterosexuality.

The critic Catharine Stimpson has explored the way the contradictory choice between "public speech" and "silence" results in the marginality of the lesbian novelist. "Being quiet enables her to 'pass.' Her silence is her passport into the territory of the dominant world. . . . Being silent signifies a subterranean belief in the magical power of language. . . . Silence can also be a tactically shrewd refusal to provoke punitive familial, social, legal and religious powers. However, its effect is antithetical to literature as public speech." This is a heightened version of the taboos, enunciated by Sandra Gilbert and Susan Gubar in *The Madwoman in the Attic*, which emerge in the female "anxiety of authorship."[8] H.D. committed a lifetime of creative effort to the "magical power of language," but may have also chosen the option of private or coded speech for some of her texts. That is to say that the conscious or tacit decision to avoid publishing such an aesthetically finished work as *HER* might have been H.D.'s resolution of the kind of contradiction which Stimpson presents. Such a decision on H.D.'s part would keep a particular text in that ambiguous place precisely to express the contradictory pressures for public speech and silence which a lesbian work might require. Such a work as *HER* might, then, indeed be finished (that is, an articulate contribution to literature as public speech) yet at the same time unpublished (silent, hardly to be revealed).

The act of writing a lesbian novel can never be "neutral"; as Stimpson wrote: "Because the violent yoking of homosexuality with deviancy has been so pervasive, little or no modern writing about it can be neutral. . . . No matter how 'irretrievably honest,' a homosexual text responds judgmentally to the perversion that has made homosexuality perverse."[9] Thus for H.D. to initiate, complete, and ready a lesbian text for publication would require a fundamental denial of culture in all its heterosexist forms. *HER* can be characterized as a lesbian text because of its critique of heterosexuality and because the marriage plot takes the form of exploring strongly articulated relations between women, relations with an erotic component.

HER deserves publication in its entirety. It is important to an understanding of H.D.'s entire canon as well as to the literary history of the modernist novel in general and the lesbian novel in particular. *HER* concerns a quest for identity which centers on the interrelated questions of vocation, marriage, and sexuality. The protagonist is Hermione Gart, nicknamed Her, and associated with two mythological Hermiones, one in Shakespeare's *The Winter's Tale* and the other, baby of Helen in Greek mythology. One is a mother; the other a daughter. H.D.'s own code penciled in on her typescript identifies the cast: Eugenia is her mother, Helen Wolle Doolitte, the Moravian music teacher from Bethlehem, Pennsylvania; Carl Gart is her father, the well-known professor of astronomy at the Flower Observatory in Upper Darby, near Philadelphia; Bert Gart is her adored older step-brother, a male double or twin for H.D. herself; George Lowdnes, the writer hounded by scandal at the school where he had taught briefly and just back from Venice, is Ezra Pound; Fayne Rabb, introduced to H.D. by a Vaumawr (Bryn Mawr) friend, is Frances Josepha Gregg, the woman for whom H.D. wrote her first published poems in 1911.[10]

The novel opens with Her in a state of crisis, her life inchoate, without focus, all of which is rendered unstintingly in a lucid, associative interior monologue. "A disappointment to her father, an odd duckling to her mother," Her has just flunked out of college by failing math and has returned home without a clue as to what she should do with her life (9). With no certain future as either scholar or wife, Her peremptorily condemns herself as a failure.[11] This crisis of vocation awakens the ambivalence of love and hate that permeates her feelings about her family and the family's black maid, Mandy. Her feels outraged and betrayed by her brother's marriage to Minnie, a conventional, carping woman whom she must call "sister" when the "sister" for whom she yearns would "run, would leap, would be concealed under autumn sumac or lie shaken with hail and wind, lost on some Lacedomonian foot-hill" (11). Disturbed profoundly that she has disappointed her father, Her nonetheless feels alienated from the masculine discourse that dominates family discussion: her father and brother "hurl things at one another across the table-cloth like two arctic explorers who have both discovered the north pole, each proving to the other, across chasms of frozen silence, that his is the original discovery" (47). Increasingly she turns to the woman-centered subtexts of the family: her mother; Minnie, her dead grandmother whose presence is still powerfully felt; and Mandy.

Eugenia, the most important of these, appears to Her in double focus. She is, on the one hand, the voice of convention who wants her daughter well married and is initially outraged that Her would have anything to do with the scandalous George Lowdnes (57). Yet when Eugenia recalls the story of Her's birth without midwife or doctor in the middle of a terrible storm, she is a mother strong as Demeter, and, Her thinks, "One should sing hymns of worship to her, powerful, powerless, all-powerful" (111). Eugenia's "hypnotizing" power as a mother and her powerlessness as a wife arouse in her daughter the ambivalence that structures many mother-daughter relationships in a patriarchy. Her tells Eugenia: "You never listen to what I say, mama. I said you ought to be guillotined. Your throat looks so pretty coming out of that ruffle . . . like a moon-flower. . . . You're round like a moon-flower with a sort of stamen pistil sort of thing, the sort of throat that you have rising out of a moon-ruffle" (110).[12]

Her's parents represent the binary opposites within which she must define a destiny: male-female, power-powerlessness, science-art, god-goddess. "What am I between them? I am broken like a nut between two rocks, granite and granite," Her thinks (111). What breaks the paralysis at home is the simultaneous arrival of two letters—one from George announcing his return and his continued passion, and one from her schoolmate inviting her to tea to meet Fayne. These letters and the meetings that follow initiate a double love plot in which Her is attracted by both a man and a woman. The novel's ensuing structure is interesting for the formal inscription of questions of sexuality which it so dramatically raises. The book is divided into two parts: *grosso modo*, George dominates the first, Fayne the second. The structure of each alternates between Her's meetings with George and Fayne, with occasional hiatuses when Her must confront her parents' changing feelings toward her relationships. Part I records the progression of her engagement with George — her agreement to marry him, her parents' opposition, then acquiescence to the impending marriage. Part II incorporates Her's growing fascination for Fayne, her disengagement from George, and the final dissolution of both relationships.

The plots of heterosexual and homosexual attraction intersect at various places with great complexity. The more involved Her becomes with Fayne, the less Eugenia objects to the marriage to George. Marriage to a writer whose mother Lillian, at least, is "respectable" is more acceptable than Her's attachment to the "unwholesome" Fayne (236). Highlighting the growing conflict between mother and daughter, however, Her matches her mother's enthusiasm with increasing discomfort at the unfolding of her conventional heterosexual romance. With George, Hermione feels trapped by a rigid sense of social and sexual scripts that inhibit her autonomy and fledgling artistic identity. She finds his demands intense and formulaic, and when he approaches her sexually, she feels both dissociated and enveloped. His smothering kisses presage a suffocation of the spirit, in which she fears that she will become the object of his poem rather than the poet. While she had hoped that their love, originally so unconventional, might transform their world into the magical forest of Arden or the "forest primeval," she concludes that their romance is the script of a "bad play," the route of banal conventionality. She is increasingly certain that she is play-acting the role of woman, like a young girl thrilled to put up her hair and wear long skirts (85). George is angry about Fayne, sides with Eugenia in labeling her "unwholesome," and warns Hermione that the two women would have been burned as witches a few centuries earlier (238). Paradoxically, the iconoclastic poet condemned by Eugenia's circle of university ladies is allied with the voices of respectability. Hermione concludes that George "wanted a Her that he called decorative [and] . . . never understood me" (230). George, in short, "could never love a Tree properly," a line that recurs, for Hermione is that "Tree" in the novel just as H.D. was "Dryad" to Pound (100[2]).[13]

Disengagement from George parallels engagement with Fayne, who tells Hermione that she only wants to marry George because she is afraid to be different. Together they read translations of Freud, about "people who loved . . . differently" (274). In Fayne, Hermione finds the "sister" for whom she had yearned, the twin soul in whose gaze Her can discover herself: "I know her. Her. I am Her. She is Her. Knowing her, I know Her. She is some amplification of myself like amoeba giving birth by breaking off, to amoeba. I am a sort of mother, a sort of sister to Her. *'O sister my sister Oh fleet sweet swallow'* " (211). The name Her has different valences in the two relationships. With George, Hermione's nickname "Her" — always grammatically awkward as a subject — signifies her object status within conventional heterosexuality. With Fayne, however, the nickname signals a fusion, one that gives birth to two selves, subject and object indistinct.

An erotic mysticism and mystical eroticism draw the "sisters" together: "prophetess to prophetess on some Delphic head-land" (241). Fayne's deprived childhood has left her with psychic abilities, and in prophetic trance she pronounces on Hermione's fate. Aroused, they merge as H.D.'s syntax obliterates the distinction between them: "Her bent forward, face bent toward Her" (217). Lines from Swinburne capture the ecstatic moment and contrast with the obliterating kisses of George: *"Curled lips long since half kissed away"* (217–18).[14] Contrasting with the conic sections of math, "Her and Fayne Rabb were flung into a concentric intimacy, rings on rings that made a geometric circle" (218). This intimacy both frees and possesses Her. It liberates her from being the "decorative" object that inspires George's poems; rather she experiences her own writing, in Fayne's words, as "the thin flute holding you to eternity" (215). So Her follows Fayne's prophetic commands to renounce her engagement. Yet Fayne's trances dominate Her just as George's kisses had earlier. "Yes, Fayne," Her passively answers to every utterance, but nonetheless Hermione is ready to renounce all convention to be with and protect Fayne. The balance has shifted from George to Fayne in spite of the troubling undercurrents.

The heterosexual and homosexual love plots are rejoined in the end by a series of double betrayals. The culturally inscribed heterosexual script breaks into the concentric intimacy of the sister-lovers just as Hermione has found the strength to abandon her conventional role in a "bad play," her impending marriage to George. In the climax of part II, Her discovers that Fayne and George have been secretly involved with each other. George has not only failed the promise of their Arden by misunderstanding her, but he has also betrayed her by loving another in secrecy. Moreover, in opting for conventional romance with George, Fayne has renounced her lesbian self and rejected the love through which Hermione had found her erotic, spiritual, and artistic identities. To add insult to injury, Fayne defends her actions by chiding Hermione with the superficiality of her love for George. Only she, Fayne, can love George properly (296). The final lines of Swinburne's song celebrating the union of sisters enter Hermione's consciousness to underline the power of the heterosexual norm: "O sister my sister o singing swallow, the world's division divideth us" (241).

Hermione's confusion, muted anger, and sense of betrayal combine to produce a physical and mental breakdown, rendered at length in an interior monologue of striking aesthetic control and structural purpose, comparable to the passages of delirium at the end of Woolf's *The Voyage Out*. The fledgling Her has been excluded from two binary sets: the parental and the erotic. Her illness, however, is the creative madness through which she must pass to discover an autonomous identity. The growth and solidification of the solitary self achieved at the end of *HER* are presented in the psyche-butterfly image familiar to readers of H.D.'s poetry, summarizing the interior structure of the novel and illustrating H.D.'s fusion of imagist craft and interior monologue:

A white butterfly that hesitates a moment finds frost to break the wavering tenuous antennae. I put, so to speak, antennae out too early. I felt letting Her so delicately protrude prenatal antennae from the husk of the thing called Her, frost nip the delicate fiber of the star-fish edges of the thing I clung to. I, Her clung to the most tenuous of antennae. Mama, Eugenia that is, Carl Gart and Lillian [George's mother] were so many leaves wrapped around the unborn butterfly. Outside a force wakened, drew Her out of Her. Call the thing Fayne Rabb. I clung to some sort of branch that wavered in the wind, something between Lillian and Eugenia, a sort of precise character, George Lowndes. Wavering by instinct toward George I found George Lowndes inadequate. He would have pulled back quivering antennae. (292)[15]

The time span of the novel is about nine months, and at the end of Psyche's gestation, Her emerges tenuously from the chrysalis of conflicting desires and intersecting betrayals. Having ordered the individuals and events which culminated in her illness, Her can tentatively imagine an identity, at least the beginning of a path. It has snowed, and a weak but no longer ill Her goes on a walk, which significantly takes her beyond her family's property into the neighboring woods where the novel began:

The whole world had been made clear like that black-board last summer. Last summer Gart lawn had been a black-board but not quite clear. Now Gart lawn and Gart forest and the Werby meadow and the Farrand forest were swept clear.
They were virginal for one purpose, for one Creator. Last summer the Creator had been white lightning brandished against blackness. Now the creator was Her's feet, narrow black crayon across the winter whiteness. (302)

So Hermione begins her autonomous life as writer by writing a track into the snow, an act which parallels the lightning flash which augured her birth. The tentativeness of that design emphasizes the newness of the path, which is nonetheless elevated by the grandeur of the romantic comparison between divine "Creator" and human creator. Her "writing" on the snow leads her at the very end of the novel to the Farrands' house where she reestablishes her friendship with some other young people who have also "got to the end of something" (316). They invite her to accompany them to Europe, and she decides to use the money set aside for her trousseau for that journey. That quest for identity will "be my marriage," she states in reference to the classic love plot and its traditional ending (317).

As is so often the case in H.D.'s work, however, the resolution that ends one set of conflicts opens into the beginning of a new process. The last sentence of the novel contains an enigma that can only be unveiled in another novel. Hermione returns home from her walk in the woods, her tea with the Farrands, and her decision about the future to hear Mandy say: "I done left Miss Fayne all alone upstairs in your little work-room" (317). The next novel in the "madrigal cycle," *Asphodel*—next, that is, in terms of the chronology of H.D.'s life—opens with Fayne and Her regarding the statue of St. Joan in Rouen and realizing that they too could have been burned as witches. In point of fact, H.D. went to Europe in 1911 with Frances Gregg and her mother, not with her neighbors. The failure of Fayne and Her to break through convention in *HER* did not end their literary or biographical existence together. *Asphodel*, part I, records their second attempt to create a life together, Frances' refusal to remain in London with H.D. with a proper "screen," Frances' sudden marriage to Louis Wilkinson, and Hermione's ambivalent acquiescence to Gerrald's (Aldington's) ardent companionship.

In her essay "Lesbian Intertextuality," Elaine Marks has suggested that the mid and late twenties were "*anni mirabili* for novels by women that depict important lesbian characters or references to women loving women."[16] Virginia Woolf, Colette, Djuna Barnes, Gertrude Stein, Natalie Barney, and Radclyffe Hall were among the more prominent whose lives and works gave visibility to an eros that was increasingly regarded with homophobia. H.D. and Bryher personally knew some of these women and avidly read all of them, most especially Woolf and Colette. The full biographical and textual tapestry of H.D.'s ties with this lesbian tradition has yet to be understood, but our initial placement of *HER* within this context will, we hope, stimulate much-needed exploration.

HER is immediately fascinating as a novel that explores lesbian passion because of its differences from other women-loving-women texts of the twenties. In *Mrs. Dalloway*, Clarissa's direct passion for Sally, expressed vividly in some three pages of the novel, is like a lesbian subtext within the text of a heterosexual life. Anchored by her marriage to Richard, Clarissa recalls with nostalgia the brief lesbian respite from courtship, but since neither she nor Sally made life choices based on that love, the novel only implicitly challenges the conventions of marriage. Further, that idyllic erotic memory is "bought" at the expense of a negative perception of Mrs. Dalloway's daughter together with Miss Kilman, a relationship called "nauseating." *HER*, in contrast, makes the issue of choice between heterosexual and homosexual love the dramatic center of Hermione's quest for identity. Woolf's *Orlando* is more direct than *Mrs. Dalloway* in challenging exclusive heterosexuality because Orlando acts upon the desire for women which Clarissa only felt. But Woolf's joyous "love-letter" to Vita Sackville-West relies on the fantastic to make "speakable" the "unspeakable" love between women.[17] H.D. in *HER* uses nothing like the distancing device of fantasy to make Hermione's rejection of George and preference for Fayne palatable to a heterocentric literary tradition.

Ladies Almanack by Djuna Barnes shares an exuberant gaiety with *Orlando*, and both may share Sterne's *Tristram Shandy* as backboard. Barnes's book has no plot to speak of. It takes its structure from the cycle of months, each celebrating lesbian couples, the nominal quest of Dame Musset, and sexual bliss. Narrative organization is not at issue. Barnes uses the conceit of the almanac, plotting the calendar and natural periodicities to create a rhetorical structure of desire so charged that any phrase seems to have an erotic meaning—and many, indeed, do. The climax of a number of the essayistic chapters is a cunningly contrived description of orgasm. Cataloguing the seductions, the little languages, and the nuances of desire, Barnes furbishes a world whose happiest secret is lesbian fulfillment. The book's charm therefore lies in its sectarian exclusiveness. In a work written for similars, Barnes has assumed an already existing sexual identity and has avoided nonlesbian society, which are precisely the central materials with which H.D.'s Bildungsroman struggles.

The indirections of modernist technique may themselves have nourished Gertrude Stein's elaborately and self-consciously constructed codes for lesbian experience. Certainly Stein's extraordinary linguistic innovations served, among other aesthetic purposes, as an obscuring device that allowed her simultaneously to reveal and conceal the forbidden. *HER* operates within a much more accessible system of coded personae, for once the biographical key for the roman à clef is discovered, the novel's disguises dissolve. H.D.'s imagistic innovations in interior monologue in no way mask lesbian passion: indeed they are clearly meant to enhance expression of desire. *HER*'s celebration of "sister love"—the fusion of twin selves, the division of separate selves from a single amoebic cell—also challenges the lesbian model that Stein and Toklas represented in their artistic milieu. Blanche Wiesen Cook has argued that it was "no accident" that a couple like Stein and Toklas came to be "the acknowledged lesbian model. . . . Heterosexist society is little threatened by a relationship that appeared so culturally determined. Stein wrote and slept while Toklas cooked, embroidered, and typed. Few feminist principles are evident there to challenge the ruling scheme of things."[18] Strongly woman-identified in its concept of love between women, *HER* does challenge the presence of hierarchy and power in any intimate relationship, but also does not flinch from ambivalence and betrayals.

In envisioning an eroticism that operates out of a self-loving female center, H.D.'s *HER* also shares little with Radclyffe Hall's *The Well of Loneliness*. To explain her hero's "difference," Hall names the girl as boy, the woman as man. She is Stephen Gordon, whose self-concept is thoroughly masculine, if indeed not entirely male. Stephen's masculine gender identity and stereotypic behavior serve as the defining core of her lesbianism. *The Well of Loneliness* presents a passionate plea for tolerance, but its very formulation, Stimpson argues, "supports the stigma [against homosexuality] through succumbing to a sense of the lesbian as deviant. . . . The narrative of *The Well of Loneliness* stresses the unhappiness of the homosexual, the morbidity of the stigma, which the politics of Heaven, not of earth, must relieve."[19] H.D., in contrast, investigates lesbian difference from heterosexual norms and presents the love between Her and Fayne as a liberating gestalt of psychic, aesthetic, and erotic passion. Cook and Stimpson both suggest that Hall's presentation of the deviant, swaggering, and tortured lesbian was partially acceptable because it fundamentally confirmed the heterosexual norm it seemed to question. H.D.'s *HER* has no such protective armor. As this brief survey suggests, the very difference of H.D.'s text from other lesbian work of the twenties made *HER* a personally difficult book for H.D. to have published.

As both Stimpson and Cook point out, Hall's portrait of Stephen Gordon gives literary expression to a number of psychological theories of homosexuality that had gained increasing acceptance since the turn of the century, particularly the "trapped soul" concept of homosexuality and Havelock Ellis's related formulations of sexual inversion. Such writers as Ellis, Richard von Krafft-Ebing, Karl Ulrichs, Edward Carpenter, and John Addington Symonds varied considerably in both theory and judgment, but all regarded homosexuality as primarily (if not entirely) biological in origin. Homosexual passion was explained as an inborn, not acquired, trait that belonged to individuals who combined the masculine and the feminine, the male and female in body and soul.[20]

H.D. was thoroughly conversant with these theories, especially with Ellis's concept of sexual inversion in the seven volumes of his *Studies in the Psychology of Sex*. H.D. and Bryher knew Ellis personally, greatly admired his work, and corresponded with him well into the thirties when their involvement with psychoanalysis had eclipsed their interest in Ellis's work. In 1919, a few months after she met Bryher, H.D. arranged for her young, deeply troubled friend to see Ellis. Bryher wrote enthusiastically to H.D. about how Ellis had clarified her problem: "Then we got on to the question of whether I was a boy sort of escaped into the wrong body and he says it is a disputed subject but quite possible and showed me a book about it. He said I should find it perhaps too difficult to read as it was very scientific. We agreed it was most unfair for it to happen but apparently I am quite justified in pleading I ought to be a boy, — I am just a girl by accident." Bryher's second autobiographical novel, *Two Selves* (1923), a fascinating, well-written text that deserves critical attention), operates out of Ellis's schema. Bryher's persona, Nancy, is a child whose inner self is a "boy," caged in the unfortunate body of a girl. Nancy's joyful discovery of a "friend" (H.D.), which serves as the novel's climax, is recompense for her fate; the novel ends on that personally happy note.[21]

Although H.D.'s influence on the imagery of *Two Selves* is everywhere apparent, H.D. did not accept for herself the explanation of lesbianism that Bryher so enthusiastically endorsed in the early twenties. As articulations of a woman-centered lesbian love, *Paint It To-Day, Asphodel,* and *HER* contrast sharply with *Two Selves* and the psychological theories on which Bryher's and Hall's works were based. H.D. did not portray Hermione's love for Fayne as an expression of masculinity, nor did she identify her persona as a "boy" in any psychological or physical sense of the word. Where Bryher's *Two Selves* bewails a biological "accident," H.D.'s texts never suggest that lesbians are congenitally different from heterosexual people. Indeed, the very structure of *HER* emphasizes the element of choice, and the role of culture in determinations of sexuality. Hermione is in love with both a man and a woman. Her movement toward Fayne results from a growing sense that her potentially magical relationship with George is doomed by the norms of traditional heterosexual romance and marriage.

Although H.D.'s extensive involvement with psychoanalysis did not begin until after *HER* was completed, the novel illustrates the beginnings of Freud's influence on H.D.'s sexual identity, one that was to take on major proportions from 1933 and 1934, when H.D. was his analysand, and enter all her subsequent work. Even in his early *Three Contributions to the Theory of Sex,* Freud had attacked the concept of congenital homosexuality and argued that most homosexuality was acquired in the process of an individual's early psychosexual interactions with the parents. His two related radical propositions were that all human beings are psychologically bisexual, not just an "intermediate sex," and that all human beings have homosexual as well as heterosexual desires. The heterosexual adult,

Freud believed, has simply repressed homosexual "object choice," love for members of the same sex. Homosexual adults, who may be "normal" in every other regard, have repressed heterosexual desire. Dreams, daydreams, works of art, and many other expressions of unconscious wishes frequently articulated the desire which had been repressed.[22] Hermione's double passion, her capacity to love in two directions, is basically consistent with Freud's view of the potential oscillations of sexual "object choice." The conflict between different loves becomes the drama of heterosexual and homosexual choice that Freud believed to be a central dynamic of everyone's psychosexual development. Anticipating Freudian disciples such as Karen Horney and Gregory Zilborg, furthermore, H.D. also recognized the role of sexual politics in the larger culture in shaping conflicting desires.

During the war decade, Freud argued that the narcissism which predominates in infants motivated (at least partially) homosexual desire. Same-sex love represents self-love, through the substitution of someone as similar as possible to the self: "in the choice of their love-object they have taken as their model not the mother but their own selves. They are plainly seeking themselves as a love object."[23] H.D. was most probably influenced by Freud's association of narcissism with homosexuality. Her lyrical and linguistic fusions of Fayne and Her give eloquent expression to Freud's ideas on narcissism. But H.D.'s vision of the twin sister-lovers, the doubling amoebic cell, contains none of Freud's normative belief that narcissistic love represents "megalomania," or "arrested" development, a libido blocked in an early stage of growth, although there is an echo of this idea in the opening pages of *HER* when Hermione thinks of her identity crisis in terms of that "conniving phrase, 'arrested development' " (1). The word "conniving" itself suggests what H.D. did to the prescriptive norm implicit in Freud's terminology. As she was to do time and again in much later works such as *Tribute to Freud*, H.D. ignored Freud's concept of a norm and thereby transformed his theories into a source of self-validation.[24]

There is some evidence to suggest, however speculatively at this point, that Freud's direct influence on H.D.'s life and art in the thirties changed her understanding (perhaps even experience) of love between women. His diagnosis of H.D.'s symptoms in 1933 and 1934 is itself a microcosm of his theoretical directions. He was convinced that her dreams and psychic experiences demonstrated a desire for union with her mother, the "phallic mother" of the pre-oedipal stage of development. In his writings on lesbianism in the twenties and thirties, Freud did not develop his ideas about narcissism but instead increasingly focused on an analysis of the "masculinity complex" and the mother-daughter relationship. In "Femininity," an essay he completed shortly before meeting H.D., Freud stated that psychoanalysts had not sufficiently understood the significance of the little girl's love for the mother *prior* to the child's discovery of anatomical sex differences. In the pre-oedipal, masculine phase, the daughter desires her mother and sees her as all-powerful. But, Freud theorized, "with the discovery that her mother is castrated," the girl feels tremendous hostility toward her mother, drops her as an object of love, and gradually attaches herself to her father. The girl who will achieve "normal femininity" sublimates all envy for the penis into a desire for a child and continues to direct love toward men. But the lesbian "regresses" to her pre-oedipal love for the still-powerful mother. This return to the mother-daughter bond of the masculine phase is coupled with a powerful envy for the penis, and by extension the power and destiny of men. The lesbian, he concluded, is a woman with an extreme "masculinity complex," attempting to play the role of the man in both erotic and intellectual dimensions of life.[25]

Freud's emphasis on the mother-daughter relationship in both theory and the specific analysis of the poet may well have contributed to the shift in H.D.'s writing about love between women. Her novels of the twenties basically portray lesbian love as a "sister-love," the narcissistic passion of twin souls for themselves in each other. As in certain contemporaneous homosexual circles, this love is set up in opposition to conventional romance and materialist values. In H.D.'s later prose and poetry, the emphasis on spirituality and difference is omnipresent, but mother love has replaced sister love as the bond that validates the woman-centered self and inspires her art. The lesbian love plot that figures so centrally in *HER* has disappeared not only from the published version of the madrigal cycle, but also from her other memoirs and novels.

The Gift, written at the beginning of H.D.'s creative explosion in the 1940s, may well be the pivotal text in this shift, attesting to Freud's possible influence in convincing H.D. that her love for Frances Gregg and Bryher had been unconsciously motivated by her desire for union with her mother. H.D. herself believed that *The Gift*, a memoir of her mother's Moravian upbringing and her own early years in Bethlehem, Pennsylvania, unlocked the floodgates of poetic inspiration and led to the *Trilogy* (1944–46). Indeed the work is completely wrought, with thematic motifs, image patterns, and repeated situations — like fire — recurring through the text. It also deserves publication in its entirety.

Much as the finalizing of divorce in 1938 probably freed H.D. to write *Bid Me to Live* in 1939, reflections on her matrilineage in *The Gift* paved the way for recovery of the goddesses or religious mother figures in the alchemy of her modernist mythmaking in the *Trilogy*. Helen Wolle Doolittle of *The Gift* bears little resemblance to the Eugenia Gart of *HER* and thereby suggests the shift in H.D.'s attitude toward her own mother and the mother figure as potential symbol in her art. Where Hermione is impatient with Eugenia and even fantasizes killing her at one point, the daughter Hilda in *The Gift* is compassionate in attempting to understand the forces that constricted her mother's creativity. In *HER*, there is a subtext of attraction to her mother and belief in Eugenia's Demeter-like power, almost as if to echo the pre-oedipal mother of Freud's theory. But the prevailing voice in *HER* expresses the daughter's contempt for what the mother has become—the arbiter of convention, the proponent of her daughter's marriage. Recognition of her mother's "gift" for life ultimately crushed by convention helps her understand why her mother failed to recognize the visionary "gift"—both spiritual and artistic—in her child. Hilda: "How could I know that this apparent disappointment that her children were not 'gifted,' was itself her own sense of inadequacy and frustration, carried a step further?" The mother, victimized by the patriarchy, cannot easily nourish her daughter to be "different." But the child finds that support in Mamalie, the grandmother who reveals the mysteries of esoteric Moravianism to the gifted child.[26]

The pattern of revelation from mother figure to daughter-poet appears repeatedly in H.D.'s later poetry, a different bond between women than H.D. expressed in *HER*. As H.D. wrote in reference to *Helen in Egypt*, "the mother is the Muse, the Creator, and in my case especially, as my mother's name was Helen."[27] In *Helen in Egypt*, Helen's search for identity leads to her identification with goddess figures all of whom cohere into the matriarchal force of Love set in opposition to the "masculine iron-ring" of War. In the *Trilogy*, the revelations of the "Lady" through dream and religious experience constitute a revisionary mythology as the poet attempts to "found a new religion" for the war-torn world—as Freud himself stated that H.D. wanted to do. In *Hermetic Definition*, the aging poet, first enthralled with a man who fills the role of "Lover" and then overwhelmed by a male poet's genius, must rely on the mother figure Isis to find her "own way." Isis draws aside the veil to reveal hermetic secrets, commands the poet to "Write, write or die," and oversees the creative pregnancy of the poet's labor to generate her poem over a nine-month period.[28]

While H.D.'s probable transformation of the lesbian sister of *HER* into the goddess figures of her later work represents a turning away from the direct affirmation of a lesbian eros, it is important to recognize the common origins of these different representations of love between women. When we understand the connection both Freud and H.D. made between her love for Gregg and Bryher and her search for the powerful mother, we can decipher the sister love that is deeply encoded in H.D.'s later works.

We have speculated that Freud's analysis of H.D.'s lesbian desire as the need for union with her mother may well have led her to encode that love so covertly that it went largely unrecognized in the published poems from the 1940s on. There are, of course, other factors. The mystical religious traditions with which she increasingly identified might also have played a significant part in forging the mother goddess and erasing the sister-lover. Perhaps also the patterns and conventions in which she could formulate her relationships were themselves biased toward heterosexuality, adultery, and certain types of betrayal. It takes a bold act of cultural critique and refabrication to construct the unconventional plots H.D. was attempting. But the power of convention, as well as the fear of exposure, could have made it very difficult for H.D. to develop further the narrative mode she had begun in *HER*.

For later works such as *Hermetic Definition, Winter Love, End to Torment*, and *Vale Ave* reproduce the drama of romantic thralldom. Taken together, they depict a woman who sought to make herself vulnerable to men — as if her attraction to them was never fulfilled until she was marginalized and rejected. The symbolic mother-daughter bond that all these works simultaneously resurrect anchored the poet precisely so that she could make these forays into the world of male-female sexuality, to search for male hierophants and lovers. Romantic love may indeed have been the bait for spiritual conversion — a bait which the poet herself ate, as well as casting to the male "fishes." H.D.'s various personae often see themselves as the martyred or betrayed priestess of a new religion, urgent to transform destructive maleness to visionary transcendence. This at any rate is Helen's achievement: with Achilles' violent hands around her neck, she calls out the name of Thetis, thereby recalling him to a gentler self, and finally serves as the agent of his rebirth as the androgynous "New Mortal." A necessary precondition for creativity in all these poems is, then, both the poet's nourishment from the mother figure and her confrontation with the male lover.

The transformation of the "sister motive" into the mother goddess mythos is embodied most concretely in *Winter Love* (1959), a coda for *Helen in Egypt* that H.D. withdrew from publication with the epic shortly before she died. At the same time, the poem is grounded in heterosexual desire. *Winter Love* records the love affair between the aging Helen and Odysseus after both have returned home from the Trojan war, an affair that is a ratification of Helen's very first seduction by Odysseus, long before the war. Not at all a source of biographical fact about H.D., the poem is nonetheless deeply personal and explores her feelings for Pound, Odysseus his most notable persona. Here, as in *End to Torment*, H.D. returned at the end of her life to the relationship with Pound which she had elaborated in *HER*, crystallizing complex meditations around him, as an unresolved and volatile figure in her life.[29] To return to Pound was to return to core questions about the male companion, the betrayer, the "lover," a figure on whom could focus the multiple white lasers that pierced her later years: passion, a sense of imprisonment, a desire for synthesis.

The contact between Ezra Pound and H.D. in the London years of early modernism is close to legendary, as he named the manner of her "first authentic verses," a gesture which, however ambiguous it eventually seemed, was a gift to H.D. at that moment, for it was an act of faith in her power as a poet.[30] Even before this, at the time of their earliest sexual and poetic contact, when Pound composed the poems in "Hilda's Book" (1905–7), he sustained two conflicting versions of her presence. When he wrote his constant variations on this theme:

> Out of thy purity
> Saint Hilda pray for me.
> . . .
> Saint Hilda pray for me
> Lay on my forehead
> Cool hands of thy blessing[31]

he had cast H.D. into a familiar iconic role, the beautiful woman as *stil novisti* muse. But Pound also visualized Hilda in another fashion, when he wrote, more rarely, about a coequal companionship between male and female poets:

> Yea in this house of thine that I have found at last
> Meseemeth a high heaven's antepast
> And thou thyself art unto me
> Both as the glory head and sun
> Casting thine own anthelion
> Thru this dull mist.
> My soul was wont to be.[32]

Thus in that 1905–7 period, Pound saw H.D. in two alternative roles—as cool, saintly advisor, above and beyond his fears, and as a hot, gold coequal. In that second image of Hilda as gloryhead (for anthelion means the luminous ring or halo around a head), Ez-Ray saw her nimbus, her power, her radiance. He desired that glory to serve a curative and inspirational function, but beyond the poem's astonishingly archaic diction, "Ver Novum" is a vision of the female as powerful inspiration *because* coequal, a "mage powerful and subtly sweet."[33]

An analysis of *End to Torment* with its evocative reflections upon these years confirms that H.D. also experienced these interestingly contradictory patterns for their earliest relationship. One pattern she valued more, and, recognizing it as an unusual paradigm for male-female relations, she named it an "uncoordinated entity." In the rather cryptic passage in which she describes their relationship and poses this issue, she remembers an image of companionate twins, based on Balzac's Séraphita-Séraphitus, in the book which Pound himself had given her to read.[34] These are male and female as coequal twin selves — indeed, as mystical versions of each other. H.D. contrasts this tie, which she did feel with Pound, with another bond, the "coordinated convention" for male-female relations: the culturally mandated love plot with its asymmetry of the sexes. In *End to Torment*, H.D. seems to recover the traumatic moment when Pound changes from being a coequal to being a "Man-Hero," whose dynamic power was stultifying, rather than enlivening. In the recovery of this time, she is able to begin transposing the relationships. While depicting him as an incandescent lover, H.D. also binds him verbally, in lambent and dramatic chains of image, association, and biographical allusion into a series of other roles. Pound is simultaneously brother, father, child, friendly counsellor (parallel to Erich Heydt). He is even associated with his most extreme antonym — the sister companion, Frances Gregg, who "came into" H.D.'s life when "Ezra left finally for Europe," and about whom H.D. says: "She completed or 'complemented' the Dryad or Druid that Ezra had evoked so poignantly."[35]

Indeed, to begin writing *End to Torment*, H.D. was able to recover her "deep love for Ezra" by being "injected" with Pound by Erich Heydt.[36] Heydt and Norman Holmes Pearson were men who deliberately cast themselves as H.D.'s helpers, and whose aid was critical: *End to Torment* simply could not have been written without them. This is not only because of their actual biographical presence as physician and correspondent, but also because their careful, even ritualized, cultivation of H.D.'s diffident need to speak made them into the companionate figures whose love and desire for her work sustained the female artist.[37] They are avatars of the figure Pound could have been during H.D.'s life, the wished-for twin companion. It is clear, however, that in reality, H.D. visualized Ezra less as sympathetic companion than as judge.

When, after *End to Torment* was completed, she sent him a copy of *Winter Love*, a poem written about Odysseus and Helen, she did not mention his presence in the poem, presumably hoping he would discover it on his own. But enclosed with the manuscript is a note which anticipates his criticism. "It might be a little divertissement to you to slash it to pieces & return — or not."[38] Less than two weeks later, she sent him the complete *Helen in Egypt*. It is again accompanied by a remarkable note, replete with her double image of herself as powerful mage and distressed woman. It is hard even to believe that we are dealing with a seventy-five-year-old major poet who had just completed several major works, when she sent the poem of mastery and at the same time skitterishly instructed Pound not to respond:

> Don't worry or hurry with the *Helen* — don't read it all —
> don't read it yet — don't bother to write of it.[39]

She recoiled from the judge and sought the lover and companion — and she played that drama out, gesture by gesture.

Sustained by the interest and attentions of Heydt and Pearson, H.D. had begun to follow Ezra's case in the late 1950s, as his release from Saint Elizabeths was exactingly negotiated. To assist her, she invited almost daily letters from Pearson, each of which, along with Heydt's salutary curiosity, triggered the dated entries of the diarylike *End to Torment*. This male permission was essential, especially as Bryher was quite angry that H.D. was following the case of Pound with such care. This anger went beyond jealousy. Bryher was thinking of her close friend Sylvia Beach, a woman who had been incarcerated during the Nazi era. Further, Bryher herself had done "war work" in Switzerland that involved her in a private network to rescue Jews threatened with extermination. Among the cases which Bryher remembers was Walter Benjamin's. She herself had smuggled visas into Vienna and Prague — a dangerous task.[40] Bryher understandably viewed H.D.'s concern with Pound as a political betrayal, even though H.D. took every care to dissociate herself from Pound's dubious epigones in that period.[41]

Given H.D.'s increasingly elaborate views of the patterns created by her relationships, one of Pound's gestures in the late period is particularly significant. Pound inscribed H.D.'s copy of *The Confucian Odes* with the phrase "clouds over Taishan."[42] If she had not already noticed, this inscription was designed to direct her attention to those lines in the Pisan sequence in which Pound calls out to her, using the name that had been hers from the beginning of their relationship, and which she still used in letters to him: Dryad.

> Δρυάς, your eyes are like the clouds over Taishan
> When some of the rain has fallen
> and half remains yet to fall[43]

In *The Pisan Cantos*, Pound evokes various women because they appeared as visionary presences to the poet — the most notable is the triple appearance of eyes in the tent. Because of H.D.'s abiding interest in psychic phenomena, articulated throughout the 1940s, and because of her own highly self-conscious and sometimes self-lacerating probing of the past, this call from Pound had to have been extremely evocative. The call to a vision of Dryad — of herself — suggested that Pound was attentive to exactly the kinds of mystical experiences she found most valuable, and it suggested, too, that she was as much a subject for his meditations as he was for hers. And indeed, H.D. responded deeply to Pound's delicate signal.

That H.D.'s *Winter Love* was directly inspired by *The Pisan Cantos* there can be little doubt. The atmosphere in *Winter Love* of intoxicating fruit, the references to apples and pomegranates allude to Pound's well-known "Pomona" lines ("This fruit has a fire within it") which H.D. greatly admired.[44] The seduction of Helen by Odysseus occurs in a passage filled with references to a section of the Lynx Canto in the Pisan sequence where the sensual virile force and the erotic natural smells ("the smell of pine mingles with rose leaves") are echoed directly by H.D., who evokes first the Dionysian presence of the lynx and then the fragrant, woody setting:

> Who has been here before?
> was it Iacchus, Dionysus, Bacchus?
> fragrance of grapes mingles with scent of cedar
>
> and apple-wood; though we have only fir-wood and dried cones,
> altar-incense — and the hiss of resin. . . .[45]

But desire, although consummated, and heterosexual betrayal, with which H.D. was quite obsessed, are neither the climax of this poem. The character who matches Odysseus-Pound in emotional importance and structural weight is the Grande Dame or Sage Femme (wise woman or midwife), who cares for Helen in her pregnancy and attends the birth of the child, playing the role that Bryher played in 1919 at the birth of H.D.'s child. While *Winter Love*, unlike the earlier *HER*, contains no sister-lover to counterbalance the troubled relationship with Pound, the sister is now encoded in the mother figure, overseeing the poet's labor to produce the child-poem. In the poem, then, that climactic child belongs as much to Sage Femme as to Odysseus. By using childbirth agony, resentment, revulsion, and ecstasy as the climax of the poem, and by making the child come equally from the insemination by man and the salvation by woman, H.D. has created a bisexual structure which gives the loved woman weight and force in her poetic universe. This makes the encoding of Bryher and Pound in *Winter Love* an extremely important consummation of the motifs and structures in *HER*.

The two works of her last years which return to Pound demonstrate, then, a development of the male figure parallel in its meaning to the development of the female figure which we have already discussed. While relationships of romantic thralldom still exist, H.D. also sought to invent and to encourage a companionate visionary male. Hence H.D.'s later work shows this double movement — of sister transposed to mother, fixed and hidden because of taboos against lesbian relationships, and a more volatile, chemically unstable series of heterosexual shiftings between romantic thralldom and two other ways of visualizing male-female companionship. H.D. could diffuse and de-fuse the "lover" into other structures, mainly a ritualistic parent-child relation between women and men, as in *Hermetic Definition*. More rarely, she visualized a coequal relation with a companion. This companionate love for men, indeed, was a source of inspiration and poetic validation.

The text of *HER* itself, alongside H.D.'s life and the transformations she has proposed, suggests the underlying reasons why she was not to develop in the direction of either exclusive lesbian or heterosexual identification in her life and art. *HER* presents its main character caught in the dilemma of choice between a man and a woman. This narrative critique of heterosexist convention, however, ends in no *choice* at all. Her decision not to choose between a man and a woman reflects H.D.'s state of mind and sexual identification. Throughout her life, H.D.'s emotional, sexual, and spiritual life was bisexual. Just as she was unwilling to give up her love of women while married to Aldington, so she explored her passion for men while bonded with Bryher.[46] In unpublished memoirs, poems, and correspondence, H.D. even identified her confusion about her desires as a major reason for seeing Freud — one of the reasons she did not identify in her public memoir, *Tribute to Freud*. Her unpublished poem "The Master," for example, refers directly to the dilemma of sexuality that structures *HER*:

> I had two loves separate;
> God who loves all mountains,
> alone knew why
> and understood
> and told the old man
> to explain
>
> the impossible,
> which he did.[47]

Freud's "explanation" certainly involved an analysis of H.D.'s love for women, but it also contained explicit discussion of her anxiety about bisexuality, which apparently was linked to the writer's block she suffered from in the early thirties. In 1934, H.D. wrote to Bryher about her sessions with Freud: "I have gone terribly deep with papa. He says, 'you had two things to hide, one that you were a girl, the other that you were a boy.' It appears I am that all-but extinct phenomena, the perfect bi-. Well, this is terribly exciting, but for the moment, PLEASE do not speak of my own MSS., for it seems the conflict consists partly that what I write commits me—to one sex, or to the other. I no longer HIDE. It is not quite so obvious as that—and no doubt, before I leave, we will come to some balance."[48] Freud's theories of psychosexual development identified a feminine heterosexual woman as one who had repressed her masculine self and lesbian desire in the unconscious; the lesbian was simply, in his view, an "inversion," repressing the feminine heterosexual self. H.D., he seemed to have said, was neither: the "perfect bi-," she repressed neither side. Her writer's block, partially a result of confusion, would disappear if she could accept both sides as valid and stop trying to hide in literary silence. H.D. was drawn to Freud because she believed that he provided her with a psychology of transcendence, the validation of her desire to synthesize all dualities, particularly the oppositions her parents represented symbolically and which she, as their child, continued to live out in her interactions with the men and women who followed her parents as objects of her love. Caught like Hermione between her father and mother, his science and her art, H.D. could not choose either one to the exclusion of the other.

Her exploration of the socially condemned category—the lesbian—was defiantly revisionist throughout her life and art; her erotic "difference," in whatever aspect of her life it found expression, served as a center of identity from which she could create. She consistently renamed and reclaimed the female, the spiritual, the lesbian within the context of a hostile world that valued the male, the material, the heterosexual. But she never adopted that "difference," particularly her sexual difference from a heterosexist society, as her whole identity. The dilemma which the open ending of *HER* illuminates is one that H.D. continued to address in different forms for the rest of her life. H.D. forged her oeuvre in persistent and profound struggles with cultural and narrative questions concerning sexuality and the domains of gender.

NOTES

Research for this paper was conducted with assistance from the Women's Studies Research Center, University of Wisconsin–Madison, and with a Temple University Summer Research Fellowship, 1980. The essay previously appeared in *Montemora* 8 (1981): 7–30.
1   The manuscripts of *Paint It To-Day, Asphodel, Pilate's Wife,* and *HER* are located in the Collection of American Literature, Beinecke Rare Book and Manuscript Library, Yale University. We would like to thank Perdita Schaffner, H.D.'s literary executor, Donald Gallup, former curator of the Collection,

and the staff of Beinecke Library for their support of our work with these and the other manuscripts to which we refer. All quotations from H.D. manuscripts and correspondence are from materials at Beinecke Library and are used with the permission of Perdita Schaffner and Beinecke Library.

2   Some scholars have recently begun to explore the impact of the films she saw, made, and wrote about on her art, among them Anne Friedberg in her "Approaching *Borderline*," *Millenium Film Journal*, nos. 7–9 (Fall/Winter 1980): 130–39 and " 'All the light within the light fascinates me': H.D.'s Film Work in Context," paper delivered at MLA, 1980; and Charlotte Mandel, "Garbo/Helen: The Self-Projection of Beauty by H.D.," *Women's Studies* 71/2 (1980), 127–35.

3   In a letter of January 16, 1935, to Bryher, H.D. referred to her submission of *Pilate's Wife* to Greenslet. For the information about Pearson, we are indebted to the French scholar Jeanne Kerblat-Houghton, who discussed Pearson's publication plans with him in 1974. A letter from H.D. to Viola Jordan suggest H.D.'s plans for at least some of her unpublished works, perhaps including *HER*: "I destroyed a barrel-full of old stuff, not destroyed really, as I finally boiled down the material and re-worked it in my War I and in my War II novels . . . But there is no hurry for publication; only, it is good to have them properly shaped and in the hands of Norman Pearson" (September 12, 1951). With H.D., Pearson played the crucial role of encouraging her to review old manuscripts and send them to him for future publication.

4   Information about her life and the composition of *Bid Me to Live (A Madrigal)* (New York: Grove, 1960) comes largely from H.D.'s *Autobiographical Notes* (34) and her correspondence with Aldington and Bryher. H.D. may well have begun the novel while in analysis with Freud in 1933 and 1934 because her letters to Bryher during this period refer to Freud's suggestions that she write of the War I period to free herself of her writer's block. H.D.'s reference to the "madrigal cycle" is in her memoir *Thorn Thicket* at Beinecke. The whole citation is pertinent to our argument: "Bryher came into the *Madrigal* cycle, July 17, 1918, but I do not bring her into the story. The story ends with the letter that Julia [H.D.] writes to Frederico or Lorenzo [Lawrence]. He had been dead 17 years" (28).

5   Frances Josepha Gregg, also mentioned in H.D.'s *End to Torment* (New York: New Directions, 1979) and *Tribute to Freud* (1956; rpt. Boston: David Godine, 1974), continued to appear at the fringes of H.D.'s artistic circles for many years. A writer herself, she published in the *Egoist*, and other little magazines. In 1926, she sent Kenneth Macpherson to H.D. H.D.'s letters to Bryher in the twenties and thirties express considerable irritation with Gregg however — for example, in an undated letter of 1930, "I may or may not see the Greggggggg again. She is really completely cracked. She tells me one thing and Egon the diametric opposite. She now speaks as in ownership of 'Kenneth's genius,' having yelled at me 'filth and slime.' She wants to break up this whole combine. Her fingers itch for it like a kleptomaniac. Yes . . . she is psychic klepto-maniac. She must get and break."

6 For discussion of romantic thralldom, see Rachel Blau DuPlessis "Romantic Thralldom in H.D.," in this volume, and "Family, Sexes, Psyche: an essay on H.D. and the muse of the woman writer," *Montemora* 6 (1979): 137–56.

7 Interview with Silvia Dobson, December 1980. For an account of the court case and surrounding events, see Vera Brittain, *Radclyffe Hall: A Case of Obscenity?* (London: Femina Books, 1968) and Una, Lady Troubridge, *The Life and Death of Radclyffe Hall* (London: Hammond, 1961).

8 Catharine Stimpson, "Zero Degree Deviancy: A Study of the Lesbian Novel," 5–6, paper delivered at MLA, 1980; Sandra Gilbert and Susan Gubar, *The Madwoman in the Attic* (New Haven: Yale UP, 1979), 45–53.

9 Stimpson, "Zero Degree Deviancy," 1.

10 In *Autobiographical Notes*, H.D. identified 1910 as the "Frances Gregg period" and said that she wrote her first poems to Frances, modeled on translations of Theocritus that Pound gave her. "I am satisfied with these poems," she noted and may have had them published in "New York syndicated newspapers" in 1910.

11 H.D.'s alteration of her actual life here is an important reminder that *HER* is not reliable as factual biography. H.D. left Bryn Mawr College in 1906, not 1910, as *HER* implies. Pound was a frequent visitor during the five years prior to her involvement with Gregg. H.D.'s cousin Francis Wolle wrote that Pound's dismissal from his position at Wabash College (1907) led H.D.'s father to forbid their meeting. She and Pound disobeyed his orders, and became unofficially engaged in 1907. Eric's wife Sara (the maligned Minnie of *HER*) allowed Pound and H.D. to meet secretly in their rooms. In 1909, with her father's backing, H.D. took an apartment in Greenwich Village to pursue her artistic development, but returned home within five months. Pound returned from Europe shortly thereafter, the point at which the story of *HER* begins. See Wolle, *A Moravian Heritage* (Boulder, CO: Empire Reproductions, 1972), 55–60.

12 For discussion of H.D.'s ambivalence toward and transformation of the mother-daughter relationship, see Susan Stanford Friedman, "Psyche Reborn: Tradition, Re-Vision and the Goddess as Mother-Symbol in H.D.'s Epic Poetry," *Women's Studies* 6.2 (1979): 147–60.

13 The collection of H.D.'s letters to Pound at Beinecke (1928–39, 1949–60) includes about ten letters from Pound to H.D. (1937–39, 1958–59) in which he frequently addressed her as "Dryad." *End to Torment* also reviews H.D.'s identification with their code name "Dryad."

14 The poem H.D. quoted here and throughout *HER* is Algernon Swinburne's "Itylus," in his *Poems and Ballads, First Series* (London: Chatto & Windus, 1904), I, 54–55. "Itylus" is a poem based on the Philomela myth and explores the tabooed erotic attraction between women. H.D.'s decision to weave lines from Swinburne's poem throughout her descriptions of the bond between Fayne and Her may well have been influenced by Havelock Ellis's identification of Swinburne as one "among poets who have used the motive of homosexuality in women with more or less boldness." See Ellis, *Studies in the*

Psychology of Sex (New York: Random House, 1905), I, 200. The sister and swallow imagery, so prominent in "Itylus," was connected not only with Gregg, but also with Bryher. Fayne Rabb may well be a composite of both Gregg and Bryher. H.D.'s lyrical description of the "sisters' " ecstatic moments may refer to experiences she shared with Bryher. The "swallow," for example, evoked for both H.D. and Bryher the magical month they spent together in Cornwall in July 1919. In a letter of June 28, 1931, to Bryher, H.D. wrote in response to a gift: "My dear . . . that SWALLOW. What could be more exquisite. It seems almost the loveliest thing that has happened, especially as it is just at about this time, that said Cornwall swallow, did its little conjuring trick . . . it is, of course . . . a sacred bird, and the symbol of Isis." The narrative of *HER* also echoes H.D.'s life in 1926–28. Bryher married Kenneth Macpherson while Macpherson and H.D. were lovers. In *Tribute to Freud*, H.D. indicated the palimpsestic nature of the two women in her life by explaining that Bryher appeared "to take the place of Frances," with whom she had been "infatuated" (152). These parallels suggest how misleading it could be to take the events of H.D.'s romans à clef as a source of biographical fact.

15   For discussions of the butterfly motif, see Susan Stanford Friedman, *Psyche Reborn: The Emergence of H.D.* (Bloomington: Indiana UP, 1981); DuPlessis, "Romantic Thralldom in H.D."; and Susan Gubar, "The Echoing Spell of H.D.'s *Trilogy*," in this volume.

16   Elaine Marks, "Lesbian Intertexuality," in *Homosexualities and French Literature: Cultural Contexts/Critical Texts*, ed. George Stambolian and Elaine Marks (Ithaca: Cornell UP, 1979), 365. In " 'Women Alone Stir My Imagination': Lesbianism and the Cultural Tradition," *Signs* 4.4 (Summer 1979), Blanche Wiesen Cook also notes the significance of the late twenties for lesbian publishing (718). We are indebted to these two important essays along with Stimpson's "Zero Degree Deviancy: A Study of the Lesbian Novel," and a number of other essays on lesbian culture, among them: Lillian Faderman, "Lesbian Magazine Fiction in the Early Twentieth Century," *Journal of Popular Culture* 11.4 (Spring 1978): 800–17; Bertha Harris, "*What we mean to say:* Notes toward Defining the Nature of Lesbian Literature," *Heresies* 3 (Fall 1977): 5–8; Blanche Wiesen Cook, "The Historical Denial of Lesbianism," *Radical History Review* 20 (Spring/Summer 1979): 60–65; Adrienne Rich, "Compulsory Heterosexuality and Lesbian Existence," *Signs* 5.4 (Summer 1980): 631–60.

17   See Adrienne Rich, "It Is the Lesbian in Us . . . ," *On Lies, Secrets and Silence: Selected Prose, 1966–1978* (New York: Norton, 1979), 200.

18   Cook, " 'Women Alone Stir My Imagination,' " 730–31. Cook also discusses Woolf and Hall.

19   Stimpson, "Zero Degree Deviancy," 26.

20   For discussions of these theories, see Barbara Fassler, "Theories of Homosexuality as Sources of Bloomsbury's Androgyny," *Signs* 5.2 (Winter 1979): 237–51; Sheila Rowbotham and Jeffrey Weeks, *Socialism and the New Life: The Personal and Sexual Politics of Edward Carpenter and Havelock Ellis*

(London: Pluto Press, 1977); Lillian Faderman, "The Morbidification of Love between Women by Nineteenth-Century Sexologists," *Journal of Homosexuality* 4.1 (Fall 1978): 73–90. We are indebted to Biddy Martin, Friedman's research assistant, for collecting these and other sources on theories of homosexuality.

21   Bryher to H.D., March 20, 1919; Bryher, *Two Selves* (Paris: Contact, 1923).

22   Sigmund Freud, *Three Contributions to the Theory of Sex* (1905), trans. A. A. Brill (New York: Dutton, 1962), 1–34. See also Freud, "Psychogenesis of a Case of Homosexuality in a Woman" (1920) in *The Standard Edition of the Complete Psychological Works of Sigmund Freud* (London: Hogarth Press, 1950), II, 202–31.

23   Sigmund Freud, "On Narcissism: An Introduction" (1914) in his *General Psychological Theory: Papers on Metapsychology*, ed. Philip Rieff (New York: Collier, 1963), 56–82. See also his "The Libido Theory and Narcissism," in *Introductory Lectures on Psychoanalysis* (1917), trans. James Strachey (New York: Norton, 1966), 412–30.

24   See Friedman, *Psyche Reborn*, for a discussion of Freud's influence on H.D. and her abandonment of his prescriptive lens embedded in his theories of sexuality, religion, and art. We do not agree with Juliet Mitchell, who argues that Freud's norms are only descriptive. See her *Psychoanalysis and Feminism* (New York: Pantheon, 1974).

25   Sigmund Freud, "Femininity" (1933) in *New Introductory Lectures*, trans. James Strachey (New York: Norton, 1965), 129–31. See also "Psychogenesis of a Case of Homosexuality in a Woman." H.D.'s *Advent* notes on her analysis, printed in the second edition of *Tribute to Freud*, comment on Freud's statement to her about the early psychoanalytic "mistake" in "not sufficiently understanding that the girl did not invariably transfer her emotions to her father" (175). In the spring of 1933, H.D.'s letters to Bryher reporting on her analysis with Freud refer excitedly to Freud's description of a recent shift in his theories of femininity.

26   H.D., "Dark Room," p. 32 of *The Gift*, manuscript at Beinecke. Mamalie's revelation to the ten-year-old child Hilda takes place in the chapter "The Secret" and serves as the spiritual climax of the memoir.

27   H.D., *End to Torment* 41.

28   H.D., *Hermetic Definition* (New York: New Directions, 1972), 7. For discussions of the goddess and the poet as mother, see Friedman, *Psyche Reborn*; Vincent Quinn, "H.D.'s 'Hermetic Definition': The Poet as Archetypal Mother," *Contemporary Literature* 18.1 (Winter 1977): 51–61; and Susan Stanford Friedman, "Who Buried H.D.? A Poet, Her Critics and Her Place in 'The Literary Tradition,' " *College English* 36, no. 7 (March 1975), 801–14.

29   Since we discuss the two works in an intertwined fashion, it would be worth simply noting that *End to Torment* is dated March 7–July 13, 1958, and *Winter Love* was written between January 3 and April 15, 1959.

30   Glenn Hughes, *Imagism and the Imagists* (Stanford: Stanford UP, 1931), 111, citing a letter from H.D.

31   Ezra Pound, "Sancta Patrona Domina Caelae," in "Hilda's Book," *End to*

Torment 83–84.

32 Pound, "Ver Novum," "Hilda's Book," *End to Torment* 72. The sun image also occurs in "Praise of Ysolt," in *Personae*.

33 Pound, "Ver Novum," "Hilda's Book," *End to Torment* 71.

34 *End to Torment* 23. In fact, the arguments in the introduction to the 1889 Boston edition of the Balzac, by George Frederic Parsons, may have had an influence on H.D.: that women are in charge of the spiritual growth of civilization and the progress of the race; that the divine deliverer for the next round of progress will be a person who has both sexes within her.

35 *End to Torment* 53.

36 H.D. to Norman Holmes Pearson, April 11, 1958; *End to Torment* 20.

37 Norman Holmes Pearson to H.D., May 10, 1958: "do keep on with private EPistles to yourself. This is the moment on paper for a kind of catharsis, the ordering and getting it down which will free you. It is the ordering, not the data which is important, and I hold your hand while *unser* [Heydt] guides your pen. The ink is from your heart."

38 H.D. to Pound, November 4, 1959.

39 H.D. to Pound, November 18, [1959].

40 Bryher, *The Heart to Artemis—A Writer's Memoirs* (New York: Harcourt, Brace and World, 1962), 276–77.

41 H.D. to Norman Holmes Pearson, April 11, 1958. "I had a terrible evening with Fido [Bryher] + [Sylvia] Beach, who both turned violently on me about poor Ezra. . . . I have been so *happy* writing the E.P. 'story'—it must not be taken away from me."

42 H.D.'s copy is held in the Beinecke Library, Yale University. *The Confucian Odes* was published in 1954.

43 Ezra Pound, *The Pisan Cantos* (New York: New Directions, 1948), 108. She is mentioned three times, and indeed in her charily marked copy of *The Pisan Cantos*, this page has been checked three times.

44 *End to Torment* 34; *The Pisan Cantos* 68.

45 *Winter Love*, in *Hermetic Definition* 108. The line from *The Pisan Cantos* occurs on p. 69.

46 Aldington wrote many love letters to H.D. from the front in 1918, attempting to explain his affairs and telling H.D. that her own affair with Gray did not change his desire to resume the marriage. On August 5, 1918, he wrote that "I want you to be happy & have lovers & girl-lovers if you want, but I don't want to lose you." These appeals ceased after H.D. became pregnant. While with Bryher, H.D. was also involved with some men, most importantly Macpherson.

47 H.D., "The Master," at Beinecke, p. 3. The poem, which has twelve sections, was probably written in 1934–35. In a November 1, 1935, letter to Bryher, H.D. angrily refused to publish it in Robert Herrings' *Life and Letters Today*. See commentary by Friedman and DuPlessis, who first published the poem in *Feminist Studies* 7 (Fall 1981): 407–30.

48 H.D. to Bryher, November 24, 1934.

CHAPTER 13

Return of the Repressed
in H.D.'s Madrigal Cycle

SUSAN STANFORD FRIEDMAN

"Things now are like Gibbon," Hermione thinks in *Asphodel* during the Great War; "The decline and Fall. This is history, I suppose" (II, 6). Paradoxically applied to the here-and-now, the phrase "this is history" suggests the past-in-the-present and the future-about-to-become-the-past, an awareness, in other words, of the chronological passage of time and the compulsion of "history" to repeat itself. "History" forces a Fall into time, into the "real" events of time and the larger patterns of time that shape the lives of individuals powerless to halt its march—like the "decline and fall" of the Roman Empire, like the "decline and fall" of European civilization in the modern world. Like so many of her generation, the great events of the modern world wrenched H.D. out of the relatively private realm of the imagination and into the public realm of "history," into the development of a historical consciousness in a postlapsarian world. Trying to "make it new," as Pound proclaimed, many of the modernists nonetheless became obsessed with "history," with their failure to awaken from the "nightmare" of "history" and with their search to discover or create some pattern of continuity and meaning in the processus of time.[1]

H.D., forced by "history" to fall from lyric into narrative, made the self-in-history the centerpiece of much of her prose. Perhaps echoing Richard Aldington's war poem "Madrigal," she called her major novel about the "cosmic, comic, crucifying times of history" *Madrigal* and only reluctantly agreed to change it to *Bid Me to Live (A Madrigal)*. Later in *Thorn Thicket*, she refers to the texts she wrote about her life during World War I—*Paint It To-Day*, *Asphodel*, and *Bid Me to Live (A Madrigal)*—as "the *Madrigal* cycle."[2] The term "madrigal" is ironic, evoking in the midst of war the image of a lyric form associated with Elizabethan love

233

songs in timeless pastoral settings. *Madrigal* is a novel about love — hetero-sexual love — caught in the monstrous cataclysm of history, what began as an out-of-time pastoral trapped in the reality of the in-time.

The Great War, ultimately war itself, both epitomizes "history" and signifies its extremis — "this is history." "Time," in *Madrigal*, is metonymi-cally a soldier's wristwatch, ticking away "inside its steel cage" (19). The spirit of the age, of the modern world, centers on a civilization caught in the war machine of death. It is concretely the guns and bombs of war that create and represent H.D.'s twentieth-century waste land, "a city of dreadful night, a city of dreadful night" (109). The devouring labyrinth is not a web of words, but "the crucifying times of history" that reduced civilization to "Ashes and death; it was the city of dreadful night, it was a dead city" (109).

For T. S. Eliot in "The Waste Land," the war is unnamed; it is the gap in the text, an absence that signifies the extremity of its horror — we wit-ness it only by regarding its devastating personal and cultural effects. The exhilaration of early modernism celebrating its break from the absolutism of the Victorian age gave way to despair, even lamentation for what had been lost. Unlike Eliot, Ezra Pound in "Hugh Selwyn Mauberley" (1918) and Aldington in volumes such as *Reverie: A Little Book of Poems for H.D.* (1917), *War and Love* (1919), and *Images of War* (1919) wrote directly about the shattering impact of the war. Like Pound and Alding-ton, H.D. felt compelled to stare her experience of the Great War in the face, even if she risked being turned to stone by its gaze. H.D.'s prose about the war mirrored Aldington's *Reverie*, the nine poems he had scrib-bled in little notebooks in the trenches. The underlying battle of these poems is between the war's attempt to destroy the soul and the poet's desire to remain spiritually alive. Love — the memory of love, the desire for love, the passion of love — is the poet's ally, the only avenue of possible escape from the spiritual death that stalks the trenches and cities of Europe. The poet alternates between images of anguish and images of a redemptive desire. He is the "faun captive," dreaming that afar off he can see "Bent poppies and the deathless asphodel" (*CP* 68–69). The poems are "madri-gals," modernist style, their pastoral passions mediated by the historical realities of war. In this landscape, ironically titled "trench idyll" in one poem, the individual is history's victim. The poet laments the power of history, embodied in the war, to engulf the individual, whose dike against the flood of circumstance is love. The lesson of the war for Aldington was that particularly at times of crisis, history penetrates the individual psyche — the barriers between public and private spheres break down. Love remained for Aldington the individual's last line of defense against the tyranny of history — love, and the poetry it inspired.

Like Aldington, H.D. believed that the power of history embodied in the war held love, poetry, and beauty in its death grip. However, H.D.'s Madrigal Cycle probes even more radically into the meaning of history. For women, the private sphere has never been a "haven in a heartless world," a respite from the great march of events in the public sphere. Rather, "home" is a point of instability, a place that oscillates between woman's potential legitimation and victimization within the social order. Like Virginia Woolf's *Mrs. Dalloway* and *Three Guineas*, H.D.'s texts show war to be a monstrous extension of the structural violence of society that governs both the public and private spheres in times of peace and war. In contrast to Aldington's *Reverie*, H.D.'s madrigals portray romantic love as a product of history, not a force outside it; as a primal enactment of war, not a flight from it. From her perspective, one that explores woman as both object of and subject in history, the war at home is also a war in the home. In addition to being a civilian's view of the war, H.D.'s madrigals examine the war at the front as it both creates and reflects the patterns of the battle on the home front.

H.D.'s novels about the war deconstruct the prevailing binary oppositions between private and public, personal and political, individual and societal to suggest that no place is immune from history because the structures of the social order and of desire correspond to and replicate each other. Superimposed and interpenetrating, each is an extension of the other. This view, which anticipates contemporary feminist formulations of the personal as political, parallels Woolf's contemporaneous critique of the patriarchal family as the structural basis of oppression and war. H.D.'s perspective also resonates with Freud's speculative hypothesis of the dual instincts—Eros and the death drive—presented mainly in *Beyond the Pleasure Principle* (1920) and *Civilization and Its Discontents* (1930).[3] *Beyond the Pleasure Principle* was Freud's answer to the challenge of the Great War. The sight of the most "advanced" civilizations engaged in a suicidal war for which there could be no real victors led him to revise his view that the drive for pleasure—the "pleasure principle"—was the only instinct in the unconscious. To the dismay of many of his disciples, he posited the existence of an opposite drive, the death wish "to return to the inanimate state," to which he linked both individual and societal aggression (32). Even more radically, however, he theorized not only the alternation of eros and thanatos, but also their interrelationship. The link, he writes in *Beyond the Pleasure Principle*, is in the dynamics of sadomasochism, in the "displacement" of the death drive into the erotic (48).

To locate the interrelationship of eros and thanatos in the interlocking scenes of love and war is a central task in H.D.'s modernist madrigals. The novels in the Madrigal Cycle repeat each other, compelled by the "crucifying times of history" to go over and over the story, as in "the compulsion to repeat." But each text in the cycle structures the interrelationship of love and death differently. Using the basic events in her life from about 1911 until 1919, the three novels remain distinct, as their different titles and authorial signatures emphasize. The first is *Paint It To-Day*, written in 1921 and signed Helga Dart, a name that fleshed out her gender-free initials and signified her lesbian self. The second is *Asphodel*, written in 1921–22, its title page unsigned. The third, *Bid Me to Live (A Madrigal)*, is a novel she called *Madrigal* and signed Delia Alton, a condensed and displaced form of her married name, Hilda Aldington. Written in 1939 and revised after World War II, *Madrigal* was published in 1960 under the name "H.D." and the title *Bid Me to Live (A Madrigal)*, changes that she strenuously protested.[4] After completing *Madrigal* in 1949, H.D. returned to the manuscripts of the earlier texts, which she decided with hindsight were inadequate "drafts" for the final text. Across the title page of *Asphodel* she wrote, "DESTROY   Draft for *Madrigal*," and in *H.D. by Delia Alton*, a meditative essay written in 1949–50 on her own work, she reflects:

> *Madrigal*, left simmering or fermenting, is run through a vintner's sieve, the dregs are thrown out. Really, this is not bad. We began on that vineyard in 1921. It was stony. We grubbed up dead roots, trimmed and pruned. But the grapes were sour. We went on. It was a pity to let that field (1914–1918) lie utterly fallow. We returned to it, from time to time. At last, winter 1949, we taste the 1939 gathering. Impossible but true. The War I novel has been fermenting away during War II. This is intoxicating, the red grapes of —
>
                         War?   Love?   (212)

    Paint It To-Day and *Asphodel* are both drafts of *Madrigal* and dramatically different novels about the same period in her life. H.D. prepared all three for publication, but she suppressed the first two, at least partially because they dealt with lesbian desire and illegitimate motherhood.[5] But instead of reading these texts as autonomous or as inadequate "drafts" that teleologically lead up to the intended and fully realized "final" text, I want to suggest that we read them as distinct parts of a larger composite "text" whose parts are like the imperfectly erased layers of a palimpsest, one whose textual and political unconscious can be read with a psychoanalytic, intertextual hermeneutic.

READING THE TEXT-AS-PSYCHE:
A PSYCHOPOLITICAL HERMENEUTIC

The Madrigal Cycle is a palimpsest that can serve paradigmatically for "the return of the repressed" in women's narratives of the modernist period.

By invoking Freud's phrase, I do not want to suggest that women's writing in general — and H.D.'s Madrigal Cycle in particular — is a symptom of history's dis-ease, but rather to propose that his hermeneutic for recovery of the repressed can be useful first for reading women's narratives as the repressed of history, and second for interpreting the repressed narratives in women's writing.[6] As the return of the repressed, women's narrative serves as the textual and political unconscious of the dominant phallocentric narrative tradition. Women's narrative has within itself as well a textual and political unconscious that can be deciphered in relation to the repression and oppression of women in history. Adapting Freud to a feminist project, I want to propose a psychopolitical hermeneutic for reading women's narratives that decodes them as articulations of what has been forbidden to women, that reads them as effects of ideological and psychological censorship, and that overinterprets them as part of an endless web of intertexts. I will begin by articulating some general principles for this approach and then show how it can be used to decode the return of the repressed narrative in textual clusters like H.D.'s Madrigal Cycle.

Literary narratives are neither dreams nor symptoms. But as indirect fictionalizations, they often share with these articulations of the unconscious the linguistic mechanisms of production that Freud associated with the grammar of the dream work and the psychodynamics of repression and desire, governed by the "censor," that mysterious personification of the force that forbids. Whether in dream or novel, narrative is a form of linguistic disguise — in Freud's terms, a manifest form that reveals latent and forbidden desire as a compromise between the conflicting needs of expression and repression. The mechanisms of the dream work that accomplish the compromise are like, according to Freud, the strategies of a political writer who must disguise dangerous content so as to fool the censor who works on behalf of the oppressive state. Both external and internal censors, Freud writes, compel "apparently innocent disguise": "The stricter the censorship, the more far-reaching will be the disguise and the more ingenious too may be the means employed for putting the reader on the scent of the true meaning" (*Interpretation of Dreams* 175–76).[7]

Freud's hermeneutic in turn fools the censor — undoes the suppression of the social order, the repression of the psyche — by a process that he names "decoding" and variously images as an archeological dig, a journey into the labyrinth, an unraveling of woven threads, a translation of pictographic runes, a detective analysis of mystery and disguise, a removal of the layers in a palimpsest — all resonant metaphors for a corresponding literary decoding. Beginning in determinacy, his method ends in indeterminacy. Dreams *have* "authors," "intentions," and "meanings" to be decoded, he affirms. But their "overdetermination" necessitates an unending "overinterpretation," an infinite regress of interpretation that ultimately leads to the threshold of mystery. "There is," Freud writes in *The Interpretation of Dreams*, "at least one spot in every dream at which it is unplumbable — a navel, as it were, that is its point of contact with the unknown" (143).[8]

As the dream's "navel," the unplumbable aporia of the dream text for Freud is the point of contact with the maternal body, the irretrievable site of origins. Freud's metaphor for the gap or knot in the dream text and the text of dream interpretation privileges woman — specifically the maternal — as origin of what is censored, what is disguised in the grammar of the dream work. Ultimately, his figurative formulation suggests, the return of the repressed is the return of woman, of that mother/other, to him forever unknown, untranscribable, untranslatable.

Freud's method for "overinterpretation" is fundamentally intertextual. He rejects what he calls the "symbolic" method of dream interpretation which analyzes the dream as an autonomous unit with interrelating parts — a method that is strikingly consonant with the theory of art that Stephen Dedalus expounded in Joyce's *Stephen Hero* and *Portrait* and that New Criticism developed into a method. Freud proposes instead his psychoanalytic method, in which fragments of the dream become departure points into a labyrinth of associations that radiate without end into the dreamer's recent and distant past, the linguistic and visual artifacts of culture, and the events of history.

Freud also breaks down the autonomy of the dream text by reading dreams in relation to other dreams, decoding a series of dreams as a composite text. In "consecutive dreams," one dream often "takes as its central point something that is only on the periphery of the other and *vice versa*" (*Interpretation of Dreams* 563). Reading serial dreams requires an analysis of the gaps in each that can be filled in by the other — the traces of displacement, condensation, and secondary revision that can be deciphered by juxtaposing and superimposing the texts in the whole series. The resonances among the dreams — the consonances and dissonances — can themselves be read for clues to undo the work of the Censor. As he writes about dreams occurring in the same night:

The content of all dreams that occur during the same night forms part of the same whole. . . . successive dreams of this kind . . . may be giving expression to the same impulses in different material. If so, the first of these homologous dreams to occur is often the more distorted and timid, while the succeeding one will be more confident and distinct. (*Interpretation of Dreams* 369)

This formulation of successive dreams anticipates Freud's concept of the repetition compulsion and transference. Repressed desires lead a person to "repeat" patterns of behavior as the person "transfers" the feelings from early childhood onto the contemporary adult scene. The analytic situation triggers the "transference": the analysand repeats with the analyst the patterns he or she once enacted with others. The goal of analysis, Freud believes, is to move the analysand from "repetition" to "remembering" by "working through" the transference. Once an adult can "remember" the past, he or she is no longer doomed to "repeat" it (*Therapy and Technique* 157–66).

Freud's intertextual hermeneutic and related concepts of transference are richly suggestive for literary analysis because writing, like dreams, can enact a negotiation between desire and repression in which linguistic disguise accomplishes a compromise between expression and suppression. When the novel is autobiographical, this negotiation—which may be conscious or unconscious—is further heightened. Like a palimpsest, both psyche and literary text are layered, with repressed elements erupting in disguised forms onto the manifest surface of consciousness, of a text. Adapting Kristeva's formulations of the text-as-psyche, critics such as Jonathan Culler, Shoshana Felman, Fredric Jameson, and Michael Riffaterre further suggest that a text has an unconscious accessible to interpretation through a decoding of its linguistic traces and effects. For Culler and Felman, this textual unconscious is located in the interaction between reader and text, which they see as a scene of transference in which the reader "repeats" the complexes of the text. For Jameson and Riffaterre, the textual unconscious resides in the text, subject to the decoding of the reader, who occupies the authoritative position of the analyst. According to Riffaterre, the surface of a novel is narrative, but it has a lyric "subtext," a "verbal unconscious" buried etymologically inside the manifest words of the text. For Jameson, texts have a "political unconscious," which he defines as the repressed narrative of class struggle which a marxist hermeneutic can interpret (20). From another perspective, Culler suggests, "the literary unconscious is an authorial unconscious, an unconscious involved in the production of literature; and the notion is thus useful for raising questions about the relation between what gets into the work and what gets left out, and about the sorts of repression that may operate in the production of literature" (369).

All these approaches to the textual unconscious are useful for reading chains of related texts intertextually. The "draft" may contain elements that are repressed and transformed by linguistic mechanisms analogous to those of the dream work as the author revises the text. In becoming more "artful," the "final" version may indeed subject the "draft" to the process of linguistic encoding analogous to the production of a dream out of the forbidden desires restricted to the unconscious. In political terms, the repression of what is forbidden in the change from "draft" to "final"

text may reflect the role of ideology as an internalized censor that allows
the revelation of a given story only if it is concealed through the mechanisms of the dream work. Existence of the "draft" potentially aids the
interpretation of what is hidden in the "final" text. The earlier text may
erupt into the gaps of the later text just as cultural and political rebellion
disrupts the social order. Textual repression can reflect cultural and political oppression. Representing "the return of the repressed," the "draft"
version may contain a powerful and forbidden critique of the social order
reflected in the "final" text.

On the other hand, a chain of drafts and texts with the same characters
invokes Freud's theory of serial dreams and repetition. Especially in autobiographical texts, *writing*, as well as reading, can be regarded as a scene
of transference. Different "drafts" of a final text or texts in a series can
be interpreted as "repetitions" in which the author is "working through"
conflicts in an effort (conscious or unconscious) to move from "repetition" to "remembering." Within this context, the earlier "drafts" might
well be the most repressed. Similarly, in a series of texts with the same
character, the early text may be the most distorted or "timid," while the
last text might represent the author's success in working through repetition to remembering.

I am suggesting, in other words, the necessity of reading a chain of
related texts "both ways"—on the one hand refusing to regard the "final"
text simply as the aesthetically superior and teleological endpoint of all
the others; on the other hand, recognizing that repression can be present
at the beginning as well as the end of the process. Rather than searching
for the "authentic" or "intended" version, I want to regard all versions
as part of a larger composite text whose parts remain distinct, yet interact
according to a psychopolitical dynamic to which we have some access with
the help of Freud's theory of repression and grammar for the dream work.
These processes may be the result of conscious decisions on the part of
the author or of unconscious negotiations of which the author was largely
unaware. Sometimes these processes can be charted empirically by reading the "drafts" and "final" text as they intersect with texts in the biographical archive. At other times, they are traceable only through an
interpretation of their effects in the texts at hand. But in either case, the
critic needs a flexible concept of intertextuality that examines the clash-
ing and blending of texts from the biographical, literary, and cultural
records.

But for writing by women, situated as they are in the subject position
as knower and knowing within a culture that denies them that status, what
could "the return of the repressed" mean? If women themselves are what
is forbidden and forbidding in their insistent return in male narratives—

as Freud's metaphor of the dream's unplumbable navel suggests—how do we decipher their own narratives? Reading women's narrative as "the return of the repressed," I want to suggest, means reading psychopolitically, seeing women's writing as an insistent record—a trace, a web, a palimpsest, a rune, a disguise—of what has not or cannot be spoken directly because of the external and internalized censors of patriarchal social order. Operating within the dialectic of speech and silence, women (or women's texts) often consciously or unconsciously negotiate a compromise between revelation and concealment of the forbidden through textual disguise. Often, the more public the text, the greater the disguise; the more private the text, the greater its revelations. Paradoxically, the price of public speech is sometimes the silence of protective distortion. The price of private speech is the silence of its absence from the public domain. Women may talk louder and more directly in the closet; but a closet is a closet is a closet.

All four concepts of the textual unconscious proposed by Jameson, Culler, Felman, and Riffaterre are useful for decoding women's narrative—*if* we set aside the marxist imperialism of Jameson's privileging of class struggle, the hermeneutic pessimism of Culler's and Felman's insistence on the reader's inevitable repetition compulsion, the reductionism of reading a text as biography. Read in relation to an author, a woman's narrative can be decoded for "what gets into the work and what gets left out"—read, in other words, with a focus on the mechanisms of censorship (both external and internal) in the production of the work. Read in relation to transference, a woman's narrative can be interpreted as a site (cite) of resistance and what Freud called "working through" the "repetition compulsion" to "remembering" (*Therapy and Technique* 157-66). Read in relation to history, a woman's narrative can be translated as a forbidden story that exists within and threatens to disrupt the social order.

Such an integrated psychopolitical hermeneutic unites considerations of oppression and repression—the very binary that according to Elaine Marks has divided the two main currents of French feminism: the psychoanalytic theorists including Hélène Cixous, Luce Irigaray, and Julia Kristeva, who variously argue that phallogocentrism has repressed the discourse of the Other, the feminine, the different; and the materialist theorists like Monique Wittig, inheritors of the existentialist-marxist feminism of Simone de Beauvoir, who argue that women are oppressed by the social construction of "femininity" by the dominant patriarchal order.[9] This integration of oppression and repression does not transcend the binary; rather it maintains the distinction to focus on the interplay of each dynamic in the narrative inscription and its translation, an integrative move fostered by Freud's own explanation of censorship.

READING THE MADRIGAL CYCLE PSYCHOPOLITICALLY

H.D.'s Madrigal Cycle read intertextually and psychopolitically is a scene of (self)censorship that represents the return of the repressed. As the site of transformation from the "raw" to the "cooked," each novel enacts the dynamic of repression and desire differently. The ingredients are the same, but the recipe is different. Read intertextually, these texts form different layers of the psyche, different surfaces of the palimpsest, each one of which erupts into the others. The gaps and omissions in one text are filled by the surface of another. One text, in other words, serves as the textual unconscious of another. The differences among the texts — interpreted with the aid of Freud's grammar for the dream work — point to ways in which all three texts constitute the political unconscious of history, the repressed narratives of forbidden female desire.

The events that H.D. transmutes in the three novels can be usefully summarized, although Jameson's warning in *The Political Unconscious* that we can approach "the Real" only through its endless textualizations reminds us that such a summary is interpretive, not "fact" in any absolute sense.[10] After her on-again-off-again engagement to Ezra Pound had essentially dissolved, H.D. left the States for Europe in 1911 in the company of the woman she loved, Frances Josepha Gregg, and Mrs. Gregg. In 1912, Gregg refused to stay in London with H.D., and shocked H.D. by marrying. In turn, H.D. fell in love with British poet Richard Aldington, with whom she translated the Greeks, wrote poetry, and traveled in Italy. They married in 1913 and as poet-companion-lovers became leaders in the imagist movement. Shortly after the Germans sank the *Lusitania*, H.D.'s first child was born dead in May of 1915, "from shock and repercussions of war news broken to me in a rather brutal fashion" (*Tribute to Freud* 40). She was told to avoid another pregnancy until after the war to save the doctors for the wounded soldiers. Aldington's affairs with other women started as early as the spring of 1916. Although he opposed the war bitterly, Aldington enlisted in the spring of 1916 and left for the front in December of 1916. He seemed to don his Tommy uniform in spirit as well as flesh, and his leaves became increasingly disastrous. Disillusioned and despairing, he mocked poetry and sought passion in the arms of Dorothy Yorke, the woman H.D. was protecting for Cournos at 44 Mecklenburgh Square. In the fall of 1917 H.D. was also sheltering Frieda and D. H. Lawrence, expelled from Cornwall for suspected spying. But her vitally important friendship with Lawrence fell apart as the affair between them that Frieda apparently fostered never materialized and as H.D.'s relationship with Cecil Gray began in early 1918. Her escape from London's bombs to Gray's house in Cornwall in March of 1918 was healing, but left her unexpectantly pregnant in July of 1918, just days after Bryher first came to visit. Aldington approved of the affair and hoped for the restoration of their marriage after the war. But he was very upset by her consequent pregnancy in August of 1918. His letters alternately expressed anger and promised support, with the constant threat of his passion for Yorke in the wings. Compounding this ambivalence was his continued enthusiasm for her talent, his adoration of her "spirit," and his passion for the "body" of Yorke.

The war continued to intensify H.D.'s personal suffering. Her brother Gilbert died in France in September of 1918; her father's subsequent stroke led to his death just weeks before the baby was due. Taking "the place" of Frances Gregg (*Advent* 152), Bryher was adoring, but suicidally in need of support. Pound, whom H.D. had barely seen in years, appeared at the nursing home to tell her that the baby should have been his. Contraction of the deadly epidemic flu in the final period of pregnancy spelled death, but mother and babe miraculously survived the birth on March 31, due in part to Bryher's devotion and promise of a trip to Greece. A shell-shocked Aldington appeared with daffodils and a plea for reunion. But when she arrived at his hotel in April, he brutally rejected her and threatened prison if she dared to register the child with his name. Emotional breakdown followed. Recovery came with Bryher on an idyllic trip to the Scilly Isles in July of 1919, where H.D. had the first of several visionary experiences in her travels with Bryher, culminating in the "writing on the wall" in Corfu in the spring of 1920. Cut off completely from the community of artists with whom she had forged her early success, she lived out the first year of the new decade with Bryher and her fatherless child. Beginning the decade as a unit of two daughters with a mother, she ended it in a family of two mothers and a daughter.

Bid Me to Live (A Madrigal), the last text in the Madrigal series, is in some ways the most condensed and displaced version of these events, which suggests that the artful disguise of the dream work has been significant in the text's production. Establishing the frame of her autobiographical account, *Madrigal* is set in London and Cornwall during 1917 and 1918, with flashbacks to scenes of an idyllic courtship in 1912–13 and the still-birth in 1915. Outside the frame of the public text is H.D.'s love for Frances Gregg and Bryher at the beginning and end of the decade. Repressed within the frame is the story of her pregnancy in 1918. The stories of the lesbian and the mother of an "illegitimate" child are repressed, censored out of a text that focuses on the story of heterosexual marriage in wartime. This textual repression of forbidden narratives reflects the oppression of mothers and lesbians within the dominant patriarchal discourses of the father. Nonetheless, *Madrigal* docs represent "the return of the repressed."

In relationship to phallocentric articulations of Love and War, *Madrigal* deconstructs the binary of public and private to examine not only the war at home faced by civilians, but also the war *in* the home, the marriage bed as battlefield of sexual politics. For Rafe, the Aldington figure in the novel, home is a refuge; love is a respite from battle. For his wife Julia, the H.D. figure, love exists in a postlapsarian world structured by violence. Rafe's kiss pours the death of battle into her lungs with the gas that never leaves him. As H.D. later reflects on herself-in-Julia, "I had accepted the Establishment. That is, I had accepted the whole cosmic, bloody show. *The war was my husband*" (*Thorn Thicket* 13).

Like Woolf in *Three Guineas*, H.D. regards the battlefields of war as extensions of the politics of the patriarchal family—not that husband and wife were implacable enemies, but rather that the configurations of desire made "Love" and "War" interpenetrating, like Freud's dialectic of eros and thanatos. As both poet and wife, Julia finds herself caught in the representations of the men who love her. Both Rafe and Rico, the Lawrence figure, divide women into minds and bodies, a version of the virgin-whore dichotomy. For them, Julia is untouchable, cerebral, spiritual; for sex, they turn to earthy, stereotypically feminine women. Julia turns to her poetry as the one loophole out of this male trap. But with her writing criticized by each man, she must also write herself out of their textual and linguistic authority. The novel concludes with a long letter to Rico, in which the abandoned Julia envisions the poem she writes as a child born in an androgynous *gloire*.

Madrigal uses the metaphor of the gap to point to the story of the mother that it has repressed. While Rafe is making love to Julia, she remembers the annihilating "wound" of the stillbirth "that gaped at her" (14). It was "a gap in her consciousness, a sort of black hollow, a cave, a pit of blackness; black nebula. . . . The greater the gap in consciousness, the more black-hole-of-Calcutta the gap; the more unformed the black nebula" (13–14). Julia's memory of the stillbirth is *Madrigal*'s black hole, an invisible source of immense power into which the stories of *Paint It To-Day* and *Asphodel* have disappeared.

Asphodel fills the black hole of *Madrigal* in two ways—by restoring the lesbian frame and by narrating the story of the poet-mother in wartime. As the most expansive and longest of the three, *Asphodel* opens with the figures of two women—Hermione and Fayne—entering Europe in 1911 and closes with two women—Hermione and Beryl—setting up house to care for the new baby. But this textualization of H.D.'s love for Frances and Bryher is not what motivates the narrative middle. Part I of *Asphodel* records the dissolution of the lesbian pair into the plots of heterosexual courtship. Part II of *Asphodel*, which parallels *Madrigal* quite closely, highlights first the stillbirth of 1915, and then the illegitimate pregnancy of 1918. The story of marriage foregrounded in *Madrigal* is still present in *Asphodel*, but muted in comparison. Reading Part II of *Asphodel* and *Madrigal* as superimposed layers of a palimpsest, we can interpret the public text as a critique of the sexual politics of marriage and the repressed text as a critique of the sexual politics of motherhood. The stillbirth is not simply the "wound" that has been covered over, as it is in *Madrigal*. Rather, it is the narrative focus—the return of the repressed narrative—a death caused by an air raid in a social order where women (re)produce cannon fodder, where mothers and soldiers "go over the top" in a symbiotic system of war and birth.[11] "Men and guns, women and babies," Hermione thinks; "she had had a baby in an air raid just like Daily Mail atrocities" (16–17). Hermione's metonymic thought—"Khaki killed it"— applies directly to the child and more figuratively to what the child represents, the lost renewal of civilization (2–4).

The choice that Hermione makes in *Asphodel* not to abort her second pregnancy marks her defiance of the death-driven war machine of modern life. Sitting Druid-like on the rocks in the clear, bright sunlight of Cornwall, Hermione identifies with the mortal women impregnated by the gods and gives her coming child a Divine Father. Witchlike, a "Morgan le Fay," Hermione speaks in a discourse of pregnancy that anticipates Kristeva's concept of the pre-oedipal "semiotic" register of language, the rhythmic discourse of the maternal body—one that deconstructs the opposition of inside/outside, container/contained; one that hypnotically weaves a web of meaning based in sound, color, and cadence instead of reference; one that refuses the pronoun distinctions that separate self and other.[12] When Hermione's interior monologue turns to her pregnancy, the semiotic modality of discourse is especially heightened. To quote a few instances of this discourse of pregnancy in the unsigned text of the repressed mother:

You tasted grape and grape and gold grape (can you imagine it?) and gold on gold and gold filled your palate, pushed against your mouth, pushed down your throat, filled you with some divine web, a spider, gold web and you wove with it, wove with it, wove with the web inside you. . . . (68–69)

I feel no difference between in and out. . . . for inside and outside are the same, God in and out, all god, gorse, pollen-dust, gold and gold of rayed light slanting across the low spikes of white orchid and fragrance in and out. . . . (87–88)

Weave, that is your metier Morgan le Fay, weave subtly, weave grape-green by grape-silver and let your voice weave songs, songs in the little hut that gets so blithely cold, cold with such clarity that you are like a flower of green-grape flowering in a crystal globe, in an ice globe for the air that you breathe into your lungs makes you too part of the crystal, you are part of the air, part of the crystal. . . . (119)

The images of pregnancy repeated in passages like these erupt into the surface of *Madrigal*, but shorn of their association with procreativity. The pregnancy in Cornwall is repressed in *Madrigal*, but its erasure is imperfect. Julia walks and sits in the same circle of Druid stones on Cornwall's harsh shoreline in *Madrigal*. *Asphodel*'s images of pregnancy—the "crystal globe," the cocoon, the Holy Spirit, the fragrance, the web, weaving, and so forth—reappear repeatedly in *Madrigal*, but cut off from their fertile referents in pregnancy. Even the name "Morgan le Fay"—Hermione's pregnant self in *Asphodel*—has been displaced in *Madrigal* onto "Morgan," the "witch" who is the first to steal Rafe in the plot of heterosexual romance. *Asphodel*'s narrative of illicit procreation is displaced into *Madrigal*'s narrative of relatively less forbidden creation—the (re)creation of the poet Julia and her child-poem out of the ashes of war. As separate texts, *Asphodel* and *Madrigal* tell different stories—one of the mother, the other of the lover. But superimposed as traces in a palimpsestic psyche, they articulate a poetics of (pro)creativity.

Asphodel, however, also has its black hole into which *Paint It To-Day*—the narrative of lesbian love—has been absorbed. As the story of desire most forbidden by the phallocentric narratives of history, *Paint It To-Day* is the textual and political unconscious of *Asphodel*. What exists as the static lesbian frame of *Asphodel* implodes into the middle to become the narrative kinesis of *Paint It To-Day*. *Paint It To-Day* cuts the frame on the events in H.D.'s life much like *Asphodel*—the novel begins and ends with a lesbian pair. But the middle movement establishes an Artemisian discourse, a lesbian wilderness of landscape and desire that is literally another world away from the material conditions of history: the heterosexual scripts of love and war. These scripts have an existence in the novel—Josepha leaves Midget to marry; Midget herself marries; and "There was a war. A cloud. Five years. . . . Time had them by the throat, shaking and shaking, evil and vicious" (V, 1). But men and war exist at the periphery of the narrative—the Pound figure scarcely has a name; he is called most often the "erstwhile fiancé," then simply "the erstwhile." At the narrative center is a wild pastoral of hyacinthian desire, imaged in the part of Hyde Park that "has been left wild and free in homage to the tall blue hyacinths [that] rise like islands in the short grass" (VIII, 9–10).

With Josepha's betrayal, Midget finds her escape from the social order through a "trick"—she leaves her body caught in the coordinates of narrative space and time and imaginatively travels to a timeless, placeless lyric state of mind governed by the spirit of Artemis. There she meets Althea, a healing projection of one part of her self in the psychodrama of this transferential text. Dressed in "tunics," with "bare upper legs," the two women battle a fierce storm in their canoe, strip off their wet clothes, and stand on a whortleberry blanket to warm their naked bodies before the "smoldering brazier" (VIII). Like maids of Artemis, the women are strong, athletic, chaste. Eroticism is covertly present, sublimated into their battle against the storm, their undressing before the fire, the pastoral landscape where the wind catches "the branches of the white rose-tree," where the "plumes of the wild willow . . . drift across Midget's shoulder" (VII, 8). Midget's task is to bring this Neo-platonic lesbian realm into the real space and time of history, to inscribe this Artemisian discourse in her art.

In the context of the dominant phallocentric narratives of history, *Paint It To-Day* represents the return of the repressed — the lesbian narrative of women's writing as the political unconscious of patriarchal cultural scripts. But in relation to writing as the scene of the author's transference, *Paint It To-Day* is only the first narrative of a story H.D. repeated again and again. To read "both ways" in an intertextual, psychopolitical hermeneutic, we should avoid privileging the earliest text as the most radical in a "political" sense. To do so would merely reverse the current practice of privileging the last text as the teleological endpoint of artistic revision. In relation to H.D.'s life, each textual (re)creation of the war decade represents a "repetition" of those events. As the writing self, H.D. was caught in the round of repetitions that signal the transference. Instead of remembering the past — gaining control over it by making an orderly story about it — the writing self gets swallowed up by the narrated self and is compelled to repeat the past. The re-vision of the story in each successive text can represent the writing self's attempt to reassert her authority by interpreting instead of repeating what she has repressed. From this perspective, we could expect that the later texts might include stories that were repressed in the earlier ones.

This is indeed the case in H.D.'s Madrigal Cycle. Her suffering during the war years made the more politically acceptable stories of mother and wife more painful to remember than the culturally tabooed story of her lesbian love. Consequently, *Paint It To-Day* represses these heterosexual episodes, which exist as mere traces or not at all in the surface of this celebration of Artemisian maidenhood. *Asphodel* confronts head-on the pain of the stillbirth and the trauma of the second pregnancy. But it does not touch the loss of Lawrence, it scarcely hints of the intense love H.D. felt for Aldington, and it only barely suggests the artistic crisis that is central to *Madrigal*. In the transferential scene of writing, H.D. moved from repeating to remembering what she had repressed.

The three texts of the Madrigal Cycle stand alone and together. As a cluster, they form a palimpsest of imperfectly erased layers. Rather than contradicting each other, they are "mutually complementary," to quote Freud on serial dreams (*Interpretation of Dreams* 369). Never the equivalent of the writing self, they nonetheless originate in H.D. and loop back to her. The wife layer, *Madrigal*, tells the familiar story of triangulated desire in an unfamiliar way, transposing the conventional interplay of love and war into an unconventional exposé of sexual politics on the home front. The mother layer, *Asphodel*, challenges the dominant narratives of history through proposing the discourse of pregnancy in opposition to the engines of war. The lesbian layer, *Paint It To-Day*, suffers the most erasure in the processes of rewriting because within the context of history, its narrative is the most forbidden. Each novel has its own challenge to pose, its own hermeneutic of history. Gender is central to each work's interpretive self-creation. But each novel genders history differently, highlighting different aspects of the gender system. In patriarchy, the stories of motherhood, lesbian love, and heterosexual love are not "autonomous texts," but rather intertextual narratives within the gender system. Taken separately and together, the composite and distinct self-portraits in the Madrigal Cycle (en)gender the historical consciousness of modernism. "This is history": the stories of love and war, creation and procreation, public and private—woven of distinct, but inseparable strands.

Reading textual clusters like H.D.'s Madrigal Cycle as the return of repressed texts suggests some basic strategies for reading the return of the repressed in women's narrative. First, the repression of women's speech and subjectivity in history means that women's narratives should be read oppositionally against and intertextually within the dominant phallocentric discourses of history. As the repressed of history, women have returned again and again to the scene of writing to make their mark, however disguised and undecipherable readers within dominant hermeneutic frames have found that writing to be. Second, women's narratives are themselves the scene of repression—they have their own political and textual unconscious to be deciphered. Reading strategies need to unravel the disguise—the interlocking psychopolitical dynamics of repression and oppression in the textualization of women's desire. We need to read, in other words, for the traces of internal and external censorship in the authors' and texts' negotiation between the desire for speech and the need for disguise. Both strategies for reading the return of the repressed in women's narratives invite an intertextual approach that integrates considerations of the author, the text, and history.

NOTES

This essay is adapted from "The Return of the Repressed in Women's Writing," *Journal of Narrative Technique* 19 (January 1989): 141–56.

1 I disagree with Hayden White's contention in "The Burden of History" that the modernists had no "historical consciousness." Some may have yearned like Stephen Dedalus to awaken from the nightmare of history. But even Joyce's famous line signifies not the lack of a historical consciousness, but the inevitability of it. See Gilbert and Gubar, *No Man's Land,* for a different examination of the relation between history and modernism.

2 See *Thorn Thicket,* in which H.D. reflects that "Bryher came into the *Madrigal* cycle, July 17, 1918, but I do not bring her into the story. The story ends with the letter that Julia writes to Frederico or Lorenzo" (28). In her reflections on her work in *Thorn Thicket,* H.D. does not specify particular texts as part of the "Madrigal cycle," but rather seems to attach the phrase to a particular point in her life — namely the time frame of World War I. Bryher was a part of that story after their meeting on July 17, 1918, and she "comes into" the texts of both *Paint It To-Day* and *Asphodel.* H.D. regarded the texts about her life during World War I as the basic layer upon which the texts about World War II were superimposed, as palimpsest. She referred to the imagist poet H.D. as the "pre-*Madrigal* H.D." In our "'I had two loves separate': The Sexualities of H.D.'s *HER*" (in this volume), Rachel DuPlessis and I included *HER* in the "*Madrigal* cycle," along with *Asphodel* and *Paint It To-Day.* I would now alter that inclusion somewhat. Although *HER* features characters with the same names as those in *Asphodel* (e.g., Hermione and Fayne), it does not deal with the war; the roman à clef focuses on the making of the "pre-*Madrigal* H.D." I think that the term "Madrigal" resonated for H.D. with the issues of war and love (love-in-war) for reasons that I touch on in this text and explore at length in *Penelope's Web.*

3 H.D. was very familiar with the works of both Woolf and Freud. Her knowledge of Freud may have gone back as far as 1910; by the early twenties, Bryher followed up on the suggestion of Havelock Ellis that she subscribe to the *International Psychoanalytic Journal,* which both women read all through the twenties and thirties. In *Tribute to Freud,* H.D. specifically mentions a number of Freud's books, as well as his theory of Eros and death. While Freud's ideas certainly reinforced H.D.'s, it would be a mistake to attribute them to Freud (or Woolf) because H.D.'s critique was strongly present in *Paint It To-Day* and *Asphodel,* written before she could have had much sustained exposure to *Beyond the Pleasure Principle* or the later *Jacob's Room* (1922) and *Mrs. Dalloway* (1925).

4 The significance of these noms de plume in relation to H.D.'s imagist lyric and narrative fiction is discussed at length in *Penelope's Web.*

5 See Friedman and DuPlessis, "Foreword"; we have published the first four

chapters of *Paint It To-Day*; Cassandra Laity will edit the complete novel. *Asphodel* is unpublished but Robert Spoo is preparing an edition to be published by Duke UP. For a discussion of H.D.'s suppression of other lesbian texts, see Friedman and DuPlessis, " 'I had two loves separate.' "

6   The phrase "the return of the repressed" appears in Freud, "Negation" (1925), reprinted in *General Psychological Theory* 111–12.

7   Only in his so-called speculative writing, in which he theorized about the connection between the psyche and society — about, in other words, the psychological dimensions of social contract — did Freud seriously consider the significance of his comparison between state censorship and the internal censor. See especially *Totem and Taboo* and *Civilization and Its Discontents*.

8   See also p. 564. Freud uses the terms "overdetermination" and "overinterpretation" throughout this volume, as well as the metaphors cited above. "Analysis Terminable and Interminable," Freud's final essay on clinical technique, stresses the indeterminacy of interpretation (*Therapy and Technique* 233–72).

9   See Marks, "Women and Literature in France," and *New French Feminisms* 28–38.

10 Particularly sensitive to the problem of textualization and subjective fictionalizations, I have built this outline mainly from H.D.'s accounts in letters, journals, memoirs, divorce papers, and (with great care) autobiographical novels. Aldington's letters from the front in 1918 provide important corroboration of H.D.'s versions of the events in this critical year. I have also found other memoirs, letters, and fictionalizations useful, especially by Aldington, Bryher, Perdita Schaffner, Robert McAlmon, Lawrence, Pound, John Cournos, and Brigit Patmore.

11 See Huston for a related critique of mothers and soldier-heroes in patriarchal ideology.

12 See Kristeva, *Revolution in Poetic Language* 22–30 and *Desire in Language* 237–70.

WORKS CITED

Aldington, Richard. *The Complete Poems*. London: Allan Wingate, 1948.

Aldington, Richard. *Reverie: A Little Book of Poems for H.D.* Cleveland: Clerk's Press, 1917.

Barthes, Roland. "The Death of the Author." *Image — Music — Text*, trans. Stephen Heath, 142–48. New York: Hill and Wang, 1977.

Culler, Jonathan. *The Pursuit of Signs*. Ithaca: Cornell UP, 1981.

Culler, Jonathan. "Textual Self-Consciousness and the Textual Unconscious." *Style* 18 (Summer 1984): 369–76.

Felman, Shoshana. *Lacan and the Adventure of Insight: Psychoanalysis in Contemporary Culture*. Cambridge: Harvard UP, 1987.

Felman, Shoshana. "Turning the Screw of Interpretation." *Yale French Studies* 55/56 (1977): 94–207.

Foucault, Michel. "What Is an Author?" *Textual Strategies: Perspectives in Post-Structuralist Criticism*, ed. Josué V. Harari, 141–60. Ithaca: Cornell UP, 1979.

Freud, Sigmund. *Beyond the Pleasure Principle* (1920). Trans. James Strachey. New York: Norton, 1961.

Freud, Sigmund. *Civilization and Its Discontents* (1930). Trans. James Strachey. New York: Norton, 1961.

Freud, Sigmund. *General Psychological Theory*. Ed. Philip Rieff. New York: Collier, 1963.

Freud, Sigmund. *The Interpretation of Dreams* (1900). Trans. James Strachey. New York: Avon, 1965.

Freud, Sigmund. *Therapy and Technique*. Ed. Philip Rieff. New York: Collier Books, 1963.

Freud, Sigmund. *Totem and Taboo* (1913). Trans. James Strachey. New York: Norton, 1950.

Friedman, Susan Stanford. *Penelope's Web: Gender, Modernity, H.D.'s Fiction*. New York: Cambridge UP, 1990.

Friedman, Susan Stanford and Rachel Blau DuPlessis. "Foreword to *Paint It To-Day*." *Contemporary Literature* 27 (Winter 1986): 440–43.

Friedman, Susan Stanford and Rachel Blau DuPlessis. " 'I had two loves separate': The Sexualities of H.D.'s *HER*." *Montemora* 8 (1981): 7–30.

Gallop, Jane. "Lacan and Literature: A Case for Transference." *Poetics* 13 (1984).

Gilbert, Sandra M., and Susan Gubar. *No Man's Land: The Place of the Woman Writer in the Twentieth Century*. New Haven: Yale UP, 1988.

H.D. (Hilda Doolittle). *Advent* (1948). In *Tribute to Freud* 113–88.

H.D. *Asphodel* (1921–22). Manuscript at Beinecke Rare Book and Manuscript Library, Yale University.

H.D. *Bid Me to Live (A Madrigal)*. New York: Grove Press, 1960.

H.D. *Collected Poems 1912–1944*. Ed. Louis L. Martz. New York: New Directions, 1983.

H.D. *H.D. by Delia Alton* (1949–50). *Iowa Review* 16 (1986): 174–221.

H.D. *Paint It To-Day* (1921). Manuscript at Beinecke Library. Chapters I–IV in *Contemporary Literature* 27 (Winter 1986): 444–74.

H.D. *Thorn Thicket* (1960). Manuscript at Beinecke Library.

H.D. *Tribute to Freud* (1956). Boston: David R. Godine, 1974.

Huston, Nancy. "The Matrix of War: Mothers and Heroes." *The Female Body in Western Culture: Contemporary Perspectives*, ed. Susan Rubin Suleiman. Cambridge: Harvard UP, 1986.

Jameson, Fredric. *The Political Unconscious: Narrative as a Socially Symbolic Act*. Ithaca: Cornell UP, 1981.

Kristeva, Julia. *Desire in Language: A Semiotic Approach to Literature and Art*. Ed. Leon Roudiez. Trans. Thomas Gora et al. New York: Columbia UP, 1980.

Kristeva, Julia. *Revolution in Poetic Language*. Trans. Margaret Walker. New York: Columbia UP, 1984.

Marks, Elaine. "Women and Literature in France." *Signs* 3 (Summer 1978): 832–42.

Marks, Elaine, and Isabelle de Courtivron, eds. *New French Feminisms*. Amherst: U of Massachusetts P, 1980.

Riffaterre, Michael. "The Intertextual Unconscious." *Critical Inquiry* 13 (Winter 1987): 371–85.

White, Hayden. "The Burden of History." *Tropics of Discourse: Essays in Cultural Criticism*, 27–50. Baltimore: Johns Hopkins UP, 1978.

CHAPTER 14

Excerpts from "Language Acquisition"

RACHEL BLAU DUPLESSIS

. . . her wavering hieroglyph . . .
—H.D., *HER*

We suggest that naming, always originating in a place (the *chora*, space, "topic,"
subject-predicate), is a *replacement* for what the speaker perceives as an archaic
mother—a more or less victorious confrontation, never finished with her.
—Julia Kristeva, *Desire in Language*

1.

This is the task of wildflower honey.
Quiet. Initiate of sound.
Poetry is about—
Is negated. All gestures of writing
Made suspect by writing.
Song leaf of pure and burnished gold
Porous at a random touch, plissé.

Began to forget "writing."

The secrets of enclosure
Set drooping.

What is first? First is voicing? Was it when we called her Renata Tebaldi
and moved the crib into her own room, separating her, because the con-
certs came too often through the night.

Or was first kitten, sheep, and animal heartless, heartbreaking bleats inside the dead of night. At first it sounds hopeless, then soon, when a
response is patterned, it sounds perpetually enraged. Now is never good
enough; satisfaction had already to have happened before.

253

Is first the chuckle, the chortle, the gurgle, that sounds like delight: that this is, that 'I' this.

Then there is sentence melody; they sing your language before any "language," any "message," any "content."[1] And for the longest time, there is da da. For a long time there is ba ba (which some translate *baby* and others *bottle*). Sometimes a sound comes in floods, then ebbs, an "l" or an "f/v" which crests and then pulls back, some tide moving far away. There are a few other words like "d-g" or "gie" (the second half of *doggie*). With these few syllables, months and months pass in which they are content. And do not (some do not) say ma ma.

These patterns may have no signifying function, but they are socially assimilated in three ways: by translation (baba means bottle), by mimicry, face close to face, to create a dialogue of la la's, and emotionally (this one will not say ma ma).

This babble, these baby melodies

"This *heterogeneousness*, detected genetically in the first echolalias of infants as rhythms and intonations anterior to the first phonemes, morphemes, lexemes, and sentences; this heterogeneousness, which is later reactivated as rhythms, intonations, glossalalias in psychotic discourse, serving as ultimate support of the speaking subject threatened by the collapse of the signifying function; this heterogeneousness to signification operates through, despite, and in excess of it and produces in poetic language 'musical' but also nonsense effects that destroy not only accepted beliefs and significations, but, in radical experiments, syntax itself. . . . We shall call this disposition *semiotic (le sémiotique)*, meaning, according to the etymology of the Greek *sémeion* (σημεῖον), a distinctive mark, trace, index, the premonitory sign, the proof, engraved mark, imprint — in short, a *distinctiveness* admitting of an uncertain and indeterminate articulation because it does not yet refer (for young children) or no longer refers (in psychotic discourse) to a signified object for a thetic consciousness. . . . Plato's *Timaeus* speaks of a *chora* (χώρα), receptacle (ὑποδοχεῖον), unnamable, improbable, hybrid, anterior to naming, to the One, to the father, and consequently, maternally connoted to such an extent that it merits 'not even the rank of syllable'. . . . It goes without saying that, concerning a *signifying practice*, that is, a socially communicable discourse like poetic language, this semiotic heterogeneity posited by theory is inseparable from what I shall call, to distinguish it from the latter, the *symbolic* function of significance."[2]

The inseparability of the two functions: that while it may sing melodies in all and nothing, we in English only hear its English. Translation and focused location occur to filter the heterogeneousness through the meaning-melody we hear, in speaking English. Yet it will always sing more than we can hear.

The semiotic abounds with signs ("mark, trace, index, premonitory sign, proof, engraved mark, imprint" "signet — as from sign, a mark, token, proof; signet — the privy seal, a seal; signet-ring — a ring with a signet or private seal . . .").[3]

What is all of this, and why is it important? Kristeva's location of two developmentally distinct registers of normal language, whose intensity and relationship are heightened in poetic language, offers a powerful picture through which certain elements of gender cruise.

2.

thay hey ho, aydee thay yo you

thay dg,

hyyyi, O, hi

This "master place" of analysis — how to be true to it and to me? What can it mean? Certainly the massive bilaterality of the system can both satisfy and distress. There are two sides, one sidelong, allusively called "maternally connoted"; the other comically, named in more absolute terms "the father." Does this mean that the genders are divided into the one that speaks and the other that cannot be intelligible? At times (as in *About Chinese Women*) Kristeva has implied that the only way a woman makes sense is through identification with the father. This is not helpful. And it is a tautology. Makes sense is a way of speaking as sense is given: a way of speaking the dominant discourses.[4]

But the maternally connoted chora is not silent: there is babble and pulse, intonation, mark and sign. There is everything of language in it but specificity and form. It is the place that could be any language. (Greek, Egyptian) If this area represents the mother, it is a mother visualized as a font of linguality, as well as a mother (they say) repressed by virtue of the transfer of power and allegiance by means of oedipalization: the learning of gender asymmetry, inequalities, one's place in a gendered order.

The "symbolic order" is thus affiliated with the political and social power of dominant discourses. The "semiotic" with the marginal, and with subversion, critique, weakening of the permutations of dominance.[5]

	speaks unheard, from margins
One speaks, the other	has spoken
	will speak

Yet the inseparability of the two functions. When this theory does its dance of naming, we are called into chora, tempted into claiming its dramas. Language in its thickness, layered, can also peel back and become a map of levels, with space behind space.[6]

The interplay of these two sides in H.D. has a particular name: palimpsest. Meaning what it conventionally does in ancient scribal practice: an overwritten page, a script under which is shadowed another script, another text. As H.D. defines this as epigraph to her novel called by that very name: one text "erased" but "imperfectly" to make "room for another" writing. Thematically, morally, textually in H.D. the erasure of the signs (mark, trace, index, imprint) of the "mother"—the text made marginal, by the signs of the "father"—the text of dominance. But imperfect erasure. Can see both writings. Can see them as interactive. Could pick and valorize one (as opposed to the other); could say lower one is original, therefore right. Could say recent one by virtue of that place, closer to now, to our sense of progress towards us, is therefore right. Or, could as well place them together as the situation of writing. Palimpsest is the feel of writing within the consciousness of the producer of poetic language.

So reading (whether choosing one side as the primary though almost eradicated source, or whether mingling both texts by reading all the layers of intercalations) is the key to H.D.'s relation to the "semiotic." And this—although reading or interpreting is, in Kristeva's terms, the precise component missing, absent from the semiotic. Reading would be, definitionally, a function of the "side" of the symbolic. The maternally connoted side would produce only UNreadable marks.

The act of reading must be slid across to the mother.

. . .

4.

It is a peculiarity of Kristeva's analysis that she is so ungiving, so unsuggestive on the subject of women writers. For if all who write are filial, they are for her, more specifically, the sons. In *Desire in Language* all examples of poetic stances and poetic careers engage only with male writers, even though a most profound, elegant, and boldest woman is herself writing. It is odd to read of things "maternally connoted" or to hear that we may "call the moment of rupture and negativity which conditions and underlies the novelty of any praxis 'feminine,' " when this still leaves a little in the air what the specific relations of a woman writer to the semiotic register could be.[7] What is the relation of the woman writer to chora, when she can be that "maternally connoted" area by being/having/wanting mother? Is the chora safe for women? Or do "women tend to move immediately to the other side — the side of symbolic power."[8]

Then, what if the writer is not a "son" but a "daughter." Even if one's preoedipal is the "same" no matter what gender, the fact that our return is mediated through gender must make (could make?) some marked difference in language.

Why (asks Kristeva) does Virginia Woolf "not dissect language as Joyce does"?[9] A question which makes me immediately defensive can be translated into a series of other questions that makes this language a question. Why must Kristeva affirm that Woolf does not dissect language as Joyce does? Why does Virginia Woolf not choose to "dissect language as Joyce does"? Why must Joyce be the standard for such activities in language, Woolf not up to that norm? What is the precise level and kind of rupturing practices that must occur for it to be said that "language is dissected"? Would Stein's be "too much"? What is the place of Woman, static, iconic Woman in Joyce's writing practice? How might that Woman function by virtue of her iconic Otherness? What happens when the writer is Other in systems of discourse? How does Otherness own, write its Otherness when it is not only otherness? How can I (a woman) read my our their his her semiotic? What is a woman writer's negotiation with the semiotic to produce poetic language?

For H.D., on the evidence of *Tribute to Freud*, the semiotic is safest when it can be interwoven with a symbolic (interpretive) function so fluid and polyvalent that it almost annexes itself to the semiotic; the semiotic is therefore safest, most satisfying not when it is glossolalia, not syntactic rupture, not invective/obscenity (Céline-Pound), but when it is expressed as signs.

. . .

9.

There is in fact a plethora of incest in H.D. One of her tasks as a writer seems to have been to naturalize, normalize that "incest" and to overwrite the emotional taboo by measured, articulate, lyric considerations of desires within the family: the depiction of Bertie and Hermione in *HER*, the depiction of the brothers in *Tribute to Freud*, the relation to the father in *Tribute to Freud*, to the mother, the mother-daughter dyad in *Helen in Egypt*

"If it is true that the prohibition of incest constitutes, at the same time, language as communicative code and women as exchange objects in order for a society to be established, *poetic language would be* for its questionable subject-in-process the *equivalent of incest. . . .*"[10]

What does it mean when you both be it (the woman/the mother) and want it (the mother/the woman)? The desire to be folded over onto herself (thus, for both H.D. and Woolf, the charge of narcissism). The desire to be both parts of the dyad at once (thus, for both Woolf and H.D., the charge of preciousness). What can lubricate this otherwise complete abrasion? What prevents a woman who writes from unreadable envelopment, unwritable envelopment?

Often, it is the sign of a reader. Often, it is a book, a reader. Someone must read or be reading. (Mrs. Ramsay is reading, and to James—yet—a tale about the boundless sea when Lily is at first inspired. Mr. Ramsay reads a book across the boundless sea, when Lily finishes.) The vision holds a book. It is an unwritten book. It is the perfect sign of exit from the engulfment of maternal incest from the perspective of a woman writer. It is a listening reader, the reader whose book is always waiting, the tolerant listener (and sometimes the demanding "Write, write, or die!") It is the vision of a Mary with the empty (always to be filled, always fillable) book. Because interpretation is always interminable. Because writing is reading. And there is a sacred triangle: writing (saying); listening (eliciting); reading (interpreting is another form of listening).   "her wavering hieroglyph"   "never finished with her"

10.

or sees an unreadable sign.

If a wall releases writing, pictures called "writing"
if a space brings up (as lighting the cyc, the backdrop, they pronounce
it "psyche"
as in "psyche it out" and it is short for cyclorama, a large curved screen
or curtain
used as a background in stage settings) writing
if a space is readied for the projection of necessities
if a space seems so possible

a hotel room, in a country called Hellas, that landscape of urgency, of
longing in a hotel room in the father-and-master country of our (Western) civilization which H.D. entered only to wedge up, prying, a fulcrum,
what lever? to see the other side, Hellas, the mother, Helen the mother,
Greek myths first learned from a teacher astonishingly named "Miss Helen"
(*Tribute to Freud* 186)
This room H.D. bore 13 years later into Freud's room, his chambers, the
room inside his room.

In another key moment of H.D.'s sorting (out) the lesbian/matrisexual
erotics of Hermione's identity, the heroine sits at the breakfast table with
her mother, trying to recall to her mother the scene in the storm of a liquid
intensity in which a flame of language is lit. She (semicomically, the novel
seems as myopic as Dorothy Richardson but it is also like *Pilgrimage* very,
very funny) chooses to read to her mother from Swinburne's "Itylus," the
poem which, throughout, indicates the passion of Hermione for Fayne
(its "swallow" evokes Bryher as well). A specific event has provoked Her's
quixotic attempt to unify by her qualified power the two forces which are
most obdurately opposed in the novel: maternal and lesbian passion. The
event? the flight of a bird. "Things out of the window, across the window
seemed to be on the window, against the window, like writing on the wall.
Things, a bird skimming across a window, were a sort of writing on a
wall."[11] Here is an evocation, written by H.D. in 1927, of the "Corfu
vision" of 1920 by its "title" which would not be used again until the Freud
experience of 1933–34 (*Tribute to Freud* 169), and then not again until
it was made the title of the Freud memoir in 1944, a title which indicates
H.D.'s entitlement. "I see by that birdflight across an apparently black
[blank?] surface, that curves of wings meant actual things to Greeks, not
just vague symbols but actual hieroglyphics . . . hieroglyphs . . ." (*HER*
125, ellipses in original, of course).

In *HER*, H.D. is clear about the sources of her writing in a reiterated, layered sense of otherness. H.D. postulated a realm of mystery, something beyond, something vitally generative for her writing, a kind of intensity, a sense of presence and power ("Words with Fayne in a room, in any room, became projections of things beyond one" [*HER* 146]). A generative space sends forth signs, and these signs are called by a name which connotes an artfully deciphered writing, distant, mysterious, cryptic, strange, of a strange culture: the hieroglyphs of ancient

~~EGYPT~~ GREECE!

Of course, the hieroglyphs of Egypt, but here she says that the Greeks read hieroglyphs, as later she said about the picture writing on the wall that they are like "Greek vase silhouettes" (*Tribute to Freud* 169), as later she will have Helen become a hieroglyph that she is, that she reads, reading the maternal name/the self, reading Greece/Egypt, ciphering (encoding the mystery)/deciphering (decoding mystery), entering a boundless space of containment (contentment) as a reader (a writer), a hero/ine (a poet), a mother (a daughter), reading Greece (the father, the brother) as Egypt (the mother). To pick out the signs from this space "a distinctive mark, trace, index, the premonitory sigh, the proof, engraved mark, imprint—in short, a *distinctiveness* admitting of an uncertain and indeterminate articulation. . . ." Coming from the old country, one of those old countries, from the mother country.

the premonitory ~~sigh~~ sign

Awakened from illness/madness by the "talking cure," Her walks into the snow, "leaving her wavering hieroglyph as upon white parchment" (*HER* 224). And doing so, she sees that the snowy embankment is a "roll from which more parchment [more space for writing] might be shaken." Writing is listening into the list(en)ing space.

. . .

12.

The chora safe for women. Why have I used the notion of safety except by the assumption that the habits of mind, emotion, and gender position of the male subject offer some secondary protection to the descent, via language and form, to the position before meaning. While female habits of mind, emotion, and gender position may look with vertigo upon the temptation to engulfment, and loss of ego. Or, with unassimilable desire.

H.D. makes the chora safe by concentration, within the semiotic, on those features most closely allied to the symbolic: (un)readable signs, with a further evocation of figures of the reader, the book, interpretation, reading—but only as the activities undertaken in the understanding that the signs remain mysteries, and wisdom is not in translation or identification but in the dark illumination of mystery, its layerings, its implications, the variety of its traces, its metamorphoses, using the sign as portal, as entrance to the area where not reading but readings will forever gush. An activity of mind, a condition of desiring.

One is reminded of Virginia Woolf's pique, anger even, at interpretations of the mark at the end of *To the Lighthouse*.[12]

And so H.D. found a key medium when she found (re-founded) the essay (*The Gift, Tribute to Freud, Compassionate Friendship*), because she makes it the medium of endless interpretation, intellectually bold—bolder indeed than "The Cinema and the Classics" (1927) and thicker, richer than the very short and early *Notes on Thought and Vision* (1919). She makes it palimpsest, she makes it plenitude.

And when she writes out her vision of the picture writing in *Tribute to Freud*, notice that, while she evokes and engages with a rare suggestiveness and multiplicity, she leaves these signs ultimately unreadable, her tribute (or gift) to Freud being first the presence-to-be-reckoned-with of this particular permutation of consciousness—her visions—and second the affirmation of (un)readability, that is, the possibility of meditating upon but never fixing or pinning any sign.

Already, when she went to Freud, she had found to her intense disappointment that she could not use ("use") any of her visions narratively, directly positioning them in a story, as she had tried to do with the Peter Rodeck material in the destroyed novel *Niké*.[13]

(She decided now not to use them, but to let them use her.)

Because in *Tribute to Freud* (despite, no, because of the nuanced intelligence, the cultural range deployed and displayed, the fact that, with such a touch in writing for exfoliation and depiction, such a writer could have done anything), H.D. does not interpret those signs. That is, while she does make local identifications (Jacob's ladder, Delphic tripod, *s*'s like question marks), the better for us to have evoked the resonance of the signs and their impact, H.D. does not narrate any story or prepare any statement that the images make, separately (as static pictures) or together

(as cinematic sequence), although the latter portion of the vision even suggests that direction because it is filmic in conception. Nor does she narrate
or interpret despite the presence of the "determinative" — which "contains"
or "helps clarify or explain" a set of hieroglyphics. She only takes the time
to reject one ("Freudian") reading of one of the hieroglyphs in which
Niké = Athene without spear = castrated woman.[14] She later says that
Freud's own theory was premised upon the nonallegorical reading of these
materials. "There are all these shapes, lines, graphs, the *hieroglyph of the
unconscious*, and the Professor had first opened the field to the study of
this vast, unexplored region. He himself — at least to me personally — deplored the tendency to *fix* ideas too firmly to set symbols, or to weld them
inexorably" (*Tribute to Freud* 93).

She says, when Freud moves in onto her Niké, that in offering her his
theory of castration, "She has lost her spear," "he might have been talking Greek" (*Tribute to Freud* 69). She would rather be talking Egyptian.

13.

What writes *Tribute to Freud*? H.D. said, "I wish to recall the impressions, or rather I wish the impressions to recall me" (*Tribute to Freud* 14).
This no longer sounds like a sentimental reversal, but a bidirectional
bridging between symbolic and semiotic. A hushed incipience, (not) already filled. Not notes, not chronology, not the invigilator but the HearD.
The shift from active forming to hushed attention will recall the "me" that
each memory could make. And H.D. does here seem to shift between the
postulate of a stable ego which may be reformulated through the clari-
ties of memory and the postulation of what Kristeva calls a "subject-in-
process," a selving (like a duckling) that can be provisionally postulated
given this kind of statement, another selving, given another kind of statement, for H.D. enjoys fragmenting herself when and if she can do this
by attending to myth (multicultural myths and stories) because these old
images are a bottom. So if she loses her ego, her stable sense of self, she
can still both gather together and disappear into a larger, more volumi-
nous story, a story with many chapters, a story whose combinations will
never conclude.

14.

. . .

What writes listens. Listening is one of the major social and intellectual
skills necessary for signification. (When they sing to themselves the "lan-

guage in the crib" is it for the pleasure of listening in the dark to their voice (pause) their voice and the difference it makes "shoes on   shoes off pants on   pants off" 21 months.)

Listening is not presignification, in the sense of lower than or prior to; it is the simultaneous sine qua non, that without which there is no significication: no talk without pauses, no dialogue without silence, no translation without the white emptiness into which bubbles parallel statement.

Holding on: that in the semiotic realm are a plethora of "hieroglyphs," of signs, of "signets" — jewels of the unnameable, that in the maternal (and sometimes elsewhere) is incipience and listening, a waiting

the passage between Mamalie and Hilda in *The Gift* in which Hilda feels she protects her grandmother by a benevolent, interested, receptive hush, protects Mamalie from waking up from her trance state; this is what allows information and a way of knowing to pass between the dyad

and thus for women (well, for a woman, for H.D. as a woman writing) the presentation of unreadable signs to herself, the lush evocation of a plurality of possible readings, the reader of hush, are the materials of primary creation.

"I hug a soft shabby doll to my heart, my Muse is an old doll."[15]

15.

In fact, after the elaborate, pensive, and solemn accumulation of statement about the pictographs (*Tribute to Freud*, sections 28–41), which replicates, in the prose, the straining and pressure of the appearance of these signs, and which offers some local interpretation, some reading, as well as some set of questions which precisely alters the position of the self from side to side of an evoked story — "Am I looking at the Gorgon head . . . Or am I myself Perseus" (52) — after the reader is awash with signs, H.D., as if it were the most natural thing to do now, simply offers more signs. "Confetti-like tokens" with "mottoes . . . short and bright and to the point" supporting Hitler (58). "Other swastikas . . . I followed them down Berggasse as if they had been chalked on the pavement especially for my benefit" (59). "Then there were rifles." These were stacked neatly, looked like "an 1860 print . . . familiar pictures of our American Civil War" (59). When she astonishingly arrives for her session at the time of the attempted Nazi Putsch it is that day when she notices the waiting room with its "framed photographs," the "diploma" from Clark University, the "bizarre print or engraving" (61). There is the sign of her coming, the sign of the gardenias she wanted to give, and the dream icon of the "snake on a brick" (64) and the finding in reality of the dream icon in a little case of signet rings at the Louvre (65). Signs, readable, unreadable, a plethora of signs, and then, in climax, the hymn to signs, section 50, based, appropriately for issues of reading, interpreting, decoding—or not—on checking "up on the word 'signet' in my Chambers' English Dictionary" (66). Upon which she discovers that her choice of name, her signature, is a "signet" proof of a royal manner, proof of (as Emily Dickinson might have said) an election: to the saturation in, the creation of, the abandonment to "sign again—a word, gesture, symbol, or mark, intended to signify something else" (66). And in this sign, "*in hoc signo . . . vinces.*" Now certainly there might be ways and ways of reading this (Christian ways, for example), but let us say this way: that the *vinces* is the victory, the Niké, and what Niké signals is then the plethora of signs, and the emotional investment in noticing them, and the intellectual and poetic energy invested in continuing them. Not in stopping, not in saying one thing, one true thing, but in the sheer continuance, the bubbling of sign after sign. Because the very dramatic structure of the writing on the wall section has meaning: its meaning is continuance—will there be energy enough, intensity enough, care and risk enough to continue to see what the signs themselves want: that "the writing continues to write itself or be written" (51).

I know that this is a somewhat tendentious, limited reading. But satisfying to the degree that the H.D. of the essay is, among other things, the H.D. of continuations, of readings, of bright hieroglyphs forever read, forever unreadable: "her wavering hieroglyph"   "the *hieroglyph of the unconscious*"

It is the H.D. who, even when an interpretation "might have led us too far afield in a discussion or reconstruction of cause and effect, which might indeed have included priceless treasures, gems, and jewels, among the so-called findings of the unconscious mind revealed by the dream-content or associated thought and memory"—might, even thus, "have side-tracked the issue in hand"—still even then continues (88).

. . .

23.

A translation that folds, that enfolds on-self back into the semiotic. H.D.'s "writing on the wall" in her writing as she writes it, as she narrates it, as she interprets it (to release it quickly back to [un]readability) opens a vast space of endless reading. A vast space endlessly accreting. With connected signs and stories, a vast space of the unreadable, which is slightly, glancingly, read before it is back, it goes back, it ebbs back into continuous signing, the never to be fully explained. Never to be fully articulated surplus. The meaning of the essay is the forever surplus signings (sighings) of ruminative pleasure and pain, of seeing the unreadable, of reading, only to have more unreadable bubble. There is no final reading the (un)readable. A perpetual (the essay) and enacted resistance to thetic meaning even in the creation of meaning; the encirclement of meaning

and to mark this process, the sign of a reader; to anchor the question, the presence of a (an ironized) master of reading (a certain Freud in *Tribute to Freud*, Kaspar the Mage in *Trilogy*, Durand as writer/judge in *Hermetic Definition* and as well St. John Perse therein, Amen as an early "read" meaning in *Helen in Egypt*). The presence of an empty book, a blank page. The blank page is (like a) gushing spring. The mother in *Trilogy* who does not carry a child/"tome"/tomb, but a "blank" and "unwritten" book.

24.

"I cannot realize it, but it goes on." Not a citation from the Corfu vision, but from Kristeva on the maternal. Becoming a mother has, the process of gestation (outside in and inside out) has so far been accounted for in only two discourses, says Kristeva. Science. And Christian theology (*cum* art). H.D., did she want to invent a third (single-handedly, as usual, and therefore she had to encrust herself with the bestudded, bestudied armor of myth)? To invent a way of bringing access to the maternal (the baby) body into . . . she said . . .[16]

the writing on the wall is gestation, is being both mother and child.

25.

In a long excursus fictionalizing an account of, offering some interior monologue about early Freud discoveries (section 59 and its surroundings), H.D. insists that Freud was both scientific (methodological) and intuitive. H.D. insists that Freud modified the Socratic (false dialogic) method: so that, instead of being "egged on" to definition and elucidation by a probing, articulate sword fighter: teacher-mentor, instead "the question must be propounded by the protagonist himself, he must dig it out from its buried hiding-place, he himself must find the question before it could be answered" (*Tribute to Freud* 84).

First, the protagonist must change the pronouns.
Then she must find her question. What is the question? Is it what is the meaning of this writing? Is it what are the meanings of these signs? Is it what is the meaning of the Niké which is the "determinative"? Is it what are the meanings of my hallucinatory experiences? Is it (how) should I read these signs? Is it what docs my desire for union with the maternal body, with the baby body, necessitate for me as a woman writer? What writes, when the writer is a woman?

> milk page
> no libation down, the page is wet but
> a cakey ground
> restrains
> an unusual train (of)
>
> thought awakened
> high engines passing and only tunnels of access.

26.

I have tried only to discuss the section *Writing on the Wall*—the "written" text—in an unsystematic way, although I have cited from *Advent*. Each text in itself deserves a complete (what a word, here) and polyphonic commentary which it has gotten only to a certain degree. This commentary needs to take into account the status of the one text as being, H.D. says, "written" (and it was also published, or, as she says, it "appeared"), and "written in London in the autumn of 1944, with no reference to the Vienna notebooks of spring 1933," which were, of course, the source of *Advent*. *Advent* is different. It was "taken direct from the old notebooks of 1933": this says to me that the writing, the physical flow of words upon the page as they had come were mainly retained in that order. But H.D. then says that *Advent* was "not assembled until December 1948, Lausanne" (*Tribute to Freud* xiv). Probably a cutting and possibly (but not likely) a rejuxtaposing process was engaged. The text of *Advent* is dated by day, and within each day, by hour (thus prefiguring in this tactic both *Sagesse* and *End to Torment*). It is not likely that H.D. would have violated that organizing principle unless a sentence or two extraneous to a certain date/time but pertinent to, illuminating of, really belonging to another date/time had surfaced and become obtrusive. In that rare case (because the very accidents and conjunctions of this text offer an endless field for speculation, not least to their author), it is plausible that H.D.'s "reassembling" would have moved such material. But basically *Advent* wants to present the raw materials of association in an enlivening, startling, silly, and even frightening matter.

H.D. describes *Advent* as "the continuation of 'Writing on the Wall,' or its prelude" (*Tribute to Freud* xiv). These two terms, both alluding to narrative formation, are of exceeding interest. First, the terms allude to very different points or positions in narrative — pre-beginning and after-ending — yet here suggest some equivalence. Both imply that the "finished" status of the Freud memoir (which "appeared in *Life & Letters Today*") has now been self-ruptured ("now" is when this doubled version of *Tribute to Freud* was first allowed by H.D. — 1956). That self-rupture is an act which, not to be tedious, could be assimilated to the strategies of "writing beyond the ending": here as a kind of self-critique, the rewriting by breaking the sequence, postulating (as "prelude" and/or as "continuation") another sequence. One might say that *Advent* was placed with *Writing on the Wall* to make sure it is remembered that what is learned from the careful (non)reading offered in the Freud memoir is precisely the necessity of continuance. Certainly if *Advent* continued (was the sequel to) *Writing on the Wall* — as it was chronologically, the one finished in 1944, the other in 1948 — the climactic status of the triumphant and sentimental ending in the Goethe poem might be seriously undercut. (In that poem it is hard — willful — to read mother for father, to say that the presence of Mignonne the baby is the desire for the baby; so it can be known as a paean to the master.) If *Advent* offered a prelude to the other work — as it did in terms of writing process, of language acquisition — it becomes the space of heterogeneousness which can never be fully explored or explained, whose fits and starts never fused with the lyrical and argumentative cunning of *Writing on the Wall*; the presence of *Advent* making us see signs bubbling up.[17] Together, the two statements published under the title *Tribute to Freud*, with their slight changes of the nuances of certain incidents, the differences in emphasis, the alternative trajectories of development, the presence of more dreams in one, of more characters in one than the other, the wayward fragmentary shifts as opposed to (as related to) the pulsing elegance of hypotactic sentences, make the most astonishing and vital palimpsest H.D. ever produced in a career of intense concentration on that word about writing, that "form": the overwriting of one erased writing by another writing: semi (un)readable signs.[18]

The idea of inscribing, reinscribing, rescribing, new scribbling, is a tribute to Stein (there is no repetition, there is only insistence) as well as to Freud. ("I said that I wished I had asked an artist friend to sketch the series [of pictographs, the "writing on the wall"] for me, so that I could have shown it to him direct. He said that would have been no use. 'There would be value in the pictures only if you yourself drew them' " [*Tribute to Freud* 173]). Not about revelation, but about representation. As much as H.D. believed in, fostered in herself the idea of revelation in order for her *to* represent.[19]

The question was in finding (what writes when the writer is a woman) the exact proportion and shiftings of reading and not-yet and yes, interpreting which would continue to generate writing precisely because such a proportion (a high degree of allegiance to the semiotic, to unreadable sign) also evoked listening, not speaking (not formulating the question but allowing the writing, the writer to "ask the question," language acquisition, language a question)

Forever read, forever beyond reading. Listening, listing, listeth, listed.

> with a debt to the presence and work of
> Beverly Dahlen, work called *A Reading*

NOTES

This essay consists of excerpts from *Iowa Review* 16 (Fall 1986): 252–83.

1   "It is frequently noted in observations on the linguistic development of the child that intonation or sentence melody is one of the earliest linguistic features acquired by a child." This necessitates "a discussion of prosody which follows. Under prosody, we include intonation, pauses and stress." Ruth Hirsch Weir, *Language in the Crib* (The Hague: Mouton & Co., 1962), 28.

2   Julia Kristeva, "From One Identity to An Other," *Desire in Language: A Semiotic Approach to Literature and Art* (New York: Columbia UP, 1980), 133–34.

3   H.D., *Tribute to Freud* (containing *Writing on the Wall* and *Advent*) (1956; Boston: David R. Godine, 1974), 66.

4   Julia Kristeva, *About Chinese Women*, trans. Anita Barrows (New York: Urizen Books, 1977), 29–30.

5   This "relational definition" emphasizes that Kristeva offers "a theory of marginality, subversion, and dissidence" which intersects with notions of the female, seen "in terms of *positionality* rather than of essences." Toril Moi, *Sexual/Textual Politics: Feminist Literary Theory* (London: Methuen, 1985), 166, 164, 166.

6   In "Stabat Mater" (1977) Kristeva offers, by parallel intertexts, each marginal, each central, a way of structurally representing the relationship of analysis and speculation. Recently translated in *Poetics Today* 6.1–2 (1985): 133–52.

7   Julia Kristeva, "From 'Oscillation du "pouvoir" au "refus," ' " in *New French Feminisms*, ed. Elaine Marks and Isabelle de Courtivron (Amherst: U of Massachusetts P, 1980), 167.

8   Ibid., 166.

9   Ibid.

10 Kristeva, "From One Identity to An Other," 136. Theoretically, if one has access to the presymbolic mother, this "incest" would be true for both male writers and female writers. Kristeva's examples again come exclusively from male writers: Sade, Artaud, Joyce, Céline. So again gender questions are aroused: since when a woman writes, a person constituted and represented as an "exchange object" who is, at the same time, the potential object of the presymbolic longings of others and who is constituted to be that, must "appropriate to itself this archaic, instinctual, maternal territory."

11 H.D., *HERmione* [*HER*] (New York: New Directions, 1982), 125.

12 As reported in Quentin Bell, *Virginia Woolf: A Biography*, Vol. II (London: Hogarth Press, 1972), 129.

13 Adalaide Morris, "The Concept of Projection: H.D.'s Visionary Powers" (in this volume), also discusses the "Writing on the Wall" in conjunction with other, repeated events of vision and projection which defined H.D.'s work.

14 For an elaboration of this moment in the analysis see DuPlessis and Susan Stanford Friedman, " 'Woman is Perfect': H.D.'s Debate with Freud," *Feminist Studies* 7.3 (Fall 1981): 417–30.

15 H.D., *Compassionate Friendship* (1955), typescript, Collection of American Literature, Beinecke Rare Book and Manuscript Library, Yale University, p. 62.

16 Kristeva, "Motherhood According to Giovanni Bellini," *Desire in Language* 237.

17 I have interpreted all this as if the main relationship explored (by one light) were not H.D.-Freud but rather H.D.-writing (her writing, her "writing on the wall," and so on). For this to have had any possibility of being written depends upon the major elucidation by Susan Friedman of the feminist and cultural meanings of the H.D.-Freud encounter, a work presupposed in the study made here. See *Psyche Reborn: The Emergence of H.D.* (Bloomington: Indiana UP, 1981).

18 This idea of the palimpsest of *Tribute to Freud* and of the plenitude of the sign was written without consulting Deborah Kelly Kloepfer's essay "Fishing the Murex Up: Sense and Resonance in H.D.'s *Palimpsest*" (in this volume), but it should probably not be read without an acknowledgment to that work.

19 Gertrude Stein on repetition and insistence occurs for a few pages of "Portraits and Repetition," in *Lectures in America* (1935; Boston: Beacon Press, 1985), 166–69.

Part IV

Prophecies

we are powerless,

dust and powder fill our lungs
our bodies blunder

through doors twisted on hinges,
and the lintels slant

cross-wise;
we walk continually

on thin air
that thickens to a blind fog,

. . .

we know no rule
of procedure,

we are voyagers, discoverers
of the not-known,

the unrecorded;
we have no map;

possibly we will reach haven,
heaven.

—H.D., *Trilogy*

CHAPTER 15

The Concept of Projection: H.D.'s Visionary Powers

ADALAIDE MORRIS

In April 1920, while staying with her friend Bryher in a hotel on the island of Corfu, H.D. had a vision which marked and measured the rest of her life. It set the aims, announced the means, and disclosed the dimensions of her great work, the visionary epics *Trilogy* and *Helen in Egypt*, and it seemed to guarantee her gift as seer and prophet. It would be twenty years from the Corfu vision to the poems that first grasp its promise, however, years of drift and anxiety in which H.D. would write and re-write the story of her vision. By the time the event achieves final formulation in the first part of *Tribute to Freud*, it is clear that, however charged the vision's imagery, the plot we are to follow, the *mythos* of the matter, is its method: the miraculous projection of the images.

As H.D. explains in *Tribute to Freud*, the images she witnessed had the clarity, intensity, and authenticity of dream symbols and yet took shape not inside her mind but on the wall between the foot of her bed and the washstand. Because it was late afternoon and their side of the hotel was already dim and because the images were outlined in light, the shapes that appeared could not have been cast shadows. Neither accidental nor random, they formed with a stately, steady purpose, one after another, and seemed inscribed by the same hand. Their abstract, impersonal, rather conventional notation—a head in profile, a chalice, a ladder, an angel named Victory or Nike—made them appear part of a picture alphabet or hieroglyphic system, a supposition reinforced by their orderly succession, their syntax. For these reasons and because of the eerie, miraculous portentousness of the moment, H.D. calls this experience the "writing on the wall."[1]

When Belshazzar witnessed the writing on his wall, he glimpsed along

273

with the letters a part of the hand that wrote them. The origin of H.D.'s writing is, if equally mysterious, less simply formulated. The agent is not a hand but a projective process: the casting of an image onto a screen. The vision's earlier images, which appear entire, are like magic lantern slides; the later ones, which draw themselves in dots of light elongating into lines, resemble primitive movies.

The path from mind to wall is direct. It at first seems to follow what H.D. calls her "sustained crystal-gazing stare" (47), an aching concentration that propels the image outward on her eyebeam. Because the vision rides on will, she must not flag: "if I let go," she thinks, "lessen the intensity of my stare and shut my eyes or even blink my eyes, to rest them, the pictures will fade out" (49). When, however, she drops her head in her hands, exhausted, the process continues, and Bryher, who has until now seen nothing, witnesses the final image. What she sees — H.D.'s Nike elevated into the sun disk — is so consistent with the preceding figures that H.D. compares it to "that 'determinative' that is used in the actual hieroglyph, the picture that contains the whole series of pictures in itself or helps clarify or explain them" (56). With the power of the poet or prophet, H.D. has not only materialized the images of her psyche but cast them onto the consciousness of another and released her audience's own visionary capacities.

The images of the vision are described as flowing from, or at least through, H.D.'s psyche, yet their origin is obscured. What creates these slides or magic transparencies? Where do they come from? The answer given in *Tribute to Freud* is ambiguous. On the one hand, the images seem little different than the clips from memories or dream scenes that H.D. had earlier compared to "transparencies in a dark room, set before lighted candles" (35). In this sense, however extraordinary, they would be "merely an extension of the artist's mind, a *picture* or an illustrated poem, taken out of the actual dream or daydream content and projected from within" (51). On the other hand, in an interpretation H.D. clearly prefers, one sanctioned by the classical belief that gods speak through dreams and oracles, the images seem "projected from outside" (46), messages from another world, another state of being.

Images as signs and warnings from her own subconscious, images as signs and wonders from another world; the artist as moving-picture machine, the artist as psychic, the artist as message transmitter: what gives this odd combination of attributes coherence, positions it within H.D.'s development, and makes it central to any interpretation of her work is the concept of projection. All the more apt for its abundant ambiguities, projection is the master metaphor of H.D.'s technique. Its operations connect the material, mental, and mystical realms and enact her belief that there is no physical reality that is not also psychic and spiritual. Without the energies of projection, H.D.'s work stalls and thins; with them, her writing has strength and brilliance. It is this excellence that the "projected pictures" at Corfu seem to promise.

The word *projection* appears throughout H.D.'s work. Though its meaning alters subtly and sometimes confusingly, it always marks an important moment in her creative process. From the verb meaning *to throw forward*, projection is the thrust that bridges two worlds. It is the movement across a borderline: between the mind and the wall, between the brain and the page, between inner and outer, between me and you, between states of being, across dimensions of time and space. The concept of projection informs H.D.'s transitions from imagist to clairvoyant, to film theorist, analysand, and prophetic poet. What does it clarify at each stage? how does it change between stages? what light does it throw on the overall strategies and strengths of H.D.'s work? These will be the questions that guide our inquiry.

Projection: the act of throwing or shooting forward

"Cut the cackle!" "Go in fear of abstractions!" "Don't be 'viewy'!"[2] Most memorable imagist statements are prescriptions against a poetic tradition condemned as rigid, overblown, and unoriginal. Cackle is the chatter of conventional verse. It fills long lines with flourishes Pound called "rhetorical bustuous rumpus": platitudes, circumlocutions, and rolling, ornamental din.[3] To theorists like Pound and T. E. Hulme, these flourishes were self-generated and self-sustained, cut off from the world they purported to present. In its eagerness to pronounce upon the world and in the vaporous grandeur of its pronouncements, cackle went in fear neither of abstractions nor of viewiness.

The cure for cackle is contact. Imagist theory privileges sight as fresh, accurate access to the exterior world. Sight is the acid bath that dissolves the sticky sludge of rhetoric. It connects us directly, so the imagists argue, with the things of this world. Bad art, for Hulme, is "words divorced from any real vision," strings of conventional locutions, abstractions, "counters" which, like x and y in an algebraic formula, replace six pounds of cashews and four Florida oranges. Formulaic words, like algebraic symbols, can be manipulated according to laws independent of their meaning. Hulme's test of good poetry is whether the words turn back into things that we can see.[4]

The major imagist theorists echo each other on this point. "Each *word* must be an image *seen*, not a counter," Hulme legislates. "Language in a healthy state," T. S. Eliot insists, "presents the object, is so close to the object that the two are identical." For Pound, "the very essence" of a writer's work is "the application of word to thing." It was Pound who discovered, through the work of Ernest Fenollosa, the ur-pattern of the word-thing: the Chinese ideogram which was assumed to be direct, visibly concrete, natural rather than conventional, a picture language within which, as Fenollosa put it, "Thinking is *thinging*."[5]

The image of a thing, set into a poem, becomes for the imagists the innocent word, the word that has somehow escaped the conventional, abstracting, mediating nature of language. The assumption of transparent expression is a correlate of the Bergsonian faith in the artist's direct intuition of the object. Where contemporary theorists hold that we see what we know, imagists insist we know what we see. They find in vision the release from a shared system of signs into spontaneous, intuitive, unmediated apprehension of essences. Whatever her subsequent elaborations — and they are many and strange — this belief in the possibility of essential intuitions, so central to imagism, remains at the core of H.D.'s projective practice.

Projection is the act of throwing or shooting forward. Though the imagists don't use the term, they depend on the concept. In the genesis of the imagist poem, a thing in the world projects its essence onto the poet's consciousness; the poet imprints the image, or record of the thing, in a poem; and the poem, in turn, projects the image onto the reader's consciousness. The model for this, the simplest form of projection, is the magic lantern show. It is Hulme's concrete display of images that "always endeavours to arrest you, and to make you continuously see a physical thing"; it is Pound's *phanopoeia*, the technique by which "you use a word to throw a visual image on to the reader's imagination."[6]

H.D.'s *Sea Garden* is full of *phanopoeia*. The reader's visual imagination is bombarded by sand, tree bark, salt tracks, silver dust, wood violets, and thin, stinging twigs — objects in a world of clear, hard-edged, gritty particularity. The images have an almost hallucinatory specificity. The view is tight, close up, almost too bright: on the beach, "hard sand breaks, / and the grains of it / are clear as wine"; in the late afternoon sun, "each leaf / cuts another leaf on the grass"; night, when it comes, curls "the petals / back from the stalk / . . . under till the rinds break, / back till each bent leaf / is parted from its stalk."[7] Break, cut, curl: these moments are doubly projective. H.D.'s images, forcibly cast onto the reader's imagination, themselves record moments in which one thing, thrown onto another, opens, releases, or transforms it. In *Sea Garden*, objects are perpetually twisted, lifted, flung, split, scattered, slashed, and stripped clear by rushing energies that enact the impact the poet wishes to exert on the reader's imagination.

The rushing energies are the sea, the sun, and the night, but in H.D.'s world these are more than fierce weather: they testify to a sacred power and promise in the universe. Unlike other of the imagists, H.D. conceived of essence as god-stuff. To her, each intense natural fact is the trace of a spiritual force; each charged landscape enshrines a deity. Thus, in *Sea Garden*, dryads haunt the groves, nereids the waves; Priapus transfuses the orchard, Artemis courses the woods; Hermes marks the crossroads, and the mysterious Wind Sleepers roam searching for their altar. The world glows with sacred energy.

This radiance, however, like a Derridean sign, marks a presence that is vanished or just vanishing. Gods do not manifest directly to mortals, but they do, like Apollo at Delphi, leave us signs,[8] the afterglow of sacred presence. The speaker in *Sea Garden* is a supplicant in search of deities that are everywhere immanent in the landscape: they beckon, stand tense, await us a moment, then surge away, leaving behind heel prints, snapped stalks, and a charged silence. The poet, like a skilled tracker, moves from sign to sign in rapt, sagacious pursuit.

As embodiments of essence, the deities might seem mere metaphors, relics of the kind of claptrap the imagists despised. H.D.'s work, however, is spare, stripped, as Pound said, of slither.[9] In it, the gods function not as the poems' ornament but as their absent center. The deities are both cause and condition of this poetry; the poems do not work if we don't posit the reality of the presence they yearn toward.

The poems in *Sea Garden* are thrown out as bridges to the sacred. They project themselves toward the gods with a plea that the gods will in return appear to us. Poems like "Sea Gods," "Hermes of the Ways," "The Helmsman," and "The Shrine" address the gods directly, compelling them from immanence to manifestation: "For you will come," H.D. presses, "you will come, / you will answer our taut hearts, / . . . and cherish and shelter us."[10] Projection as *phanopoeia*, a poetic technique, here, in H.D.'s first important modification, broadens into a technique of meditation or prayer: an imaging used to summon a being from another world.

*Projection: a representation on a plane surface of any part
of the celestial sphere*

Except for three brief reviews in the *Egoist*, H.D. took little part in the barrage of imagist treatises and evaluations. Contrasting strongly with the polemics she later wrote for the cinema, this silence had several sources. She was a new poet, unused to literary disputation, and, until the arrival of Amy Lowell, she was the only woman in a contentious group of men. In addition, she held a constricted position in the movement: if Hulme was its principal theorist and Pound its chief publicist,[11] H.D. was from the first the imagiste extraordinaire, the movement's most effective practitioner. Her poems stimulated and exemplified positions held by others.

A third, more significant source of H.D.'s silence, however, lies in her hesitations about imagist doctrine. Her *Egoist* review of John Gould Fletcher's *Goblins and Pagodas*, for example, makes an obligatory bow to imagist principles but is compelled by something else. "He uses the direct image, it is true," H.D. writes, "but he seems to use it as a means of evoking other and vaguer images — a pebble, as it were, dropped into a quiet pool, in order to start across the silent water, wave on wave of light, of colour, of sound." Fletcher attempts "a more difficult and, when successfully handled, richer form of art: not that of direct presentation, but that of suggestion."[12] The goblins and pagodas that title his volume testify to visionary capacities. His art pursues not the solidity of physical things so much as the spiritual enigmas that radiate from them.

The next stage of H.D.'s development furthers her own shift from pebbles to their radiating rings; from the objects of this world to the phantasms of light, color, and sound surrounding them; from our three dimensions to the largest ring of all, the fourth dimension or celestial sphere surrounding us. In 1919, after her bonds with Pound, Aldington, and the other imagists had cracked, after her alliance with Bryher had begun and her daughter Perdita had been born, H.D. had a series of intense psychic experiences. The visions of 1919 and 1920 undid any remaining traces of imagist empiricism, affirmed a privileged role for the woman poet, and demonstrated H.D.'s clairvoyant powers. Applied to these experiences, the term *projection* registers not the poet's design on the reader or on the gods but rather the dynamics of clairvoyance. To this end H.D. extends the term by borrowing a metaphor from the art of cartography.

In the language of mapping, projection is the representation of a sphere on a flat surface. Like most figuration, projection simplifies, here reducing a curve to a plane. Two methods of charting the heavens clarify the distinction between general and cartographic projection. In the first sense, as Robert Duncan in *The H.D. Book* observes, we make the night "a projected screen" by casting our mythologies into the heavens and rendering "the sky-dome above . . . the image of another configuration in the skull-dome below."[13] Cartographers reverse this movement and project intersecting coordinate lines from the sky down to our earthly charts. This entry of another dimension into our familiar figuration is the equivalent in H.D.'s work of the process by which material from the celestial or astral planes manifests on the earthly plane. It is this that haunts and compels her.

H.D. experienced what she felt was an inrush of material from other dimensions at least four times in 1919–20, all after surviving her near-fatal childbirth and all in the steadying company of Bryher. The first, in late spring 1919, involved "the transcendental feeling of the two globes or the two transparent half-globes enclosing me" (*Tribute to Freud* 168); the second was the apparition of an ideal figure on the voyage to Greece in 1920; the third and fourth, in the hotel room at Corfu, were the projected pictures and a series of dance scenes conjured up for Bryher. Each of these seemed, as H.D. affirmed, "a god-send,"[14] an irradiation of the world of ordinary events and rules by an extraordinary grace.

The first of these experiences is described in *Notes on Thought and Vision*, a document composed for Havelock Ellis, whom H.D. and Bryher had been consulting and who subsequently accompanied them to Greece. Though rough and sometimes contradictory, these notes describe a matrix of creativity she calls the "jelly-fish" or "over-mind" state (19). The self is divided into body, mind, and over-mind. The artist-initiate begins, like the neophyte in the Eleusinian mysteries, with the body's desires and the brain's sensitivities, but the aim is to transcend these consciousnesses in the over-mind, the receptacle of mystical vision.

Like Ellis, H.D. begins her exposition with sexuality. All humans need physical relationships, she argues, but creative men and women crave them "to develop and draw forth their talents" (17). The erotic personality, suffused with sympathetic, questing, and playful energies, is the artistic personality par excellence, a hypothesis Ellis and H.D. both exemplify by evoking Leonardo da Vinci.[15] Ellis, however, separates sexuality's primary reproductive function from a secondary spiritual function of "furthering the higher mental and emotional processes."[16] H.D. counters this separation with a theory derived partly from the Eleusinian mysteries and partly from her own recent childbirth.

Complementing the "vision of the brain" is a force H.D. calls "vision of the womb" (20). The term underscores the artist's receptive/procreative role. In the womb-brain, thoughts from another realm are received, nourished, brought to form, then projected out into the barrenness H.D. calls "the murky, dead, old, thousand-times explored old world" (24). This model rewrites conventional phallic metaphors for creativity[17] by depicting visionary consciousness as "a foetus in the body" which, after "grinding discomfort," is released in the miracle the mysteries celebrated as Kore's return. "Is it easier for a woman to attain this state of consciousness than for a man?" H.D. asks. Though both sexes possess this capacity, her formulation privileges her own particularly female experience of integration and regeneration (19–20).

Notes on Thought and Vision provides many explications of visionary consciousness, but the most pertinent to H.D.'s developing notion of projection are three ocular models. H.D.'s fascination with optics came from watching her father the astronomer and her grandfather the botanist gaze through lenses into a teeming world where before there had been only a blank. Each of her models postulates two kinds of vision, womb vision and brain vision, and each invents a way to adjust them so as to transform void to plenitude.

H.D.'s initial formulation describes the jellyfish state as enclosure in two caps or diving bells of consciousness, one over the forehead and one in the "love-region." Each is a sort of amniotic sac, "like water, transparent, fluid yet with definite body, contained in a definite space . . . like a closed sea-plant, jelly-fish or anemone." This sac holds and nurtures the delicate, amorphous life of the over-mind, but it has a further function. Like a diver's mask or aquarium glass, the over-mind allows us to see the usually invisible inhabitants of the watery depths: here, H.D. explains, "thoughts pass and are visible like fish swimming under clear water" (18–19).[18]

The second formulation transforms these caps into dual lenses for a pair of psychic opera glasses. These, "properly adjusted, focused . . . bring the world of vision into consciousness. The two work separately, perceive separately, yet make one picture" (23). What they see is the whole world of vision registered by the mystic, the philosopher, and the artist.

In the last and most evocative formulation, these lenses merge into a complexly constituted third eye. "The jelly-fish over my head," H.D. explains, "had become concentrated. . . . That is, all the spiritual energy seemed concentrated in the middle of my forehead, inside my skull, and it was small and giving out a very soft light, but not scattered light, light concentrated in itself as the light of a pearl would be" (51). Like a crystal ball, this eye both receives and emits the force H.D. calls "over-world energy" (47). It draws in, concentrates, then projects outward "pictures from the world of vision" (50). This receptive/transmissive eye is the gift of vision, the pearl of great price.

The jellyfish eye opens the skull-dome. Into, out of, through this rupture pours all the prophetic soul-energy scientific materialism would deny and H.D.'s visions and visionary poetry affirm. Archetypal memories, dreams, the Corfu pictures all exemplify this projected vision, but a more excessive, startling instance is the sudden apparition of Peter Van Eck at the ship rail of the *Borodino*.

For more than twenty years, H.D. struggled to tell the story of Peter Van Eck, her code name for Peter Rodeck, architect, artist, spiritualist, and fellow passenger on the voyage to Greece. It formed the heart of a much rewritten novel entitled *Niké*, finally jettisoned in 1924. The most ample remaining accounts are in the pseudonymous short story "Mouse Island," published in 1932; in the analysis notebooks of 1933, published as part of *Tribute to Freud*; and in the unpublished autobiographical novel *Majic Ring*, written in 1943–44.

It was sunset, neither day nor night, and the ocean was suffused with a soft violet-blue glow. The ship was approaching the Pillars of Hercules between the outer waters of the Atlantic and the inner sea of the Mediterranean. "We were crossing something," H.D. explains — a line, a boundary, perhaps a threshold (*Tribute to Freud* 156). Alone at the rail of the *Borodino*, she stood "on the deck of a mythical ship as well, a ship that had no existence in the world of ordinary events and laws and rules."[19] The sea was quiet, the boat moved smoothly, and the waves broke "in a thousand perfectly peaked wavelets like the waves in the background of a Botticelli" (*Tribute to Freud* 160). When she turned to search for Bryher, she saw a three-dimensional figure at the rail, a man who both was and was not Peter Van Eck. Taller, clearer, brighter than Van Eck, without his disfiguring scar and thick-rimmed glasses, this apparition summoned a band of leaping dolphins and disclosed, on the ship's seaward side, a chain of hilly islands. At the peak of the moment, H.D. reports, "his eyes, it seemed now, were my eyes. I was seeing his vision, what he (though I did not of course, realize it) was himself projecting. This was the promised land, the islands of the blest, the islands of Atlantis or of the Hesperides."[20]

Was this a hallucination, a holographic illusion, an epiphany? If the latter, who was the being who directed or even impersonated Peter Van Eck? H.D. gives no consistent answer. *Majic Ring* suggests it was "Anax Apollo, Helios, Lord of Magic and Prophecy and Music"; the letters to Silvia Dobson imply he was an astral double; the story "Mouse Island" compares him to Christ at Emmaus.[21]

Whatever he was, all accounts agree he was a "projection" from another dimension into this one, a phenomenon for which "Mouse Island" gives the most extensive — and mechanical — explication. If each being is composed of two substances, "platinum sheet-metal over jelly-fish" or body over soul, Van Eck's appearance was a "galvanized projection": soul-stuff shocked into form, transmitted through the third-eye opening in his skull, perceived through the opening in hers. "The inside could get out that way," the story tells us, "only when the top was broken. It was the transcendentalist inside that had met [Van Eck] in the storm on deck, when [Peter Van Eck] was downstairs in the smoking room."[22]

The terminology is awkward, the physics creak, but the experience was real and haunted H.D. all her life. Van Eck's three-dimensionality was a kind of psychic *phanopoeia* — not at all what Pound meant but very much H.D.'s technique in her later poetry. The visionary figures of *Trilogy*, the hordes of souls thronging *Helen in Egypt*, the angelic forces of *Hermetic*

Definition, all are figures entering the imagination from another dimension and carrying with them the mysterious radiance by which H.D. gratefully remapped our "dead, old, thousand-times explored old world."

Projection: the display of motion pictures by casting an image on a screen

When H.D. once again broached the Greek material in the 1940s, she reported that "the story, in its new form, began unwinding itself, like a roll of film that had been neatly stored in my brain, waiting for a propitious moment to be re-set in the projector and cast on a screen."[23] This new twist to the term *projection* emerged from extensive experience. She had taken an exhilarating step into the technology of the cinema.

In spring 1929, when asked by the *Little Review* what she most liked to do, H.D. had no trouble answering. "I myself have learned to use the small projector," she replied, "and spend literally hundreds of hours alone in my apartment, making the mountains and village streets and my own acquaintances reel past me in the light and light and light."[24] The projector belonged to POOL Productions, a company run by Bryher and Kenneth Macpherson, H.D.'s companions in film work in the late 1920s and early 1930s. H.D. wrote for their journal *Close Up*, acted in their films, did montage for one and publicity for two, and, finally, filled her contemporary poetry and fiction with images of light, focus, superimposition, and projection.[25]

Most of H.D.'s film theory is in a series of essays composed for the first issues of *Close Up* and titled "The Cinema and the Classics." By "classics" H.D. meant, specifically, Greek culture and, more narrowly, the Greek amalgamation of the beautiful and the good.[26] Despite Hollywood's fixation on "longdrawn out embraces and the artificially enhanced thud-offs of galloping bronchoes" and despite "the gigantic Cyclops, the American Censor" who prettifies beauty and homogenizes goodness,[27] cinema offers our best opportunity to recapture Greek wisdom. In the hands of the avant-garde, film repossesses the visionary consciousness of Athens, Delphi, and Eleusis. Here, at last, "miracles and godhead are *not* out of place, are not awkward"; it is "a perfect medium . . . at last granted us."[28]

The word *medium* resonates through H.D.'s meditations. Film is an artistic medium, one occupying a medial position between the filmmaker's visual imagination and our own, but for H.D. it also functions as a psychic medium externalizing and making perceptible invisible inward intentions and coherencies. The announcement of the POOL film *Wing Beat*, starring H.D. and Kenneth Macpherson, promises "Telepathy and attraction, the reaching out, the very edge of dimensions in dimensions."[29] Film reads and reveals the far reaches of our minds, and this connects it for H.D. with the Delphian dictate "Know Thyself."[30] The mediumship, however, is more than telepathic. Cinema discloses the thoughts of the gods, their power, knowledge, and beauty. It may even, finally, disclose their very being, for here "Hermes, indicated in faint light, may step forward, outlined in semi-obscurity, or simply dazzling the whole picture in a blaze of splendour. Helios may stand simply and restrained with uplifted arm."[31]

Because film calls together in a dark room witnesses of charged hieratic images, images that make manifest what was mysterious, because it brings light to darkness and conveys the will of beauty and goodness, cinema is to us what the church was to H.D.'s ancestors and what the Delphic oracle was to the Greeks. The long two-part poem H.D. entitled "Projector" and published alongside her essays in *Close Up* names the Delphian Apollo as god of the cinema and envisions him reasserting his domain on a ray of image-bearing, world-creating light:

> This is his gift;
> light,
> light
> a wave
> that sweeps
> us
> from old fears
> and powers.

Just as Apollo claimed the power of prophecy at Delphi by slaying the monster Python, this projector-god destroys squalid commercialism and makes Hollywood into a "holy wood" where "souls upon the screen / live lives that might have been, / live lives that ever are."[32]

H.D.'s ecstatic poem greets Apollo as he begins his miracles. The poem's clipped, incantatory lines and detailed invocation of the Delphic paradigm, however, suggest something more than simple salutation. H.D.'s advocacy asserts a place and function for herself. Apollo at Delphi works through his oracle, the Pythoness, who is a medium between the god and the seeker. She has what *Notes on Thought and Vision* calls "womb vision," for it is she who receives, brings to form, and throws forth his knowledge. As the transmitter of the prophetic message, her position precedes and predicts H.D.'s. Who, then, is the poem's "Projector"? It is Apollo, light-bearer; it is his Delphic oracle; it is H.D. herself, the projector-poet; and perhaps it is also the machine in her apartment which, in a coincidence that doubtless delighted H.D., rested, like the Pythoness herself, upon a tripod — symbol of prophecy, prophetic utterance, occult or hidden knowledge.

Projection: a defense mechanism in which the individual attributes
            an impulse of his own to some other person or object in
            the outside world

Close Up did not push a particular doctrine. It contained accounts of
German and Russian cinema, translations of Eisenstein, reviews of film
exhibitions and avant-garde screenings, vituperations against Hollywood's
censor, advice on the newest cameras and projectors, and assorted editorial pronouncements. As Anne Friedberg notes, however, one consistent strain in its pages is psychoanalytic theory.[33] Many of the writers cite
Freud; Dr. Hanns Sachs, Bryher's analyst and a member of Freud's inner
circle, and lay analysts Barbara Low and Mary Chadwick contribute
essays; and editor Kenneth Macpherson frequently elaborates his positions with psychoanalytic concepts. This interest illuminates Macpherson's
own most ambitious project, the full-length film *Borderline*, in which
H.D., disguised in the credits as Helga Doorn, plays a character caught
between conscious and unconscious pressures. Her work on *Borderline*
provides a glimpse into H.D.'s preoccupations some three years prior to
her analysis with Freud.

Macpherson intended to take the film "into the labyrinth of the human
mind, with its queer impulses and tricks, its unreliability, its stresses and
obsessions, its half-formed deductions, its glibness, its occasional amnesia,
its fantasy, suppression, and desires."[34] The plot is a tangle of desire,
murder, and bigotry. Astrid, the sensitive and worldly neurotic played by
H.D., comes with her alcoholic husband Thorne to a small Swiss border
town; in this limbo, she becomes obsessed with Pete, a giant, half-vagrant
black man played by Paul Robeson, and is stabbed to death by Thorne
in a crime for which the town persecutes Pete. The frayed atmosphere
is exacerbated by the movie's silence, by the camera's raking of symbolic
landscapes and faces gouged with light, and, finally, by Astrid's staring
into the camera — as if she were emptying her mind out onto the screen,
or, even more uncomfortably, as if she were attempting a direct transfer
of her psychic content into the mind of the viewer.

The unsigned, thirty-nine-page publicity pamphlet, almost certainly
written by H.D., reminds us that "Astrid, the woman, terribly incarnated,
is 'astral' in effect."[35] The earthly/astral border is only one more in a film
deliberately situated on every possible margin: physical, social, racial,
sexual, mental, even, since Macpherson and his company were displaced
and uncredentialed, professional. The film's terrain is the limbo that
H.D.'s projection — imagist, clairvoyant, cinematic, or prophetic — always
traversed.

If the stark, otherworldly sequences that punctuate *Borderline* have a hieroglyphic portentousness, it is because they in fact originated in picture writing. As the pamphlet explains, Macpherson drew 910 pen-and-ink sketches giving detailed directions for each shot. Each was a light sculpture, a dream scene, a hieroglyph designed for projection, a "welding of the psychic or super-normal to the things of precise everyday existence."[36] For H.D. this places *Borderline* in the same psychic category as the Corfu pictures and the charged dreams of her accounts of analysis: "For myself," she writes in *Tribute to Freud*, "I consider this sort of dream or projected picture or vision as a sort of halfway state between ordinary dream and the vision of those who, for lack of a more definite term, we must call psychics or clairvoyants" (41).

"Borderline" is, of course, a psychoanalytic term designating the halfway state between neurosis and psychosis. H.D. would know the term from Bryher, who in the late 1920s was both studying and undergoing analysis, from lectures she and Bryher attended in Berlin during these years, from the general theoretic climate of *Close Up*, and, finally, from the fact that Macpherson in titling his film doubtless had the technical term in mind. While playing on all its other nuances, however, the pamphlet shuns the psychoanalytic meaning and resituates the borderline so that it lies not between the neurotic and the psychotic but between the neurotic and the psychic. This gesture typifies H.D.'s complex attitude toward psychoanalysis.

"*Borderline* is a dream," the pamphlet pronounces, entering its summation, "and perhaps when we say that we have said everything. The film is the art of dream portrayal and perhaps when we say that we have achieved the definition, the synthesis toward which we have been striving."[37] For H.D., dream was always interior projection, a cinematic exhibition of the mind's submerged content. Like *Borderline* and the Corfu pictures, dreams display "the *hieroglyph of the unconscious*." It is for "open[ing] the field to the study of this vast, unexplored region" (*Tribute to Freud* 93) that H.D. would be forever grateful to Freud.

Accounts of dreams are, as it were, projections of projections, and H.D. was justly proud of her command of this intricate transmutation. It was not simple. "The dream-picture focussed and projected by the mind, may perhaps achieve something of the character of a magic-lantern slide and may 'come true' in the projection," H.D. explains in *The Gift*, but to make it do so demands all the equipment developed by Freud: free association, command of the parallels between individual, biological, and racial development, and mastery of concepts like condensation, displacement, dramatization by visual imagery, superimposition, distortion, and screen memory. An admonitory passage from *The Gift* conveys H.D.'s delight in her descriptive skill:

The dream, the memory, the unexpected related memories must be allowed to sway backward and forward, as if the sheet or screen upon which they are projected, blows and is rippled in the wind of whatever emotion or idea is entering a door, left open. The wind blows through the door, from outside, through long, long corridors of personal memory, of biological and of race-memory. Shut the door and you have a neat flat picture. Leave all the doors open and you are almost out-of-doors, almost within the un-walled province of the fourth-dimensional. This is creation in the truer sense, in *the wind bloweth where it listeth* way.[38]

Her delight was matched — perhaps even sparked — by Freud's joy in the intense and haunting dreams of her two periods of analysis in 1933 and 1934. "[Freud] has embarrassed me," H.D. writes Bryher in April 1933, "by telling me I have a rare type of mind he seldom meets with, in which thought crystalizes out in dream in a very special way." In their sessions they pour over dream after enigmatic dream, Freud complimenting her on their "very 'beautiful' construction," their invention of symbols, their "almost perfect mythological state."[39] The fact that so much of H.D.'s post-analysis writing places her before a luminous dream that she both creates and analyzes, participates in and watches, surely repeats the exhilarations of her contact with Freud.

In the analysis of her dreams, H.D. and Freud are colleagues who heed, adjust, and validate each other's interpretations, but much of the analysis material indicates another kind of relationship. Here H.D. is a small, confused seeker and Freud is the wise Hermit on the edge of the Forest of the Unknown (*Tribute to Freud* 13), Asklepios the blameless healer (50), Herakles struggling with Death (74), Jeremiah discovering the well of living water (83), St. Michael who will slay the Dragon of her fears (109), even "the infinitely old symbol" weighing Psyche the soul in the Balance (97), even the Supreme Being (16, 63). These formulations, as Freud taught us, call on another sort of projection: transference, or the process by which the patient directs toward the physician an intensity of feeling that is based on no real relation between them and can only be traced back to old fantasies rendered unconscious.

The first step in analysis, the establishment of transference, H.D. took easily, if somewhat ambiguously. To H.D., Freud became papa, the Professor, his study, like Professor Doolittle's, cluttered with erudite writings and "old, old sacred objects" (25); to Freud, however, transference made him the gentle, intuitive mother. Both were right, for as Susan Stanford Friedman points out, "in an ultimate sense, he became both mother and father to her as he fused her mother's art and her father's science in the mysteries of psychoanalysis."[40] Her transference love for Freud enabled H.D. to affirm herself as poet and visionary, release her blocked creativity, and write with passion and continuity throughout the rest of her life.

There was another, murkier transference in the analysis, however, one subject not to resolution but to repetition. This rendered every figure in her life a stand-in for someone else, every love a deflection, every trauma a replay of earlier disaster. The records of analysis swarm with formulae as Freud and H.D. decipher originary patterns beneath a palimpsest of repetition. Ellis as father, Freud as mother; Aldington as father, Bryher as mother; Rodeck as father, Bryher as mother; her "ideal" brothers Rodeck, Frances Gregg, and Bryher; her "real" brothers Pound, Aldington, and Macpherson[41] — the list goes on and on. One fevered letter to Bryher in March 1933 indicates both the exuberance and the suspicion of futility beneath all this activity:

My triangle is mother-brother-self. That is, early phallic-mother, baby brother or smaller brother and self. I have worked in and around that, I have HAD the baby with my mother, and been the phallic-baby, hence Moses in the bulrushes, I have HAD the baby with the brother, hence Cuthbert [Aldington], Cecil [Gray], Kenneth etc. I have HAD the "illumination" or the back to the womb WITH the brother, hence you and me in Corfu, island = mother. . . . Well, well, well, I could go on and on and on, demonstrating but once you get the first idea, all the other, later diverse-looking manifestations fit in somehow. Savvy?????? It's all too queer and at first, I felt life had been wasted in all this repetition etc. but somehow F. seems to find it amusing, sometimes.[42]

Until the end of her life, H.D. deluged near strangers with intensities of feeling belonging not to them but to their forerunners or even to the forerunners of their forerunners. Here transference was a condition not of cure but of compulsion.[43]

Dreams and transference are projective in a general sense, but psychoanalytic theory, of course, defines the term *projection* precisely: as a defense mechanism that causes us to attribute an interior wish to a person or object in the exterior world. This charged term formed an exemplary site for the disagreement between Freud and H.D. about the nature of reality, and here H.D. took Freud on, if not directly, nonetheless deftly.

The word *projection* occurs frequently in *Tribute to Freud*, but, like "borderline" in the movie pamphlet, not once with its Freudian denotation. The "projected picture" (*Tribute to Freud* 41), images "projected" from the subconscious mind or from outside (46), the strain of projection (49), the impact that "projected" a dream sequence (72): each use of the term points to the Corfu vision. Of all the events that could have titled H.D.'s original account of analysis, her choice, "Writing on the Wall," privileges and gives biblical sanction to the vision at Corfu. The phrase draws our attention from the analytic to the mystical and prepares our confrontation with the main question raised by the Corfu pictures. Were they, as Freud maintained, a "dangerous 'symptom' " (41), or were they rather an upwelling of creativity, an inspiration, and a promise?

In Freud's use of the word, the "projected pictures" reduce to defensive exteriorizations of unconscious material. In this sense they would be desperate strategies of containment. By H.D.'s definition, however, the projected pictures are precisely the opposite: they open the boundaries of the self to another, higher reality, not in order to deny its operations but in order to claim and be claimed by them. The pictures predict — or project into the future — not a repetition of palimpsestic transferences but a transcendence, a breakthrough into a new dimension. In her final image, the angel Nike moving through a field of tents, H.D. recognizes the aftermath of the next world war: "When that war had completed itself," she writes, "rung by rung or year by year, I, personally (I felt), would be free, I myself would go on in another, a winged dimension" (*Tribute to Freud* 56). This vision of 1920, recalled and reaffirmed through analysis with Freud, predicts the transmutations wrought two decades later in the great poem H.D. would call her War Trilogy.

Projection: the casting of some ingredient into a crucible; especially in alchemy, the casting of the powder of the philosopher's stone (powder of projection) *upon a metal in fusion to effect its transmutation into gold or silver*

H.D.'s notes on her recent writings, composed in 1949 for Norman Holmes Pearson, stress the generation of *Trilogy* out of the ravages of World War II. Throughout the Nazi air assault, H.D. had remained in London, close to the Hyde Park anti-aircraft batteries and in the thick of incendiary raids. Bombs — buzz bombs, fly bombs, oil bombs, doodlebugs, and low, close V-1 rockets — in often nightly bombardments tore open apartments, leveled buildings, lodged unexploded shells in areaways and under pavements, and threw the survivors into unregistered dimensions of terror and powerlessness.[44] "The actual fire has raged round the crystal," H.D. reported to Pearson. "The crystalline poetry to be projected, must of necessity, have that fire in it. You will find fire in *The Walls Do Not Fall, Tribute to the Angels* and *The Flowering of the Rod. . . . Trilogy*, as we called the three volumes of poetry written during War II, seemed to project itself in time and out-of-time together. And with no effort."[45]

After agonized blockage, H.D. was writing with assurance and speed, her typewriter clacking across the noise of the raids. In the last eight months of 1944 alone she composed three of her finest works: May 17 to 31, *Tribute to the Angels*; September 19 to November 2, *Writing on the Wall*;

December 18 to 31, *The Flowering of the Rod*. The Freud memoir slid easily between the last two parts of *Trilogy*, for *Trilogy* performs, in its way, a kind of analysis. If, as Robert Duncan suggests, "in Freudian terms, the War is a manifestation of the latent content of the civilization and its discontents, a projection of the collective unconscious,"[46] *Trilogy* works to surface the terrors and redirect savage impulses to sublimer ends.

As in analysis, dream is the agent of transmutation. *Trilogy*, however, builds on a distinction made in *Writing on the Wall* between "trivial, confused dreams and . . . real dreams. The trivial dream bears the same relationship to the real as a column of gutter-press news-print to a folio page of a play of Shakespeare." The enigmas of revelatory dreams emerge not from extravagantly repressed desire but from "the same source as the script or Scripture, the Holy Writ or Word" (*Tribute to Freud* 35–36). Dream is the active force of the sacred in human life. "Now it appears very clear," H.D. writes, "that the Holy Ghost, // childhood's mysterious enigma, / is the Dream":

> it merges the distant future
> with most distant antiquity,
>
> states economically
> in a simple dream-equation
>
> the most profound philosophy,
> discloses the alchemist's secret
>
> and follows the Mage
> in the desert.[47]

Each of the three parts of *Trilogy* generates a real dream, a vision of eternal beings who reappear with the recovery of "the alchemist's secret," the process through which destruction precedes and permits new, more perfect life.

War executes a horrifying reverse alchemy. Rails are melted down and made into guns, books are pulped for cartridge cases, the Word is absorbed in the Sword, and people become "wolves, jackals, / mongrel curs" (*Trilogy* 3, 16, 17, 47). Casting back to "most distant antiquity" in order to project "the distant future," H.D. turns to the early alchemists. Though our culture cartoons them as greedy bunglers struggling to turn dung into gold, alchemists were scholars of spiritual transformation. Alchemical formulas and philosophy structure *Trilogy* and give the metaphor of *projection* its final precise and complex elaboration.

Until modern chemistry's mechanical and quantitative postulates replaced alchemy's organic, qualitative theory, four tenets seemed self-evident.[48] The universe, alchemists believed, was everywhere alive, all matter possessing body, passion, and soul. Because substances appear, grow, decay, diminish, and disappear, secondly, transmutation is considered the essence of life. Third, all transmutation moves toward perfection: the seed becomes a tree, the worm turns into a butterfly, grains of sand round into pearls. In this process, the seed splits, the worm bursts, the sand vanishes, thus demonstrating the fourth alchemical tenet: the belief that all creation requires an initial act of destruction.

Projection is the final stage of an alchemical transmutation, the act that precipitates new, more perfect form. All *Trilogy* moves toward the moment of projection, but to understand this moment we must look briefly at the alchemists' explication of transformation. Like Aristotle, they believed that each substance consists of indeterminate prime matter and specific form impressed into it like a hot seal in wax. Changing a substance, therefore, was simply a matter of altering its "form." Ingredients were cast into a crucible, heated, and, in a process alchemists called "death" or "putrefaction," reduced to prime matter; then, after many intricate maneuvers — calcination, distillation, sublimation, fermentation, separation, and more — the specific form of a finer substance was projected into the crucible and new shape sprang forth. However audacious or even preposterous this procedure might now appear, to the alchemists it merely hastened a natural, universal process.

The magical act — or, as H.D. would remind us, the act of the Mage — was the making of the seed of perfection called the philosopher's stone or the elixir of life. Formulas were inherited, debated, obfuscated, adulterated, encoded, translated and mistranslated into and out of a dozen different languages, but the basic schema remained the same. To effect what was called "the alchemical marriage," sulphur, the male element, and mercury, the female element, were fused in the crucible and this union generated the philosopher's stone, "the Royal Child" which, like Christ, redeemed all life to its highest form. H.D.'s spiritual challenge in *Trilogy* is no less than the reawakening of this transmuting, projecting power: "the alchemist's key . . . / the elixir of life, the philosopher's stone" which "is yours if you surrender // sterile logic, trivial reason" (40).

Nearly every image in *Trilogy* enacts a transmutation meant to convince us of the universality of the process and to draw our perception along a continuous line from the poem's smallest event to its largest. These images are holograms or discrete cells of the poem containing in code the plan of the whole. The archetypal alchemical transformation, for example, the changing of lead to gold, reappears in a casually inserted icon as "corn . . . enclosed in black-lead, / ploughed land." Washed by earth's waters, heated by sun's fire, and strewn with seed, black-lead land becomes gold corn (56). "This is no rune nor riddle," H.D. reiterates; "it is happening everywhere" (84). In alchemical crucibles, under pressure, again and again, metamorphosis occurs: the mollusc shell holds a sand grain, the eggshell an egg; the heart shell lodges a seed dropped by the phoenix; the cocoon houses a caterpillar, the shroud a worm preparing resurrection (8, 9, 35, 12). Even the brain in its skull case ferments and distills, dissolving sterile logic, generating new vision.

These images prepare our understanding of the poem's larger sweep. With properly cryptic encoding, the sections together retell the story of the making of the philosopher's stone. Each section contains a crucible, a purifying fire, and a double movement of destruction and creation; each moves us backward through time and inward across logic and custom, closer and closer to the culminating miracle of projection.

In *The Walls Do Not Fall*, part 1 of *Trilogy*, the crucible is the city of London, flattened by ceaseless pounding, filled with the shards of civilization, flaming with "Apocryphal fire" (4). London's ruin makes it "the tomb, the temple" (3), a matrix of death and rebirth in which Old Testament wrath and vengeance yield to a higher form of being. In a dream-vision, H.D. witnesses the reborn god whom she calls "Ra, Osiris, *Amen*":

> he is the world-father,
> father of past aeons,
>
> present and future equally;
> beardless, not at all like Jehovah.
>
> (25)

This slender figure is the anointed son, the Christos, whose luminous amber eyes shine like transforming fire. With his entry into the poem, H.D. has half the alchemical formula, traditionally represented as the sun, fire, sulphur, the fathering principle.

In *Tribute to the Angels*, part 2 of *Trilogy*, the crucible becomes the poem-bowl and the shards the word-fragments that survive as traces of the great traditions of female divinity.[49] After proper invocations, with reverence for her materials and awe at the powers they hold, H.D. the poet-alchemist begins:

> Now polish the crucible
> and in the bowl distill
>
> a word most bitter, *marah*,
> a word bitterer still, *mar*,

sea, brine, breaker, seducer,
giver of life, giver of tears;

Now polish the crucible
and set the jet of flame

under, till *marah-mar*
are melted, fuse and join

and change and alter,
mer, mere, mère, mater, Maia, Mary,

Star of the Sea,
Mother.

(71)[50]

This alchemical transaction creates a pulsing green-white, opalescent jewel which lives, breathes, and gives off "a vibration that we can not name" (76). After distilling, purifying, and refining this force, after witnessing intermediate manifestations and meditating on "the moon-cycle . . . the moon-shell" (92), H.D. has a dream-vision that closes this stage of her alchemy. It is an epiphany of the Lady, stripped of her myriad old forms— Isis, Astarte, Aset, Aphrodite, the old Eve, the Virgin Mary, "Our Lady of the Goldfinch, / Our Lady of the Candelabra" (93)—and released into new, as yet unnamed power. She is without the bridegroom, without the child; she is not hieratic; she is "no symbolic figure" (104). The book she carries "is not / the tome of the ancient wisdom" but "the unwritten volume of the new" (103). This as yet uninscribed essence is the renewed stuff of the other half of the alchemical formula, traditionally represented as the moon, mercury, the mothering principle.

In *The Flowering of the Rod*, part 3 of *Trilogy*, the crucible is not a place or a poem but the legend of resurrection: "a tale of a Fisherman, / a tale of a jar or jars," an ancient story which in its Christian form is "the same—different—the same attributes, / different yet the same as before" (105). What the poet-alchemist must break down here is the familiar racist and misogynist reading of the scriptures that dismisses Kaspar as a dark heathen and Mary Magdalene as a devil-ridden harlot, making both peripheral to the real story. In H.D.'s rewriting, they are central. The first two parts of *Trilogy* precipitated a new male and female principle; now, in part 3, they meet in alchemical marriage to effect the miraculous transformation. Kaspar, who might be Abraham or an Angel or even God (140), is here a somewhat forgetful and fallible philosopher, dream interpreter, astrologer, and alchemist from a long line of Arabs who knew "the secret of the sacred processes of distillation" (133). He carries with him a sealed jar of myrrh exuding a fragrance that is the eternal essence "of all flowering things together" (172): the elixir of life, the seed of resurrection.

Kaspar was traveling to "a coronation and a funeral," like all alchemical transmutations "a double affair" (130), when found by Mary Magdalene, avatar of H.D.'s "mer, mere, mère, mater, Maia, Mary, // Star of the Sea, / Mother." When he momentarily abandons his patriarchal stiffness and, assuming a posture of reverence, stoops to pick up Mary's scarf, he is granted a vision that reaches back to "the islands of the Blest" and "the lost centre-island, Atlantis" (153) and forward to "the whole scope and plan // of our and his civilization on this, / his and our earth" (154). The spell he hears recovers the lost matriarchal genealogy, identifies Mary as heritor of *Lilith born before Eve / and one born before Lilith, / and Eve* (157, italics in original), and convinces Kaspar to yield her the precious myrrh. This act — in H.D.'s astonishing rewriting — seeds the resurrection.[51] When Mary washes the feet of Christ, she anoints him with the elixir of life and insures that his crucifixion will be the first step in triumphant regeneration. Consecrated by Mary, Christ himself becomes the legendary philosopher's stone: the resurrection and the life.

Mary Magdalene's washing of the feet of Christ is the act of the alchemist: the projecting of the Mage's elixir onto substance prepared for transmutation. Behind the story of Kaspar and Mary is the old tale of sulphur and mercury; ahead of it is the work of the poet-alchemist who wanted to give us, through her combinations and recombinations of lost spells and legends, the power to transmute our own damaged civilization. The ultimate, audacious hope of *Trilogy* is that it might itself become an elixir of life, a resurrective power.

The mechanical philosophy that superseded alchemy posits a world of dead matter, matter without passion and without soul. This world of objects has often proved for its inhabitants a place of subjection, dejection, abjection, rejection — a place of energy twisted, repressed, or subverted. The nurturing universe H.D. glimpsed from the beginning of her career is profoundly different, a world of immanence and immediacy that could be called a projective universe. As the glow of radium with its puzzle of energy resident in matter led Marie Curie through her discoveries, the image of projection served as a conceptual and aesthetic focus for H.D.'s developing inquiries. An instrument of verbal organization and a source of intellectual and spiritual energies, projection was an act, an intuition, and an integration. It opened into, achieved, and helped to maintain the coherence and direction of her lifelong redemptive quest.

NOTES

This essay previously appeared in *Contemporary Literature* 25 (Winter 1984): 411–36.

1   *Tribute to Freud* (New York: McGraw-Hill, 1974), 3.
2   Herbert Read, quoted by William E. Baker, *Syntax in English Poetry, 1870–1930* (Berkeley: U of California P, 1967), 118; Ezra Pound, *Literary Essays of Ezra Pound,* ed. T. S. Eliot (New York: New Directions, 1958), 5, 6.
3   Pound, *Literary Essays* 202.
4   T. E. Hulme, *Further Speculations*, ed. Sam Hynes (Lincoln: U of Nebraska P, 1962), 77–78.
5   Ibid., 79; T. S. Eliot, quoted by Hugh Kenner, *Selected Essays* (New York: Harcourt, Brace & World, 1950), 285; Pound, *Literary Essays* 21; Fenollosa, quoted in Lawrence W. Chisolm, *Fenollosa: The Far East and American Culture* (New Haven: Yale UP, 1963), 168.
6   T. E. Hulme, *Speculations: Essays on Humanism and the Philosophy of Art*, ed. Herbert Read (London: Routledge and Kegan Paul, 1924), 134; Ezra Pound, *ABC of Reading* (New York: New Directions, 1960), 37.
7   H.D., *Collected Poems, 1912–1944*, ed. Louis L. Martz (New York: New Directions, 1983), 37, 19, 33.
8   See H.D., *Notes on Thought and Vision* (San Francisco: City Lights, 1982), 38.
9   Pound to Harriet Monroe about H.D.'s poetry, *The Letters of Ezra Pound, 1907–1941*, ed. D. D. Paige (New York: Harcourt, Brace, 1950), 11.
10 *Collected Poems* 31.
11 John T. Gage, *In the Arresting Eye: The Rhetoric of Imagism* (Baton Rouge: Louisiana State UP, 1981), 6. I am indebted to Gage's consistently sharp overview of imagist theory.
12 *Egoist* 3 (1916): 183.
13 Robert Duncan, *The H.D. Book*, Chapter 1 of Part II, *Nights and Days, Sumac* 1.1 (Fall 1968): 101, 102.
14 H.D., *Majic Ring*, typescript in the Collection of American Literature, Beinecke Rare Book and Manuscript Library, Yale University, p. 150. This and other unpublished H.D. materials are cited with the generous permission of Perdita Schaffner and the Beinecke Library.
15 Havelock Ellis, *The Dance of Life* (Boston: Houghton Mifflin, 1923), 113; H.D., *Notes on Thought and Vision* 18.
16 Havelock Ellis, *The Play Function of Sex* (London: J. E. Francis, 1921), 1.
17 See Sandra M. Gilbert and Susan Gubar, *The Madwoman in the Attic: The Woman Writer and the Nineteenth-Century Literary Imagination* (New Haven: Yale UP, 1979), 3–44, for an account of the traditional metaphors for creativity that H.D.'s "womb vision" radically revises.
18 This passage may be the origin of the code Bryher and H.D. use in the correspondence to talk about psychic manifestations (fish matters), psychic foresight (fish-eye), psychic mobility (fish-tail), the guide to the psychic realms (the always-capitalized Fish), even the psychic era to come (the Fish-age,

Pisces). See correspondence of Bryher and H.D., Beinecke Rare Book and Manuscript Library, passim.

19 *Majic Ring* 152.

20 Ibid., 163.

21 Ibid., 156; "A Friendship Traced: H.D. Letters to Silvia Dobson," ed. Carol Tinker, *Conjunctions* 2 (Spring/Summer 1982): 118; "Pontikonisi (Mouse Island)," by Rhoda Peter [H.D.], *Pagany* 3.3 (July–September 1932): 7.

22 "Pontikonisi (Mouse Island)," 1, 7, 8.

23 *Majic Ring* 127.

24 *Little Review* 12.2 (May 1929): 38.

25 For an account of H.D.'s film experience, see Anne Friedberg's "Approaching *Borderline*," *Millenium Film Journal*, nos. 7–9 (Fall–Winter 1980–81): 130–39.

26 "The Cinema and the Classics, I: Beauty," *Close Up*, July 1927, 27.

27 Ibid., 23, 24.

28 "The Cinema and the Classics, II: Restraint," *Close Up*, August 1927, 36, 35.

29 "Beauty," 58.

30 "The Cinema and the Classics, III: The Mask and the Movietone," *Close Up*, November 1927, 27.

31 "Restraint," 35.

32 "Projector II (Chang)," *Close Up*, October 1927, 37, 42–43. Rpt. *Collected Poems* 354, 358.

33 Friedberg, "Approaching *Borderline*," 131.

34 Macpherson, *Close Up*, November 1930, 294.

35 *Borderline* (London: Mercury Press, 1930), 38.

36 Ibid., 38.

37 Ibid., 31.

38 "The Dream," Chapter 3 of *The Gift, Contemporary Literature* 10.4 (1969): 605–6. This key passage was unfortunately excised from the New Directions edition of *The Gift* (New York: New Directions, 1982).

39 H.D. to Bryher: April 22, 1933 (p. 2); April 28, 1933 ("The Dream," 2); April 25, 1933 (p. 1); May 26, 1933 (p. 2).

40 Susan Stanford Friedman, *Psyche Reborn: The Emergence of H.D.* (Bloomington: Indiana UP, 1981), 153.

41 H.D. to Bryher: March 10, 1933 (p. 2); November 19, 1934 (pp. 2–3); December 7, 1934 (p. 1).

42 H.D. to Bryher: March 23, 1933 (p. 2).

43 See Rachel Blau DuPlessis, "Romantic Thralldom in H.D.," in this volume, for an excellent summary of the repetitive pattern of H.D.'s relationships with men.

44 For a detailed and moving account of the period, see Bryher, *The Days of Mars: A Memoir, 1940–1946* (New York: Harcourt Brace Jovanovich, 1972).

45 *H.D. by Delia Alton, The Iowa Review* 16.3 (1986): 186.

46 Robert Duncan, *The H.D. Book*, Chapter 5 of Part II, *Nights and Days, Stony Brook Review*, nos. 3–4 (Fall 1969): 337.

47 H.D., *Trilogy* (New York: New Directions, 1973), 29.

48 My summary here is indebted to Allison Coudert's interesting book, *Alchemy: The Philosopher's Stone* (Boulder: Shambhala, 1980).
49 See Susan Gubar's fine essay "The Echoing Spell of H.D.'s *Trilogy*," in this volume, for an extended discussion of this section of *Trilogy*.
50 H.D., *Trilogy*. Copyright ©1973 by Norman Holmes Pearson. Reprinted by permission of New Directions Publishing Corporation.
51 H.D.'s novel *Pilate's Wife*, in typescript at the Beinecke, also attributes Christ's resurrection to the intervention of a woman.

CHAPTER 16

The Echoing Spell of H.D.'s Trilogy

SUSAN GUBAR

In a wonderful children's story called *The Hedgehog*, H.D. focuses on a little girl called "Madge" or "Madgelet" whose name "isn't a name at all" and whose nationality is both English and American, although "You would think she was French too, or Swiss, when you heard her speak."[1] Understandably, she is termed "Madd" by the natives of Leytaux who find it difficult to pronounce her name or understand her language. She, too, has problems understanding them; indeed, her quest in the story is an attempt to discover the meaning of the word "*hérisson*." A wild little girl in flight from the rules and regulations of the adult world, such as the demand that she wear horrid thick boots outdoors in the garden, Madge is at the point in her life when she begins to experience self-consciousness. She is fleetingly but frighteningly aware of her separateness from the rest of creation, and it seems fitting that she is searching for an animal whose body provides a kind of natural fortress — armored protection against the slings and arrows of misfortune. This little girl's confusion at the meaning of cultural signs and her identification with the natural world recall a number of wild romantic children who are first lost and then found, but her story — which was, appropriately, written by H.D. for her daughter, Perdita — is a paradigm of a uniquely female quest for maturation that would also concern H.D. in her most ambitious poetic narratives.

Madge learns the secret meaning of the word *hérisson* only after she finds an educated man who owns and interprets for her a book on classical lore that explains how *hérissons* were used by the warriors of Mycenae to make caps and by the Athenians for combing wool. Madge's dependency on Dr. Blum recalls not only H.D.'s subsequent reliance on Dr. Freud, but also her mystification as a child when she "could . . . scarcely distinguish the shape of a number from a letter, or know which was

297

which" on the pages of writing she saw on her father's desk.[2] Sure, then, that her father possessed "sacred symbols,"[3] H.D. was conscious ever after that mythic, scientific, and linguistic symbols are controlled and defined by men. She repeatedly describes her alienation from a puzzling system of inherited symbols which do, nevertheless, finally reveal a special meaning to the female initiate. For Madge, the classical references and the successful completion of her quest lead to a joyously personal experience of her own powers which she articulates in her subsequent hymn to the moon, Artemis, who "loved girls, little girls and big girls, and all girls who were wild and free in the mountains, and girls who ran races just like boys along the seashore" (75–76).

What undercuts the traditional Freudian interpretation of this tale as a little girl's search for the phallus she presumably lacks[4] is precisely this vision of Artemis, embodying Madge's distinctively female joy and her sense that she contains multitudes, that she exists in both the mythic past and the secular present. Far from seeking so-called "masculine" forms of power, Madge manages to create out of the enigmatic, recalcitrant signs of her culture a new and sustaining story of female freedom. In her fascination with ambiguous signs and stories with "double sorts of meaning" (20), Madge resembles her creator, whose initials stand not only for Hilda Doolittle but also for the *Hermetic Definitions* that would intrigue her with secret meanings made accessible only to those who experience either themselves or their culture as alien. One of H.D.'s most coherent and ambitious poetic narratives, her war *Trilogy*, explores the reasons for her lifelong fascination with the palimpsest. Like Madge, H.D. presents herself as an outsider who must express her views from a consciously female perspective, telling the truth, as Dickinson would say, "slant." Inheriting uncomfortable male-defined images of women and of history, H.D. responds with palimpsestic or encoded revisions of male myths. Thus, like Madge, she discovers behind the recalcitrant and threatening signs of her times a hidden meaning that sustains her quest by furnishing stories of female strength and survival. In the *Trilogy*, through recurrent references to secret languages, codes, dialects, hieroglyphs, foreign idioms, fossilized traces, mysterious signs, and indecipherable signets, H.D. illustrates how patriarchal culture can be subverted by the woman who dares to "re-invoke, re-create" what has been "scattered in the shards / men tread upon."[5]

While there is rarely any question for H.D. that she can avoid reinvoking or recreating, such a posture implies that she never expects to find or make a language of her own. It is significant, I think, that H.D. sees in her famous vision at Corfu a tripod, symbol of "prophetic utterance or occult or hidden knowledge: the Priestess or Pythoness of Delphi sat on the tripod while she pronounced her verse couplets, the famous Delphic utterances which it was said *could be read two ways*" (italics mine).[6] Throughout her career, H.D. wrote couplets which have been read only one way. Placed in exclusively male contexts, the poetry of Freud's analysand, Pound's girlfriend, and D. H. Lawrence's Isis has been viewed from the monolithic perspective of the twentieth-century trinity of psychoanalysis, imagism, and modernism.[7] While none of these contexts can be discounted, each is profoundly affected by H.D.'s sense of herself as a woman writing about female confinement, specifically the woman writer's struggle against entrapment within male literary conventions. Furthermore, the fact that H.D. wrote her verse so it could be read two ways demonstrates her ambivalence over self-expression: she hides her private meaning behind public words in a juggling act that tells us a great deal about the anxieties of many women poets. Reticence and resistance characterize H.D.'s revisions in the *Trilogy*, where we can trace her contradictory attitudes toward communication: in *The Walls Do Not Fall*, H.D. demonstrates the need for imagistic and lexical redefinition, an activity closely associated with the recovery of female myths, specifically the story of Isis; in *Tribute to the Angels*, she actually begins transforming certain words, even as she revises apocalyptic myth; finally, H.D. translates the story of the New Testament in *The Flowering of the Rod*, feminizing a male mythology as she celebrates the female or "feminine" Word made flesh.

Written in three parts of forty-three poems each, primarily in unrhymed couplets, H.D.'s *Trilogy* was completed between 1944 and 1946, and it deals initially with the meaning of World War II. The title of the first volume, *The Walls Do Not Fall*, reveals the primacy of spatial imagery in H.D.'s analysis of a splintered world where "there are no doors" and "the fallen roof / leaves the sealed room / open to the air" (*WDNF* 1). All of civilized history has failed to create forms that can protect or nurture the inhabitants of this wasteland, and the "Apocryphal fire" threatens even the skeleton which has incomprehensibly survived. The poet is especially vulnerable in a world that worships coercion, for the sword takes precedence over the word. Such so-called nonutilitarian efforts as poetry are deemed irrelevant as books are burned, and the poet who identifies herself as a member of a fellowship of "nameless initiates, / born of one mother" (*WDNF* 13) realizes that only a shift in perspective can redeem this landscape of pain: then the fallen roofs, absent doors, and crumbling walls will be, paradoxically, transformed from houses into shrines. Furthermore, because "gods always face two-ways" (*WDNF* 2), H.D. considers the possibility of scratching out "indelible ink of the palimpsest" to get back to an earlier script on the still-standing walls. However, she knows that her search for "the true-rune, the right-spell" will be castigated as "retrogressive" (*WDNF* 2). In a world dominated by a God who demands *"Thou shall have none other gods but me"* (*WDNF* 37), the entire culture castigates the beauty of "Isis, Aset or Astarte" as the snare of "a harlot" (*WDNF* 2). But from the beginning, H.D. senses that the jealousy of this monotheistic God actually affirms the reality of those "old fleshpots" (*WDNF* 2).[8] Therefore she seeks "to recover old values," although her attempt will be labeled heretical and her rhythm will be identified with "the devil's hymn" (*WDNF* 2).

It is only in the context of her psychological and physical dispossession that H.D.'s famous poem about the spell of the seashell can be fully understood. In her first attempt to "recover the Sceptre, / the rod of power" associated with the healing powers of Caduceus (*WDNF* 3), H.D. portrays herself in the image of the "master-mason" or "craftsman" mollusc within the seashell (*WDNF* 4). No less an emblem of defensive survival in a hostile world than the hedgehog, the mollusc opens its house/shell to the infinite sea "at stated intervals: // prompted by hunger." But, sensing its limits, it "snap[s] shut // at invasion of the limitless" in order to preserve its own existence. Managing to eat without being eaten, the mollusc serves as an object lesson when the poet advises herself and her readers to "be firm in your own small, static, limited // orbit" so that "living within, / you beget, self-out-of-self, // selfless, / that pearl-of-great-price." Self-sufficient, brave, efficient, productive, equipped to endure in a dangerous world, H.D.'s mollusc recalls Marianne Moore's snail whose "Contractility is a virtue / as modesty is a virtue," and Denise Levertov's "Snail" whose shell is both a burden and a grace.[9] Hidden and therefore safe, the mollusc is protected in precisely the way the poet craves asylum: neither fully alive nor fully dead, half in and half out, the mollusc in its shell becomes for H.D. a tantalizing image of the self or soul safely ensconced within the person or body, always and anywhere at home.

But the fascination goes much further, because the "flabby, amorphous" mollusc not only protects itself with such impenetrable material as "bone, stone, marble" but also transforms living substance into formal object, and thereby mysteriously creates the beautiful circular patterns of its house and also the perfectly spherical pearl. Shells are associated traditionally with art because the shell is a musical instrument expressing the rhythm of the waves, and H.D. would know that it was Hermes who scooped out the shell of a tortoise, converting it into a lyre which he gave, under duress, to his brother Apollo. Hermes, who later in the *Trilogy* becomes associated with alchemy, reminds us of the transformative power that creates art out of natural objects and that caused the shell to become an important dream symbol for Wordsworth, who hears through it

A loud prophetic blast of harmony;
An Ode, in passion uttered, which foretold
Destruction to the children of the earth
By deluge, now at hand.

(*The Prelude*, v, 95–98)

Created within the watery world that threatens to overwhclm all of civilization, Wordsworth's shell warns of a return to the beginning in a flood that will cleanse and baptize the earth. H.D.'s shell also forecasts apocalypse; however, she characteristically emphasizes not the onrushing deluge but the paradoxical powerlessness of the infinite waves which cannot break the closed-in "egg in egg-shell."

The self-enclosed, nonreferential completeness of pearl and shell recalls H.D.'s own earlier imagistic poems, but the limits of imagism are what emerge most emphatically since the mollusc can combat the hostile powers of the sea only by snapping shut "shell-jaws." As Gaston Bachelard so brilliantly puts it, while "the animal in its box is sure of its secrets, it has become a monster of impenetrable physiognomy."[10] H.D. has spoken of the power of her verse to "snap-shut neatly,"[11] and the analogy implies that these tidy, enclosed poems may be unable to communicate or unwilling even to admit a content. Imprisoned within what amounts to a beautiful but inescapable tomb of form, the mollusc will not be cracked open or digested, but instead remains "small, static, limited," just as H.D.'s early poems refuse any interaction with the external world when they reproduce images that seem shaped by a poet rigidly and self-consciously in control of herself and her material. Far from representing the ultimate statement of her poetics, the seashell poem is a very limited statement, altered and superseded by transformations of this image as the *Trilogy* progresses.[12]

While H.D. discusses her craft in terms of the crafts*man* mollusc, clearly she was drawn to the shell and pearl because of their feminine evocations. Associated iconographically with Venus and the Virgin, the shell is also said to represent the female genitals.[13] It may represent pregnancy, since the pearl is a kind of seed in the womb of the shellfish, or a hope of rebirth, as in the traditionally termed "resurrection shells." This association is supported by the mythic story that Hermes created the lyre from the shell on the very day of his birth,[14] as well as the occasional identification of the seashell with the eggshell. H.D. was careful to elaborate on these aspects of her initial self-portrait in succeeding images of female artistry. But as the poet progresses in her identification with overtly feminine forms of creation, shells become associated with "beautiful yet static, empty //
old thought, old convention" (*WDNF* 17) as she drags her old self around

after her like a "dead shell" (*WDNF* 14). She wants not a shell into which she can withdraw but, on the contrary, an escape from entrapment: "my heart-shell // breaks open" (*WDNF* 25), she proclaims ecstatically when a grain, instead of a pearl, falls into the "urn" of her heart so that "the heart's alabaster / is broken" (*WDNF* 29). The locked-in image of female sexuality and creativity provided by male culture, complete with its emphasis on purity and impenetrability, is finally a "jar too circumscribed" (*WDNF* 31), and the poet renounces "fixed indigestible matter / such as shell, pearl, imagery // done to death" (*WDNF* 32) in her attempt to forge more liberating and nourishing images of survival.

In her next attempt to recover the scepter of power that is Caduceus, H.D. wittily decides not to become the rod itself, which is transformed into an innocent blade of grass, but the snake/worm which travels up the rod in a circuitous spiral toward heaven. Small, parasitic, and persistent, the worm can literally eat its way out of every calamity and sustain life even in the overwhelmingly large world that is its home. Although people cry out in disgust at the worm, it is "unrepentant" as it spins its "shroud," sure in its knowledge of "how the Lord God / is about to manifest" (*WDNF* 6). The enclosing shroud of the worm is a shell that testifies to its divinity since it adumbrates regeneration: the winged headdress, we are told, is a sign in both the snake and the emerging butterfly of magical powers of transformation, specifically of the mystery of death and rebirth experienced by all those who have endured the worm cycle to be raised into a new, higher form. Wrapped in the "shroud" of her own self (*WDNF* 13), the poet feels that she is a part of a poetic race who "know each other / by secret symbols" (*WDNF* 13) of their twice-born experience. Crawling up an "individual grass-blade / toward our individual star" (*WDNF* 14), these survivors are "the keepers of the secret / the carriers, the spinners // of the rare intangible thread / that binds all humanity // to ancient wisdom, / to antiquity" (*WDNF* 15).

It is significant that Denise Levertov centers her discussion of H.D.'s poetry on this sequence of worm poems, voicing her appreciation for poetry which provides "doors, ways in, tunnels through." When Levertov explains that H.D. "showed us a way to penetrate mystery . . . *to enter into* darkness, mystery, so that it is experienced," by darkness she means "not evil but the other side, the Hiddenness before which *man must shed his arrogance*" (italics mine).[15] In Levertov's poetry, woman is described as "a shadow / . . . drawn out / on a thread of wonder," and this "thread of wonder" links woman to "the worm artist," who tills the soil and thereby pays homage to "earth, aerates / the ground of his living." Levertov makes explicit the relationship between woman and worm artist when she describes one of the "signs" under which she has been living and writing —

a "Minoan Snake Goddess" who muses as she stands between two worlds, a symbol of female wisdom and regeneration.[16]

Of course, women from the Fates to Madame Defarge have traditionally been associated with the spinning of fate, the weaving of webs, the ensnaring of men with serpentine allies or embodiments. But H.D. and Levertov reinvent the Lamia-Eve, testimony to modern defilement of Isis, in the innocuous form of the lowly worm who recalls the speaker of Psalm 22: after crying out, "I am a worm and no man; a reproach of men, and despised of the people," the petitioner in the Psalm asks that the God "who took me out of the womb" provide a loving substitute for that loss. Both H.D. and Levertov emphasize the ways in which the worm, like the woman, has been despised by a culture that cannot stop to appreciate an artistry based not on elucidation or appropriation but on homage and wonder at the hidden darkness, the mystery. Both emphasize the worm's ability to provide another womb for its own death and resurrection. With visionary realism, both insist that the only paradise worth seeing exists not behind or beyond but within the dust. While "the keepers of the secret, / the carriers, the spinners" of such "Earth Psalms" are surely men as well as women, they are all associated with traditionally female arts of weaving, with uniquely female powers of reproducing life, and with a pre-Christian tradition that embraces gods (like Ra, Osiris, Amen) who are "not at all like Jehovah" (*WDNF* 16).

The "other side, the Hiddenness" which H.D. and Levertov seek to penetrate consists precisely of those experiences unique to women which have been denied a place in our publicly acknowledged culture, specifically the experiences of female sexuality and motherhood. Told that they embody mystery to men, even if they are indifferent to their bodies' miraculous ability to hide, foster, and emit another life, women may very well experience their own concealed sex organs as curiously mysterious, separate from their consciousness. Furthermore, the abrupt and total biological shifts that distinguish female growth from the more continuous development of men may be one reason why the worm cycle has fascinated women. In describing the fears of growing girls, Simone de Beauvoir says, "I have known little girls whom the sight of a chrysalis plunged into a frightened reverie."[17]

Confronting approving images of women that are equally degrading because they trivialize, Emily Dickinson redefines the ornamental butterfly by describing its potential for flight. She experiences confinement as her "Cocoon tightens," realizing that "A dim capacity for Wings / Demeans the Dress" she wears.[18] We see the same conflict portrayed in Judy Chicago's recent portraits of creative women in which what she calls the "butterfly-vagina"[19] struggles in its desire for "easy sweeps of Sky" against the enclosing geometrical boxes and scripts that attempt to contain it in the center of the canvas. Dickinson articulates this sense of contradiction:

> So I must baffle at the Hint
> And cipher at the Sign
> And make much blunder, if at last
> I take the clue divine.

The need for self-transformation creates a dilemma for Dickinson not dissimilar to H.D.'s confusion when she feels ready "to begin a new spiral" (*WDNF* 21) but finds herself thrown back on outworn vocabularies and the terrible feeling that she has failed to achieve metamorphosis. Like Dickinson, who "must baffle at the Hint," H.D. blunders over an "indecipherable palimpsest" (*WDNF* 31) which she cannot read. Floundering, "lost in sea-depth / . . . where Fish / move two-ways" (*WDNF* 30), overwhelmed by confusion at her own "pitiful reticence, // boasting, intrusion of strained / inappropriate allusion" (*WDNF* 31), H.D. admits the failure of her own invocations.

Perhaps she has failed because she has tried to evoke Ra, Osiris, Amen, Christ, God, All-father, and the Holy Ghost, all the while knowing that she is an "initiate of the secret wisdom, / bride of the kingdom" (*WDNF* 31). The "illusion of lost-gods, daemons" has brought, instead of revelation, the "reversion of old values" (*WDNF* 31) which inhibits, denying as it does the validity of her female perspective. Specifically, she recalls now that the spinners who keep the secret that links humanity to the ancient wisdom are aspects of the female goddess, Isis. She must remain true to her own perspective — "the angle of incidence / equals the angle of reflection" (*WDNF* 32) — and to her own needs and hungers, so she now entreats a new energy: "Hest, // Aset, Isis, the great enchantress, / in her attribute to Serqet, // the original great-mother, / who drove // harnessed scorpions / before her" (*WDNF* 34).

Seeking the "one-truth," to become as wise as "scorpions, *as serpents*" (*WDNF* 35), H.D. can now read her own personal psychic map to find the external realities. Specifically, she can now reevaluate "our secret hoard" (*WDNF* 36). The stars toward which the worm moves in its slow spiral toward the sky are also "little jars . . . boxes, very precious to hold further // unguent, myrrh, incense" (*WDNF* 24). They contain a promise of revelation not very different from shells and cocoons, which can also disclose secret treasures. Modern words, too, may reveal hidden meanings, thereby relinquishing their alien impenetrability, if the poet can somehow perceive their coded, palimpsestic status. Fairly early in the *Trilogy*, H.D. manages to take some small comfort in the bitter joke wrapped in the pun "*cartouche*": for her contemporaries, it might mean a gun cartridge with a paper case, but she knows that it once signified the oblong figure in an Egyptian monument enclosing a sovereign's name (*WDNF* 9). This kind of irony offers potential consolation when the poet realizes that it might still be possible to disentangle ancient meanings from corrupt forms, for instance the "Christos-image . . . from its art-craft junk-shop / paint-and-plaster medieval jumble // of pain-worship and death-symbol" (*WDNF* 18). Finally the poet knows and feels

> the meaning that words hide;
>
> they are anagrams, cryptograms,
> little boxes, conditioned
>
> *to hatch butterflies* . . .
> > (*WDNF* 39; italics mine)

H.D. learns how to decipher what that other H.D. — Humpty Dumpty — called "portmanteaus," words which open up like a bag or a book into compartments.[20] By means of lexical reconstruction, she begins to see the possibility of purging language of its destructive associations and arbitrariness. Viewing each word as a puzzle ready to be solved and thereby freed not only of modernity but also of contingency, H.D. begins to hope that she can discover secret, coded messages. Surely these must be subversive to warrant their being so cunningly concealed by her culture.

Now *The Walls Do Not Fall* can end in a hymn to Osiris because the poet has managed to "recover the secret of Isis" (*WDNF* 40). Just as H.D. is sure that the destructive signs surrounding her can be redefined for her own renewal, in the ancient myth Isis gathers together the scattered fragments of her lost brother/husband's body and reconstructs him in a happier ending than that to be enacted by the King's men for Humpty Dumpty. The resurrection of Osiris and the reconstruction of the magical power of the Word testify to the healing, even vivifying powers of the poet-Isis who can now see the unity between Osiris and Sirius. Since Sirius is the star representing Isis come to wake her brother from death, such an equation means that the poet glimpses the shared identity of the sibling lovers Osiris and Isis. Approaching this "serious" mystery, H.D. asks, "O, Sire, is" this union between the god and the goddess finally possible (*WDNF* 42)? She can even connect "Osiris" with the "zrr-hiss" of war lightning.[21] The poet who uses words with reverence can release the coded messages contained or enfolded within them. She has found the "alchemist's key" which "unlocks secret doors" (*WDNF* 30). Although the walls still do not fall, continuing to testify to the divisions and barriers between people, between historical periods, within consciousness itself, they also preserve remnants of written messages — anagrams and cryptograms — which, by providing the link from the present back to the past, allow H.D. to evade the destructive definitions of reality provided by those who utilize the word for modern mastery.

The poet's response in the subsequent volumes of the *Trilogy* to the shattered fragmentation of her world is stated in the first poem of *Tribute to the Angels*: dedicating herself to Hermes Trismegistus, patron of alchemists, H.D. undertakes not merely the archeological reconstruction of a lost past, but also a magical transfiguration not unlike Christ's creation of the sustaining loaves and fishes or the transubstantiation of bread and water into body and blood. Since alchemical art has traditionally been associated with fiery purification that resurrects what is decomposing in the grave into a divine and golden form,[22] even the destructive lightning and bombs can now be associated with melting that fuses a new unity, heat that transforms the contents of the dross in the alchemist's bowl into the philosopher's stone. The seashell of *The Walls Do Not Fall* becomes a testimony to such displacement, reappearing as a bowl which is cauldron, grave, and oven, yet another womb in which a new jewel can be created. Now the poet sees the function of the poem/bowl as the transformative redefinition of language itself. Thus she gives us the recipe by which she endows "a word most bitter, *marah*" and a word denigrated, "*Venus*," with more affirmative nurturing meanings: "marah" becomes "Mother," and "Venus" is translated from "venery" to "venerate" (*TA* 8, 12). Similarly, she seeks a way of evading names that definitely label the word-jewel in the bowl: "I do not want to name it," she explains, because "I want to minimize thought, // concentrate on it / till I shrink, // dematerialize / and am drawn into it" (*TA* 14). Seeking a noncoercive vocabulary, a new language that will consecrate what has been desecrated by her culture, H.D. tries to reestablish the primacy of what masculine culture has relegated to a secondary place as "feminine."

Implicitly heretical, Hermes' alchemy is associated with "candle and script and bell," with "what the new-church spat upon" (*TA* 1), and H.D. does not evade the challenge her own alchemical art constitutes to the prevailing Christian conception of the Word. On the contrary, in *Tribute to the Angels* she self-consciously sets her narrative in the context of the Book of Revelation, quoting directly from it in numerous poems in order to question John's version of redemption while offering her own revision. In many poems she seems to be arguing with John directly because his vision appears warped: H.D. quotes John's assertion of the finality of his own account, his admonition that "*if any man shall add // God shall add unto him the plagues*," even as she determines to alter his story, dedicating herself to making all things new (*TA* 3). She realizes that "he of the seventy-times-seven / passionate, bitter wrongs" is also "he of the seventy-times-seven / bitter, unending wars" (*TA* 3), and she questions the severity and punishing cruelty of John's apocalypse, with its vengeful version of the hidden future. While John sings the praises of seven angels whose seven golden bowls pour out the wrath of God upon the earth, H.D. calls on seven angels whose presence in war-torn London is a testament to the promise of rebirth that her bowl holds. While "*I John saw*" a series of monstrosities and disasters on the face of the earth, H.D. claims that "my eyes saw" a sign of resurrection: "a half-burnt-out apple-tree / blossoming" (*TA* 23) is the fulfillment of her hopes at the beginning of the *Trilogy* to recover the scepter, the lily-bud rod of Caduceus, which is now associated with the Tree of Life that links heaven and earth, the Cosmic Tree which represents the mysterious but perpetual regeneration of the natural world, the tree that miraculously lodges the coffin of the dead Osiris or the tree on which Christ was hung to be reborn. Aaron's rod which made the bitter (marah) waters sweet when it blossomed in the desert for the wandering children of Israel is converted from a sign of Moses' control to an emblem of a Lady's presence.

Most significantly, H.D. contrasts the final vision of the holy Jerusalem — a city with no need of the sun or the moon because lit by the glory of God, a city which John imagines as the bride of the Lamb — with her own final revelation of redemption. H.D. first describes a Lady in a bedroom lit by the "luminous disc" of the clock by her bedhead, ironically commenting that this room has "no need / of the moon to shine in it" (*TA* 25). But this appearance is only a dream adumbration of the vision of this same Lady who appears when H.D. is "thinking of Gabriel / of the moon-cycle, of the moon-shell, // of the moon-crescent / and the moon at full" (*TA* 28). Far from seeking a place with no need of moonshine, H.D. celebrates a Lady who is actually the representative of lunar time and consciousness. Furthermore, the poet is careful to remind us through a whole series of negatives that this Lady, whom we recognize from the various portraits of the female as she has been worshipped by various cultures, is like none of these previous representatives or incarnations. "None of these / suggest her" as the poet sees her (*TA* 31). H.D.'s vision of the Lady is not hieratic or frozen: "she is no symbolic figure." While she has "the dove's symbolic purity," and "veils / like the Lamb's Bride," H.D. is insistent that "the Lamb was not with her / either as Bridegroom or Child"; not He, but "*we* are her bridegroom and lamb" (*TA* 39; italics mine).

The miraculous transformation in the alchemical bowl and the equally mysterious flowering of the rod find their culmination in this revelation of the muse who is not only the veiled goddess, Persephone, the *Sanctus*

Spiritus, Santa Sophia, Venus, Isis, and Mary, but most important the
female spirit liberated from precisely these mystifications:

> but she is not shut up in a cave
> like a Sibyl; she is not
>
> imprisoned in leaden bars
> in a coloured window;
>
> she is Psyche, *the butterfly*,
> *out of the cocoon*.
>   (*TA* 38; italics mine)

Unnamed and elusive, the Lady recalls in her flight the hatched and winged
words of H.D. herself, if only because this visionary Lady carries a book
which "is our book" (*TA* 39). Whether this "tome of the ancient wisdom"
whose pages "are the blank pages / of the unwritten volume of the new"
(*TA* 38) is "a tribute to the Angels" (*TA* 41) or a "tale of a jar or jars"
(*TA* 39) that will constitute the next volume of the *Trilogy*, H.D. closely
identifies this new Eve who has come to retrieve what was lost at the apple
tree with her own liberating revisions of the past. Whatever volume of
the poem she may carry or inspire, the Lady reflects H.D.'s hope that her
narrative is a "Book of Life" (*TA* 36).

As she evokes and thereby reinterprets the inherited signs of her culture which are said to contain the secret wisdom necessary for the attainment of paradise, H.D. implies that "the letter killeth but the spirit giveth
life" (2 Corinthians 3:6). It is life that she sees finally created in the crucible "when the jewel / melts" and what we find is "a cluster of garden-
pinks / or a face like a Christmas-rose" (*TA* 43). In the final book of the
Trilogy, the escaping fragrance of such flowering within the pristine glass
of a jar represents the poet's success in finding a form that can contain
without confining. No longer surrounded by splintered shards, H.D. makes
of her jars symbols of aesthetic shape not unlike those of Wallace Stevens
or Hart Crane, beautiful and complete objects but also transparencies
through which a healing content is made manifest. Purified of their opac-
ity, shell, bowl, and box are now ready to reveal their previously secret
and therefore inaccessible hoard. This promise of release is realized fully
in *The Flowering of the Rod*: dedicated to the Lady who has escaped
conventionally defined categories, the poet readies herself for flight as she
asks us to "leave the smouldering cities below" (*FR* 1), the place of deathly
skulls, to follow the quest of Christ, who was "the first to wing / from
that sad Tree" (*FR* 11) and whose journey is similar to that of the snow
geese circling the Arctic or the mythical migratory flocks seeking paradise.

Not only does H.D. move further back in time in this third volume of *Trilogy*, but her initial focus on seemingly insignificant animals and her subsequent naming of angelic powers seem to have made it possible for her finally to create human characters as she retells the story of the birth and death of Christ from the unexpected perspective of two participants in the gospel — Kaspar the Magian and Mary Magdala. Furthermore, after two sequences of poems progressing by allusive associations, complex networks of imagery, and repetitive, almost liturgical invocations, the final book of the *Trilogy* embodies the emergence of the poet's sustained voice in a story — if not of her own making — of her own perspective. She takes an unusual stance toward the ancient story to distinguish her vision: claiming to see "what men say is-not," to remember what men have forgot (*FR* 6), she sets out to testify to an event known by everyone but as yet unrecorded (*FR* 12).

Like Christ, who was himself "an outcast and a vagabond" (*FR* 11), and like the poet who is identified with the thief crucified by His side, both Kaspar and Mary are aliens in their society. The inheritor of ancient alchemical tradition, Kaspar owns the jars which hold "priceless, unobtainable-elsewhere / myrrh" (*FR* 13), a "distillation" which some said "lasted literally forever," the product of "sacred processes" which were "never written, not even in symbols" (*FR* 14). As a heathen, he represents prebiblical lore that acknowledges the power of "daemons" termed "devils" by the modern Christian world. His education, however, is a patrimony in an exclusively male tradition that assumes "no secret was safe with a woman" (*FR* 14). Kaspar is shown to be a bit of a prig and something of a misogynist, so it is highly incongruous that Mary Magdala comes to this Arab stranger in his "little booth of a house" (*FR* 13) behind the market. Unmaidenly and unpredictable, Mary is as much of an outcast as Kaspar, if only because of her ability "to detach herself," a strength responsible for her persistence in spite of Kaspar's statement that the myrrh is not for sale: "planted" before him (*FR* 15), Mary identifies herself first as "Mary, a great tower," and then explains that, though she is "Mara, bitter," through her own power she will be "Mary-myrrh" (*FR* 16). Clearly, the coming together of Kaspar and Mary implies the healing of the poet's own sense of fragmentation. Before the jar actually changes hands, however, H.D. dramatizes the discomfort of Simon, who views Mary at the Last Supper as a destructive siren. This "woman from the city" who seems "devil-ridden" to the Christian is recognized by Kaspar as a living embodiment of the indwelling daemons of "Isis, Astarte, Cyprus / and the other four: // he might re-name them, / Ge-meter, De-meter, earth-mother // or Venus / in a star" (*FR* 25).

Only after we have recognized the seemingly antithetical wise man and

the whore as common representatives of reverence for the ancient principles of female fertility and creativity does H.D. return to the scene in the
booth behind the market to fully describe the vision granted to Kaspar
through the intervention of Mary. Here, at the climax of the *Trilogy*,
Kaspar recalls the poet's experience with the Lady, for he is graced with
a remembrance of "when he saw the light on her hair / like moonlight
on a lost river" (*FR* 27). In a fleck or a flaw of a jewel on the head of
one of three crowned ladies, Kaspar discovers "the whole secret of the
mystery" (*FR* 30). He sees the circles of islands and the lost center island,
Atlantis: he sees earth before Adam, Paradise before Eve. Finally, he hears
a spell in an unknown language which seems to come down from pre-
historical times as it translates itself to him:

> *Lilith born before Eve*
> *and one born before Lilith,*
> *and Eve; we three are forgiven,*
> *we are three of the seven*
> *daemons cast out of her.*
>
> (*FR* 33)

This is an extremely enigmatic message, but it does seem to imply that
a matriarchal genealogy had been erased from recorded history when this
ancient female trinity was exorcized as evil, cast out of human consciousness by those who would begin in the Garden with Eve. Since Lilith is
a woman who dared pronounce the Ineffable Name and who was un-
abashed at articulating her sexual preferences, her presence among the
crowned or crucified queens seems to promise a prelapsarian vision quite
different from that of Genesis: Lilith, Eve, and the unnamed daemon are
three of the seven who establish a link back to Kaspar's pagan daemons;
together they promise a submerged but now recoverable time of female
strength, female speech, and female sexuality, all of which have mysteriously managed to survive, although in radically subdued ways, incarnate
in the body of Mary Magdala. As a healer, a shaman of sorts,[23] Kaspar
has in a sense recaptured Mary's stolen soul, her lost ancestors; he has
established the matriarchal genealogy that confers divinity upon her.

Reading Mary like a palimpsest, Kaspar has fully penetrated the secret
of the mystery. H.D. then reverses the chronology of his life, moving
backward from his confrontation with this Mary over the jars of myrrh
to his delivery of the gift of myrrh to the Virgin Mary. When Kaspar thinks
in the ox stall that "there were always two jars" (*FR* 41) and that "*some-
day* [he] *will bring the other*" (*FR* 42), we know that his prophecy has
been or will be fulfilled: as he gives the myrrh to the Virgin, we know
that he is destined to give the other jar to Mary Magdala, thereby authen-

ticating his vision of the female trinity—his knowledge that the whore is the mother and that Isis, who has been labeled a retrogressive harlot, is actually the regenerative goddess of life. Through the two Marys, Kaspar recovers the aspects of Isis retained by Christianity—the lady of sorrows weeping for the dead Osiris and the divine mother nursing her son, Horus.[24] When marah is shown to be mother the translation is complete, and the poem can end with a new word, as the gift is miraculously appreciated by a Mary who might know that the blossoming, flowering fragrance is the commingling of the magical contents of the jar, the myrrh in her arms, and perhaps even the baby in her lap.

Dramatically ending at the beginning, moving from Apocalypse to Genesis, from death to birth, from history to mystery, H.D. illustrates the cyclical renewal she personally seeks of dying into life. Calling our attention to her own narrative principles, H.D. proclaims: "I have gone forward. / I have gone backward" (*FR* 8). And as we have seen, her point is precisely the need of going backward in time to recover what has been lost in the past, for this justifies her own progress backward in chronological time throughout the *Trilogy*: proceeding from the modern times of London in *The Walls Do Not Fall* to the medieval cities of *Tribute to the Angels* and back to the ancient deserts of Israel in *The Flowering of the Rod*, she dedicates herself to finding the half-erased traces of a time "When in the company of the gods / I loved and was loved" (*WDNF* 5). Such a discovery, as we have seen, involves not a learning but a remembering. However, instead of moving backward in a linear, sequential manner, she chooses three time bands that seem to be relatively self-contained, like ever-narrowing circles enclosing some still point of origin. Furthermore, she calls our attention to the disconnectedness of her three time spheres by isolating each within a book of the *Trilogy*. These three distinct periods in time, when taken in themselves, are senseless and directionless, each repeating the other:

> you think, even before it is half-over,
> that your cycle is at an end,
>
> but you repeat your foolish circling—again, again, again;
> again, the steel sharpened on the stone;
>
> again, the pyramid of skulls.
>
> (*FR* 6)

The senseless wheeling within each of these foolish cycles, caused by the lack of vision that cannot see "then" as an aspect of "now," is fittingly experienced as a tornado (*WDNF* 32). It can produce only war.

On the other hand, each moment of time in each of these historical cycles is, at least potentially, related to a prehistoric origin, just as all points on the circumference of a circle are related to its center. The poet who understands the palimpsestic symbols of the past in today's imagery can interpret the "mysterious enigma" that merges "the distant future / with most distant antiquity" (*WDNF* 20). Similarly, seeing down the "deep, deep-well // of the so-far unknown / depth of pre-history," Kaspar realizes "a *point* in time — // he called it a fleck or a flaw in a gem" on a circlet of gems on a lady's head (*FR* 40). Since historical time is envisioned as a series of circles enclosing a prehistoric center, H.D. can describe how Kaspar heard "an echo of an echo in a shell" (*FR* 28), a language he had never heard spoken and which seems translated "as it transmuted its message // through spiral upon spiral of the shell / of memory that yet connects us // with the drowned cities of pre-history" (*FR* 33).

That Kaspar hears "an echo of an echo in a shell" recalls not only the importance of the seashell earlier in the *Trilogy*, but also the fascination of Madge in *The Hedgehog* with Echo, who always answers her caller "Echo":

Or sometimes just O, O, O, just the same O, getting thin and far and far and thin like the sound of water. Echo melts into the hill, into the water. Now she is a real person. . . . Echo is the answer of our own hearts, like the singing in a sea-shell. (44)

What tantalizes Madge about Echo's response, just as it informed her curiosity about *hérisson*, is the recalcitrance of the word, its refusal to yield up meaning, its emptiness of signification, as well as its ambiguous status as silent sound, the voice of nature, a living remnant of ancient Greece, an aspect of her own voice returned from a far distance, a female utterance of completion and circularity. In *Tribute to Freud*, H.D. returns to the image of the echoing shell when she describes how her unspoken expressions of gratitude go on singing

like an echo of an echo in a shell — very far away yet very near — the very shell substance of my outer ear and the curled involuted or convoluted shell skull, and inside the skull, the curled, intricate, hermit-like mollusk, the brain-matter itself.[25]

Clearly the spiraling echoes of the shell are a way of recognizing the intimate yet convoluted relationship between a central origin and its distant reaches. Hearing "the echoed syllables of this spell" (*FR* 33), Kaspar remains unsure about the status of his revelation: is it "a sort of spiritual optical-illusion" (*FR* 40) — the answer of his own heart? Or could the echoing shell also contain the secret revealed in *Hermetic Definition* — a sound like that of water, "*Grande Mer*" or "*Mère*"?[26]

Echo, we should remember, was punished for her only "failing," her fondness for talk, by being deprived of the power of speaking first. In this respect, she serves as a paradigm of the secondary status of women who have traditionally been reduced to supporting, assuaging, serving, and thereby echoing the work, wishes, and words of men. Specifically, she serves as a model for H.D.'s sense of her own belatedness as she repeats the warped words she experiences as prior authorities on her own spiritual and psychic experiences. Echo does manage, however, to express her desires, even as she mocks the speech of those she mimics. Like Echo, H.D. felt cursed because she was denied control over her own speech, destined to repeat the language of another's making, and therefore hidden, if not obliterated, from her own creations. However, just as Echo manages to express her desires, even making sexual advances by dropping certain words and altering her inflection, H.D. manages to get her secrets sung, making of her echoes a personal response to the literary and linguistic conventions she inherits. Moreover, as a symbol of retreat from the danger of meaning into protective obscurity, the echoing shell is an understandably attractive image for H.D., who can define her art as "merely" derivative. Using the language of another's creation is, after all, a foolproof defense against being defined by one's verse and thereby confined within the prisonhouse of language. H.D.'s story is always "different yet the same as before" (*TA* 39), and therefore "only" a repetition. Herein lies both the strength and the weakness of her art, as well as the reason why the echo is yet another infinitely decipherable (and therefore indecipherable) palimpsest.

Whether derivative or transmuted sound, however, the spiraling echo of the shell makes all of the enclosures of the first two poems comprehensible as metamorphoses of the circle. The shell with its spherical pearl, the bowl containing the gold, the boxes hatching butterflies, even the jars are circles surrounding a magical potent center. In an evocation of the spiraling turns of the worm approaching its star, the migratory geese of *The Flowering of the Rod* seek paradise by circling "till they drop from the highest point of the spiral / or fall from the innermost center of the ever- / narrowing circle" (*FR* 5). Their drowning would be a welcome end for the poet, who feels now that "only love is holy and love's ecstasy // that turns and turns and turns about one centre, / reckless, regardless, blind to reality" (*FR* 6). The islands encircled by water, especially the lost center island of Atlantis, become a fitting symbol of the time of prehistoric eternity. The poet seeks this center because it can serve as an escape from the repetitions of history and because it is an entrance to creative stasis. Such a center is neither temporally nor spatially bound: its potential for unfolding gains it extension in space as it detemporalizes the present into an emblem of both the past and the future.[27]

Finally we see the circumference as a flower which, contained in the grain or seed,

> opened petal by petal, a circle,
> and each petal was separate
>
> yet still held, as it were,
> by some force of attraction
>
> to its dynamic centre;
> and the circle went on widening
>
> and would go on opening
> . . . to infinity.
>
> (*FR* 31)

Participating in a mystical literary tradition that extends from Dante to Roethke, H.D. evokes the unbroken, unfolding circle to satisfy her longing to "equilibrate" (*FR* 5) the antagonisms between desert and arctic, spring and winter, silence and sound, to heal the struggle between father and mother, thereby establishing a harmony dramatized by the recognition of commonality between Kaspar and Mary Magdala and by the image of the androgynous center of the flower. Seeking to be drawn into the center, H.D. finds in resurrection "a sense of direction" taking her "straight to the horde and plunder, / the treasure, the store-room, // the honeycomb," to "food, shelter, fragrance" (*FR* 7). While H.D. never denies the place of men in such an origin, she does end the *Trilogy* with an emphasis on the feminine that extends Kaspar's consciousness of prelapsarian time as a time of woman worship: she celebrates the baby or myrrh cradled in the arms of a woman whose sex is represented as a circle on a stem ♀ — the sacred *ankh* which is the symbol of life in Egypt.[28] The medieval definition of God as the sphere whose center is everywhere and whose circumference is nowhere has been radically feminized by a writer who sees the outstretched wings of the butterfly or the beauty of the "lunar rainbow" (*WDNF* 32) as alternative examples of the "arc of perfection" (*TA* 43). Here again H.D. serves as a paradigm for other women writers, such as Marge Piercy, whose sequence of poems entitled "The Spring Offensive of the Snail" celebrates encircling, blossoming lovers; Monique Wittig, who makes the circle an emblem of her Amazon utopia; Margaret Atwood, who focuses on circularity in her revision of the myth of Circe's island; and Adrienne Rich, who circles around the wreck with a book of outworn myths.[29]

H.D. would not and does not deprive the center of its inaccessible mystery or the circumference of its distance from origin. On the contrary, as one of Jung's precursors, she testifies to the continued need for approaching the center, for retelling and rewriting and adding to a palimpsest even as she realizes that such an approach is a regression, and that — as the word "re-cover" implies — she hides what she seeks to reveal. Denise Levertov celebrates just this reverence for the unknowable in H.D.'s poetry when she explains that H.D. went "further, further out of the circle of known light, further in toward an unknown center."[30] This center is the secret; for example, the final transaction between Kaspar and Mary Magdala which is never represented in the *Trilogy* or even adequately explained. If in some ways Kaspar the Magian was right that "no secret was safe with a woman" (*FR* 14), he nevertheless failed to realize that the woman who models her speech on that of Echo or Sibyl, or (less hopefully) Cassandra or Philomel, would be telling a secret that retains the power of its hidden mystery. Singing a spell which conforms to none of the words she had ever heard spoken, H.D. reveals the ways in which one woman mythologizes herself and her gender, asserting herself as the center of the universe in a radical reversal and revision of the inherited images she so brilliantly echoes.

NOTES

This essay previously appeared in *Contemporary Literature* 19 (Spring 1978): 196–218.

1 H.D., *The Hedgehog* (London: Brendin Publishing Co., 1936), 1 and 3. Parenthetical page references in the text refer to this edition.

2 H.D., *Tribute to Freud, Writing on the Wall, Advent* (Boston: David R. Godine, 1974), 19.

3 Ibid., 25.

4 Norman N. Holland, *Poems in Persons: An Introduction to the Psychoanalysis of Literature* (New York: W. W. Norton, 1975), 32.

5 H.D., *Tribute to the Angels*, in *Trilogy* (New York: New Directions, 1973), #1. Subsequent references to poems in *Trilogy* will be parenthetically indicated in the text by capitalized initials of the volume and number of the poem.

6 *Tribute to Freud* 51.

7 A very fine discussion of the limitation of male-dominated criticism of H.D. appears in Susan Friedman's "Who Buried H.D.? A Poet, Her Critics, and Her Place in 'The Literary Tradition,' " *College English* 36.7 (March 1975): 801–14, although she seems to ignore some of the exceptionally sensitive insights of Joseph N. Riddel in "H.D. and the Poetics of 'Spiritual Realism,' "

Contemporary Literature 10.4 (Autumn 1969): 447–73. For earlier criticism of the *Trilogy*, see Vincent Quinn, *Hilda Doolittle* (New York: Twayne Publishers, 1967), 116–26 and Thomas Burnett Swann, *The Classical World of H.D.* (Lincoln: U of Nebraska P, 1962), 163–73.

8   H.D. would seem to agree with the secret gnostic gospels that celebrate God in masculine and feminine terms. These gospels and their social implications for religious women are examined by Elaine H. Pagels in "What Became of God the Mother? Conflicting Images of God in Early Christianity," *Signs* 2.2 (Winter 1976): 293–303.

9   Marianne Moore's quest for defensive protection to prevent personal exposure is explored by Suzanne Juhasz, *Naked and Fiery Forms: Modern American Poetry by Women, A New Tradition* (New York: Harper Colophon Books, 1976), 33–56. I have quoted Moore's "To a Snail" from *Complete Poems* (New York: Macmillan Co./Viking Press, 1967), 85. Denise Levertov's "Snail" is in *Relearning the Alphabet* (New York: New Directions, 1970), 77.

10 Gaston Bachelard, *The Poetics of Space*, trans. Maria Jolas (Boston: Beacon Press, 1969), 134. Bachelard's chapter "Shells," 105–35, illuminates H.D.'s use of the image.

11 Norman Holmes Pearson quotes her phrase in his "Introduction" to the *Trilogy* viii.

12 See H.D., "The Poet," in *The Poet and the Dancer* (1935; rpt. San Francisco: Five Trees Press, 1975), #3: "Yes / it is dangerous to get out, / and you shall not fail: / but it is also / dangerous to stay in, / unless one is a snail." Significantly, this poem contrasts the shell to the "butterfly [who] has antennae, / is moral / and ironical too." I am indebted to Pat Fishman for a copy of this little-known volume of H.D.'s.

13 In *The Poetics of Space* Bachelard discusses the conch of Venus that represents a woman's vulva, as well as representations in the shell museum of the toothed vagina (114); in *The Second Sex*, trans. H. M. Parshley (New York: Bantam, 1961), Simone de Beauvoir describes how "feminine sex desire is the soft throbbing of a mollusk" (362); the medieval alliterative poem *Pearl* is one of many works of literature to tap the patristic convention associating the pearl with female purity. And, of course, Botticelli was not the first to portray Venus emerging from the sea on a shell.

14 Bachelard, *The Poetics of Space* 117; Benjamin Boyce, "Sounding Shells and Little Prattlers in the Mid-Eighteenth-Century English Ode," *Eighteenth-Century Studies* 8.3 (Spring 1975): 245–64.

15 Denise Levertov, "H.D.: An Appreciation," *The Poet in the World* (New York: New Directions, 1973), 246.

16 The phrases quoted are from Levertov's "Stepping Westward," "The Earth Worm," and "The Postcards: A Triptych," which appear in *The Sorrow Dance* (New York: New Directions, 1967), 15, 16, and 69.

17 Beauvoir, *Second Sex* 285. Significantly, one of the more recent women's journals is entitled *Chrysalis*.

18 Emily Dickinson, #1099, *The Complete Poems of Emily Dickinson*, ed. Thomas H. Johnson (Boston: Little, Brown, 1960), 496.

19 Lecture delivered at Indiana University on October 24, 1975; Judy Chicago also discusses flower imagery as a representation of women's sexuality in *Through the Flower: My Struggle as a Woman Artist* (Garden City, NY: Doubleday, 1975).

20 Lewis Carroll, *Alice in Wonderland*, ed. Donald Gray (New York: W. W. Norton, 1971), 164.

21 I am referring here to poems 40–43 that conclude *The Walls Do Not Fall*. The significance of the Isis-Osiris myth to H.D. is at least partially explained by Arthur Weigall, *The Paganism in Our Christianity* (New York: G. P. Putnam's Sons, 1928), 124–34, a book that Mr. Pearson describes as "a favorite" of H.D.'s in his "Introduction" to the *Trilogy* vii.

22 This association, exploited by Renaissance poets like Jonson, Greene, Nashe, and Donne, is explained with some fine background information on alchemy by Edgar H. Duncan in "Donne's Alchemical Figures," *ELH* 9 (1942): 257–85.

23 See the discussion of shamanism in *Myths, Rites, Symbols: A Mircea Eliade Reader*, ed. Wendell C. Beane and William G. Doty (New York: Harper Colophon Books, 1975), II, 262–82. The magical identification with dead ancestors achieved by the shaman, his trance as he is carried away to learn the secrets of the gods, his healing role in the community, and his ability to speak in secret languages make him a paradigm of the kind of artist H.D. sought to become.

24 Weigall, *Paganism in Our Christianity* 129.

25 *Tribute to Freud* 90.

26 H.D., *Sagesse*, in *Hermetic Definition* (New York: New Directions, 1972), #18, p. 75.

27 To understand how this places H.D. in a romantic tradition encompassing Tieck, Fichte, Novalis, Coleridge, and Goethe, see Georges Poulet, *The Metamorphoses of the Circle*, trans. Larley Dawson and Elliott Coleman (Baltimore: Johns Hopkins UP, 1966), 91–118.

28 In *Tribute to Freud*, H.D. calls a magnifying glass stolen by her Promethean brother, with its "circle and the stem of the circle," a sacred symbol: "This is the sacred *ankh*, the symbol of life in Egypt" (25). In *The Flowering of the Rod*, Kaspar sees the prehistoric city as if it were "enlarged under a sunglass" (#32, p. 155).

29 Marge Piercy, *To Be of Use* (Garden City, NY: Doubleday, 1973); Monique Wittig, *Les Guerrillères*, trans. David Le Vay (London: Peter Owen, 1971); Margaret Atwood, "Circe/Mud Poems," *You Are Happy* (New York: Harper and Row, 1974); Adrienne Rich, *Diving into the Wreck* (New York: W. W. Norton, 1976).

30 Levertov, "H.D.: An Appreciation," 247.

CHAPTER 17

Re-Membering the Mother:
A Reading of H.D.'s Trilogy

ALBERT GELPI

Shortly before her death in 1925, Amy Lowell began a monologue about the melancholy situation of women poets with these lines:

> Taking us by and large, we're a queer lot
> We women who write poetry. And when you think
> How few of us there've been, it's queerer still.
> I wonder what it is that makes us do it,
> Singles us out to scribble down, man-wise,
> The fragments of ourselves. Why are we
> Already mother-creatures, double bearing,
> With matrices in body and in brain?[1]

Although the question is left hanging in the air, the suggestion is that the woman poet ought ideally to be a double mother "with matrices in body and in brain." But if the challenge or the circumstances of patriarchy prove too daunting, can she be a mother in brain, if not in body? Can her poems become the parthenogenetic offspring of her "man-wise" powers which proclaim her at once mother and daughter and virgin? H.D.'s *Trilogy* offers an instance of such a parthenogenesis, remarkable in the history of women's poetry.

H.D.'s prematurely titled *Collected Poems* (1925) summed up her imagist phase, in which Ezra Pound, Richard Aldington, and D. H. Lawrence were powerful but threatening presences. *Red Roses for Bronze* (1931) gathered together the poems of the previous six years, but showed the poet in an agitated and uncertain state about herself and her work. Then no volumes of poems until *The Walls Do Not Fall* (1944), followed by *Tribute to the Angels* (1945) and *The Flowering of the Rod* (1946), the first written in 1942 and the other two in separate fortnights in May and December of 1944. The sequences were closely related to one another, but were first published together as *Trilogy* only posthumously in 1973.[2] Nonetheless, *Trilogy* marks the opening of the late, great phase of H.D.'s poetry and must be ranked with *Four Quartets* and *The Pisan Cantos* as the major poems in English to come out of the war.

There had been less writing during the thirties than in previous and subsequent decades. The war clouds that hung over H.D.'s sessions with Freud broke, as she feared, and drove her and Freud separately to London for shelter. Freud died — fortunately, H.D. came to feel — before the blitz which at times rained daily terror but which she refused to escape through asylum in America. As with the First War, when she refused Aldington's suggestion that she return to her family in Pennsylvania, she resolved to stick it out. The political upheaval of the twentieth century had again put her sense of self and cosmos to the incendiary test, and she knew instinctively that she had somehow to meet the test.

Robert Duncan charted H.D.'s development from her early Greek imagism as a deepening engagement with the metaphysics of the Image, which connected the riddle of the psyche with the mystery of the universe:

H.D. had come to be concerned . . . with finding out the gods in levels of many meanings, as personae of states of mind, but also as guides in reading the message of the universe. Here, the Image is also a Sign . . . Image and Fact are now Logos, revelations that we must receive. The Universe is a book of what we are and asks us to put it all together, to learn to read.

Early on "the Image was the nexus of the individual consciousness and the Presence," and "the *sense* (awareness as feeling) of Presence was all." But "now [in the forties] H.D. must search out the sense anew in the meaning *sense* has of import (awareness as knowledge of meaning): she must read the message the Presence presents."[3]

H.D. saw the mystery cults which interpreted that message running from Greece to Provence, as Pound did, and then from "a branch of the dispersed or 'lost' church of Provence, the Church of Love that we touch on in *By Avon River*,"[4] to the Moravian Brotherhood which established her hometown of Bethlehem, Pennsylvania. When in old age she revisited her mother's family's church, where as a girl she had attended the love feasts, she certified her continuing identification by signing the register "Baptized Moravian" ("Foreword," v).

Simultaneously her growing interest in the Egyptian mysteries drew her by the 1940s to their formulation in Rosicrucianism. Again as with Pound, various elements — Greek and Egyptian, Jewish and Christian — intermingled in her mind as they had for centuries in the ancient world. In the process, as her close friend Norman Holmes Pearson put it, "like many Freudians, she became quasi-Jungian and could bring the cabala, astrollogy, magic, Christianity, classical and Egyptian mythology, and personal experience into a joint sense of Ancient Wisdom." In World War II London she and Bryher held seances at H.D.'s insistence regularly, often daily, with Arthur Bhaduri, a Eurasian medium, and his mother. They soon found a tripod in H.D.'s possession which had once belonged to William Morris more effective than a table for receiving the messages tapped out from the other world. An unpublished manuscript entitled *Majic Ring* gives an account of the messages she received from slain RAF pilots. When she heard Lord Hugh Dowding, the retired air marshal of Britain, who had been responsible for the heroic defense of the homeland, lecture in October 1943 about his own spirit messages from some of his dead airmen, H.D. took the coincidence of their initials as a sign of their deep personal affinity. To Hugh Dowding's bafflement she sought him out as her soul mate and fictionalized him as Lord Howell in *Majic Ring* ("Foreword," vi).[5] By the time of the writing of *Trilogy*, therefore, H.D. was thoroughly steeped in the occult: a fact which made for the eclectic theology, but also for the compelling religious and imaginative vision of the poems.

Like each of the other two poems in *Trilogy, The Walls Do Not Fall* consists of forty-three sections of varying length, written in pairs of free-verse lines which accommodate language ranging from the colloquially discursive to the intricately rhythmic and densely associative. *Walls* is dedicated to Bryher, who spent the war years with H.D. in London. The opening section overlays the bombed-out city with the ruined temple at Karnak which the two women had visited in 1923; now night fires lit the sky outside their windows, and day broke on ruins which seemed to announce apocalypse. Bryher's memoirs of these years would come later in *The Days of Mars* (1972), but H.D.'s were recorded on the spot in *Trilogy*, the unpublished autobiographical fictions, and *Tribute to Freud*.

H.D.'s initial reaction to the explosion of war is to withdraw into the psyche as protective shell. In a poem early in *The Walls* she becomes a shellfish, not now a rare murex but a lowly oyster or clam or mollusc, whose cunning contrives survival in the jaws of Leviathan:

> I sense my own limit,
> my shell-jaws snap shut
>
> . . .
>
> so I in my own way know
> that the whale
>
> can not digest me:
> be firm in your own small, static, limited

orbit and the shark-jaws
of outer circumstance

will spit you forth:
be indigestible, hard, ungiving.

(9)

It was a strategy she first learned during the other war, yet learned too that "there is a spell . . . in every sea-shell" which allows "that flabby, amorphous hermit" to quicken and flourish (8). So the shellfish becomes an "egg in egg-shell" (9), and the imagery of female gestation in *The Walls Do Not Fall* goes on to include the cocoon (anticipating *Tribute to the Angels*) and the myrrh jar (anticipating *The Flowering of the Rod*). The enclosure is hermetic in a double sense: sealed and magical. The shell becomes an alchemical crucible within which "you beget, self-out-of-self, / selfless, / that pearl-of-great-price" (9). So in the course of the poem the hermetic crucible splits in birth, as "my heart-shell / breaks open" (35) to deliver the pearl, the precious oils, the bird, the butterfly—all images of the parthenogenetic self.

Trilogy enacts the phases of that parthenogenesis: in *The Walls Do Not Fall*, through H.D.'s "man-wise" identification with the male scribes of antiquity; in *Tribute to the Angels*, through her self-identification as Virgin Scribe (her astrological sign was Virgo); in *The Flowering of the Rod*, through her self-identification as Virgin Mother. So this account of self-mothering begins not so paradoxically—with her masculine initiators, paternal and sibling, autobiographical and mythical. In the paternal line Professor Freud, the "blameless physician," had succeeded Professor Doolittle: among her siblings, Pound and Aldington and Lawrence would give way to Lord Dowding. But collectively they served to define for H.D. her "man-wise" powers, personified in her animus. His Scepter, the flowering "rod of power" (cf. "A sceptre / and a flower-shaft" in "The Mysteries" earlier) is the Caduceus of Hermes the Greek healer, of his Egyptian counterpart Thoth, and of the Roman Aesculapius. She had told Freud of a girlhood dream wherein she saw a stone divided into halves into which were incised a coiled, erect serpent and a thistle; in *Tribute to Freud* she associated the glyphs with Moses' staff, Aaron's rod, and Aesculapius' caduceus, and associated the serpent's *S* with Sigmund and with the tau-cross of Thoth. Years later she found that precise image on a Greco-Roman signet ring in the Louvre and, still later, in writing the Freud book, finally associated it with "H.D."[6] Those male symbols and hieroglyphs inscribed her own hermetic signet.

There were many reasons why Hermes came to stand with Helios in H.D.'s pantheon. In addition to healing, Hermes was a heroic explorer—

again like Freud and like her father, whom she also acclaimed as "a path-finder, an explorer."[7] The key to Hermes' multiple powers is that he acts as an agent of change. True to his Roman avatar, his nature is mercurial, and H.D. was struck by the astrological fact that her sun sign Virgo was ruled by Mercury. Moreover, Hermes was a messenger of the other gods, and the Greek root of "angel" as "messenger" allowed H.D. to link Hermes with the archangel Michael, "Captain or Centurion of the hosts of heaven." And finally the hermetic messenger becomes a word-mage in his com-munication with humans: in various guises, Thoth the inventor of hiero-glyphs, Hermes Trismegistus the alchemical scribe, Amenhotep the pha-raoh scribe, Christos the divine Logos, St. John the author of Revelation (*Tribute to Freud* 109).[8]

Healer, pathfinder, messenger, mystic, scribe: such were the male gods and demigods. But in her own life Doctors Doolittle and Freud, awesome as their power might be, restricted their area of exploration and refused to submit human reason to the realm of mystery. Her father was a pro-fessor of astronomy, not an astrologer; it was her mother who as Mora-vian, musician, and artist was the daughter's covert link with the world of mystery. In the first "happiness of the quest" on which Freud was set-ting her, she wanted to believe that his psychology was a "philosophy" which could reconcile "my father's science and my mother's art" (*Tribute to Freud* 145). Unlike Professor Doolittle, the surrogate father seemed to have an aesthetic sense and might admit the woman's powers to the family group and encourage them. But further experience forced her to recognize that Freud's aesthetic sense — unlike her mother's — did not ex-tend to the religious: "About the greater transcendental issues, we never argued. But there was an argument implicit in our very bones" (13). The difference never came to argument because Freud refused to theorize about such matters; he "shut the door on transcendental speculations" and limited his study to the "personal reactions, dreams, thought associations or thought 'transferences' of the individual human mind. It was the human individual that concerned him. . . ." Freud's denial of "this dream of heaven, this hope of eternal life," H.D. came sadly to believe, doomed him to a "courageous pessimism," and it pained her that his agnostic dis-belief in personal immortality afforded him "little hope for the world" (102–3).

No more than her father, then, could Freud be hermetic; there were some messages that neither could deliver or decipher. One of the princi-pal matters she had come to Freud to discuss was what she called "the writing on the wall" — not writing, really, but an astonishing succession of images of light, which she had seen on the wall of a hotel room on Corfu in the spring of 1920 with Bryher. The series of archetypal images began with the head and shoulders of a soldier or airman, unrecognized but suggestive of Aldington and her brother ("dead brother?" H.D. mused; maybe, but also "lost friend"). He was followed on the wall by light images of a goblet or mystic chalice, a tripod like the one used by Apollo's priestess at Delphi (and later by H.D. in her seances), a ladder spanning heaven and earth, and a figure like Nike, Athene triumphant. The intensity of the experience overwhelmed H.D. at this point, and she averted her eyes. But Bryher, who though present had till then seen nothing, now began to see the double image which completed the vision: Helios in his sun disc "reaching out to draw the image of a woman (my Nike) into the sun beside him." H.D. did not insist that it had been a supernatural revelation and entertained the possibility that the vision was "merely an extension of the artist's mind, a *picture* or an illustrated poem." But she knew that the apparition was in any case of enormous symbolic significance, and she was disappointed and dismayed when Freud warned that such an experience was a "dangerous" symptom, perhaps her only dangerous symptom (*Tribute to Freud* 44–56).

So Freud could not heal her wholly. The antique figures on Freud's desk and in his glass cases he loved not as gods but as artifacts. Though she did not argue with the professor at the time, H.D. insisted that the art of healing went beyond the terms he set. After all, Hermes was called "Psychopompos," mediator of the underworld, where psyche and Spirit met, where human shades mingled with deities. As psychopomp Hermes was affiliated with the artist; by devising the lyre he made possible Apollo's song. His Egyptian predecessor Thoth was also the god of learning who invented all the arts and sciences: not only doctor and healer, mathematician and astronomer, but musician and writer — in fact, specifically the creator of the hieroglyphs and the scribe of the gods. Long before her sessions with Freud, Pound and Aldington and Lawrence, sibling-poets, had introduced her to the hermetic world, but in breaking the parental bonds they had separated her from mother as well as father. The assimilation of the animus-scribe's hermeticism in *The Walls Do Not Fall* permits the rediscovery of the scribe's feminine and then maternal character in the other two sequences. Such is the subtending impulse and secret meaning of *Trilogy*.

But first physical survival requires the invocation of Hermes and Thoth against the fiery rain of the blitz:

> Thoth, Hermes, the stylus,
> the palette, the pen, the quill endure,
>
> though our books are a floor
> of smouldering ash under our feet. . . .

(16)

H.D. wrote to Norman Holmes Pearson that she had been stung into writing *The Walls Do Not Fall* as a "vindication of the writer, or the 'scribe' "
in response to letters from an acquaintance which doubted the efficacy
of literature in crises of war and survival.[9] H.D.'s response to the damning question was unequivocal:

> so what good are your scribblings?
> this—we take them with us
>
> beyond death; Mercury, Hermes, Thoth
> invented the script, letters, palette;
>
> the indicated flute or lyre-notes
> on papyrus or parchment
>
> are magic, indelibly stamped
> on the atmosphere somewhere,
>
> forever. . . .
>
> (17)

The "smouldering ash" of burned books requires the reinscription for which
she assumes responsibility in the present crisis; she will stand among the
remaining walls against the war. Her correspondent's word "scribblings"
demeans the power of the word, but the pun which makes the "word"
mightier than the "sword" is meant to assert the power of language over
physical force. For that reason the Egyptian scribe "takes precedence of
the priest, / stands second only to the Pharaoh" (15)—that is, she told
Pearson, "stands second only to God" ("Foreword," vii).

St. John and Christos the Word, the scribe and his God. The sections
of *The Walls Do Not Fall* interweave the Christian references with invocations of ancient male scribes and deities, with the "Amen" of Amenhotep's name as the punning link. In the remarkable dream of section 16,
"Ra, Osiris, *Amen* appeared" in the "spacious, bare meeting-house" where
as a girl H.D. worshipped with her mother's Moravian family. The god
is first identified as "the world-father, / father of past aeons / present
and future equally," but then is surprisingly described as "beardless, not
at all like Jehovah." The unapproachable Father—Ra, Jehovah—manifests Himself as the Son, Christos, Osiris, Amen: "upright, slender, /
impressive as the Memnon monolith" (25).

Moreover, in section 21 the transformation of the Father into the Son
is effected through the connection of the masculine with the feminine:

> Splintered the crystal of identity,
> shattered the vessel of integrity,

till the Lord *Amen*,
paw-er of the ground,

bearer of the curled horns,
bellows from the horizon:

here am I, Amen-Ra,
Amen, Aries, the Ram;

time, time for you to begin a new spiral,
see — I toss you into the star-whirlpool;

till pitying, pitying,
snuffing the ground,

here am I, Amen-Ra whispers,
Amen, Aries, the Ram,

be cocoon, smothered in wool,
be Lamb, mothered again.

(30)

"Amen-Ra" is the archetypal father; the pun on "paw-er" as "father" links
Ra with the Ram, the "bearer of curled horns." But "a new spiral" brings
metamorphosis, summed up in the pun on "smothered/mothered"; the
Ram becomes mother ("cocoon, smothered in wool") and so Son ("Lamb,
mothered again"). In the next section, the alchemical wordplay (worm/
warm, fleece/grass, sun/son) runs through H.D.'s prayer that the father
bear her as Hermes, Helios/Christos:

Now my right hand,
now my left hand

clutch your curled fleece;
take me home, take me home,

my voice wails from the ground;
take me home, Father:

pale as the worm in the grass,
yet I am a spark

struck by your hoof from a rock:
Amen, you are so warm,

hide me in your fleece,
crop me up with the new-grass;

let your teeth devour me,
let me be warm in your belly,

the sun-disk,
the re-born Sun.

(31)

The refrain "Take me home, Father" means "take me home to Mother."
H.D. had hoped that her visits to Freud, whose office felt like "home,"
would effect reconciliation with her lost father and mother, so that she
might come to a sense of her own identity. The late poetry voices the effort to return home as the place of rebirth; in her beginning would be
her end. "Take me home, Father"; let me be smothered/mothered in the
father's fleece, "let me be warm in your belly" and in the name of the
Sun/Son let the daughter be born again to the mother who in life had
favored her sons to the daughter. As sibling-poet, Pound had rescued
the daughter from that bruising domestic situation and initiated her into
womanhood in the Sunship/Sonship of the scribes. But some essential
connection had been obscured, and now the alchemy of the word seeks
to restore her psychologically to the mother she missed in life.

As we can already see, the punning throughout *Trilogy* is no mere trick
or game. It makes a language appropriate to a world in which there are
meanings within meanings, meanings beyond meanings. In the concluding sections of *The Walls Do Not Fall* the personal and psychological synthesis is characteristically merged into the cosmic design. The play on
"O-sir-is or O-Sire-is" fuses the names of Osiris and his sister-wife Isis
in a cyclic pattern of death and rebirth which constitutes the recurrent
manifestation of "the One in the beginning": "Fosterer, Begetter, the
Same-for-ever / in the papyrus-swamp / in the Judean meadow" (54–55).
Perhaps intentionally H.D. indicated the American source of the Neo-
platonism she shared with Pound in her use of Emerson's epithet "the
over-soul" (42), whose immanence confers on everyday objects a sacra-
mental significance:

grape, knife, cup, wheat

are symbols in eternity,
and every concrete object

has abstract value, is timeless
in the dream parallel

whose relative sigil has not changed
since Nineveh and Babel.

(24)

Play on the names of Osiris and Isis points to their ultimate union: "O, Sire, is this the path? . . . drawn to the temple-gate, O, Sire, / is this union at last?" (57). Since the ruins of London still stand like the remnants of the temple at Karnak, *"possibly we will reach haven, / heaven"* (59). These last words of the poem conjoin the maternal haven with the paternal heaven, but the prospect still lies in the future. In the second poem of *Trilogy* the question will recur for further resolution:

> what is this mother-father
> to tear at our entrails?
>
> what is this unsatisfied duality
> which you can not satisfy?
>
> (72)

Tribute to the Angels was written in a fortnight during "a wonderful pause just before D-Day" as "a sort of premature peace poem" ("Foreword," ix). The unexpected epiphany which generated this spring poem occurred on a London bus when H.D. glimpsed a charred apple tree flowering again amidst the rubble of a burned-out square. Hermes Trismegistus (Thoth) and St. John are still present at the beginning of the sequence. However, Hermes leads to Aphrodite; Christos, to Mary. Their animus-inspiration directs the poem through the divination of the angels to an astonishing manifestation of the feminine.

The angels of St. John's Revelation who attend the divine throne appear as emissaries, and four of the seven have been named and addressed — Raphael (Birth), Gabriel (Change), Azrael (Death), and Uriel (the fire of God's judgment and will) — before the first premonition of the archetypal feminine, whose appearance is rendered as alchemical "Transubstantiation" (87):

> Now polish the crucible
> and in the bowl distill
>
> a word most bitter, *marah*,
> a word bitterer still, *mar*,
>
> sea, brine, breaker, seducer,
> giver of life, giver of tears;
>
> Now polish the crucible
> and set the jet of flame
>
> under, till *marah-mar*
> are melted, fuse and join

and change and alter,
mer, mere, mère, mater, Maia, Mary,

Star of the Sea,
Mother.

(71)

The bitter and destructive sea, nature's womb and tomb, becomes the
virgin-mother goddess. "Star of the Sea," an epithet from the Litany of
the Blessed Virgin, precipitates the association of Mary with "Venus,
Aphrodite, Astarte," who appears in double aspect as a star, "Phosphorus
/ at sun-rise, / Hesperus at sun-set" (73). This evocation of the feminine
calls forth the fifth angel, Annael, the peace of God, designated by H.D.
as the Mohammedan Venus, and linked in turn with the Hebrew Anna,
Hannah, or Grace ("Foreword," ix). Moreover, she appears in a syzygy
with Uriel, the angel of God's fiery breath; the pair intimates the Sancta
Spiritus: "So we hail them together, / one to contrast the other" (80). After
this annunciation God's bride blooms in war-torn London: "We see her
visible and actual, / beauty incarnate" in the miraculous spring flowering
of the scorched tree in a garden square behind a demolished house (82–83).

Then all unexpected, the vision of the Lady, first in a dream in which
she appeared to H.D. and two women friends. Remembering perhaps the
triune goddesses in "Triplex," the poet wonders whether "we three together"
could summon the supernatural, "yet it was all natural enough, we agreed"
(90). For when the poet wakens from the dream the Presence is "there
more than ever, / as if she had miraculously / related herself to time here"
(91). Who is this Lady? Earlier in the poem, when

my patron [Freud or Bryher or both] said, "name it";

I said, I can not name it,
there is no name;

he said,
"invent it."

(76)

So here, the patron's voice in her head tells her that if she cannot define
the Lady by name she can at least invent images. Though the Lady be
a Presence and "no rune nor riddle" (84), the scribe suggests her mysterious charisma in rich details from the Renaissance painters and their Pre-
Raphaelite imitators:

Our Lady of the Goldfinch,
Our Lady of the Candelabra,

> Our Lady of the Pomegranate,
> Our Lady of the Chair;
>
> we have seen her, an empress,
> magnificent in pomp and grace,
>
> and we have seen her
> with a single flower
>
> or a cluster of garden-pinks
> in a glass beside her;
>
> we have seen her snood
> drawn over her hair,
>
> or her face set in profile
> with the blue hood and stars;
>
> we have seen her head bowed down
> with the weight of a domed crown,
>
> or we have seen her, a wisp of a girl
> trapped in a golden halo. . . .
>   (93)

H.D. goes on to designate the voice which delineates these images, gorgeous though they are, as "you" — not her truest voice, but Bryher's or Freud's voice in her mind, turning her to aesthetic inventions for the Lady. Without taking back any of the gorgeous images, the voice of "I," H.D. speaking for herself, insists that the Lady, far from being "a hieratic figure, the veiled Goddess" (as "you would have her") is more human and approachable: a Vestal, perhaps, of the *Bona Dea*, but in any case a living reality, no mere art image. In fact, as it turns out, "she is Psyche, the butterfly, / out of the cocoon" at last (103).

The Lady is, then, the apotheosis of the Self. Her specific character, as she manifested herself at H.D.'s bedside that night in 1944, is disclosed when she is paired with the sixth angel, Michael, earlier linked to Thoth and Hermes and here "regent of the planet Mercury" (99). H.D. suggested to Pearson that "she is the Troubadour's or Poet's Lady" ("Foreword," ix), but in fact she is something more than muse. She is H.D.'s archetype: the troubadour as woman, the woman as troubadour, the woman-troubadour herself. In her arms the Lady bears no Son ("the Child was not with her" [97]; "the Lamb was not with her" [104]) but instead her writings: "she looked so kindly at us / under her drift of veils, / and she carried a book" (100). The Madonna anticipated earlier ("Star of the Sea /

Mother") turns out to be the Virgin-Scribe. What's more, "her book is our book" (105), is in fact H.D.'s poem in the reader's hand:

> She carried a book, either to imply
> she was one of us with us,
>
> or to suggest she was satisfied
> with our purpose, a tribute to the Angels. . . .
>   (107)

Just as the revelation of the masculine as scribe and psychopomp in *The Walls Do Not Fall* opened the way to the revelation of the Virgin-Scribe in *Tribute to the Angels*, so the Virgin-Scribe makes possible a fuller exfoliation of the feminine archetype in *The Flowering of the Rod*, and preparation for that further exfoliation summons the masculine once more. The seventh and last angel is Zadkiel:

>   regent of Jupiter,
> or Zeus-pater or Theus-pater,
>
> *Theus*, God; God-the-father, father-god
> or the Angel god-father,
>
> himself, heaven yet at home in a star. . . .
>   (108)

Such is the scribe's witness: "*I John saw, I testify*" (109). The final address to Zadkiel specifically foreshadows the third poem in the image of the Lady's "face like a Christmas-rose" (110). So the spring poem of the angels and the Lady grows into a Christmas poem, *The Flowering of the Rod*, dated December 18–31, 1944. It is the book the Lady holds. Though the Lady's book is blank when she appears in *Tribute to the Angels*, it is announced as "a tale of a Fisherman / a tale of a jar or jars" (105), the third sequence of *Trilogy*.

The tale of the Fisherman and the two jars of Kaspar—the jar the Wise Man presented to Mary and the Christ child at His birth and the twin jar Mary Magdalene later used to anoint Him for His death—is both traditional and heterodox. Jesus and the two Marys: but the episodes are held told in inverted chronological order. The poem first presents the anointing by Magdalene the reformed courtesan and then ends with the stable at Bethlehem, but the narrative order corresponds to H.D.'s deepening engagement with the mother archetype. The alienation from the mother with whom she felt deep religious and artistic affinity had thwarted her psychological realization of herself as woman and mother. She brooded over her miscarriage of Aldington's baby during the war; when she bore

Cecil Gray's child in 1919, she called her Perdita, the lost one, and had difficulty in assuming and fulfilling the mothering role. On Corfu the year after Perdita's birth she took Athene Nike, the motherless maiden-daughter of Zeus, as "my own especial sign or part of my hieroglyph" (*Tribute to Freud* 56).

In *Hippolytus Temporizes* and *Red Roses for Bronze* the Artemis and Athene in H.D. had contended with the Aphrodite. The Lady in *Tribute to the Angels* is explicitly the Virgin but not the lover or mother; though she is "innocent / and immaculate . . . like the Lamb's Bride," "the Lamb was not with her either as Bridegroom or Child" (104). Now *The Flowering of the Rod* presents the two Marys as versions of Aphrodite and Artemis — but with paradoxical complications: Magdalene's passion is purified, and the Virgin bears a child. Mary the courtesan, redeemed of sexual sin and preparing the Redeemer for His death, is succeeded by and assimilated into the Mary whose immaculate flesh incarnates God. Because the burgeoning of the blasted tree images not death from life but rebirth from death, in this telling crucifixion precedes nativity. The Old English "rood" links the Cross with the Tree of Life. The Easter mystery, alluded to in the references to Jesus' transfiguration, crucifixion, and resurrection, is subsumed in the Christmas Mystery. The flowering of the rood is a Christmas rose: Deus manifest in Mater, material spirit.

H.D. recalled in the Freud memoir written in the same year as this poem that "the Professor translated the pictures on the wall, or the picture-writing on the wall . . . in Corfu . . . as a desire for union with my mother" (*Tribute to Freud* 44). The Mediterranean world H.D. sought was a substitute homeland; Hellas, she came to see, stood for Helen, and Helen had accompanied her to the Mediterranean in 1923. Now we can see why the surrogate father's acknowledgment of the primacy of the mother seemed to H.D. a "coming home," and why Freud's office seemed a "home" she associated with "father-mother" (*Tribute to Freud* 146). The plea "Take me home, Father" opened the way to the advent of the Lady, and the psychological breakthrough from her visitation carried H.D. past Greece all the way back to Bethlehem and Mother. For just as the Greece of *Sea Garden* was the lost America of her childhood memories, so now Bethlehem is as much in Pennsylvania as in Palestine. In one session when H.D. was reminiscing about her hometown, Freud made the connection: "Bethlehem is the town of Mary" (*Tribute to Freud* 123) — yes, and the town where Helen bore Hilda.

The mystery of Mary, then, is the culmination of the poem, and her metamorphosis is reflected in the puns on her name. The playing upon "Marah" (bitter), "mar" (sea), and "mere" (mother) in *Tribute to the Angels* is extended by the linking of "myrrh" and "Mary," as H.D. articulates her parthenogenesis: "through my will and my power, / Mary shall be myrrh," "(though I am Mara, bitter) I shall be Mary-myrrh" (135); "*I am Mary, the incense-flower of the incense-tree, / myself worshipping, weeping, shall be changed to myrrh*" (138). The blasted tree blossoming amidst the blitz yields the woman-flower, "face like a Christmas rose" (110). Her burgeoning, like that of Yeats's "great-rooted blossomer," enfolds the cycle of birth, death, and resurrection. Her precious oils are bitter to the tongue but incomparably sweet in the nostrils. The Myrrh vessels are crucibles in an alchemic sublimation, for alchemy was, as Jung demonstrated, the science — or art — of psychological and spiritual transformation.

Kaspar with his two fabled jars of myrrh provides H.D.'s fictional link between the two Marys; one he gives to Mary Magdalene, and the other he presented years before in Bethlehem. In *The Walls Do Not Fall* Love was identified as a "Mage, / bringing myrrh" (10). In H.D.'s version the Mage is the man with woman-wisdom, the woman-wise man who matches and mirrors the man-wise woman. Kaspar understands the old goddesses as "unalterably part" of Mary: "Isis, Astarte, Cyprus," "Ge-meter, De-meter, earth-mother," "Venus / in a star" (145). For him the "Star of the Sea" is one with the Star of Bethlehem. In his encounter with Mary Magdalene Kaspar is granted a vision of the three primordial mothers: Eve, and before her Lilith, and even before her a nameless mother from the lost paradise of Atlantis. The feminine is symbolized as a flower opening, petal on petal, circle on circle, both backward and forward through time and infinity (cf. 153–57). Her full revelation includes origin and fall and redemption: Paradise, Paradise lost, Paradise regained.

Kaspar gives Magdalene the jar to anoint the Christ for His death because in her he recalls the other Mary, the second Eve at the nativity. For what he knelt to in the stable at Bethlehem was not the Spirit-Father, the I-Am or Jehovah, but God as Son of Mary: "the Holy-Presence-Manifest," "the Great Word" (170). Kaspar wordlessly offers Mary myrrh, but she speaks:

> she said, Sir, it is a most beautiful fragrance,
> as of all flowering things together;
>
> but Kaspar knew the seal of the jar was unbroken,
> he did not know whether she knew
>
> the fragrance came from the bundle of myrrh
> she held in her arms.
>
> (172)

In personal terms Hilda has found herself as Helen in Bethlehem, but that discovery has profound and far-reaching implications for herself and for her readers. The poems of *Trilogy* have led to the widening and cumulative revelation of the scribe, the Virgin with Book, and the Madonna with Child. In the sequence of things the Madonna with Child subsumes the Virgin with Book. Or rather the Virgin-scribe writes the book of the Virgin-mother. The "bundle of myrrh / she held in her arms" is the Child and the poem, the Child in the poem, the poem as Child. The poet-mother cradles the bundled flowers and leaves of *Trilogy*, and as readers we kneel with Kaspar at the Epiphany: "her book is our book" (105). In our patriarchal society this is perhaps the closest a woman poet has come to claiming the prophetic representativeness of *Leaves of Grass*.

Two contemporary poets — a man and a woman — offer separate glosses on the poet as mother. Robert Duncan described the irresistible pull of Poetry — backwards and forwards at once — as a need to re-member the Mother:

Back of the Muses, so the old teaching goes, is Mnemosyne, Mother of the Muses. Freud, too, teaches that the Art has something to do with restoring, re-membering, the Mother. Poetry itself may then be the Mother of those who have destroyed their mothers. But no. The image Freud projects of dismembering and remembering is the image of his own creative process in Psychoanalysis which he reads into all Arts. Mnemosyne, the Mother-Memory of Poetry, is our made-up life, the matrix of fictions. Poetry is the Mother of those who have created their own mothers.[10]

In Duncan's convolutions mother and child are almost indistinguishable; the poet and the poem are each both mother and child of the other. Marilyn Farwell has found the basis for an organic feminist criticism in Adrienne Rich's growing concern with motherhood and in her consequent emphasis on the "relational" aspect of art.[11] Farwell argues that Rich has rejected the notion of art as a depersonalized "creation," projected by the "creative" artist (as male criticism tends to conceive it), because such an attitude regards the artwork as an object existing in and of itself, beyond change and outside the flux of experience. However, for Rich or Duncan or anyone who views art organically as inseparable from the flux of experience, the art object, the text of the poem has no significance or meaning except in its "relational" function, as the artist or reader engages and experiences it. "Creation" from this point of view is not a completed act but an ongoing process of gestation, which extends even to the reader: Duncan's notion of the poet's being his or her own mother and child. Moreover, such a conception of art determines form as well as substance. Rich has observed of her own development:

Today, I have to say that what I know I know through making poems. Like the novelist who finds that his characters begin to have a life of their own and to demand certain experiences, I find that I can no longer go to write a poem with a neat handful of materials and express those materials according to a prior plan: the poem itself engenders new sensations, new awareness in me as it progresses. Without for one moment turning my back on conscious choice and selection, I have been increasingly willing to let the unconscious offer its materials, to listen to more than the one voice of a single idea. Perhaps a simple way of putting it would be to say that instead of poems *about* experiences I am getting poems that *are* experiences, that contribute to my knowledge and my emotional life even while they reflect and assimilate it. In my earlier poems I told you, as precisely and eloquently as I knew how, about something; in the more recent poems something is happening, something has happened to me and, if I have been a good parent to the poem, something will happen to you who read it.[12]

In the early 1960s, when Rich wrote this, she used the neutral term "parent," but there is no question that today she would seek to be a good "mother" to the poem and in a certain sense expect the reader, male as well as female, to be so too.

Certainly for H.D. the re-membering of the Mother required a new kind of poetry. Those who prefer the imagist poems find the long later sequences looser, more associative, more opaque. But Denise Levertov is correct in seeing the continuity of the work in its differences. For her, "the icily passionate precision of the earlier work, the 'Greek' vision, had not been an *end*, a closed statement, but a preparation" for the long works of the later years. As a matter of fact, a rereading of *Collected Poems* convinced Levertov that even "the poems I had thought of as shadowless were full of shadows, planes, movement: correspondences of what was to come."[13] H.D. herself resented the critical view, reflected in anthology selections, that treated her as though she had ceased writing or developing in 1925. She pointedly and proudly proclaimed *Trilogy* "runic, divinatory" — "not the 'crystalline' poetry that my early critics would insist on."[14] For H.D. the stylistic differences beneath the thematic continuities running through her work were important because the difference in language and stance indicated a deepening of the psychological and spiritual comprehension of those thematic materials. The later work — not just the work centered in World War II (*Trilogy, Tribute to Freud, Bid Me To Live, By Avon River*), but the long poems of her last decade — are unashamedly more personal and religious, more autobiographical and mystical than the more modernist manner of her imagist phase.

To return to Duncan's distinction which introduced this discussion of *Trilogy*, H.D.'s early Images which were "personae of states of mind" often appeared as male, but the Images which served as "guides in reading the message of the universe" tended more and more to constellate themselves around the figure of the mother. It was a long way from the lean, hardtorsoed athlete of *Sea Garden* to the Madonna of *The Flowering of the Rod*, but it was the way she was seeking from the beginning.

NOTES

This essay first appeared in *H.D.: Woman and Poet*, ed. Michael King (Orono, ME: National Poetry Foundation, 1986), 173–90.

1 *The Complete Poetic Works of Amy Lowell*, ed. Louis Untermeyer (Boston: Houghton Mifflin, 1955), 459.

2 H.D., *Trilogy* (New York: New Directions, 1973). Parenthetical references are to pages in this edition.

3 Robert Duncan, Part I, Chapters 3 & 4 of *The H.D. Book, TriQuarterly* 12 (Spring 1968), 97.

4 Norman Holmes Pearson, "Foreword," *Hermetic Definition* (New York: New Directions, 1972), v.

5 The typescript of *Majic Ring* is at the Beinecke Library, Yale University. Cf. also the typescript of *Compassionate Friendship* there, pp. 47, 78, 79, 81, and *Notes on Recent Writing* 14, 18, 22–23.

6 H.D., *Tribute to Freud* (Boston: David R. Godine, 1974), 87–90, 64–66, 101.

7 H.D., "The Dream," from *The Gift, Contemporary Literature* 10.4 (Autumn 1969): 618.

8 Susan Friedman has an extensive commentary on H.D.'s involvement with the occult in *Psyche Reborn: The Emergence of H.D.* (Bloomington: Indiana UP, 1981), 157–207.

9 Norman Holmes Pearson, "Foreword," *Trilogy* vi–vii.

10 Robert Duncan, Part I, Chapter 2 of *The H.D. Book, Coyote's Journal* 8 (1967): 27.

11 Marilyn R. Farwell, "Adrienne Rich and an Organic Feminist Criticism," *College English* 39.2 (October 1977): 191–203.

12 "Poetry and Experience: Statement at a Poetry Reading," *Adrienne Rich's Poetry*, ed. Barbara Charlesworth Gelpi and Albert Gelpi (New York: W. W. Norton, 1975), 89.

13 Denise Levertov, "H.D.: An Appreciation," *Poetry* 100.3 (June 1962), 183–84.

14 *Notes on Recent Writing* 22.

No Rule of Procedure:
The Open Poetics of H.D.

A L I C I A   O S T R I K E R

My topic is a dimension of H.D.'s writing which is of the deepest importance and without which we would not be reading her at all: the beauty
of her poetic music; that mysterious, exquisite, "crystalline" yet fluid movement of her versification; her ear. And our ears, listening. For poetry is
first of all and most magically a tissue of sound, "words set in delightful
proportion," as Sir Philip Sidney puts it. This is what we mean when we
say that poetry ravishes us; and as T. S. Eliot in writing of the auditory
imagination remarks, the poet in the act of composition is commonly preoccupied more with "the arrangement of metric and pattern" than with
a conscious exposition of ideas.[1] At the opening of his classic study of
prosody in English, *Poetic Meter and Poetic Form*, Paul Fussell observes,

Poetic meter is a prime physical and emotional constituent of poetic meaning.
The great moments of perception in English poetry — *Paradise Lost,* "The Rape
of the Lock," *Songs of Innocence and Experience*, "The Rime of the Ancient
Mariner," "Mauberly," "The Waste Land" — have constituted moments of metrical
discovery: they all reveal an excitement with meter almost as an object of fundamental meaning in itself.[2]

I wish to add *Trilogy* to that list, and to remark further that we cannot
confine the significance of discoveries in prosody merely to literary history. If poets need new ways to make sound run in the listening ear, it
is because they find themselves taking a new stance toward reality, toward
society. "When the music changes, the walls of the city tremble," says
Plato; the reverberations of prosody are inevitably political as well as
aesthetic. I hope to suggest, then, that the uniqueness of H.D.'s versification is inseperable from her radical stance as visionary and modernist poet.

The vulgar conception that free verse, free love, and freethinking are somehow connected is not far off the mark. For all formal verse of any value depends on a balance between recurrent elements which gratify the reader by providing a sensation of reassuring predictable order, and variations which give us the vitality of the unpredictable, the spontaneous, the unpremeditated. "Repetition makes us feel secure and variation makes us feel free," as Robert Hass says in a recent essay on the psychic significance of pattern and variation in poetry, noting also that "because rhythm has direct access to the unconscious, because it can hypnotize us, enter our bodies and make us move, it is a power. And power is political."[3] In the formal life of poetry as in the psychic life of individuals or the political life of the state, we might roughly say that health depends on continual adjustments between the demands of control and the demands of liberty; and that of course the proportions in the history of art as in the history of a self or a nation are not constant but various.

In the history of English poetry, periods of social and political conservatism have tended to be registered in highly constrained, closed verse forms dominated by orderly pattern in rhetoric as well as rhyme. The shining instance is the heroic couplet of Dryden and Pope, the "smoothness" or "harmony" of which was understood by its practitioners and their critics to reflect the rationality and morality of the maker and to predispose readers toward sound conduct. Johnson, commending Dryden, declares "the rectitude of [his] mind" demonstrated by his "rejection of unnatural thoughts and rugged numbers."[4] By the same token, poets who offer themselves as radicals, rule breakers, revolutionaries, or renewers of human feeling tend to do so in deliberately looser, less constricted rhythms. Blake's "Preface" to the prophetic poem *Jerusalem* at once justifies the poet's prosodic innovations and announces that "Poetry Fetter'd Fetters the Human Race."[5] Behind the rhythmic flexibility of Wordsworth and Coleridge, Shelley and Keats, lies a comparable if less plainly stated anti-authoritarian impulse which locates poetic and moral value within the human heart rather than with external regulation. The perennial dialogue between classicism's insistence on human self-restraint and romanticism's insistence on human spontaneity is in its prosodic dimension a dialogue between elements of fixed form and elements of unpredictability in a poem's rhythms, the tidiness of Pope's "Know then thyself, presume not God to scan, / The proper study of mankind is Man," against the turbulence of Shelley's "Be thou, spirit fierce, / My spirit! Be thou me, impetuous one!"

When we leap the Atlantic, we find Emerson writing a proto–free verse and Walt Whitman as a conscious prosodic inventor for whom prosody and politics were indistinguishable.[6] Emily Dickinson in her way was another; editors who smoothed the meters of the few poems she published in her lifetime infuriated her in ways we can fully understand only when we look at the facsimile versions of her poems with their extraordinary irregularities of punctuation and lineation.[7] "To break the pentameter, that was the first heave," says Ezra Pound;[8] and we know that he is talking about breaking the hold of what he considers a moribund society over its artists. Twentieth-century poetics is full of pronouncements about versification, many of which are simultaneously pronouncements about psychic and institutional control and constraint, and the poet's need to discard them. On the other hand, when Frost delivers his famous line about free verse resembling playing tennis with the net down, we are listening to a profoundly pessimistic man who feels serious dread at the prospect of loss of control, in individuals and societies.

Yet as Eliot and others have observed, the term "free verse" is a misnomer: "no *vers* is *libre* for the man who wants to do a good job."[9] Among the alternative terms which have been proposed to designate poetry composed improvisationally, which is to say not without form but without *fixed* form, the most relevant to H.D.'s work is what Charles Olson in the influential essay "Projective Verse" calls "open form, or composition by field." Olson assumes as axiomatic the idea that "form is never more than an extension of content," and that the essence of open form is process—"one perception must immediately and directly lead to a further perception . . . keep moving, keep in, speed, and nerves, their speed, the perceptions, theirs, the acts, the split second acts." He further demands that we attend to the syllable ("it is by their syllables that words juxtapose in beauty, by these particles of sound as clearly as by the sense of the words which they compose"), the line, the play of syntax, and the use of space and spacing on the page. These are dicta which will resonate for the reader of H.D., as should Olson's announcement that the "field" of the poem which departs from closed form is mysteriously more than words on the page: "A poem is energy transferred from where the poet got it (he will have some several causations), by way of the poem itself to, all the way over to, the reader."[10]

The foregoing constitutes an extremely brief introduction to a complicated and technical subject. I should add that people who write about prosody tend to disagree vehemently with one another; there is no guarantee that what one says about any poet's form and music will have "objective" validity. With this caveat I would like to point out at least a few rudimentary facts about H.D.'s versification, and make a few speculative proposals regarding qualities of prosodic meaning in her poetry—suggesting how what we perceive sensually, as recurrence of sound and shape, becomes a portion of her work's total significance.

The poem I will try to describe is *Trilogy*, that breakthrough work in which H.D. sets herself alongside her major modernist cohorts to compose a long poem which will grapple with the giant issues of twentieth-century poetry: the need to recover a coherent idea of self and society from the shards of social fragmentation, the apocalyptic horror of war, and the confusion and distress arising from changing gender relations; the need to construct or invent some grounds of spiritual faith in a world dominated by materialism and doubt; and the need to redefine the nature and uses of poetry and the imagination. I will compare the formal strategies of *Trilogy* partly with H.D.'s own earlier work, partly with the techniques in comparable poems by others.

The primary determining fact about *Trilogy* is that it is a long poem, philosophical and discursive, partly narrative, ultimately visionary, belonging to a line that includes, for example, Dante's *Commedia*, Blake's visionary poems, and Wordsworth's *Prelude*. In its own period, as Cyrena Pondrum has demonstrated, it most powerfully parallels the *Four Quartets*,[11] although we might also see it as a sequence which moves from doubt to faith as if it were a combination "Waste Land," "Ash Wednesday" (likewise centered on the figure of a Lady), and *Four Quartets*. It has obvious affinities as well with such poems as Pound's *Cantos* and Williams' *Paterson*.

The art of *Trilogy* technically involves a balance between a sense of confident order on the one hand and on the other a sense of improvisation which we experience as seeking and questing, as hesitation and testing, as confusion and as play; between a sensation of crisp clarity and one of fluidity; between the closed and the open.

Formally we have a series of numbered individual lyrics, of varying length but usually no longer than a page. There are three long poems each containing forty-three sections. Three is of course a magic number, recurrent in folktales and children's rhymes, the number of the Trinity, and the number of parts in the *Commedia*, among other things. Multiples of four, as the author of *Four Quartets* also knew, refer us to the four seasons, the four elements, the four tarot suits, and numerous other hermetic sequences. Each of the lyrics is designed to be read as if it were a single sentence composed of multiple linked segments, as we see if we look at the poet's punctuation. Commas, colons, semicolons, even question marks retain us as readers in suspension, while full stops occur only at conclusions of individual sections or lyrics. The opening lyric of *The Walls Do Not Fall* is in triplets, and thereafter all are in couplets. Here then is a fairly high degree of formal order, experienced visually on the page and audibly in the mind's ear primarily as a regular succession of couplet units, steady throughout the poem. In this respect *Trilogy* resembles the pre-twentieth-century poems in its meditative tradition, all of which rely on continuous form, and differs from poems of its own era like the *Cantos*, "The Waste Land," or *Paterson*, notable for their disorderly prosodic conduct. It also differs from H.D.'s own earlier lyric work, in which stanzas of a single poem are typically of uneven length and unpredictable shape. H.D. thus in *Trilogy* is making at least one decision which is the same as Dante's, Milton's, Wordsworth's—that for the long haul of the long poem you need at least one fixed, stable, unchanging prosodic element. Insofar as all poetic form is mimetic, a reassuringly predictable form implies an ultimately reassuring, habitable cosmos. The reader of such a poem knows from the outset that the poem's goal is some sort of closure or resolution, and experiences confidence and certitude that the universe of this poem will be ultimately coherent.

This predictability, however, is balanced by a constantly varying element: the individual lines in *Trilogy* are cadenced but they are distinctly nonmetrical. As a general rule the two lines of a couplet are close in length, but this rule is broken fairly often, and from couplet to couplet the line lengths fluctuate unpredictably. What we have then is a form that is neither fixed nor free, but a combination.

And what of rhyme? Here again there is a balancing, and this is one of the poet's most important and subtle techniques. *Trilogy* is, one might say, a poem that is neither rhymed nor not-rhymed. To the casual reader it will not sound rhymed, for there is no consistent rhyme scheme in it, no recurrent *abba* or whatever, and because H.D. is a mistress of the inconspicuous off-rhyme, as well as of all sorts of interior sound linkages. What escapes notice, in a swift reading, is the extraordinary weaving of sounds together to create a unified web within which we are, as it were, impalpably lapped. Here for example is the opening lyric of *The Walls Do Not Fall*, quoted in full, with one of the off-rhymes which runs through it indicated by italics:

> An incident *here* and *there*,
> and rails gone (for guns)
> from *your* (and my) old town *square*:
>
> mist and mist-grey, no col*our*,
> still the Luxor bee, chick and *hare*
> pursue unalterable purpose
>
> in green, rose-red, lapis;
> they continue to prophesy
> from the stone papyrus:

there, as *here*, ruin opens
the tomb, the temple; *enter*,
there as *here*, there are no *doors*;

the shrine lies open to the sky,
the rain falls, *here, there*
sand drifts; eternity end*ures*:

ruin every*where*, yet as the fallen roof
leaves the sealed room
open to the *air*,

so, through our desolation,
thoughts *stir*, inspiration stalks us
through gloom:

una*ware*, Spirit announces the Presence;
shivering overtakes us,
as of old, Samuel:

trembling at a known street-*corner*,
we know not nor are known;
the Pythian pronounces — we pass on

to another *cellar*, to another sliced wall
where *poor* utensils show
like *rare* objects in a museum;

Pompeii has nothing to teach us,
we know crack of volcanic *fissure*,
slow flow of terrible lava,

pressure on heart, lungs, the brain
about to burst its brittle case
(what the skull can *endure*!):

over us, Apocryphal *fire*,
under us, the earth sway, dip of a *floor*,
slope of a pavement

where men roll, drunk
with a new bewilderment,
sorcery, bedevilment:

the bone-frame was made *for*
no such shock knit within *terror*,
yet the skeleton stood up to it:

the flesh? it was melted away,
the heart burnt out, dead *ember*,
tendons, muscles shattered, outer husk dis*membered*,

yet the frame held:
we passed the flame: we *wonder*
what saved us? what *for*?[12]

Among the many threads of sound, the *here-there* off-rhyme slips imperceptibly through the lyric, gradually altering its tone from a neutral to an intense shade. The first six stanzas contain *here, there, square, colour, hare, enter, doors, endure, everywhere*. Conceptually these terms, some of them repeated and balanced against each other, give us a rather abstract ground-tone, not unlike the repeated term "time" at the opening of "Burnt Norton." That the "here" and "there" which at first feel rather casual and spatial will turn out to refer to desolations vastly separate in both space and time is only gradually apprehended. Beginning in stanza 9 and continuing to the lyric's close the sound resumes: *corner, nor, cellar, poor, rare, fissure, pressure, endure, fire, floor, terror, ember, dismembered, wonder*, and what *for*; here the sound comes to reinforce the motif of struggle, fear, and disorientation. But notice now the contrasting sound-and-meaning cluster of *purpose, lapis, papyrus . . . stalks us, overtakes us*, and *teach us*, which introduce the motif of spiritual survival through material forms; and again *tomb, room*, and *gloom* as against the Luxor *bee, prophesy, sky, eternity*. Among the alliterative and assonantal clusters we have *gone/guns*, *pursue/purpose*, *prophesy/papyrus*, *tomb/temple*, *shrine/sky*, *ruin/roof/room/gloom*. In the second half of the lyric a set of plosive *b*'s implies the apocalyptic horror of the bombing of London — "the *b*rain / a*b*out to *b*urst its *b*rittle case; *b*ewilderment/*b*edevilment/*b*one-frame/*b*urnt-out, dead em*b*er" — against the frighteningly smooth *f*'s of *f*ire, *f*loor, *f*rame, *f*lesh, *f*rame, *f*lame, what *f*or, making the reverberation of bombshell and the sound of steady flame the sensory background of this first image of spiritual initiation.

In a key lyric of *Tribute to the Angels* (*TA* 38) we find a subtle play of end-rhymes, some adjacent, some at a distance from each other, underlying the irony of the poet's tone as she responds to her interlocutor's interpretation of the Lady:

O yes — you understand, I say,
this is all most satisfactory,

> but she wasn't hieratic, she wasn't frozen,
> she wasn't very tall;
>
> she is the Vestal
> from the days of Numa,
>
> she carries over the cult
> of the *Bona Dea*,
>
> she carries a book but it is not
> the tome of the ancient wisdom,
>
> the pages, I imagine, are the blank pages
> of the unwritten volume of the new;
>
> all you say, is implicit,
> all that and much more;
>
> but she is not shut up in a cave
> like a Sibyl; she is not
>
> imprisoned in leaden bars
> in a coloured window;
>
> she is Psyche, the butterfly,
> out of the cocoon.

Here we have *say*/satisfactor*y*, *tall*/Ves*tal*, *Numa*/Bona *Dea*, *pages*/ *cave*, and *wisdom*/*window* as well as *new*/*dow*, *more*/*bars*, *not*/*implicit*/ *not*; and the run of repeated phrases *she wasn't . . . she wasn't . . . she wasn't . . . she is . . . she carries . . . she carries . . . she is not . . . she is not . . . she is*. Repeated sounds, simply as sounds, weave the lyric into a unit. The final two end words *butterfly* and *cocoon* at the lyric's climax feel to the ear as if they are appropriately outside of any pattern, although butter*fly* faintly but significantly echoes *say* and *satisfactory* and coc*oon* significantly echoes fro*zen*.

With a number of exceptions and variations, and with varying degrees of intensity, this is the technique throughout *Trilogy*: there are chains of end-rhymes which may be local or may run through whole lyrics, but which are always inconspicuous and unpredictable in frequency, and which are reinforced by interior sound echoes of all sorts. The reader experiences this, I believe, not as rhyme but (without having to think about it) as beauty and coherence. And this sound-play, I believe, is a formal correlative of the poem's premise that order, beauty, and meaning remain permanently present in our shattered world but not permanently obvious, and that the way to recover them is not through rational effort but through the receptive psychic states of dream and vision which are prior to the semantic Word as the Word is prior to the Sword (*WDNF* 11, 20). Hearing (without thinking about it) these sound connections is like knowing (below the level of argument) that god exists, that paradise exists. It is precisely this kind of knowledge, softly but firmly opposed to the world of rationalism and violence, to which the poet wishes to lead us. Or, rather, the poet is reminding us of what we already know, of spiritual capacities we already possess. Interpreting her own dream of Osiris as a dream of Christ, she turns to the reader:

> I assure you that the eyes
> Of Velasquez' crucified
>
> now look straight at you,
> (*WDNF* 19)

and then turns to further discovery:

> Now it appears very clear
> that the Holy Ghost,
>
> childhood's mysterious enigma
> is the Dream;
>
> that way of inspiration
> is always open
>
> and open to everyone.
> (*WDNF* 20)

At least part of the magic of H.D. as a poet is her capacity to affirm radically antinomian spiritual principles without theological argument, without rhetoric, merely by creating a pattern of cadences and sounds that perform the work of persuasion. We see what she wants us to see, in part thanks to the complex off-rhymes of "*eyes*" and "cruci*fied*," "ass*ure you*," "*cru*cified," and again "*you*," the monosyllabic simplicity of "now look straight at you," the play of "app*ears*," "*clear*," and "myst*er*ious," "*way*" and "al*ways*," and the quiet assertion through an inconspicuous sound echo of what all churches, schools, scriptures, and orthodoxies are bound to deny: "inspira*tion*," "op*en*," "op*en*," "every*one*."[13]

A second essential characteristic of the versification of *Trilogy* is its lightness. If you hold one of the great monuments of meditative poetry in English up to your mind's eye — *Paradise Lost* or *The Prelude*, say — you see solid blocks, pillars of language, weighty looking, mighty looking, distinctly intimidating. If you hold them to the mind's ear, you hear blank verse paragraphs. Organ tones. Sententious sentences. A strong, energetic, relentless flow of verse in the long line, the pentameter line, which since the late sixteenth century has been the standard vehicle for public poetry in English. This is the line in which tragedy, serious narrative, and moral discourse of all sorts take place. It is the line, in sum, of poetic authority. If we look and listen to H.D.'s male cohorts the visual solidity has broken up but the sound of power and authority remains, the sea surge modulating into the didact in Pound, the liturgical, magisterial tones of Eliot.[14]

Now hold H.D. up to the eye and ear and we have something quite different, something which includes a great deal more space, more silence around the words as if pausing were as important as speaking; something neither thunderous nor magnificent but rather like a still small voice. H.D.'s voice and verse are not authoritative but intimate. For the lines are first of all short and slight, having three stresses to the line, sometimes four, quite often only two, seldom (until relatively late in the poem) five. The verse is commonly closer to triple rhythms than to iambs, and it frequently uses feminine endings, so that unstressed syllables tend to outnumber the stressed ones, enhancing the air of slightness. In the lyric quoted earlier, for example, even if one reads with heavy emphasis in order to produce a maximum degree of stress, the lines remain buoyant:

> she carries a book but it is not
> the tome of the ancient wisdom,
>
> the pages, I imagine, are the blank pages
> of the unwritten volume of the new;
>   . . .
> she is Psyche, the butterfly,
> out of the cocoon.

We associate lines like this with lightweight lyric poetry, and we are not at all intimidated by them, not overwhelmed, they do not spell power and authority. The voice has a definite forward momentum ("persistence," it tells us in *WDNF* 6, is its virtue) in its run-on lines and enjambed leaping of stanza breaks, as well as its long suspended sentences, but it is also full of pauses, hesitations, little loopings of repetition and qualification.

What does this aspect of *Trilogy*'s music—the combination of forward momentum with lightness and hesitation—contribute to the poem's meaning? First, we have to recognize that given the history of poetic form in English it was as bold for H.D. to undertake writing a major philosophical poem in these slender lines as it was to undertake writing one while inhabiting a slender woman's body. Second, it seems to me that the poem's lightness connects with the poet's insistence on a poetics, and a politics, of openness, which conveys itself in a number of ways.

Part of the quality of openness in *Trilogy* derives from its imagery. We have, for example, that astonishing sequence of enclosure images which turn out to be generative opening wombs: the mollusc that begets its pearl-of-great-price, the words that are boxes conditioned to hatch butterflies, the poet's heart-shell breaking open and a tree of faith growing from it, a crucible in which words melt, transforming itself into a Lady freed from a cocoon who is also flowers bursting from a half-burnt-out apple tree. In *The Flowering of the Rod* we have a jar of myrrh which is also Mary, perhaps two Marys, perhaps also Christ, and the speck of light in a head-band's jewel which opens out like an infinite petaled flower into a revelation of paradise. *Trilogy* is a poem about things which seem closed and resistant until they open and are infinite. Just so, the poet implies, to the materialist, rationalist, or militarist sensibility the world itself will remain closed; to the receptively spiritual self it will open.

Another source of openness in the poem is the unique way it relates to its audience. "An incident here and there / from your (and my) old town square," and "we" are immediately among the initiates of destruction: "Pompeii has nothing to teach us . . . over us, Apocryphal fire, / under us, the earth sway, dip of a floor . . . we passed the flame: we wonder / what saved us? what for?" This is of course unlike any pre-twentieth-century bardic utterance. It is also different from T. S. Eliot's partially comparable gestures of inclusion. "Let us go then, you and I. . . . Till human voices wake us, and we drown," the famous opening and closing lines of "The Love Song of J. Alfred Prufrock," retain a mysterious resonance in part because the person addressed is never named. As in "Prufrock," H.D.'s "you" in the opening lyric of *The Walls Do Not Fall* may be the reader, an unnamed person in the poem, or a portion of the poet's self; the significance of the poem in both cases is deepened by this indeterminacy. In *Four Quartets* Eliot again conspicuously reaches for the reader: "My words echo / Thus, in your mind. But to what purpose / Disturbing the dust on a bowl of rose-leaves / I do not know."[15] The passage is succeeded by the "garden" episode of "Burnt Norton" in which the poet guides the reader into "our first world," the analogue of paradise, having first inquired politely, "Shall we follow / The deception of the thrush?" In "East Coker," the author-reader relation is again evoked at the outset of Eliot's lecture on the Via Negativa:

You say I am repeating
Something I have said before. I shall say it again.
Shall I say it again? In order to arrive there,
To arrive where you are, to get from where you are not,

You must go by a way wherein there is no ecstasy.
In order to arrive at what you do not know,
You must go by a way which is the way of ignorance.

Through much of *Four Quartets* Eliot uses "I" and "we" relatively interchangeably, thus inviting the reader to identify with the poet's meditations, or to be instructed by them. In *Trilogy* the author-reader relationship is far more complicated and fluctuating. During many passages H.D. plays, like Eliot, the role of generic poet whose "I" and "we" blur together. There are also moments of advisory remonstrance such as the shell passage: "be indigestible, hard, ungiving, / so that, living within, / you beget, self-out-of-self, / selfless, / that pearl-of-great-price" (*WDNF* 4), or the introduction of the resurrection theme at the opening of *The Flowering of the Rod*: "do not think of His face / or even His hands, // do not think how we will stand / before Him" (*FR* 1). H.D. like Eliot is at times the confident spiritual instructor of her reader. But there are also distinctions and ambivalences in H.D. which are absent in Eliot. "We," for example, at various moments in the poem may include all readers, or all Londoners, or only initiates, spiritual seekers like herself. "I" at times distinguishes itself defensively from "you others" — skeptics and materialists — or from "those others" to whom she cries, "yours is the more foolish circling, / yours is the senseless wheeling" (*FR* 6), who may also be the reader. At times "I" seems at once a single defined self able to say things like "I am so happy," and in the next line an undefined being who declares, "I am the first or the last," with suspicious resemblance to the "I am Alpha and Omega" of Revelation (*FR* 8). "You" in a single lyric may shift from "It is no madness to say / you will fall, you great cities," to the casualness of "it is, if you like, a lily / folded like a pyramid . . . a lily, if you will" (*FR* 10). Pronouns, in fact, continually slip and slide throughout *Walls, Tribute,* and the opening of *Flowering,* as if to imply that the capacity each individual has to be either subject or object, ally or antagonist, singular or plural, defined or indefinable is an essential principle of any spiritual progress we hope to make.

In *WDNF* 38 the poet's self-criticism takes the form of a dialogue with an imagined interlocutor against whom or for whom she defends herself: "my mind (yours), / your way of thought (mine), / each has its peculiar intricate map." The device of parenthesis here instantly recalls H.D.'s initial image of "your (and my) old town square," enlisting our sense that human experience is simultaneously, mysteriously, both unique to each of us and common to all of us. "Chasm, schism in consciousness / must be bridged over; // we are each, householder, / each with a treasure" (*WDNF* 36). To find the truth, then, the poet's quest is exemplary but not determining: we have each our own truth, equally valuable, which we must learn to see. Hints, clues, texts, sacred images which have survived from the shattered past abound, and yet none is a substitute for our own act of engaged perception. Thus before the vision of the Lady comes the sight of the May-tree in *TA* 21:

> This is no rune nor riddle,
> it is happening everywhere;
>
> what I mean is—it is so simple
> yet no trick of the pen or the brush
>
> could capture that impression;
> music could do nothing with it,
>
> nothing whatever; what I mean is—
> but you have seen for yourself
>
> that burnt-out wood crumbling . . .
> you have seen for yourself.

In the history of meditative poetry there is no such distance-collapsing gesture before this. The poet's earnest address, which depends on believing that we are a real part of her community, is analogous to the appeal she makes to us. As she turns directly to us, like an actor pausing in the midst of a play to address the audience from the proscenium, breaking the theatrical illusion, so we are urged to turn directly to ourselves. Authority finally becomes irrelevant. Ultimately we are being invited to trust not a still point outside of ourselves, transcending this world, but our own interiority. As with the transfer of power and priority from Sword to Word, and from Word to Vision, the subversion of pronomial fixities which draws us toward recognition that the self is an entity of boundless spiritual potential produces a radically open form of teaching.[16]

A final feature of the prosody in *Trilogy* as in all of H.D.'s poetry is the very high degree of repetition she employs. In the passage I have just quoted, for example, there is the sequence "This is . . . it is . . . what I mean is . . . it is . . . what I mean is," "nothing . . . nothing whatever," "but you have seen for yourself . . . you have seen for yourself." Unlike her use of rhyme, which is typically inconspicuous, her use of repeated phrases at close quarters is a strongly foregrounded device. H.D.'s penchant for repetition takes multifoliate rhetorical forms, and has multiple effects on the poetry's meaning.

Most obviously, repetition has the function of intensifying emotion. A little less obviously, repetition as H.D. tends to use it suggests the mind ruminating over and over a thing, a word, an idea. The reader is made privy to the poet's mental process rather than being given a finished product. The attempt to represent the process rather than the result of the mind's activity is of course a feature of much modernist writing in both prose and poetry; what is unique perhaps about H.D.'s method is the sense it gives us of a mind working, specifically, on a *problem* it is attempting to solve, and the vision it gives us of how far the problem-solving motions of the mind are from logic, how close they are to trance. Further, in the many crucial passages where H.D. plays with etymology and phonic overlap, repetition functions as an agent of transformation: *Osiris* can be *Sirius* and *O-Sire-is* (*WDNF* 40–42), *marah* and *mar* can melt and fuse to become *Mary* (*TA* 8), *Mary* can be *myrrh* (*FR* 16). Words for H.D. are like material substances capable of alchemic refinement; they are like organisms which evolve over time, taking new forms in new generations; they are like the bodily casings which "conceal" (*WDNF* 8) or "hide" (*WDNF* 39) spiritual substances. Even so, it is implied, are certain divine beings who appear to die only to be reborn, and even so are we ourselves. The surface effect of repetition in H.D. thus becomes at times an objective correlative for the spiritual power of metamorphosis and rebirth which the poet in her poem is attempting to recover and is recommending to us.

Finally there is the physical phenomenon of echo itself, which H.D. consistently uses to suggest a reality that emanates from a mysterious source, endures through transformations, and may ultimately communicate to the receptive ear a sacred truth. Kaspar's moment of revelation in *FR* 33 is partly visual, partly auditory. What he sees is the infinite unfolding flower within which is paradise. What he hears is

> the echo
> of an echo in a shell,
>
> words neither sung nor chanted
> but stressed rhythmically;
>
> the echoed syllables of this spell
> conformed to the sound
>
> of no word he had ever heard spoken,
> . . .
> it translated itself
> as it transmuted its message
>
> through spiral upon spiral of the shell
> of memory that yet connects us
>
> with the drowned cities of pre-history.

If we assume, as is reasonable, that H.D. means Kaspar to stand not only for Freud, or for patriarchy, but also as surrogate for and representative of the reader, then we are being told what is happening to us in the act of reading her poem. The "shell" through which sound reverberates and changes is at once a musical instrument, the spiral passages of the inner ear and, as it were, the still more spiral and convoluted passages of that other inner ear which connects us to the mythic past. To "echo" is to repeat while changing, or to change while repeating, so as to be understood. The "words neither sung nor chanted / but stressed rhythmically" are words of poetry, as distinguished from the more fixed and formalized words of music or ritual. In this passage H.D. has described her prosody, its intention, and its radically open dependence on our capacity to listen. Who has ears, let her hear.

NOTES

This essay first appeared in *Agenda* 25 (Autumn/Winter 1987–88): 145–54.

1   Quoted in Paul Fussell, Jr., *Poetic Meter and Poetic Form* (New York: Random House, 1965), 3–4.

2   Ibid., 3.

3   Robert Hass, "Listening and Making," *Twentieth Century Pleasures* (New York: Ecco Press, 1984), 108, 115.

4   Samuel Johnson, *Lives of the English Poets*, ed. George Birkbeck Hill (Oxford, 1905), I, 421. Paul Fussell, *Theory of Prosody in Eighteenth-Century England* (New London: Connecticut College Monograph No. 5, 1954), examines in detail the moral dimension of prosodic regularity in this period.

5   William Blake, *Complete Poems*, ed. Alicia Ostriker (New York: Penguin Books, 1977), 637.

6   See, e.g., in Whitman's open letter to Emerson, printed in the second edition of *Leaves of Grass* (1856): "Poets here, literats here, are to rest on organic different bases from other countries; not a class set apart, circling only in the circle of themselves, modest and pretty, desperately scratching for rhymes, pallid with white paper, shut off. . . . Lands of ensemble, bards of ensemble! Walking freely out from the old traditions as our politics has walked out. . . ." Quoted in *The Poetics of the New American Poetry*, ed. Donald Allen and Warren Tallman (New York: Grove Press, 1973), 9–10.

7   Thomas H. Johnson's edition of Dickinson's poetry, first published in 1955, reproduces the poet's idiosyncratic spelling, capitalization, and punctuation. To see the often highly irregular lineation of the manuscripts, however, one must consult *The Manuscript Books of Emily Dickinson*, ed. R. W. Franklin (Cambridge: Harvard UP, 1981).

8   Ezra Pound, Canto LXXXI. *The Pisan Cantos*, in *The Cantos of Ezra Pound* (New York: New Directions, 1948), 96.

9 Quoted by Pound, "Re Vers Libre" (1917). In Allen and Tallman, *Poetics of the New American Poetry* 46.

10 Charles Olson, "Projective Verse" (1950), in ibid., 148–49.

11 Cyrena Pondrum, "*Trilogy* and *Four Quartets*: Contrapuntal Visions of Spiritual Quest," *Agenda* 25, 3–4 (Autumn–Winter 1987–88).

12 Subsequent parenthetical references are to poem numbers in *Trilogy*.

13 Compare Olson: "It would do no harm, as an act of correction to both prose and verse as now written, if both rime and meter . . . were less in the forefront of the mind than the syllable, if the syllable, that fine creature, were more allowed to lead the harmony on . . . The dance of the intellect is there, among them." Allen and Tallman, *Poetics of the New American Poetry* 50–51. Compare also T. S. Eliot, in "Reflections on 'Vers Libre' ": "But it is possible that excessive devotion to rhyme has thickened the modern ear. The rejection of rhyme is not a leap at facility; on the contrary, it imposes a much severer strain upon the language. When the comfort of rhyme is removed, success or failure in the choice of words, in the sentence structure, in the order, is at once more apparent. Rhyme removed, the poet is at once held up to the standards of prose. Rhyme removed, much ethereal music leaps up from the word, music which has hitherto chirped unnoticed in the expanse of prose. . . . And this liberation from rhyme might well be a liberation *of* rhyme. Freed from its exacting task of supporting lame verse, it could well be applied with greater effect where it is most needed. There are often passages in an unrhymed poem where rhyme is wanted for some special effect, for a sudden tightening-up, for a cumulative insistence, or for an abrupt change of mood." *Selected Prose*, ed. Frank Kermode (New York: Harcourt Brace Jovanovich, 1975), 36.

14 Robert Bly discusses the advantages of the long line for public poetry, as against the "tentative probing" of the free verse short line, in the essay "Whitman's Line as a Public Form," *Selected Poems* (New York: Harper and Row, 1986), 194–98. Of Whitman's line he observes that the poet "aimed at rhetorical power in the sense that Milton, Homer, Shakespeare and the prophets did. The English line created by the translators of the King James Bible, and altered by Whitman's ebullient energy, is a line of authority and power that unfolds, unrolls, or catapults into the outer world." It is precisely such "authority and power" that H.D.'s verse is designed to subvert.

15 T. S. Eliot, *Four Quartets*, *Complete Poems and Plays* (New York: Harcourt Brace Jovanovich, 1952), 117.

16 Play with pronouns, and unconventional ways of addressing the reader which are designed to alter the usual author-reader relationship, may be characteristic of women poets. In *Stealing the Language: The Emergence of Women's Poetry in America* (Boston: Beacon Press, 1986), 202–9, I discuss "the poem that resists the closure of artifact to become a communal transaction," as well as devices of reader involvement in poets such as Anne Sexton, Diane Wakoski, Adrienne Rich, Denise Levertov, and Judy Grahn. Indeterminate pronouns, and especially the slippery uses of "you" in Emily Dickinson, Marianne Moore, and Elizabeth Bishop, would be worth examining.

CHAPTER 19

The H.D. Book: *Part II, Chapter 10*

ROBERT DUNCAN

March 25, Saturday

What is the truth of the matter. The gospel truth. For the truth of what actually happened we need a jury, "the recollection of adults," which Freud in the early essay *Screen Memories* would call upon to test the truth of childhood memories. Fact is one kind of truth of the matter. But the facts of memories, Freud began to suspect, have been reassembled into a fiction of the living. Each psyche strives in its account of the facts to present its peculiar experience; here the facts are not true in themselves but become true as factors of the fiction to which they contribute. When we have assembled from a group of witnesses — Matthew, Mark, Luke and John — an account of the facts, only an ardent faith can coordinate the historical evidence in which every recounted fact is gospel truth of an actuality and the spiritual evidence in which every parable and revelation is gospel truth of a dogmatic reality.

*

The life experience of any individual is not simply a matter of its actualities but of its realities. The man who would present himself without the dimensions of dream and fantasy, much less the experience of illusion and error, who would render the true from the false by voiding the fictional and the doubtful, diminishes the human experience. In the extreme state of such an anxiety for what truth can be held with certainty, he has left only the terms defined by logical positivism with which to communicate; the rest is poetry, the made-up world — the forging of the conscience of his race.

*

In classifying "the various worlds of deliberate fable"—the world of the *Iliad*, of *King Lear*, of the *Pickwick Papers*—with the various worlds of faith—the Christian heaven and hell, the world of the Hindoo mythology, the world of Swedenborg's *visa et audita*—William James proposes that such fictions must each be "a consistent system" within which certain definite relations can be ascertained. "It thus comes about that we can say such things as that Ivanhoe did not *really* marry Rebecca, as Thackeray *falsely* makes him do. The real Ivanhoe world is the one which Scott wrote down for us. *In that world* Ivanhoe does *not* marry Rebecca." It is curious, given his pluralism, that just here James cannot allow that after the Ivanhoe world of Sir Walter Scott another Ivanhoe world could have reality. The history of Christianity is a history of bloody persecutions and wars waged in the high mania of true against false doctrines of what Jesus was and what the Christ was.

In the classical case, there is a strong tradition in Greek thought that Homer falsified the story of Helen. The poet Stêsichorus was blinded (blind like Homer to the truth) after writing his *Helen* and wrote then a recantation of *Palinôdia of which only a fragment remains: "That tale was never true! Thy foot never stepped on the benched galley, nor crossed to the towers of Troy."* Whereupon, as the legend goes, he recovered his sight. The historian Herodotus tells us that he learned from the priests in Egypt that Helen was given refuge at the court of Proteus in Memphis thruout the war. "Within the enclosure stands a temple, which is called that of Aprhodite the Stranger," Herodotus testifies: "I conjecture the building to have been erected to Helen, the daughter of Tyndarus." And at the conclusion of the Egyptian account, Herodotus proceeds to give his own reasons as an historian for finding this tradition convincing. So too, Helen in Euripides' great drama testifies that she was never at Troy: *"Let me tell you the truth / of what has happened to me."* (Following here Richmond Lattimore's translation that carries into our tongue something of high poetry):

> But Hera, angry that she was not given the prize,
> made void the love that might have been for Paris and me
> and gave him, not me, but in my likeness fashioning
> a breathing image out of the sky's air, bestowed
> this on King Priam's son, who thinks he holds me now
> but holds a vanity which is not I.

Euripides does not recant the Homeric account of Troy but imagines in his drama the fiction of an historical Helen and a spiritual Helen, the one in Egypt and the other in Troy, the one the real body and the other an eidolon.

*

Yet James would stress the definite and consistent within each system of reality. "Neptune's trident, e.g., has no status of reality whatever in the Christian heaven; but within the classic Olympus certain definite things are true of it, whether one believe in the reality of the classic mythology as a whole or not." "The various worlds themselves, however, appear to most men's minds in no very definitely conceived relation to each other," he continues, speaking here of the larger subuniverses of reality—the world of sense, the world of science, the world of ideal relations, as well as the world of creative fictions: "and our attention, when it turns to one, is apt to drop the others for the time being out of its account." But even within the world of fictions, as James's own trouble with Thackeray's Ivanhoe exhibits, men find it difficult to entertain contradictory accounts it would seem, much less to imagine new syntheses in which all accounts can be seen as contributing to the truth. Both the historical telling of Jesus and the spiritual account of the Christ in the New Testament present inconsistencies that must be held in one system, and a Robert Graves who is obsessed with reducing the variety of realities to what really happened must labor to establish a true Nazarene Gospel by clearing away what he would persuade us is false in the texts of Matthew, Mark, Luke and John.

*

In the same year of James's *Psychology* (1890), Sir James Frazer in *The Golden Bough* began to advance another sense of supernatural systems, where in place of separate and discrete worlds or churches, nations or races of the spirit and mind, incomparable truths, self-consistent, he raised the picture of a field of religious order where Neptune's trident was no longer assumed to have no status of reality whatever in the Christian heaven. To the consternation of such a view, Frazer was to look for Neptune and trident in all other orders—"emblem of Hittite thunder-god, emblem of Indian deity . . ."—composing a language of persona, symbol, image and emblem that would dissolve the pluralism of cultures and civilizations in the monism of a larger language of human meanings.

*

The exclusive truth that defines any individual order, in what it excludes, may be seen as false to the larger fabric of orders. Every factor of human experience has its own truth in its potency. It is more fluid, more interwoven with other realities than James allows. Neptune's trident that had no status of reality in the Christian heaven rose from the same ground, was child, as Heaven was, of man's imagination become most real. Toynbee in his *Study of History*, some fifty years after James's *Psychology* would trace the Kingdom of Heaven back to the idea of a cloud kingdom as it appears in Aristophanes' fantasy of Cloudcuckooland. And if we look not in the upper world of Christian belief but in the lower world, we may find Neptune's trident in the pitchfork among the instruments of Hell's monitors.

*

Besides things as facts, there is another aspect of things as information, what sets up those widening circles of meaning and influence, what rings true. Neptune's trident that once seemed discordant, out of mode or system, now is heard in another, larger or higher sense of scale to be true. By the inspired subscription of the Council of Nicaea in 325 A.D. it is true and only it is true of Christ that he was the only begotten Son of God and was of the substance of God, who was incarnate, made Man, and suffered the Crucifixion. But by the inspired testament of *The Acts of John* the Lord not only suffered but he did not suffer. The Christ of this gnostic gospel is a Heraklitean Christ and His revelation is the suffering of the cross that is also the playing upon the Cross of the Contraries. "For you I call this cross of light," He says to Saint John: "now logos, now spirit, now Jesus, now Christ, now door, now way, now bread, now seed . . ." "God and the World," Whitehead proposes in *Process and Reality*, "are the contrasted opposites in terms of which Creativity achieves its supreme task of transforming disjoined multiplicity with its diversities in opposition, into concrescent unity, with its diversities in contrast."

*

I take the poem, any poem, as a product of this "Creativity" as the individual experiences it in language, to convey the transformation of a multiplicity of impressions into a unity of expression, that now becomes in its own order part of a new multiplicity of what poetry is, a pending material of the need for a new transformation.

*

Here, the poet's sense of the truth of his matter is not that it belongs to some previous system, that it happened or didn't happen in history, that it is defined as orthodox or heretical, but that it belongs to the work in which he is engaged. Here, his responsibility to the truth is to test the action of sound and sense in the process of its creation of its own definition. He must recognize what is going on. In his *Maximus*, Charles Olson insists the ear must listen, and he speaks in terms of sea depths: *"a peak of the ocean's floor he knew so well the care / he gave his trade, his listening / at 17 to Callaghan (as Callaghan, / at 17, to Bohlen, / Bohlen to Smith) Olsen,"* as Olson in the language could,

> could set his dories out
> as a landsman sows his fields
>
> and reap such halibut . . .

*

Gloucester, for Olson, is not a small town boundary for the mind, but a locus of the Earth. The continent and the sea are real, or elemental to the great reality. The nation or state of mind is another thing, a project of certain men to exploit the communities of other men. So there is "perjorocracy"; there is ownership of utilities — the sea or land or language — proprietorships men would make over truth or means to close off — the wondership, Olson calls it — the freedom any man has to take thought and to create in what he is.

*

"Evil was active in the land," is, in *The Walls Do Not Fall* not only the War-Rule, usurping the creative will from each individual and forcing all action and language into its own terms, but it is also *"tricked up like Jehovah,"* the Puritan ethos or its descendant the capitalist ethos or its ancestor the monotheistic ethos. *"They were angry when we were so hungry / for the nourishment, God"* refers not only to the Laws of Moses that ban certain actual foods, but to the banning of some food of the soul, of some experience. *"They snatched off our amulets."*

*

> they whine to my people, these entertainers, sellers
> they play upon their bigotries (upon their fears
> *Maximus* cries.

*

At the end of the nineteenth century, when William James was writing his *Psychology* and James Frazer his *Golden Bough*, even intelligent men, men with something larger than small-town minds, still thought, not of all men being civilized in a variety of civilizations, but of "civilized" men and of "primitives" or savages, and of "advanced" civilizations and "retarded" civilizations. It was a late version of the old Christian sense of the City and the wilderness — heathen land or pagany; or back of that of the older division between the City and the barbarian world.

But today there are some, men in every field of thought and feeling who begin to picture in their work a species of humanity, a "we" where Australian bushman and Manhattan cityman each have community, where mud beehive forms and concrete tower forms are differing, contrasting but not opposing, expressions of being men. "There is no more striking general fact about language," Edward Sapir writes in 1921 in *Language*, "than its universality. One may argue as to whether a particular tribe engages in activities that are worthy of the name of religion or of art, but we know of no people that is not possessed of a fully developed language. The lowliest South African Bushman speaks in the forms of a rich symbolic system that is in essence perfectly comparable to the speech of the cultivated Frenchman. . . . Scarcely less impressive than the universality of speech is its almost incredible diversity. Those of us that have studied French or German, or, better yet, Latin or Greek, know in what varied forms a thought may run."

THE CHRIST AS PERSON OF THE POEM

Helen is at Troy; Helen is in Egypt. The spectral Helen in Marlowe's *Doctor Faustus* is desire *"performed in twinkling of an eye,"* Beauty that would draw a man's soul forth from him. The Helena of Goethe's *Faust* is an intelligence, where Joy and Beauty are known in one and lost. One Helen *is* the other Helen. Herodotus will be concerned to find the historical Helen: the truth was, he tells us, she was in Egypt. The Trojan Helen was a wraith of men's minds. But the poetic truth has to do with the existence of a real unity or creation seeking its fullness in many personae, in many places, in many times. We will never understand the power of the mistress of Simon Magus if we believe her to be only a whore from Tyre, for it is an important part of her meaning that she is also the great Helen who was born from the egg of Leda, and was daughter of Zeus.

*

So too the *persona* of the Christos is continually created in the imagination. *Mythos* and *drômenon*, gospel and rite, are events first of poetry. This god Christ will not rest in an historical identity, but again and again seeks incarnation anew in our lives. The religious will takes the Divine as given, "uncreated," and seeks to use the god as an authority against any further creation of the idea of the god, drawing upon the spell of magic voice and action in which the Christ is real to convert, yet working thruout to establish prohibition and dogma to limit the creative energy to the immediate purpose. The powers that a Paul must use to set up one Church or one authoritative Christ in the place of many meanings and images, against the authors, come not from an historical Jesus where the truth of things can be located and done with but come from the fullness of a person that is hidden in the creative life, from a dangerous source. Creation and persuasion contend in the use. The cause must be drawn from the expression.

"Yet every cause," Burckhardt writes in *Force and Freedom*, "is in some way alienated and profaned by being expressed." "In the course of time, religion realizes how freely free art is behaving, moulding its material." The Church seeks to impose an unfree style, "the function of which is to represent only the sacred aspect of things, i.e., it must abandon the totality of the living object."

*

"Art is the most arrant traitor of all, firstly because it profanes the substance of religion," he continues. For the artist there is no established Truth, but events, ideas, things have their truth hidden in a form yet to be realized. "Secondly, because it possesses a high and independent selfhood, in virtue of which its union with anything on earth is necessarily ephemeral and may be dissolved at any time. And those unions are very free, for all that art will accept from religion or any other themes is a stimulus. The real work of art is born of its own mysterious life."

*

It is in the mystery-life of poem and novel, picture and drama, that Helen and Christ emerge as eternal persons of our human spirit, and again and again must be drawn from their conventions into their own life. Here the high and independent selfhood of each work of art is the vehicle of the reincarnation. H.D. working anew the Christos-Amen of her *War Trilogy* must free her figure from the predispositions of old ideas towards a life of its own. "*The Christos-image / is most difficult to disentangle*," she writes in *The Walls Do Not Fall*

> from its art-craft junk-shop
> paint-and-plaster medieval jumble
>
> of pain-worship and death-symbol.

The difficulty of the separation coming into the operation of the poem, the medieval jumble and even the junk shop have been brought up and must haunt the picture then as a negative image. So Fitts finds his after-impression that the poem is "pseudo-medieval."

*

The Christ that is *"the Presence . . . spectrum-blue, / ultimate blue ray"* is not medieval but belongs to the Alexandrian orientalizing Greek world, to Gnostic doctrines of the Light Body and to Neo-Platonic theories of the soul being moved spiritually through the senses. This world of thought was revived by the Renaissance Platonists, following Pletho and Ficino. Sound was thought of as spiritually effective because it had movement, but color, though it came second to sound in order, was not primary because it was thought of as a static appearance. Following Newton's demonstration that white light could be broken up by a prism into the spectral colors red, orange, yellow, green, blue, indigo and violet, theosophists identified the seven colors with the seven archangels, as before they had so identified the scale of seven tones. And following the early nineteenth century theories of color as vibration, the whole world of spirit was identified with a world of vibrations in which now color and sound were equally primary as spiritual forces. Kandinsky in *Concerning the Spiritual in Art* speaks theosophically as well as psychologically when he tells us that in the color blue "We feel a call to the infinite, a desire for purity and transcendence. *Blue is the typical heavenly color*; the ultimate feeling it creates is one of rest." *"Rare as radium,"* H.D. describes her blue ray, *"as healing."*

It is a rarefied Christ H.D. would evoke here, the power of a pure color, the presentation of a dream where *"deftly stage-managed"* the bare, clean meeting-house interior suggests the spirituality of innerness, the language of inner light of the Moravian communion stript bare of the morbid fascination with the wounds and blood of the Crucified. At last, it is the image from Velasquez that emerges and here where the terror and agony that would "Stun us with the old sense of guilt" is hidden by lowered eyelids, in the remove of high art, the figure is accepted.

*

But, "most difficult to disentangle," in its high and independent selfhood, the persona is haunted thruout by past lives. Long before the art-craft junk-shop of the nineteenth and twentieth centuries, before the dolls of Christ with up-rolled eyes, leaking piety from nailed palms, there was another Image that appeared in the Gothic world of Christ in torment. In a Christendom torn by savage wars of church against church and church against heresy the very ground of Christ was one of abject and evil suffering. With the great plagues of the fifteenth and sixteenth centuries, sweeping the crowded populations of the new cities, not only wounds but sores ran from the Image. Is it against such Images, as if they were not true — against the Christ of Perpignan in the fifteenth century or the Christ of Grünewald in the sixteenth century — that H.D. would avoid the "medieval jumble / of pain-worship and death-symbol" and pose the Image of the Velasquez crucifixion?

*

If we compare the *Christ Carrying the Cross* of Bosch, contemporary with the crucified Christ of Grünewald, we see in the sixteenth century the expression of two contrasting images — the heterodox Quietist Master of Bosch and the orthodox Catholic Man of Grünewald. In the wholeness of the imagination they are magnetic alternates of one Image, having their life each in each. In their high and independent selfhood they are dependent upon each other. They exist in the rage of a higher union, as, we may begin to see, H.D.'s Christos, rightly, exists in the disentangling she feels necessary, in the difficulty.

*

"And Heraclitus rebukes the poet who says, 'would that strife might perish from among gods and men.' They understand not how that which is at variance with itself agrees with itself. There is an attunement of opposite tensions, like that of the bow and the harp."

*

The crucifixion was not only a punishment (as those who judged Him saw it), not only a sacrifice, passion and endurance, in the name of the world's sin (as the cult of pain-worship saw it), not only a compassion (as the cult of the Redeemer saw it), but also not a punishment, not a suffering, but, if one saw it as a thing in itself, a drama enacted, it was a play of revelation, or a dance. "To each and all it is given to dance," the Christ tells John at Ephesus: "He who joins not in the dance mistakes the event."

*

The eighteenth century Christ of the dream in the War Trilogy has Its origins in the very figure we see in the work of Bosch and in the gnostic Christ of St. John at Ephesus, in the heterodox tradition. The critical opposition — where those of orthodox persuasion considered the War Trilogy at all — had its origins too in the contentions raised against such a Christ of the Eternal Present, as if the truth of Grünewald's Christ must mean the falsity, the "irresponsible even perverse" and "naive" counter of Bosch. For the heretic sects, as often for mystics within the environs of the established Catholic and Protestant churches, the pain, death and judgment of Christ were a dramatic reality in their own persecution, a ground for vision and meaning. He was a persona not of a contention in history but of an eternal event. The Christ of Bosch is not a victim but an actor in a mystery.

*

It is against the very idea of the Eternal that the critics of the War Trilogy strike. Jarrell's quip that "H.D. is History and misunderstands a later stage of herself so spectacularly that her poem exists primarily as an anachronism," Fitts' outrage at the incantation (the music of the dance), knowingly or unknowingly echo the outrage and contempt of Church Fathers for deviate ideas of Christ outside the History of the Church.

Attacking the "Myth" of H.D.'s Christos-Amen, H. H. Watts wrote: "Whatever, then, the sources of the poet's view, it amounts to this: any man may, in his life, draw the inspired circle with a full sense that it coincides exactly with other circles drawn by past men, since they too were touched by the Vision that came from the Healer" — a view of H.D.'s sense of the past at work within the present that would seem to dismiss without consideration her insistence that each experience *"differs from every other / in minute particulars."* But Watts is concerned to dismiss, not to explore, the mythopoeic ground of H.D.'s thought. Having established to his satisfaction that her method is mistaken, Watts expresses his contempt in his conclusion: "Very moving, if there be such a composite figure as Amen-Christos, such a fixed point, such an as-if. But one does not put a roof to bare ruined walls by means of an intensely felt metaphor or, to be quite fair, an emotional *aperçu* that is apparently the product of serious, extensive reading in comparative religion." Is there back of this the outrage of a man who in his own belief knows the true Christ, the one that really is, against the false images of the Christ that the human creativity raises? Or is there the outrage of the rational atheist who will have no traffic with things of the imagination at all?

*

H.D., Pound, and Lawrence, in their poetic vision saw the art-craft image as the god played false. Where what had been a passion is reduced to a lynching or a martyrdom as the social realist imagination sees the man as a victim, Christ beatnik or Christ under-dog. What goes false here is that these figures made real for the one-way literal mind, cleared of all intensely felt metaphor or as-if, act to block further activity of the imagination. The art-craft junk-shop and the scholastic criticism (biblical or literary) concur in their stand against the possibility of resonance and meaning.

*

This is not "our" Christos, H.D. insists. Her generation had a distaste for the warped emotionality of the cultivated sense of sin and suffering in the generation preceding theirs. The very aesthetic of the modern with its clean line and direct image was a reaction against morbidity. "This more or less masochistic and hell-breeding belief is always accompanied," Pound wrote in *Cavalcanti* of the prejudice against the body, "by bad and nig-gled sculpture (Angoulême or Bengal)."

*

They drew from everywhere it seemed, from "extensive reading in com-parative religion," cooperative with many sources, to create a new compo-sition that would stand against the public culture and its images. As Augustine had brought his City of God to stand in place of the actual Rome, they brought inner images and evocations of the divine world to stand against the actual megapolis. Not only H.D., but Lawrence, Pound, Joyce, and, for all his claim for orthodoxy, Eliot, strive for a composite art to embody the individual composite. "A man in himself is a city, beginning, seeking, achieving and concluding his life in ways which the various aspects of a city may embody," Williams proposes in *Paterson* and, for all his claim for the local against the international, Williams's America is a composite of times and places: "if imaginatively conceived — any city, all the details of which may be made to voice his most intimate convictions."

*

The Christs of public worship then that embody the convictions of

Roman Catholic power or of Protestant capitalism, the art-craft gods of the manufacturers and consumers of commodities are false to the inner convictions of the poet. Pound and Joyce avoid Christ entirely, and Lawrence and H.D. must recreate Him. But the Christ of Lawrence and H.D. is of the same order as the Helios or the crystal body of Aphrodite in Pound's cantos, or the Living God of Lawrence's last poems. The Divine Beings of our poets are presentations of their most intimate conviction— the creative imagination. Aphrodite and Pomona attend Pound in his Pisan cell as a higher reality. *"I assure you that the eyes / of Velasquez' crucified,"* H.D. tells us,

> now look straight at you,
> and they are amber and they are fire.

I

She had "gay blue eyes," William Carlos Williams tells us, and the Priestess of Isis in Lawrence's *The Man Who Died* who looks up at him "with her wondering blue eyes" may recall H.D. Not only readings in comparative religion but scenes from actual life enter into the composite to become the matter in which the divine presents itself. H.D., in picturing the confrontation of Mary Magdalene and Kaspar, and Lawrence, in picturing the confrontation between his Man-Who-Died and the priestess, may each draw from their own confrontation in the Bloomsbury days, creating from each his model a new reality.

*

"Has Isis brought thee home to herself?" the woman asks the Christ of Lawrence's story. "I know not," he says.

"But the woman was pondering that this was the lost Osiris," Lawrence continues: "She felt it in the quick of her soul. And her agitation was intense." It was Orpheus that H.D. in her agitation saw Lawrence as; but Orpheus too was torn into many fragments and scattered.

*

It is Christ-Osiris in the War Trilogy whose eyes open, as in Lawrence's novella the eyes of the Man-Who-Died open "upon the other life, the greater day of the human consciousness." "To charge with meaning to the utmost possible degree," Pound had asked of the poem. For Lawrence, as for H.D. and Pound, the revulsion for the Christ as Sin-Bearer is a revulsion for the way He sees life. The Man Who Died rises from nausea and disillusion. The Christ-life had been a sickness, of soul and body: "I wanted to be greater than the limits of my hands and feet, so I brought betrayal on myself. And I know I wronged Judas, my poor Judas . . . But Judas and the high priests saved me from my own salvation." For Lawrence, the revelation was not in the Passion on the Cross but in the Man re-born. The priestess of Isis had been told: "Rare women wait for the re-born man. For the lotus, as you know, will not answer to all the bright heat of the sun. But she curves her dark, hidden head in the depths, and stirs not. Till, in the night, one of these rare, invisible suns that have been killed and shine no more, rises among the stars in unseen purple."

II

Pound in the early period of *The Spirit of Romance* and the Cavalcanti essay, perhaps in his close association with Yeats, is concerned with an art that would "revive the mind of the reader . . . with some form of ecstasy, by some splendor of thought, some presentation of sheer beauty." In the Cantos, Cypris-Aphrodite, Dionysos, Kuthera and Kore attend at Pisa, and in *Thrones*, "the boat of Ra-Set moves with the sun," but he will not let Christ move. Pound, mentor and monitor of *Kulchur*, bending his mind to furnish his "Chronology for school use," avoids the question of Christ and of the ecstatic.

*

In 1916 his mind was more open. "Christianity and all other forms of ecstatic religion," Pound writes in *Psychology and Troubadours*, "are not in inception dogma or propaganda of something called *one truth* . . . their general object appears to be to stimulate a sort of confidence in the life-force." In *Cavalcanti* he writes again: "There is a residue of perception, perception of something which requires a human being to produce it. Which even may require a certain individual to produce it. This really complicates the aesthetic. You deal with an interactive force: the *virtu* in short."

*

Lawrence's Man Who Died and H.D.'s "over Love, a new Master" are creative projections, new images of a force or *virtu*, imagined along the line of interaction between the poet and the inspiring world, a life-force between percept and concept.

*

The personification that for Hulme was a literary device related to the conceit to heighten impression, to remove the thing seen from its common associations and to render it divergent and interesting—

> And saw the ruddy moon lean over a hedge
> Like a red-faced farmer

—for H.D. or for Lawrence was something quite different, coming into being along the route of a conversion, a feeling towards the deeper reality of the thing seen. They sought not originality but to recover a commune of spirit in the image. The "Make It New" that Pound took as his motto could stand for the old renewed as well as for the new replacing the old. Not only the experiment for novelty but also the psyche in its metamorphosis and the phoenix.

*

The truth here is the truth of what feeds the life of the organism where *"prompted by hunger, / it opens to the tide-flow"* but in its openness conservative of the poet's range of feeling. *"But infinity? no,"* H.D. warns: *"of nothing-too-much: I sense my own limit."* As in *The Man Who Died*, Lawrence's persona resolves, "Now I know my own limits. Now I can live without striving to sway others any more. For my reach ends in my fingertips, and my stride is no longer than the ends of my shoes."

*

We sense it right away when a poet or painter is using a doll of Christ to project a given attitude, for the figure postures to present suffering or brotherly love and has no other life of its own. Even a master like El Greco, obsessed with attitude, will lose the persona. The doll of Christ becomes the occasion of a sanctified grievance that can easily be allied with the sanctions the artist or his patron would give to his own grievance. The exchange or interaction within What Is is closed off, and an inflation of attitude is drawn from the hubris involved.

In the exchange, the man makes a place for the God to be. In himself—the stigmata of a Saint Francis appear in the intensity of the compassion. Or the man as artist makes a place in his work for the God to be.

In the inflation, the man makes a place for his self, his grievance or guilt, to be deified in the doll.

*

We know the difference between the gods of vanity and the gods of desire. But my sense here is that in every event of his art man dwells in mixed possibilities of inflation and inspiration. Hence the constant warnings Dante must receive from Virgil and then from Beatrice. The locus of the Vision must be clearly given at the opening. The dark wood, the she-wolf, the leopard and the lion may be allegorical figures of Dante's own times, of the Papal See, the city of Florence, and the Royal House of France; but they are also, most certainly, real figures of Dante's own psyche, his acknowledgment of his own limits.

*

Dante's sense of his own place is the foundation of the Dream, the locus of its Truth. "Thou art my master and my author," he addresses Virgil — it is the Permission of the poet Dante in the man Dante. The glory is to be universal, not personal. The poet must not — it is the commandment of vision — usurp authority in his office. This is what Blake in turn means when he tells us "the authors are in eternity." Dante's master and author, Blake's authors, are counterparts of Thoth and the New Master, not only over Love but over the Poem, in H.D.'s trilogy. These things, the poet testifies, I did not see by my own virtues, but they were revealed to me.

*

In the tenth circle of the *Inferno*, where the falsifiers of word and coinage contend, Dante loses his locus as poet. "I was standing all intent to hear them," he tells us — he had been lost in the contests of the damned; some personal wish of his feeding upon the wrathful spectacle: "when the Master said to me: 'Now keep looking, a little longer and I quarrel with thee!' " "*For the wish to hear it,*" Virgil adds, "*is a vulgar wish.*"

*

All Paradise and Saint Peter wax red in a famous scene of the *Paradiso* at the thought of how Boniface VIII uses the Office of Pope as a personal power. "He who usurpeth upon earth my place, my place, my place," Peter exclaims: "*il loco mio, il loco mio, il loco mio.*" It is the wrath of the Office misused.

*

Dante is about to witness in the Office of the Poet the splendor of

God, the Rose Itself, and there may be a warning in this reminder of *il loco mio* that the poet too is to most remember his place. But the author and master of the Divine Comedy, the poet, has also his locus — it is the work itself. And Dante, to know his own place, but writes the work in service of, as agent of, that author.

III

March 28, Tuesday

There is, then, not only the order of *Paterson* and the *Cantos* in which we may consider the *War Trilogy* as a vision of our own times; but there is another order of dream or vision-poem disclosing the soul's journey from this world through "Apocryphal fire," leaving "the-place-of-a-skull/ to those who have fashioned it" — How Virgil has to warn Dante to let Hell be — and coming at last into the presence of God in which works as various as *The Divine Comedy* or Bunyan's *Pilgrim's Progress* may be of a kind with H.D.'s trilogy.

*

Dante, the heir of a cult in Christendom of Amor; Bunyan, a preaching seventeenth century Protestant convert, certainly no heir of a high poetic tradition; and H.D., late Imagist, versed in a Hermetic-Christian lore of the twentieth century. But to each the order or worth of this world is revealed in the light of another world. Man's spirit is seen more ardent, more in need. Angelic and daemonic spirits attend, and the narrative is in the terms of a religious convention the story of the individual soul's trials or stations in consciousness towards an authority or author who is God.

*

Each is a Dream-Vision. "I cannot rightly tell how I entered it," Dante tells us, "so full of sleep was I about the moment that I left the true way." The *selva oscura* is a dark passage of the Life-Dream, and the poet is moved by what Dante in the close of the Comedy calls his high fantasy.

*

In Bunyan's case he had, he tells us, set about to write an allegory. Well, no . . . he says:

> And thus it was: I writing of the Way
> And Race of Saints, in this our Gospel Day
> Fell suddenly into an Allegory
> About their Journey and the way to Glory.

*

To "fall into" an Allegory is, in this case, like falling in love or falling into a revery, to be compelled in the Work by a creative force—"*in Eternity*," Blake said that force was. Where what the imagination sees is acknowledged to be, not an unreal thing, nor an invention of the poet, but a higher reality revealed. The book itself becomes the Way. The journal, the daily return to the imagination of the book, becomes the journey.

*

"*In the similitude of a DREAM,*" Bunyan subtitles the Progress.

*

Then there is, as in a fairy tale, the primary condition that the soul has lost the straight way and finds itself bewildered, having no way out except its angel or daimon direct. "Through the wilderness of this world," Bunyan has it. "*So,*" H.D. tells us, "*through our desolation / thoughts stir.*" "*And they again began to multiply*," Bunyan testifies, "*Like sparks that from the coals of fire do fly.*"

*

It is like a dream but not a dream, this going out into the world of the poem, inspired by the directions of an other self. It has a kinship too with the seance of the shaman, and in this light we recognize the country of the poem as being like the shaman's land of the dead or the theosophical medium's astral plane. In the story of Orpheus there is a hint of how close the shaman and the poet may be, the singer and the seer.

*

Hermes in the old lore guides the poet in the underworld, as Virgil guides Dante in the Inferno. Briefly, in the Cantos, Plotinus appears to rescue Pound from the hell-mire of politicians and dead issues, but Pound is eager to interrupt the inspiration of his poem and to direct its course.

It is the originality of Pound that mars his intelligence. The goods of the intellect are communal; there is a *virtu* or power that flows from the language itself, a fountain of man's meanings, and the poet seeking the help of this source awakens first to the guidance of those who have gone before in the art, then the guidance of the meanings and dreams that all who have ever stored the honey of the invisible in the hive have prepared.

IV

March 29, Thursday

From Bunyan's *Apology to Pilgrim's Progress*:

> Would'st read thy self, and read thou know'st not what
> And yet know whether thou art blest or not
> By reading the same lines? O then come hither,
> And lay my Book, thy Head, and Heart together.

—from this verse of Bunyan's we may go on to the close of H.D.'s poem *Good Friend*, where H.D. calls upon Shakespeare as her author, with "Avon's Trinity":

> When one is Three and Three are One,
> The Dream, the Dreamer and the Song.

This piece first appeared in *Ironwood* 22 (1983): 47–64.

Part V

Rescriptings

I think I see clearly at last,

the old pictures are really there,
eternal as the painted ibis in Egypt,
the hawk and the hare,

but written in marble and silver,
the spiral-stair, the maze
of the intricate streets,

each turn of the winding
and secret passage-ways
that led to the sea,

my meanderings back and forth,
till I learned by rote
the intimate labyrinth

that I kept in my brain,
going over and over again
the swiftest way to take

through this arched way or that,
patient to re-trace my steps
or swift to dart

past a careless guard at the gate;
O, I knew my way,
O, I knew my ways. . . .

        —H.D., *Helen in Egypt*

CHAPTER 20

Creating a Women's Mythology: H.D.'s Helen in Egypt

SUSAN STANFORD FRIEDMAN

For if Chloe likes Olivia and Mary Carmichael knows how to express it she will light a torch in that vast chamber where nobody has yet been. It is all half lights and profound shadows like those serpentine caves where one goes with a candle peering up and down, not knowing where one is stepping.

—Virginia Woolf, *A Room of One's Own*

We know of no rule
of procedure,

we are voyagers, discoverers
of the not-known,

the unrecorded;
we have no map;

possibly we will reach haven,
heaven.

—H.D., *The Walls Do Not Fall*

The half lights and profound shadows Virginia Woolf called women writers of the future to explore are the unrecorded territory of women's experience and perspectives. The polarization of men and women in most societies and the economic, intellectual, and cultural dominance of one over the other, Woolf eloquently argued, have created a mystery, an untold story whose forms and visions have yet to be fully determined. H.D., the American artist who assumed a leadership role in the short-lived, tremendously influential imagist school of poetry, incorporated that story into

373

her search for spiritual reality in a war-torn century overwhelmed and atomized by its destructive, scientific technologies. H.D.'s voyage into the "not-known, the unrecorded" produced work in many genres—novel, poetry, drama, film, translation, memoir, and essay—in an impressive career that spanned the years between the publication of her first poems in 1913 and her "Cantos," as she called *Helen in Egypt*, the epic-length poem published in the year she died, 1961.

Woolf predicted that it would take another hundred years before women poets could speak in their own distinct voice, one true to the historically different experience of women.[1] However, as Suzanne Juhasz convincingly argued in *Naked and Fiery Forms: Modern American Poetry by Women: A New Tradition*, a female poetic tradition is rapidly coming into existence.[2] H.D.'s poetry, most particularly the seldom-studied long poems she wrote between 1942 and 1961, is a crucial link in the creation of a rich poetic tradition that will serve as the springboard of continuity and context for future generations of Shakespeare's sisters. H.D.'s special contribution lies in the clarity with which she understood the need and process of transformation: the metamorphosis of the woman as "other" to authentic selfhood. Her long poems are all narratives in which the traditional female object of the artist's quest (Dante, *Paradiso*; Keats, "La Belle Dame Sans Merci"; Williams, *Paterson*; Crane, *The Bridge*; Joyce, *Portrait of the Artist*, etc.) is simultaneously and self-consciously the subject and the creator. In reference to current women's poetry, Adrienne Rich has written that "woman is becoming her own midwife, creating herself anew."[3] Along with Rich, H.D. understood that creation of selfhood for women involves not only a new expression of women's experience, but also a transformation of the androcentric cultural tradition which has shaped and often thwarted that experience in the first place. Rich writes: "Revision—the act of looking back, of seeing with fresh eyes, of entering an old text from a new critical direction—is for us more than a chapter in cultural history: it is an act of survival. Until we can understand the assumptions in which we are drenched we cannot know ourselves. And this drive to self-knowledge for woman, is more than a search for identity: it is part of her refusal of the self-destructiveness of male-dominated society."[4] The birth of the new woman does not come ex nihilo, just as the traditional images of woman did not exist in a vacuum, but emerged out of a slowly evolving ideology tied to the institutions of patriarchy. For H.D., the quest for identity involves the reexamination of existing cultural traditions and the rediscovery and creation of a women's mythology.

By a "women's mythology," I do not mean a set of myths that deal only with women or that have meaning only for women. In some societies, such as the various groups of Australian aborigines described in Mircea Eliade's

Rites and Symbols of Initiation, men and women do indeed have separate mythologies and accompanying rituals that serve as the ideological component of rigidly polarized and hierarchical sex roles.[5] It would be a grave distortion of H.D.'s poetry to see her work as that kind of separate mythology. Instead, H.D.'s epic heroes quest for vision and selfhood against the same cultural backdrop of various religions, psychologies, and literary traditions that their male counterparts in Pound, Yeats, Williams, and Crane do. As with these poets in the male poetic tradition, H.D.'s motivating concern that ultimately leads her to a women's mythology is what she saw as the general crisis of the fragmented and drifting twentieth century: the fact of war, the destruction by progress, the mortality of individuals and civilizations, the fact of time and death itself. *The Walls Do Not Fall* (1944), the first of her long poems, expresses in the objective correlative of a very real war the spiritual despair that motivates her search:

> we are powerless,
>
> dust and powder fill our lungs,
> our bodies blunder
>
> through doors twisted on hinges,
> and the lintels slant
>
> cross-wise;
> we walk continually
>
> on thin air
> that thickens to a blind fog.[6]

This journey through the spiritual wasteland of a war-torn century produces a different mythology from Pound's Confucian fascism or Eliot's Anglican conservatism. From her perspective as a woman in a man's world, H.D. resurrects matriarchal values and literally restores the desecrated Goddess (Isis-Aphrodite-Astarte-Aset, etc.) to her original position of veneration (*Trilogy* 5, 73–75). Her purpose is to counterbalance what she views as the masculine "whirlwind" of destruction. Her work constitutes a "women's mythology" because she utterly transforms the psychoanalytic and mythological traditions she works within by a perspective based fundamentally on the value of qualities historically associated with women and the experience of women. In the *Trilogy*, her characterization of poets as "initiates / born of one mother" (21) is no ornamental metaphor, but is expressive of the female origins to which she returns and from which she believes civilization has wandered disastrously. Her "women's mythology" is thus simultaneously a restoration of a worldview buried and degraded by patriarchal tradition and a new mythology which she believes can reshape the "sand-heap maze / of present-day endeavour" (23). Because this revisionist mythmaking offers a rich source of personal and cultural transformations from a woman's perspective, it makes an important contribution to the female poetic tradition. Simultaneously, it helps to reshape *the* poetic tradition to which all groups, with their different historically determined experiences and perspectives, contribute.[7]

Although the *Trilogy, Tribute to Freud, Winter Love* (1972), and *Hermetic Definition* (1972) are all crucial to understanding H.D.'s canon within the context of her total contribution to the female poetic tradition, *Helen in Egypt* brings into sharp focus her place within that tradition. Her choice of a mythological persona through which to explore contemporary realities is the first clue to H.D.'s understanding of the conditions of quest for the woman hero. H.D.'s hero is the Greek Helen, symbol throughout centuries of mythology and literature of the twin images of woman — beauty and evil. Helen in the patriarchal tale is a Greek Eve. Tempted by the delights of the flesh, she leaves her husband Menelaus, king of Sparta, and goes to Troy with Paris. Because of her (and the goddess of sexual love, Aphrodite, who directs her), Troy and Greece are doomed, victors as well as victims. To write an epic of genuinely female quest, H.D. goes directly to the heart of the patriarchal mythology of woman's nature — woman as representative of the flesh who tempts mankind to evil and death through her sexuality.[8] This woman becomes the center of consciousness in an epic aimed at revising both mythology and the concept of woman's selfhood.

Helen is H.D.'s "everywoman," and the starting point of her quest is the recognition of what she stands for in others' eyes. Helen thinks to herself, as the epic opens, "Helena, Helen hated of all Greece";[9] others call her "this evil philtre / this curse of Aphrodite" (4); heroes, both Trojan and Greek, will be "cursing Helen through eternity" (4). Like more contemporary heroes, such as Edna Pontellier and Nora Helmer, Helen cannot begin to construct a new selfhood until she has come to terms with the identity created by the perceptions and expectations of the dominant tradition.

To eradicate the image of Helen as a guilty Eve figure, H.D. constructs an "apologia" or defense of Helen and, by extension, all women. This modern "pallinode" (literally a "song against," in Greek) revises the dominant tradition by reviving and redefining the buried tradition of Helen's innocence. In the prose passage that opens the epic, H.D. reminds her readers of the precedents for revisionist mythmaking in Greek literature itself:

We all know the story of Helen of Troy but few of us have followed her to Egypt. How did she get there? Stesichorus of Sicily . . . was said to have been struck blind because of his invective against Helen, but later was restored to sight, when he reinstated her in his Pallinode. *Euripides, notably in* The Trojan Women, *reviles her, but he also is "restored to sight." The later, little understood* Helen in Egypt, *is again a* Pallinode, *a defense, explanation or apology.*

According to the Pallinode, *Helen was never in Troy. She had been transposed or translated from Greece into Egypt. Helen of Troy was a phantom, substituted for the real Helen, by jealous deities. The Greeks and the Trojans alike fought for an illusion.* (1)[10]

H.D.'s choice of the Helen myth predates and parallels contemporary feminists' fascination for Lilith and the unnamed "Eve" in the first version of the Judeo-Christian creation myth (Genesis 1:27)—these legends whose egalitarian message about women has been erased in time from the consciousness of the culture because they have been out of step with the dominant masculine values. The growth of new identities requires the creation of new mythologies; and Helen's personal search for self-knowledge and selfhood stands as one link in that new chain of being.

But H.D.'s pallinode is a far more complicated critique of tradition than Euripides' and Stesichorus' revisions of the Helen myth. They both established Helen's innocence by seeing her as a modest and chaste Penelope figure who waits patiently in Egypt for her husband to reclaim her. H.D., on the other hand, bases her defense of Helen on a redefinition of innocence that calls into question the male-dominated system of values victimizing Helen in the first place. In a way highly reminiscent of Woolf's *To the Lighthouse*, H.D. portrays an enormous chasm between the traditionally overvalued "masculine" world and the undervalued "feminine" world. Helen's actions become defensible within the context of her discovery of a dialectical confrontation between matriarchal and patriarchal worldviews ultimately leading to an androgynous synthesis. Helen's understanding of these opposing worldviews and her consequent search for wholeness take a complex narrative form that operates on two levels simultaneously: a linear journey through space and time and an inner journey into the layers of dreams and memory, and the out-of-time dimension of "enchantment."

Let me clarify the story line that H.D. creates out of variant myths, her syncretist religious researches, and her own imagination before analyzing the dialectical opposition of masculine and feminine values that form the symbolic backdrop of Helen's quest. The epic is divided into three parts, each of which takes place in a different locale and in a definite sequence of time. Part I, the "Pallinode," centers on Helen in Egypt and her gradual realization that she has suppressed all memories of being in Troy with Paris. At the beginning of the "Pallinode," she is alone in Egypt. With Stesichorus and Euripides, Helen believes that her father (the male divinity whose Greek, Egyptian, and Judeo-Christian identities are merged and variously called "Amen," "Zeus," and "God") long ago brought her to the peace and protection of the temples of Egypt. Here the woman "hated of all Greece" studies the sacred script of holy Egypt: "there is mystery in this place / I am instructed, I know the script, / the shape of this bird is a letter, / They call it the hieroglyph" (13–14). Her peace of certain innocence is shattered by the sudden appearance of Achilles who is shipwrecked, lost and limping from the fatal wound in his heel. When Achilles recognizes the hated Helen whom he used to watch in fascination and anger as she walked the ramparts of Troy, he calls her "Hecate," "witch," and tries to strangle her. Helen's first response is overwhelming guilt: "How could I hide my eyes? / How could I veil my face? / with ash or charcoal from the embers?" (16). She appeals to his mother, Thetis, the goddess of the sea who is linked in the poem with the other female deities, Isis, Aphrodite, and Astarte. Achilles' violence changes to love as the name of the goddess recalls him to a former self that knew nothing of killing "and the clang of metal / and the glint of steel" (26).

Achilles' presence cracks the whole original thrust of the "Pallinode" because he keeps asking Helen "which was the dream, which was the veil of Cytheraea?" (36). Was Helen at Troy or in Egypt? The electric meeting of their eyes at Troy caused his fatal negligence in fastening the greave at his ankle. Did he exchange a magnetic glance with a phantom? Is Helen guilty or innocent? Helen treats Achilles with great ambivalence because his questions destroy the peace of easy innocence. She draws him back with her magic and sends him away: "and do I care, / do I care greatly / to keep him eternally? / I was happier alone, / why did I call him to me? / Must I forever look back? . . . O do not turn, do not turn [back to her], / go, follow the ways of the sea" (36). Certainly she is resisting his questions within the psychoanalytic sense of the term "resistance," but she also fears that she will be sucked into his worldview, thereby losing her identity: His *charm or enchantment is . . . so strong that she must fight for her identity, for* Helena," H.D. explains. "Helena? who is she? . . . I must fight for Helena" (37), Helen thinks. In the "Pallinode" Helen comes to understand that she herself is the primary hieroglyph that needs deciphering.[11] The epic is a love story, of sorts. But before Achilles and Helen can be united on the island of Leuké, as the variant myth has it, Helen must discover who she is.[12] Achilles leaves Egypt for Leuké, and Thetis tells Helen to follow. Helen, however, remains alone to remember earlier selves without succumbing to the hated-Helen image. The "Pallinode" which begins in an affirmation that Helen was never in Troy ends by pushing her deep into *"the so far suppressed memory"* (109).

Part II, "Leuké," and part III, "Eidolon," are structured primarily by Helen's inner confrontation with the past. Narrative based on identifiable action is scanty and often like a dream sequence in its shifting time and locale. As "Leuké" opens, a skiff brings Helen to Leuké where she awakes not to Achilles, but to the memory of a "familiar fragrance, / late roses, bruised apples; / reality opened before me, / I had come back; I retraced the thorny path / but the thorns of rancour and hatred were gone / . . . I was laughing with Paris" (116). Space has become time as she remembers her "first rebellion," the joy of young love. The alchemy of her memory draws Paris to her, and together they relive the years of the war in Troy. Paris tells Helen that she really died as the walls of Troy fell and that he died not long after when his first love Oenone refused to heal his poisoned wound. Paris reminds Helen of their vows and denounces Achilles — "I say he never loved you" (144) — but Helen leaves Paris. Still, she is not ready to go to Achilles because of the conflict between her dual selves: "Helen Dendritis," the young Helen who loved Paris, and the older Helen of Egypt. "Who is Helena?" The old question is still with her. Now *"baffled and buffeted and very tired,"* she arrives "blown by the wind, the snow" (151, 147) at the home of Theseus, her first lover. Theseus as mythic psychoanalyst kindly helps Helen sort through the past to reconcile her various fragmented selves.

Part III, "Eidolon," records that slow process of synthesizing dual selves in the search for wholeness. As Helen wakes up to a new "dawn" uniting through cyclical process all oppositions, she is ready to join Achilles on Leuké. This union and the subsequent birth of their child Euphorion, however, is not the climax of the epic. Instead, the emphasis is on Helen's own sense of who she is. Helen, overwhelmed by everyone's hatred for her, has become Helen, at peace with a fully healed self.

Helen's inner journey follows a free-associational structure reminiscent of H.D.'s psychoanalysis and *Tribute to Freud* because past, present, and future are melded together in what often seems like "the dream parallel." But the narrative of space and time does not itself make clear H.D.'s redefinition of Helen's fundamental innocence. Helen's defense emerges out of her discovery of the meaning of the Trojan War. The origin of this war is the polarization of love and death or "L'Amour and La Mort." H.D. associates love with the women's world and death with the men's. Helen's reflections on her newly recovered memories center on the chasm between these worlds, and her "pallinode" rests finally on an understanding that it is only from the perspective of the man's world that she is the source of evil. The war was caused not by Helen, nor even Aphrodite, but by the opposition of the force of life and love and the force of death and strife. The "Pallinode" in particular abounds in descriptions of the two opposing forces that Helen discovers at work in her family history. Contrasting the two worlds, for example, Helen wonders about Achilles just after his arrival in Egypt:

> does he dare remember
> the unreality of war,
> in this enchanted place?
>
> his fortress and his tower
> and his throne
> were built for man, alone;
>
> no echo or soft whisper
> in those halls,
> no iridescent sheen,
>
> no iris-flower,
> no sweep of strings,
> no answering laughter,
>
> but the trumpet's call;
>
> (30–31)

This imagist rendering of two worlds seems to be operating on the basis of traditional qualities associated with the "masculine" and the "feminine" — strength, power, war, heroism with the "masculine" and softness, flowers, gaiety, music, beauty, interiors with the "feminine." But like Woolf in *To the Lighthouse*, H.D.'s careful building of the values connected with the man's and woman's world revises the familiar connotations greatly. In H.D.'s schema, the women's values (she never uses the word "feminine") constitute a powerful force for love, birth, regeneration, growth, peace, order, joy, and the fertile happiness symbolized by flowers, harvest, light, laughter, music, and "shimmering" glances. Isis, Aphrodite, Astarte, Ishtar, Nepthys, Artemis, and most of all Thetis are protean forms of the Goddess, the embodiment of the powerful love force. The "masculine" world — and here H.D. does use the word "masculine" and the phrase *"the purely masculine 'iron-ring'"* (55) — is the negation of life and love. Personified by the destructive "whirlwind" monster Typhon and his Egyptian equivalent Set, god of the desert winds, the masculine world is also powerful; but it is associated with darkness, disorder, steel, iron, weapons, clanging sounds, fortresses, ice, cold, might-makes-right morality, hate, pride, will, tyranny, rape, and above all death and war. The two worlds are always shown in head-on conflict.

The images and language used to describe the "masculine" world intensify even more the negative, life-denying qualities of Achilles' world. "We were an iron-ring / whom Death made stronger," Achilles tells Helen. In the "timeless-time, / here in the Amen-temple," Helen sees demonic images of war:

> the rasp of a severed wheel
>
> seemed to ring in the dark,
> the spark of a sword on a shield,
> the whirr of an arrow,
>
> the crack of a broken lance,
> then laughter mingled with fury,
> as host encountered host.
>
> (39)

This "laughter" is no "answering laughter" as in the halls of the women's world because it is the one-sided battle cry of the victor who feeds upon the destruction of others. Another contemporary pattern of images is superimposed on the Homeric gear of battle. At one point, H.D. infuses her prose description of the "purely masculine iron-ring" and Achilles' following explanation to Helen with words that come directly out of the wars in her own century:

This is the Achilles of legend, Lord of the Myrmidons, indisputable dictator with his select body-guard, the seven, of whom he, the eighth, received the directives of campaign. Technically, he shares the Command, as he calls it, with Helen's discredited husband, Menelaus and with Agamemnon, the husband of her sister. There is also, Odysseus, with whom we gather, there has been some plot or compromise. . . . There is evidently a bribe, some counter-burgaining. . . . But there is some secret agreement. If Odysseus succeeds in his designs [with the "iron-horse"], Achilles will be given Helen and world-leadership. This is contrary to the first agreement of the allies.

> I had broken the proud
> and re-moulded them to my whim;
> the elect, asleep in their tents,
>
> were my slaves, my servants;
> we were an iron-ring, unbreakable
> . . .
> into the ring of our Immortality,
> there came with a clamour of arms,
> as a roar of chargers, answering the trumpeter,

The Command; no swerving, no wavering
. . .
let Odysseus unfold his plan
of the iron-horse,
. . .
the Towers will fall;
Helen will be your share
of the spoils of war;

what is a promise given?
this is the iron-ring,
no Grecian or other king

may contest or disobey;
within the iron-circle of your fame,
no more invisible,

you shall control the world...

(51-52)

"Dictator," "body-guards," "directives," "campaign," "world leadership," "secret agreement," "allies," "Command," etc., are modern war words. But H.D.'s intent, I think, was broader than to remind us that ancient Greece is a palimpsest of modern Europe. Some of these words have distinctly fascist overtones—"elect," "dictator," and the "cult" of total obedience, "the Command" (German chiefs of staff were known as the "High Command" during World War II)—and the promise of "world-leadership" to Achilles is, I think, a direct reference to Hitler. H.D. is attacking the "purely masculine" worldview as tyrannical, elitist, and death-centered. Its social system requires war and a dictator to fulfill the masculine mystique of total power and command. Coming directly out of the historical period which saw the demonic rise of German, Italian, Spanish, and Japanese fascism, H.D. is suggesting that the most extreme forms of "masculine" values are tantamount to fascism. Her "Cantos" recall Pound's *Cantos* in more ways than one: her attack on fascism as a "death-cult" is perhaps an answer to Pound's espousal of fascism in Italy and his celebration of the patriarchal, Confucian worldview.[13]

Once again, parallel to but years before the contemporary women's movement, H.D. is linking the masculine mystique with hierarchical terror-based, death-centered social systems. In fact, "link" is probably too weak a word; H.D. seems to take as the defining characteristic of the Greek world its patriarchal nature. She explains that *the Command or the adamant rule of the inner circle of the warrior caste was 'bequest from the past.'* The Achilleses, Agamemnons, Hitlers, and Mussolinis of the world are not freak accidents of history; they are part of a patriarchal chain structuring a social system. As Achilles explains to Helen:

> The Command was bequest from the past,
> from father to son,
> the Command bound past to the present
>
> and the present to aeons to come,
> the Command was my father, my brother,
> my lover, [his male friend Patroklos], my God.
>
> (61)

H.D. carefully delineated the position of women within this "warrior caste." As possessions prized for their beauty and sexual potential, the women were the "spoils of war"; the most beautiful, Helen, would go to the world leader, Achilles.[14] The theme of female sacrifice to the masculine "warrior cult" reappears many times throughout the epic. Helen explores the power structures of her world by seeing the common pattern underlying the fates of other women: Cassandra, Polyxena, Briseis, Chryseis, and most of all, the women in her own family. In reliving the story of her twin sister, Clytaemnestra, and her niece, Iphigenia, Helen comes to a full realization of the conflict between polarized worlds. When Helen is able to visualize *"her own fate in terms of that of her twin sister"* (74), she takes the first step in her inner quest to recover and accept her role at Troy.

The story of her sister clarifies for Helen the values of the woman's world as well as the patriarchal state and family which oppose it. Like Helen, Clytaemnestra was "hated by all Greece." Her name became synonymous with women's treachery and evil because she took a lover while her husband Agamemnon was in Troy and then killed him when he came home victorious with his concubine Cassandra. Deep in family history, however, Helen finds the motivations for Clytaemnestra's violence as her defense of the woman's world. Clytaemnestra's wedding day defines for Helen that world. In contrast to the metallic world of war, it is characterized by the ascendance of peace and harmony. The Goddess rules through the Word, not the Sword, as humankind exists in organic relation to nature. The marriage (like the *komos* or wedding party with which all Greek comedy ends) is holy, incarnating in the real world the force of life. Helen recalls:

> She was a bride, my sister,
> with a bride's innocence,
> she was a lover of flowers

and she wound in her hair,
the same simple weeds
that Iphigenia wore;

she stepped forward,
they stood together
as one, before the altar;

O Word of the Goddess,
O Harmony and Grace,
it was a moment

of infinite beauty,
but a war-Lord
blighted that peace.

                    (74)

The altar of marriage is literally transformed into the altar of sacrifice
as Agamemnon destroys the rule of the Goddess. Because the Greeks violated the sacred hunting grounds of Artemis, Apollo holds back the winds
needed by the Greeks to send their warships to Troy. H.D. tells us that
Calchas, the priest of Apollo, becomes *"a substitute or double of the
original Command,"* the prophet for the "death-cult" and "warrior caste"
who hands down the "dictate" to the Greek leaders: *"The ships shall never
leave Aulis, / until a virgin is offered / to Artemis"* (87). The confrontation of two value systems becomes family history. The "virgin" is Iphigenia,
who is *"summoned to Aulis, on the pretext of a marriage to Achilles"* (72).
Representative of the patriarchal family and state, Agamemnon sacrifices
his daughter. Clytaemnestra's murder of Agamemnon is her revenge.
Representative of a matriarchal value system, Clytaemnestra strikes back
in fury at the world of men. As the first step in her own defense, Helen
creates a "pallinode" for her sister:

what did she care for the trumpet,
the herald's cry at the gate,
war is over;

it is true she lay with her lover,
but she could never forget
the glint of steel at the throat

of her child on the altar;
Artemis snatched away
the proffered sacrifice,

but not even Artemis could veil
that terrible moment,
could make Clytaemnestra forget

the lure, the deception, the lie
that had brought her to Aulis;
"we will pledge, forsooth, our dearest child

to the greatest hero in Greece;
bring her here
to join hand with hand

in the bridal pledge at the altar";
but the pledge was a pledge to Death,
to War and the armies of Greece.

(72–73)

The powerlessness of the woman's world to overcome the treachery of
the masculine iron ring at this moment does not mean that H.D. associated passivity or helplessness with the Goddess or her human embodiments.
The female world is at times defeated, but not at all passive or accepting
in the face of the death cult.[15] *"Their* [Iphigenia, Clytaemnestra] *divinity
is stronger than all the material forces gathered against them,"* H.D. explains. The poem continues with a marvelous reversal on the image of
the swan Zeus raping Leda; Clytaemnestra and Iphigenia are the swans:

Have you ever seen a swan,
when you threaten its nest —
. . .
the wings of an angry swan
can compass the earth,

can drive the demons
back to Tartarus,
can measure heaven in their span;

one swan and one cygnet
were stronger than all the host.

(76)

The power of the Swan-mother is only one manifestation of a pervasive pattern. The power of the Goddess herself confronts the Command.
Achilles' explanation of the Command as patriarchal "bequest from the
past" is immediately followed by a description of the opposing power of
the Goddess:

it was not the Command that betrayed
   [Achilles],
it was Another;
She is stronger than God, they say,

She is stronger than Fate
and a chaffing greave,
loose at the ankle.

(61)

Achilles continues to tell Helen how the Goddess led him to renounce world leadership, the Command, and the masculine ring of war. As with Clytaemnestra, the Goddess operates through her human counterpart. Helen on the ramparts of Troy holds Achilles in a potent glance just as he stoops to fasten his armor:

I stooped to fasten a greave
that was loose at the ankle,

when she turned; I stood
indifferent to the rasp of metal,
and her eyes met mine.

(54)

In this moment, Achilles turned his back forever on the masculine world of war to become absorbed into the power of the woman's world view. Paris' arrow soon after killed Achilles through his one mortal spot, his ankle, and thus sealed the defeat of the Command. Achilles' story of the glance that caused his death and subsequent rebirth as the "new Mortal" in Egypt and Leuké is H.D.'s own. Her variation on the classical myth underscores her focus on the polarization of male and female worlds.

The power of Helen's glance operates through the defining quality of the women's world — Love or Eros. At one point in the "Pallinode," Helen is "deified" as Love: "The Lords have passed a decree / . . . / Helena, reads the decree, / shall be shrined forever; / in Melos, in Thessaly / they shall honour the name of Love" (95). This deification may at first glance seem like a new form of a very old image — that women are concerned only about love while men turn to philosophy, art, and the conquering of the forces of nature. But I think such a reading of H.D.'s work is to take her concept of love out of the context of her broader argument about the polarized worldviews. By love, she does not refer narrowly to a relationship between adult men and women; she is writing about the life force which infuses all organic and spiritual things with the power of growth, synthesis, and resurrection. Familiarity with her potential source material is, I think, helpful. J. J. Bachofen, whom she might have read, and Robert Graves, whom she definitely read, believed without question in an early matriarchal period of human history. They did not see this ancient culture as a simple reversal of patriarchy. Instead, Bachofen described matriarchal culture as based in the same values H.D. assigns to the Goddess in her epic: "it operates in a world of violence as the divine principle of love, of union, of peace."[16] Matriarchies, he argued, were classless societies based on cooperation and common ownership of material goods. Competition, hierarchies of power, ownership of property, and war characterized the patriarchal cultures that destroyed the matriarchies. While Bachofen saw the ascendance of the male as "progress," H.D. associates the same "masculine" values with destructive fascism.

Bachofen insisted that classical mythology records the uneasy transition from matriarchal to patriarchal societies. For Freud, the history of the individual psyche recapitulates the history of the race recorded in myth. Late in life, Freud posited the existence of two warring instincts in the unconscious. H.D.'s portrayal of the worlds of love and war closely parallels Freud's description of Eros and the "death instinct": "After long doubts and vacillations we have decided to assume the existence of only two basic instincts, *Eros* and *the destructive instinct* . . . the aim of the first of these basic instincts is to establish ever greater unities and to preserve them thus—in short, to bind together; the aim of the second on the contrary, is to undo connections and so to destroy things. We may suppose that the final aim of the destructive instinct is to reduce living things to an inorganic state. For this reason we also call it the death instinct."[17] H.D. accepts these definitions but adds a crucial new element that is inconsistent with Freud's theory of the libido: she associates a woman's worldview with Eros and a man's worldview with the death instinct.

The voice of Thetis, heard only once in the poem, tells Helen near the end of the "Pallinode" about the kind and extent of women's power. It is not violent or aggressive; it is intangible, invisible, omniscient, and operating without might but with magic, the power of Isis:

Phoenix, the symbol of resurrection has vanquished indecision and doubt, the eternal why of the Sphinx. It is Thetis (Isis, Aphrodite) who tells us this, at last, in complete harmony with Helen.

Choragus:
(Image or Eidolon of Thetis)

> A woman's wiles are a net;
> they would take the stars
> or a grasshopper in its mesh;

they would sweep the sea
for a bubble's iridescence
or a flying-fish;

they would plunge beneath the surface,
without fear of the treacherous deep
or a monstrous octopus;

what unexpected treasure,
what talisman or magic ring
may the net find?

frailer than spider spins,
or a worm for its bier,
deep as a lion or a fox

or a panther's lair,
leaf upon leaf, hair upon hair
as a bird's nest,

Phoenix
has vanquished
that ancient enemy, Sphinx.

$$(93-94)^{18}$$

To some extent, H.D's use of the word "wiles" is ironic. She refers to the familiar image of deceptive, childish, coquettish woman embedded in the cliché "feminine wiles" as well as to the net in which Clytaemnestra trapped Agamemnon in Aeschylus' play. The net of power in the poem with its "catch" of the earth, the stars, the sea (representing here, as they often do in H.D.'s poem, all of nature, spiritual heights, and unconscious depths) is a total contrast to the weak, powerless woman who uses deceptive "wiles" to wheedle some little favor out of her man. The ultimate "catch" of the female power is in fact the vision of resurrection, the Phoenix. But in another sense, H.D. uses the connotations of "wiles" to make another point about the power of the woman's world and the nature of the values its stands for. H.D. expresses, I believe, a strongly pacifist view in the next few sections and rejects any idea that women should become like men or use the weapons of men in their fight against the death cult. Helen decides that Clytaemnestra's fate was a dark one because she became her opposite in the defense of the woman's world:

Clytaemnestra struck with her mind,
with the Will-to-Power,
her Lord returned with Cassandra,

and she had a lover;
does it even the Balance
if a wife repeats a husband's folly?

never; the law is different;
if a woman fights,
she must fight by stealth,

with invisible gear;
no sword, no dagger, no spear
in a woman's hands

can make wrong, right.

(97)

Linda Wagner refers to this passage as evidence that H.D. urged women to accept and not rebel against their men.[19] But I think H.D. is much closer to an argument in the women's movement today which insists that women should not simply become "masculinized women," accepting and profiting from all the values of a competitive, hierarchical, class society. The epic argues that the qualities of the woman's world are life-affirming and should be restored to culture if civilization is to survive the destructiveness of the male ethos. For H.D., who abhorred war, this change had to come through peaceful means, through the intangible net of the life force and the transforming power of love, if the cycle of violence was ever to stop. As a poet, H.D.'s contribution to that change is her revaluation of a female worldview and a restitution of a woman's mythology.

Helen's psychic and mythic explorations into family history and revised mythology prepare her to remember her past love affairs by releasing her from guilt. Seen in the context of contrasting matriarchal and patriarchal values, her love of Paris becomes her rebellion against the iron ring of the death cult, a revolt that parallels her sister's darker revenge. The defense of the "Pallinode" complete, "Helena has withstood / the rancour of time and hate" (96), and she is now ready to recapture the lost Helen of Troy. "Leuké" opens with her memory of the trip to Troy and a warning that the image of Helen down through the ages is still not the real Helen, whom she is just now free to discover:

I am not nor mean to be
the Daemon they made of me;
going forward, my will was the wind,

(or the will of Aphrodite
filled the sail, as the story told
of my first rebellion;

> the sail, they said,
> was the veil of Aphrodite),
>
> . . .
>
> let them sing Helena for a thousand years,
> let them name and re-name Helen,
>
> I can not endure the weight of eternity,
> they will never understand
> how, a second time, I am free;
>
>   (109–10)

Helen recognizes that she bears the weight of patriarchal images but now she no longer internalizes those images so that she is free to reflect fully on her past and future.

For H.D., women give birth to a new self by first destroying the false self created by the culture. The songs that "name and re-name Helen" have called her either virtuously chaste (Helen in Egypt) or destructively evil (Helen of Troy). As she greets Paris in Leuké to relive her Trojan experience, Helen has erased that traditional duality of woman as angel or demon. But she has not eliminated duality itself. In "Leuké" and "Eidolon," her inner journey reveals a conflict of opposites and a multiplicity of selves that bring pain and confusion. Once the censor of suppressed memories opens the door to past selves, Helen can at first find no pattern or certainty in the quicksand succession of identities: Helen, daughter of Zeus and child of worldly Sparta; Helen, the kidnapped child bride of Theseus; Helen, the wife and mother in Sparta; Helen Dendritis in springtime love with Paris in Troy; Helen alone, in the timeless dimension of sacred Egypt; Helen, the older (perhaps even dead) lover of Achilles; Helen as Persephone, bride of death; Helen, seeking the healing of self-acceptance with Theseus; Helen of Leuké, alone, yet also together with Achilles and the child Euphorion. Helen's quest becomes the search to reconcile the seemingly contradictory selves of daughter, wife, mother, lover, and person alone.

As H.D. herself discovered in her analysis with Freud, recovery of hidden selves is often painful. But H.D. agreed with Freud that self-knowledge brings liberation from the crippling scars of the buried past.[20] Freed by the process of the "Pallinode," Helen is able to confront each of those selves. The last experience to resurface is her first step outside the traditional role: her desertion of her husband Menelaus and baby Hermione. The memory comes now, however, with a recognition of why she left and without the urge to blacken her face in shame:

> now I remember, I remember
> Paris before Egypt, Paris after;
> I remember all that went before,

> Sparta; autumn? summer?
> the fragrant bough? fruit ripening
> on a wall? the ships at anchor?
>
> I had all that, everything,
> my Lord's devotion, my child
> prattling of a bird-nest,
>
> playing with my work-basket;
> the reels rolled to the floor
> and she did not stoop to pick up
>
> the scattered spools but stared
> with wide eyes in a white face,
> at a stranger — and stared at her mother,
>
> a stranger — that was all,
> I placed my foot on the last step
> of the marble water-stair
>
> and never looked back;
> how could I remember all that?
> Zeus, our-father was merciful.
>
> (227–28)

Helen's statement is a stark, timeless expression of the potential invisibility and hollowness of women within the satin cage of a "happy marriage" as wife and mother ("I had all that, everything"). H.D. captures in the technique of tableau Helen's first step on the threshold beyond the patriarchy. Helen's quest for self begins as she leaves the isolation of a nuclear family of strangers for the unknown.

Like many other rebellious women heroes (Edna Pontellier, Madame Bovary, Anna Karenina, Julia Martin, etc.), Helen's "first rebellion" took the form of an "illicit" love relationship with another man. The sensual awakening of love however proved ultimately inadequate; Helen left Paris to begin a search for selfhood that included relationships with men, but she was not dependent on those lovers for self-definition. The rhythm of encounters that structures the epic includes time alone for Helen. In contrast to so many women heroes who are afflicted with despair, passivity, and suicide when they are alone, Helen uses this separate space to translate the hieroglyph of her own nature. Helen is not only with Paris in Troy, Achilles in Egypt, Paris in Leuké, Theseus in Greece, and Achilles in Leuké; but she is also alone in each of these places. Separateness does not preclude relationship; love does not exclude independence.

The inner rhythm of quest that makes possible both independence and

love is itself structured around Helen's attempt to find unity in the multiplicity of awakened selves. Helen succeeds in discovering the healing pattern in two different ways: the first focuses on the matriarchal values of
the woman's world; and the second places those values within the context
of an androgynous ideal. To make these patterns viable for Helen, H.D.
must revise the traditions on which they are based in order to allow full
humanity for her woman hero. The summation of the two patterns is a
woman's mythology that both constitutes H.D.'s contribution to the female
poetic tradition and substitutes a new mythology to replace the inade-
quacies of the old.

The first unifying pattern that Helen discovers involves her growing
understanding that she herself incarnates the various aspects of the Goddess who rules the women's world of peace and harmony. To translate
this into contemporary terms, Helen must find herself as a *woman*, distinct from man, before she can move to a final personhood. Helen arrives at Theseus' door desperately in need of spiritual help as symbolized
by the driving wind and snow and her wounded feet. The source of this
"heart-storm" (159) is a feeling of total fragmentation of selves. Having
recovered her experience in Troy, she now cannot reconcile the contradictory selves within. "*How reconcile Trojan and Greek? It is Helen's old
and Helen's own problem*" (157), H.D. comments. Helen restates the
problem in terms of the stages of her life:

> Paris was my youth — don't you see?
> must youth and maturity quarrel
> but how reconcile
>
> the magnetic, steel-clad Achilles
> with the flowering pomegranate?
> in Rhodes (Paris said) they called me
>
> *Dendritis*, Helena of the trees;
> can spring forget winter?
>
> (181)

The winter of her maturity foreshadows the third identity she discovers
in talking with Theseus. If Achilles is "death" or Typhon in his association with the "death-cult" of men, then she must be Persephone, the
bride of Hades and a goddess of death (195). How can this be reconciled
with herself as Thetis ("Pallinode") or her youthful identity with Paris
("Leuké")? The answer lies in the Protean nature of the Goddess, as H.D.
redefined her various forms in ancient religious tradition. H.D.'s most
direct source is Robert Graves's *The White Goddess*, as her notebook of
background material for *Helen in Egypt* makes clear. H.D. develops

Graves's theory that the goddesses of mythology appear in the phases of the moon. H.D.'s notes on Graves's summary of the white goddess in her three phases read: "the New Moon is the white goddess of birth and growth; the Full Moon, the red goddess of love and battle; the old Moon, the black goddess of death and divination."[21] Helen sees the pattern structuring her shifting identities. As the white goddess of birth and growth, Helen of Troy was Aphrodite with her young lover Adonis (159). As the red goddess of love and battle, Helen was identified with Thetis as mother in her relationship with Achilles that began in Troy and moved to Egypt. And finally, as the black goddess of death and divination, Helen was Persephone, the bride of Achilles-Dis, or Koré, the daughter of the goddess Demeter and seed of the rebirth to come.

The fragments of Helen's life are structured by the pattern of the life process from youth to old age. The essence which infuses the parts with a single wholeness is the Goddess who can take many shapes. In this epic, she is called *"Thetis who (like Proteus) 'can change her shape'"* (193). In Apuleius' *Golden Ass*, which H.D. was reading either directly or indirectly through Graves,[22] the Goddess is Isis; in *Hermetic Definition*, H.D.'s last poem, Isis is both Goddess and muse commanding the poet to "write, write, or die."[23] H.D. probably chose to use Thetis because she was the mother of Achilles, but the name of the Goddess is unimportant. What Helen's quest reveals is an argument for the necessity in women's search for identity to resurrect the female divine spirit, the Goddess of the matriarchal traditions. As the epic opens, Helen feels safe in a cocoon of forgetfulness under the guidance of the "all-father," the male Proteus who takes many shapes. In the process of quest, Helen discovers her identity as a woman in her recovery of the "Eidolon," the image of Thetis that dominates part III. The essence of H.D.'s "pallinode" or defense of Helen is the growing understanding and acceptance of the power and values of the women's worldview.[24] This resurrection of the Goddess, "regent of heaven and the star-zone," "Empress and lure of the sea" (253), against the backdrop of conflicting male and female worlds is a later version of the alchemy in the *Trilogy* that restores the original potency and purity to the Goddess. It is, as Riddel says of the *Trilogy*, a "deliberate mythmaking in the present."[25] But the "spiritual realism" of the new myth is in part a correction of the patriarchal traditions with which H.D. works. Where Pound's mythmaking called for a "rectification" of the language, H.D.'s focused on the "rectification" of the traditions themselves. Certainly the dualism of male and female is a cornerstone of both the religious-mythological and psychoanalytical schools H.D. is revising. But H.D. radically changes the qualities and values traditionally associated with men and women. Freud's theories about women are well known today, but unrecognizable in H.D.'s poetry. In "Femininity," for example, Freud warns against too easily equating "femininity" with "passive" and "masculinity" with "active." However, his whole theory of girls' psychosexual development rests on his assumption that psychic qualities are analogous to biological ones. Freud's subjective perception of biological "facts" — that the sperm actively attacks the passive egg and the aggressive male assaults the waiting female in sexual intercourse — leads him to conclude that "normal femininity" is characterized by passivity, masochism, and the narcissism which is a compensation for the girls' recognition of male "superior equipment." As a result of their oedipal development, girls do not develop strong superegos (sense of morality, ideals, etc.), and their contributions to the growth of civilization are consequently limited to the discovery of weaving, which they did as a symbolic compensation to cover their genital inferiority.[26] The aim of analysis with women, Freud later explained, was to draw a woman away from her envy of the penis and into "submissive" acceptance of her "castrated" state.[27] H.D.'s recreation of the woman's world has none of this passivity or yielding will and none of the shame Freud saw as central to the female psyche. Or, to be more precise, Helen does begin with a sense of shame created by her early internalization of the dominant culture's hatred and scorn; but the process of quest which brings her to an acceptance of herself as woman dissolves the original shame and reveals to her an identification with the Protean Goddess. In H.D.'s reversal of Freud's valuation of women, the woman's world embodies the powerful force of synthesis through love and a life force. And finally, the masculine iron ring is the force that destroys civilization, while the female divinity is the presence which creates civilization. It is Thetis who insists that Achilles forget the "lure of war" to learn "the laws and the arts of peace" (286). And it is the divinity as mother, not father, which becomes the object of quest.

    H.D.'s erasure of the bias against women in psychoanalysis is not so surprising — Freud's theories are so patently androcentric and misogynist. Much more subtle is her transformation of various mystical, mythological traditions. The underground current of both Judaism and Christianity for centuries recognized a female divine spirit as part of the religion. The Manichean, Gnostic, and Kabbalistic traditions in which H.D. was well versed[28] all posited an androgynous, Divine One — the En-Soph of Kabbalistic lore. This divine spirit incorporated all existence within itself as latent potential with no material existence. The creation was understood to be a fall from unity into the diversity of material forms. In the process of becoming manifest, the Divine One split into a series of dualisms, the pairs of opposites that are a familiar part of many mythologies: sun-moon, light-dark, day-night, good-evil, spirit-body, fire-water, white-black, right-left, active-passive, positive-negative, reason-emotion, male-female. Robert Ambelain, the French syncretist whose comparative religious research formed a major source of H.D.'s late poetry, summed up the traditional dualism in a book H.D. read and carefully marked: "The traditional symbol of Light is the Sun — the male principle, which is positive and the image of the Day, of the Father, of Man. The symbol of Darkness is the Moon — the female principle, which is negative and the image of the Night, of the Mother, of Woman. Here are the two origins of patriarchy and matriarchy, of the phallic and yonic cults, of Osiris and Isis (the 'dark virgin')."[29]

H.D. does indeed establish a kind of patriarchy and matriarchy in perpetual conflict in the course of the epic, but she does not create a goddess or female spirit that corresponds to the negative darkness of patriarchal tradition. The "feminine principle" that Ambelain and so much of mythological tradition postulates is itself a reflection of a masculine ethos. In an act of creative mythmaking, her "masculine principle" is death centered, the "*Absolute of negation*" (195), destructive, dark, and fiery in spite of its symbolic association with the sun (51). Her "feminine principle" is potent, life-giving, and never the equivalent of matter, sexuality, and mortality. Similarly, the Goddess in H.D.'s work never has the ambivalence of the mother goddesses in recent attempts to restore the female to the divine pantheon. Joseph Campbell, Erich Neumann (*The Great Mother*), and even Robert Graves see the Goddess as both devouring and life-giving. The Jungians in particular would agree with H.D. that the "feminine principle" personified in the anima has been greatly undervalued in the rationalistic, technological West. But Jung's disciple Neumann sees the positive womb of the Great Mother balanced by the terrifying toothed vagina of the castrating "Terrible Mother."[30] This balance of apocalyptic and demonic images of the Goddess in various cultures is in reality an intensified form of the dual image of woman that pervades Judeo-Christian religion and secular mass culture — woman is either a saint or a seductress, a loving wife or a castrating bitch, Mary or Eve. In contemporary advertising images or campaigns like the "Total Woman" phenomenon, the woman often tantalizingly combines the sexpot and saint images, but the category human does not exist as a real potential for women. What parades as restitution of women's value is in reality a constricting "feminine principle" that limits the growth of women and reflects a deep-seated ambivalence toward them.

This androcentric ambivalence toward the goddesses of tradition is totally absent from H.D.'s work. The whole demonic aspect of the "feminine" image in fact never appears. The completely positive nature of the divine female principle underlines the creatively alchemical process in

H.D.'s poetry: to borrow an image from the *Trilogy*, she will erase the "corrosive sublimate" of patriarchal versions of the Goddess and restore the image of woman to its original purity. She never uses the term "matriarchy," but *Helen in Egypt* represents an attempt to resurrect a matriarchal ethos.

Helen's discovery of her shared identity with the Goddess is not the end of her quest, however. While the Protean forms of the Goddess in the life cycle bring unity to the multiplicity of selves, Helen is still confused by the basic duality of male and female, love and death, war and peace. In her meditations on the Trojan War, on Greece and Egypt, and on herself and Achilles, she is not content to accept a Manichean worldview of unending separation and conflict. To do so would be tantamount to writing an unqualified celebration of a biologically based "feminine principle." Such an argument would operate, like Freud's, through an analogy of psychological and biological characteristics. Anatomy would be destiny. Of course, H.D.'s perception of biological "fact" would be radically different from Freud's: the life-giving spirit of Thetis-Isis-Aphrodite-Helen could be based on the metaphoric extension of the creative process of the womb, not on the supposed passivity of the egg. But H.D. does not foster such dangerous biological determinism that ultimately denies the power of socialization and the historical origins of women's "femininity."[31] Helen's understanding of herself as woman coexists with her growing perception of the dialectical interrelationship of the male and female worlds. Helen comes to see a psychic bisexuality or androgyny operating both on a societal level and in an individual psychic dimension. She reconciles the duality that posed her original conflict by understanding that each pole contains within itself the potential to become its opposite. Helen's revelation in "Eidolon" is her final recognition that this dynamic process of opposition can become synthesis. The wholeness that incorporates all conflicting forces ultimately transcends the duality of a sexually polarized world. H.D. bases Helen's vision of mythic and psychic wholeness on the androgynous ideal inherent in mysticism and possibly on Jung's model of bisexual "integration." But just as she revises patriarchal traditions of female divinity, so she eliminates the sexism that permeates much of the androgynous tradition.[32]

Marilyn Farwell's important article "Virginia Woolf and Androgyny" makes a cogent argument for the careful use of the term "androgyny." She divides recent uses of the term into those which stress the "balance" or "interplay" of distinctly male and female psychic attributes and those which emphasize the fusion of what is traditionally known as the "masculine" and the "feminine."[33] Her distinction is a useful one for understanding H.D.'s complex use of the concept on two different levels—the individual search for wholeness and the parallel transcendence of duality in the patterns of society itself.

Like both Jung and Freud, H.D. portrayed the psyches of her representative male and female heroes as bisexual. Helen discovers a pattern within herself and Achilles that reconciles duality: the dynamic interplay of the "masculine" and "feminine." And for both, the epic concludes with the fusion of the dual selves into androgyne. Achilles' quest to become fully human is quite similar to the integration into consciousness of the anima (the inner "feminine" soul), as described in Jung.[34] Achilles' initial attraction to Helen on the ramparts has its origin in the buried image of his mother (anima) and his sense of the incompleteness of the purely masculine iron ring "of the 'warrior caste.' " Like Mr. Ramsay in *To the Lighthouse*, Achilles at Troy suffers from the inadequacy and lifelessness of the "masculine" worldview. In Egypt, he tells Helen not to feel guilty by explaining to her what she meant to him: " 'I can see you still, a mist / or a fountain of water / in that desert; we died of thirst' " (48). Achilles' exchange of glances with Helen ends his life as a warrior, but opens up for him a new identity. H.D. doesn't call Achilles an androgyne; she uses the term the "new Mortal." The arrow of love, of Paris, that kills Achilles destroys only the rigid warrior and "frees the man." In complaining that Achilles here has none of his shining glory, Thomas Swann[35] has missed the significance of Achilles' resurrection as androgyne:

> some said a bowman from the Walls
> let fly the dart, some said it was Apollo,
> but I, Helena, know it was Love's arrow;
>
> the body honoured
> by the Grecian host
> was but an iron casement,
>
> it was God's plan
> to melt the icy fortress of the soul,
> and free the man;
> . . .
> God had summoned me hither [Egypt],
> until I saw the dim outline
> grown clearer,
>
> as the new Mortal,
> shedding his glory,
> limped slowly across the sand.

(9–10)

Achilles' achievement of "New Mortal" status is possible only because of an original androgynous identity that has been perverted by the "lure of war" and the Command. Thetis, his sea mother, had been an inner voice or quality which had once been dominant in his childhood (286–87). This part of his selfhood was personified in the "eidolon" of Thetis he treasured secretly and then put on the prow of his warship. It was the "sea-enchantment" in his eyes that Helen saw as Achilles began to attack her. Her appeal to Thetis awoke the Thetis side of his identity and destroyed the extreme of his Typhon self. In psychoanalytic terms, Achilles succumbs to the infantile oral wish to merge with his mother. But in H.D.'s religious and protofeminist terms, Achilles is resurrected to a new selfhood by the recovery of his own inner qualities, human potentials, that originated in his mother and are associated with the women's worldview. Achilles too has been on a meditative quest. Before he can be ready for love on the island of Leuké, he must restore a creative balance between the "masculine" and "feminine" within himself and achieve a fusion of these dual voices in rebirth as the "New Mortal."

Where Jung could not offer the same model of integration to women,[36] H.D. shows Helen's discovery of her inner duality as the first step toward a parallel rebirth. Helen is first drawn to Achilles by a sense of his difference only to discover those qualities within herself. If she is the "fountain of water," he is the fire, associated with the Sun and the Son (the Egyptian Horus, son of Isis and Osiris; and Jesus). He is "the Star in the night" (77), the "flash in the heaven at noon / that blinds the sun" (100), "the blazing focus / or the sun-blade, the ember, / Achilles in Egypt" (205). Helen Dendritis, the young Aphrodite with her "spring-love" Adonis-Paris, must be renounced on Leuké because it is only one phase of a whole identity. The older goddess must come to terms with Death and somehow be united with it (155, 181, 200). Helen's desire for the fire of Achilles is not exactly parallel to the inadequacy of the male however. Helen, along with Thetis and Isis, is never presented as lacking—H.D. clearly seems to favor the woman's worldview. Instead, Helen comes to realize that she is magnetically tied to Achilles because the life force she embodies contains within itself its opposite. Theseus helps her to hear "the voice within . . . *an heroic voice, the voice of Helen of Sparta*" (175–76). The voice of Helen's origins in Sparta is a voice of war: "O, the rage of the sea, / the thunder of battle . . . O, the beauty of arrows / each bringing surcease, release; / do I love war? is this Helena?" (177). Part of Helen's early identity was a love of battle, a longing for death ("surcease, release"). Helen Dendritis was balanced by "*Helen, loved of War*" (178). Having recovered this part of herself, Helen as the new moon goddess enters a new phase of Koré, the goddess of death. The "masculine" and "feminine" worldview are contained androgynously within Helen's own psyche.

Her discovery of inner duality overlaps with her recognition of identity with the Goddess.

The unity of multiple selves and dual voices is achieved gradually in her discussions with the ancient avatar of H.D.'s own analyst, Sigmund Freud. Helen continually asks Theseus how to "reconcile" all the parts of herself and all the opposites interwoven in the dualism of love and death. Theseus himself fuses the qualities of *"power and tenderness"* as H.D. explains (206) and by his healing example holds out a promise of the ideal. At the same time that he recounts to Helen his quest as an Argonaut, he exhibits the greatest care for her welfare. He offers her fleece-lined shoes before a warm fire and calms her "heart-storm." He is mother and father — traditional nurturer and hero fused into one. As androgynous parent he oversees her rebirth into a new life and identity, one that parallels Achilles' status as the "New Mortal." With Theseus, she is "wavering / like a Psyche / with half-dried wings." He is "half-way to that Lover" beyond all the dualisms of her past (Achilles-Paris, Greek-Trojan) (165–66). As a reborn soul who has recaptured her past without shame, understood her identity as a woman, and perceived the dualities inherent in herself as well as the polarized world, Helen is ready to join Achilles on Leuké. The *"miraculous birth"* of their child Euphorion is a symbol of their transcendence and the union of death-in-life and life-in-death (288–90).

The parallel quests of Helen and Achilles for human selfhood are not contained solely in the personal dimension however. For H.D., the inner reality reflects the outer; the same pattern shapes the individual, the interpersonal, the societal, and the mythic. Helen's discovery of her own dual identity is intertwined with a recognition that the conflicting polarized worlds of love and death relate to each other dialectically as well as confrontationally. Each struggle between the human incarnations of the life force and death force results in the one becoming its opposite. This is what Helen means by her constant refrain that "it was love's arrow" that killed Achilles. Paradoxically, love becomes a destroyer as it overpowers the forces of destruction. Helen, representative of peace and love, becomes the killer as she draws Achilles away from the Command. The victimizer becomes the victim as Typhon the Destroyer is himself destroyed. His thirst for life brings his death. But the dialectical process continues the interplay of opposites. Achilles' death in Troy evolves into his resurrection as a New Mortal limping along the beach in Egypt. At the sight of his destroyer, Helen, Achilles reacts in hate and violence. Helen's appeal to Thetis, the love principle within Achilles himself, transforms Achilles' attack into love.

This kind of androgynous interplay of love and death operates only because Helen and Achilles themselves each contain their opposites in identities that balance the two elements of the polarized world. Helen translates this pattern of alternating opposites within herself and Achilles by linking them to the whole history of the Trojan War and to "all myth, the one reality" (151). It is, in fact, H.D.'s vision of the fundamental design underlying the personal and universal. The Egyptian myth of Isis, Osiris, Set, and Horus establishes the mythic pattern to which the family history of Clytaemnestra, Agamemnon, Hecuba, and Paris is applied. The love of Isis and Osiris symbolizes the power of the life force (*eros*); Set, the masculine destroyer, kills Osiris (*eris*, or strife). Isis revives Osiris just enough to become pregnant with Horus (*eros*); Horus defeats Set as the victimizer becomes the victim, and Horus himself now represents the force of *eris*. This alternation of *eros* and *eris* results in the synthesis of joint rule in Egyptian religion: Isis over the living and Osiris over the dead.[37] Interplay of opposites becomes fusion into Oneness as Helen perceives that "the dart of Love / is the dart of Death" (303).

The androgynous ideal H.D. portrays in the epic is not the kind of androcentric "fusion" Farwell critiques in religious tradition. Man as the representative of light, reason, and spirit all too often absorbed and thereby saved the "feminine," representative of darkness, matter, and mortal flesh. H.D. substitutes a new polarity that places the women's world at the center of the life force. From this perspective, Helen is able to wipe out the patriarchal images of women that destroy her potential selfhood. Freed from the negative burden of distorted tradition, Helen can simultaneously understand her particularity as woman and her universality as human. Helen as the Goddess and Helen as the androgyne merge to transform "Helena, hated of all Greece" into reborn "Psyche." Freed from the sterility of his iron invincibility, Achilles can abandon the Command and follow the "sea-enchantment" of the Goddess. Achilles as the "Star in the Night" and Achilles as the child of Thetis fuse to become the "New Mortal." In H.D.'s epic, authentic selfhood for both women and men involves a rewriting of patriarchal traditions and a creation of a women's mythology.

NOTES

This essay previously appeared in *Women's Studies* 5 (1977): 163–97.

1 Virginia Woolf, *A Room of One's Own* (1929; rpt. New York: Harcourt Brace, 1957), 80, 98.
2 Suzanne Juhasz, *Naked and Fiery Forms: Modern American Poetry by Women: A New Tradition* (New York: Harper and Row, 1976).
3 Adrienne Rich, "When we dead awaken: Writing as Re-Vision," *College English*

20.1 (October 1972): 18–25; also in *Adrienne Rich's Poetry*, ed. Barbara Gelpi and Albert Gelpi (New York: Norton, 1975), 98.

4   Ibid., 90.

5   Mircea Eliade, *Rites and Symbols of Initiation: The Mysteries of Birth and Rebirth*, trans. Willard Trask (New York: Harper and Row, 1958), 1–40.

6   H.D., *Trilogy* (1944, 1945, 1946; rpt. New York: New Directions, 1973), 58; all following quotations from the *Trilogy* will be from this edition and will be identified by page number within the text. See particularly H.D.'s *Tribute to Freud* (1956; rpt. Boston: Godine, 1974), written and published serially during and right after World War II, though not published as a volume until 1956. This important book contains not only her reevaluation of Freud's contribution, but also the key that unlocks the psychoanalytic and occult influences on her late poetry. See also my dissertation, "Mythology, Psychoanalysis and the Occult in the Late Poetry of H.D." (DAI34A-6638; University of Wisconsin-Madison, 1973).

7   Juhasz's concluding chapter on the female poetic tradition is an eloquent statement of the need for women poets to write *as women*. But I disagree with the implication that being a part of a female poetic tradition separates the poet from "the" poetic tradition in general. "Separation" and "integration" are paradoxically not mutually exclusive. The new discipline of women's studies, for example, insists that by understanding the experience of women, a reevaluation of all human knowledge will become possible. Similarly, the creation of a distinct female poetic tradition will simultaneously change the hitherto male poetic tradition that has falsely worn the mask of universality.

8   I highly recommend H. R. Hays's *The Dangerous Sex: The Myth of Feminine Evil* (New York: Putnam, 1964) and Rosemary Ruether's "Misogynism and Virginal Feminism in the Fathers of the Church" in her *Religion and Sexism* (New York: Simon and Schuster, 1974), for excellent discussions of the cultural equations of women with sexuality, mortality, and evil.

9   H.D., *Helen in Egypt* (1961; rpt. New York: New Directions, 1974), 2. All following quotations are taken from this edition and will be identified within the text.

10 This opening prose passage is characteristic of the final form of the poem. H.D. first wrote the epic entirely in verse (each part has seven books; each book has eight separate poems). Then she wrote the italicized prose explanations that precede each short poem. The result is a strikingly new epic form with two voices, one somewhat discursive reflecting on the earlier metaphoric one.

11 Freud and H.D. both used the metaphor of the hieroglyph to represent the hidden meaning of the buried self. Freud's whole theory of the "dream-work" is based on an analogy to hieroglyphs—the dream-work puts latent impulses and instincts into a visual language that the analyst and analysand must translate into rational terms. See especially his *General Introductory Lectures*, trans. Joan Riviere (1924; rpt. New York: Doubleday, 1956), 181–82, 241. See also H.D.'s reference to the "hieroglyph of the unconscious" in *Tribute*

to Freud 93. H.D.'s use of the hieroglyph image in *Helen in Egypt* should be read in the context of Freud's discussion of translating the unconscious and not as an instance of her desire to change her body into something "hard" as a kind of penis substitute, as Norman Holland reads it in his "H.D. and the 'blameless physician,' " *Contemporary Literature* 10.4 (Autumn 1969): 476, 501.

12 *New Larousse Encyclopedia of Mythology*, trans. Richard Aldington (New York: Prometheus, 1968), notes two variant myths which place Helen and Achilles after death on the island of Leuké in the Black Sea. This volume with its beautiful illustrations of ancient art and its accurate text is an excellent companion to H.D.'s poems even though she explains most mythological allusions.

13 H.D. read each of his "cantos" as they were published. She occasionally commented upon them in her twenty-odd-year correspondence with Viola Jordan. She had at one time been very close to Pound, even engaged to him before he went to Europe in his youth. Sometime in the late thirties, however, she broke off contact with him. Occasionally she would mention to Viola how disturbed she was with Pound's politics (see especially letter of May 1, 1941, Beinecke Library Collection, Yale University). Long after the war she resumed correspondence with Pound and was particularly moved by his Pisan cantos based on his confinement in a mental institution. Her reflections on her relationship with Pound are to be found in *End to Torment*.

14 This variant story of Achilles' potential world leadership is probably H.D.'s own; it does not appear in any of the standard reference works in Greek mythology. In fact it changes significantly the masculine honor code permeating the Homeric world: Menelaus' honor was violated by the theft of his wife. The Trojan War was fought to restore the king's honor by returning Helen to him and destroying his male rivals. H.D.'s change of Homeric tradition brings out more starkly the naked power structure of the fascist, masculine world she depicts.

15 See Linda Welshimer Wagner, "*Helen in Egypt*: A Culmination," *Contemporary Literature* 10.4 (Autumn 1969): 527, 529–30. Wagner argues that Helen is one of H.D.'s "terrifying passive women," that she represents the woman as acceptor and comforter of men. Much to her credit, Wagner is the only critic who has published any discussion of specifically male and female identities in the epic. But I do think she has taken a few episodes out of the context of H.D.'s broader argument and Helen's changing sense of identity.

16 J. J. Bachofen, *Myths, Religion and Mother Right: Selected Writings of J. J. Bachofen*, trans. Ralph Manheim (Princeton: Princeton UP, 1967), 79. No volume of Bachofen was present in Norman Holmes Pearson's partial collection of H.D.'s library. However, the ideas of Bachofen were as generally known by H.D.'s contemporaries as the works of James Frazer and Jane Harrison. Robert Graves's *The White Goddess* (1948; rev. ed. New York: Noonday, 1969) H.D. did own, carefully mark, and take notes on as she was writing *Helen in Egypt*. She may also have read Freud's *Totem and Taboo* (1913), which accepts Bachofen's theories.

17 Sigmund Freud, *An Outline of Psychoanalysis*, trans. James Strachey (1939; rpt. New York: Norton, 1949), 20. See also "Analysis Terminable and Interminable" (1937) reprinted in *Therapy and Technique* (New York: Collier, 1963), 258–65 for a discussion of Empedocles' theory of dual instincts, love and strife. H.D. referred directly to Freud's ideas on love and the death instinct in *Tribute to Freud:* "*Eros* and *Death*, those two were the chief subjects — in fact the only subjects — of the Professor's eternal preoccupation," 103. Her use of the punning opposites "L'Amour" and "La Mort" comes from another highly influential book that she read and marked many times, Denis de Rougemont's *Love in the Western World* (1940; rpt. New York: Pantheon, 1956).

18 H.D.'s associations of the Phoenix with female resurrection and the Sphinx with the male probably comes from Graves's *The White Goddess*. He writes that "the Egyptian Sphinx became masculine like the Assyrian winged bull; the Pharonic cult being patriarchal, though also matrilinear" (417). The Phoenix, as a symbol of resurrection, is sometimes born in the palm-tree, linked with the Tree of Life in Eden and therefore Ishtar or Ashtaroth, according to Graves (190). H.D. took notes for *Helen in Egypt* from various sources in a small red notebook which is now part of the Beinecke Collection. There are many pages of notes from Graves, including a notation on the Phoenix and its connection with the goddess symbol of the myrrh egg (*White Goddess* 413).

19 Wagner, "*Helen in Egypt*," 530.

20 See *Tribute to Freud* 72–73.

21 See p. 15 in H.D.'s red notebook for *Helen in Egypt* and Graves, *White Goddess* 70.

22 See p. 14 of the *Helen in Egypt* notebook for notes on Apuleius.

23 H.D., *Hermetic Definition* (New York: New Directions, 1972), 7.

24 Psychoanalytic interpretations have been offered for H.D.'s return to the mother in this epic and other poems. Norman Holland in "H.D. and the 'blameless physician' " (474–506) argues that H.D.'s poetry originated in part out of an oral wish to fuse with her mother and in part out of the phallic desire for the penis that was "missing." Freud himself told H.D. that she had come to him to find her mother (this mother transference on the part of H.D. and many other analysands "surprised" and shocked Freud: " 'I feel so very masculine,' " *Tribute to Freud* xxxvii) and that she went to Greece to find her mother (xxxvii, 17, 65). Helen in the epic does find her mother (H.D.'s mother's name was Helen) in the broad sense of the female divinity. But this return to origins must be seen in a broader context than H.D.'s personal life. As Freud himself taught H.D., individual patterns reproduce mythic ones.

25 Joseph N. Riddel, "H.D. and the Poetics of 'Spiritual Realism,' " *Contemporary Literature* 10.4 (Autumn 1969), 469. Riddel's article contains some excellent discussions of H.D.'s mythmaking, but it is unfortunately riddled with the blatant distortions of phallic criticism.

26 Sigmund Freud, "Femininity," in *New Introductory Lectures*, trans. James Strachey (New York: Norton, 1964), 112–35.

27 Freud, "Analysis Terminable and Interminable," 270. While this statement

is consistent with his theory of women's psychosexual development, it is not at all characteristic of his treatment of H.D. in therapy.

28   H.D.'s correspondence with her American friend Viola Jordan and her collection of extensively marked occult books demonstrate H.D.'s involvement in numerology, astrology, cult of St. Theresa, spiritualism, and theosophical séances, Martinism, Kabbalah, Moravian mysticism, syncretist studies of Near Eastern religions. See my dissertation for a full discussion.

29   Robert Ambelain, *Adam Dieu Rouge* (Paris: Editions Niclaus, 1941), 127–28. My translation. See also L. S. Dembo's fine discussion of the "dynamic dualisms" in *Helen in Egypt* in his *Conceptions of Reality in Modern American Poetry* (Berkeley and Los Angeles: U of California P, 1966), 24–41. H.D. intertwines a complex tapestry of dualisms in the epic — all are in some way related to the conflict of love and death: Egypt-Greece; Troy-Greece; Achilles-Paris; Mysteries-intellect or reason; slayer-slain; Phoenix-Sphinx; Typhon-Osiris; Eleusis-Egypt, etc.

30   Neumann, *The Great Mother: An Analysis of the Archetype*. Trans. Ralph Manheim (Princeton: Princeton UP, 1955), 168. For Jung's discussion of the imbalance of Western civilization, see *Modern Man in Search of a Soul*, trans. W. S. Dell and Cary Baynes (New York: Harcourt, 1933). Pearson told me that H.D. lived in a Zürich sanitorium just down the road from Jung during the last years of her life; he also said that she undoubtedly read a great deal of Jung, but out of loyalty to Freud, never met him.

31   Mary Ellman's brilliant discussion of the images of women argues that all notions of woman's psychological nature supposedly based on her biology are rationalizations in the language of "fact" for the subjective ideas about women; see *Thinking about Women* (New York: Harcourt Brace Jovanovich, 1968), 2–26. See also James Hillman's brief history of the scientific belief in the inferiority of woman based on biased observations of her biology, in *The Myth of Analysis* (Evanston: Northwestern UP, 1972), 215–99.

32   For a discussion of sexism in the androgynous tradition, see the special issue on androgyny of *Women's Studies: An Interdisciplinary Journal* 2 (Fall 1974). See especially articles by Gelpi, Secor, Harris, and Stimpson. Each shows how androgynous traditions often extend the "feminine" to men without legitimizing women's attempt to incorporate the "masculine." Men can become "human"; but women remain women — separate, subordinate, and "other."

33   Marilyn Farwell, "Virginia Woolf and Androgyny," *Contemporary Literature* 16.4 (Autumn 1975): 433–51.

34   See for example, C. G. Jung, *The Relations between the Ego and the Unconscious* (1928) in *The Basic Writings of C. G. Jung*, ed. Violet de Laszlo (New York: Modern Library, 1959), 158–82.

35   Thomas Burnett Swann, *The Classical World of H.D.* (Lincoln: U of Nebraska P, 1962), 177.

36   See Jung, *Relations* 176–81. Jung and his disciple M. Esther Harding feared that women would lose their femininity if their animus (opinionated, masculine inner voice) were not held in proper check. Jung intended for his model to be reversible for men and women, but he did not carry through on his

ideas with women. Jungians like James Hillman and Jane Singer (*Androgyny: Toward a New Theory of Sexuality*) are attempting to eliminate the sexism in Jung's theory of the anima and the animus.

37 H.D. develops the same dialectical pattern in the Trojan and Greek families and in the war itself: (1) Trojan War: wedding (*eros*)→Apple of Discord, labeled "To the fairest" (*eris*)→war (*eris*)→synthesis in Helen and Achilles (*eros/eris*). (2) Trojan family: love of Hecuba and Priam (*eros*)→Hecuba's abandonment of Paris, her son (*eris*)→love of Paris and Helen (*eros*)→destruction of Troy (*eris*). (3) Greek family: love of Agamemnon and Clytaemnestra (*eros*)→sacrifice of Iphigenia (*eris*)→love of Clytaemnestra and Aigisthus (*eros*)→murder of Agamemnon (*eris*).

CHAPTER 21

Romantic Thralldom in H.D.

RACHEL BLAU DUPLESSIS

In her life's work, H.D. returned constantly to a pattern of personal relations that she found perplexing and felt to be damaging to herself and
other women: thralldom to males in romantic and spiritual love. In her
later writing, she invented a number of strategies to transform this culturally mandated and seductive pattern of male-female relations.[1] Romantic thralldom is a feature of many literary plots because of conventions
surrounding love and marriage, quest and vocation, hero and heroine.
These conventions could be termed "scripts" for both literary plots and
personal relations. In order to transform these psychocultural scripts, H.D.
had to invent in her works patterns for male-female relationships less
damaging than, but equally as satisfying as, those she and other women
had experienced.

Romantic thralldom is an all-encompassing, totally defining love between unequals. The lover has the power of conferring self-worth and
purpose upon the loved one. Such love is possessive, and while those
enthralled feel it completes and even transforms them, they are also enslaved. The eroticism of romantic love, born of this unequal relationship
between the sexes, may depend for its satisfaction upon dominance and
submission. Thralldom insists upon the differences between the sexes, encouraging a sense of mystery surrounding the motives and powers of the
lover: thus it begins with and ends in sexual polarization. Viewed from
a critical, feminist perspective, the sense of completion or transformation
that often accompanies thralldom in love has the high price of obliteration and paralysis, for the entranced self is entirely defined by another.
I do not need to emphasize that this kind of love is socially learned and
that it is central in our culture.

Female thralldom occurs with startling, even dismal frequency throughout H.D.'s published and unpublished works. In particular, H.D. was

vulnerable to the power of what she termed the *"héros fatal,"* a man whom she saw as her spiritual similar, an artist, a healer, a psychic.[2] Again and again this figure that she conspired to create betrayed her; again and again she was reduced to fragments from which her identity had once more to be painfully reconstructed. She states, for instance, that one famous *"héros"* — D. H. Lawrence — "conditioned me to deception, loss, destruction," and that another, "Lord Howell," "was the perfected Image" of this former lover.[3] Though H.D. lived for many years as the companion of Winifred Bryher, her work returned obsessively to the *héros* figure and to the damage she suffered in her relations with him. Whatever personal and sexual arrangements she made could not obliterate the culturally reinforced plot of thralldom. She had to remake this psychocultural pattern in her writing in order fully to break with it.

The impact of sexual subordination on H.D. as woman and artist can be seen in two autobiographical novel-memoirs written about her early adulthood: the unpublished *HER* (c. 1927), an ungainly but interesting work which justifies H.D.'s decision not to marry Pound, and the more serious and desperate *Bid Me to Live* (1960), a roman à clef about the London Bohemian set during the First World War. In tandem, these works describe the situation of a woman of artistic leanings and achievements within a male-dominated society in the early part of this century. In every role in which she is cast, the woman is unsatisfied and tormented: as courtesan, as deceived wife, as muse, as consort. She is prevented from claiming the end to that torment: equality.

On the title page of the typed manuscript of *HER*, H.D. has obligingly noted the correspondence between coded names and actual people, beginning with the heroine Her (short for Hermione), who is the poet. Only one character is not decoded; this woman, named Fayne, represents both love and inspiration for the main character, who tries to find some definition of her identity and vocation.[4] Morose after a failing year at college, moping about in a midsummer heat wave, Her ends a season of love (wooed by George, alias Ezra Pound) and a season of breakdown (involved with Fayne) with one clear decision: Her will go to Europe, unmarried. This decision, though important in H.D.'s life, seems anticlimactic in the novel, which does not really close but merely stops with the convenient discovery of some companions with whom to make that journey.

The novel concerns a classic dilemma for woman: the necessity to choose between being a muse for another and being an artist oneself. Although intrigued and fascinated by George, and, caught up in the willing annihilation of thralldom, hoping he would define her and decide everything for her, Her suddenly realizes that his kisses "smudge out" her identity (100). George, she discovers, seeks a muse and consort to complete a picture of himself. "He wanted Her, but he wanted a Her that he called decorative" (230). This fact is analyzed in a long passage which contrasts the temptation of female roles metaphorically presented as pageantry, with the deeper authenticity of selfhood which Her seeks. The passage functions as an unmasking of romantic thralldom by a critique of its archaic, costume-party trappings:

George, regarding Her, was saying "You are so decorative." There was something stripped of decoration, something of somewhat painful angles that he would not recognize. George saying "choriambics of a forgotten Mellic" [his comment on her poems] was flattering her, tribute such as some courtier might pay to a queen who played at classicism; he did not proffer her the bare branch that was the strip of wild naked olive or the tenuous oleander. George saw Her at best as some Florentine page or some Florentine girl dressed for a pageant as the Queen Diana. To George, Her was Dian or Diana, never Artemis. To George, she was the Queen of Love, never white Aphrodite. (230)

The heroine's authentic identity, indicated in the image of a tree which recurs throughout the novel, and, as above, in the contrast between austere Greek and sensual Roman pantheons, is mirrored and intensified by Her's relationship with Fayne. Fayne represents self-love, self-identification, and a twinship between spiritual sisters. Through Fayne, Her makes contact with herself and her vision. Instead of being George's muse, she takes Fayne as her inspiration.

The name "Her" has a particular meaning bound up with the image of Fayne. Whenever H.D. writes "Her realizes" or "Her says," she is using the wrong form of the pronoun in subject place; and every time this ungrammatical usage occurs, one is jarred into a recognition of the situation of generic woman. Though "Her" is the object form, the very ungainly quality of the name used as the subject of a verb ("Her does," "Her realizes") suggests that we are in the presence of some resistant, stubborn matter which will not be captured. The contradictory features of this striking nickname are brought into focus and then resolved as Her strokes Fayne's forehead with "healing hands" and says, "I will not have her hurt. I will not have Her hurt. She is Her. I am Her. Her is Fayne. Fayne is Her. I will not let them hurt HER."[5] By identifying with another wounded woman, the heroine perceives her own hurt and her own capacity for self-protection. The heroine must love herself through another woman as a sign of selfhood. However, the novel does not deal directly with the alternative loves which are so clearly delineated within it. In any case, thralldom to males has been only temporarily rejected. *HER* is a first skirmish in the almost endless battle of H.D.'s psychic life.

At the end of her life, H.D. returned to this formative World War I period in her novel *Bid Me to Live*.[6] The title epigram, from Herrick, wittily presents the life of the emotions as a playful religion of love:

> Bid me to live, and I will live
>   Thy Protestant to be:
> Or bid me love, and I will give
>   A loving heart to thee. . . .

The poem refers to the time in a relationship when adoration is mutual and commands are not burdensome. The novel explores the attempt by Julia and Rafe Ashton to sustain such a "blithe arrangement."[7] But equal comradeship and romantic love appear to be contradictory states. The circumstances faced by the couple—the war, the birth of a dead child—make it difficult, even impossible, to sustain equality and interdependence. She becomes vulnerable, neurasthenic, needy; he is bluff, willful, callous. They fall into stereotypic behavior, their needs at cross-purposes. Therefore the woman in *Bid Me to Live* feels completely inadequate—a sexual failure and a professional anomaly within the group of male artists that surrounds her.

Julia Ashton has had a stillborn child before the novel begins. That grief and her consequent feelings of sexual and maternal failure permeate the whole book. Her husband, home from the front on brief leaves, is having an affair with a passionate but shallow woman. At one point, they make love in the Ashton marriage bed, and Julia discovers them there. Sexual despair combined with depression over the war paralyzes Julia, and her sense of failure is exacerbated when the two men in her life, her husband Rafe (Richard Aldington) and fellow artist Rico (D. H. Lawrence), exploit her need for their love to hurt her as an artist.

Both men attack her writing. Rico's attack occurs in a letter which Rafe discovers; Rafe's comes in his response to that letter. Rico writes: "I don't like the second half of the Orpheus sequence as well as the first. Stick to the woman speaking. How can you know what Orpheus feels? It's your part to be woman, the woman vibration, Eurydice should be enough. You can't deal with both" (51). Although Julia disagrees with the absolute sexual division upon which Rico insists, his opinions are bold, his presence charismatic. Julia sees that he has given himself permission to write of both women and men, but has snappishly denied her the parallel and complementary right to "enter into the feelings of men" (62). Rico's desire to control her range or breadth censors and controls her artistic work. Her aesthetic options (of voice, subject, sexual perspective) are not freely chosen but are shaped by her personal need to please him, or scarred by her struggle to write in ways that he has explicitly forbidden. Her vulnerabilities, perhaps based on a need to retain what she viewed as a female identity, did not allow her to reject these impositions from men. Later, having sent her seductive messages, Rico refuses Julia's tentative sexual advance. This too is an act which asserts his sole power of definition, and one of the rejections presented in the book that shatter her identity as poet and woman.

The same demands for artistic and sexual dominance are made by Julia's husband. He is jealous of her correspondence with Rico, and, finding she is writing under his inspiration, Rafe demands to see the rough drafts of the poem. All his remarks are critical and judgmental: "Not so good," "A bit dramatic," "It's Victorian." " 'You might boil this one down,' he said, 'about one quarter the length and cut the *clichés*' " (54, 56). Defensive, wounded, unable to talk to Rafe about Rico's status as a muse, Julia responds evasively to his criticism. Rafe implicitly threatens her with further loss of his love because of his discovery that she has been inspired to write by another man. The encounter leaves her feeling trapped:

"There aren't eight furies and why unglorified furies?" he said [in reference to the draft]. There were eight furies, there were eighty furies, everything was unglorified. She didn't say anything. It didn't really matter.
"It doesn't really matter."
"What doesn't matter?"
"Why, what I told you, I told you it was only preliminary scribbling."
There was no taut nerve in her that wanted to spring forward, she had no tragedy-queen desire to stand, facing him, hand dramatically held forward to seize the maligned page. She felt no Muse. (54)

The pain of such self-negation pervades the book. The extent of Julia's confusion becomes clear when Vane, her third companion, calls her "Person" in an effort to be sexually neutral, and Julia fears that he might mean the French *personne*, that is, "no one." Without the entrapment of sexual and spiritual thralldom, she questions whether she has any existence at all.

The draft discussed in this letter may well have become H.D.'s long poem "Eurydice," a reconstruction of myth which puts the woman into the center of the story.[8] Orpheus, in the act the whole of Western culture has called love, enters hell to bring his dead wife back to earth, winning her from death by his power of song. In his eagerness, however, he turns to see her before the journey has been completed and thus loses her. H.D. shifts the perspective of this familiar myth. Her Eurydice is fated to suffer an arousal to life and then to be compelled back into death because to be annihilated by the act of another is a fate which defines this mythic woman *as* a woman. But her lack of choice has angered her. She accuses Orpheus peremptorily of seeking her in order to appropriate her presence, to create an aggrandized Orpheus and a diminished, virtually nonexistent Eurydice:

> and you who passed across the light
> and reached
> ruthless;

you who have your own light,
who are to yourself a presence,
who need no presence. . . .[9]

Eurydice has been betrayed by his arrogant act of trying to save her; but
she regains her identity in response to his act. She asserts her own dis-
tinctness: she is the woman of hell, a place that she has been compelled
to assume as her own. She is stung by male egotism and arrogance to claim
a separate territory.

At least I have the flowers of myself,
and my thoughts, no god
can take that;
I have the fervour of myself for a presence
and my own spirit for light;

and my spirit with its loss
knows this;
though small against the black,
small against the formless rocks,
hell must break before I am lost;

before I am lost,
hell must open like a red rose
for the dead to pass.[10]

The mysterious last lines, with their glancing reference to the Christian
harrowing of hell, focus on the idea of resistance rather than passivity.
Hell must open voluntarily and naturally, "like a red rose," rather than
being forced. Eurydice declares that she is autonomous, tending the small
flame of her otherness, lighting her own way. The end of this poem can
be read as proud acceptance of the classical destiny of the figure "Eurydice" — being the dead woman within hell — or it can be read as an appropriation of territory. Locked in that space, defined within it, she declares
it to be not the space of rejection, negation, and loss, but the splendor
of her essential life. That life will persist until hell opens without force,
and the dead pass to a new life. A number of H.D.'s early poems concern
the sort of hard-edged beauty created by resistance to a devastating force.
Often these beautiful things are flowers, the very image of the feminine
in our cultural iconography.[11]

In Julia's encounters with Rico and Rafe, we confront the unedifying
spectacle of male poets compelling a female poet to curtail her ambition,
to dissolve the complete world she strove for, to concentrate on the item,
not on the oeuvre. While there is both justice and satisfaction in seeing
Eurydice placed squarely in the center of the myth, it is not pleasant to

consider that this poem might have been born in a demand extrinsic to the idea toward which H.D. aspired. *Bid Me to Live* shows male poets limiting the shape and force of a woman's material by using sexual and personal acceptance as a weapon. Julia's response reveals the internalization and acceptance of these demands, which diminished her ambition and limited or negated her power. The issue is larger than the relationship of these three writers. The encounter raises the question whether male writers, in complicity with prescribed roles for women, have helped create poetesses where there could have been poets. This is the issue underlying the censorship with which H.D. grappled. The stakes were poetic achievement itself. Thralldom to male power had to be attacked; yet it was the most difficult thing to attack. For the pain of thralldom seemed to fire H.D.'s creativity even as it undercut the conditions necessary for her fullest, uncensored flowering.

While resistance is one solution to thralldom, H.D. also tries to articulate a creative and psychic power transcending the claims of romantic love. In a letter to Rico that is never sent, Julia articulates a second path for the solving of the conflicts between man and woman:

> You might be angry with me. You might shrivel my hope. You might say I had no business writing of old shoes, ladies-bed-straw and the roots of the furze bushes you grubbed up and stacked under the stairs. There are still a few left.
>
> Perhaps you would say I was trespassing, couldn't see both sides, as you said of my Orpheus. I could be Eurydice in character, you said, but woman-is-woman and I couldn't be both. The *gloire* is both. (176)

The *gloire* is spiritual vision, which sees the aura of objects, the magnetism of things, their numinous flamelike quality. All of this is familiar in modern and postmodern poetics. But more interestingly, the *gloire* is identified as a way to avoid that direct confrontation of male and female which is characteristic of the Eurydice voice. H.D. is opting for another path, conceding the field, but taking up the question in a transposed form: "What did Rico matter with his blood-stream, his sex-fixations, his man-is-man, woman-is-woman? That was not true. This mood, this realm of consciousness [i.e., *gloire*] was sexless, or all sex, it was child-consciousness, it was heaven. In heaven, there is neither marriage nor giving in marriage" (62).

The spiritual quest for this special realm of consciousness occurs above and beyond the cultural institutions of heterosexuality. The biblical echo ("neither marriage nor giving in marriage") signifies that H.D. was trying to construct some perspective that avoided the constant subordination of the woman to the man in normal sexual and cultural life. In her view, men and women are equals in the spiritual realm, not seeking the distinctions of fixed sex roles, but rather a mutual suffusion of insight and wisdom.

The spiritual dimension termed *gloire* is the inner radiance set forth by an object or experience, substance beyond dualism. It is compared to a child "before it is born," before it falls into sexual division.[12] H.D. feels Rico can achieve this poise and magnetism in his work only if he gives up the sexual polarities for which he so eagerly and didactically proselytized. Nondualistic thinking appears in one of H.D.'s rare general aesthetic statements, the manuscript *Notes on Thought and Vision*, written in 1919; that is, almost contemporaneous with the events of *Bid Me to Live*, though not with the novel's composition. While concerned that men develop this consciousness, her metaphors reveal that she was especially interested in women's ability "to think with the womb and feel with the brain."[13] The third consciousness — neither body nor mind but a fusion — is fixed within the self "like a foetus in the body."[14] Here women's biology, the capacity to nourish a growing soul, is a metaphor for the monism beyond the sexual polarities of thralldom. Child and mother are not opposites or extremes; they are separate but fused. This vision will recur in the psyche madonna.

However, among Aldington, Lawrence, and Pound, H.D. received no support in her attempts to resist, reconstruct, defy, or transform that sexual thralldom from which it is clear her male lovers benefited. Julia's attempt to seduce Rico might be viewed not only as a search for sexual reassurance but also as a desire to engage him in her ideas about the *gloire* that transcended damaging sexual polarities and scripts of subordination. Yet she was powerless to convince him that in the case of the artist, "the woman was man-woman, the man was woman-man. But Frederico, for all his acceptance of her verses, had shouted his man-is-man, his woman-is-woman at her; his shrill peacock-cry sounded a love-cry, death-cry for their generation" (136). Startling critical, she here states that sexual polarity is death.

H.D.'s profound psychic damage from sexual and spiritual thralldom continued to torment her. The kinds of rejections she suffered were coupled in her mind with the First World War as linked aspects of that destructive force which shattered the possibility of a cultural life. Yet the themes of the first war recurred to be resolved during World War II, which H.D. spent, by choice, in the London of the Blitz. In her inner patterning of these events, the first war was death, and the second was rebirth.[15] The long-awaited consummation of her poetic force did occur; the evidence can be seen in the brilliance of *Trilogy*, for its symbols of resurrection, its vision of a new city, and its invention of the role of Mary Magdalene constitute the materials of a psychic and cultural reconstruction. At the same time, however, H.D. returned to the forms of sexual polarization and entrapment represented by the thralldom of women to men.

It is difficult without letters, without a biography or even analytic considerations of H.D.'s life, to understand the compulsions of that return.[16] It is clear that she continued to construct painful, even lacerating hopes for companionship based on equality between women and men — painful because they always failed, and she was always rejected. Let me suggest some possible reasons. Perhaps her strong desire for a companionship of the spirit led her to keep testing different men, hoping that one would succeed in becoming that companion, and that the metaphoric "child" of their relationship would transform world consciousness. Perhaps she felt guilty to be so happily involved in a world made up of women exclusively — she, her daughter Perdita, and Bryher appear as a kind of triple goddess in some of her late dreams — and had to compensate by torturing herself with thralldom to men. Perhaps she felt that men needed to be converted to spiritual insight, and that she was a sacrificial leader-sufferer, capable of aiding them.[17] Or perhaps she felt that she needed to be excessively, almost parodically feminine, investing her emotional life in various men as a way of experiencing indirectly (but also evading) the impact of her own poetic power and psychic gifts.[18] She may indeed have been brought up to aver that to be female was to be inferior, and to go against these paternal and fraternal orders of understanding involved strategies of doubleness in which she apparently subsumed herself in a man but in reality held back. Telling and retelling these stories of defeat and manipulation, playing and replaying the events of the past in diary and memoir, and studying the overlay of other events from a further past helped H.D. control her experience.

The strategy of outright resistance to and confrontation of male by female forces is not paramount in H.D.'s poetry.[19] The transposition of conflicts to a spiritual area beyond conflict (like the *gloire*) sometimes makes H.D. lose contact with her materials. I surmise that these exits from the script of thralldom do not wholly succeed for H.D., although the transposition of conflicts into a spiritual area of unification remains an important end in her writing. The first option represents conflict and defiance, the second represents sheer resolution, unity by the suppression of conflict. Only in the final solution to romantic thralldom — what I term the sufficient family — do both conflict and resolution exist in a complex and nuanced balance, with a full account both of the engendering conflict and of the transpositions that create resolution. This solution, paramount in *Helen in Egypt*, builds a new structure of relationships to substitute for thralldom.[20]

A specific "case" of thralldom is associated with the beginning of *Helen in Egypt*: "That summer, we began the long *Helen* sequence, our attempt, not unsuccessful, to retain a relationship materially 'ditched.' "[21] The poem was begun because she had been thrown over by a man. In *End to Torment*, H.D. draws a parallel between herself and La Martinelli, minor poet, artist, and hierophant of the Pound circle. During Pound's incarceration in St. Elizabeths, La Martinelli remained loyal and expected to return with him to Italy. However, when Pound was released, he extricated himself from the woman, who felt cast off, deceived, and broken. She protested that "the male just can't go about like that ditching a spirit love."[22] H.D. identified wholeheartedly with La Martinelli's grief because she too had been cast off—by Lord Dowding, Britain's air marshal, with whom she had briefly corresponded. She had written him about being in communication with dead RAF pilots, a psychic event which he too had experienced, thinking that their mutual experience made them spiritual equals. However, far more familiar male-female patterns intervened. He insisted to her that his dead pilots came from a higher order of the spirit realm and had better and more complete authority than her dead pilots, thus denying the import and validity of the messages she had received. She suffered acutely from his rebuff.[23] When she writes that *Helen in Egypt* was an "attempt . . . to retain a relationship materially 'ditched,' " it is to this relationship and rebuff that she refers.

The second part of *Helen in Egypt* (a poem composed in stages) was also provoked by a feeling of being ditched. Erich Heydt, her friend at Küsnacht, quarreled with her over her claim to be a medium.[24] Heydt, who becomes the figure of Paris, could not believe in or sympathize with H.D.'s stories of dead RAF airmen communicating with her and Lord Dowding. Having seen Heydt as a possible convert or adept, H.D. was very hurt.[25] The pattern is clear: H.D. wrote this poem in the aftermath of strong spiritual and psychic attraction to men on whom she had depended for some kind of self-justification. She suffered rejection; her response is the poem. But although the poem was provoked by rejection, within it the pattern of thralldom is broken: the same needs are met by different relationships, and nurturance and vision are achieved without sexual or spiritual damage from men.

Helen in Egypt is engaged with one particular literary "order of reality," a prominent myth of Western culture.[26] H.D. has not precisely displaced the *Iliad* or the story of the war following an abduction; that tale is taken for granted as the plot that precedes this new alignment of characters and actions. But criticism of the epic realm is present, if indirect. Before the poem begins, H.D. has replaced the sexually centered woman and her bellicose lover with two liminal figures, wavering between worlds of fragmentation and wholeness: Achilles, the vulnerable "New Mortal," and an

incubating psyche, still in chrysalis but nonetheless fully winged (Helen-
Thetis). H.D. chooses her characters not because of their capacity for
sensual love or savage war but because of their visionary ability to crystallize the dissolved or latent meanings hidden in the former story. The
characters act as catalyzing precipitants of nonepic material already "dissolved" in culture. By postulating that another shape to traditional stories
occurs necessarily, H.D. mutes the critique she is making. In her view,
stories are not created but recovered; they are not new-made but really
old. *Helen in Egypt* is the archeological site where those recovered stories
are found:

> the flame
> of thoughts too deep to remember,
>
> that break through the legend,
> the fame of Achilles,
> the beauty of Helen,
>
> like fire
> through the broken pictures
> on a marble-floor.
> (258–59)

Helen in Egypt primarily concerns the "flame of thoughts" excluded
from the traditional story:

> none of these
> came into the story,
>
> it was epic, heroic and it was far
> from a basket a child upset
> and the spools that rolled to the floor. . . .
> (289)

In contrast, this story will be different, untraditional, unheroic, even eerie
where the epic was direct. It will draw on

> the million personal things,
> things remembered, forgotten,
>
> remembered again, assembled
> and re-assembled in different order. . . .
> (289)

In *Trilogy* too there is a tension between sameness and difference: the
affirmation of the traditional story and the break with it through the dis-

covery of a hidden, even hermetic, pattern. The blank pages held by the madonna, "the unwritten volume of the new," might reveal a familiar story: "the same—different—the same attributes, / different yet the same as before."[27] H.D., like other women writers, had difficulty establishing an authority sufficient to remake a culturally sanctioned story. So the story is "the same"—the old legend—when she felt her own authority most weakly, and "different"—the "flame of thoughts"—when she could plumb the depths of her desire for critique and transformation. But neither feeling ever appears to the exclusion of the other. H.D. seems to want the traditional and the transformed stories to exist simultaneously.

The form of *Helen in Egypt* also dramatizes the question of the poet's authority to remake this story, and that question becomes part of the strain of remaking it. There are prose passages preceding every poem which summarize the contents of that section.[28] This is helpful, because the material is difficult and obscure. But the prose also has the effect of making the events seem more elusive, challenging both their place in time and their reality. Sometimes the prose passages make a statement implying that something has happened, while the poetry which comes later poses the same fact as a question. After having read the two statements, the reader is unsure whether or not something has occurred. While generally the prose and poetry are simple retellings of the same events, at other points a degree of difference is emphasized: the event is first present, then absent or obscured.

The poem concerns the parallel quests of Helen and Achilles which are not journeys to each other, but quests for access to the unifying mother. Helen's quest is emphasized, but both have found Thetis at the end; this is what finally unites them. The poem is constructed to confirm Helen's act of intuition at the moment when Achilles attacks and almost strangles her in direct, rapacious male rage at what she represents: the old Helen of Troy, "Goddess" of the polarized and deformed male-female relations in the system of romantic thralldom. At that moment, around which the whole of part I reverberates, Helen cries out the one word capable of stopping Achilles: "Thetis," the mother of Achilles in the traditional myth.

In part I, H.D. presides over the imaginative reconstruction of the hero, which had begun during the Trojan War and is recorded in Achilles' retrospective meditations. From being a "Destroyer" (26), a member of the "iron-ring" of warriors (51) in the "death-cult" (99), Achilles breaks with conventional, cultural patterns of maleness. He is "at odds with the Command" (53), speaking in the querying, pensive, uncertain voice typical of the questing characters in this work. Although Achilles is based on Lord Dowding, it is possible to associate him with the Aldington of the World War I era, viewing the character as a rescue operation performed on the memory of the terrible masculine husband who enjoyed returning to the front. During the war, Achilles had looked to Helen (or to her image) for a sign about some proposal already decided upon by his male companions; by this act he questioned Command. For breaking this explicitly described patriarchal chain from father to son and brother, Achilles is shot (61). His estrangement from the male world of force and obedience, and his entrance into the female world of quest and wavering, love and death mark the working out within him of his inheritance from Thetis, the sea mother. Achilles becomes a postheroic man, vulnerable and questing:

> the new Mortal,
> shedding his glory,
> limped slowly across the sand.
>
> (10)

In the second part of the poem, H.D. begins with a contrast between Achilles and Paris, the original lover of Helen. Paris is the character who evokes the lyricism of erotic love. During this part of *Helen in Egypt*, Paris views Helen as his possession, and wants to seduce her once again. By trying to win her from Achilles, Paris simply repeats without transformation his role in the traditional myth. Paris has a glimpse of an intimate, sensual bond:

> this fragrance of pine-knots,
> this small room,
> no blaze of torches,
>
> no trumpet-note, no clamour of war-gear,
> this haven, this peace, this return. . . .
>
> (140)

This is a vision upon which he cannot act because he feels rivalry, jealousy, and the old enmity of male versus male (142–43). Because of these attitudes he cannot listen to what Helen tells him about her sustaining love for Achilles: that they are doubles on one journey. He sees Helen only as she once was, "suave" and silver-sandaled (146). Because he does not acknowledge her quest or change, he is "defeated even upon Leuké," the magical white-island setting of this book (143). Thus Helen walks barefoot away from him and vanishes, escaping from the old myth which Paris persists in believing.

Yet at the same time, Paris—remember that he is based upon her critical friend—challenges some basic structures of Helen's understanding of herself. Helen had feared to acknowledge that great rout of the female represented by the Trojan War, for after dwelling in part I upon the stories of her sister and Iphigenia, she had been instructed by the male godhead to "Grieve not for Clytaemnestra" in order to proceed on her quest (105). In contrast, Paris has a flash of recognition about male force and its female victims—Polyxena, Briseis, Chryseis, Cassandra—whom Helen is ritualistically told to remember. As well as being sensuous and seductive, he helps a woman see her difficulties with men.

Not only Paris, but all the males in *Helen in Egypt*—Achilles, Paris, and Theseus (the figure of Freud)—have begun to form a postheroic personality, and all give Helen permission to make her quest, which must include understanding herself as a postromantic woman.[29] The granting of permission by all three males is a female fantasy, based on extraordinary need for male approval and fear of male judgment. All the male characters know of and approve of her desire for reintegration within Thetis, the mother: all instruct her in one way or another to "call on Thetis" (213). Yet they want different Helens. She must avoid the polarized roles which the two lovers give her while at the same time retaining their approval. She struggles with the antagonism of Greece and Troy (Achilles and Paris): one insists on the spiritual initiate, Helen in Egypt (in part I of the poem), associated with the soul, death, and Eris (discord); the other prefers the sensual fertility figure, Helen Dendritis (in part II), associated with the body, life, and Eros. These multiple identities indicate her own lack of inner integration. This dilemma is solved when she transcends these opposites through the healing mediation of Theseus in part II, who "reparents" her, acting as both mother and father and healing the divisions found in the traditional nuclear family. She becomes Helen-Thetis in part III, uniting Troy and Greece and uniting her own torn consciousness in love and death.

Making Achilles and Helen into fellow questers is the first move in H.D.'s strategy for breaking the script of romantic thralldom. The lover and woman are imagined as brother-sister questers, so that totally spiritual, not sexual, forces define the relationship. The quests of Helen and Achilles are finally not journeys toward love for each other, but a single quest to identify the source: the mother. Further, Helen avoids a replay of the drama of sexual thralldom by asking Paris, too, to join her on a brother-sister quest. Paris then emerges as Helen's child by Achilles; for the lover, displaced from dominance in the plot of thralldom, can return in the role of a child. The sibling questers seem to have been successful as a solution to thralldom only when buttressed either by the presexual powers of reparenting or by the postsexual source of power represented by the psyche madonna. For although the brother-sister quest is central to this poem, it is dangerously close to the structure of dominance and subordination in romantic love; Dowding's brush-off was a revelation that conventional sexual politics operate even in the spiritual realm, which H.D. had thought was exempt.

The character Helen unites, comprises, and needs all the variants of the sufficient family:

> father, brothei, son, lover,
> sister, husband and child;
>
> beyond all other, the Child,
> the child in the father,
> the child in the mother,
>
> the child-mother, yourself. . . .
>   (187)

This chant is the mystery of the nenuphar or water lily. This flower-beacon is the hieroglyphic sign given to Helen to decode, for "she herself is the writing" (22, 91). When she decodes the hieroglyph, she discovers her identity. "She herself is the writing" encapsulates the situation of women writers who begin to review and reinterpret the culturally sanctioned stories that contain them. Helen is at once the old story that must be displaced and the hidden story that must be recovered. As in the poem "Eurydice," H.D. has attempted to give a voice to one of the female figures long left voiceless within our culture or ascribed a damaging meaning which the poem deconstructs. Traditionally, Helen is sex, temptation, allure, the possessed and the possessing: a one-dimensional love goddess, victim of romantic thralldom and the victimizer of others. In this poem, Helen is multidimensional, far beyond the sexual category, possessed by her history and her visionary experiences. She is a kind of thought thinking itself whose veil always wavers in the wind and eludes capture. She is a seeker trying "to unravel the tangle / that no man can ever un-knot" (298). She is a broken sandal strap and a limp of vulnerability, a sister quester to Achilles with his vulnerable heel. Far from being centered on sex and beauty, she is concerned with the possibility of achieving transformation and wholeness. To accomplish this quest she must sift, seek, and mull, acting as the historian of her own unrecorded — indeed never before recorded — emotions.

In the quest for Helen's unfragmented identity, whiteness is often an image of the integrated self, the place where prismatic colors fuse. The image of whiteness in the little shells on a beach has become her sign for the story as she has experienced it, beyond the legends made by others about her: "I only remember the shells, whiter than bone, / on the ledge of a desolate beach . . ." (224). This is an unrecorded fact, one of "the million personal things" that Helen must touch to find herself (289). And these shells are themselves fragments of a greater and more inclusive shell: the egg from which Helen, daughter of Leda and the swan, originally came, and to which she will now return. At dead center in the poem Helen re-enters the white world-egg, assisted by the paternal and maternal figure of Theseus, acting as midwife and inseminator. The incubating isle of Leuké is the chrysalis for Helen as a psyche figure.

For the decoding and discovery of Helen's self, H.D.'s metaphor is the chrysalis with its psyche or soul. If Achilles is a New Mortal, Helen is the embryonic, dazed psyche: H.D. attempts throughout, with fascinating violence to the biological process, to incorporate the butterfly and the chrysalid in one constantly liminal unit. Helen is characterized, for instance, as

> wavering
> like a Psyche
> with half-dried wings.
>
> (166)

She is unable to fly because her wings are not yet ready, and is thus held in transition between two forms.

In *Helen in Egypt*, Freud appears in the role of the psychopomp or soul guide, Theseus. He has instructed Helen to incubate in the cocoon which he has woven for her out of the "bright threads" of his own accomplished quest:

> here is soft woven wool;
> wrapped in this shawl, my butterfly,
>
> my Psyche, disappear into the web,
> the shell, re-integrate,
> nor fear to recall
>
> the shock of the iron-Ram,
> the break in the Wall,
> the flaming Towers,
>
> shouting and desecration
> of the altars; you are safe here;
> remember if you wish to remember,
>
> or forget. . . .
>
> (170–71)

The metamorphosis of caterpillar to butterfly is not, of course, reversible. A butterfly does not reenter a cocoon. But because H.D. wanted to evoke the amount of "backward" integration necessary to move the soul forward, she has Theseus tell Helen the butterfly to reenter the cocoon because her formation needs extra dimensions, or because her formation is not complete. This corresponds to the mingling of backward-moving memory and forward-moving quest in the structure of the poem.

This combined maternal/paternal figure with his cocoon of nurturance and his inseminating insights provides ecstatically received reparenting for the questing soul. This reparenting is another component of H.D.'s strategic solution to romantic thralldom, that major destroyer of female identity. The wounded woman is saved by taking the form of a child, subsumed under a caring mother or father.[30] The solution of reparenting is only one aspect of the total familial structure H.D. invented, but it is crucial, for in several ways romantic love and reparenting are parallel. In both structures, the woman has less power than a larger, controlling figure. But when she is subsumed as a child under a benevolent power, she is protected and nurtured, and may gather strength to leave the parental figure or to absorb its lessons. In the plot of thralldom, on the other hand, the woman is exposed and destroyed. There are undeniable psychic advantages to being small and protected, rather than diminished and broken. Reparenting also allows the woman to begin anew, as a fresh complete soul filled with promise, while romantic thralldom fractures her identity, and deadens her contact with her own inner strength. If sexuality and the system of thralldom provide only a negative space charged with frustration and paralysis, reparenting, in contrast, occurs in a neutral, unencumbered space, or in a positive, womblike space in which one need no longer be afraid of speech or memory.

Helen in Egypt ends with the appearance of a mother-child chain: Helen as avatar of the mother, Thetis; Helen as mother of the son, Paris; Helen as a girl child in the arms of the goddess who is also herself. Most often in H.D.'s poems, the child is male. Only in *Helen in Egypt* is the child both female and male, an additional complexity that parallels Theseus' dual role as father and mother. In later poems, such as *Hermetic Definition*, the boy child is the place where the exasperating lover has been put;[31] such a son/consort, while fascinating, cannot dominate or entrap the woman. She has contained his sexual power by demoting him generationally.

In another version of this mother-child dyad, the lover totally disappears, incorporated into and displaced by the female power of fertility and maternity. This occurs in *Winter Love*, the final Helen poem in which the hero and lover—quite evidently Pound, for H.D. echoes his sensual lynx cantos—disappears in the middle. Similarly, in *End to Torment*, H.D. imagines the fruit of their short sexual and long spiritual friendship as a baby whose solar brilliance does not express itself sexually.

The third section of *Helen in Egypt* is dominated by a little wooden idol of Thetis which Achilles had carved when a boy. This idol is also a psyche figure. Like Helen in the Theseus section, the eidolon or image of Thetis is portrayed both as a pupa and as a butterfly. Thetis is both the swaddled soul and her own psychopomp, or soul bearer. That is the mystery of the psyche figure who, according to the old myth, is pregnant on her quest of soul making. She is bearing both herself and her child, a double incubation. The psyche madonna transforms the mother along with the child, making one birth the sign of the other.[32] Thetis can be aroused only by profound cries of need from the brother and sister questers Achilles and Helen:

> true, the world knows her name,
> the world may bring her
> marble to build her walls,
>
> and ships for her harbours;
> but her wings are folded about her
> and her wings only un-furl
>
> at the cry of the New Mortal,
> or the child's pitiful call. . . .
>
> (300)

What H.D. embodies within Helen-Thetis is the recurrent mystery of birth as resurrection: "Phoenix, the symbol of resurrection has vanquished indecision and doubt, the eternal *why* of the Sphinx. It is Thetis (Isis, Aphrodite) who tells us this, at last, in complete harmony with Helen" (93). This is a secret power beyond all others which women possess: the power of reproduction. During a portion of her quest, Helen, like Psyche, is pregnant with Achilles' child: "a treasure beyond a treasure . . . the gift I forced from him" (282–83). This little jewel is imagined in fertility images of vulnerability and strength:

> frailer than spider spins,
> or a worm for its bier,
> deep as a lion or a fox
>
> or a panther's lair,
> leaf upon leaf, hair upon hair
> as a bird's nest,
>
> Phoenix
> has vanquished
> that ancient enemy, Sphinx.
>
> (93–94)

Birth is a gift of love, and the capacity for love is the basis of this complex mother. Rather than themselves being united in a *Liebestod*, Achilles and Helen have both found Thetis, the power of death and love. What joins them at the end is "one secret, / unpronounceable name, / a whisper, a breath" (279) — Thetis. Their promised child turns out to be two, images of themselves as children (288). Generation is the true secret of this poem, not heroism or romance. "For her, we are One, / not for each other" (269).

The "child-mother, yourself" is a way of moving beyond both war and romantic love, beyond the strains of the heroic and romantic scripts. Helen is both the Great Mother, avatar of Thetis, and the baby in her mother's arms. "Helen in Hellas forever" is the climactic, reverberating phrase which suggests an ongoing exchange of force in the closed circuit of mother-child-mother (190). This closure solves for H.D. the needs and themes of her major work — the needs for undamaging nurturance and undamaging powers.[33] Helen is the complete family represented by the petals of the nenuphar, but most particularly she is "the child in the father, / the child in the mother," the child-mother herself (187).

By this set of solutions, H.D. was attempting to end her submission to male power, constructing from available male and female roles, especially from parent and child roles, some set of relationships that would be less emotionally damaging to her as a woman than those she had actually experienced with men. To do this she creates a female quest whose final answer is the central revelation of mother and child, flanked by father and brother; "the thousand-petalled lily" contains and presents all the relations of the sufficient family (104).

Tribute to Freud and the work of Norman Holland give us the material for a strictly autobiographical reading of this poem. H.D.'s family, comprising an austere father, overloved brothers, and an ambivalent mother, certainly led her to focus on the family as a place where transformations were necessary.[34] And in order to solve the contradictions she felt within, H.D. draws in as many of these figures as possible — siblings, lovers, parents, children — to fuse an identity she often felt has been lost. The damaging or unsatisfactory relations with men that women artists can often experience in artistic communities — never sure whether they are to be courtesans or creators — have a clearly autobiographical origin. But although this material comes from one woman's life, the patterns in it are familiar to many. Through the sufficient family H.D. was trying to construct a set of relationships that would sustain her. The transformative structures of *Helen in Egypt* and other of H.D.'s later poems link her both to other women and to other women writers.

Through the superficially bizarre connections among her characters,

H.D. constructed an answer to thralldom to male power, inventing relationships that would make specific kinds of transformations of that damaging script. In the hieroglyph of the sufficient family, a strict division
of sexual roles is often retained, but female insight is approved of and
assisted as if it were a valued cultural and personal resource. Under the
system of romantic thralldom, love, care, and nurturing come with a very
high price: sexual bitterness and despair. But in the system of the sufficient family, the father or mother figure, and more rarely the brother,
give care and nurturing to the female character without exacting the debilitating price which the male lover always seemed to extort.

Further, in the system of thralldom which H.D. experienced, male power
always stood first, and female power was unequal to it. This meant that
a man expected a woman to be subsumed under him and to experience
a loss of identity, as in *HER*, while the woman at once desired to be equal
and experienced guilt about that desire. Certainly it is an old story. Within
the sufficient family, rather than being subsumed in an unequal power
relation, the woman has two special sources of force—in biological creation (as the mother through the child) and in self-creation (as the child
through herself as mother)—on the psyche quest.[35]

While the sufficient family composed of brother-sister questers, reparenting fathers and mothers, and the psyche madonna is not the product
of any social or political analysis, this family could nonetheless be taken
as an accurate postulation of all the relationships that would have to be
transformed in order for a new kind of male-female sexual and spiritual
relation to exist; that is, in order to end romantic thralldom. Some sense
of the enormity of the task of cultural reconstruction is revealed by the
immense changes that H.D. makes in her poetic family. Since psychocultural patterns are learned within the family, it must surely be recast in
order to change our images of women, culture, and society.

NOTES

Research for this paper was supported wholly by a Faculty Summer Research
Fellowship from Temple University. This paper previously appeared in *Contemporary Literature* 20 (Summer 1979): 178–203.
1   H.D. had two "careers" as a writer—one associated with the First World War
    and one associated with the Second. The second career completes and trans-
    forms central issues from the first, as I hope to show here. Her analysis with
    Freud (1933–34) and her divorce from Richard Aldington (1938), from whom
    she had long been separated, both played a role in the unblocking which she
    experienced.

2   *Compassionate Friendship* (1955), uncatalogued typescript, 30. This and
    other unpublished materials cited here are among the Hilda Doolittle-Norman
    Holmes Pearson papers in the Collection of American Literature, The Bein-
    ecke Rare Book and Manuscript Library, Yale University. I would like to
    express my thanks to Mr. Donald Gallup, Curator of the Collection of Ameri-
    can Literature, for permission to consult the H.D. papers, and to express my
    deepest gratitude to H.D.'s daughter, Mrs. John Schaffner, for very gener-
    ously allowing me to cite this and other unpublished material. Previously
    unpublished material by H.D. is published by permission of Mrs. John Schaff-
    ner and New Directions, Agents.

3   *Compassionate Friendship* 36. "Lord Howell" is H.D.'s name for Lord Hugh
    Dowding, Air Marshal during the Battle of Britain.

4   *HER* (circa 1927), uncatalogued typescript. Page references will hereafter be
    given parenthetically in the text. Susan Friedman helped me identify Fayne
    as Frances Josepha Gregg Wilkinson. The name Fayne has a suggestive con-
    stellation of meanings: "feign"—to contrive, to make fictions; "fain"—prefer-
    ably, gladly, willingly; and "fay"—to join tightly (v.), fairy, sprite, or elf (n.),
    and faith (n.).

5   *HER* 241, 244. The lower-case and upper-case material is not accidental, for
    the typescript has everywhere been carefully revised.

6   *Bid Me to Live (A Madrigal)* (New York: Grove Press, 1960). Copyright ©1960
    by Norman Holmes Pearson. Reprinted by permission of New Directions.
    Parenthetical page references in the text will be to this edition.

7   *Bid Me to Live* 11. The lyric poem "Heliodora," originally published in 1924,
    is about two male poets working together in emulation and friendly compe-
    tition and might be viewed as an ideal projection of the kind of companion-
    ship which H.D. sought. *Collected Poems of H.D.* (New York: Boni and
    Liveright, 1925), 222–26. Copyright ©1925, 1953 by Norman Holmes Pear-
    son. Excerpts reprinted by permission of New Directions.

8   "Eurydice," *Collected Poems of H.D.* 74–80.

9   *Collected Poems* 78. There are a number of parallels between this poem and
    Lawrence's desire, in *Bid Me to Live*, to speak for men and women both,
    while compelling H.D. to speak only for women.

10 *Collected Poems* 79–80.

11 Examples are the following lines from "Sea Rose": "Stunted, with small leaf
    / you are flung on the sand"; from "Sea Lily": "Yet though the whole wind
    / slash at your bark, / you are lifted up"; and from "Garden": "You are clear
    / O rose, cut in rock, / hard as the descent of hail," *Collected Poems* 3, 17,
    34. It is impossible not to think of Georgia O'Keeffe's hard-edged, sensuous
    flower paintings, roughly contemporaneous with H.D.'s poems. These paint-
    ings come to mind as a parallel appropriation of forms iconographically
    associated with the feminine, in order to transform them into icons of female
    power. O'Keeffe's flower paintings are statements of grandeur, for they are
    so massive that they preempt the whole field of vision, excluding everything
    that is not flower. H.D., in contrast, is acutely aware of the shaping, sculpt-
    ing force against which these flowers are poised.

12 *Bid Me to Live* 177. H.D.'s use of the term *gloire* may have drawn on D. H. Lawrence's title "Gloire de Dijon," in his collection of poems *Look! We Have Come Through!* (New York: B. W. Huebsch, 1918).

13 H.D., *Notes on Thought and Vision*, typescript, 2.

14 Ibid.

15 During the Second World War, H.D. recorded a striking dream of the dead self released and a new self born in "She is Dead": "I am sustained through the day. . . . I have only to think 'She is dead, she is dead' and a wave of joy and hope sustains me. I have carried her with me, I think, almost my whole life. She was a stalactite-self, she was neatly fitted in myself, it seems, her coffin. She was wrapped in the layers of my growing self, like a nun in her enveloping garments." *Stories* (1940–41), unpublished typescript, 2.

16 One part of her life and art that needs to be explained is the "prose period" represented in works like *Kora and Ka* (Dijon: Darantière, 1934), and *Narthex, The [Second] American Caravan: A Yearbook of American Literature*, ed. Alfred Kreymborg, Lewis Mumford, and Paul Rosenfeld (New York: Macaulay, 1928). In these works several liminal male and female personalities fuse and exchange identities. The effect is both haunting and haunted. Androgyny and/or bisexuality is experienced primarily as damaging, blurring the identity of the central character. However positively the works end, their tone is quite uneasy.

17 The problem with arguing that H.D. sought to convert only males is that Bryher too rejected H.D.'s visionary and occult interests during World War II. Despite her participation in the Corfu experience (1920) chronicled in *Tribute to Freud* during which she saw and completed H.D.'s vision, Bryher was constantly concerned by the apparent instability that H.D. exhibited in the practices of spiritualism and mediumship.

18 This argument is influenced by Robin Morgan's "The Politics of Sado-Masochistic Fantasies," *Going Too Far: The Personal Chronicle of a Feminist* (New York: Random House, 1977), 227–40.

19 As Susan Gubar shows, H.D.'s resistance to male-defined myths is also an indication of ambivalence about her own power. "The Echoing Spell of H.D.'s *Trilogy*," in this volume.

20 H.D., *Helen in Egypt* (New York: New Directions, 1961). Copyright ©1961 by Norman Holmes Pearson. Excerpts reprinted by permission of New Directions. Parenthetical page references in the text will be to this edition. The significant study of this poem is Susan Friedman's "Creating a Woman's Mythology: H.D.'s *Helen in Egypt*," in this volume. L. S. Dembo has a brief but fruitful section on the poem in *Conceptions of Reality in Modern American Poetry* (Berkeley: U of California P, 1966), chap. 2.

21 *End to Torment* (1958), uncatalogued ts., p. 73. H.D. uses the editorial "we."

22 Ibid.

23 The evidence occurs in *The Sword Went Out to Sea (Synthesis of a Dream)* [late 1940?], typescript, pp. 173, 177 and in *Compassionate Friendship* 78–79.

24 Though Heydt was an analyst, he and H.D. did not have a doctor-patient relationship. In the words of Perdita Schaffner, "They contracted a great friendship" (Personal communication, May 9, 1978).

25 She felt, in fact, that he had betrayed their "compassionate friendship."
    "Erich did very well as my model for Paris, in the second part of my *Helen*
    sequence. I only began writing the poems, as a continuation of the first Helen,
    after he had gone away . . . leaving me with a quarrel or half-quarrel on my
    hands," she wrote in 1953. *Compassionate Friendship* 78.

26 The phrase is from Ellen Moers, *Literary Women* (Garden City, N.Y.: Double-
    day, 1976), 123.

27 H.D., *Trilogy* (New York: New Directions, 1973), 103, 105. Subsequent paren-
    thetical references are to page numbers in this edition. *Tribute to the Angels* —
    Copyright ©1945 by Oxford University Press. Excerpts reprinted by permis-
    sion of New Directions.

28 This tactic was suggested by Norman Holmes Pearson, but enthusiastically
    picked up by H.D. "Norman Holmes Pearson on H.D.: An Interview," con-
    ducted by L. S. Dembo, *Contemporary Literature* 10.4 (Autumn 1969): 440.

29 Pearson identifies Theseus as Freud in the *Contemporary Literature* inter-
    view, 443.

30 In the ecstatic reparenting at the end of *Tribute to Freud*, H.D. uses "Mi-
    gonne," the girl child in a Goethe novel, to celebrate the quest of the baby
    soul under the guardianship of a purely paternal Father Protector. The child
    in *The Hedgehog*, a children's story by H.D., is at once protected from and
    released into quest by a large, brilliant, almost Jamesian paternal figure. Pro-
    tection from a Great Mother is an equally powerful image for H.D. A most
    extraordinary version occurs in the unpublished memoir of her childhood,
    The Gift. The water and flowers of a long ago trip to a waterlily pond are
    lyrically evoked as the "secret body" of the Mother: she rocks, pushed for-
    ward in a little boat, "into the fragrant enclosed organ of the flowering water."
    The Gift (1943), typescript, 34, 36.

31 This poem is discussed by Susan Friedman in "Who Buried H.D.?" *College
    English* 36.7 (March 1975): 801–14, and by Vincent Quinn in "H.D.'s 'Her-
    metic Definition': The Poet as Archetypal Mother," *Contemporary Litera-
    ture* 18.1 (Winter 1977): 51–61.

32 More Psyche images occur in *Trilogy* 53 and 103. There the madonna is
    "Psyche, the butterfly, / out of the cocoon."

33 The fusion Helen-Hellas is analyzed by H.D. as an amalgam of a fourfold
    woman: "Helen is my mother's name + Hellas is Greece + Bryher, Perdita
    [H.D.'s daughter] + I." Hirslanden-Zürich notebook 3 (1957), autograph MS,
    p. 27.

34 *Tribute to Freud* (1956; rpt. Boston: David R. Godine, 1974); Norman N.
    Holland, *Poems in Persons: An Introduction to the Psychoanalysis of Litera-
    ture* (New York: W. W. Norton, 1973).

35 Women writers often show a family in their work from which an autobio-
    graphical daughter figure emerges, the solution of a dialectical struggle be-
    tween male and female represented by father and mother. Lily Briscoe in
    Woolf's *To the Lighthouse* and the granddaughter Jeannie in Tillie Olsen's
    "Tell Me a Riddle" both perform this function. The authors of these works,

represented in a central character, pass through the family represented in order to be reborn. *Helen in Egypt*, in rather occult fashion, follows this motif of the second family and is equally autobiographical. The authors weave the family as their cocoon, in order to emerge as artists in some articulated space beyond patriarchy.

CHAPTER 22

Imaginary Images: "H.D.," Modernism, and the Psychoanalysis of Seeing

ELIZABETH A. HIRSH

In more ways than one, H.D. was in a unique position to recognize the special relation that exists between women and images. Born, or rather baptized, Hilda Doolittle, she was rechristened "H.D." by her friend Pound, who appended this signature to her earliest publications along with the fashionably French epithet that — until recently — defined her reputation: *Imagiste*. Following Pound's cue, critical legend made "H.D." "the perfect Imagist," not only *an* example, but *the* example, the exemplar, the veritable Image of Imagism. And since *Imagisme* has itself long been recognized as what T. S. Eliot called "the *point de repère* for the beginning of modern poetry," "H.D." was accorded a certain place in the history of literature — but only to the extent that she embodied, perfectly, fully adequately and with nothing left over, a certain *theory* of the Image, which was not her own. For as one historian of imagism remarks, "H.D. was no theorist" (Coffman 163).

"H.D." was no theorist — only an example of a theory, an image, her images, presented in evidence for a male-authored truth. In this way a naive reading practice reinscribed as history what was, after all, only a theory: that the poetic Image, in a timeless moment of aesthetic perception, could effect an adequation of seeing and knowing, appearance and reality, outside and inside. But just as feminist criticism has dislodged "H.D." from her place of (no) honor in the literary history of men, so has feminist theory analyzed the Imaginary logic that put her there in the first place.[1] Turning Jacques Lacan's critique of the Imaginary against his own discourse, the French feminist Luce Irigaray suggests that the constitution of psychoanalytic knowledge — and beyond this, the constructions of masculine self-knowledge reflected throughout philosophical tradition —

begins with the erasure of female images as such, their fetishization as evidence or incarnation within a certain order of visibility. Film theory, meanwhile, demonstrates that within the conventions of classic cinema, "images of women" are likely to function as sites of epistemological crisis or self-verification, as prostheses or fetishes, in a masculine imaginary. (In fact, one contemporary filmmaker, Peter Gidal, suggests that within the order of cinematic representation as it now exists there is no way to photograph women that is not in effect pornographic, since *images* of women can never be images of *women*.) The fate that befell "H.D." in the history of modernism — being robbed of an image even as she was reduced to one — was then no accident, but recapitulated the fate of woman in Western thought.

In linking the sense of sight, the eye, to the constitution of the Ego or I, "French Freud" indicts both as instruments for the repression of *différance*. But if in feminist criticism more or less frenchified inscriptions of "difference" have succeeded in evicting America's native "images of women" school, French modes of thought have hardly met with universal acceptance by American feminists. And to a significant degree the Franco-American feminist controversy repeats the ongoing debate within the academy at large concerning the value of engaging with "theory" at all. In fact, one recent site of struggle between "the theorists" and "the historians" (we are dealing, for the moment, in types) has been none other than the modernist poetic Image, specifically considered in its role as the proverbial *point de repère* for the beginning of modern poetry, and by extension, since lyric is the paradigmatic mode of modernist writing, of modernism itself. Poststructuralist critics have sought to reclaim the Image as rubric from the vocabulary of a visualist and spatialist reading of modernist poetics — a usage inherited, they suggest, from the New Critics — in favor of their own temporalizing and antiformalist readings. They point out that in advancing terms like "spatial form," New Critical type criticism privileged the classicizing, reactionary strains of so-called High Modernism, recuperating modernist texts as "timeless" artifacts and self-sufficient objects of aesthetic contemplation. In this interest lyric was privileged and the decline of representation equated with the elevation of abstract form. Obviously, such an understanding also entails a privilege granted to the mind's *eye*. As antidote, critics like Paul Bové, Joseph Riddel, and William Spanos offer readings of modernist texts that mobilize, for example, Heideggerian notions of interpretation and historicity, the indeterminacy of Derridean spac*ing*, and the constitution of identity in *différance*. In some cases deconstructive or destructive impulses are attributed to the practices (if not to the theories) of the modernist writers themselves, in some cases the deferred action of interpretation is invoked, but in every case one effect of such rereading is to obscure (perhaps I should say, to defer) any distinction between the "modern" and the "postmodern."[2]

Like Irigaray's feminist deconstruction of Western theory, the poststructuralist revision of Anglo-American modernism is framed as a critique of formalism. Explicitly at stake in both—and implicitly at stake in the competing claims of "history" and "theory," "French" and "American," "modern" and "postmodern"—is the problem of the Image, denoting, in one case, the primordial Platonic *eidos* from which the dominant traditions of Western philosophy descend (itself understood as the theoretical equivalent of the Imaginary mirror image of Lacanian psychoanalysis); and in the other, what might be seen as an effect of that philosophical hegemony, a totalizing-formalist theory of the literary text. What Irigaray's *Speculum* demonstrates is that in Western theoretical tradition woman has always appeared *as* image, the reflection or re-presentative of man, the em-bodiment of *his* form or intelligence, with the result that the image as such assumes a "feminine" character; and she argues that it is the logic of representation per se that enacts this repression/assimilation of any actual feminine difference. In relation to poststructuralist revisions of modernism, then, *Speculum* would suggest that a thoroughgoing critique of formalism must also be a feminist critique: one that analyzes the connection not only between philosophical formalism and the poetic Image, for example, but also between imagist poetics and the ideology of gender. This the poststructuralist critics have not done—have not perhaps been able to do if, as Irigaray indicates, the master discourses that enable their critique do not necessarily escape the formalism they analyze.

Thus Joseph Riddel, who reinterprets the Poundian Image and the ideogrammic method in de(con)structive terms, elsewhere also subjects "H.D."'s prose memoir *Tribute to Freud* to an orthodox Lacanian analysis, reading her text, in the manner of "The Purloined Letter" as read by Lacan, as a self-referential allegory that pays (its) "tribute" to the Phallus as the signifier of signifiers, the coin of the realm (Riddel 1979). But "H.D." herself said of Freud, "there was an argument implicit in our very bones," and her "tribute" to him must be understood in a double, an ironic sense, playing upon the meaning of "tribute" as praise but also as payoff, extortion, blackmail: in short, a canny acknowledgment of his power partly veiled by/as an expression of indebtedness. Similarly, the ironic ambiguity involved in naming a poem about Freud "The Master" is obvious. American feminists like Shari Benstock and Sandra Gilbert and Susan Gubar, meanwhile, are increasingly insistent upon the importance of gender difference in a historical and sociological sense to the emergence of Anglo-American modernism.

What the "example" of "H.D." makes clear, however, is that in the construction of literary histories appeals to "evidence" always proceed by way of a certain practice of reading, and reading itself by way of a certain theory of the text. As David Carroll has said, literary form "is never 'present' in itself, without the intervention of some theory to make it present" (Carroll 27). On the other hand, poststructuralism compels the recognition that every "theory" is itself a writing and/or a reading practice within which the signifier stubbornly works. In order to escape the phallacy of the self-evident, the sexual metaphysics of precept and example, what seems needed in feminist deconstructions and reconstructions of literary history is a reading practice that will be exercised as a mode of theoretical inquiry, and conversely, a theory that does not disavow but enjoys its own fate as practice. In the essay to follow, "H.D." 's career-long and indeed posthumous involvement with the problem of the Image will be at once the subject of and a guide to such a method (if method it be). Focusing particularly on *Helen in Egypt* I will read the poem as a belated allegory of Woman and/as Image that specifically reworks "H.D." 's own relation to imagism, to modernism, and to psychoanalysis. In "H.D." 's later writings psychoanalysis and modernist poetics not only intersect but actively interrogate one another. What results is both feminist critique and a precocious mode of feminine *écriture* in some ways akin to more contemporary feminism(s). As Irigaray re-vised Lacan from a feminist angle, *Helen* revises both Freud and Pound, anticipating the feminist critique of formalism in discerning the affinity of the psychoanalytic phallus and the modernist poetic Image. For this reason there could be no better place for a feminist revision of modernism to begin (again) than with "the perfect Imagist," and especially with her carefully veiled autobiography, *Helen in Egypt*.

Pound's originary and Svengali-like gesture in signing (for) "H.D., Imagiste" finds a telling parallel in the institutional and intellectual history of psychoanalysis (much as Pound loathed all that "vile Freud bunk" and urged "H.D." to abandon it). To the extent that psychoanalysis begins with the theory and treatment of hysteria, with Freud's revision of Charcot, it begins by making (mute) female images "speak" theoretical truths—a phenomenon answerable to Pound's famous formula, "the Image is itself the speech." This appropriation is literally registered in the photographs of the *Iconographie photographique de la Salpêtrière*, beautiful images which through the discipline of Charcot's theoretical labels become illustrations of beautiful truth. In this connection, Joan Copjec makes the case that the alienating image of Lacan's Imaginary intrudes itself *as* alien into any such attempt to make the image of seeing or perception coextensive with (its) meaning. And yet, for Lacan no less than for Charcot, "the cure" works in essence by making the fascination of the (female) image yield to the Law of the word/Symbol (the *"nom du père"*).[3] This survival from the prehistory of psychoanalysis — however alien the language of cure might otherwise seem to Lacanian discourse — is apparent in Lacan's now-famous distinction between the Symbolic and the Imaginary.

Lacan theorized the genesis of the ego as a series of alienating identifications inaugurated by the subject's assumption of his own specular image during the Mirror Stage. In part his theory develops Freud's suggestion in *The Ego and the Id* that "the ego is first and foremost a bodily ego," which, Freud says, "may be considered a mental projection of the surface of the body," as well as Freud's consistent characterization of the Ego as the first psychic organization and agent of psychic synthesis. For Lacan, it is "the total form of the body" that provides the nucleus of the ego, and this "total form" first emerges in the Mirror Stage. In his theory the specular image functions as a kind of prosthesis, a pseudototality that permits the subject, by a fantasmatic detour, to evade the lack congenital to his human-being. At the same time, in subject-ing him to the gaze that returns his look in the mirror, the Mirror Stage prefigures the moment when castration will propel the subject into the order of the Symbol (and vice versa). But despite this interesting turn of events, and especially in Lacan's early work, the image as such remains tainted with associations of narcissistic bad faith, insofar as it spells the "scotomization" of absence or lack. "Our experience shows that . . . the function of *méconnaissance* . . . characterizes the ego in all its structures," Lacan writes (1977: 6), invoking Anna Freud's *The Ego and the Mechanisms of Defense*. The ego is in essence a defensive formation that shares in the paradoxical nature of the symptom as Freud defined it, a structure that at once masks and betrays — betrays by masking — the lack it is meant to re(ct)ify. Thus, as paradigm of the ego, the image is also a pseudopresence in the sense that it can escape its status as substitute only fantasmatically, that is, in "the function of *méconnaissance*." The disavowal embodied in the symptom recapitulates the *méconnaissance* of the Mirror Stage. The genetic relation that obtains between image, ego, and symptom in Lacanian theory is most readily apparent in the case of the fetishist, which Lacan uses to elucidate his distinction between the Imaginary and Symbolic orders:

The imaginary is decipherable only if it is rendered into symbols. Harry's [a fetishist's] behavior at this moment is not; rather, he is himself drawn in by the image. This imaginary captation (*captation of and by the image*) is the essential constituent of any imaginary "reality" . . . experience in analysis proves that instead of giving reality to the symbol, the patient attempts to constitute *hic et nunc*, in the experience of the treatment, that imaginary point of reference which we call bringing the analyst into his game. (Lacan and Granoff 1956: 269–70)[4]

Lacan's hierarchical opposition between Image and Symbol participates in a distrust of the Image as such, amounting almost to a kind of iconophobia, which is endemic to Western tradition. Psychoanalysis suggests that it is a constitutive and not an incidental part of this tradition that the Image is identified with the female (in the Lacanian scenario, with the appearance of the body of the mother) and its opposite or antidote with the Father; like all binary oppositions, this one bears the marks of gender. Irigaray's critique of Lacan moots the distinction between Image and Symbol, indicating that the prestige of the (symbolic) Phallus derives from, precisely, its *visibility*, not in an empirical but in an ideal sense. That is, the Phallus as master trope endows the field of language with its own singularity, totality, and self-identity, preserving in a sublimated form the same dream of symmetry projected in the Image. Where in Lacan's genealogy of the Ego an Other (the mirror image exterior to the subject) passes itself off as a self, in Irigaray's exposé a selfsameness (the Law of the Symbolic Order) passes itself off as an Other. In both operations, cognition implies seeing — empirical and ideal — and seeing connotes the containment of feminine difference by an image of the selfsame.

The elevation of the Image as "self-evident" — a form or appearance coextensive with its own meaning, subsuming the function of reference in a state of full presence — is but the inverse of its denigration in the dominant theoretical traditions of the West as prelinguistic, the hallmark of infantile incapacity, neurotic fixation, intellectual passivity. The relationship between the "perfection" or self-sufficiency ascribed to the Image by the former, and the "poverty" ascribed to it by the latter, in this way replicates the complementarity women have come to recognize between the idealization of the feminine on the one hand (the pedestal) and the subjection of women on the other. To be relegated to exemplary status as bearer of a male word, or to accede to a speech and subjectivity gendered male, is a difference that doesn't amount to much.

The idea of "perfection," a dream of symmetry and totality, is one that haunts the imagination of "H.D., *Imagiste*" and informs the intersection of poetics and femininity in her work. In "H.D." 's memoir of her therapy sessions with Freud in 1932–33, *Tribute to Freud*, for example, her "argument" with the father of psychoanalysis comes to focus on a statue of Nike which Freud describes as "perfect," a comment that "H.D." meditates at length:

when he said, *she is perfect*, he meant not only that the little bronze statue was a perfect symbol, made in man's image (in woman's, as it happened), to be venerated as a projection of abstract thought, Pallas Athene, born without human or even without divine mother, sprung full-armed from the head of her father, our-Father, Zeus . . . he meant as well . . . it is *perfect*, a prize, a find of the best period of Greek art, the classic period in its most concrete expression, before it became top-heavy with exterior trappings and ornate detail. This is a perfect specimen of Greek art, produced at the moment when the archaic abstraction became humanized but not yet over-humanized. (70)

Nike is at once identified with the figure of woman as the pure (indeed motherless) reflection of man (specifically of his *form*), and implicitly with the poetic Image of Imagism, the *point de repère* for the beginning of modernist neoclassicism. What "H.D." especially fixes on, though, is Freud's suggestion that Nike's perfection is compromised because she "has lost her spear" (the text first italicizes, then capitalizes these words). The obvious reference to woman's "castration" is countered by "H.D." in "The Master," where another female figure, a dancer, is described in conjunction with the repeated theme "woman is perfect." In a real sense, "H.D." 's argument with Freud resolves itself into a question of how Nike is to be seen, a question of what it is to see. Walter Schmideberg's insistence, the echo of Freud's own, that psychoanalysis is based strictly on the "accumulated data of scientific observation" (*Tribute to Freud* 77) is a suggestion that "H.D." finds resistible, but one that associates Freud with a whole series of fathers: her "Papalie" or grandfather, who with a microscope "sees what's invisible" (*Gift* 9); her father, an astronomer armed with his telescope; and Pound, the anointed father of modern poetry, who repeatedly advances an analogy between scientific observation and artistic perception, perhaps most famously in the parable of Agassiz and the fish from *The ABC of Reading*. For "H.D.," on the other hand, poetry was more like psychoanalysis and psychoanalysis more like poetry than either one was like science.

But to insist that "woman is perfect" — identifying her with the fullness and imaginary perfection of the Image — merely reinscribes the logic of castration that deems (a) woman "no theorist" because putatively mired in (the illusion of) presence. It is a response that bears comparison with "H.D." 's comment, reported by Barbara Guest, that "Mstn. ["H.D." 's euphemistic shorthand for "masturbation"] with me only breaks down the perfection, I have to be perfect, I get that in my writing" (Guest 218). As in Rousseau's *Confessions* as read by Derrida, it seems, masturbation is a "dangerous supplement" (it breaks down perfection) that "cannot be separated from [the] activity" of writing, its implied substitute in "H.D." 's psychic economy (Derrida 1974: 155). (Un)Willing to "touch herself," "H.D." instead hallucinates a "moving finger" that inscribes, on the wall of a hotel room in Corfu, a new script, a form of picture writing that will become the master trope of her postimagist writing. Because these hallucinations occur in Greece, in Hellas (which "H.D." had considered her "spiritual" home), Freud interprets them as denoting a desire for union with her mother, Helen (Wolle) (*Tribute to Freud* 44)—thus, a *material* home. But then "to return home to mother" would be to break down the motherless formal perfection of Nike with the materiality of writing, specifically of a picture writing that contests the entrenched opposition between Image and Symbol, or the closely related opposition between signifier and signified. Such an exploration of the borderline/between (opposites) in fact constitutes the most radical impulse of "H.D." 's writing practice, one that was often at odds with her desire to be perfect. Thematized in the title of the film in which she appeared with Paul Robeson during the thirties, the "Borderline" might be expressed in the moving finger and picture writing of Corfu, or in the light writing of the cinema itself.

The dream of writing perfect poems, of being perfect, was an imagist dream, and as several critics have suggested, imagism was a straightjacket from which "H.D." had to escape. This she did with considerably more difficulty than Pound, and in a radically different way. Within the evolution of Pound's poetic the impressionistic Image of early statements like "In a Station of the Metro" is sublimated to a (Phallic) principle of Form that makes it possible to compose a long imagist poem: thus, the "Ideogrammic method" of the *Cantos*, describing what Hugh Kenner aptly called "the intelligible form" of the poem. "H.D." 's ideo-grammatology, by contrast, perpetually crosses the border between categories that Pound was at pains to keep distinct: presence and representation, form and ornament, origin(al) and mimesis, masculine and feminine. From psychoanalysis "H.D." derived a kind of literalism or *lettrisme* which could then be redirected against the formality of Phallus and Image alike (rather than erected as an absolute value, as in Lacan's elevation of the Signifier). "Thoughts were things," she writes of Freud's method in *Tribute to Freud* (14); Nike, then, was also a thing, in "H.D." 's word a "doll," neither the (im)perfect embodiment of an ideal form, nor something to be sublimated into/as "evidence," but a thing implicitly *to be played with*. In the unfolding of this poetic, "H.D." 's identification with the Image plays a complex and sometimes contradictory role, debilitating in some ways, suggestive in others. Of interest here is her involvement with photography and the new art of the cinema (media Pound always disdained as slavishly mimetic), which marked out not a repudiation of but a new stage in her career as *Imagiste*. This involvement, incidentally, was substantial: she appeared in three films; wrote for *Close Up*, the film journal coedited by her friend Bryher which was the first English-language journal to treat film as "art"; and at one point seriously considered a career as a film actress, inspired, perhaps, by her strong identification with Greta Garbo. (Dietrich's was another image with which she identified.)

Hellenic hallucinations and moving pictures aside, the single most important development distinguishing the imagist and the postimagist "H.D." was her experience with Freud and psychoanalysis. For "H.D." as for many contemporary feminists, psychoanalysis seemed to expose the meshing of gears between the machinery of gender and that of representation, even when it also served to fuel the operation of that machinery. What is striking in several prose works written by "H.D." in the forties and fifties — *The Gift* (written ca. 1941–43), and *End to Torment* (1958), for example, as well as *Tribute to Freud* (1944) — is, in general, an obsession with problems of seeing and their relation to the constitution of subjectivity, and in particular, a reconceptualization of the Image in terms of a structure of deferred interpretive action, a kind of psychic writing, that is very much at odds with the imagism of Pound (or Hulme, or Bergson).

In *The Gift*, for example, "H.D." recreates her memory of a childhood episode which she says elsewhere had been lost to her for thirty-five years prior to her treatment with Freud (*Tribute to Freud* 139). In this scene, her father turns up at the door one night badly injured from a streetcar accident. Emphasizing the trauma of *seeing without recognizing* him in this state, she writes in a chapter titled "What It Was": "What it was, was not appreciable at the moment," and, "was this a drunk man? I looked at him . . . and I looked at him" (*Gift* 106). The (re)construction of this childhood memory is in turn related to "H.D." 's initiation by her grandmother into the arcana of Moravian tradition, particularly the hermetic knowledge of a scene at "Wunden Eiland" ("Wounded Island" in the polyglot tongue of the Moravians) in which "the unbaptized king of the Showanese gave his beloved and only wife to the Brotherhood," thus uniting the "ancient secrets" of Europe and America. In the recollective-associative method of "H.D." 's text, both scenes of "wounding" are linked to the mysteries of copulation, childbirth, and death, so that seeing itself becomes a kind of wounding, a trauma of initiation. Obviously relevant to the method of the work is Freud's theory of the primal scene, a doctrine that helped posthumanist thought to displace the theoretical primacy of perception and consciousness. (Pound's imagism in part represents a rearguard action against this development.) The primal scene is neither primal nor a scene, except insofar as these terms are placed under erasure, but describes a process of deferred action in which the "witnessing" of a traumatic event is retroactively installed in the subject. The importance of the primal scene is that literal perception or cognition is no longer regarded, as in the *Studies in Hysteria*, as a psychogenic agent, but is instead seen to depend on a structure of *re*-cognition, deferral, or *différance*. And while the paradigmatic content of the primal scene as elaborated in *The Wolf Man* is the wounding of the female by the male in copulation, the structure of deferred action which it describes will come to be identified as the essential force of "castration" — again helping to displace scene, event, or perception as privileged terms.[5] The displacement of the origin(al) effected in the primal scene is in this sense anticipated in Freud's blurring of the distinction between primary text and secondary revision in the structure of dream interpretation, a blurring to which *Helen in Egypt* will repeatedly allude.

"H.D." 's "imagist" and "postimagist" modes correspond approximately to the two "modernisms" — the "spatializing" or "New Critical," and the "temporalizing" or poststructuralist that would "cure" it — as well as to the two "psychoanalyses" proffered by Stephen Heath and Jacqueline Rose respectively, and finally to "the two feminisms," American and French, as we have grown accustomed to thinking of them. In considering the historical and theoretical relation of femininity and (post)modernism I think it important to bear in mind not only the authoritarian ideology of modernist writing, but also the fact that some of the most authoritarian texts of modernism are antiformalist, vitalistic, and mimetic with a vengeance, futurism being an obvious case in point. Perhaps in their very opposition the contemplative, idealizing elevation of abstract form and the overt aggression of an iconoclastic mimesis both swear allegiance to the eye/I. And as Jane Gallop observes, "writing a non-phallomorphic text" is a rather "common modernist [in Anglo-American parlance, postmodern] practice" which in my terms may be poststructuralist but protofeminist. That is why Irigaray *adds* to her deconstruction of phallomorphism another discourse, marked by what Gallop calls "the gesture of a troubled but nonetheless insistent referentiality," an illusion of reference embodied partly in a vulvomorphic imagery that has often led to her misrecognition as "Essentialist" (Gallop 83). But as Margaret Homans observes, "Irigaray does not so much answer as rewrite the question of essentialism" (Homans 13).

To write and rewrite, rather than to answer, a question — the question of "essentialism," the question of female identity — also aptly describes the project of *Helen in Egypt*, the three-hundred-page pseudoepic that "H.D." wrote partly as a rejoinder to Pound's *Cantos*. The *Cantos'* pantheon of Real Life Heroes, manly figures drawn from the annals of History, finds its correlative in the realism, the essentialism, of Pound's Image, and later in the "ideogram," where a collocation of particulars theoretically forces some more general truth to appear, as it were, "in person": not as an abstraction but as it, in itself, really is. As if by way of contrast to this factual atomism, "H.D." devises a heroine whose status as nothing more nor less than a textual effect is insistently emphasized. "She herself is the writing," we are repeatedly told, her identity palimpsestically inscribed by several hands in several variant narratives. In this sense the text takes as its subject the condition of its own existence as fiction or myth, a problem it will ultimately assimilate, through the "figure" of Helen, to the problem of femininity itself. For if Helen is writing she is also and emphatically Image—the most beautiful, the most perfect woman in the world—the Image of beauty and for "H.D." therefore the Image of imagism. Throughout modernist writing, from Symons' "Modern Beauty" (1905) to Yeats and the *Cantos*, Helen was commonly cited not only as a paragon but as the paradigm of beauty as such; at the same time, of course, her deadly effect on men was invoked. In "H.D." 's text we see Helen diversely reflected in the eyes of several men, each of whom narrates a history that constructs a tableau in which he "sees" and "inscribes" his very own "Helen." Thus, "H.D." 's Achilles, Theseus, and Paris might be compared to Stesichorus, Homer, Euripides, Goethe, and their anonymous precursors, each of whom narrated a tale of "Helen." Collectively these male figures repeat "inside" the text the process of mythmaking that constitutes its "outside" or context, that is, of mythmaking conceived as a culture's collective writing and rewriting of a tale which thereby acquires the force of (psychological and cultural) fact. For "H.D." as for Freud, myth is the collective correlative of individual phantasy.

The title of the poem refers to a pre-Homeric variant of the Helen myth by Stesichorus of Sicily, which claims, as "H.D." 's copious gloss to the poem says, that "Helen was never in Troy. She had been transposed or translated from Greece into Egypt. Helen of Troy was a phantom, substituted for the real Helen, by jealous deities" (*Helen in Egypt* 1). The purpose of this variant was to vindicate "the real Helen" by making her remain faithful to Menelaus throughout the Trojan War, stowed away in Egypt under the protection of its virtuous King Proteus. This *division* of the female image is a familiar expedient which becomes an implicit target of "H.D." 's satire. But even in *her* text, Helen, swamped as she is by masculine narratives that contradictorily define her and unable to construct an image or truth scene of her own, is a thing of naught, a blind reflection of the sighted male. Thus the multiplicity or fragmentation of Helen's text/identity is initially posed not as an antidote to her captation by a collective masculine Imaginary, but rather as the result of it.

In response there emerges what might be called the Helen of "American feminism"—the "images of woman" Helen—in quest for an authentic self-perception, a true account of her being and experience. At the beginning of the poem, Helen is in Egypt, believing herself the virtuous and maligned woman of Stesichorus' *Palinode*, but only because she has repressed all memory of her involvement with Paris and the war, which she will shortly begin to recollect. The action of the poem is wholly "interior" or interpretive, comprising Helen's laborious efforts to reconstruct crucial scenes from her past so as to arrive at an accurate account of her personal history and thereby a determination of her true identity, *evident*, as it were, in these scenes. At this level the text presses toward the amnesiac Helen's recognition of the complementary duality of her own nature as both human and divine, and toward the derivation of her contradictory identities from a single source, the "great white mother goddess" of comparative mythography, whose power as (m)other can oppose that of the death-dealing patriarchal order. But finally "H.D." 's text will simply not sustain any such attempt to add up the two (or the several) Helens, the good and the bad, the real and the apparent, into some kind of well-balanced totality. Instead, "H.D." *multiplies* Helens, images, variant myths and narratives, superimposing these in such a way that there can no longer be any question of which represents "the original" or authoritative *one*. In *Helen in Egypt*, it is not only, not so much, that the expatriate Helen wanders from place to place, as that place itself, the topography of the text and the text as topo-graphy, wanders, will not stay in place. Especially in part III of the poem, as in the echoing *antre/entre* of Irigaray's *Speculum*, the echoing, querying voice(s) of the text—chiefly of "Helen" and of the narrator who doubles her—effect a spatiotemporal dislocation and cognitive regression that suggest a return to the womb (figured in *Helen* as the Ledean egg), and suggest further that this continual passage *entre* places, languages, and identities is woman's very "self," her only "home."

"H.D." 's conception for *Helen* was informed by the second part of Goethe's *Faust*, in which Mephistopheles calls up the ghost of Helen of Troy at Faust's bidding, because he, Faust, wishes to marry the most beautiful woman in the world, even if only in a kind of make-believe. Evil as he is, Mephistopheles can't resist tormenting Helen, a phantom brought back from the dead, a mere semblance who, happily oblivious to her lack of ontological status, believes herself to be real. Mephistopheles can't tell Helen the truth outright, but he undermines her by hinting at it, recollecting the Stesichorus myth about the phantom Helen, and demanding of her a question he knows she can't answer: which was the real? The effect of the bizarre scene is wonderfully pathetic, a triumph and an allegory of art in which we *feel* for Helen even though we know she exists only as a figment of the Imagination, that is, doesn't exist. A triumph, then, like Mephistopheles', of trompe l'oeil.

Substituting for the real but absent Helen, Goethe's/Mephistopheles' phantom shares the same status of nonentity as the simulacrum of Stesichorus, the statue-image which is called, in both Goethe and Euripides, *eidolon*, "painted image" or "cloud image"; she remains equally subject, as his creation and mouthpiece, to the requirements of the male artist/

magician. To the extent that Goethe recognizes a kind of pathos in the situation of the woman/phantom his conception begins to approach that of *Helen in Egypt*, for as I have suggested it too is an allegory of art, an allegory of the woman as artwork, but one told, as it were, from the point of view of the work. As such it becomes also an allegory of feminine identity or self-knowledge. For the "Helen" of *Faust* there can be no solution for the usurpation of her identity; for that of Stesichorus and Euripides, the solution lies in distinguishing between the true and the false, the chaste and unchaste, Helens (with much play, in Euripides, on the power of appearances to deceive); but for the "Helen" of *Helen in Egypt* the "real"/chaste Helen is no less an image, a projection/reflection of male wants, than is her phantom counterpart.

The problem of feminine identity cannot, thus, be formulated in terms of a decision to be taken between the one/true and the false/double woman — whether from a masculine or from a feminist perspective. What, indeed, would or could it mean to recover a true "Helen" within a context where identity itself is conceived as a fictional/mythic projection? The question Mephistopheles puts to Helen — which was the real? — expresses the same desire for a determination of female identity as Freud's famous question, "What does a woman want?" But as Irigaray says, "It is . . . useless to trap women into giving an exact definition of what they mean . . . they desire at the same time nothing and everything" (1985b: 29). Thus, "in a culture that claims to enumerate everything, cipher everything by units, inventory everything by individualities," women will represent "a mystery," being in Irigaray's words, *"neither one nor two"* (26). Initially "trapped" by the dualistic/monolithic form of the question that Achilles (echoing both Mephistopheles and Freud) puts to her — "Which was the real?" — the "Helen" of *Helen in Egypt* struggles painfully to satisfy his demand for the truth with an answer/statement that will "stop" the question, close and complete its "gaping" form. But this proves futile, as in the course of Helen's interior quest what emerges is rather a bewildering multiplicity of selves, a multiplicity obscured by the singularity of the proper name, "Helen." Ultimately, it is only in the home-coming of her own quest(ion)ing, only in the shelter of such an opening, that the heroine's identity rests: an (ir)resolution that contrasts with the restoration of family and state in which the questing of masculine heroes, however elaborately digressive, must finally conclude.

Thus if the Stesichorus myth is an alternative to the dominant tradition of Homer, the myth of feminine identity represented in *Helen in Egypt* must be considered an alternative to that alternative. As Froma Zeitlin and others have shown, in Homeric tradition the figure of Helen bears connotations of eroticism, disguise, and deception that associate her with the art of poetry and more simply with art as such, but she also bears the suggestion of divinity and thus of a "truth beyond fiction."[6] Stesichorus then "analyzes" this ambiguity into a clear and distinct duality that erects an absolute distinction between truth and trope, rehabilitating the figure of Helen by stripping her of her figurality, transferring or projecting all her erotic/poetic properties onto a "bad"/external simulacrum of the real woman. He proposes, in short, that Helen should recover her good or proper "name" by forswearing all the potency implied by her status as image, imposter, or mime. But Stesichorus cannot escape the irony that in formulating his *Palinode* he must himself have recourse to the arts of fiction or rhetoric, the art, thus, of the Sophists who Plato said exhibited "painted images" or *eidola* of things in order to make the speaker seem wise; according to Plato, in fact, the Sophist Gorgias set out to rehabilitate the figure of Helen using the power of rhetoric alone, simply to prove that it could be done (Zeitlin 324).

The *eidola* or tropes of the Sophist and the *eidolon* or cloud image of Helen devised, in one version of the Stesichorus myth, by Zeus, the cloud gatherer, are both fashioned to deceive; yet the Greek word *eidos*, from which *eidolon* derives, is also and more famously translated from the text of Plato as "form." In fact, the word *eidolon* has what Freud called an "antithetical sense," and can mean both form and image, can designate a sacred manifestation or icon of a god, or can have the sense of a forgery, a "mere" copy or image. In *Helen in Egypt*, the heroine's anamnesis is paralleled by that of her leading man, Achilles, which culminates in the recovery, in effect the uncovering, of a certain *eidolon*, the memory of an image. Here the so-called *eidolon* is a wooden doll representing Achilles' mother, the goddess Thetis, that was cherished by the boy in her absence but that he abandoned when his military training began. In the mythic idiom of the poem, the repudiated mother substitute or Thetis *eidolon* is associated not only with the Helen *eidolon* of Stesichorus, but also with the figure of Helen Dendritis, described by Robert Graves as "an orgiastic goddess" whose cult was centered at Sparta, and whose ritual involved the use of wooden dolls, often hung from fruit trees, that helped to increase fertility. In "H.D." 's psychologizing of "Helen," Helen Dendritis becomes a repressed aspect of the heroine's identity that must be recovered along with the lost memory of her part in the Trojan War, and it is Achilles' recovery of the primal *eidolon* — also the title of the final book of the poem — that links "Helen" 's recovery with that of the repudiated mother (and with the repudiated divinity or potency of the mother-as-goddess).

But insofar as the Thetis *eidolon* is itself a substitute, a doll signifier that usurps the potency of "the real" in Achilles' psychic economy, its

unveiling, like the psychomythic archeology of "Helen" 's identity, can only
lead to further revelations, further questions. And if the "veil" or "garment" of style is traditionally the trope of rhetoric, the trope of tropes,
Helen in Egypt literalizes this trope by making "Helen" 's veil her defining attribute in the poem, a metonym of the figure of "Helen" herself.
More precisely, as a (literal) "image" (*eidolon*), the veil plays a crucial part
in the plot and scenography of the poem, including several dramatic scenes
recollected by Paris, Achilles, and Helen; while as symbol or signifier
("veil") it suggests the deceptive and alluring properties associated with
the Helen *eidolon*. Indeed, if the *eidolon* proves to be a "veil," the veil
in turn proves to be an *eidolon*. Thus *Helen*'s reinscription of the Image
as veil*ing* must be distinguished not only from the imaginary self-evidence
of a Poundian Image, but also from any concept of reading as explication. As Irigaray demonstrates in her retraversal of Plato's cave allegory
in part 3 of *Speculum*, the traditional structure of *allegoresis* and of trope
in general depends upon distinguishing, deciding between, an outside (the
literal sense or vehicle) and an inside (the figurative, nonsensible "sense,"
or tenor) in order to arrive, through such judicious deliberation, at the
unveiling of a singular truth/scene. "Interpretation" on this model is thus
a process that pleasurably recapitulates the primordial self-constitution
of the specular ego in the action of *placing outside*, of articulating a (bad
or inessential) outside and a (good, essential) inside, meaning or truth.
But *Helen* not only calls into question any distinction between (its) "inside" and "outside"; as allegory, it emerges only in/out of this quest(ion)-
ing. Thus, *Helen*'s "allegorical" "veil," though in one scene torn or rent,
is otherwise represented as many-folded — endlessly self-implicating and
finally in-ex-plicable.

It is because of "H.D." 's tendency to read psychoanalysis as an interminable dialectic of (un)veiling that her writing can be characterized by
Riddel as anticipating Lacanian psychoanalysis. But Riddel's reading of
"H.D." is inscribed wholly within the same Lacanian problematic that
simultaneously subordinates the female image to the phallic "word," and
upholds the form of the phallus in its place. Thus, when Lacan speaks
of the "kaleidoscopic" structure of imaginary space, he underlines both
the formal/aesthetic properties of that beautiful (*kalos*) form (*eidos*), the
Ego, and its purely spectral or illusory nature (1977: 27). It is, again, the
subject's narcissistic interest in the integrity of his own form that ultimately
impels him to "imagine the [Phallic] Symbol" and so pass beyond the state
of "captation to the Image." Irigaray's analysis of the cave allegory is in
effect an extended allusion to Lacan's account of the passage from the
Imaginary to the Symbolic, in which she indicates that like the *eidos*/form
of Platonic philosophy, the Lacanian "Phallus" is ironically yet definitively

set *beyond* the field of vision — "the [Phallus] can play its role only when veiled" (that is, only *as* trope or signifier), according to Lacan (1977: 288) — precisely in order that it should function in that "beyond" as the truth reserve, the guarantee of the visible/knowable/re-presentational world. For Irigaray, the difference between the Imaginary Ego/*eidolon* and the Symbolic Phallus/*eidolon* therefore doesn't amount to much: the formality of the Symbolic Order and the singularity of its Phallic *differentia* continually return (in) the Symbolic to the specularity of male narcissism or "hom(m)osexualité," as Irigaray puts it. Unlike the phallic structure of Lacanian trope (and the tropological structure of the Lacanian Phallus), which privileges absent sense, *Helen*'s "veiling" resembles the Derridean "hymen" of *Spurs*, that indeterminate place/word ("hymen" signifies both marriage and virginity) that separates/joins inside and out. The hymen/veil also epitomizes the problem of Helen's female identity: chaste? (in-tact?) or (de)spoiled? — these being the two narrow parameters that traditionally have defined feminine (im)possibilities.

As Irigaray draws from Lacan a critique of formalism that reflects on his own psychoanalysis, *Helen*'s reworking of the Image/*eidolon* draws out Pound's critique of representation in a way that implicates his own aesthetic. Just as the traditional structure of a well-made trope is divided into an essential/inside and an inessential/outside part, more recently called a tenor and a vehicle, so, for Pound, trope in general was divided into two kinds, which he called decorative metaphor on one hand, and interpretive metaphor on the other. To eschew decoration was of course among the cardinal principles of imagism, which from the first exhorted its followers, "don't be viewy," and "use no word which does not contribute to the presentation" of the object, "whether subjective or objective." But for Pound "interpretive metaphor" was another matter. Whereas decorative metaphor merely *copied*, *re*-presented, or embellished a preexisting sense — belonged, in short, to the despised order of "mimesis" — interpretive metaphor *created* the sense which it incarnated, and was in this sense presentational, admitting of no distinction between vehicle and tenor. In Saussurean terms, it was a motivated sign. Pound's commentary on Fenollosa argues, in a manner reminiscent of Shelley's *Defense of Poetry*, that the self-renewing processes of language as such are, in the interpretive sense, metaphoric; in contrast to the arbitrary phonetic symbols of the West, the Chinese ideogram "bears its metaphors on its face," and so prevents their unheeded degeneration into abstraction, or a merely conventional relation between symbol and symbolized, their degeneration, that is, into dead or decorative metaphor. Thus it is of the essence of interpretive metaphor to embody an act of cognition and not recognition; to incarnate new knowledge rather than to repeat or vary something already

known; and this epistemological value is inseparable from its phenomeno-
logical mode of being as a full yet significant presence.

Ideogrammic metaphors are "interpretive," oddly enough, because they
require no interpretation or reading, being self-evident, visible, pictorial;
they embody and do not refer or represent. And even when Fenollosa says
that the ideogram is a visible bridge to the invisible — a more traditional
definition of metaphor or analogy — this "invisible" is that which inheres
in the directly observable relations of the ideogrammic structure, what
Kenner calls its "intelligible form." Seeing, the discernment of form, remains the privileged metaphor of cognition and of metaphor *as* cognition; while in all essentials, Pound's characterization of the ideogram —
ontology, epistemology, and aesthetics — remains wholly consistent with
that of the Image. Where decoration suggests that which distracts and
(merely) amuses the eye, contributing nothing to knowledge, the ideogrammic method is a mode of writing that permits the antidecorative
principle of imagism to be applied to a long poem. Both imagism and the
ideogram express Pound's deeply felt aversion to "decoration" as the antithesis, the obscurer, and potentially the corrupter, of (good) form.

It is largely as such, no doubt, that decoration has long been associated
with the feminine; psychoanalysis suggests that woman's love for self-
adornment is a form of self-disguise or veiling that proceeds from her
inherent "lack," and Irigaray identifies this "lack" as, above all, the lack
of (a) (good) form. Pound, of course, deplored not only decoration but
also the effete serenity of Greek "form," which especially in his vorticist
phase he regarded as a sham of true, dynamic form. To the vorticists the
color and primitive energy of Egyptian art represented the opposite of
the Greek aesthetic, and in many accounts of Pound's poetic development
vorticism therefore marks an essential transition from the static confines
of the Image to the dynamic inclusiveness of the *Cantos'* (theoretically)
ideogrammic method. The opposition between Greek and Semite which
in this way was so important to vorticist rhetoric is called into question
by the elusive figure of "Helen in Egypt," as by James Joyce's equally
elusive "Jewgreek" or "greekjew," Leopold Bloom; in both figures, "extremes meet" (cited in Derrida 1978a: 153). But the impact of this meeting in *Helen in Egypt* is not that of a marriage or dialectic of force and
form, a formula that some critics have recently proposed as capturing the
essence of modernism. Rather, just as *Helen*'s undecidable veil/*eidolon*
reinscribes the Poundian Image, its/her Egyptian "hieroglyphics" transmute the "ideogrammic method" into a mode of writing that oscillates
perpetually between symbol and image, decoration and genesis, spectacle
and sense.

For "H.D.," dreams and visions were "the hieroglyphics of the Unconscious," and thus the ancient ground of consciousness and the ego, which

in this scheme would correspond to the rational "form" of the Greeks. Freud called dream interpretation "the royal road to the Unconscious," and "hieroglyphics of the Unconscious" suggests a script to-be-deciphered, an art of interpretation which in Lacanian terms must depend upon the opposition of image and symbol/signifier. It is in connection with Freud's *Interpretation of Dreams* that Lacan insists there can be, strictly speaking, no such thing as picture writing:

Freud shows in every possible way that the value of the image as signifier has nothing whatsoever to do with its signification, giving as an example Egyptian hieroglyphics . . . even in this writing, the so-called "ideogram" is a letter. (1977: 159)

The *interpretation* of dreams and the unconscious, whether regarded as terminable or interminable, thus entails the same sort of *Aufhebung* that, in the passage from the Imaginary to the Symbolic, conscripts the (female) image in service to the *nom du père*. In this sense Lacan's distinction recapitulates the passage from polytheism, the worship of images, to the unified rule of the father-god and concomitant banning of images, as described by Freud in *Moses and Monotheism*.

The very term "hieroglyphic," however, inscribes an uncertainty concerning its own nature similar to that of the *eidolon*, for the *glyphe* in question here, from Greek *glyphein*, to carve, can designate either a symbolic "figure" or character carved in relief or an ornamental groove in a Doric frieze, that is, a purely decorative element that bespeaks no other value. Both antithetical senses speak together in *Helen in Egypt*, a text that might just as well be named "Egypt in Hel(l)en(e)," where the gaudy hieroglyphs of Egypt are associated not only with an art of interpretation but also with a script of "silent," purely decorative images that "H.D." identified as a particularly feminine art.[7] Thus in one moment the variable Helen longs to be like Achilles, master of the "Star Script," in "untangling the riddle" of her identity; but in another, she "flings away knowledge," preferring instead to dwell on/in the beauty of the holy picture-writing, preferring pleasure to desire. Not incidentally, "H.D." (like Dorothy Richardson) regarded the silent cinema as a feminine medium which lost this character when it began to "talk." "The screen image, a mask, a sort of doll or marionette was somehow mechanized," she wrote in *Close Up*; "I didn't really *like* my old screen image to be so improved (I might almost say imposed) on . . . Haven't we been just a little hurt and disappointed that our dolls have grown so perfect?" ("Cinema," 20). The light writing or photography of the silent cinema also came to be associated with the protracted hallucinations "H.D." experienced while visiting on Corfu, and which later served as partial inspiration for *Helen*. Moreover, the silent script beheld in *Hellas* became a kind of mother tongue akin both to the silent cinema and to the decorative images painted by "H.D." 's mother, Helen Wolle, amateur creations whose decorative nature and domestic content were ridiculed by the youthful Pound.

It was not only the conventional character of Helen Wolle Doolittle's paintings but also their representational or referential nature that Pound disdained, as he would later disdain photography, cinema, and "decorative metaphor." Riddel says that Pound's "presentational" poetic consisted essentially in removing the "re" from "representation" through the elevation of interpretive metaphor. But in his well-founded determination to displace the orthodoxy of Kenner's modernism, Riddel does not acknowledge the degree to which the radical force of Pound's gesture was contradicted by its historical and ideological context. After all, Kenner's Pound is also to a great extent Pound's Pound. For the illusion(ism) of referentiality, the illusion of the presence of something actually absent, Pound sought to substitute the real presence of the Image/ideogram as form, a form incarnate in the text as perfected through the poetic regimen of "Imagism." "H.D.," the living doll, the spitting Image of Imagism, responds with a "hieroglyphic" text that, on the one hand, reinterprets the Image in light of psychoanalysis, as a mode of hermeneutic veiling that restores the centrality of reading, and on the other, suggests a purely decorative or "silent" picture writing that prefers the pleasurable illusion of a feminine presence over the desire for knowledge.

In this way "H.D." 's writing touches that of Irigaray and also constantly touches or implicates itself, not as verbal artifact but in its own (un)veiling. Lacan indicates that subjectivity is structured by two glances — the glance of specular self-recognition and the glance that spots a hole — one constituting and the other forever breaking a psychocorporal totality. Yet, as a developmental fiction the Imaginary folds back on itself, implicitly barring the possibility of identifying any such "moment of origin" for the subject.[8] Thus, charges of Imaginary captation leveled against this position or that one necessarily implicate themselves, as we all are implicated, in the Imaginary, that is, by *believing* in it. Feminism should analyze but cannot purge itself of Imaginary effects because feminism depends on Imaginary effects for its putative existence and perpetually reinscribes them. This is a situation I see reflected in the text of *Helen in Egypt*.

Finally, psychoanalysis motivates but will not necessarily authorize such a reading practice. But perhaps feminist psychoanalysis will always have to be "wild." That was Freud's term for psychoanalysis undertaken by amateurs, a practice he regarded as a grave danger both to the patient and to the doctrine of psychoanalysis. Perhaps "H.D." 's wild inventiveness with psychoanalytic doctrine was attributable to the fact that she was Freud's patient and "student," as he called her, but was not actually psychoanalyzed by him. Freud told her he saw " 'from signs' " that she did not want to be analyzed, and perhaps this was because, as "H.D." herself said, "[his] explanations were too illuminating, it sometimes seemed" (*Tribute to Freud* 30).

NOTES

This essay is adapted from an article of the same title in *Discontented Discourse: Feminism/Textual Intervention/Psychoanalysis*, ed. Richard Feldstein and Marleen Barr. Champaign-Urbana, 1989.

1   The first book-length study to approach "H.D." 's work in a noncondescending spirit was Friedman's, which established the importance of "H.D." 's encounter with Freud. Her discussion of "H.D." 's particular conflation of dream images and poetic ones informs the present essay. Subsequently several illuminating feminist discussions of "H.D." have been published, including DuPlessis' recent book, which like the present essay considers "H.D." 's affinity with "French Feminism."

2   " 'Modernism' in Western literature — and the New Critical and, more recently, structuralist hermeneutics it has given rise to — is grounded in a strategy that spatializes the temporal process of existence . . . It is no accident that the autotelic and inclusive circle, that is the circle as image or Icon, is the essential symbol of high Modernism . . . and of the New Criticisim and Structuralism" (Spanos 116). Spanos proposes a reading that substitutes a postmodern-Heideggerian hermeneutic circle for the modernist circle as image. For lyric as the paradigm of modernist writing see Riddel 1978: "the theory of the lyric is indeed the model for modern poetry, because it is a theory that undoes its own closure and therefore all the spatial metaphors which reify its 'form' " (466), and "after de Man and Derrida, it is probably wise to use the terms modern and postmodern with caution, if not to abandon them altogether" (470).

3   This suggests that psychoanalysis may be seen as at one level antivisualist (contra Stephen Heath) and at the same time or at another level phallomorphic, that is, tied precisely to an order of ideal visibility which (contra Jacqueline Rose) it simultaneously unveils and upholds.

4   In another essay, Lacan connects the body *imago* or "imaginary Anatomy" with the "laws of *gestalt*," which he says are "exhibited" in the forms taken by hysterical symptoms. "The fact that the penis is dominant in the shaping of the body-image / . . . may shock the sworn champions of the autonomy of female sexuality," he writes, "but such dominance is a fact and one moreover which cannot be put down to cultural influences alone" (1953: 13). The "relation of the subject to his own body" is mediated by his identification with this penis-shaped *gestalt* or *imago*, which Lacan here goes on to associate with both the mirroring function of the cerebral cortex and "Aristotle's idea of *Morphe*," an idea "discarded by experimental science" which "we psychoanalysts are here reintroducing" in terms of the theory of narcissism. Additional comments on the relation between the Imaginary, the Symbolic, and the Real

are scattered throughout Lacan's writings; see especially "The Mirror Stage as Formative of the Function of the 'I' " and "Aggressivity in Psychoanalysis" in *Ecrits*.

5 The fact that *The Gift* identifies the primal scene in part with the wounding of the father is an interesting turn, but one whose implications are unclear to me.

6 Zeitlin reads Helen as an expression of Greek ambivalence toward both art and the feminine.

7 Susan Stanford Friedman and Adalaide Morris also emphasize the feminine character of the Image as it was reinterpreted by "H.D."

8 Jacqueline Rose argues that Lacan's later writing exhibits a shift of emphasis from the early notion of the ego as Gestalt to a later one which retheorizes the ego/image as a structure of linguistic insistence or repeated difference — thus hardly distinguishable from the Symbolic (Rose 1981).

WORKS CITED

Benstock, Shari. *Women of the Left Bank: Paris 1900–1940*. Austin: U of Texas P, 1986.

Boundary 2 (Winter 1976, Fall 1979, and Spring/Fall 1984).

Bové, Paul. *Destructive Poetics: Heidegger and Modern American Poetry*. New York: Columbia UP, 1980.

Buck, Claire. "Freud and H.D. — Bisexuality and a Feminine Discourse." *M/F* 8 (1983): 53–66.

Carroll, David. *The Subject in Question*. Chicago: U of Chicago P, 1982.

Copjec, Joan. "*Flavit et dissipati sunt.*" *October* 18 (Fall 1981): 20–40.

Coffman, Stanley K., Jr. *Imagism: A Chapter for the History of Modern Poetry*. Norman: U of Oklahoma P, 1951.

Derrida, Jacques. *Spurs: Nietzsche's Styles*. Trans. Barbara Harlow. Chicago: U of Chicago P, 1978b.

Derrida, Jacques. "Freud and the Scene of Writing." In *Writing and Difference*, trans. Alan Bass. Chicago: U of Chicago P, 1978a.

Derrida, Jacques. *Of Grammatology*. Trans. Gayatri Chakravorty Spivak. Baltimore: Johns Hopkins UP, 1974.

DuPlessis, Rachel Blau. *H.D.: The Career of That Struggle*. Bloomington: Indiana UP, 1986.

DuPlessis, Rachel Blau, and Susan Stanford Friedman. " 'Woman is Perfect': H.D.'s Debate with Freud." *Feminist Studies* 7 (Fall 1981): 417–30.

Friedman, Susan Stanford. *Psyche Reborn: The Emergence of H.D.* Bloomington: Indiana UP, 1981.

Friedman, Susan Stanford. "Hilda Doolittle (H.D.)." In *Dictionary of Literary Biography*, Vol. 45: *American Poets 1880–1945*, ed. Peter Quartermain. Detroit: Gale Research, 1986.

Gallop, Jane. "*Quand nos lèvres s'ecrivent*: Irigaray's Body Politic." *Romanic Review* 74 (1983): 77–83.

Gilbert, Sandra, and Susan Gubar. *No Man's Land,* Vol. 1: *The Place of the Woman Writer in the Twentieth Century.* New Haven: Yale UP, 1988.

Guest, Barbara. *Herself Defined: The Poet H.D. and Her World.* New York: Doubleday, 1984.

H.D. "The Cinema and the Classics, Part III." *Close Up* 1.5 (November 1927): 19–20.

H.D. *Helen in Egypt.* New York: New Directions, 1961.

H.D. *Tribute to Freud and Advent.* New York: New Directions, 1956, 1974.

H.D. *The Gift.* New York: New Directions, 1982.

Heath, Stephen. "Difference." *Screen* 19.3 (Fall 1978): 51–112.

Homans, Margaret. "Reconstructing the Feminine." *Women's Review of Books* 3.6 (March 1986): 12–13.

Irigaray, Luce. *Speculum of the Other Woman.* Trans. Gillian C. Gill. Ithaca: Cornell UP, 1985a.

Irigaray, Luce. *This Sex Which Is Not One.* Trans. Catherine Porter with Carolyn Burke. Ithaca: Cornell UP, 1985b.

Kenner, Hugh. *The Poetry of Ezra Pound.* London: Faber and Faber, 1951.

Lacan, Jacques. *Ecrits.* Trans. Alan Sheridan. New York: W. W. Norton, 1977.

Lacan, Jacques, and Wladimir Granoff. "Fetishism: The Symbolic, the Imaginary and the Real." In Sandor Lorand and Michael Balint, eds., *Perversion: Psychodynamics and Therapy.* New York: Random House, 1956.

Lacan, Jacques. "Reflections on the Ego." *International Journal of Psychoanalysis* 34 (1953): 11–17.

Mitchell, W. J. T. *Iconology: Image, Text, Ideology.* Chicago: U of Chicago P, 1986.

Pound, Ezra. *The ABC of Reading.* New York: New Directions, 1934.

Pound, Ezra. Translation of Ernest Fenollosa's *The Chinese Written Character as a Medium for Poetry.* London: Stanley Nott, 1936.

Riddel, Joseph. "A Somewhat Polemical Introduction: The Elliptical Poem." *Genre* 11 (Winter 1978): 459–77.

Riddel, Joseph. "H.D.'s Scene of Writing—Poetry As (And) Analysis." *Studies in the Literary Imagination* 12.1 (Spring 1979): 41–59.

Riddel, Joseph. " 'Neo-Nietzschean Clatter'—Speculation and/on Pound's Poetic Image." In Ian P. Bell, ed., *Ezra Pound: Tactics for Reading,* 187–220. London: Vision and Barnes and Nobel, 1982.

Rose, Jacqueline. "Introduction." In Rose & Juliet Mitchell, eds., *Feminine Sexuality: Jacques Lacan and the Ecole Freudienne.* New York: W. W. Norton, 1980.

Rose, Jacqueline. "The Imaginary." In Colin McCabe, ed., *The Talking Cure.* London: Routledge and Kegan Paul, 1981.

Schwartz, Sanford. *The Matrix of Modernism.* Chicago: U of Chicago P, 1985.

Smith, Paul. *Pound Revised.* London and Canberra: Croom Helm, 1983.

Spanos, William V. "Heidegger, Kierkegaard and the Hermeneutic Circle: Towards a Postmodern Theory of Interpretation as Dis-closure." *Boundary 2* (Winter 1977): 115–48.

Zeitlin, Froma I. "Travesties of Gender and Genre in Aristophanes' *Thesmophoriazousae.*" *Critical Inquiry* 8.2 (Winter 1981): 301–27.

Selected Bibliography

BOOKS BY H.D.: PUBLISHED

Sea Garden. London: Constable, 1916.

Choruses from Iphigeneia in Aulis. London: Egoist Press, 1916.

The Tribute and Circe: Two Poems. Cleveland: Clerk's Private Press, 1917.

Choruses from the Iphigeneia in Aulis and the Hippolytus of Euripides. London: Egoist Press, 1919.

Hymen. London: Egoist Press, 1921.

Heliodora and Other Poems. Boston: Houghton Mifflin, 1924.

Collected Poems of H.D. New York: Boni & Liveright, 1925.

H.D. Ed. Hughes Mearns. New York: Simon & Schuster, 1926.

Palimpsest. Paris: Contact Editions, 1926.

Hippolytus Temporizes. Boston: Houghton Mifflin, 1927.

Hedylus. Boston: Houghton Mifflin, 1928.

Narthex. In *The Second American Caravan,* ed. Alfred Kreymborg, Lewis Mumford, and Paul Rosenfeld, 225–84. New York: Macaulay, 1928.

Borderline—A Pool Film with Paul Robeson. London: Mercury, 1930.

Red Roses for Bronze. London: Chatto & Windus, 1931.

Kora and Ka [*Kora and Ka*; *Mira-Mare*]. Dijon: Darantièrc, 1934.

The Usual Star [*The Usual Star*; "Two Americans"]. Dijon: Darantière, 1934.

Nights, by John Helforth. Dijon: Darantière, 1935.

The Hedgehog. London: Brendin, 1936.

Euripides' Ion. London: Chatto & Windus, 1937.

What Do I Love. London: Brendin, 1944.

The Walls Do Not Fall. London: Oxford UP, 1944.

Tribute to the Angels. London: Oxford UP, 1945.

Writing on the Wall. Life and Letters Today 45 (April–June 1945): 67, 137–54; 46 (July–September 1945): 72, 136–51; 48 (January–March 1946): 33–118.

The Flowering of the Rod. London: Oxford UP, 1946.

By Avon River. New York: Macmillan, 1949.

For their generous help, I am grateful to Louis H. Silverstein, Rachel Blau DuPlessis, Michael King, Mary Mathis, Eileen Gregory, and Thomas Jackson—S. S. F.

Tribute to Freud [*Writing on the Wall*]. New York: Pantheon, 1956.

Selected Poems of H.D. New York: Grove Press, 1957.

Bid Me To Live (A Madrigal). New York: Grove Press, 1960.

Helen in Egypt. New York: Grove Press, 1961.

Palimpsest. Rev. ed. Carbondale: Southern Illinois UP, 1968.

Two Poems by H.D. ["Star of Day"; "Wooden Animal"]. Berkeley: ARIF Press, 1971.

Hermetic Definitions [pirated edition]. West Newberry, MA: Frontier Press, 1971.

Hermetic Definition. New York: New Directions, 1972.

Temple of the Sun. Berkeley: ARIF Press, 1972.

Trilogy [*The Walls Do Not Fall*; *Tribute to the Angels*; *The Flowering of the Rod*]. New York: New Directions, 1973.

Tribute to Freud. Boston: David R. Godine, 1974.

Advent. In *Tribute to Freud*. Boston: David R. Godine, 1974.

The Poet & The Dancer. San Francisco: Five Trees Press, 1975.

The Mystery [Chapters 3, 14–19]. In *Images of H.D.*, by Eric W. White. London: Enitharmon Press, 1976.

End to Torment: A Memoir of Ezra Pound. With *Hilda's Book*, by Ezra Pound. Ed. Norman Holmes Pearson and Michael King. New York: New Directions, 1979.

Hedylus. Rev. ed. Redding Ridge, CT: Black Swan Books, 1980.

HERmione [*HER*]. New York: New Directions, 1981.

The Gift [abridged]. New York: New Directions, 1982. Unabridged: Chapter 1 ("The Dark Room"), *Montemora* 8 (1981): 57–72; Chapter 2 ("The Fortune Teller"), *Iowa Review* 16 (Fall 1986): 14–41; Chapter 3 ("The Dream"), *Contemporary Literature* 10 (Winter 1969): 605–26.

Notes on Thought and Vision & The Wise Sappho. San Francisco: City Lights Books, 1982.

Vale Ave. In *New Directions in Prose and Poetry 44*, ed. James Laughlin et al., 18–68. New York: New Directions, 1982.

The Collected Poems, 1912–1944. Ed. Louis L. Martz. New York: New Directions, 1983.

Bid Me To Live (A Madrigal). Redding Ridge, CT: Black Swan Books, 1983.

Priest and A Dead Priestess Speaks. Port Townsend, WA: Copper Canyon, 1983.

Hippolytus Temporizes. Redding Ridge, CT: Black Swan Books, 1985.

Ion: A Play after Euripides. Redding Ridge, CT: Black Swan Books, 1986.

Nights. New York: New Directions, 1986.

Paint It To-Day [Chapters 1–4]. *Contemporary Literature* 27 (Winter 1986): 444–74.

H.D. by Delia Alton. *Iowa Review* 16 (Fall 1986): 174–221.

Borderline—A Pool Film with Paul Robeson. *Sagetrieb* 7 (Fall 1987): 29–50.

"Two Americans." In *New Directions 51*, ed. James Laughlin, 58–150. New York: New Directions, 1987.

Selected Poems. Ed. Louis L. Martz. New York: New Directions, 1988.

The Hedgehog. New York: New Directions, 1988.

Within the Walls. Iowa City: Windhover Press, 1990.

By Avon River. Redding Ridge, CT: Black Swan Books, 1990.

H.D.'S UNPUBLISHED WORK[1]

(List does not include miscellaneous short manuscripts; portions of some have been published.)

NOVELS

Paint It To-Day (1921)
Asphodel (1921–22)
Pilate's Wife (1924, 1929, 1934)
Majic Ring (1943–44)
The Sword Went Out to Sea (Synthesis of a Dream) (1946–47)
White Rose and the Red (1947?–48)
The Mystery (1949, 1951)
Magic Mirror (1955 or 1956?)

MEMOIRS/JOURNALS

"Paris Diary" (1912)
The Gift. Unabridged, with Notes (1941, 1943, 1944)
"Dante Notebooks" (1948)
Autobiographical Notes (1949?)
"Zinzendorf Notebooks" (1951)
"*Helen in Egypt* Notebooks" (late 1940s–early 1950s?)
Compassionate Friendship (1955)
Hirslanden Notebooks, I–IV (1957–59)
Thorn Thicket (1960)
"Lionel Durand Diary" (1960–61)

SHORT STORIES

Four Stories: "Uncle David," "The Pretend Child," and "Monsieur's Princess,"
    by Edith Gray; "The Suffragette," by J. Beran (1907–13?)
Seven Stories: "Hesperia" (1923), "AEgina" (1932), "The Moment" (1926),
    "Jubilee" (1935), "The Last Time" (1936), "The Death of Martin Presser" (?),
    "The Guardians" (1945–46). Also titled *The Seven* and *The Moment* (6 or
    7 stories)

ESSAYS

Notes on Euripides, Pausanius, and Greek Lyric Poets (1916?–20)
"Wing-Beat" (1927/28?)

MANUSCRIPT COLLECTIONS

Manuscripts for H.D.'s unpublished and some published works are in the Collection of American Literature, Beinecke Rare Book and Manuscript Library, Yale

---

1. Unpublished works by H.D. that are being prepared for publication include: *Asphodel*, ed. Robert Spoo, for Duke University Press (1991); *Paint It To-Day*, ed. Cassandra Laity; and *Notes on Euripides, Pausanius, and Greek Lyric Poets*, ed. Robert Babcock.

University. Most of H.D.'s correspondence is at Beinecke, but letters can also be found at the Bibliothèque Jacques Doucet (Sorbonne); the Berg Collection (New York Public Library); Firestone Library (Princeton University); Houghton Library (Harvard University); Lilly Library (Indiana University); Lockwood Library (State University of New York–Buffalo); Rosenbach Collection, Rosenbach Foundation in Philadelphia; Huntington Library (Los Angeles); and the libraries of the University of Texas–Austin, University of Southern Illinois, University of Arkansas, UCLA, and Bryn Mawr College. Beinecke also holds an index file of the books H.D. owned that she left to Norman Holmes Pearson, many volumes of which are at Beinecke. Perdita Schaffner has established a library, open to scholars and students, of the books Bryher collected at Villa Kenwin. This collection includes many of H.D.'s books (see Virginia Smyers, "H.D.'s Books in the Bryher Library." *H.D. Newsletter* 1 [Winter 1987]: 18–25; 2 [Spring 1988]: 25–26).

LETTERS FROM H.D. (PUBLISHED)[2]

Dobson, Silvia. " 'Shock Knit with Terror': Living through World War II." *Iowa Review* 16 (Fall 1986): 232–45.

H.D. to Margaret Anderson (1929?). Published as " 'H.D.,' Hilda Aldington." *Little Review* 12 (May 1929): 38–40. Rpt. in *Little Review Anthology*, ed. Margaret Anderson, 364–66. New York: Hermitage House, 1953.

H.D. to Richard Johns, March 14, 1932. In *A Return to Pagany: The History, Correspondences, and Selections from a Little Magazine, 1929–1932*, ed. Stephen Halpert, with Richard Johns, 444. Boston: Beacon Press, 1969.

H.D. to Norman Holmes Pearson, December 12, 1937. Published as "A Note on Poetry" in *The Oxford Anthology of American Literature*, ed. William Rose Benét and Norman Holmes Pearson, 1287–88. New York: Oxford UP, 1938. Rpt. in *Agenda* 25 (Autumn/Winter 1987–1988): 64–70.

Hollenberg, Donna Krolik, ed. "Art and Ardor in World War One: Selected Letters from H.D. to John Cournos." *Iowa Review* 16 (Fall 1986): 126–55.

Pondrom, Cyrena N., ed. "Selected Letters from H.D. to F. S. Flint: A Commentary on the Imagist Period." *Contemporary Literature* 10 (Autumn 1969): 557–86.

Tinker, Carol T., ed. "A Friendship Traced: H.D. Letters to Silvia Dobson." *Conjunctions* 2 (Spring/Summer 1982): 115–57.

Zilboorg, Caroline, ed. "Across the Abyss: The H.D.–Adrienne Monnier Correspondence." *Sagetrieb* (1990).

RECORDINGS OF H.D.

H.D. Readings from *Helen in Egypt*. Watershed Tapes, P.O. Box 50145, Washington, D.C. 20004.

---

2. Editions of correspondence in preparation include: H.D.–Bryher, 1933–34 (Susan Stanford Friedman); H.D.–Norman Holmes Pearson (Donna Krolik Hollenberg and Louis Silverstein); H.D.–Richard Aldington (Caroline Zilboorg); H.D. to Silvia Dobson (Diana Collecott).

BIBLIOGRAPHIES ON H.D.

Boughn, Michael. "The Bibliographic Record of H.D.'s Contributions to Periodicals." *Sagetrieb* 6 (Fall 1987): 171–94.

Boughn, Michael. "The Bibliographic Record of Reviews of H.D.'s Works." *H.D. Newsletter* 2 (Spring 1988): 27–47.

Bryer, Jackson R., and Pamela Roblyer. "H.D.: A Preliminary Checklist." *Contemporary Literature* 10 (Autumn 1969): 632–75.

Mathis, Mary S. *H.D.: An Annotated Bibliography, 1913–1986.* Boston: Garland, 1991.

Mathis, Mary S., and Michael King. "An Annotated Bibliography of Works about H.D.: 1969–1985." In *H.D.: Woman and Poet*, ed. Michael King, 393–512. Orono, ME: National Poetry Foundation, 1986.

MEMOIRS, POEMS, SKETCHES, AND ROMANS À CLEF
FEATURING OR FOR H.D.

(List includes only texts by people who knew H.D. personally; question marks indicate uncertainty of attribution.)

Aldington, Richard. *Reverie: A Little Book of Poems for H.D.* Cleveland: Clerk's Press, 1917.

Aldington, Richard. *Images Old and New.* London: Egoist, 1919.

Aldington, Richard. *Death of a Hero, A Novel.* 1929. London: Hogarth, 1984.

Aldington, Richard. *Life for Life's Sake: A Book of Reminiscences.* 1941. London: Cassell, 1968.

Bryher, Winifred. *Arrow Music.* London, 1922.

Bryher, Winifred. *Two Selves.* Paris: Contact, 1923.

Bryher, Winifred. *West.* London: Jonathan Cape, 1925.

Bryher, Winifred. *The Heart to Artemis — A Writer's Memoirs.* New York: Harcourt, Brace & World, 1962.

Bryher, Winifred. *The Days of Mars: A Memoir, 1940–1946.* New York: Harcourt Brace Jovanovich, 1972.

Capper, Jessie. *Severed Faces* (193?). No publication information.

Collins, H. P. *H.D.* (196?). Manuscript at Beinecke Library, Yale University.

Cournos, John. *Miranda Masters.* London: Knopf, 1926.

Cournos, John. *Autobiography.* New York: Putnam, 1935.

Dobson, Silvia. "A Friendship Traced: Letters to Silvia Dobson and a Poem." Ed. Carol Tinker. *Conjunctions* 2 (Spring/Summer 1982): 115–57.

Dobson, Silvia. " 'Shock Knit with Terror': Living through World War II." *Iowa Review* 16 (Fall 1986): 232–45.

Dobson, Silvia. "Woof and Heave and Surge and Wave and Flow." In King 37–48 (*see under* Books on H.D.).

Dobson, Silvia. "Cloud of Memories: Books H.D. Shared with Me, 1934–1960." *H.D. Newsletter* 1 (Winter 1987): 26–41.

Dobson, Silvia. "For H.D." *Agenda* 25 (Autumn/Winter 1987–88): 125.

Dobson, Silvia. "Remembering H.D." *Agenda* 25 (Autumn/Winter 1987–88): 126–44.

Duncan, Robert. "After Reading *Barely and Widely*." *The Opening of the Field* 88–92. New York: Grove Press, 1960.

Duncan, Robert. "A Sequence of Poems for H.D.'s Birthday, September 10, 1959. Finishd [*sic*] October 24, 1959"; "Two Presentations"; "After Reading H.D.'s *H*ermetic *D*efinitions"; and "Doves." *Roots and Branches* 10–16, 73–76, 81–84, 86–88. New York: Charles Scribner's Sons, 1964.

Duncan, Robert. "Achilles' Song." *Ground Work: Before the War* 3–5. New York: New Directions, 1984.

Ellis, Havelock. *The Fountain of Life: Being the Impressions and Comments* 355–61. Boston: Houghton Mifflin, 1930.

Gregg, Frances Josepha. "La Mendiante" (?). *Forum* 46 (December 1911): 681–83.

Gregg, Frances Josepha. "Dreams" (?). *Forum* 48 (October 1912): 390.

Gregg, Frances Josepha. "To H.D." and "Pageant" (?). *Poetry* (October 1914– March 1915): 165–66.

Gregg, Frances Josepha. "Quest" (?), "Hermaphroditus" (?), and "Iris" (?). *Others* 1 (November 1915): 75–77.

Lawrence, D. H. *Aaron's Rod*. London: Heinemann, 1922.

Lawrence, D. H. *Kangaroo*. London: Heinemann, 1923.

Lawrence, D. H. *The Man Who Died*. New York: Knopf, 1931.

McAlmon, Robert. *Some Have Their Moments* (1936?). Manuscript at Beinecke Library, Yale University.

Macpherson, Kenneth. *One*. Manuscript at Beinecke Library, Yale University.

Macpherson, Kenneth. *Poolreflection*. Territet, Switzerland: Pool, 1927.

Patmore, Brigit. *This Impassioned Onlooker*. London: Robert Holden, 1926.

Patmore, Brigit. *No Tomorrow*. London: Century, 1929.

Patmore, Brigit. *My Friends When Young*. London: Heinemann, 1968.

Pearson, Norman Holmes. Notes for a Biography. File of notes Pearson kept from the late 1940s to the 1970s. Beinecke Library, Yale University.

Pearson, Norman Holmes. "Norman Holmes Pearson on H.D.: An Interview." Conducted by L. S. Dembo. *Contemporary Literature* 10 (Autumn 1969): 435–46.

Pound, Ezra. (?) "De Aegypto," "Au Jardin," "Ortus," "Dance Figure," "Tempora." *Personae*, in *The Collected Shorter Poems*. 1926; New York: New Directions, 1931.

Pound, Ezra. Cantos LXXVI, LXXXI (?), LXXXIII, LXXIX (?). *The Pisan Cantos* (30, 98, 108, 62–70), in *The Cantos (1–95)*. New York: New Directions, 1956.

Pound, Ezra. *Hilda's Book*. In *End to Torment* 67–84. New York: New Directions, 1979.

Rachewiltz, Mary De. "For H.D." In King 35–36 (*see under* Books on H.D.).

Schaffner, Perdita. "Merano, 1962." *Paideuma* 4 (Fall/Winter 1975): 513–18.

Schaffner, Perdita. "Sketch of H.D.: The Egyptian Cat." *Hedylus* 142–46. Redding Ridge, CT: Black Swan Books, 1980. Also in this volume.

Schaffner, Perdita. "Pandora's Box." *HERmione* vii–xi. New York: New Directions, 1981.

Schaffner, Perdita. "Unless a Bomb Falls . . ." *The Gift* ix–xv. New York: New Directions, 1982.

Schaffner, Perdita. "A Profound Animal." *Bid Me to Live (A Madrigal)* 185–94. Redding Ridge, CT: Black Swan Books, 1983.

Schaffner, Perdita. "Keeper of the Flame." In King 27–36 (*see under* Books on H.D.).

Schaffner, Perdita. Introduction. *Nights* ix–xvi. New York: New Directions, 1986.

Schaffner, Perdita. "Running." *Iowa Review* 16 (Fall 1986): 7–13.

Schaffner, Perdita. Introduction. *The Hedgehog* vii–xiii. New York: New Directions, 1988.

Schaffner, Perdita. "They Lived to Write." *New Directions for Women* 18 (July/August 1989): 18–19.

White, Eric Walter. *Images of H.D./From the Mystery*. London: Enitharmon Press, 1976.

Wilkinson, Louis. *The Buffoon*. New York: Knopf, 1916.

Williams, William Carlos. *The Autobiography* 67–70 and passim. New York: New Directions, 1951.

Williams, William Carlos. "Letter to N. H. P. concerning Hilda Doolittle and Her Mother and Father (11 July 1955)." *William Carlos Williams Newsletter* 2 (1976): 2–3.

Wolle, Francis. *A Moravian Heritage* 55–60. Boulder, CO: Empire Reproduction & Printing Co., 1972.

BOOKS ON H.D.

(List includes books on or substantially on H.D. that are published or in press. It does not include the many books on H.D. under contract and in progress.)[3]

Bloom, Harold, ed. *Modern Critical Views: H.D.* New York: Chelsea House, 1989.

Burnett, Gary. *H.D. between Image and Epic: The Mysteries of Her Poetics*. Ann Arbor: UMI Research P, 1990.

DuPlessis, Rachel Blau. *H.D.: The Career of That Struggle*. Brighton: Harvester, 1986.

Friedman, Susan Stanford. *Psyche Reborn: The Emergence of H.D.* Bloomington: Indiana UP, 1981.

Friedman, Susan Stanford. *Penelope's Web: Gender, Modernity, H.D.'s Fiction*. New York: Cambridge UP, 1990.

Friedman, Susan Stanford, and Rachel Blau DuPlessis, eds. *Signets: Reading H.D.* Madison: U of Wisconsin P, 1990.

Fritz, Angela DiPace. *Thought and Vision: A Critical Reading of H.D.'s Poetry*. Washington, DC: Catholic UP, 1988.

---

3. Books under contract nearing completion (as of November 1989) include works by Claire Buck, Dianne Chisolm, Diana Collecott, Robert Duncan (a University of California-Berkeley Press edition of *The H.D. Book*), Cassandra Laity, Rose Lucas, and Adalaide Morris. Many others are in progress, including studies by Raffaella Baccolini, Marina Camboni, Eileen Gregory, Elizabeth A. Hirsh, and Donna Krolik Hollenberg.

Guest, Barbara. *Herself Defined: The Poet H.D. and Her World*. Garden City, NY: Doubleday, 1984.

Holland, Norman. *Poems in Persons* 4–163. New York: Norton, 1973.

King, Michael, ed. *H.D.: Woman and Poet*. Orono, ME: National Poetry Foundation, 1986.

Kloepfer, Deborah Kelly. *The Unspeakable Mother: Forbidden Discourse in Jean Rhys and H.D.* Ithaca: Cornell UP, 1989.

Link, Franz H. *Zwei amerikanische Dichterinnen: Emily Dickinson und Hilda Doolittle*. Berlin: Duncker & Humboldt, 1977.

Mathis, Mary S. *H.D.: An Annotated Bibliography, 1913–1986*. Boston: Garland, 1991.

Quinn, Vincent. *Hilda Doolittle*. New York: Twayne, 1967.

Robinson, Janice S. *H.D.: The Life and Work of an American Poet*. Boston: Houghton Mifflin, 1982.

Swann, Thomas Burnett. *The Classical World of H.D.* Lincoln: U of Nebraska P, 1962.

SPECIAL JOURNAL ISSUES ON H.D.

Agenda 25 (Autumn/Winter 1987–88). Ed. Diana Collecott.

Contemporary Literature 10 (Autumn 1969). Ed. L. S. Dembo.

Contemporary Literature 27 (Winter 1986). Ed. Susan Stanford Friedman and Rachel Blau DuPlessis.

H.D. Newsletter (1987–). Ed. Eileen Gregory.

(HOW)ever 3 (October 1986). Ed. Kathleen Fraser.

Iowa Review 16 (1986). Ed. Adalaide Morris.

Poesis 6 (Fall 1985). Ed. Thomas H. Jackson.

Sagetrieb 6 (Fall 1987). Ed. Rachel Blau DuPlessis.

San Jose Studies 13 (Fall 1987). Consulting Editor: Alan Soldofsky.

SELECTED ARTICLES AND BOOK CHAPTERS ON H.D.

(List focuses on criticism published after 1969; for additional criticism and reviews published prior to 1969, see Jackson R. Bryer and Pamela Roblyer, "H.D.: A Preliminary Checklist" (*Contemporary Literature* 10 [Autumn 1969]: 632–75). Articles in Michael King's *H.D.: Woman and Poet* and special journal issues on H.D. are included; book reviews are not included.)

Arthur, Marilyn. "Psycho-Mythology: The Case of H.D." *Bucknell Review* 28 (1983): 65–79.

Baccolini, Raffaella. "Pound's Tribute to H.D., 1961." *Contemporary Literature* 27 (Winter 1986): 435–39.

Baccolini, Raffaella. "*Hermetic Definition* di H(ilda) D(oolittle): La Tradizione del *Kunstlerroman*, Creazione e Pro-Creazione." In *Ritratto dell'Artista come Donna: Saggi sull'Avanguardia del Novecento*, ed. Lilli M. Crisafulli Jones and Vita Fortunati, 19–42. Urbino: Quattro Venti, 1988.

Beck, Joyce Lorraine. "Dea, Awakening: A Reading of H.D.'s *Trilogy*." *San Jose Studies* 8 (Spring 1982): 59–70.

Benstock, Shari. *Women of the Left Bank, Paris, 1900–1940* 311–56. Austin: U of Texas P, 1986.

Bergman, David. "The Economics of Influence: Gift Giving in H.D. and Robert Duncan." *H.D. Newsletter* 2 (Spring 1988): 11–16.

Bernikow, Louise. *Among Women* 155–92. New York: Harper & Row, 1980.

Boone, Bruce. "H.D.'s Writing: Herself a Ghost." *Sagetrieb* 6 (Fall 1987): 17–20.

Boughn, Michael. "Elements of the Sounding: H.D. and the Origins of Modernist Poetics." *Sagetrieb* 6 (Fall 1987): 101–22.

Brown, Chris. "A Filmography for H.D." *H.D. Newsletter* 2 (Spring 1988): 19–24.

Bruzzi, Zara. " 'The Fiery Moment': H.D. and the Eleusinian Landscape of English Modernism." *Agenda* 25 (Autumn/Winter 1987–88): 97–112.

Bryer, Jackson R. "H.D.: A Note on Her Critical Reputation." *Contemporary Literature* 10 (Autumn 1969): 627–31.

Buck, Claire. "Freud and H.D. — Bisexuality and a Feminine Discourse." *M/F* 8 (1983): 53–65.

Burnett, Gary. "A Poetics Out of War: H.D.'s Responses to the First World War." *Agenda* 25 (Autumn/Winter 1987–88): 54–63.

Burnett, Gary. "H.D. and Lawrence: Two Allusions." *H.D. Newsletter* 1 (Spring 1987): 32–34.

Bush, Douglas. *Mythology and the Romantic Tradition in English Poetry* 497–506. Cambridge: Harvard UP, 1937.

Camboni, Marina. "H.D.'s *Trilogy*, or the Secret Language of Change." *Letteratura d'America* 6 (Spring 1985): 87–106.

Campbell, Bruce. "H.D.'s 'Hermetic Definition' and the Order of Writing." *American Poetry* 5 (Spring 1988): 24–31.

Carruth, Hayden. "Poetry Chronicle." *Hudson Review* 27 (Summer 1974): 52–65.

Chisholm, Dianne. "H.D.'s Auto*hetero*graphy." *Tulsa Studies in Women's Literature* 9 (Spring 1990): 79–106.

Coffman, Stanley K., Jr. *Imagism — A Chapter for the History of Modern Poetry.* Norman: U of Oklahoma P, 1951.

Collecott, Diana. Introduction. *The Gift* vii–xix. London: Virago, 1984.

Collecott, Diana. "Remembering Oneself: The Reputation and Later Poetry of H.D." *Critical Quarterly* 27 (Spring 1985): 7–22.

Collecott, Diana. "Mirror-Images: Images of Mirrors . . . in poems by Sylvia Plath, Adrienne Rich, Denise Levertov and H.D." *Revue Française d'Etudes Américaines* 30 (November 1986): 449–60.

Collecott, Diana. "Images at the Crossroads: The 'H.D. Scrapbook.' " In King 319–68 (*see under* Books on H.D.). Revised version in this volume.

Collecott, Diana. "A Double Matrix: Re-reading H.D." *Iowa Review* 16 (Fall 1986): 93–122.

Collecott, Diana. "Memory and Desire: H.D.'s 'A Note on Poetry.' " *Agenda* 25 (Autumn/Winter 1987–88): 64–70.

Collecott, Diana. "H.D. & Mass Observation." *Line* 13 (Spring 1989).

Collins, H. P. *Modern Poetry* 154–202. London: Jonathan Cape, 1925.

Cutler, Carolyn. "Words and Images in H.D.'s *Tribute to Freud*." *Psychoanalytic Review* 76 (Spring 1989): 107–13.

Crawford, Fred D. "Approaches to Biography: Two Studies of H.D." *Review* 7 (1985): 215–38.

Crawford, Fred D. "Misleading Accounts of Aldington and H.D." *English Literature in Transition, 1880–1920* 30 (1987): 48–67.

Creeley, Robert. "H.D." *Sagetrieb* 6 (Fall 1987): 15–16.

Dahlen, Beverly. "Homonymous: A Meditation on H.D.'s *Trilogy*." *Sagetrieb* 6 (Fall 1987): 9–14.

Davis, Dale. "*Heliodora*'s Greece." In King 143–56 (*see under* Books on H.D.).

Davis, Dale. "The Matter of Myrrhine for Louis." *Iowa Review* 16 (Fall 1987): 165–73.

Dembo, L. S. *Conceptions of Reality in Modern American Poetry* 20–47. Berkeley: U of California P, 1966.

Dembo, L. S. "H.D. *Imagiste* and Her Octopus Intelligence." In King 209–26 (*see under* Books on H.D.).

DeShazer, Mary K. *Inspiring Women: Reimagining the Muse* 67–110 passim. New York: Pergamon P, 1986.

DeShazer, Mary K. " 'A Primary Intensity between Women': H.D. and the Female Muse." In King 157–72 (*see under* Books on H.D.).

Diepeveen, Leonard. "H.D. and the Film Arts." *Journal of Aesthetic Education* 18 (Winter 1984): 57–65.

Doyle, Charles. "Palimpsests of the Word: The Poetry of H.D." *Queen's Quarterly* 92/93 (Summer 1985): 310–21.

Doyle, Charles. *Richard Aldington: A Biography*. Carbondale: Southern Illinois UP, 1989.

Duncan, Robert. "From the Day Book." *Origin* 10 (July 1963): 1–47.

Duncan, Robert. "Beginnings: Chapter 1 of the H.D. Book, Part 1." *Coyote's Journal* 5/6 (1966): 8–31.

Duncan, Robert. "The H.D. Book, Part I: Chapter 2." *Coyote's Journal* 8 (1967): 27–35.

Duncan, Robert. "Rites of Participation." *Caterpillar* 1 (October 1967): 6–34.

Duncan, Robert. "Rites of Participation, II." *Caterpillar* 2 (January 1968): 125–54.

Duncan, Robert. "Two Chapters from *H.D.*" *TriQuarterly* 12 (Spring 1968): 67–98.

Duncan, Robert. "From the H.D. Book: Part 1: Beginnings, Chapter 5: Occult Matters." *Stony Brook Review* 1/2 (Fall 1968): 4–19.

Duncan, Robert. "Nights and Days." *Sumac* 1 (Fall 1968): 101–46.

Duncan, Robert. "The H.D. Book, Part 2, Nights and Days: Chapter 2." *Caterpillar* 6 (January 1969): 16–38.

Duncan, Robert. "The H.D. Book, Part 2, Nights and Days: Chapter 4." *Caterpillar* 7 (April 1969): 27–60.

Duncan, Robert. "The H.D. Book, Part 2, Nights and Days, Chapter 9." *Io* 6 (Summer 1969): 117–40.

Duncan, Robert. "From the H.D. Book, Part II, Chapter 5." *Stony Brook Review* 3/4 (Fall 1969): 336–47.

Duncan, Robert. "Glimpses of the Last Day: From Chapter 2 of the H.D. Book." *Io* 10 (1971): 212–15.

Duncan, Robert. "From the H.D. Book: Part 2, Chapter 5." *Credences* 2 (August 1975): 50–95.

Duncan, Robert. "The H.D. Book: Part 2: Nights and Days, Chapter 9." *Chicago Review* 30 (Winter 1979): 37–88.

Duncan, Robert. "From the H.D. Book." *Montemora* 8 (1981): 79–116.

Duncan, Robert. "From the H.D. Book. Book II, Chapter 10." *Ironwood* 22 (1983): 47–64. Also in this volume.

Duncan, Robert. "The H.D. Book: Outline & Chronology." *Ironwood* 22 (1983): 65.

Duncan, Robert. "The H.D. Book: Book II, Chapter 6." *Southern Review* 21 (January 1985): 26–48.

Duncan, Robert. "H.D.'s Challenge." *Poesis* 6 (1985): 21–35.

Duncan, Robert. "From the H.D. Book, Part II, Chapter 5." *Sagetrieb* 4 (Fall/Winter 1985): 39–86.

Dunn, Margaret M. "Altered Patterns and New Endings: Reflections of Change in Stein's *Three Lives* and H.D.'s *Palimpsest*." *Frontiers* 9 (1987): 54–59.

DuPlessis, Rachel Blau. "Romantic Thralldom in H.D." *Contemporary Literature* 20 (Summer 1979): 178–203. Also in this volume.

DuPlessis, Rachel Blau. "Family, Sexes, Psyche: an essay on H.D. and the muse of the woman writer." *Montemora* 6 (1979): 137–56. In King 69–90 (*see under* Books on H.D.).

DuPlessis, Rachel Blau. "A Note on the State of H.D.'s *The Gift*." *Sulfur* 9 (1984): 178–82.

DuPlessis, Rachel Blau. *Writing Beyond the Ending: Narrative Strategies of Twentieth-Century Women Writers* 66–83, 116–21. Bloomington: Indiana UP, 1985.

DuPlessis, Rachel Blau. "Language Acquisition." *Iowa Review* 16 (Fall 1986): 252–83. Also excerpted in this volume.

DuPlessis, Rachel Blau, and Susan Stanford Friedman. " 'Woman is Perfect': H.D.'s Debate with Freud." *Feminist Studies* 7 (Fall 1981): 417–30.

Eder, Doris. "Freud and H.D." *Book Form; An International Transdisciplinary Quarterly* 1 (1975): 365–69.

Engel, Bernard F. "H.D.: Poems that Matter and Dilutions." *Contemporary Literature* 10 (Autumn 1969): 507–22.

Faery, Rebecca Blevins. " 'Love Is Writing': Eros in H.D.'s *HERmione*." *San Jose Studies* 13 (Fall 1987): 56–65.

Fields, Kenneth. Introduction. *Tribute to Freud* xvii–xliv. Boston: Godine, 1974.

Firchow, Peter E. *American Writers: A Collection of Literary Biographers*. Supplement I, Part I, 253–75. Ed. Leonard Unger. New York: Charles Scribner's, 1979.

Firchow, Peter E. "Rico and Julia: The Hilda Doolittle-D. H. Lawrence Affair Reconsidered." *Journal of Modern Literature* 8 (1980): 51–76.

Flem, Lydia. *La Vie quotidienne de Freud et de ses patients*. Paris: Hachette, 1986.

Freeman, Lucy, and Herbert Stream. *Freud and Women* 117–20. New York: Ungar, 1981.

Freibert, Lucy. "Conflict and Creativity in the World of H.D." *Journal of Women's Studies in Literature* 1 (Summer 1979): 258–71.

Freibert, Lucy. "From Semblance to Selfhood: The Evolution of Woman in H.D.'s Neo-Epic *Helen in Egypt.*" *Arizona Quarterly* 36 (Summer 1980): 165–75.

Friedberg, Anne. "Approaching *Borderline.*" *Millenium Film Journal*, nos. 7/8/9 (Fall–Winter 1980–81): 130–39. Expanded version in King 369–90 (*see under* Books on H.D.).

Friedberg, Anne. "On H.D., Woman, History, Recognition." *Wide Angle: A Film Quarterly of Theory, Criticism, and Practice* 5 (1982): 26–31.

Friedberg, Anne. "The POOL Films: What They Are, Where They Are, How to See Them." *H.D. Newsletter* 1 (Spring 1987): 10–11.

Friedman, Susan Stanford. "Who Buried H.D.? A Poet, Her Critics and Her Place in 'The Literary Tradition.' " *College English* 36 (March 1975): 801–14.

Friedman, Susan Stanford. "Creating a Women's Mythology: H.D.'s *Helen in Egypt.*" *Women's Studies* 5 (1977): 163–97. Also in this volume.

Friedman, Susan Stanford. "Psyche Reborn: Tradition, Re-Vision, and the Goddess as Mother-Symbol in H.D.'s Epic Poetry." *Women's Studies* 6 (1979): 147–60.

Friedman, Susan Stanford. " 'Remembering Shakespeare always, but remembering him differently': H.D.'s *By Avon River.*" *Sagetrieb* 2 (Summer–Fall 1983): 45–70. Shorter version: H.D., *By Avon River* (Redding Ridge, CT: Black Swan Books, 1990).

Friedman, Susan Stanford. " 'I go where I love: An Intertextual Study of H.D. and Adrienne Rich." *Signs* 9 (Winter 1983): 228–46. Expanded version: *Reading Adrienne Rich: Reviews and Re-Vision, 1951–1981.* Ed. Jane Roberta Cooper. Ann Arbor: U of Michigan P, 1984.

Friedman, Susan Stanford. "Palimpsest of Origins in H.D.'s Career." *Poesis* 6 (1985): 56–73.

Friedman, Susan Stanford. Review Essay of H.D.'s *Hedylus. Sagetrieb* 4 (Fall/Winter 1985): 325–34.

Friedman, Susan Stanford. "A Most Luscious Vers Libre Relationship: H.D. and Freud." *Annual of Psychoanalysis* 14, 319–44. Madison, CT: International Universities P, 1986.

Friedman, Susan Stanford. "Gender and Genre Anxiety: Elizabeth Barrett Browning and H.D. as Epic Poets." *Tulsa Studies in Women's Literature* 5 (Fall 1986): 203–29.

Friedman, Susan Stanford. "Emergences and Convergences." *Iowa Review* 16 (Fall 1986): 42–56.

Friedman, Susan Stanford. "Hilda Doolittle (H.D.)." In *Dictionary of Literary Biography*, Vol. 45: *American Poets, 1880–1945*, 1st Ser., ed. Peter Quartermain, 115–49. Detroit: Gale Research, 1986.

Friedman, Susan Stanford. "Against Discipleship: Intimacy and Collaboration in H.D.'s Analysis with Freud." *Literature and Psychology* 33 (1987): 89–108.

Friedman, Susan Stanford. "H.D. Chronology: Composition and Publication of Volumes." *Sagetrieb* 6 (Fall 1987): 51–56. Updated version in this volume.

Friedman, Susan Stanford. "Exile in the American Grain: H.D.'s Diaspora." In

Women's Writing in Exile, ed. Mary Lynn Broe and Angela Ingram, 87–112. Durham: U of North Carolina P, 1989. Shorter version: *Agenda* 25 (Autumn/Winter 1987–88): 27–50.

Friedman, Susan Stanford. "The Writing Cure: Transference and Resistance in a Dialogic Analysis." *H.D. Newsletter* 2 (Winter 1988): 25–35.

Friedman, Susan Stanford. "The Return of the Repressed in Women's Narrative." *Journal of Narrative Technique* 19 (January 1989): 141–56. Expanded version in this volume.

Friedman, Susan Stanford. Editor's Introduction to H.D.'s *Notes on Thought and Vision*; *Borderline*; Reviews of Marianne Moore, Yeats, and *Joan of Arc*; and selected letters to Amy Lowell and Moore. In *The Gender of Modernism*, ed. Bonnie Kime Scott. Bloomington: Indiana UP, 1990.

Friedman, Susan Stanford. "A Portrait of the Artist as a Young Woman: H.D.'s Rescriptions of Joyce, Lawrence, and Pound." In *Writing the Woman Artist*, ed. Suzanne Jones. Philadelphia: U of Pennsylvania P, 1990.

Friedman, Susan Stanford, and Rachel Blau DuPlessis. " 'I had two loves separate': The Sexualities of H.D.'s *HER*." *Montemora* 8 (1981): 3–30. Also in this volume.

Friedman, Susan Stanford, and Rachel Blau DuPlessis. Foreword. *Paint It To-Day* (Chapters I–IV). *Contemporary Literature* 27 (Winter 1986): 440–43.

Gage, John T. *In the Arresting Eye: The Rhetoric of Imagism*. Baton Rouge: Louisiana State UP, 1981.

Gelpi, Albert. Introduction. *Notes on Thought and Vision & The Wise Sappho* 7–16. San Francisco: City Lights Books, 1982.

Gelpi, Albert. "Hilda in Egypt." *Southern Review* 18 (Spring 1982): 233–50.

Gelpi, Albert. "Re-membering the Mother: A Reading of H.D.'s *Trilogy*." In King 173–90 (*see under* Books on H.D.). Also in this volume.

Gelpi, Albert. *A Coherent Splendour: The American Poetic Renaissance, 1910–1950* 253–320. Cambridge: Cambridge UP, 1987.

Gibbons, Kathryn. "The Art of H.D." *Mississippi Quarterly* 15 (Fall 1962): 152–60.

Gilbert, Sandra M. "H.D.? Who Was She?" *Contemporary Literature* 24 (Winter 1983): 496–511.

Gilbert, Sandra M., and Susan Gubar. *No Man's Land: The Place of the Woman Writer in the Twentieth Century*, Vol. III: *Letters from the Front*. New Haven, Yale UP, 1990.

Goheen, Cynthia J. "By Impression Re-Called." *San Jose Studies* 13 (Fall 1987): 47–55.

Gould, Jean. *American Women Poets: Pioneers of Modern Poetry* 151–76. New York: Dodd, Mead, 1980.

Grahn, Judy. *The Highest Apple: Sappho and the Lesbian Poetic Tradition* 49–57, 102–9, 135. San Francisco: Spinsters, Ink, 1985.

Greenwood, E. B. "H.D. and the Problem of Escapism." *Essays in Criticism* 21 (October 1971): 365–76.

Gregory, Eileen. "Rose Cut in Rock: Sappho and H.D.'s *Sea Garden*." *Contemporary Literature* 27 (Winter 1986): 525–52. Also in this volume.

Gregory, Eileen. "Scarlet Experience: H.D.'s *Hymen*." *Sagetrieb* 6 (Fall 1987): 77–100.

Gregory, Eileen. "Ovid and H.D.'s 'Thetis' (*Hymen* Version)." *H.D. Newsletter* 1 (Spring 1987): 29–31.

Gregory, Eileen. "Falling from the White Rock: A Myth of Margins in H.D." *Agenda* 25 (Autumn/Winter 1987–88): 113–23.

Gregory, Eileen. "Virginity and Erotic Liminality: H.D.'s *Hippolytus Temporizes*." *Contemporary Literature* 31 (Summer 1990): 133–60.

Gubar, Susan. "The Echoing Spell of H.D.'s *Trilogy*." *Contemporary Literature* 19 (Spring 1978): 196–218. Also in this volume.

Gubar, Susan. "Sapphistries." *Signs* 10 (Autumn 1984): 43–62.

Guest, Barbara. "The Intimacy of Biography." *Poesis* 6 (1985): 74–83.

Hamilton, R. S. "After Strange Gods: Robert Duncan Reading Ezra Pound and H.D." *Sagetrieb* 4 (Fall/Winter 1985): 225–40.

Hanscombe, Gillian, and Virginia L. Smyers. *Writing for Their Lives: The Modernist Women, 1910–1940* 14–46. London: Women's Press, 1987.

Harmer, J. B. *Victory in Limbo: Imagism, 1908–1917*. London: Secker and Warburg, 1975.

Hatlen, Burton. "Recovering the Human Equation: H.D.'s 'Hermetic Definition.' " *Sagetrieb* 6 (Fall 1987): 141–70.

Healey, Claire. "Hilda Doolittle." In *American Women Writers: A Critical Reference Guide from Colonial Times to the Present*, Vol. 1, ed. Lina Mainiero, 523–26. New York: Frederick Ungar, 1979.

Hirsh, Elizabeth A. " 'New Eyes': H.D., Modernism, and the Psychoanalysis of Seeing." *Literature and Psychology* 32 (1986): 1–10.

Hirsh, Elizabeth A. "Imaginary Images: 'H.D.,' Modernism, and the Psychoanalysis of Seeing." In *Discontented Discourses: Feminism/Textual Intervention/Psychoanalysis*, ed. Richard Feldstein and Marleen S. Barr, 141–59. Champaign-Urbana: U of Illinois P, 1989. Also in this volume.

Holland, Norman N. "H.D. and the 'Blameless Physician.' " *Contemporary Literature* 10 (Autumn 1969): 474–506.

Howdle, Andrew. "Feminine Hermeticism in H.D.'s *Trilogy*." *Studies in Mystical Literature* 4 (January 1984): 26–44.

Hughes, Glenn. *Imagism and the Imagists*. Stanford: Stanford UP, 1931.

Jackson, Brendan. " 'The Fulsomeness of Her Prolixity': Reflections on 'H.D., Imagiste.' " *South Atlantic Quarterly* 83 (Winter 1984): 91–102.

Jaffe, Nora Crow. " 'She herself is the writing': Language and Sexual Identity in H.D." *Literature and Medicine* 4 (Fall 1985): 86–111.

Jones, Alan. "The Writing on the Wall." *Arts Magazine* (October 1988): 21–22.

Jones, Peter. *Imagist Poetry*. London: Penguin, 1972.

Kerblat-Houghton, Jeanne. "*Helen in Egypt*: Variations sur un thème sonore." *G.R.E.S.* 2 (April 1978).

Kerblat-Houghton, Jeanne. "The Rose Loved of Lover or the Heroines in the Poems of the Twenties." *G.R.E.N.A.* (1982): 45–64.

Kerblat-Houghton, Jeanne. "Après la guerre de Troie." *C.A.R.A.* Université de Provence (March 1982): 201–13.

Kerblat-Houghton, Jeanne. " 'Ce que recèlent les mots' dans *The Walls Do Not Fall*." *Revue Française d'Etudes Américaines* 7 (Novembre 1982): 373–81.

Kerblat-Houghton, Jeanne. "But Am I Wrong?: A Study of Interrogation in *End to Torment*." In King 259–78 (*see under* Books on H.D.).

King, Michael. Foreword. *End to Torment* vii–xii. New York: New Directions, 1979.

King, Michael. "Williams, Pound, H.D.: A Modern Triangle." *Library Chronicle of the University of Texas at Austin* 29 (Winter 1984): 11–33.

King-Smyth, Rosie. "The Spell of the Luxor Bee." *San Jose Studies* 13 (Fall 1987): 77–87.

Kloepfer, Deborah Kelly. "Flesh Made Word: Maternal Inscription in H.D." *Sagetrieb* 3 (Spring 1984): 27–48.

Kloepfer, Deborah Kelly. "Mother as Muse and Desire: The Sexual Politics of H.D.'s *Trilogy*." In King 191–208 (*see under* Books on H.D.).

Kloepfer, Deborah Kelly. "Fishing the Murex Up: Sense and Resonance in H.D.'s *Palimpsest*." *Contemporary Literature* 27 (Winter 1986): 553–73. Also in this volume.

Knapp, Peggy A. "Women's Freud(e): H.D.'s *Tribute to Freud* and Gladys Schmitt's *Sonnets for an Analyst*." *Massachusetts Review* 24 (Summer 1983): 338–52.

Kolokithas, Dawn. "The Pursuit of Spirituality in the Poetry of H.D." *San Jose Studies* 13 (Fall 1987): 66–76.

Kunitz, Stanley J. *A Kind of Order, A Kind of Folly: Essays and Conversations* 204–9. Boston: Little, Brown, 1975.

Laity, Cassandra. "H.D.'s Romantic Landscapes: The Sexual Politics of the Garden." *Sagetrieb* 6 (Fall 1987): 57–76. Also in this volume.

Laity, Cassandra. "H.D. and A. C. Swinburne: Decadence and Modernist Women's Writing." *Feminist Studies* 15 (Fall 1989): 461–84.

Larson, Jeanne. "Myth and Glyph in *Helen in Egypt*." *San Jose Studies* 13 (Fall 1987): 88–101.

Levertov, Denise. "H.D.: An Appreciation." *Poetry* 100 (June 1962): 182–86.

Lowell, Amy. *Tendencies in Modern American Poetry* 235–43. New York: Macmillan, 1917.

Lynch, Beverly. "Love, Beyond Men and Women: H.D." In *Lesbian Lives: Biographies of Women from The Ladder*, ed. Barbara Grier and Colletta Reid, 259–72. Baltimore: Diana P, 1976.

McNeil, Helen. Introduction. *Bid Me to Live* vii–xix. London: Virago P, 1984.

McNeil, Helen. Introduction. *HER* v–xi. London: Virago P, 1984.

Mandel, Charlotte. "Garbo/Helen: The Self-Projection of Beauty by H.D." *Women's Studies* 7 (1980): 127–35.

Mandel, Charlotte. "The Redirected Image: Cinematic Dynamics in the Style of H.D. (Hilda Doolittle)." *Literature/Film Quarterly* 11 (1983): 35–45.

Mandel, Charlotte. "Magical Lenses: Poet's Vision beyond the Naked Eye." In King 301–18 (*see under* Books on H.D.).

Mandel, Charlotte. "H.D.'s 'Projector II' and *Chang*, A Film of the Jungle." *H.D. Newsletter* 1 (Winter 1987): 42–45.

Martz, Louis L. Introduction. *Collected Poems, 1912–1944* xi–xxxvi. New York: New Directions, 1983.

Martz, Louis L. Introduction. *Selected Poems* vii–xxv. New York: New Directions, 1988.

Materer, Timothy. "H.D., Serenitas, and Canto CXIII." *Paideuma* 12 (Fall/Winter 1983): 275–80.

Meyers, Jeffrey. "H.D. and D.H." *Hudson Review* 35 (Winter 1982–83): 628–32.

Milicia, Joseph. "*Bid Me to Live*: Within the Storm." In King 279–300 (*see under* Books on H.D.).

Milicia, Joseph. "H.D.'s 'Athenians': Son and Mother in *Hedylus*." *Contemporary Literature* 27 (Winter 1986): 574–94.

Montefiore, Jan. " 'What Words Say': Three Women Poets Reading H.D." *Agenda* 25 (Autumn/Winter 1987–88): 172–90.

Moody, A. D. "H.D., '*Imagiste*': An Elemental Mind." *Agenda* 25 (Autumn/Winter 1987–88): 77–96.

Morley, Hilda. Review of *Collected Poems, 1912–1944. Ironwood* 13 (Spring 1985): 159–75.

Morris, Adalaide. "Reading H.D.'s 'Helios and Athene.' " *Iowa Review* 12 (Spring–Summer 1981): 155–63.

Morris, Adalaide. "The Concept of Projection: H.D.'s Visionary Powers." *Contemporary Literature* 25 (Winter 1984): 411–36. Also in this volume.

Morris, Adalaide. "Autobiography and Prophecy: H.D.'s *The Gift*." In King 227–36 (*see under* Books on H.D.).

Morris, Adalaide. "A Relay of Power and of Peace: H.D. and the Spirit of the Gift." *Contemporary Literature* 27 (Winter 1986): 493–524. Also in this volume.

Morris, Adalaide. "Science and the Mythopoetic Mind: The Case of H.D." In *Chaos and Order: Complex Dynamics in Literature and Society*, ed. N. Katherine Hayles. Chicago: U of Chicago P, 1991.

Morris, Adalaide. "H.D." In *Modern American Women Writers*, ed. Elaine Showalter, A. Walter Litz, and Lea Bacchler. New York: Charles Scribner's Sons, 1991.

Newlin, Margaret. " 'Unhelpful Hymen': Marianne Moore and Hilda Doolittle." *Essays in Criticism* 27 (July 1977): 216–30.

Ogilvie, D. Bruce. "H.D. and Hugh Dowding." *H.D. Newsletter* 1 (Winter 1987): 9–17.

Ostriker, Alicia. "The Thieves of Language: Women Poets and Revisionist Mythmaking." *Signs* 8 (Autumn 1982): 68–90.

Ostriker, Alicia. *Writing like a Woman* 7–41. Ann Arbor: U of Michigan P, 1983.

Ostriker, Alicia. "What Do Women (Poets) Want?: H.D. and Marianne Moore as Poetic Ancestresses." *Contemporary Literature* 27 (Winter 1986): 475–92.

Ostriker, Alicia. "No Rule of Procedure: The Open Poetics of H.D." *Agenda* 25 (Autumn/Winter 1987–88): 145–54. Revised version in this volume.

Pearson, Norman Holmes. Foreword. *Hermetic Definition* v–viii. New York: New Directions, 1972.

Pearson, Norman Holmes. Foreword. *Trilogy* v–xii. New York: New Directions, 1973.

Peck, John. "Passio Perpetuse H.D." *Parnassus* 3 (Spring–Summer 1975): 42–74.

Pondrom, Cyrena N. "H.D. and the Origins of Imagism." *Sagetrieb* 4 (Spring 1985): 73–100. Also in this volume.

Pondrom, Cyrena N. "*Trilogy* and *Four Quartets*: Contrapuntal Visions of Spiritual Quest." *Agenda* 25 (Autumn/Winter 1987–88): 155–65.

Pondrom, Cyrena N. "Marianne Moore and H.D.: Female Community and Poetic Achievement." In *Marianne Moore: Woman and Poet*, ed. Patricia C. Willis, 1–32. Orono, ME: National Poetry Foundation, 1990.

Pratt, William, ed. *The Imagist Poem* 11–39. New York: Dutton, 1963.

Quinn, Vincent. "H.D.'s 'Hermetic Definition': The Poet as Archetypal Mother." *Contemporary Literature* 18 (Winter 1977): 51–61.

Rasula, Jed. "A Renaissance of Women Writers." *Sulfur* 7 (1983): 160–72.

Ratner, Rochelle. *Trying to Understand What It Means to Be a Feminist: Essays on Women Writers* 1–9. New York: Contact II, 1984.

Retallack, Joan. "H.D. H.D." *Parnassus* 12–13 (Spring–Winter 1985): 67–88.

Revell, Peter. *Quest in Modern American Poetry* 171–98. New York: Barnes and Noble, 1981.

Riddel, Joseph N. "H.D. and the Poetics of 'Spiritual Realism.' " *Contemporary Literature* 10 (Autumn 1969): 447–73.

Riddel, Joseph N. "H.D.'s Scene of Writing—Poetry as (and) Analysis." *Studies in the Literary Imagination* 12 (Spring 1979): 41–59.

Robinson, Janice S. "What's in a Box? Psychoanalytic Concept and Literary Technique in H.D." In King 237–58 (*see under* Books on H.D.).

Rode, Judith. "Myrrh: A Study of Persona in H.D.'s *Trilogy*." *Line* 12 (Fall 1988): 63–110.

Roessel, David. "H.D. and Lawrence: Two More Allusions." *H.D. Newsletter* 1 (Winter 1987): 46–50.

Romig, Evelyn M. "An Achievement of H.D. and Theodore Roethke: Psychoanalysis and the Poetics of Teaching." *Literature and Psychology* 28 (1978): 105–11.

Rosenberg, Samuel. *Why Freud Fainted* 62–63, 74–79, 90–93, 175–76, 179. New York: Bobbs-Merrill, 1978.

Rosenmeier, Rosamond. "Doolittle, Hilda (H.D.)." In *Notable American Women: The Modern Period*, ed. Barbara Sicherman et al., 198–201. Cambridge: Harvard UP, 1980.

Satterthwaite, Alfred. "John Cournos and 'H.D.' " *Twentieth-Century Literature* 22 (December 1976): 394–410.

Schoeck, Richard. "Listening to Stones: Reflections on H.D.'s *The Walls Do Not Fall*." *H.D. Newsletter* 2 (Winter 1988): 15–24.

Schweik, Susan. *A Gulf So Deeply Cut: American Women Poets and the Second World War*, chap. 9. Madison: U of Wisconsin P, 1991.

Scupham, Peter. "H.D." *Agenda* 12 (Autumn 1974): 40–44.

Shinck, Annette Kreis. "*We are voyagers, discoverers*": H.D.'s Trilogy *and Modern Religious Poetry*. Heidelberg: Carl Winter Verlag, 1990.

Sievert, Heather Rosario. "H.D.: A Symbolist Perspective." *Comparative Literature Studies* 16 (March 1979): 48–57.

Silverstein, Louis H. "Reveries of a Cataloguer." *Iowa Review* 16 (Fall 1986): 156–64.

Silverstein, Louis H. "The H.D. Papers at Yale University." *H.D. Newsletter* 1 (Spring 1987): 7–9.

Silverstein, Louis H. "Nicknames and Acronyms Used by H.D. and Her Circle." *H.D. Newsletter* 1 (Winter 1987): 4–5.

Silverstein, Louis H. "Planting the Seeds: Selections from the H.D. Chronology." *H.D. Newsletter* 2 (Winter 1988): 4–14.

Silverstein, Louis H. "Herself Delineated: Chronological Highlights of H.D." In this volume.

Smith, Martha Nell. "Not Each in Isolation." *H.D. Newsletter* 2 (Spring 1988): 48–51.

Smith, Paul. *Pound Revised* 110–33. London: Croom Helm, 1983.

Smith, Paul. "H.D.'s Identity." *Women's Studies* 10 (1984): 321–38.

Smith, Paul. "H.D.'s Flaws." *Iowa Review* 16 (Fall 1986): 77–86.

Smith, Penny. "Hilda Doolittle and Frances Gregg." *Powys Review* 6 (1988): 46–51.

Smyers, Virginia. "H.D.'s Books in the Bryher Library." *H.D. Newsletter* 1 (Winter 1987): 18–25.

Spoo, Robert. " 'Authentic Sisters': H.D. and Margaret Cravens." *H.D. Newsletter* 3 (Spring 1989).

Thurley, Geoffrey. *The American Moment: American Poetry in the Mid-Century* 109–25. London: Edward Arnold, 1977.

Travis, S. "A Crack in the Ice: Subjectivity and the Mirror in H.D.'s *HER*." *Sagetrieb* 6 (Fall 1987): 123–40.

Tylee, Claire. *Great War and Women's Consciousness* 224–49. Iowa City: Iowa UP, 1990.

Wagner, Linda Welshimer. "*Helen in Egypt*: A Culmination." *Contemporary Literature* 10 (Autumn 1969): 523–36.

Wagner-Martin, Linda W. "H.D.'s Fiction: Convolutions to Clarity." In *Breaking the Sequence: Women's Experimental Fiction*, ed. Ellen G. Friedman and Miriam Fuchs, 148–60. Princeton: Princeton UP, 1989.

Walker, Cheryl. "H.D. and Time." In *Taking Our Time: Feminist Perspectives on Temporality*, ed. Frieda Forman. New York: Pergamon P, 1988.

Wallace, Emily Mitchell. "Afterword: The House of the Father's Science and the Mother's Art." *William Carlos Williams Newsletter* 2 (1976): 4–5.

Wallace, Emily Mitchell. "Athene's Owl." *Poesis* 6 (1985): 98–123.

Wallace, Emily Mitchell. "Hilda Doolittle at Friends' Central School in 1905." *H.D. Newsletter* 1 (Spring 1987): 17–28.

Walsh, John. Afterword. *Hedylus* 147–56. Redding Ridge, CT: Black Swan Books, 1980.

Walsh, John. Afterword. *Bid Me to Live (A Madrigal)* 195–203. Redding Ridge, CT: Black Swan Books, 1983.

Walsh, John. Afterword. *Hippolytus Temporizes* 139–51. Redding Ridge, CT: Black Swan Books, 1985.

Walsh, John. Afterword. *Ion* 120–30. Redding Ridge, CT: Black Swan Books, 1985.

Walsh, John. "H.D., C. G. Jung & Küsnacht: Fantasia on a Theme." In King 59–68 (*see under* Books on H.D.).

Walsh, John. Afterword. *By Avon River*. Redding Ridge, CT: Black Swan Books, 1990.

Watts, Emily Stipes. *The Poetry of American Women from 1632–1945* 152–58. Austin: U of Texas P, 1977.

Watts, Harold H. *Hound and Quarry* 209–22. London: Routledge and Kegan Paul, 1953.

Weatherhead, A. Kinsley. "Style in H.D.'s Novels." *Contemporary Literature* 10 (Autumn 1969): 537–56.

Zajdel, Melody McCollum. "Hilda Doolittle (H.D.)." In *Dictionary of Literary Biography: American Writers in Paris, 1920–1939*, Vol. 4, ed. Karen Lane Rood, 112–20. Detroit: Gale Research, 1980.

Zajdel, Melody McCollum. " 'I See Her Differently': H.D.'s *Trilogy* as Feminist Response to Masculine Modernism." *Sagetrieb* 5 (Spring 1986): 7–16.

Zajdel, Melody McCollum. "Portrait of the Artist as a Woman: H.D.'s Raymonde Ransome." *Women's Studies* 13 (1986): 127–34.

Zilboorg, Caroline. "H.D. and Richard Aldington: Early Love and the Exclusion of Ezra Pound." *H.D. Newsletter* 3 (Spring 1989): 26–34.

Zilboorg, Caroline. "A New Chapter in the Lives of H.D. and Richard Aldington: Their Relationship with Clement Shorter." *Philological Quarterly* 68 (Spring 1989): 241–62.

Zilboorg, Caroline. "H.D.'s Influence on Richard Aldington." In *Richard Aldington*, ed. Charles Doyle. Victoria: U of Victoria P, 1990.

DISSERTATIONS ON (OR SUBSTANTIALLY ON) H.D.

1959   Kaufman, J. Lee. "Theme and Meaning in the Poetry of H.D." Indiana U.
1961   Swann, Thomas Burnett, Jr. "The Classical World of H.D." U of Florida.
1967   Holland, Joyce M. "H.D.: The Shape of a Career." Brown U.
1972   Milicia, Joseph, Jr. "The Fiction of H.D. (Hilda Doolittle)." Columbia U.
1973   Friedman, Susan Stanford. "Mythology, Psychoanalysis, and the Occult in the Late Poetry of H.D." U of Wisconsin.
       Robinson, Janice Stevenson. "H.D.'s *Helen in Egypt*: A Recollection." U of California–Santa Cruz.
1978   Desy, Peter Michael. "H.D. and the Search for the Absolute." Kent State U.
       Steele, Joy Cogdell. "Time and American Autobiography: Four Twentieth-Century Writers." U of Iowa.
1979   Zajdel, Melody McCollum. "The Development of a Poetic Vision: H.D.'s Growth from Imagist to Mythologist." Michigan State U.
1980   Bock, Layeh Aronson. "The Birth of Modernism: 'Des Imagistes' and the Psychology of William James." Stanford U.
       Cramer, Carmen Kay. "The New Democratic Protagonist: American Novels and Women Main Characters, 1960–1966." Texas Christian U.
       Croweel, Joan T. "A Study of H.D.: Her Life and Work." Dalhousie U.
       Levine-Keating, Helane. "Myth and Archetype from a Female Perspective:

An Exploration of Twentieth-Century North and South American Women Poets." New York U.

1982 DeShazer, Mary K. "The Woman Poet and Her Muse: Sources and Images of Female Creativity in the Poetry of H.D., Louise Bogan, May Sarton, and Adrienne Rich." U of Oregon.

Fritz, Angela DiPace. "The Thematic Development in the Poetry of H.D." Washington State U.

Scoggan, John William. "De(con)structive Poetics: Readings of Hilda Doolittle's *The War Trilogy*." U of British Columbia.

1983 Boles, Joseph David. "Clio in Crisis: The Historiographic Impulse in the Writings of H.D." Rutgers U.

Friedberg, Anne. "Writing about Cinema: *Close Up*, 1927–1933." New York U.

Funt, Karen Lorraine Bryce. "Reading, Psychoanalysis, Dialectics." State U of New York at Buffalo.

Gardner, Frieda. "H.D.'s Palimpsests." U of Minnesota.

King, Rosalie Anne. "Bee, Angels, Myrrh: Studies in H.D.'s *Trilogy*." U of California–Santa Cruz.

Kloepfer, Deborah Kelly. " 'Companions of the Flame': The Relationship between the Mother and Language in Jean Rhys and H.D." State U of New York at Buffalo.

Miller, Marie Celeste. " 'Seeking Similar Fundamentals': The Relationship between Painting and Poetry of American Early Moderns." Emory U.

Schultz, Steven Paul. "The Imagination of H.D.: Hilda Doolittle and 'Hermetic Definition.' " State U of New York at Buffalo.

1984 Combellick, Katherine Ann. "Feminine Forms of Closure: Gilman, Deming and H.D." State U of New York at Binghamton.

Shapiro, Daniel. "The Shape of Poetry 1910–1920." U of Toronto.

Van Gerven, Claudia Blood. " 'But to an Outcast and a Vagabond': Authority and Rhetoric in the Poetry of H.D." U of Colorado–Boulder.

1985 McKay, Belinda Jane. "H.D.: Her Life and Work." Oxford U.

Sievert, Heather Rosario. "H.D.: A Symbolist Perspective." New York U.

1986 Hollenberg, Donna Krolik. "Nursing the Muse: The Childbirth Metaphor in H.D.'s Poetry." Tufts U.

Shikina, Seiji. "The Adaptation of the Haiku Form in the Poetry of the Imagists." U of Southwestern Louisiana.

Wasserman, Rosanne. "Helen of Troy: Her Myth in Modern Poetry." City U of New York.

1987 Dunn, Margaret. " 'The Inevitable Triad': Self and Other in the Fiction and Poetry of H.D." Indiana U.

Kerblat-Houghton, Jeanne. "La création poètique dans l'oeuvre de H.D. (Hilda Doolittle)." U of Paris (Sorbonne nouvelle).

Meggison, Lauren Louise. "Keepers of the Flame: Hermeticism in Yeats, H.D., and Borges." U of California–Irvine.

Phelan, Margaret. "I. H.D. and Marianne Moore: Correspondences and Contradictions. II. Yvonne Rainer's 'Journeys from Berlin/1971' and 'The

Man Who Envied Women': Narrative, Image, Sound. III. Discovery Time in Shakespeare's 'The Tempest.' " Rutgers U.

1988   Augustine, Jane. "Annotated Edition of H.D.'s *The Mystery*." City U of New York.

Baccolini, Raffaella. "Scrittura, Revisione, Sopravvivenza: H(ilda) D(oolittle) fra le Tradizioni." U of Bologna.

Burnett, Gary. "The Mysteries between Image and Epic: H.D.'s Poetry and Poetics in Transition." Princeton U.

1989   Baccolini, Raffaella. "Tradition, Identity, Desire: H.D.'s Revisionist Strategies in *By Avon River, Winter Love*, and *Hermetic Definition*." U of Wisconsin–Madison.

Chisolm, Dianne. "H.D.'s Freudian Poetics: Psychoanalysis in Transition." Oxford U.

Hirsh, Elizabeth A. "Modernism Revised: Formalism and the Feminine (Irigaray, H.D., and Barnes)." U of Wisconsin–Madison.

Kreis, Annette. " 'We are voyagers, discoverers': H.D.'s *Trilogy* and Modern Religious Poetry." University of Zürich.

Lucas, Rose. "Imag(in)ing the Mother: Transformative Images in H.D.'s Epic Poetry." Monash U.

Notes on Contributors

Diana Collecott teaches British and American literature and co-directs the Basil Bunting Poetry Centre at the University of Durham, England. She edited the special H.D. issue of *Agenda*, introduced the Virago edition of H.D.'s *The Gift*, and contributed essays on H.D. to other centennial publications and symposia. She has also written on other American writers, such as Henry James, William Carlos Williams, and Denise Levertov. She is completing a book entitled *The Unborn Story: H.D. and Women's Writing* and is at work on another called *H.D. and Her London*.

Robert Duncan, whose poetic career began in the 1940s, was the author of pivotal works of contemporary American poetry: *The Opening of the Field* (1960), *Roots and Branches* (1964), *Bending the Bow* (1968), *Ground Work I: Before the War* (1984), and *Ground Work II: In the Dark* (1987). His essays are collected in the volume *Fictive Certainties* (1985). *The H.D. Book* was begun as a birthday gift for H.D., but extended into a decades-long meditation about American modernism and the nature of poetry, portions of which have appeared in little magazines since the 1960s. The University of California Press has scheduled *The H.D. Book* for publication in 1991.

Rachel Blau DuPlessis, Professor at Temple University, is the author of *Writing Beyond the Ending: Narrative Strategies of Twentieth-Century Women Writers* (1985), *H.D.: The Career of That Struggle* (1986), and *The Pink Guitar: Writing as Feminist Practice* (1990). Her poetry is collected in *Wells* (1980) and *Tabula Rosa* (1987), and she is the editor of *The Selected Letters of George Oppen* (1990).

Susan Stanford Friedman is Professor of English and Women's Studies at the University of Wisconsin–Madison. She is the author of *Psyche Reborn: The Emergence of H.D.* (1981), *Penelope's Web: Gender, Modernity, H.D.'s Fiction* (1990), and articles on women's writing and narrative theory, psychoanalysis, poetics, and genre. She is at work on *Portrait of an Analysis with Freud: The Letters of H.D., Bryher, and Their Circle, 1933–1934* and *Return of the Repressed in Modernist Narratives*.

Albert Gelpi is the Coe Professor of American Literature at Stanford University and editor of Cambridge Studies in American Literature and Culture for Cambridge University Press. His books include *Emily Dickinson: The Mind of the Poet* (1966), *The Tenth Muse* (1975), *A Coherent Splendour: The American Poetic Renaissance, 1910–1950* (1987), and, with Barbara Charlesworth Gelpi, *Adrienne Rich's Poetry* (1975). He has published a number of essays on H.D., including the Introduction to H.D.'s *Notes on Thought and Vision*.

Eileen Gregory has published essays on H.D. and is the founding editor of the *H.D. Newsletter*. She has also written on mythic themes in *Summoning the Familiar: Powers and Rites of Common Life* (1983), as well as articles on Southern literature. An Associate Professor of English at the University of Dallas, she is at work on a book entitled *Transmission, Translation, Transcription: Classical Texts in H.D.'s Writing*.

Susan Gubar has co-edited, with Sandra M. Gilbert, The *Norton Anthology of Literature by Women* (1985) and co-authored *The Madwoman in the Attic: The Woman Writer and the Nineteenth-Century Literary Imagination* (1979), as well as *No-Man's Land: The Place of the Woman Writer in the Twentieth Century*, a three-volume literary history that includes *The War of the Words* (1988), *Sexchanges* (1989), and *Letters from the Front* (forthcoming). She teaches in the English Department and the Women's Studies Program at Indiana University.

Barbara Guest, the poet, novelist, and biographer, is the author of *Herself Defined: The Poet H.D. and Her World* (1984) and the novel *Seeking Air* (1978). She has written *Poems* (1962), *The Blue Stairs* (1968), *Moscow Mansions* (1973), *The Countess from Minneapolis* (1976), and *Biography* (1980). Her most recent book of poems is *Fair Realism* (1989).

Elizabeth A. Hirsh is at work on a book entitled *Modernism Revised: Formalism and the Feminine*, a reading of woman writers in modernist poetics. She has published essays on Victorian language theory, women's experimental fiction, and feminist theories. She currently teaches at Swarthmore College.

Deborah Kelly Kloepfer teaches English at the State University College at Buffalo. She has published various essays on modernist women's fiction and poetry and is the author of *The Unspeakable Mother: Forbidden Discourse in Jean Rhys and H.D.* (1989).

Cassandra Laity is Assistant Professor of English at the University of Oregon. She is currently completing a book entitled *H.D. and the Turn of the Century: Gender, Modernism, and Romantic Influence*. She has published essays on gender and modernism in Yeats and H.D. and will edit H.D.'s *Paint It To-Day*.

Adalaide Morris is Professor of English at the University of Iowa. She is the author of *Wallace Stevens: Imagination and Faith* (1974), a co-editor of *Extended*

Outlooks: The Iowa Review Collection of Contemporary Women Writers (1982), and the editor of the H.D. centenary issue of *The Iowa Review*. In addition to her work on H.D., she has published essays on Emily Dickinson, Adrienne Rich, and the contemporary American canon. She is completing a book entitled *H.D.'s Lexicon*.

Alicia Ostriker is a poet-critic whose writing on women's poetry includes *Writing like a Woman* (1983) and *Stealing the Language: The Emergence of Women's Poetry in America* (1986). She has published seven volumes of poetry, most recently *The Imaginary Lover* (1986) and *Green Age* (1989). She is Professor of English at Rutgers University.

Cyrena N. Pondrom is Professor of English and Women's Studies and Director of the Women's Studies Research Center at the University of Wisconsin–Madison. Her books include *The Road from Paris: French Influence on English Poetry, 1900–1920* (1974) and, with L. S. Dembo, *The Contemporary Writer: Interviews with Sixteen Novelists and Poets* (1972). She has written on a variety of modern figures and is currently at work on a volume entitled *Women and the Rise of Modernism*, a study of H.D., Moore, Stein, Virginia Woolf, Dorothy Richardson, and Edith Sitwell in the context of the modernist movement.

Perdita Schaffner is H.D.'s daughter and literary executor. She has written a number of biographical essays about H.D. and the literary milieu in which she grew up. She is the author of introductions to several of H.D.'s works, as well as book reviews and articles for the *East Hampton Star* and *New Directions for Women*.

Louis H. Silverstein is a principal catalog librarian on the Yale University Library's Rare Book Team. He was largely responsible for the organization and cataloging of the H.D. Papers at Beinecke Rare Book and Manuscript Library at Yale. The author of several articles on H.D., he is currently co-editing the correspondence between H.D. and Norman Holmes Pearson. He organized and mounted the 1986 exhibition "H.D.: A Life Observed" at Beinecke. He is also a freelance bibliographer, concentrating on modernist literature, and is at work on *The H.D. Chronology*, parts of which have been published in the *H.D. Newsletter*.

Index of Works

481

Index

Abel, Elizabeth, 112
Aldington, Catherine, 45
Aldington, Frances Perdita. *See* Schaffner, Perdita
Aldington, Richard, 16, 33–46 *passim*, 55, 319, 323; H.D.'s marriage to, 34, 95, 186, 226, 242, 278; affair with Fallas, 35; affair with Yorke, 36, 116, 120–21, 242, 243; return to London (1919), 37; affair with Brigit Patmore, 40; marriage to Netta Patmore, 41; H.D.'s letters to, 43, 46; and Perdita, 56; as one of H.D.'s "initiators," 67–68, 323; and imagism, 86–100 *passim*, 318; H.D.'s relationship with, and the man-boy relation in "Hyacinth," 116, 122; "To a Greek Marble," 156; photographs of, in "Scrapbook," 170; and *Bid Me to Live*, 207, 233, 409; and the Great War, 234, 235; and H.D.'s affair with Gray, 243; H.D.'s love for, and *Asphodel*, 247; and H.D.'s miscarriage, 330; and romantic thralldom, 413; and *Helen of Egypt*, 417–18
Altman, Meryl, 176
Ambelain, Robert, 42, 394–95
Anderson, Margaret, 85
Antipater of Sidon, 193
Aristotle, 290, 449*n4*
Atwood, Margaret, 314

Bachelard, Gaston, 301
Bachofen, J. J., 387
Balzac, Honoré de, 32, 223
Barnes, Djuna, 38, 174, 214, 215
Barney, Natalie, 214
Bart, Dan, 39
Barthes, Roland, 164
Beach, Sylvia, 38, 85, 224
Beauvoir, Simone de, 241

Benjamin, Walter, 224
Benstock, Shari, 432
Bergson, Henri, 100, 108*n30*, 276
Bhaduri, Arthur, 42, 320
Bhaduri, May, 42
Blake, William, 110, 337, 339, 368
Bloom, Harold, 111, 113
Bloom, Leopold, 446
Bogan, Louise, 129, 130
Botticelli, S., 122, 123, 124
Bottome, Phyllis, 34
Bové, Paul, 431
Bowen, Elizabeth, 5, 42
Bridges, Robert, 91
Brigman, Anne, 174
Brigman, Elizabeth, 174
Browning, Elizabeth B., 129
Browning, Robert, 90, 200
Bryher (Annie Winifred Ellerman), 4, 19, 27, 36–45 *passim*, 156, 207–8, 220, 278, 407; *Two Selves*, 36, 217; and Ellis, 37, 216–17; marriage to McAlmon, 38, 39, 53, 208; marriage to Macpherson, 39–40, 53, 56, 156, 162, 208; and Perdita, 39–40, 55, 56, 69, 77, 225; and psychoanalysis, 39, 40, 284, 285; *Life and Letters Today*, 41; and H.D.'s illness, 69, 243, 279; H.D.'s relationship with, and the homoerotic myth, 116; and H.D.'s "Scrapbook," 157–75 *passim*; *West*, 158, 174; in *Palimpsest*, 197, 198, 200; and H.D.'s relationship with Pound, 224; and H.D.'s passion for men, 226; and POOL Productions, 282; *The Days of Mars*, 320; and H.D.'s visions, 322, 323, 414; H.D.'s letters to, 17, 36, 46, 51*n3*; and financial arrangements, 54; on H.D.'s analysis with Freud, 162–63, 226–27, 286